MICHAEL BURLEIGH is the author of nine well-received books, including *Earthly Powers*, *Sacred Causes* and *The Third Reich*, for which he was awarded the Samuel Johnson Prize.

From the reviews of *Moral Combat*:

'Magnificent … A work of erudition, vast practical knowledge and abundant common sense, beautifully written, and packed with insight. Even if one has read hundreds of books on the War, one finds Burleigh in this work filling gaps in understanding that in retrospect appear vast. No-one with an interest in the Second World War should be without this book; and indeed nor should anyone who cares about how our world has come about, or how nations in the grip of war handle themselves. In a field packed with competitors, Burleigh has written one of the great books on this compelling, and endlessly pervasive subject'
Daily Telegraph

'Outstanding. More than any book I have read on the war, it confronts us with the ethical questions millions of people faced in their daily lives. Extraordinarily powerful … Closely researched and splendidly written'
DOMINIC SANDBROOK, *Sunday Times*

'Burleigh is a master of significant detail unearthed in microscopic research … As always the colour and power of Burleigh's prose is outstanding. When it comes to evoking the smell of a place he is far and away our best history writer. The bloodiest and most wrenching account of the war I can recall'   GEORGE WALDEN, *Observer*

'Stunning. Michael Burleigh has set out to examine the moral dilemmas faced by the warlords, combatants and civilians in the dark barbarism of the Second World War and delivered a remarkable tour-de-force. He combines razor-sharp analysis, compelling writing and superb character portraits with character and understanding'
SIMON SEBAG MONTEFIORE, *Mail on Sunday*

'Magnificent. One of the most significant books on the Second World War in recent years … Military history does not get better than this'
TES

By the same author

Prussian Society and the German Order
Germany Turns Eastwards: A Study of Ostforschung in the Third Reich
The Racial State: Germany 1933–1945
Death and Deliverance: Euthanasia in Germany 1900–1945
(ed.) Confronting the Nazi Past
Ethics and Extermination: Reflections on Nazi Genocide
The Third Reich: A New History
Earthly Powers: The Conflict between Religion & Politics
from the French Revolution to the Great War
Sacred Causes: Religion and Politics from the
European Dictators to Al Qaeda
Blood and Rage: A Cultural History of Terrorism

MORAL COMBAT

A HISTORY OF WORLD WAR II

Michael Burleigh

Harper
Press

Harper*Press*
An imprint of HarperCollins*Publishers*
77–85 Fulham Palace Road
Hammersmith, London W6 8JB

Visit our authors' blog at www.fifthestate.co.uk

This Harper*Press* paperback edition published 2011

1

First published in Great Britain by Harper*Press* in 2010

A catalogue record for this book is
available from the British Library

ISBN 978-0-00-719577-0

Typeset in Minion with Janson and Trajan display by
G&M Designs Limited, Raunds, Northamptonshire

Printed and bound in Great Britain by
Clays Ltd, St Ives plc

Mixed Sources
Product group from well-managed
forests and other controlled sources
www.fsc.org   Cert no. SW-COC-001806
© 1996 Forest Stewardship Council
FSC

FSC is a non-profit international organisation established to promote the
responsible management of the world's forests. Products carrying the FSC
label are independently certified to assure consumers that they come
from forests that are managed to meet the social, economic and
ecological needs of present or future generations.

Find out more about HarperCollins and the environment at
www.harpercollins.co.uk/green

CONTENTS

war ad romanum — see Lindqvist

Infidels, rebels, savages = no protection on bombing

need to exercise humanity, discrimination and proportionality while waging war.

These religious and philosophical exhortations often gelled with the severely practical outlook of warriors on ancient, medieval or early modern battlefields who knew that getting a substantial ransom was better than having a dead prisoner. Throughout, however, there was an extreme alternative – of war *ad romanum* – where the enemy and his population could be enslaved and killed, allegedly in line with what was thought to be ancient Roman practice. Sometimes in the Middle Ages a red banner would be flown to indicate that chivalric norms were cancelled and that the type of war visited on infidels or rebels would ensue. As an excellent collection of essays edited by Michael Howard and others reveals, even by the mid-seventeenth century men at arms knew what constituted decent practice in warfare. While I do not think any war has ever been good, the Second World War, which killed fifty-five million people, was a necessary war against at least one regime which, uniquely, modernised barbarism into an industrial process, and another that visited cruelty and savagery on the many peoples of East Asia, from the Chinese to indigenous tribes on remote Pacific islands. That does not diminish the war against Italian Fascist imperialism or the moral problems raised by the Western alliance of desperation with the Soviet Union, which imposed Communist tyranny on half of liberated Europe. Nor does it seek to excuse Allied war crimes, although those should not be elided with what are uncharmingly called collateral casualties, which were not the objectives of an operation. To construe the D-Day landings as anything other than a noble enterprise, which the vast majority of French people welcomed, because various Allied bombardments killed tens of thousands of their compatriots, seems perverse. The British cabinet had grave reservations about this. But when they consulted the Free French general Pierre Koenig, he replied that lives are lost in any war, and this was the price to be paid for liberation of his country.

Around the margins there have been attempts to revise our general perceptions of the conflict. Some conservatives claim that Britain and the US should have let Hitler and Stalin slog it out, so that the victor – assuming they both did not lose – would have been too exhausted to take over either the whole or half of the European mainland. This line of argument reflects mutual Anglo-American animosities, to the effect that Churchill (and Roosevelt) somehow tricked the US into war against Germany, or that the war's ultimate beneficiaries were the Soviets and the Americans who liquidated the British Empire and dominated a divided Europe. It also adopts a narrowly strategic view of the issues involved, taking realism to the level of amoralism. Now while I have sympathy with the view that in some foreign policy circles it is always 1938 – with even clowns like Venezuela's President Hugo Chávez compared with Hitler – this argument ignores the existential threat Nazism posed to the human spirit as a whole. Was our rich civilisation supposed to culminate in that abnegation of everything decent, humane or joyous in our condition, ushering in an era of heroic scientising barbarity? Given Hitler's fanatic volatility, it is also unlikely that he would have left the Anglo-Saxons alone, once he had secured mastery of the Soviet Union up to the Urals. As this book tries to show, the Nazis (and their partners in crime) tried fundamentally to alter the moral understanding of humanity, in ways that deviated from the moral norms of Western civilisation. They did this by locating their murderous depredations beyond law, but within a warped moral framework that defined their purifying violence as necessary and righteous.

While this strategic revisionism reflects an extreme isolationist agenda, a more pervasive fear of armed force has resulted in a dubious moral relativism, exemplified by Nicholson Baker's pacifist tract *Human Smoke*, in which all belligerents were as bad as one another. *Human Smoke* involves cutting, pasting and juxtaposing random snippets of historical evidence to insinuate this conclusion, generally impressing critics who have no knowledge of what they are reviewing. He implies that because Churchill may have drunk too much, or because Eleanor Roosevelt was an anti-Semitic snob in her youth, they were on a par with a dictator who murdered six million Jews. The leaders of the English-speaking democracies allegedly went to war to benefit a sinister arms-manufacturing military–industrial complex, a view which much appealed to extreme US isolationists in the 1930s, and which resonates with the international left nowadays. This exercise in extreme moral relativism (and crude conspiracy theory) is sometimes excused on the grounds that the author is a novelist daringly experimenting with forms that resemble a child's scrapbook. In reality, any half-competent historian would have no difficulty assembling a small book in which Hitler appeared to be defending (German) human rights, or a directory of every leading Nazi's best Jewish friends. This would be meaningless as history, which involves evaluating complex streams of evidence in their overall context and then exercising discrimination (and taste) regarding events and persons. For rather more local reasons, some German historians are bent on inculpating Allied bomber crews in war crimes by the not very subtle method of allowing the German terminology of mass murder to leach into this context. Japanese conservatives have for a long time practised what they call 'anti-masochistic history' which insists that from 1931 to 1945 Japan sought to liberate Asia and the Asians from European colonialism, when in fact they enslaved them. Partly for these reasons, I find myself defending the Allied war effort, whatever reservations one may have about the conduct of the Soviets. Some patriotic myths are not only useful but true; so were the virtues which accompanied them. These issues are not easy, and all I have tried to do is to provide a rough map through intractable terrain, which others may wish to pursue with greater refinement.

I have never got the hang of employing research assistants. However, at an advanced stage Hugh Bicheno offered to check facts and to help unravel some of the more tortuous sentences. This editorial work proved incredibly helpful, especially since he is a bona-fide military historian who knows more about TMPFFGGH than I will ever do, even though my late father was a wing commander in the wartime RAF. (That's trim, mixture, pitch, fuel, flaps, gills, gyro and hydraulics for fellow non-initiates.) I am privileged to be one of the foreign members of the Academic Advisory Board of the Institut für Zeitgeschichte in Munich, Germany's leading contemporary history research centre, where Drs Johannes Hürter and Christian Hartmann kindly kept me abreast of their important researches on the German army. The admirable Professor James Kurth of the US Naval War Academy reminded me not to neglect the navy, though I may not have done it justice.

I have benefited from the suggestions of George Walden, Max Hastings and Frederic Raphael. Max let me have an advanced draft of his book on Churchill, and probed me with an embarrassing range of interesting questions which I struggled to answer. George gave me his book on morality and foreign policy, which became a model of how to approach these issues. Freddie kept up a running correspondence on appeasement, with a sort of bracing ferocity. From the academy I received some very useful bibliographical recommendations from Professors Christopher Coker, Robert Gellately and David Stafford. The staff at both the Imperial War Museum and the London Library helped find materials that were relevant to the book.

Arabella Pike, Annabel Wright, Helen Ellis, Peter James and Tim Duggan at HarperCollins have my gratitude for making my last four books happen smoothly on both sides of the Atlantic, as does my agent Andrew Wylie, to whom I return *un' abbraccio*. James Pullen has been an exceptionally good point man in dealing with foreign publishers. This is the fifth book Peter James has fine tuned, with his characteristic attention to detail. Cathie Arrington expertly found some arresting illustrations.

Last but not least, I owe so much to my adorable wife Linden, who has successfully created an environment in which I can do this work over sustained periods. Sadly, after enriching my understanding of the imaginative literature of this period, my dear friend Adolf Wood died before seeing many of his suggestions in print.

I wrote this book a few hundred yards from the rectory where Field Marshal Bernard Montgomery grew up. It is separated by a road from the park where on 15 October 1940 over a hundred Londoners were killed when their waterlogged trench shelters took a direct Luftwaffe hit. This bomb was one of the 2,500 which rained down on Lambeth to cut bridges and railway lines across the Thames but which damaged or destroyed four-fifths of housing stock, too. In the wake of this single incident, only forty-five bodies were recovered intact; the remains of the rest are still under the park. The railings around the adjacent junction are made from steel stretchers kept for such an eventuality, although the Underground station was being used to store barbed wire rather than as a shelter. They are a tangible reminder of the Second World War, not as patriotic myth but as grim reality, as much for so many civilians as the uniformed combatants.

Michael Burleigh
Kennington
September 2009

MAPS

THIRD REICH CONQUESTS
(1940–42)

Norway
(April–June 1940)

Sweden
(neutral)

North Sea

Denmark
(April 1940)

Battle of the
Atlantic
1939–45

Ireland
(neutral)

United
Kingdom

Berlin

German Reich

Netherlands
(May 1940)

Belgium
(May 1940)

Occupied France

Bohemia
& Moravia

France
(May–June 1940)

Switz.
(neutral)

Bay of
Biscay

Vichy France

Adriatic S

Portugal
(neutral)

Spain
(neutral, sent troops
to Eastern Front)

Corsica
(Vichy)

Italy
(German ally)

Ligurian Sea

Sardinia
(Italy)

Sicily
(Italy)

Spanish Morocco

Tunisia
(Vichy)

Malta
(British)

Morocco (Vichy)

Algeria (Vichy)

Finland
(German ally)

Leningrad

Deepest German advance 2 December 1941

Demyansk

Rzhev

Moscow

U.S.S.R.

Soviet winter offensive

Army Group North

BARBAROSSA
22 June 1941

Army Group Centre

Kursk

CODE BLUE
28 June 1942

Stalingrad

Deepest German advance 18 November 1942

Kharkov

General Gouvernement

...akia

Army Group South

Hungary
(German ally)

Sevastopol

Caucasus

Black Sea

Romania
(German ally)

...oslavia
...1 1941)

Bulgaria
(German ally)

Turkey
(neutral)

Albania
(Italy)

Greece
(April 1941)

Aegean Sea

Syria (Vichy)

Occupied by British
June-July 1941

Lebanon
(Vichy)

...editerranean Sea

Crete
(June 1941)

British Palestine
& Trans-Jordan

0   250   500 miles
0   400   800 kms

AXIS ARMY REACHES EL ALAMEIN IN EGYPT JULY 1942

© Hugh Bicheno

THE FINAL SOLUTION
INFRASTRUCTURE

□ Concentration Camp

T4 *Euthanasia centre*

✡ Major Ghetto

✗ Major massacre site

▨ Extermination Camp

kilometres
0   100   200   300   400
0   125   250
         miles

Norway
□ at Bardufoss, Berg
Bredtvet, Falstad,
Grini, Ulven.

Sweden

Horserod □

North Sea

Denmark

Neuengamme □   Ravensbrück □

□ Westerbork   Bergen- □   □ Sachsenh...
Belsen

England   Amersfoort □   Arbeitsdorf □   ● **BERLIN**
Neth.   Mittelbau-Dora   *Brandenburg*
□ Herzogenbusch   □   **T4**
T4 *Bernberg*
Breedonk □   □ Mechelen   Niederhagen
Belg.   Buchenwald □

Alderney   □ Breitenau   Ther...
□   Royallieu □   *Hadamar* **T4**   Sonnenstein **T4**

PARIS ●   □ Drancy   □ Hinzert   □ Lety   Bo...
□ Romainville   Flossenbürg □   &
□ Pitheviers

Occupied France   □ Natzweiler-   *Harthei...*
Struthof   Dachau   **T4**
T4 *Grafeneck*   □   Mautha...
Ebensee □

Switz.   Öst...

Bolzano □

Bozen...
San Sabba
□

Vichy France

□ Asti   Fossoli
□

□ Gurs   **Italy**

Vernet □   Milles □

□ Rivesaltes   Servigliano □

Spain   *Mediterranean
Sea*   ● **ROME**

© Hugh Bicheno

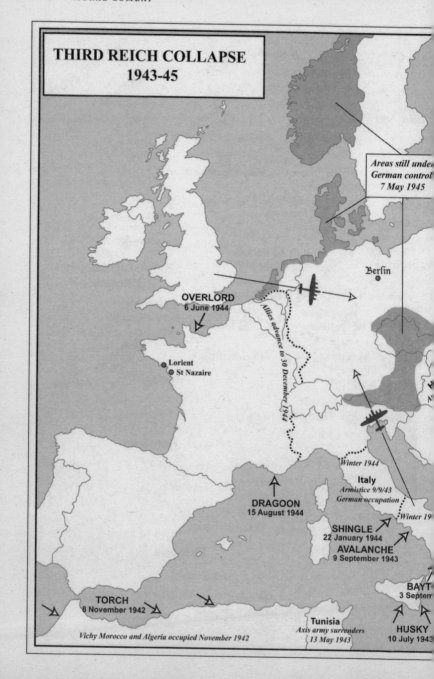

THIRD REICH COLLAPSE
1943-45

Areas still under German control 7 May 1945

Berlin

OVERLORD
6 June 1944

Allies advance to 30 December 1944

Lorient
St Nazaire

Winter 1944

DRAGOON
15 August 1944

Italy
Armistice 9/9/43
German occupation

Winter 19

SHINGLE
22 January 1944
AVALANCHE
9 September 1943

BAYT
3 Septem

TORCH
8 November 1942

Vichy Morocco and Algeria occupied November 1942

Tunisia
Axis army surrenders
13 May 1943

HUSKY
10 July 1943

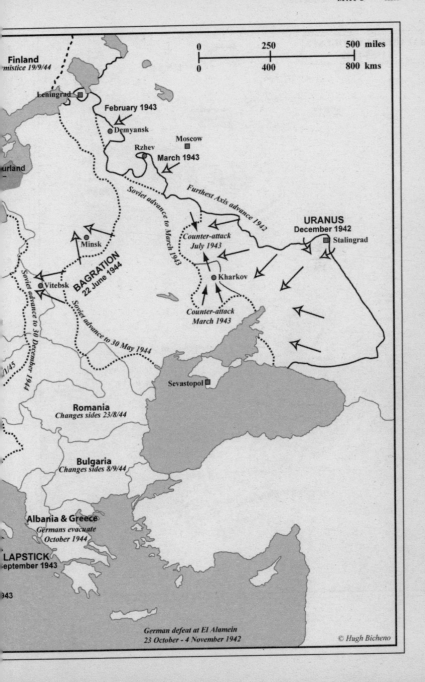

0   250   500 miles
0   400   800 kms

Finland
rmistice 19/9/44

Leningrad

February 1943

Demyansk

Moscow

Rzhev

March 1943

urland

Furthest Axis advance 1942

URANUS
December 1942

Stalingrad

Minsk

Soviet advance to March 1943

Counter-attack
July 1943

BAGRATION
22 June 1944

Vitebsk

Soviet advance to 30 December 1944

Soviet advance to 30 May 1944

Kharkov

Counter-attack
March 1943

1/45

Sevastopol

Romania
Changes sides 23/8/44

Bulgaria
Changes sides 8/9/44

Albania & Greece
Germans evacuate
October 1944

LAPSTICK
eptember 1943

943

German defeat at El Alamein
23 October - 4 November 1942

© Hugh Bicheno

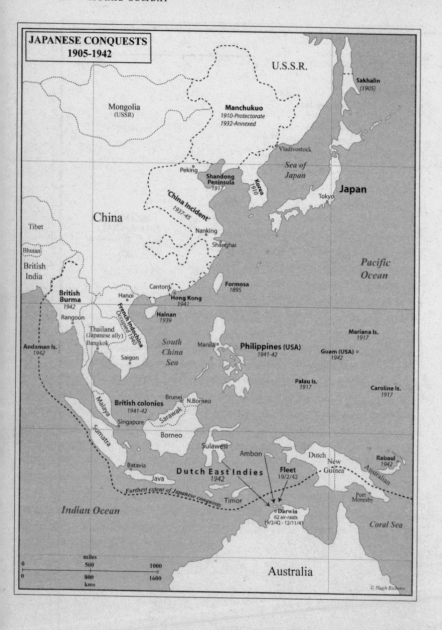

**JAPANESE CONQUESTS
1905-1942**

U.S.S.R.

Sakhalin
(1905)

Mongolia
(USSR)

Manchukuo
1910-Protectorate
1932-Annexed

Vladivostock

Peking

*Sea of
Japan*

**Shandong
Peninsula**
1917

Korea
1910

Tokyo

Japan

China

'China Incident'
1937-45

Nanking

Shanghai

Tibet

*Pacific
Ocean*

Bhutan

**British
India**

**British
Burma**
1942

Hanoi

Cantons

Formosa
1895

Hong Kong
1941

Rangoon

French Indochina
Occupied 1940

Hainan
1939

Thailand
(Japanese ally)

Bangkok

*South
China
Sea*

Manila

Mariana Is.
1917

Philippines (USA)
1941-42

Guam (USA)
1942

Andaman Is.
1942

Saigon

Malaya

British colonies
1941-42

Brunei

N.Borneo

Palau Is.
1917

Caroline Is.
1917

Sumatra

Singapore

Sarawak

Borneo

Batavia

Java

Sulawesi

Ambon

Dutch East Indies
1942

Fleet
19/2/42

Dutch
New
Guinea

Rabaul
1942

Australian

Furthest extent of Japanese conquests

Timor

Port
Moresby

Indian Ocean

Darwin
62 air-raids
19/2/42 - 12/11/43

Coral Sea

miles

500

1000

800

1600

kms

Australia

© Hugh Bicheno

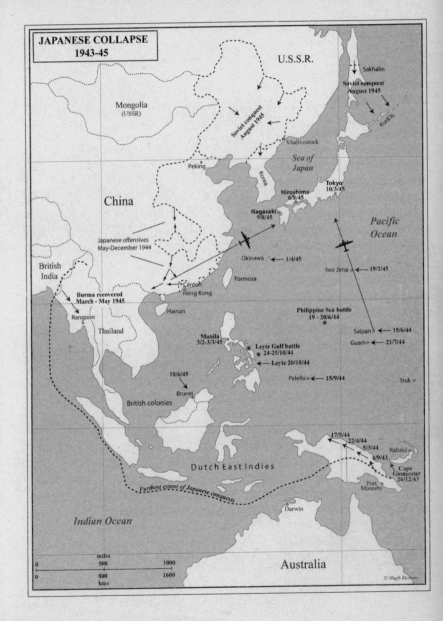

JAPANESE COLLAPSE 1943-45

U.S.S.R.

Mongolia
(USSR)

Sakhalin

Soviet conquest
August 1945

Kuril Is.

Vladivostock

Soviet conquest
August 1945

Peking

Sea of
Japan

Korea

Tokyo
10/3/45

Hiroshima
6/8/45

China

Nagasaki
9/8/45

Pacific
Ocean

Japanese offensives
May-December 1944

Okinawa   ← 1/4/45

Iwo Jima ○ ← 19/2/45

British
India

Canton
Hong Kong

Formosa

Burma recovered
March - May 1945

Rangoon

Hainan

Thailand

Philippine Sea battle
19 - 20/6/44
*

Saipan ○ ← 15/6/44

Guam ○ ← 21/7/44

Manila
3/2-3/3/45

* Leyte Gulf battle
* 24-25/10/44

← Leyte 20/10/44

10/6/45

Peleliu ○ ← 15/9/44

Truk ○

Brunei

British colonies

Dutch East Indies

17/5/44

22/4/44

5/3/44

Rabaul

1/9/43

Cape
Gloucester
26/12/43

Port
Moresby

Furthest extent of Japanese conquests

Darwin

Indian Ocean

miles
500   1000
0
0
800   1600
kms

Australia

© Hugh Bicheno

CHAPTER 1

The Predators

I NEW ROMAN EMPIRE

Europe's newly wrought post-war frontiers were first breached by the ageing poet Gabriele D'Annunzio, a flamboyant icon of Italian nationalism, when he seized the Adriatic city of Fiume. Fiume had been part of the multinational Austro-Hungarian Empire before the Great War, but its status had been left undefined in the post-war settlement negotiated at Versailles. It remained a predominantly Italian outpost set amid a Slavic sea, and was salt in the wound of what the Italian nationalists called a 'mutilated victory', their beggars' reward for belatedly joining the Entente side in 1915.

On 12 September 1919, D'Annunzio arrived overland at the head of 120 war veterans, whom he called his 'legionnaires', to forestall US President Woodrow Wilson's wish to designate Fiume a free city. The local contingent of Allied occupation troops, under the command of an Italian officer, tamely surrendered the city to D'Annunzio. The seizure of Fiume resonated among the Italian population, and the Radical Party government of Francesco Nitti in Rome judged it prudent to acquiesce in the spectacle of the old poet and his volunteer band endeavouring to rewrite Europe's post-war settlement.

D'Annunzio sought to refashion the lives of the fifty thousand inhabitants of Holocaust City, as he dubbed his new domain. He addressed admiring crowds from a balcony, crowds which bayed 'A noi!' ('the world belongs to us') or the meaningless chant 'Eia, eia, eia, alalà!' Along with the wartime shocktroops' anthem 'Giovinezza', these would pass into the repertory of Italian Fascism. So, in more elaborate ways, did his attempt to reconcile a new national religion with traditional Catholicism, and at least the idea of a corporatist state based on group vocation.

Thirteen months later, the Kingdom of Italy and the Kingdom of Serbs, Croats and Slovenes signed the Treaty of Rapallo, which created the Free State of Fiume, promptly recognised by the USA, France and Britain. D'Annunzio, however, refused to accept the treaty and had to be evicted from the city by the Italian army, in what entered Fascist mythology as the Bloody Christmas of 24–30 December 1920.[1] *Yes*

This ageing 'man of will' had a younger epigone in Italy's turbulent post-war domestic politics. The introduction of universal male suffrage in 1913, which gave the vote to Italy's many adult illiterates, disrupted the previous system based on rival elites alternating in power to dispense pork-barrel rewards to their clienteles. The largest of the new mass political parties were the Catholic Democrats and the Marxist Socialists, although the latter soon split with the formation of a new Italian Communist Party. The Great War had created a sense of mass entitlement, a feeling that all the death and suffering had to be for something. Among those who had been exempt from the war, industrial unrest blighted the factories of the northern Milan–Turin–Genoa triangle, even as swathes of the northern countryside were also blighted by agrarian militancy, which translated into Socialist gains in municipal elections. Landlords quaked as red flags were hoisted on modest municipal buildings. The Red Years (*biennio rosso*) of 1919–20 provided an opportunity for Italy's nascent Fascist Party, founded in Milan on 23 March 1919 by Benito Mussolini, a former teacher, Socialist agitator and war veteran. Mussolini, who dared to extend his reading habits beyond the prescribed texts to such infidels as Nietzsche, had finally broken with the comrades in 1915, over his insistence that Italy abandon its wartime neutrality. His Fascist movement was like a faith whose heretical spirit combined the virtues of aristocrats and democrats, excluding the stolidly prudent bourgeois virtues between.[2]

The spectre of red revolution transformed Mussolini's deracinated band of black-shirted students, bohemians and war veterans into the willing tool of powerful interests. In the absence of salvation by the state, landowners hired Fascist squads, consisting of thirty to fifty men under a leader known by the Abyssinian term *Ras* (chief), to rough up, or kill, Socialist/Communist activists, and to wreck the physical infrastructure of the leftist parties and their labour unions. Bernardo Bertolucci's movie *1900* gives a very vivid sense of these depredations. In mid-1921, a parliamentary commission reported the destruction in the previous six months of 119 labour exchanges, 59 cultural centres, 107 co-operatives and 83 offices used to co-ordinate day labourers, as well as libraries, print shops and self-help societies.[3]

Accustomed to absorbing and emasculating populist firebrands, Italy's old elites were confident that Fascism was a tool they could use to forestall red revolution, following which it would be merely a matter of political fireworks: after a puff of smoke and a whiff of sulphur, nothing would remain. For his part, Mussolini realised that the Italian liberal state was a façade, 'a mask behind which there is no face, scaffolding behind which there is no building, a force without a spirit'. In that climate of mutual cynicism, the ruling elites tried to co-opt the Fascists into the dominant liberal-nationalist bloc by offering Mussolini first the deputy premiership, then the premiership itself. They believed he would be content to be a figurehead, while they would continue to govern Italy by tried and tested methods.

They failed. Although the Fascists were sparingly represented in the Italian parliament, the illusion of strength, especially in the north where they took over entire towns, and doubts about the loyalty of the army, led King Victor Emmanuel III to invite Mussolini to form a government in October 1922, after the King had declined to introduce martial law to crush the insurgent black-shirts. Initially, Mussolini and three colleagues were the sole Fascists in a cabinet of fourteen. As was true throughout the Fascist period, the three traditional sources of power remained intact: the royal armed forces, the Catholic Church and the monarchy. In important respects they also acted as checks on Mussolini's desire to make the Mediterranean an Italian (or Roman) sea and to break out of what he saw as a geopolitical cage, whose bars were Gibraltar and Suez.

Mussolini made sure there were not many other domestic restraints. Fascism abolished the freedom of the press and political pluralism. It created a not especially effective or numerous secret police, which institutionalised the use of paid informers and wiretapping. But after the regime nearly fell over the slaying of Socialist Deputy Giacomo Matteotti, opponents were sent into internal exile rather than killed. To bolster his hold on power, Mussolini also intruded a Fascist Grand Council and a 300,000-man black-shirted militia, the Milizia Volontaria per la Sicurezza Nazionale (MVSN), into the state apparatus. Belligerence was the signature of Fascism. Angry war veterans were prominent, but so were those who for reasons of age had missed the war experience, united in the belief that political violence was cleansing and ennobling. Discipline was celebrated and fetishised, while entire swathes of life were militarised through metaphorical battles for births, drainage, the lira or grain, and by enveloping some 6,700,000 children and youths of both sexes within paramilitary formations.[4] Mussolini had been a leading Socialist journalist. Surely the preeminent British historian Alfred Cobban was right when in 1939 he described Italian Fascism as 'government by journalism', meaning a rather desperate seeking after public opinion?[5]

What Catholic intellectuals like Luigi Sturzo dubbed Fascism's idolatrous veneration of the state was designed to counteract the pervasive *campanilismo* of a society where most people's horizons did not rise beyond the elegant church towers of their village or town and the 'amoral familism' practised by the clans living in their shadows. It also sought to reforge human nature, an uphill task in the land of *bella figura*. Mussolini was openly contemptuous of what he called this 'army of mandolin players'. Instead he wished to shape a race of armed barbarians with the single-mindedness of medieval Dominican friars, to bring about a latterday Roman Empire, the obvious historical template, although his historical metaphors were surely mixed. However, attempts to fanaticise Italians through the cults of Fascist movement martyrs and of the omniscient Duce (leader/guide), or through membership of totalitarian organisations, ran into pervasive loyalties to the Church and the family, as well as the localised client networks of each town or region. The movement's attempts to create a 'new man' by exhortation were also derided by the pragmatic cynicism of Italy's self-styled *brave gente* or fine people, and Fascist meritocracy soon dissolved into the pervasive corruption and nepotism.

As a sub-species of nationalism, war was the chosen means for making Italians into Fascists and for achieving great-power status. As Mussolini said during the Spanish Civil War, 'When Spain is over, I'll think of something else: the character of the Italians must be re-created through battle.' For Mussolini, nothing could beat combat in transforming consciousness, while the rigours of new colonies would consolidate and perpetuate this martial spirit. Fascism itself was always activist and aggressive, while charismatic leadership required regular *coups de théâtre* to counteract the impression of mere management of affairs. War and imperialism were seen as the means of forging the elusive 'new man', who would enable Mussolini to complete his domestic revolution which had compromised with the old elites. But the elites who cramped the dictator's ability to implement the society he desired also checked his wilder foreign-policy gambits when they courted the risk of war. The core dynamic of the Fascist period was that Mussolini believed international war would enable him to carry out a domestic revolution – against those who had installed him to preclude one.[6]

Italy, backward
Africa

For over a decade, Fascism's uniformed swagger was not reflected in Italian foreign policy, which was conducted by the traditional diplomatic elite from their new home in the Palazzo Chigi. The need to consolidate the regime at home, and Italy's dependence on imported coal, oil, iron ore and chemical fertilisers, inhibited military adventures. This was a backward peasant country, with only a fifth of the total industrial potential of Germany and half that of Japan. A third of the population were illiterate or semi-literate, while at tertiary level there was a marked preponderance of arts graduates over engineers. When war did eventually break out there was a mass exodus into the universities, which sheltered young middle-class men from conscription until the age of twenty-six. True, in 1923 the Italian navy bombarded and occupied Corfu after the Greek government had prevaricated over the murder of four Italians engaged in resolving a border dispute between Greece and Albania. But after a threatened British naval intervention Mussolini accepted Greek financial reparations and withdrew his troops. Although Italy regained Fiume and concluded a friendship treaty with the new, multinational Kingdom of Yugoslavia, the city remained a primary object of Fascist animosity. Covert subversion was conducted by supporting Macedonian and Croat Fascist exiles based in Italy, since the Italian elites feared that overt aggression would involve Yugoslavia's patron France.

Another outlet for Fascist aggression was in Africa. In the mid-1920s, Italian forces pushed out from the narrow coastal strip of Tripolitania, taken from the Ottoman Turks in 1912, to conquer what, in conscious echo of the Romans, became known as Libya. Desert concentration camps were used to isolate from the rest of the population guerrillas who were resisting the Italians. Similar brutality was used to ensure control of Italian Somaliland in the Horn of Africa. At the same time, Mussolini kept Italy at the European top table. At Locarno in 1925, Italy became one of the co-guarantors of Germany's western frontiers with France and Belgium. In March 1933 the Duce floated a four-power directorate to regulate European affairs without the diffuse involvement of the League of Nations, founded after the Great War, a scheme intended to win leeway for further aggression in Africa.

For Mussolini, the appointment of Hitler as German chancellor in 1933 represented both a threat and an opportunity. It was a threat because Nazi machinations in Austria menaced the authoritarian Dollfuss regime, which looked to Italy (and the Papacy) for ideological inspiration, while raising the ominous prospect of German armies at the Brenner Pass. The opportunity chiefly lay in seeking licence for overseas aggression in return for collaborating with the other powers in containing Germany. Hitler and Mussolini first met in Venice on 14 June 1934. It was not a meeting of minds, largely because Mussolini dispensed with an interpreter for sessions in a language he only intermittently grasped when delivered in Hitler's guttural south German accent. Despite Hitler's pleasantries about the subtle light in Italian Renaissance paintings, Mussolini grew weary of an interlocutor he compared with a gramophone that played only seven tunes.

Hitler came away mistakenly convinced that Mussolini had granted him a free hand in Austria, and a month later Austrian Nazis, acting with Hitler's connivance, murdered Chancellor Engelbert Dollfuss. Mussolini had to inform Dollfuss's wife and children, who were staying with him, what had happened to her husband and their father. Privately, the Duce referred to Hitler as a 'sexual degenerate', associating him with the homosexual leaders of Germany's brown-shirted Sturmabteilung (SA), murdered on Hitler's orders shortly after that Venice meeting. This was the Röhm purge of stormtroopers disgruntled with Hitler's dispositions. But his public comments were restrained and he sent only a token detachment of troops to the Brenner Pass. Then, seemingly seeking support to prevent *Anschluss*, the term for Austro-German union, forbidden under Article 80 of the Treaty of Versailles, Mussolini turned to the French. Foreign Minister Pierre Laval hurried to Rome, despite the fact that in October 1934 Italian intelligence had connived at the murder, in Marseilles, of the Yugoslav King Alexander by Croatian Fascists, an incident in which Laval's predecessor, Louis Barthou, had been a collateral fatality.

This led to the so-called Stresa Front, an agreement made on 14 April 1935 in the town of that name on the banks of Italy's Lake Maggiore by Mussolini, Laval and British Prime Minister Ramsay MacDonald. The declaration reaffirmed the Locarno Treaties and declared that the independence of Austria 'would continue to inspire their common policy'. The signatories also agreed to resist any future attempt by the Germans to change the Treaty of Versailles – a unified front promptly undone by the British, who concluded a naval agreement with Germany that sanctioned an expansion of its fleet beyond the limit set at Versailles. So eager was Laval to strike a deal that he readily conceded what Mussolini was really seeking, the go-ahead for Italian military aggression in the Horn of Africa. There Italy had been massing large-scale forces in its East African colonies of Eritrea and Somaliland, bordering on Abyssinia. Mussolini also, mistakenly, believed he had secured British complicity on the basis of peripheral soundings at Stresa. It was an easy mistake to make. When a journalist at Stresa asked Ramsay MacDonald about Abyssinia, he replied, 'My friend, your question is irrelevant.' In a sense it was, for the conference had been primarily convened to forge a common front against Hitler in Europe. But that was not what Mussolini understood.[7]

Mussolini took 'irrelevant' to mean that the British did not care about Abyssinia. After all, they had not done anything about Japanese adventurism, from which Mussolini (and Hitler) learned the trick of not declaring war, while presenting aggression as defensive in purpose. When, following the Italian invasion of Abyssinia, the British deployed reinforcements to the Mediterranean Fleet, an outraged Mussolini ranted about going to war with Britain, much to the horror of King Victor Emmanuel and his service chiefs. By contrast, although Germany (and Japan) had previously been arming the Abyssinians, Hitler declared his neutrality in the Italo-Abyssinian war, while publicly forswearing any ill intent towards Austria. He even offered to supply Italy with coal should the League of Nations impose sanctions.

French refusal to support British military action led to a policy of more carrot than stick. Britain's mixed signals reflected various contradictory concerns. There was a sober refusal to dissipate forces that might one day be needed in any one of three possible global theatres. Britain also wished to engage Mussolini in any potential alliance against the more substantial threat represented by Hitler. On the other hand, while the British public were opposed to war, they believed in the League of Nations and insisted that infractions of international law should be punished, while remaining passionately opposed to rearmament. The French and British tried to assuage Mussolini's appetites by offering him stretches of empty desert, which he dismissed as 'lunar landscapes' and 'sandpits'. Next, the League of Nations suggested that Abyssinia become a League mandate, with recognition of special Italian interests – but mere sops could not divert Mussolini from his chosen course of action.[8]

Mussolini could plausibly present the invasion of Abyssinia, along with Liberia the only remaining independent state in Africa, as being a resumption of a catch-up quest for empire. It was also revenge for the humiliating defeat Italy had suffered at Adowa in 1896 when an Italian army had been wiped out by Abyssinian tribesmen. 'Cost what it may, I will avenge Adowa,' Mussolini informed the French ambassador to Rome.[9] Using more contemporary arguments, Mussolini claimed that Abyssinia would absorb the Italian rural poor, hitherto lost to North America at an alarming rate, who would feed themselves and generate a surplus for the Italian metropolis. These landless labourers and sharecroppers would become lords of all the coffee, cotton and wheat they surveyed, with Abyssinians doing the hard labour. There were even rumours of oil, which was never found but, ironically, lay undiscovered beneath the Italian colony of Libya.[10]

There was also talk of a civilising mission, of bringing order out of tribal chaos, a view that resonated with Evelyn Waugh and other conservative Roman Catholics beyond Italy. Although in reality it had been Emperor Haile Selassie's success in forging a centralised state, in defiance of rival warlords, that inclined Mussolini to act sooner rather than later, the Italians claimed they were going to liberate Abyssinia's slaves and also to deliver the country's six million Muslims from Christian tutelage. During the war, Radio Bari pumped out pro-Muslim propaganda, while afterwards Mussolini built a Grand Mosque in Addis Ababa and sponsored Abyssinian Muslims on the hajj to Mecca, to reward the thirty-five thousand Muslim troops who had fought for the Italians. One hundred thousand troops crossed from Eritrea into Abyssinia on 3 October 1935, and fifty members of the League of Nations condemned Italian aggression against one of their number. Half-hearted sanctions were imposed, which excluded the trucks the Italians needed for the invasion, as well as oil without which they could not move at all. The British also declined to close the Suez Canal to Italian shipping.

The invasion of Abyssinia did not disillusion those who thought that Mussolini could be used to restrain Hitler's excesses. Three months into the campaign, the French press revealed secret talks between the British Foreign Secretary Samuel Hoare and his French opposite number Laval, to agree on a scheme devised by the Foreign Office's Robert Vansittart, which offered Mussolini two-thirds of Abyssinia, while leaving Haile Selassie with a rump state and a corridor to the sea. These terms, devised without consulting the Abyssinians, were to be backed up with petroleum sanctions if Italy refused them. Fortuitously for Mussolini, Laval and Hoare were compelled to resign when details of the scheme became public. Vansittart fulminated against the self-indulgent moralism that had scuppered his attempt to keep the two European dictators apart.

Mussolini decided to accelerate the Italian campaign by replacing the over-cautious local commander with General Pietro Badoglio, who in 1922 had wanted to deploy the Italian army against the Fascist threat to march on Rome. Badoglio was instructed to use any means to destroy Abyssinian resistance, including large stockpiles of chemical weapons that had been shipped, via the Suez Canal, to Eritrea and Somaliland. Three types of chemical weapon were used: yperite, arsine and phosgene gas, all illegal under the 1925 Geneva Protocols. They were delivered in artillery shells, or dropped as bombs, or sprayed from aircraft. They either seeped beneath the skin to cause internal lesions or suffocated the respiratory systems. They contaminated the ground, plants, lakes, rivers and livestock. An Abyssinian leader, Ras Imru, reported that:

> On the morning of 23 December … we saw several enemy planes appear. We were not unduly alarmed as by this time we were used to being bombed. On this particular morning, however, the enemy dropped strange containers that burst open almost as soon as they hit the ground or the water, releasing pools of colourless liquid. I hardly had time to ask myself what could be happening before a hundred or so of my men who had been splashed with the mysterious fluid began to scream in agony as blisters broke out on their bare feet, their hands, their faces. Some who rushed to the river and took great gulps of water to cool their fevered lips, fell contorted on the banks and writhed in agony that lasted for hours until they died. Among the victims were a few peasants who had come to water their cattle and a number of people who lived in nearby villages. My chiefs surrounded me, asking wildly what they should do, but I was completely stunned. I didn't know what to tell them. I didn't know how to fight this terrible rain that burned and killed.[11]

In justification, Italian propagandists broadcast stories of atrocities committed against Italian prisoners. These exaggerated instances of crucifixion and emasculation, as well as the use of dum-dum bullets (named after the arsenal in British India where they were first developed) and the misuse of Red Cross symbols to camouflage arms dumps and troop concentrations. Thus empowered, the Italians bombed Red Cross facilities with relative impunity, killing a number of international aid workers.[12] Within seven months, the Italians proclaimed the conquest of Abyssinia, but in reality local resistance went on for many expensive years. It also proved remarkably difficult to lure Italian peasants as colonists, and the conquered kingdom cost much more to maintain than it ever produced. Ten million Italians volunteered their wedding rings to make up for the gold bullion draining away to keep a huge army in the wastes of Abyssinia.

Mussolini then compounded the problem through his active support of the Nationalist side in Spain's Civil War. He had multiple reasons for doing so, which went beyond Hitler's more straightforward approach of exchanging support for strategic raw materials. To Mussolini, a Nationalist victory was ideologically preferable to the elected government, which was dominated by Socialists – although he made no great efforts to bolster the Fascist elements in the Nationalist coalition. A sympathetic Nationalist Spain would ensure Mussolini's navy free passage through the Straits separating Gibraltar from Spanish Morocco. Finally, at a time when Britain and Germany were exploring a durable rapprochement, Italian (and German) aid to the Nationalists would wreck the Anglo-French-inspired non-intervention framework, and thereby further polarise the powers into hostile ideological camps. This would leave Italy, so Mussolini believed, considerable room for profitable manoeuvre.

German and Italian military assistance was co-ordinated through so called advisers based in Spain. Germany's Condor Legion acquired a reputation for ruthlessness after it bombed the historic Basque capital of Guernica, killing two or three hundred people. Thanks to Pablo Picasso's great chiaroscuro painting of the atrocity, it has received more notice than Italian air raids on Barcelona in March 1937, which killed a thousand people and left two thousand more injured.[13] The Italians made a more substantial contribution than the Germans, sending not only aircraft, but also ships and fifty thousand Fascist militia and regular army troops posing as volunteers. After the Italians had been humiliated in the Battle of Guadalajara that March, Mussolini directed his submarines to wage what amounted to a campaign of piracy against all shipping in Spanish waters, regardless of what flag they sailed under. Deniability could be preserved only by abandoning the survivors of torpedoed ships to their fate.

Italy's multiple breaches of international law, whether in Abyssinia or Spain, and their condemnation by the western powers, convinced Mussolini that humanitarian arguments were being used hypocritically to inhibit the legitimate rise of the virile nations of Italy and Germany. Through a 'gentlemen's [sic] agreement', Italy recognised Germany's right to dictate Austrian foreign policy, and Germany recognised Italy's conquest of Abyssinia. High-level contacts between Germany and Italy quickened even as Hitler despatched Joachim von Ribbentrop as ambassador to London, seeking to draw Britain into the alliance with Germany that Hitler wanted. While there was an obvious ideological congruity between the two dictators, cold-blooded calculations prevailed on both sides. Hitler needed Mussolini's Mediterranean antics to distract Britain and France from his ambitions in central Europe, where Versailles had helpfully created a patchwork of weak states, while Mussolini needed Germany to complicate central Europe so that they would tolerate his activities in the Mediterranean.

In October 1936 the two leaders embarked on a series of agreements which came to be known as the Rome–Berlin Axis, after a speech Mussolini delivered on 1 November in which he spoke of Germany and Italy as 'an axis around which all European states, animated by a desire for collaboration and peace, can revolve'. He was not the first to coin the term, but his use of it has ensured its future employ to describe all such sinister affinities. The Italian armed forces adopted a version of the German goose-step, which Mussolini claimed was really the *passo Romano*, and the regime augmented racial legislation, pioneered in Abyssinia, with measures against Italy's tiny Jewish minority, despite the fact that a third of Italian adult Jews, as members of the Italian bourgeoisie, were themselves enthusiastic Fascists.

The emergence of an anti-democratic bloc was not restricted to Europe, for in November 1937 Italy joined the Anti-Comintern Pact, concluded a year earlier by Germany and Japan and directed against the Communist International. Anything that disrupted the status quo was good, like a blast of cold air into a torpid room. The Italian regime more explicitly hoped that Japan would dissipate and neutralise the global strength of Britain's navy, to which end Italian propagandists hastened to Tokyo to explain the Fascist regime and to counter the Japanese elite's Anglophilia, while Foreign Minister Count Ciano whetted Japan's interest in negotiations by supplying it with stolen plans for Britain's Far Eastern bastion of Singapore.

In December 1937, the same month when Germany and Italy formally switched their support from the Chinese Nationalists to the Japanese, Italy belatedly followed Germany's 1933 withdrawal from the League of Nations. Although these were not military alliances, they did represent the further self-definition, and self-isolation, of a general ideological camp that held the democracies in contempt, acknowledged no rules, other than those of the jungle, and had a track record of aggression that included egregious breaches of international law.

Japan

II RISING SUN

The twenty-five-year-old Prince Hirohito succeeded to the Japanese imperial throne in the early hours of 25 December 1925. Born to rule and
comprehensively educated for the role, in the previous six years Hirohito
had acted as regent owing to his father Taisho's dementia. The malevolent
associated Taisho's neurological degeneration with Japan's parallel transformation into a democratic, modern society and a respected member of
the international order in East Asia. After Taisho's death, the young
Emperor took possession of the three sacred regalia, a sword, jewelled
necklace and mirror, signifying courage, benevolence and wisdom. Days
later he adopted the era-signifying name of Showa (meaning 'illustrious
peace'). Would that it had been auspicious.

Three years later, in November 1928, over US$7 million was spent trans-
forming this slight, stooped enthusiast of bridge, golf and marine biology into the living god of Shinto mythology, the statist version of
Buddhism that had been assiduously propagated after the mid-nine-
teenth-century Meiji Restoration. The emperor was not like the old
European monarchs who ruled by divine right, but a god who had
assumed human form within the privileged and pure local cosmos of
Japan. Hirohito himself was more enamoured of the British constitutional
monarchy of George V, which he had witnessed on a European tour. But
in Kyoto he dutifully lay down in a foetal position, to merge mystically
with the sun goddess Amaterasu Omikami, the mythical progenitor of
the Japanese imperial line. Dutifully, because from the age of twenty the
rationalist Hirohito had expressed scepticism about whether he or his
ancestors were living deities; he suppressed these youthful doubts in the
interests of what Plato called a noble lie.

Likewise, although educated Japanese knew about theories of evolution, they also subscribed to the idea of the divine origin of the Yamato
race. The divine emperor was the focus of the *kokutai*, the cardinal principles which bound Japan's state and society together, and which, because
the Japanese were the most morally pure and selfless people on earth,
elevated them above other, lesser races. A little bit of that imperial divinity was invested in them all by virtue of the devotion and loyalty they
showed to the emperor. Hirohito was also the armed forces' commander-
in-chief, a role that complicated his relations with civilian politicians.
Although a mass conscript army had been created to obliterate endemic

local warlordism in the nineteenth century, paradoxically the military was suffused from top to bottom with old-fashioned samurai values.[14]

A taciturn man who employed his high-pitched voice sparingly, Hirohito was far removed from the populist demagogues coming into their own in post-war Europe. Mussolini and Hitler were mob orators, who relied on the illusion of speaking for the inner spirit of their mass audiences; by contrast, Hirohito never spoke to his own subjects, who were expected to cast down their eyes when he passed, even when he was travelling by car or train. Fastidious rituals, impeccable taste and exquisitely crafted poetry contrasted with the odour of sweat that clung to the vulgar European dictators.

In some respects, imperial Japan better resembled the Germany of Wilhelm II rather than Hitler, in so far as it enjoyed the rule of law and had a functioning Diet or parliament. On the other hand, like the Nazis, the Japanese regime glorified war and the rural past, even though the military strength of both societies was a reflection of their modern, industrial economies. Both also entertained myths of racial purity, although they applied their racism to each other. Even when they were allied, the Japanese still saw the Germans as *gaijin*, while Hitler and his associates subscribed to every cliché about 'little yellow men'. Both powers had barged their way on to the big stage with stunning military victories that defined national identity. Imperial Germany fought three very successful wars between 1862 and 1871, and held off the Triple Entente of Britain, France and Russia until 1918; Japan defeated China in 1894–5 and Russia in 1904–5, and made stunning gains in northern China in 1931–2 and 1937–8. Both societies had a long history of inordinate respect for martial virtues and had overcome internal divisions by revolutions from above.

In the Japanese case, there was an aristocratic House of Peers and a Diet elected by universal male suffrage after 1925, although a tiny group of elder statesmen, the Genro, advised the emperor on who should be prime minister, of whom there were nine between 1937 and 1945, to co-ordinate the competing bureaucratic, business, army and navy elite factions. These elites were in turn bound by complex aristocratic clan structures and had to pay lip-service to public opinion. The army was based on the Prussian model (a spell in Germany was *de rigueur* for young officers), while the more prestigious navy copied the British. Generally speaking, in these years Japan was open to Western influences and a dedicated player in the complex diplomacy of East Asia and the Pacific. But there were also accumulated resentments. During the Great War, Japan had learned that conflict paid as it picked off German colonies, only to discover afterwards the temporary nature of the indulgence it had been shown by Germany's European enemies.

Thereafter the Japanese were treated with condescension (and sometimes hostility) by Westerners, who sought to deny this 'Asian Prussia' the hemispherical hegemony that the US claimed for itself in the Americas. The greatest provocation was that the West seemed determined to frustrate Japan's ambitions in what the Japanese regarded as the vast failed state of China, wracked by endemic warlordism. The Japanese attitude towards mainland China was marked by a cultural inferiority cum racial superiority complex, vaguely reminiscent of how the English used to view the French. The Chinese may have had a finer culture, but they were lacking in martial spirit.[15] All of these Japanese sentiments had both domestic and foreign implications at a time marked by economic troubles, labour unrest, rapid urbanisation and the emergence of socialism and female emancipation in a historically hierarchical and patriarchal society.[16]

Modernity, invariably associated with foreign influences, was always going to unsettle a deeply conservative rural society, however much it might have benefited from imported industrial technology. An angrily righteous, reactionary right, generously represented in the officer corps, railed against every manifestation of Westernised decadence and Western dominance, and against the wealthy political and business elites that it regarded as corrupt and unpatriotic. The Imperial Way sect within the officer corps believed that their incorruptible selves should replace the political parties and the Emperor's self-interested advisers. Their worldview had other moralising elements focused on Japanese society as a whole. These austere army officers – they were paid little more than were clerks in Japan's corporate combines – viewed with horror the 'eroticism, grotesquery and nonsense' that gained ground in Japan during the 1920s and 1930s. These social evils were symbolised by the short-skirted and bobbed *modarn-garu* or *mogu* (flapper) and her male *moba*, with whom the girls held hands and kissed in public.[17]

Rightist ideologues such as Kita Ikki combined imperial ultra-loyalism with militarism and state socialism. Kita propagated the need for an overseas empire beyond Formosa, Korea and the toehold Japan had secured in southern Manchuria in north-eastern China as a solution to a future population crisis he estimated at 250 million. He was executed by the secret police in the wake of a failed coup in 1937. Rich in coal and other resources, Manchuria was a big, bleak place, roughly the size of France and Germany combined. Many Japanese nationalists saw it as the answer to chronic rural overpopulation in the Japanese home islands. Instead of a mass Fascist-style party, hundreds of secret societies proliferated with sinister names like the Blood Pledge League. Their anger mounted when the Depression forced cutbacks in Japan's military budget, an anger fed by demeaning US (and Australian) immigration restrictions against Asians in general, which the Japanese bitterly resented. If the white nations were not going to allow Japanese immigration, then they could hardly object if the Japanese 'emigrated' to China. Lastly, the Depression simultaneously hit the agricultural sector, from which the army drew most of its recruits, while diminishing the great powers' ability to react to unilateral Japanese action in China, which the army saw as the solution to Japan's economic plight.[18]

One outpost of radical right sentiment was among the officers of the Kwantung Army stationed in Manchuria, who felt they were the living executors of the eighty thousand men who had perished fighting the Russians in Manchuria in 1904–5. They were garrisoned in a small coastal enclave to protect Japanese commercial interests and a six-hundred-mile railway line that stretched north into the interior. It was the sort of remote, lonely location where wild schemes incubated. The Kwantung soldiers sensed an opportunity in the simultaneous breakdown of international co-operation over China and that country's descent into chaos. They deemed it necessary to act in the window of opportunity before the Nationalist forces grew too powerful and while the great powers were turned inward on their own economic problems.

The Chinese resisted all attempts by the increasing number of Japanese and their subject Koreans settled in Manchuria to exploit the area's economic resources in an organised way. Irritation at Chinese attempts to frustrate Japanese domination mounted. In the summer of 1928, Kwantung officers blew up a train conveying a powerful Chinese warlord. The Japanese scattered the corpses of some Chinese prisoners around the scene to misattribute authorship of the assassination, a tactic the Nazis would subsequently employ in Poland. Although this plot failed to achieve its wider goals, Emperor Hirohito played a worrying part in covering up what amounted to an act of unilateral aggression by insubordinate army officers in a remote outpost.

Further clashes in which the Chinese were alleged to have harassed Koreans and Japanese reignited tension a couple of years later. In September 1931, two senior members of the Kwantung Army, Colonel Itagaki and Lieutenant Colonel Ishiwara, caused small explosions at a major junction on the southern Manchurian railway, near a Chinese military base at Mukden (or Shenyang). Its innocent denizens were falsely blamed for the incident. The Japanese government sent an intelligence officer to rein in the army, but he managed to forget his mission in the course of extended visits to a restaurant and a geisha house in the company of one of the main plotters. The Kwantung Army pressed ahead with its rampage, going on to bomb and occupy the industrial centre of Chinchow. The Emperor explicitly sanctioned these acts of military insubordination, which also involved the despatch of reinforcements from Korea, even though the plotters had an obvious domestic agenda. The agenda was: 'when we return to the homeland this time we shall carry out a coup d'état and do away with the party political system of government. Then we shall establish a nation of National Socialism with the Emperor as the centre. We shall abolish capitalists like Mitsui and Mitsubishi and carry out an even distribution of wealth. We are determined to do so.'

Encouraged by the mass media, the Japanese public were swept by war fever. Especially popular were the three Kwantung Army troopers who blew themselves up to destroy a strategically crucial section of barbed wire, although their officers may simply have equipped them with inadequate lengths of fuse. Six films were made about this incident, which was also fêted in innumerable 'three human bombs' songs. The deceased men also adorned 'human bomb' brands of sake and bean-paste sweets.[19] Partly because Japanese fatalities in Manchuria were very low, there was much scope to dwell on individual acts of heroism, as well as on the alleged cowardliness of the Chinese. Manchurian Incident _Bidan_, or epic tales of heroism involving Mukden, lauded men like Commander Koga as exemplars of bushido, the way of the samurai warrior. Koga led his men into a series of ever more suicidal actions, many of them designed to rescue the imperial flag from capture by the Chinese, whom he slaughtered in droves. The sacrifices of humble women on the rural home front were the female analogue of these stirring tales of the Japanese officer class.

Next, in 1932, the Japanese organised a sideshow to distract outraged Chinese attention from their own activities in the north. They employed Chinese criminal gangs to attack five Japanese Buddhist monks in Shanghai, to justify landing Marines in China's largest city. When Chinese forces resisted, the Japanese sent in bombers and nearly fifty thousand reinforcements. On one day alone, they dropped 2,500 bombs, a spectacle witnessed by the city's large number of Western residents. After the Chinese forces withdrew, the Japanese went berserk, destroying property and bayoneting captives at a racecourse. Five hundred thousand Chinese temporarily fled the city, which, after international mediation, was demilitarised when the Japanese withdrew. While world attention was distracted by the plight of Shanghai, the Japanese installed Puyi, the last Qing emperor of China, as ruler of what they dubbed Manchukuo, although one American suggested it should have been called Japanchukuo.

Many ordinary Japanese thought that the 'Manchurian treasure house' was vital to Japan itself, for fashionable imperatives of economic self-sufficiency underlay the rhetoric about blood spilled in earlier wars. Manchukuo joined the yen bloc and received enormous Japanese inward investment, which went into a burgeoning military–industrial complex. During the 1930s more expansive ambitions were popularised by such organisations as the Great Asia Association, founded in early 1933. Using the deceptive language of restoring harmony, this envisaged a much larger Japanese-dominated Asian bloc in which raw materials imported from liberated European colonies would be turned into manufactured goods exported by the Japanese metropolis. While the army was principally concerned with China and the Russian threat from Mongolia, the imperial navy had long been obsessed with its fuel supplies. This problem led the navy to view the US as the primary potential opponent in the wider Pacific region.[20]

The army's unilateral action in Manchuria enabled its leaders to tilt the balance in Japanese domestic affairs away from civilian political parties. In the 1930s, governing was a risky affair. Acts of terrorism by radical young officers and their ultra-nationalist civilian admirers were a useful tool in this process, for the army and navy leaders could claim that only they could keep these hotheads in check. Assassinations and attempted coups, in which the Blood Pledge League and the more benign-sounding Cherry Blossom Society were leading players, enabled the military to marginalise the political party presence within successive cabinets. Threats of resignation by the service ministers were used to deconstruct cabinets they did not like. From May 1932 onwards, civilian politicians were relegated to minor roles when senior military figures installed an admiral as prime minister in a cabinet that contained only five representatives of the parties, against ten senior officers and bureaucrats. Thanks to a devaluation of the yen, exports boomed and successive governments increased military spending until it was twelve times higher in 1938 than in 1931.[21]

Ineffectual condemnation by the League of Nations of Japan's aggression in China only heightened Japanese outrage at what it saw as foreign arrogance. Common images included that of a samurai warrior severing the restrictive ball and chain of the League of Nations, much as the Germans railed against the shackles of Versailles. Limp League condemnations of Japanese actions, and the possibility of sanctions, were portrayed as acts of white aggression, permitting the Japanese to pose as racial victims. This contributed to Japanese self-isolation, with a corresponding urge to break out through further acts of defiant violence. Interestingly, even Hitler's Germany condemned the Japanese invasion of Manchuria and, as late as 1936, General Walter von Reichenau was in China negotiating a US$100 million barter arrangement based on the exchange of raw materials for arms, iron and steel.[22]

Japan left the League of Nations in March 1933 rather than bow to what was piously called the 'organised moral opinion of the world'. The Kwantung Army struck southwards in May, first into the province of Jehol between Manchukuo and the Great Wall of China, and then further south towards Beijing. As part of his strategy of appeasing the Japanese in order to fight the Chinese Communists, Generalissimo Chiang Kai-shek agreed to the Tanggu Truce, a deal whereby Beijing would not be attacked in return for the Chinese demilitarisation of a huge area containing six million inhabitants. Chinese officials concluded the truce with the guns of two Japanese destroyers trained on the building where they stood.

Four years later, in July 1937, Japanese forces took advantage of a further incident with the Chinese to launch a full-scale punitive invasion of north-western China. The use of the euphemistic term 'incident' was deliberate, because, by not admitting it was a war, the Japanese hoped that the US would continue to supply Japan with oil. In the eyes of the Japanese, they were entitled to occupy and rule any bits of China they managed to detach. The Emperor himself resolved that 'Along with its present duties, the China Garrison Army shall chastise Chink forces in the Peking–Tientsin area and pacify strategic points.' The absence of any clear national authority in China was adduced to absolve the Japanese from observing the laws of war. On 5 August, an under-secretary in the Army Ministry issued a decree saying: 'It is inappropriate to act strictly in accordance with various stipulations in "Treaties and Practices Governing Land Warfare and Other Laws of War".' The decree soon bore evil fruit.[23]

Several hundred thousand Japanese troops were moved to China in pursuit of an ill-defined quest for a knock-out blow, knowing they were not bound by the rules of war. Many of them were reservists in their thirties and early forties, who had long lost the habit of military discipline,

Killing: obey officers, the
Nanking
Servants of emperor

which in the Japanese army invariably took the form of slaps in the face. By late October, the Japanese had bombed and shelled Shanghai into surrender. Its defenders and fearful civilians fled to the Nationalist capital of Nanking, about 180 miles along the Yangtze, pursued by Japanese soldiers who, without proper logistical support or sufficient military police, provisioned themselves from the despised civilian population. They started killing civilians long before they reached Nanking. The day before the city fell, Japanese pilots strafed a US gunboat called the *Panay*, which was being loaded with American diplomats and residents for evacuation down the Yangtze to Shanghai. A day later, Japanese troops entered Nanking after the opium-addicted Chinese commander had ordered his troops to vacate the city, with himself the first to leave, through suburbs he ordered to be set on fire. There were lantern parades in Tokyo when the news of the fall of China's capital arrived. Bereft of leaders, Chinese troops tried to surrender, sometimes after hastily exchanging their uniforms for ill-assorted civilian garb.

Once inside the city, the Japanese disregarded any distinctions between combatants, civilians and prisoners of war (which they rarely took anyway) and proceeded to indulge in an extended orgy of violence. For three months they were allowed to burn, murder, pillage and rape in Nanking and its outlying villages. Looting was the most explicable crime, since the peasant soldiers of the Japanese army were poor and wanted things to send back home, and the seventeen military policemen in the city were hardly in a position to stop it. The killing is less easy to understand. Although Japanese soldiers had a sense of right and wrong, there was no transcendental moral code to offset the absolute dictates of officers, who in turn were the unquestioning servants of the Emperor. If they said kill, you killed. On one night alone some seventeen thousand men and boys were slaughtered to ensure that a military parade attended by Hirohito's fifty-year-old uncle, Prince Asaka, would pass off without incident. Massed Japanese troops shouted 'Banzai' (meaning ten thousand years) in the Prince's honour outside the former Kuomintang nationalist HQ. Chinese were killed in every conceivable manner, including being crucified, savaged by dogs, bayoneted to save ammunition or beheaded. Officers competed to see who could kill the largest numbers before their swords became too blunt.

Lapidary Japanese reports said that such and such a unit had 'disposed of' thousands of prisoners, failing to note that they were often tied up with telegraph wire in batches of fifty, to make it easier to bayonet, burn or shoot them. Racism towards the 'Chinks' was compounded by the view that their surrender had been absolutely dishonourable. Also Japan's peasant soldiers were themselves so routinely abused by their officers and NCOs that the extreme violence may have been like the venting of accumulated frustrations.[24] Moreover, a society which treated women as third-class citizens was unlikely to have any regard for women from inferior races, who were there to be abused, especially if the Japanese were drunk, which they often were. On one night alone, approximately a thousand women, of all ages, were gang-raped by Japanese soldiers and then killed with no more emotion than one would bring to despatching farm animals. This practice was halted only by the wholesale importation of prostitute 'comfort women', mainly from Korea. Chinese and Japanese statistics for the victims of this massacre range from two to over three hundred thousand, although a more recent estimate is in the region of one hundred thousand or fewer.[25]

Japanese diplomats protested to Tokyo, concerned about the international condemnation the massacre had provoked, and even Germany expressed concern about the 'Hunnic storm' that the 'yellow peril' had unleashed.[26] But orders from the War Ministry and from the commander-in-chief, General Iwane Mutsui, made not the slightest impression on the middle and junior officers in Nanking. Shamefully, Mutsui and eighty of his staff officers were themselves transferred back to Tokyo for having tried to stop the genocide.

In the wake of these conquests, the Japanese decided on regime change in China by unilaterally refusing to recognise the government of Chiang Kai-shek, which had moved to Hankow. This precluded an early resolution of the Chinese–Japanese war. In a further sign that the conflict was about to be internationalised, the British and Americans commenced secret naval staff talks. Abandoning long-standing German assistance to the Chinese Nationalists, Hitler recognised Manchukuo in 1938.

Germany and Japan had been drawing closer since 25 November 1936, when they had agreed the Anti-Comintern Pact, although they had nothing to fear from domestic Communist subversion, and in the end the German Foreign Minister Konstantin von Neurath forgot to sign it. The agreement was the brainchild of Ribbentrop and his friend Lieutenant Colonel Hiroshi Oshima, the military attaché in Berlin who had developed open admiration for Nazism long before he became Tokyo's ambassador to Germany. As Germany abandoned its support for China, recalling military advisers and ending arms shipments, so Japan began to revise its view of Germany, especially in the wake of the *Anschluss* and the 1938–9 Czechoslovak crisis.

Yet Japan refused to join the May 1939 Italo–German Pact of Steel and was appalled by that August's Molotov–Ribbentrop Pact reconciling Germany and Russia, which it learned about only at the eleventh hour. Although Japan subsequently joined Germany and Italy in the Tripartite Alliance in September 1940, it was an alliance with few practical consequences, and in April 1941 it was Tokyo's turn to shock the Germans when it concluded a neutrality pact with the Soviet Union. This effectively signalled that Japanese sights were fixed southwards, towards the colonies of the European nations conquered by Hitler, whose helplessness made them tempting targets, despite the risk of war with the US. Like Germany and Italy, Japan acted according to its own national interests – a stance fully reflected in the virtual absence of military co-ordination between Germany and Japan during the Second World War.[27]

III THE RESTLESS REICH

Like the Italian Fascists and Japanese militarists, the German National Socialists regarded war as a release from what they called the 'lingering disease of peace', a peculiarly pathological view of the condition most human beings aspire to. They would have agreed with the great Prussian historian Heinrich von Treitschke, who claimed that war was morally sublime. It was where the enthusiastic hurrahs of patriotic boys were transformed into the steely determination of men – for Hitler's own reminiscences of the trenches, dictated nearly a decade after the event, abounded with literary clichés, even if they were much the same as those used by the future long-serving British Foreign Secretary and, briefly and disastrously, post-war Prime Minister Anthony Eden. Hitler had served as a runner, clattering along the slippery duckboards of the Western Front before being blinded in an Allied gas attack and invalided to a Pomeranian hospital.

In that eastern backwater, Hitler experienced the emotional deflation of Germany's capitulation, the primordial catastrophe that shaped his vengeful destiny. It was more than a defeat for, in his view, the collapse had been brought about by internal subversion. In the minds of many cultural pessimists, this was the culmination of an erosion of values characteristic of the modern industrial urban era in general.[28] But this collapse was simultaneously an opportunity to inaugurate a new era in which the laws of nature would reign supreme, and collective considerations would supersede the bounds of custom, Church and family. Ideology and morality, the private and the political, were to be subsumed into a single imperative based on the community, whose core values were ethnically specific and expressed through such atavistic notions as 'healthy popular instinct'. This would replace the Judaeo-Christian concept of conscience, and there would be no more subversion based on the thinking of the Jews Marx, Freud and Einstein. To make this seem less revolutionary, traditional values like bravery, diligence, duty, honour, loyalty, obedience, sacrifice and soldierly fortitude were enlisted to support it.

The mythologised legacy of Prussia was used to conjure up an ideal of state building. In *Mein Kampf*, Hitler wrote: 'Prussia, in particular, demonstrates with marvellous sharpness that ideal virtues alone, not material qualities, make possible the formation of a state ... The material interests of man can always thrive best as long as they remain in the shadow of heroic virtues ... Prussia, the germ cell of the Reich, came into being through resplendent heroism and not through financial operations or commercial deals, and the Reich itself in turn was only the glorious reward of aggressive political leadership and the death-defying courage of its soldiers.'[29] Starting with the Day of Potsdam on 21 March 1933, Hitler would have himself depicted as the lineal successor of Frederick the Great and Bismarck, neither of whom would have warmed, one strongly suspects, to the vulgar little Austrian corporal.[30]

All these appeals to traditional values and historical example were the tasty sauce that disguised the smell of the rancid meat beneath.[31] The Treaty of Versailles had imposed on Germany constraints that patriotic Germans and nationalist fanatics like Hitler regarded as tantamount to the degradations of a colony. This gained a nasty racist edge when the French deployed 'black' colonial troops in the Rhineland to break local resistance, although most were North African Arabs and Vietnamese. Loyalty became the supreme honour of the SS man, as his belt buckle proclaimed. A term like shame could also be given specific accents so that it became race shame or, less literally in English, race defilement (*Rassenschande*), that is the pollution of a superior race through sexual congress with another, and in particular the Jewish other. This was also reflected in a reversion to public punishment, as race-defilers were forced to go about with placards round their necks, or were denounced on the poster columns of the vile Nazi magazine *Der Stürmer*. Soldierly virtue was perverted into the fanatical belligerence of SS 'political soldiers', who became 'soldiers of destruction', a transformation of values that leached into the regular army and police.[32] Finally, although Nazism sought to transcend both utilitarianism and what was often referred to as the 'swindle' of humanitarianism, it was responsible for the crassest utilitarian calculations about the social cost of human life, which gave rise to sterilising or murdering people according to a eugenic calculus.[33]

Sharp-eyed officers saw some use in the corporal, who otherwise resembled a lost dog in the aftermath of the Great War. Fluency with spoken words, all vehemently expressed, ensured that Hitler was never psychologically demobilised, as he wrapped the war's ghosts around him like a metaphorical cloak. His first job was to give political talks to decontaminate restive soldiers who were turning to radical socialism. The vital experience of discovering his unique demagogic voice smoothed his path into extreme nationalist politics, where previously a crankily professorial type of speaker had addressed meetings in a style more appropriate to academic seminars.[34] After resolving a few uncertainties regarding desirable alliances, by the early 1920s Hitler had decided that Germany needed *Lebensraum*, in the east, that is land and material resources to support a dynamic, racially homogeneous population fitted for the fight for survival against other races. The war confirmed a bleak outlook that had already been formed on the mean streets of Habsburg Vienna, notably that a conscience or guilt were impediments to seeing the underlying processes of existence starkly.[35] Hitler's desire to conform human existence to the laws of nature, cruelly conceived, had inevitable ethical implications:

No one can doubt that this world will someday be exposed to the severest struggles for the existence of mankind. In the end, only the urge for self-preservation can conquer. Beneath it so-called humanity, the expression of the mixture of stupidity, cowardice, and know-it-all conceit, will melt like snow in the March sun. Mankind has grown great in eternal struggle, and only in eternal peace does it perish.[36]

Some call the basic axioms that emerged a worldview, but that probably over-dignifies a mind littered with crudely understood aspects of Darwin or Nietzsche, refracted through the prism of the violent subjective prejudices of a personality in arrested adolescence. Underlying the whole was what contemporaries called 'active nihilism'. Central to his outlook was the quest for space in which the Aryan-German race would thrive. That would inevitably entail war without end, as other powers were hardly likely to be passive spectators. Besides, if he simultaneously introduced philo-progenerative policies, state-subsidised attempts to boost the birth rate, then these additional, space-deprived Aryan-Germans would surely require more territory, necessitating further wars. A policy based on such racial demographics would never be satisfied merely by restoring the 1914 status quo ante, as most German conservative nationalists desired.[37]

In another break with the old right, Hitler abandoned the Wilhelmine quest for places in the sun, where he felt the white man would atrophy. Traditional imperialism only engendered conflicts with the British, with whom Hitler sought an amicable division of the global spoils. Similarly, he sacrificed the Tyrolean Germans to win Italy as an ally in the Mediterranean. He also categorically rejected another episodic gambit of the right under the 1918–33 democratic Weimar Republic, namely that the two pariah states of Germany and Russia should club together at the expense of Poland, arguing that a tree does not ally itself with the mistle-toe that will kill it.[38] For Hitler was certain that expansion must be towards the wider 'German East', conquered and settled by Germans in the Middle Ages, before the space was engulfed by a Slavic flood.

A simulacrum of what Hitler desired had briefly arisen in the wake of the 1917 Russo–German Treaty of Brest-Litovsk, but this had fallen victim to imperial Germany's supposedly mysterious collapse in 1918.[39] A mystery, that is, until one introduces what Hitler regarded as a supra-national force more powerful than any single state: international Jewry. The Jew, as Hitler invariably had it, was the shape-shifting force behind every deleterious development imaginable, from high finance via Bolshevism to prostitu-tion and white slavery. Although Hitler was haunted by fears of bodily fluids, blood, miscegenation and putrefaction, combating the Jew as cosmic maggot was a noble matter of 'doing the Lord's work', for the Führer had a growing sense of providential mission that compensated for the nullity of his existence.

The solutions he envisaged were correspondingly surgical. In April 1920 he announced his 'inexorable resolve to strike the evil at its root and exter-minate it root and branch', adding a year later, 'one prevents the Jewish corruption of our people, if necessary by confining its instigators to concentration camps'. This was the core of his domestic agenda, defined by the need for a dictatorship to ensure that Germany's racially determined wartime collapse of morale was never repeated. But the Jews had also taken over Russia, displacing the thin Germanic ruling classes. Although Hitler held the Jews responsible for the murderous regime of terror by Lenin's Bolsheviks, he also thought 'this scum of humanity' had no ability to organise the predominantly Slav population to resist Germany's drive towards a continental empire.[40]

While as a full vicious ensemble these manias were extreme and marginal throughout most of the 1920s, elements of them were commonplace among nationalistically minded Germans, who increasingly rejected the republican system. The Weimar Republic's fragile stability was destroyed by worsening economic conditions, which exposed irreconcilable differences of outlook between the major parties and the interests they represented over how to deal with them. While successive governments floundered, the predominantly Protestant middle classes lurched to the right, collapsing both liberal parties, as well as the plethora of single-issue protest parties that had multiplied in the wake of the hyperinflation crisis of the early 1920s. Nazi electoral support rose as the economic crisis deepened, reaching 18 per cent of the vote in September 1930 and 37 per cent in July 1932. Fear of social demotion was as potent as, indeed perhaps more potent than, having hit rock bottom in the soup kitchens and dole queues.

By now the Nazis' use of political violence had reached its apogee, with eighteen dead and sixty-eight wounded following a clash known as Bloody Sunday between Nazis and Communists in Hamburg-Altona.[41] Communist violence enabled the Nazis to pose as defenders of public order against a firebrand-bearing Bolshevik menace, even though their own muscular cadres in the brown-shirted SA relished a brawl. They also publicly rhapsodised about 'Jewish blood spurting from a knife-wound' or shouted 'Germany awake! Let Jewry croak!' Although the Nazis played the democratic electoral game, their attitude towards even the most heinous activities was symbolised by Hitler's vow to pardon five SA stormtroopers who, in August 1932, were convicted of kicking a Communist miner to death in front of his mother in the Silesian town of Potempa. After the failure of successive establishment figures to solve the deepening economic and political crises, Germany's elites engineered Hitler's ascent to the chancellorship, confident that they could contain him and the revolutionary forces he represented – just as their peers in Italy had believed a decade earlier.

The Nazis' final electoral surge reflected their success in depicting their movement as a natural force, uniquely capable of overcoming Germany's bitter domestic divisions as the necessary prelude to righting its humiliating international position. A fringe party, led by a naturalised foreigner, managed the feat of making the Republic itself seem alien, artificial, corrupt and decadent, the tool of the country's enemies, who in their latest scheme, the 1929 Young Plan regulating reparations payments, sought to keep Germany in hock until 1988.

Something more profoundly irrational was also abroad, beneath sinister manipulations of language that in the interim has become the common coin of democratic politicians.[42] The Nazis' use of drum and trumpet, light and luridly coloured symbols resulted in what the satirist Karl Kraus called 'cerebral concussion'. A sophisticated modern society reverted to the habits of fire-worshippers, beating their tom-toms around a tribal chief who expressed dangerous thoughts they could not articulate themselves.[43] Hitler presented the Germans with transgressive temptations, which many of them grasped with eager hands.[44] Carefully constructed propaganda, and his own vaulting rhetoric, ratcheted this relationship up to a more exalted plane, as the Führer did nothing to discourage the view that he was the race-nation's Redeemer or Saviour, godlike if not actually a god like Hirohito in Japan. Several Germans testified to the miracle-working effects of his glance or touch, while significant numbers of Protestants were prepared to remodel Jesus as an honorary Aryan.[45] Hope sprang eternal as Hitler presented an autographed photograph of himself to a school for the blind, which was doubtless eager to receive it.[46]

Although the Nazi Party had its thuggish paramilitary element, it also appealed to the sober Protestant middle classes, who had experienced the catastrophe of inflation and concomitant family and social breakdown earlier in the 1920s. Though they formed the critical and decisive mass of Nazi supporters, they construed themselves as individuals of culture and ethical refinement, even as they were groomed into militarised professions. Being a lawyer or physician no longer entailed being an individual with a vocation in an autonomous, self-regulating profession; now it meant being a servant of the *völkisch* national-racial collective, with good and evil determined by whatever bolstered or subverted its interests as defined by the Führer. Mere ambition was often responsible for an auto-radicalisation that was difficult to distinguish from outward conformity.

Consider, for a moment, the young Sebastian Haffner's experiences at an 'ideological training camp' for aspirant lawyers at Jüterbog, a garrison town in Brandenburg, which he attended in the autumn of 1933. Attendance was compulsory if one sought a career in law, a grail-like ambition in such middle-class circles. Life in the camp seemed to have no rhyme or reason, beyond endless cleaning and marching, long periods of boredom interspersed with sudden cranks on the big mechanical wheel by which they were trapped. Students who belonged to the SA and wore its brown uniform set the collective tone, so that even anti-Nazis were soon marching around singing anti-Semitic songs. The aspirant lawyers found songs derived from the anti-monastic *Klostersturm* of the 1525 Peasant War especially rousing: 'We want to cry out to the Lord God in heaven, heia hoho! That we want to beat the priests to death, heia hoho!! Up and down, man for man, place the red cock on the monastery roof!'

One evening Haffner and his colleagues were listening to the radio when, as he put it, the marching band halted with boots poised in mid-air. The programme was interrupted to announce that Germany had left the League of Nations. Under a large portrait of Hitler, one by one the law students stood as the national anthem and the Nazi 'Horst Wessel Lied' were played, each extending his arm in the Hitler salute. Although he and a few others had the taste of doing something 'disgustingly degrading', Haffner duly raised his arm like the rest. He began to mouth the words that the others sang with gusto, like someone in church who does not know a hymn, 'every one a Gestapo man to the other'.[47]

The guilty pleasure of identifying prominent Jews bubbled to the surface of public life. Even so fastidious a figure as the soon-to-be-exiled author Thomas Mann found himself half approving the sudden denial of oxygen to Jewish writers and critics:

> The Jews ... it is no great misfortune after all that [exiled critic Alfred] Kerr's brazen and venomous Jewish-style imitation of Nietzsche is silenced, nor that the Jewish presence in the judiciary has been ended. Secret, disquieting, intense thoughts. Nonetheless things that are revoltingly malevolent, base, unGerman in a higher sense remain. But I am beginning to suspect that the process could well be of that kind that has two sides.

A few days later he wrote: 'I could to some extent go along with the rebellion against the Jewish element, were it not that the Jewish spirit exercises a necessary control over the German element, the withdrawal of which is dangerous: left to themselves the German element is so stupid as to lump people of my type in the same category and drive me out with the rest.'[48]

Germans who were not thugs needed things expressed in terms of moral and religious restoration after the cultural and sexual indulgences of the Republic, when the youth of Germany had allegedly gone to hell in a handcart. The absence or death of fathers in the war contributed some substance to this charge, as did the well-known artistic excesses of the capital. Tedious low-grade provocation, sometimes involving homosexuality or transvestism, rebounded on its authors, for whom it was truly 'Goodbye to Berlin', the title of a contemporary novel by the camp English author Christopher Isherwood. In Hitler's first national broadcast after assuming the chancellorship, he declared:

> The National Government will therefore regard its first and foremost duty to re-establish the unity and spirit and will of our *Volk*. It will preserve and defend the foundations upon which the power of our nation rests. It will extend its strong, protecting hand over Christianity as the basis of our entire morality, and the family as the germ cell of the body of our *Volk* and State ... It will establish reverence for our great past and pride in our old traditions as the basis for the education of our German youth. Thus it will declare merciless war against the spiritual, political and cultural nihilism. Germany must not and will not drown in anarchistic Communism.[49]

Nazi Germany's opening foreign-policy gambits emphasised legitimate national grievances such as the abused human rights of several ethnic German exclaves and a continued desire for international peace. They could do little else, given the country's enforced lack of armaments and such strategic vulnerabilities as the demilitarisation of the Rhineland under articles 42 and 43 of the Versailles Treaty. Hitler was not inclined to continue in the tradition of the Republic's dogged attempts to renegotiate Versailles. He made this clear by his approach to the Geneva Disarmament Conference, ongoing when he came to power and the most neuralgic issue since the 1932 resolution of reparations by the American Young Plan. In May 1933, Hitler airily proclaimed that 'We view the European nations as a given fact' and that he 'had no desire to turn French or Poles into Germans'. But then he chronicled the miseries inflicted on Germany since Versailles, claiming that there had been 224,000 suicides in the years 1918–33, and preposterously attributing all of them to national humiliation. Turning to the issue that concerned him, he argued that either the other powers should disarm, as they were obliged to do under the League of Nations Covenant, or Germany should be allowed to rearm, to redress the glaring anomaly. 'The German government will reject no ban on arms as being too drastic, if it is likewise applied to other nations,' he said. But, he warned, should the other powers seek to coerce Germany with threats of sanctions or talk of war, then he would have no hesitation in withdrawing from the League of Nations. This was his firm intention anyway, but it played well in formerly imperial Prussian Potsdam to wrap his design in the self-pitying rhetoric employed by his Weimar predecessors.

In October, Hitler withdrew Germany from both the disarmament talks and the League of Nations, timing the decision for a Saturday when he assumed his European counterparts would be away at country-house parties. A plebiscite on Germany's 'peace policy' won an overwhelming popular majority, cunningly using international criticism of his actions to justify an appeal for a popular mandate.[50] By these means, Hitler's manoeuvres not only consolidated domestic support at the expense of the Social Democrats, but also laid the grounds for rapid rearmament. In a decisive break with the entire thrust of Weimar foreign policy, Hitler next concluded a ten-year non-aggression pact with Poland. While the pact was notionally aimed at the Soviets, its main – and intended – effect was to weaken France's influence in eastern Europe. Unilateral pacts were useful to disrupt the alliance structures of others, and could always be abrogated later. The pact with Poland was particularly startling, as it tacitly recognised the borders that sundered Germany from East Prussia, as well as Polish possession of large parts of Pomerania, the former Prussian heartland.

Not everything went smoothly. Hitler and Mussolini were rivals for the political affections of different constituencies in Austria, namely the Austrian Nazis and the clerical-authoritarians gathered around Chancellor Engelbert Dollfuss. For many Austrians, the Dollfuss regime presented them with the familiar dilemma of supporting, or tolerating, a lesser evil to forestall something infinitely worse. After the Dollfuss government had deported the Nazi party's star lawyer, Hans Frank, for subversive activities, Hitler tried to undermine the Austrian winter tourist trade. Simultaneously, Austrian Nazis embarked on a year-long terror campaign involving multiple bombings of such targets as a jewellery store, cinemas, coffee houses and trains, as well as a hand-grenade attack on a Christian youth organisation.

In July 1934 Hitler tacitly supported an Austrian Nazi putsch, in the course of which the charismatic young Austrian chancellor was slain. Only the previous month Hitler had publicly taken responsibility for killing the leadership of his brown-shirted SA followers, as well as the former chancellor Kurt von Schleicher and sundry Catholic opponents, and anyone who happened along when the murderers struck, and he was widely believed to have had a remote hand in the assassination of Dollfuss. The Austrian government's nationwide crackdown on Nazi activists – 4,700 of whom were interned in a camp at Wöllersdorf (alongside 550 Socialists) – fuelled Hitler's indignation, even as his own domestic opponents disappeared into his new network of concentration camps.

International suspicions were further raised when Germany's 1934 budget revealed a 90 per cent increase in spending on armaments, including provision for an air force prohibited by the Versailles Treaty. Funds were also provided to create a peacetime army based on mass conscription, which was also banned. Instead of trying to conceal these measures, as his Weimar predecessors had done by concentrating on a covert professional nucleus and dispersing key military activities to the Soviet Union, Hitler exaggerated his achievements, so that his opponents would not dare attack him. He was not concerned about the diplomatic repercussions, which included French attempts to revive a Little Entente in east-central Europe, and Russia's mutual-assistance pacts with France and Czechoslovakia. In fact he used the Franco-Russian agreement to argue that the Locarno Treaties had been vitiated by one of the main signatories.

At the same time, the expiration of the League of Nations' fifteen-year mandate over the coal-producing Saarland removed the one major lever it had over Germany, after a plebiscite produced an overwhelming vote for the Saar to revert to Germany. With the Saar safely in German hands, Hermann Göring could boastfully exaggerate the power of the German air force, while on 16 March 1935 Hitler introduced conscription for an army that had now risen to over half a million. The League of Nations met to condemn Germany's actions, and even contemplated sanctions. However, although the British protested, they did not cancel or even postpone a visit to Germany by Foreign Secretary Sir John Simon and his under-secretary Anthony Eden, who accepted false reassurances by the Führer at face value.

Nonetheless, at Stresa the British joined France and Italy in vowing to oppose 'by all appropriate measures any unilateral cancellation of treaties', a warning that encompassed any remilitarisation of the Rhineland, a vital part of the Franco-German frontier settlement at Locarno that had been guaranteed by Britain and Italy. Hitler immediately succeeded in weakening this Stresa Front by concluding a naval treaty with the British that allowed Germany to tear up the limits imposed on its fleet at Versailles.

The new treaty permitted him to triple existing naval tonnage to 35 per cent of the British. The Stresa Front was pronounced 'dead' by Mussolini in January 1936, after the outbreak of the Italo-Abyssinian war, an opportunity taken by Hitler, as we have seen, to reoccupy the Rhineland on Saturday 7 March 1936.

The timing of Hitler's *coup de théâtre* was influenced by reports of domestic unrest about rising food prices, the result of allocating foreign currency to buy arms-related raw materials. It has become commonplace to argue that this was the moment when the British and French could have stopped Hitler in his tracks, especially as his troops had hardly any ammunition and had to be augmented with policemen wearing military uniform. Leaving aside the fact that the Rhineland was indeed Germany's backyard, intervention was never realistically on the agenda, even of those who later advertised themselves as anti-appeasers like Labour's foreign affairs spokesman Hugh Dalton. The French were not prepared to act alone, and the British lacked the means to join any military action, even had they possessed the will. What little will there might have been was undermined when Hitler immediately offered twenty-five-year non-aggression pacts to France and Belgium, while suggesting he might rejoin the League of Nations. To round off his bloodless victory, an election was held on the sole issue of approval of the recovery of national sovereignty, which resulted in a 98.9 per cent 'yes' vote.[51]

Joint intervention in the Spanish Civil War brought warmer relations with the Italians, with Foreign Minister Ciano and Hitler signing secret October Protocols in Berlin in 1936. Although Hitler was cautious about the depth of German military involvement in Spain, he dominated the partnership from the outset, exaggerating the Bolshevik ideological affinity of leftist Popular Front governments in Spain and France. Since the Anglo-German naval agreement had not developed into the deeper understanding Hitler had hoped for, he despatched Ribbentrop as ambassador to London, in the belief that this more dynamic emissary could secure a wide-ranging accord.

But while Ribbentrop sought to persuade the British to give Germany carte blanche in eastern Europe in return for non-interference in their empire, Hitler simultaneously explored other options. The most important of these was the November 1936 Anti-Comintern Pact with the Japanese. Once Hitler realised that Britain was not going to abandon France for a 'special relationship' with Germany, he dismissed the two nations as being alike in their decadent weakness, a view nurtured by every report from

Ribbentrop in London, especially after losing what the Nazis hoped would be their trump card when the well-disposed King Edward VIII abdicated to pursue the *demi-mondaine* Wallis Simpson. Hitler concluded that there was more long-term value in his relationship with Fascist Italy; he could not have both, because any alliance with the British would have propelled Italy into the arms of the French.

The rapid build-up of the German army between 1934 and 1936 was accompanied by a reorientation in thinking about how it might be deployed in future, a change influenced by the greater availability of tanks, and officers who had thought about how to use them. In a memorandum drawn up in December 1935, General Ludwig Beck argued: 'Strategic defence can only be successful if it can also be carried out in the form of an attack. For this reason an increase in offensive capacity represents a simultaneous strengthening of defensive capacity.' In addition, Beck noted the importance of armour to 'ambitious targets', where the infantry would race to consolidate what the tanks had won.[52] What those 'ambitious targets' might be was broached by Hitler in a long and tense meeting on 5 November 1937 with Foreign Minister Neurath, War Minister Werner von Blomberg and the three service chiefs: Werner von Fritsch for the army, Hitler's henchman Göring for the air force, and Erich Raeder for the navy.

Notes taken by Hitler's military adjutant, Colonel Count Friedrich Hossbach, recorded how Hitler turned a meeting intended to resolve disputes about funding allocations into a lengthy *tour d'horizon* of grand strategy, where he felt more comfortable. This was not, however, before concentrating minds by ruling out both autarchy and reintegration into the world economy, in favour of expanding the economic base for re-armament through an expansion of 'living space' or *Lebensraum*. Although his musings did not correspond with how events eventually unfolded, and soft-pedalled his fundamental aim of winning 'living space' at the expense of Russia, they began with the throwaway hypothesis that 'force with its attendant risks ... [is] the basis of the following exposition'. He went on to explain the drawbacks of waiting until the rearmament programme bore full fruit in 1943–5 before launching wars of aggression, without putting a precise chronology on action for the more proximate future. Contingencies 2 and 3 involved an opportunistic strike against Czechoslovakia alone, or Austria as well, should France become preoccupied either by civil strife or by a war with another neighbour. The point of these ventures was to 'improve our politico-military position' by the acquisition of additional resources and military manpower, especially as 'three million people' would be subject to 'compulsory emigration'. Hitler saw Contingency 3 arising as early as 1938 from a possible Anglo-French war with Italy in the Mediterranean.[53]

Generals Blomberg and Fritsch raised so many objections that sullen annoyance began to show on their leader's face. A few weeks later, Foreign Minister Neurath also objected that such a policy could 'lead to world war' and that the goals could just as well be achieved through diplomacy. Hitler brushed this aside with claims that 'he had no more time', an allusion to his fear that he might soon die of cancer. After being reassured by the Führer that at all costs he would avoid a two-front war, German military planners went back to the map tables. Operation Red against France was down-graded in favour of Operation Green, a strike into Austria and Czechoslovakia, with a smaller force taking up a defensive posture in the west. Ribbentrop encouraged Hitler to believe that he might pursue such an option, as the ambassador was convinced that the British would not 'risk a fight for the existence of its world empire for the sake of a local central European problem'. France would not act if it lacked British backing.

In February 1938, Hitler took advantage of a sexual scandal to replace Blomberg and appointed himself commander-in-chief. He also got rid of Fritsch, leaving Göring as the most powerful service chief, and replaced the nervous Neurath with Ribbentrop, who shared his own sense of urgency. While Hitler took upon himself the delicate handling of Mussolini, with the results we have seen, he delegated to Göring the task of undermining Austrian Chancellor Kurt von Schuschnigg, Dollfuss's successor. Under the July 1936 Austro-German agreement, which Schuschnigg imagined was definitive, Austria was supposed to act broadly in accordance with Germany's interests, while taking due cognisance of the views of Austria's 'national [that is, Nazi] opposition'. In February 1938, Schuschnigg agreed to desist from 'persecuting' Austria's Nazis and to appoint their chief spokesman, the Viennese lawyer Arthur Seyss-Inquart, to the key portfolio of interior minister. Seyss-Inquart was known to travel regularly to Berlin for instructions, and Schuschnigg bravely – or rashly – decided to risk a sudden plebiscite to give popular backing to Austria's continued desire for independence. Given that those under twenty-four years of age were disfranchised, to exclude the generally Nazi-supporting student population, Hitler had grounds for concern that the vote would not go Germany's way.

While Prince Philipp of Hesse was despatched to secure Mussolini's complicity, Göring threatened Schuschnigg until he resigned in favour of

Seyss-Inquart. While the Austrian president prevaricated over his appointment, Seyss-Inquart sent a telegram, which Göring had drafted for him, inviting a German occupation. The telegram arrived in Berlin almost an hour after Hitler had already ordered Operation Otto – the fraternal invasion of his homeland. Arriving in his hometown of Linz, an emotionally overwrought Hitler authorised the *Anschluss*, an immediate union with Germany. Appalling cruelties were openly committed against Jews by triumphal and vengeful Nazis. So many Jews committed suicide in Vienna that the municipal gas company temporarily interrupted supplies to Jewish customers.

A week before, on 3 March 1938, Hitler had received the elegant figure of Sir Nevile Henderson, Britain's ambassador to Berlin. The ambassador epitomised everything Hitler disliked about the British, with his tasteful suits, claret-coloured pullover and trademark red carnation. Henderson brought what the British thought Hitler wanted, namely colonies in return for a deal in central Europe. He slyly cautioned that the Belgians, French, Italians and Portuguese should not learn about the substance of these discussions; wisely, for most of the colonies he was offering were in fact French. In addition to indicating an 'understanding' over Austria and Czechoslovakia as a means of pacifying central Europe, the British were prepared to carve up Africa so that Germany would have colonies, although not those it had ruled under the Wilhelmine Empire.

To Henderson's dismay, a scowling Hitler dismissed Britain's attempts to 'interfere' in central Europe – he would not presume to interfere over Ireland, he said – and then expressed an honest indifference to the prospect of colonies, adding that the issue had caused too much fuss with Britain and France already.[54] The interview convinced Hitler that he might be able to extract more from such willing interlocutors. Perhaps he recalled an earlier interview in November 1937, with the future Foreign Secretary Lord Halifax, in which the noble lord had signalled British willingness to countenance changes in the Versailles settlement, provided they were 'reasonable agreements, reasonably reached'.

CHAPTER 2

Appeasement

I STATES OF MIND

The Anglo-French statesmen and diplomats who had to respond to the aggressions of the predators were haunted by the mass carnage they had witnessed during the Great War, and by the prospect of cities being razed by indiscriminate bombing. Nightmare visions of Verdun and the Somme, albeit translated into Allied corpses floating in the Channel, would continue to haunt statesmen and generals until D-Day. Even before the Great War, the German-Jewish painter Ludwig Meidner had depicted the bombardment of cities; in its aftermath, novelists, with H. G. Wells's *Shape of Things to Come* (1936) among the most popular works, ratcheted up these anxieties further. Newspaper and especially newsreel coverage of bombing in Barcelona or Chinchow gave substance to such foreboding. Guilt and fear shaped the Anglo-French policy of appeasement, though not in the sense evoked by *Guilty Men*, a contemporary polemic that was published only after the policy's failure became manifest. (Its authors included the future MP Michael Foot, whose Labour Party opposed re-armament. The team's agent absconded with the royalties.)

Survivor guilt was pervasive among those who experienced the wastage of youthful promise and talent, a view that inadvertently accorded greater salience to poets and sculptors than to clerks and butchers' boys. Modern war involved mass conscript armies rather than professionals paid to assume such risks on society's behalf, exacting a human cost on sectors of society that had never paid it before. The heaviness of the burden was apparent in the case of Neville Chamberlain, the conscientious ministerial workhorse who, as chancellor of the exchequer from 1931 onwards, strongly influenced British defence and foreign policy even before he became prime minister in May 1937. When he recalled Norman Chamberlain, his cousin, best friend and fellow Birmingham councillor, killed with his entire company in 1916, Chamberlain wrote, 'I feel a despicable thing beside him'.[1] But war service, or the sadness of losing relatives and friends to the carnage, was not an infallible guide to how politicians and others viewed policy choices, or the prospect of war, as the examples of the veterans Hitler, Mussolini and Churchill indicate. The Austrian and the Italian exulted in war as a means of national or racial regeneration; but while Churchill was still stirred by the drama of war, after his brief period of service in France he was mindful of 'the Hell where youth and laughter go'.[2]

A view of war as an instrument of regeneration was unthinkable to the leaders of the democracies, for whom war was a catastrophe for civilisation as a whole. Chamberlain resorted to unusually strong language – 'hateful' and 'damnable' – when he spoke, reluctantly, of the need for rearmament, at the expense of 'the alleviation of suffering … the opening out of fresh institutions and recreations … the care of the old … the development of the minds and bodies of the young'. All the amenities that a liberal civilisation was capable of bestowing would be wasted on inert grey metal and brass casings, whose ultimate function was to kill and maim.[3] Since one in four British and Irish peers and their sons died in the war, it is hardly surprising that many members of the aristocracy were anxious for Anglo-German reconciliation, quite apart from a minority, epitomised by Lord Londonderry, who more explicitly admired Nazism's discipline or shared its fear of Bolshevism and anti-Semitism – though only 'Benny', the Duke of Westminster, cherished a secret book called *The Jews Who's Who*.[4]

A sense of guilt extended to the former wartime enemy, although Chamberlain had showed no signs of it when he caught sight of savage-looking German prisoners in their cages on a four-day trip he made to the Somme after the war. While many had agreed with the call that 'the Hun must pay', with Edward Wood, the future Lord Halifax, a firm advocate of tough terms, the continuation of the naval blockade after the Armistice, which had starved German civilians to secure compliance with Allied peace terms, inclined some to feel pity for the defeated foe. The political economist John Maynard Keynes wrote an influential polemic on the wider economic effects of Versailles, which gave some factual basis to that view. Sympathy for the vanquished Germans was joined by mounting disgust at the apparently vindictive French, who tenaciously sought to disable German might, despite that country's transition from autocracy to republican parliamentary democracy.[5] Winston Churchill was one of the few to point out that the Allies' treatment of Germany in 1919 contrasted favourably with the terms Imperial Germany had dictated to Russia at Brest-Litovsk two years earlier, when the boot was on the other foot.[6]

Then there was the future. The desire to avoid war was conditioned by widespread fear of bombing that resembled, in its irrational terror, a later generation's dread of nuclear weapons. Literary fictions with titles like *War over England* reflected the usually amiable Prime Minister Stanley Baldwin's gloomy certainty, aired in 1932, that the Channel was no longer a bulwark, and 'the bomber would always get through'. Figures were extrapolated wildly from the modest casualties that bombing had caused in the Great War, and then exaggerated further by multiples based on new technical capabilities and projected on to inflated figures for German aircraft production, without regard to the fact that Luftwaffe bombers were primarily designed to provide tactical support for armoured formations. In fact, it was not until 1940, when the Nazis acquired forward air bases in occupied France, that they could launch the air attacks that Britons dreaded throughout the 1930s. Fear of a single massive strike, delivered by waves of aircraft eclipsing the sun, and the mass panic this would cause on the ground, was widespread. When it came, the Blitz was more like a damp squib than the annihilation subsequently visited on German cities.

Although they never admitted their error or took responsibility for the consequences, pacifist organisations irresponsibly propagated lurid visions of bombs and chemical weapons wiping out entire populations. Although in 1938 Germany was not capable of doing any such thing, this nightmare fantasy haunted Chamberlain as he flew back from his second meeting with Hitler at Bonn-Godesberg, where he had just pleaded that if the Führer invaded Czechoslovakia he should not bomb Prague. According to Secretary of State for India Lord Zetland, 'I remember him saying ... that as he saw spread out like a map beneath him the mile upon mile of flimsy houses which constituted the East End of London, he could not bear to think of their inmates lying a prey to bombardment from the air.'[7] It is important to remember the feelings of dread, as well as sheer nervous exhaustion, which afflicted the participants in the drama of appeasement. As one of its opponents in cabinet, Duff Cooper, recorded in his diary: 'Every morning one wakes up with a feeling of sickening anxiety, which gradually gives way to the excitements of the day.' Chamberlain had to take pills to enable him to sleep more than a few hours each night, and came close to a nervous breakdown at the height of the Munich crisis, when war seemed a couple of hours away.[8]

II A POPULAR POLICY

Appeasement is indivisibly associated with Chamberlain, its most obdurate proponent, although many rats had to get off the sinking ship to leave the captain in such splendid isolation. A passive form of appeasement shaped the collective outlook of the governing class of the day, before hardening into the active policy that Chamberlain pursued to the point where it had all the inflexibility of an ideological conviction or religious belief. It evolved from longer traditions and habits of mind, the instinctive preference of a satiated imperial nation for which mere maintenance of Empire came at a cost, which regarded peace as indispensable to commerce, and whose people, having gained their democratic voice, expected social progress rather than war. The Great War had discredited conventional balance-of-power politics based on alliances. The public mood was one of no more wars, a sentiment that extended into such veterans' associations as the British Legion, together with its French and German counterparts.[9] The Church of England recanted its jingoist excesses in 1914–18 with the wholesale adoption of militant pacifism. An antipathy to rearmament, and naive belief in collective security, as symbolised by the League of Nations, was especially evident on the left of the political spectrum. The left may have deplored what the Nazis did to the Social Democrats, but so powerful was their detestation of merchants of death and militarism that they opposed even prudent rearmament while declaiming against Fascism – thus demonstrating a conceptual failure to grasp what was uniquely vicious about Nazism. When Labour and the Marxist left passionately adopted the cause of the Spanish Republicans, they managed to advocate, as a more sceptical Hugh Dalton pointedly remarked, 'Arms for Spain, but no arms for Britain'. Dalton would shortly outwit the Labour leftist Stafford Cripps, thereby ensuring that the party belatedly supported rearmament, although until early 1939 it opposed even a modest degree of conscription.[10] The conservative right had its own problems, including those who saw only the positive side of the new order in Germany, such as keeping bumptious or Bolshevik Jews in their place. All of which is to say that Chamberlain was captive to popular sentiment rather than a leader like Churchill, who bore grim things.

III A 'REALISTIC', WRONG POLICY

The 1920s were characterised by belief that with its Empire Britain could be semi-detached from Europe, its role confined to that of a part-time umpire in a game of cricket that continentals had never played.[11] Since the RAF's aerial policing could deal with colonial insurgents on the cheap, there could be major cuts in spending on the army and navy. The overall defence budget fell from £519 million in 1920 to £123 million in 1929, when Chancellor Winston Churchill perpetuated the Ten-Year Rule, introduced in 1919, which assumed that no major war would take place for ten years, and which became the basis for decisions by the Committee on Imperial Defence. By extending it for a further ten years, he was able to justify swingeing cuts in the navy.[12] Such economies were intended to realise a wider peace dividend, in the form of improved education, health, pensions and public housing, designed to cauterise domestic labour unrest, or as tax cuts for the industrious middle classes. Defence cuts appealed to those who passionately believed in disarmament as the key to a safer world, even if it was fiscal conservatives rather than League of Nations zealots who wielded the knife. The other side of the coin was the promiscuous moralising of the League's supporters, the bane of British service chiefs who did not want to be dragged into endless wars through the League lobby's manipulation of public sentiment. Finally, the onset of the Depression served to focus loyalties on the dependable cocoon of Empire, with Britain opting for imperial preference trade tariffs at the 1932 Ottawa Conference, further distancing itself from Europe's endemic quarrels.

In an ideal world, the Austro-Hungarian Empire would never have been supplanted by a patchwork of quarrelsome successor states to which neither Britain nor France was prepared to offer military assistance, just as no one looking at the mess of the Middle East would so casually have wished away the Ottoman Empire. That lack of interest was also natural for a governing class that often knew more about the Afrikaner, Masai or Pathan than about Britain's geographic neighbours, among whom they merely holidayed, soaking up the glorious past and ignoring the contemporary reality of everyone but hoteliers and waiters. It was also the view from the self-governing Dominions, whose leaders could point to the massed graves of Australians, Canadians and South Africans to caution against Britain going to war over a minor European country. Although Australia had only five million people, it had suffered more Great War dead than the USA. Moreover, both Canada, with its Quebeçois, and South Africa, with its white-majority Afrikaners, had to negotiate delicate domestic political issues before they could contemplate realising the doctrine of 'common belligerence'.[13]

But then there was Britain's nearest neighbour and former wartime ally. After failing to receive an Anglo-American guarantee of security against Germany, France's leaders fitfully attempted to bolster the League of Nations, before reverting to the view expressed by Foreign Minister Louis Barthou that 'It's alliances that count.' Specifically, the French hoped that a cluster of alliances with four of the eastern European successor states – Czechoslovakia, Poland, Rumania and Yugoslavia – would compensate for the loss of their pre-war alliance with Tsarist Russia. In fact, these alliances were contradictory and untidy, as well as riddled with revanchist animosities, and were never accompanied by any serious joint military planning for an eastern front.[14] The effectiveness of these alliances was substantially undermined when the 1925 Locarno Treaties guaranteed western European frontiers without securing those of Germany's eastern neighbours. Continuing in the heady spirit of Locarno, in 1928 French Foreign Minister Aristide Briand and a less enthusiastic US Secretary of State Frank B. Kellogg persuaded several states to sign up to a declaration against sin: the Treaty for the Renunciation of War as an Instrument of National Policy. Meanwhile, France's relative demographic decline, which became glaring in the 1930s as the loss of young men in 1914–18 made itself felt in a declining birth rate, led to the construction of the Maginot Line from 1929 onwards, a vast system of fortifications, tunnels, railways and gun emplacements covering the Franco-German border, intended to permit the field armies to achieve greater concentration.

Such a tangible statement of a defensive mentality led France's eastern European allies to doubt its willingness to act should Germany attack them. Finally, domestic fears of Communism meant that the 1932 non-aggression pact with the Soviets never developed into military co-operation. Barthou, its most committed exponent, died alongside the King of Yugoslavia when the latter was assassinated in 1934. Belated attempts to re-involve Russia in eastern Europe always broke down because of the unwillingness of France's local allies, especially Poland and Rumania, to allow Soviet forces transit for a lunge against Germany. Once in, they would never be got out. Domestic turmoil also impacted on foreign policy. When Hitler sent troops into the Rhineland in March 1936, France had the misfortune of a caretaker cabinet led by the elderly Radical Albert Sarraut.

The cabinet met to listen to General Maurice Gamelin expatiate about the strength of Germany's armed forces, even as Germany's generals trembled at the thought of French reprisals.[15]

The advent in 1936 of a Popular Front government encompassing Socialists and Radicals, and propped up by the Communists, may have resulted, despite pervasive pacifism, in increased arms spending to fight international Fascism. But the domestic chaos and strife that the coalition presided over led many on the political right to espouse the facile formula 'Better Hitler than Blum' the moderate French socialist leader. After the demise of the Popular Front government, the Radical Edouard Daladier made the fateful choice of dropping Foreign Minister Joseph Paul-Boncour, who had a clear-eyed understanding of the threat from Germany. His replacement, Georges Bonnet, may have been intelligent, but many thought him devoid of a moral centre in an age when politicians were supposed to have one. A self-styled realist, Bonnet believed that the eastern alliances might drag France into war. Soon after his appointment, he revealed his essential views in an interview with *Paris-Soir*:

> Don't let us go in for heroism; we are not up to it … The English will not follow us … As foreign minister I am determined to play my part fully, and it consists of finding a solution before the minister of war has to take one. France can no longer allow herself a bloodletting like that of 1914. Our population figures are going down every day. And finally the Popular Front has reduced the country to such a state that it must get ready for a sensible convalescence – a rash movement might be fatal.[16]

Britain faced the most widespread potential conflicts, with Japan in the Far East, Italy in the Mediterranean and Germany over central Europe. The cardinal principle, as starkly stated by the Defence Requirements Committee, was to avoid a situation in which Britain might simultaneously clash with all three. Worldwide British interests were not matched by the resources to defend them, especially after the leaders of the self-governing Dominions emphasised that they were not going to be dragged into a war over some obscure European country. That view was shared by the British government. Following the assassination of Dollfuss in 1934, Foreign Secretary Sir John Simon said: 'Our foreign policy is quite clear; we must keep out of troubles in Central Europe at all costs. July twenty years ago [the assassination of Archduke Franz Ferdinand, which lit the fuse to the Great War] stands out as a dreadful warning.' While Germany was recognised to be the most dangerous long-term enemy, in the shorter term Japan and Italy were the more immediate threats, especially as these were naval powers capable of menacing vital British overseas interests.

In Western eyes, Japanese aggression in Manchuria came at the worst possible time – in the depths of the Great Depression. The lawless chaos of China meant that many in the US and Britain, who were not overtly sympathetic to Japan, were disposed to a 'six of one, half a dozen of the other' view. Japan was modernising Manchuria, where it was a bulwark against the Soviets. Where else was it supposed to range? Australia? The Japanese cunningly described their actions in Manchuria as self-defence, while continuing to subscribe to the wider Washington Treaty system governing relations in the Pacific region. Western acquiescence in Japanese actions weakened with the bloody feint in Shanghai – which literally made Japanese aggression visible from the rooftops of the International Settlement enclave – and the proclamation of an independent Manchukuo, a flagrant violation of the status quo.

There was also an inherent tension between the ideals of the League of Nations and the great powers' insistence on retaining regional spheres of special interest. What the Japanese were doing in Manchuria was little more than what the US practised in Cuba, Mexico or Nicaragua. The US may have been loud in its moral condemnations of Japanese aggression, but President Herbert Hoover set policy: 'These acts [by Japan] do not imperil the freedom of the American people, the economic or moral future of our people. I do not propose ever to sacrifice American life for anything short of this ... We will not go along on war or any of the sanctions, either economic or military, for those are roads to war.'[17] While the US Secretary of State Henry Stimson demanded that the League, to which the US did not belong, should be vocal in condemning Japan, the British recognised that although their material interests in the Far East were greater than the Americans', they lacked the local forces to defend them. The nearest major fleet would have to steam from Malta, into seas all too likely to be dominated by Japan. In these circumstances, the British opted for the thankless policy of trying to retain the goodwill of China, Japan, the League of Nations and the US.

The British also hoped that the face-sensitive Japanese might bow to the force of international public opinion rather than suffer ostracism. Britain endeavoured to support Chinese requests that the League do something, but not to the extent of precluding a liberal turn in the Japanese government, a non-existent possibility promoted by Britain's pro-Japanese ambassador in Tokyo. The 1932 Lytton Report, commissioned by the League, condemned China for harming Japanese interests, and Japan for illegal changes to the territorial status quo. As a compromise solution, the report proposed an autonomous Manchuria, but with generous representation of Japanese advisers in its government. As a token rap on the knuckles, the British supported a four-week arms embargo declared by the League against both nations, at which the Japanese withdrew their ambassador from the League's Geneva headquarters. The US did not manage even a brief embargo, and kept arms and oil flowing to Japan.[18]

Foreign Secretary Simon's less than glorious handling of this Far Eastern crisis, and a public perception that the League had been betrayed, resulted in Baldwin replacing him with Hoare, while Eden was appointed minister of state for League Affairs.[19] British conservatives often admired Mussolini, although Churchill was being Machiavellian when he dubbed him the 'Roman genius' and the 'greatest lawgiver among living men'. Unlike Hitler, whose fitful charm did not conceal lurking resentments that power never assuaged, the Duce was socially vivacious.[20] Apart from their indulgent view of the Italian dictatorship's prodigies of domestic efficiency, British politicians regarded Mussolini as indispensable to the Stresa framework for constraining Hitler. There was a price to pay. In return for his co-operation, Mussolini assumed he had British and French tacit consent for his ambitions in Abyssinia. He may have been right about Pierre Laval, whose keenness on an understanding with his fellow lapsed socialist was already reflected in the Franco-Italian Rome Agreements of January 1935. Throughout the subsequent period, France was probably more concerned with Italian aggression in the Mediterranean than it was about Hitler.

While many British politicians were contemptuous of Abyssinia – Tory Foreign Secretary Simon's wife was a vociferous campaigner against its slave trade – public sentiment meant that they could not explicitly support Italian aggression. Enthusiasm for the League of Nations, as manifest in the League-organised 1935 Peace Ballot, was largely responsible for the Baldwin government's support for League coercion of Mussolini after the Italian invasion of Abyssinia, even though the British fervently hoped that the French would not co-operate in imposing sanctions. Unfortunately, the sinuous Laval did co-operate, and the League duly mandated sanctions. In the Foreign Office, the permanent under secretary Robert Vansittart hastened to ensure that they did not include denying Italy oil, fearing that Mussolini might launch some retaliatory 'mad dog' attack on the British.[21]

Simon's successor Samuel Hoare and Laval met secretly in Paris to plot how best to sell out Abyssinia, in the tradition of great powers disposing of the territory of lesser nations, but they were forced to resign when details of their talks were exposed in the French and British press. Public opinion had fully ingested the doctrine of national self-determination, foisted on Europe by President Woodrow Wilson at Versailles, and the US press also lambasted the deal, choosing to overlook the fact that US oil exports to Italy had surged since the war started. Britain now contrived to aggravate Mussolini by threatening oil sanctions, then dropping them when the French tried to link their support for sanctions to the maintenance of a demilitarised Rhineland.[22] As we have seen, Hitler was to take advantage of Anglo-French disarray following the 1935 Anglo-German naval agreement to ignore the advice of his generals and to send troops into the Rhineland.

The Nazis have become so synonymous with absolute evil that it requires considerable effort to understand how foreign statesmen reacted to them at the time. Diplomats provided the equivalent of Kremlinology in their regular assessments of who was up or down, moderate or rabid in the regime. Following two British ambassadors who disliked the Nazis, Nevile Henderson was sent to Berlin. He was judged something of an expert on dictators because of experience in monarchical Yugoslavia, but he was also chosen because he was a good shot, a shared interest that led to a friendship with Göring.[23] The Nazis also raised the perennial problem of how far the domestic character of a regime should influence the way other states reacted to it. British statesmen may have deplored the persecution of the Jews, or, as in Chamberlain's case, merely registered that it was happening; but even Churchill, who spoke on this issue more than most, was adamant that a country's internal affairs were its own.

The realities of the case, however, did not fit into the tidy internal–external dichotomy. German persecutions created the international problem posed by Jewish refugees, in Britain's case exacerbating tensions in its mandate of Palestine.[24] An even more difficult problem was the extent to which a nation's international conduct could be predicted from its domestic policies, hardly an exact science, despite the certainty with which historians sometimes dress up hypothetical reconstructions of alternative outcomes. British statesmen believed that if Hitler tore up Versailles in a controlled and consensual way Germany would then become a (powerful) member of the European Concert. At worst, if *Mein Kampf* was to be believed, he might at some future point turn on Russia, which senior conservatives like Baldwin did not regard as a disastrous outcome.

Britain's power was still considerable, as acknowledged by the alliance Hitler offered it. It seemed inconceivable that he would turn on Britain itself.

British policy towards Germany after the advent of a Nazi regime was dominated by the ongoing question of disarmament, which had survived the change of government. Such talks are invariably characterised by deception and hypocrisy, with obsolescent arms offered up while potent weapons are retained. The Geneva talks, commenced in 1932, continued until October 1933, when, for the second time, Germany withdrew. The British were sympathetic to German arguments about the unfairness of unilateral arms limitations, despite general agreements to disarm. Hence they wanted Germany to be allowed limited rearmament, while urging France to scale down its own forces.[25] The French refused to do this without security guarantees that the British were not prepared to give.

Churchill was among those who wholly agreed with the French, seeing a strong France as essential to Europe's peace. He liked Lord Grey's witticism that, though 'armed to the teeth, France was pacifist to the core' (the first part of that proposition was in fact false). A year before the Nazis came to power, Churchill had wondered what spirits animated 'all these bands of sturdy Teutonic youths, marching through the streets and roads of Germany, with the light of desire in their eyes'. He doubted whether they were interested in the abstruse formulas of disarmament negotiators. The capacity to imagine the diabolic, which perhaps required having a little of the devil in himself, was one virtue that distinguished Churchill from his more grounded colleagues; they were like electric plugs equipped with the obligatory green earth, incapable of sparking. Before the Great War, he had been forcibly struck by the engine-like movements of the German army on manoeuvres he attended. Later, he explicitly drew attention to the dictatorial nature of the new German government and the public pugnacity it encouraged, and expressed fear of the use to which it might put the prodigies of Krupp of Essen, the armaments manufacturers. His perception was accurate: the Germans used the talks as a convenient cover to begin the first, and most risky, expansion of their own armaments, and abandoned them once the period of vulnerability had passed.[26]

After Hitler had sent troops into the Rhineland, Baldwin attributed as much blame to the persistently intransigent French as to the Germans, while invoking Charlemagne to illustrate the elasticity of frontiers. Anthony Eden took the lead in discerning higher objectives within a new situation he affected to call 'deplorable'. This was 'the appeasement of

Europe as a whole that we constantly have before us'. In other words, long before Chamberlain became prime minister, British leaders had adopted the view that Hitler's violations of treaties could be overlooked in the interests of the greater good of a general peace. They were supported by public opinion, which could not see why German troops should not enter Cologne or Essen.[27] As a taxi driver told Eden, 'I suppose Jerry can do what he likes in his own back garden, can't he?' In fact, the British army was in no position to act, and the mood in the Commons was 'anything to keep out of war'. As Baldwin said of the Tory backbenchers, 'The boys won't have it.' Labour and Liberal 'boys' agreed. Echoing the government's tendency to put an optimistic spin on every strategic defeat, the headline in *The Times* was 'A Chance to Rebuild'.[28] Under its editor Geoffrey Dawson, *The Times* became the government's claque, suppressing stories that exposed the duplicitous nature of the dictators.[29]

Hitler's own tactics made it difficult to respond decisively. The moment he had moved his troops – not overtly against the French, be it noted – the Führer immediately expressed his desire for an air pact, non-aggression pacts and Germany's return to the League of Nations, and raised the prospect of negotiations about a new demilitarised zone to which Germany would contribute territory along with Belgium and France.[30] Equity dominated another area of policy, for many of the British could not grasp why Germans should be denied the Wilsonian principles of national self-determination that the Allies had enshrined elsewhere. Quite apart from the sinister nature of its government, this was to regard Germany's physical size, economic might and population as if they were of little or no account. Since the British prided themselves on the moral underpinnings of their foreign policy, they were peculiarly susceptible to appeals couched in the rhetoric of human rights, a language Hitler knew how to manipulate, although this is often forgotten in the cold light of his colossal inhumanity. He, too, could express abhorrence about bombing babies, although he was to have hundreds of thousands of them murdered.

The susceptible included Ambassador Henderson, a man who always emphasised the moral aspect of policy-making, even if he took his role of 'getting beneath Germany's skin' too literally. He conceived his responsibility to include selling the virtues of Nazi Germany to Britain, although the only virtue he could find to sell was the discipline and physical fitness of young people in Labour Front camps. Regularly thwarted in his quest for a personal meeting with Hitler, Henderson struck up a friendship with Göring, hunting horns evocatively lowing over the twilit corpses of deer they had shot. He was also full of sympathy for the German predicament after Versailles. In a retrospect written in 1940, shortly before his death from cancer, he wrote:

> The basic fault, in my humble opinion, of the Versailles Treaty was its failure to accord Germans the same right of self-determination which it granted Poles, Czechs, Yugoslavs, and Rumanians. At that time the Austrians and Sudeten Germans had clamoured for union with Germany, but the higher moral principles were waived in favour of political and strategic considerations which could not admit of any accretion of territory for a defeated but always potentially dangerous Germany.[31]

IV CHARACTER

It would be wrong to pretend that crucial changes in personnel did not have a bearing on the transformation of appeasement from a cast of mind into a doctrine or dogma, or from a passive reflex into an active policy. Britain acquired a prime minister with little direct experience of foreign affairs, but with considerable pretensions to expertise in them. Aged sixty-eight on succeeding, without a general election, to the highest office, Neville Chamberlain was unlikely to change his views. His manner has attracted much criticism from middle-class historians, who ape the snobbery of Chamberlain's upper-class contemporary detractors. The unkind compared him with a coroner, although his shy manner was surprisingly well suited to the conversational style of the newsreel interview, where the chilliness and contempt he exhibited in parliamentary debates was temporarily abandoned, and he became what *Lilliput* magazine called 'a beautiful llama' – an accurate description of his face when viewed full-on.

Everything in Chamberlain's career, as lord mayor of Birmingham, as minister of health and as the chancellor of the exchequer who had shepherded his country through the Depression, made him reluctant to gamble the 'emoluments' of peace for the risks of war, even the fuddy-duddy language being revealing. Perhaps competition with a rich, famous and successful father, and with his half-brother Austen, who in 1925 had won the Nobel Peace Prize for his achievements at the Locarno summit, explained Chamberlain's iron belief in the virtues of dogged hard work based on mastery of each brief – an approach that carries many to the point where rarer gifts are needed than those he possessed. His role in Britain's longer-term defence is often cited in mitigation, but the short-term weaknesses – which surely counted in this context – were at the root of his foreign policy.[32]

Compared with German's speed in rearming, Britain was slow to leave the starting line and to decide fundamental priorities. As chancellor, Chamberlain had a keen appreciation that financial stability was a strategic asset in itself, especially as the US refused to give credit to countries that had defaulted on Great War loans. Indeed, so little did he esteem the windy moralising of the US that in 1934 he believed Britain should ally itself with Japan. He had an understanding of the dynamic nature of modern armaments, for what was the point of spending huge sums of money on stockpiling weapons that could rapidly become obsolete? Chamberlain believed strongly in the deterrent effects of air power, to which he insisted on devoting the lion's share of the resources that a public disinclined towards rearmament were prepared to allot. But there was a catch, for that stance also necessitated a reduction of meaningful continental military commitments. In 1935 and 1937 the Treasury, which ultimately called the shots in Whitehall, decreed two sets of cuts in the budgets of the infantry forces that might be deployed to the continent.[33]

A point seldom made in Chamberlain's defence is that he did not share Churchill's belief that Britain should seek to match Germany bomber for bomber, to achieve a purely deterrent effect. Instead, Chamberlain switched resources to building up a fighter force, a defensive measure that could be more easily sold to the public and which, compared to bombers, came in at a quarter of the cost per aircraft. This would ward off an initial German onslaught before both sides fought a long war of attrition, which imperial Britain would win because of its superior economic resources. In reality, both he and Baldwin were too much in dread of a largely imaginary German bomber onslaught, which the Luftwaffe was certainly not capable of launching from German bases at the time they pursued the policy of appeasement. Ironically, the main proponent of bombers, although for imperial deployment, was Lord Londonderry, Baldwin's Air Minister, who has gone down in history as an upper-class crypto-Nazi.[34]

Appeasement was the corollary of this belated attempt at rearmament – something to tide the country over the 'danger period' identified by its defence and intelligence chiefs. It had something of the making-do, unsystematic approach that appeals to the English temperament, although it also evolved into fashionable opinion across the entire range of the British Establishment, from All Souls via the Church of England to *The Times* newspaper. Beyond this was the smart London society of Channons and Cunards, with their cynically silly flirtations with such scintillating charlatans as the German ambassador Ribbentrop, a man most top Nazis regarded as an idiot, given the London posting to get him away from Berlin. After one London cocktail party had relocated to Berlin, they joked that SS chief Heinrich Himmler resembled a department manager at Harrods, unaware that they themselves were lightweight jetsam bobbing towards a catastrophe.

Foreign policy was not such a precise science as structuring a country's armaments or economy for war; therefore it was the stage to which many politicians aspired. In the view of his detractors, Chamberlain never lost the air of a provincial seeking to shine in the big city. However, even allowing for envious snobbery, there was a great deal of truth in Duff Cooper's characterisation of Chamberlain's outlook: 'The Dictators of Germany and Italy were like the Lord Mayors of Liverpool and Manchester, who might belong to different political parties and have different interests, but who must desire the welfare of humanity and be fundamentally reasonable, decent men like himself. This misconception lay at the root of his policy and explains his mistakes.'[35]

Chamberlain argued, correctly, that in a totalitarian system it made sense to speak to the man at the top. What he could not see was that his mastery of municipal politics, or of a complex ministerial portfolio like public health, took him only from A to B rather than to Z when it came to dealing with personalities and forces that lay completely beyond his comprehension. Although Chamberlain's diaries show he was fully aware that Hitler and Mussolini were political desperadoes, his belief that people of goodwill everywhere fundamentally desired peace led him to imagine that the dictators must, deep down inside, share such sentiments. Everything could be resolved, he once told the Soviet ambassador, by sitting round a table going through Germany's grievances with a pencil, a view which failed to encompass Hitler's wider geo-racial vision. He dismissed the view that 'they were entirely inhuman. I believe this idea to be quite erroneous.' There was, however, no consistency in this belief, nor was it prudent to use diplomacy to discover Hitler's inner humanitarian. One minute Hitler was 'a lunatic', the next he was someone Chamberlain could do business with, and whose flattery he courted.[36]

Churchill's view, derived from such informed observers as Frederick Voigt of the *Manchester Guardian*, that Nazism involved 'the fetish worship of one man', could not be reconciled with Chamberlain's unimaginative rationalism.[37] Of course, like many rationalists, he was not devoid of his own irrational beliefs. He invested extraordinary faith in dubious evidence that ordinary Germans or Italians did not want war any more than the British, discounting the fact that in dictatorships their views would usually be registered only by the secret police. 'We are all members of the human race and subject to the like passions and affections and fears and desires,' he said. 'There must be something in common between us, if only we can find it.' Chamberlain's faith in reason as the universal panacea led him to believe that if reasonable demands were made, then they could be reasonably accommodated. Unfortunately, the dictators 'reasoned' that the reasonable would also meet outrageous demands, as they duly did, going on to make the further assumption that the reasonable were decadent and would never confront them.[38]

Foreign Secretary Eden resigned in February 1938 after three years in the post, over being second-guessed about policy towards Mussolini. The BBC chose not to broadcast an interview with him afterwards, lest it upset the policy of appeasement that seems to be written into the corporation's DNA. Thenceforth Chamberlain effectively shared the role of foreign secretary with Lord Halifax, who could speak only in the Upper House. They had been co-ordinating their own alternative foreign policy, especially whenever Eden was absent on official business, preferring such dubious emissaries as Austen Chamberlain's widow Ivy, or Chamberlain's *éminence grise* Sir Horace Wilson, to reach out to Mussolini. The Unitarian Prime Minister trusted the High Anglican peer, whose gravedigger's face suggested honour and high-mindedness, a man truly born to rule, with all the expectations this large assumption entailed under the social codes of the time.

Halifax rebuked one of the few bishops, Hensley Henson of York, who dared to criticise Archbishop Cosmo Lang's persistent faith in Mussolini despite the Abyssinian venture. Little or nothing in Halifax's smooth progress to the top equipped him to deal with Europe's *déclassé* dictators either. He was sincerely sly – they had the cunning of Al Capone. His memoirs describe with pious, self-deprecating smugness his smooth ascent, via Eton, All Souls and Delhi, where he was viceroy, all achieved through luck and nepotism, and padded with the usual tedious Oxbridge legends of deaf college porters and solecisms handling the port which make Englishmen seem like retarded bores. These witty banalities of a man in arrested adolescence have more immediacy and insight than his pedestrian accounts of the events leading to war.[39] Rather revealingly, whereas Halifax routinely forwarded the letters of Nazi sympathisers to Special Branch, he always exempted those written by members of his class such as the Marquis of Tavistock.[40]

The cabinet's 'big four' of Chamberlain, Halifax, Hoare and Simon were routinely supported by the majority of 'yes-men', as Duff Cooper called them, around the cabinet table. The fact that both Simon (1931–5) and Hoare (June–December 1935) had themselves been foreign secretary added further weight to their views.[41] Chamberlain's own flaws are abundantly evident from his contemporaneous diaries, although they went predictably unremarked by the royal family, who were among his greatest admirers. Trite nursery-room maxims, such as 'if at first you don't succeed, try, try again', 'hope for the best, prepare for the worst', were combined with belief in his own mission as Europe's saviour. This last conceit, which translated into his lone voyages to Germany, may have been connected with his awareness that at some point before autumn 1940 he would have to venture a general election, and a foreign policy triumph might have clinched victory.[42] The testy logic with which he defended his views immunised him from criticism. He viewed the maverick Churchill as erratic and unstable, Eden as a vain glamour-boy and the Foreign Office as a narrow caste that spent too much time with foreigners. There was also an unattractive vanity that sought solace in every carefully noted fan letter, be it from a king or a credulous old lady requesting a chip of his umbrella to insert in her reliquary. An old man's vanity partly explains why he made so many basic mistakes, although the people colluded with him.

In June 1937, a few weeks after he had become prime minister, Chamberlain outlined his views on British foreign policy for representatives of the Dominions, who were invariably a constraint on Britain's ability to commit itself in Europe. As a former chancellor, with a businessman's faith in the ameliorative powers of trade, Chamberlain argued that Germany might welcome measures to ease its current economic difficulties, problems largely caused by breakneck rearmament. He had high hopes of Hjalmar Schacht, the German Finance Minister. Typically he invested in Schachts when Schachts were on the way down, a view that conformed with that of the City of London which sought to protect the money it had invested in Germany. He thought that Germany's ambitions were limited to reunion with Austria and the deliverance of ethnic Germans marooned in the uncongenial environments of Czechoslovakia, Lithuania and Poland. These were large assumptions, based on accepting the ethnic rationalisations for Hitler's policies, without considering the possibility that the Führer might covet the arms industries and labour of these countries for further acts of aggression, an odd oversight in a man with a background in business and economics.

That October he (and the Foreign Office) encouraged Halifax to see Hitler, after he had received an unrelated invitation to a hunting exhibition. Halifax conveyed the crucial message that 'we were not necessarily concerned to stand for the status quo as today ... If reasonable settlements could be reached with the free assent and goodwill of those primarily concerned we certainly have no desire to block.' The term 'primarily concerned' held an ominous ambiguity for Hitler's smaller neighbours. At lunch the former Viceroy of India became dimly aware of incompatible values as Hitler's rambling conversation drifted from his favourite film – Gary Cooper in Henry Hathaway's Lives of a Bengal Lancer – to the problem of Indian nationalism, perhaps seeking to connect with a guest he thought looked like an English parson. 'Shoot Gandhi,' Hitler said, 'and if that does not suffice to reduce them to submission, shoot a dozen leading members of Congress; and if that doesn't suffice, shoot 200 and so on until order is established.' Halifax claimed he 'gazed at Hitler with a mixture of astonishment, repugnance and compassion' and did not strain himself to disagree, before dutifully returning home to put indirect pressure on newspaper cartoonists who had attracted Hitler's ire.[43] Armed with Halifax's assessment of the Führer, in November Chamberlain expressed the essence of his government's approach in a weekly letter to his sister Ida: 'I don't see why we shouldn't say to Germany "Give us satisfactory assurances that you won't use force to deal with the Austrians & Czecho-Slovakians & we will give you similar assurances that we won't use force to prevent the changes you want if you can get them by peaceful means."'[44]

If appeasement was an alternative to US-style isolationism, an easier option when two oceans rather than the English Channel intervened, then it also meant Britain behaving like a busy-bodying schoolmistress, a national flaw that has endured beyond the precipitate diminution of British power since Suez. Thus Britain came to practise third-party diplomacy, ultimately denying representation to those whose fate was being determined. Although the British affected the stance of an umpire, the long-held view that no single power should dominate the continent meant that Britain also became a player. Its attempts to stipulate the rules of the game in central Europe were accompanied by a refusal to contemplate alliances or the use of military force to ensure that Hitler acted with the respect for the international proprieties the rules sought to uphold. Unlike Churchill, the appeasers refused to accept that Hitler was pursuing a deliberate plan of aggression, concentrating his sights on a single limited target at a time, but always seeking ultimate domination of central Europe. Unlike Churchill, too, many of the appeasers were disdainful of the League of Nations as a possible forum for frustrating, rather than merely denouncing, outright aggression. They saw themselves as realists, although their own chimerical quest for a general European peace settlement, without alliances or threats of war to strengthen their own hand, was incredibly idealistic too – what Churchill would call the pursuit of 'futile good intentions'.[45]

V NAZI GERMANY ON THE MARCH 1938–1939

The tactics Hitler was prepared to employ towards an independent foreign state became abundantly evident with the *Anschluss* of 10–11 March 1938, when, as it happened, official London was entertaining the former ambassador Ribbentrop, newly promoted to foreign minister. Filled with accumulated hatred of the British, Ribbentrop must have savoured the moment. Even the accommodating Halifax had been moved to protest against Germany's denying Schuschnigg the right to hold a plebiscite in his own country, and had warned that 'if war should start in central Europe, it was quite impossible to say where it might end, or who might not become involved'. After lunch on the 11th, Chamberlain emphasised to Ribbentrop his 'sincere wish for an understanding with Germany'. His mood changed when incoming cables reported that Schuschnigg had caved in to intimidation and would resign. Later that day Halifax remarked: 'What was happening was an exhibition of naked force, and the public opinion of Europe would inevitably ask ... what there was to prevent the German Government from seeking to apply in similar fashion naked force to the solution of their problems in Czechoslovakia or to any other where else they thought it might be useful.'[46]

Chamberlain was drawing a slightly different conclusion, although the loyal Halifax would help him reach it. 'Master' Hitler's use of intimidation and force in securing the *Anschluss* led Chamberlain to contemplate the sort of rebuke one might have delivered to a schoolboy who had stolen, rather than asked for, an apple from an orchard:

> We gave you fair warning that if you used violence to Austria you
> would shock public opinion to such an extent as to give rise to the
> most disagreeable repercussions. Yet you obstinately went your way
> and now you can see for yourself how right we were ... but it is no use
> crying over spilt milk and what we have to do now is to consider how
> we can restore the confidence you have shattered.

By any measure, even the tone of this admission was pathetic.[47]

While aware, at some conscious level, that a bullying Germany understood only force, Chamberlain pursued such will o' the wisps as Italian co-
operation in restraining Hitler. This approach lost him Eden, who was also
alienated by the Prime Minister's disdain for US President Franklin D.
Roosevelt's guarded offers to involve the US in European affairs.
Chamberlain's policy took little cognisance of how events and ideological
affinity were drawing the two dictators together, as the Duce's enthusiastic sanctioning of the *Anschluss* demonstrated, with the further prospect
that smaller states would be drawn to the Axis like iron filings to a magnet
every time the democracies advertised their own weakness. The alternative
strategy, most forcefully represented by Churchill, was to form a grand
anti-Nazi alliance, based on Britain and France, Czechoslovakia, Bulgaria,
Greece, Rumania and Turkey, with the Soviets presumed as members. This
would enforce compliance with the League of Nations Covenant, a document to which Churchill attached great importance.[48] His approach had
practical drawbacks, notably the reluctance of neighbouring states to allow
the Red Army transit rights over their territory. But these were not the
objections that most concerned Chamberlain and Halifax, who, having
identified the likely course of events, proceeded to frustrate the wisest reaction to them.

At a meeting of the cabinet's Foreign Policy Committee on 18 March
1938, Chamberlain supported Halifax's view that such an alliance would
fuel German fears of being encircled, dismissing the view that German
'hegemony over central Europe' would be the prelude to 'picking a quarrel with France and ourselves'. Writing to his sister, Chamberlain resented
having been 'badgered and pressed' by opponents both in and outside his
own party to 'give a clear, decided, bold, unmistakable lead, show "ordinary
courage" and all the rest of the twaddle' – pressures designed to 'vex the
man who has to take the responsibility for the consequences'. While no
one should underestimate the pressures Chamberlain was under, such
burdens are borne for a purpose. Chamberlain prided himself on his intel-

lectual dexterity. He had thought of Churchill's scheme before the latter had even broached it with him. Emphasising his own practical disposition, he asked if Churchill had studied any maps. Following the *Anschluss*, Czechoslovakia was beyond salvation, while Russia was a hundred miles away. He would not guarantee Czechoslovakia, or underwrite French guarantees to it either. It was better to go back to Hitler to establish exactly what he wanted from Czechoslovakia, a state Chamberlain thought had been cobbled together from 'scraps and patches'.[49]

Chamberlain's focus on Czechoslovakia was warranted, as within two weeks of Hitler's glorious introitus into Austria he was plotting the Czech state's piecemeal disintegration.[50] A Czech-language German radio station called Truth Prevails (the motto of the Czech state) beamed anti-Semitic and anti-Czech propaganda from what had been Austria towards Czech peasant supporters of the Agrarian Party, which shared many of the ethnic Germans' prejudices towards Prague. These three and a half million Sudeten Germans were the largest minority in a successor state that included Magyars, Poles and Ruthenes as well as the dominant Czechs and Slovaks. All four minorities exhibited the national egoism that the Czechs themselves had visited upon the Habsburg Empire before 1914.

Germany was not the only neighbour casting a greedy eye over Czechoslovakia, which was why Hitler entertained the Hungarian regent, Admiral Miklós Horthy, on a five-day official visit to Germany in late August 1938, on the pretext of attending the launch of the heavy cruiser *Prinz Eugen* at Kiel. What Hitler actually intended was to whet the Hungarian's appetite for part of Czechoslovakia. Although the Czechs had their British aficionados, they did not inspire the British imagination in the way the more 'romantic' Poles did. Seeking to inspire sympathy for the threatened nation, even Churchill had to dredge up Good King Wenceslas from his otherwise capacious historical repertory. Chamberlain was not alone in regarding Czechoslovakia as an artificial construct, although at least he got its name right, unlike some Tory MPs who in their interventions referred to 'Czechoslovenia'. A British political class that had wrestled with Irish nationalism for over a century affected a lofty incomprehension towards issues of national identity and minority rights in central Europe.

The Sudeten Germans were discriminated against in petty ways by the Czechs, although they tended to attribute structural weaknesses in their regional economy exclusively and unfairly to 'alien' rule from Prague. Their glass and textiles were hit more severely by the Depression among the neighbouring states than Czechoslovakia's industrial core. As leader of a state with eighty million people, Hitler worked himself into a rage at the thought of three and a half million ethnic Germans being pushed around by seven million Czechs, although it was the belief that Czechoslovakia was a geopolitical spear at Germany's back that really concerned him.

The leader of the Sudeten German Party, Konrad Henlein, was Hitler's chosen local instrument – his 'viceroy', as the Führer put it with imperial pretentiousness, although Henlein's objectives were initially restricted to regional autonomy rather than embracing pan-Germanism. This stance gradually became irreconcilable with Czech nationalism and democracy.[51] By the late 1930s, Henlein's orders came from the German Foreign Ministry via Ernst Eisenlohr, Berlin's minister in Prague, who might have done his job with less enthusiasm had he known that Hitler was prepared to have him assassinated to justify German intervention. Henlein's role vis-à-vis the Czechs, according to secret instructions, was always to 'demand so much that we can never be satisfied'.[52] In other words, egged on by Hitler, the Sudeten Germans always negotiated in bad faith with a Czech government that also strung talks along in the hope of an external deliverance that never came.

Ethnic German demands were given a plausibly humanitarian gloss in the resolutions of the Sudeten German Party at a conference in Carlsbad, but their insatiable scope was apparent beneath that surface. As well as calling for regional autonomy, the conference sought 'complete freedom to profess adherence to the German element and German ideology'. In a letter to his sister, Chamberlain bleakly gave every reason why it was impossible to defend the Czechs against German aggression. During discussions with the French in Downing Street in April 1938, Daladier talked up the military capabilities of the Czechs, while countering Halifax's claim that Stalin's purges of his officer corps had emasculated the Soviet armed forces – they still had a vast air force, he said. In response, Chamberlain warned of the perils of bluffing at cards: 'It might be true that the chances against war were a hundred to one, but so long as that one chance existed we must consider carefully what our attitude must be, and how we should be prepared to act in the event of war.' After adding that British public opinion would not countenance any move that might risk war, Chamberlain ended on a personal note: 'The Prime Minister had taken part in one war, and he had seen how impossible it was for anyone to come out of a war stronger or happier. It was therefore only in the case of unavoidable necessity that one should submit to it.' Double negatives abounded in Britain's final evasive assurances to the French. While Germany would be warned of the dangers of violent action, both Britain and France were to exert pressure on the Czechs to accommodate reasonable Sudeten German demands.[53]

In May, unfounded rumours of German military activity near the Czech border resulted in Czech forces deploying to fortifications in the Sudetenland. Two Sudeten Germans fleeing Eger on a motorbike were shot dead by Czech frontier guards. The chance coincidence of a large group of British diplomatic personnel taking a train from Berlin to go on home leave triggered rumours of imminent war. France and the Soviet Union reasserted their commitments to the Czechs, with Britain leaving its options opaque. False claims in the foreign press that Hitler had given way to threats of war, rescinding movements that had never taken place, brought his long-harboured hatred of the Czechs to boiling point. He reversed an earlier decision not to use force against the Czechs, resolving: 'I am utterly determined that Czechoslovakia should disappear from the map.' Moreover, he instructed his naval chiefs to augment their forces rapidly with ships and submarines that could be used to deter Britain, while ordering infrastructure supremo Fritz Todt to rush construction of a West Wall designed to neutralise the Maginot Line. Hitler had resolved to attack the Czechs by 1 October, before the autumn mud sucked down his armour and winter nights impeded the scope of the Luftwaffe.

The conflict between Germany and the Czechs over the Sudeten Germans was among the first to be covered by live international radio broadcasters, and was a feature of the David and Goliath duel between Radiojournal in Prague and the massive resources of Deutsche Rundfunk. Indeed it has been plausibly argued that the Czechs were negligently tardy in setting up a German-language station to counteract the tidal waves of hysterical propaganda which German Propaganda Minister Joseph Goebbels's men beamed towards the Sudeten Germans. Elegant talks by the now exiled Thomas Mann, broadcast by a German-language station called Urania, managed by enthusiastic Jews in Prague, was not the best way of influencing the farmers and workers of the Sudetenland.[54] The Czechs were also too indolent to charm the hordes of foreign correspondents who came to their capital; by contrast, the Sudeten German press chief was a former jewellery salesman who spoke English with a Cockney accent. When there was some obscure contretemps in a remote village, he would immediately be on the telephone spinning the story to credulous foreign journalists. The Germans deployed sentiment's entire armoury – including fake atrocities and streams of pathetic refugees – to blackmail the

British and French into putting more pressure on the Czechs to give way: 'What a grotesque sight it was to see soldiers with bayonets, carrying ladies' coats and cushions, typewriters and other office material, all tied to their rucksacks, as they march through the streets like peddlers …'[55] No sooner would Radiojournal report that German university administrators in Prague had *not* been forced at gunpoint to sign declarations of loyalty to the state than Goebbels's propagandists would have invented a fresh incident. As Edward R. Murrow, who covered these events for CBS, remarked, this was the age when nation hurled invective unto nation.

In this atmosphere of mounting crisis, which he had single-handedly engineered, Hitler was the first to despatch a personal envoy, his wartime company commander Captain Fritz Wiedemann, to London bearing promises of peaceful intent. The mission came to nothing, but the tactic proved catching. In August 1938 Chamberlain sent the retired industrialist Viscount Runciman on what was described as a fact-finding mission to Czechoslovakia, but of which an American journalist wrote: 'the hangman with his little bag came shuffling through the gloom'. The hangman also brought his wife along. Within minutes of detraining, Lady Runciman was heard to fulminate against Bolshevik influence in Czechoslovakia, a bad omen for the success of the mission. That Runciman was immediately courted by the Sudeten German aristocracy did not bode well either, as there were few facts to find while fishing and shooting on their estates. Runciman's real purpose was to pressure the Czechs into promptly meeting Sudeten German demands.[56]

In that same month, Henderson informed Halifax of ever larger German military exercises, as well as other measures indicating that the country was going on a war footing. Meanwhile, British opponents of appeasement were receiving a stream of unofficial German visitors disillusioned with the Nazi regime. The latest representative of German opponents of Hitler was Ewald von Kleist-Schmenzin, a deeply religious conservative Pomeranian Junker who with his co-conspirators, including General Ludwig Beck, thought that Hitler was driving the army into a European war it could not win. One of Kleist-Schmenzin's remarks flew in the face of British suppositions about moderates and extremists in the Nazi regime: 'There is only one real extremist and that is Hitler himself. He is the great danger and he is doing it on his own.' The problem with Kleist, and for that matter an earlier visitor, Carl Goerdeler, was that their revisionist demands – especially towards Poland – seemed more extreme than Hitler's. These men seemed to epitomise the Prussian militarists whom the British were all too familiar with from the Great War. As Sir Alexander Cadogan, permanent under secretary in the Foreign Office, noted of Goerdeler: 'He had already sent us a "programme", which we couldn't subscribe to – too much like "Mein Kampf" – and that rather put me off him.'[57]

The German opposition were, naturally enough, contrastingly vague about concrete plans for an anti-Nazi coup. Chamberlain retreated to his official residence at Chequers to ponder conduct that lay outside his moral horizons. He quickly dismissed Kleist and his fellow resisters as being like 'the Jacobites at the court of France in King William's time', although he simultaneously confessed to feelings of generalised unease about the turn events had taken. What he did next reflected his conviction that Britain was not militarily ready to fight Germany, a view confirmed by his defence advisers. Since he could not stop Hitler invading Czechoslovakia, there was little prospect of a successful German conservative coup, as Hitler would be basking in a military triumph, a view that took no account of how the German people actually regarded the prospect of war.[58]

Had the Czech crisis really been about minority rights, it should have been resolved when President Eduard Beneš called the Germans bluff by conceding the Carlsbad demands. Of course, this was not what Hitler wanted. Henlein was immediately instructed to break off further talks with Prague. He used as a pretext a minor riot in Moravská Ostrava, during which a policeman had hit a Sudeten German politician. All eyes at this point were focused on the Nazi Party rally in Nuremberg, as it happens the last ever held. Henderson was in attendance, helpfully warning the British government that Hitler was so mad he might do anything, useful information if one were planning to do nothing by way of response. Göring set the mood on 10 September, calling the Czechs 'a vile race of dwarves without any culture – nobody knows where they come from … and behind them, together with Moscow, there can be seen the everlasting face of the Jewish fiend!' Hitler waited until the concluding session to deal with the Czechoslovak crisis:

> The situation in this state has become unbearable, as is well known. In a political context, three and a half million people there are robbed of their right to self-determination in the name of the right to self-determination as construed by a certain Mr Wilson. In an economic context, these people are being ruined methodically and hence are subject to a slow but steady extermination. The misery of the Sudeten

Germans defies description. [The Czechs] desire to destroy them. In a humanitarian context they are being oppressed and humiliated in an unprecedented fashion.[59]

He professed to be livid about this, and about the 'intolerable impertinence' of the May war scare, adding, 'I am a National Socialist and as such I am accustomed to strike back at any attacker.' This speech indirectly triggered riots in the Sudetenland, which led the Czechs to impose martial law. The Sudeten Germans demanded a plebiscite to resolve their existential dilemma, a suggestion that had been aired in *The Times* – the house organ of appeasement – a week before in a leader that regarded the disintegration of an artificial Czechoslovakia with equanimity. Some weeks before, Chamberlain had decided upon what he melodramatically termed his 'Z plan', although in the initial version he planned to despatch Runciman to see Hitler rather than going himself. Runciman wisely demurred. With the intensification of the crisis, Chamberlain sent a message to Hitler: 'I propose to come over at once to see you with a view to try to find a peaceful solution. I propose to come across by air and am ready to start tomorrow.' He presented this bizarre gambit to the cabinet as a fait accompli.

VI GENTLEMEN AND GANGSTERS

At Heston aerodrome, Chamberlain told the BBC, 'The Führer's ready acceptance of my suggestion encourages me to hope my visit to him will not be without results.' He landed in Germany on 15 September after what had been his first major flight, at nearly seventy years of age. That week he had been reading a biography of George Canning, written by one of his own academic admirers. This led him to conclude that one should issue no threats until they could be carried out, the view of his own military advisers. Against the urgings of Churchill to declare war if Hitler used force, Chamberlain had resolved that the most vital decision he might ever take should not be passed 'into the hands of the ruler of another country and a lunatic at that'.[60] After a long train and car journey to the Berghof, the Führer's Alpine retreat at Berchtesgaden, the vista from the lunatic's vast window, which had impressed ex-Prime Minister Lloyd George a few years before, proved disappointing because of low-lying mist. In the letters he used as a diary, Chamberlain made a series of predictable private observations about Hitler's nondescript physical appearance, incorrectly comparing him with 'the house painter he once was'. Here he followed a snobbish trend established by Halifax, who had once nearly mistaken Hitler for a footman, letting the lazy optic of social class substitute for thinking hard about such a dangerous opponent.[61]

There was no ice-breaking small talk, because Hitler was more the master of the tirade and the monologue. The two men talked alone except for Schmidt the interpreter, which meant Chamberlain lacked an independent record, in an austerely furnished salon with a couple of bottles of mineral water on the table that Hitler did not offer his elderly guest. Hitler knocked Chamberlain straight off course by claiming that, since three hundred Sudeten Germans had been killed by the Czechs, he could not agree to Chamberlain's wish to defer the local – Czechoslovakia – in favour of Anglo-German generalities. After the German dictator had expressed his indifference to the prospect of war, Chamberlain conceded Hitler's right to incorporate the Sudeten Germans into Germany. Even though Chamberlain thought he was merely conceding a theoretical principle, this was to stray far beyond the matter of autonomy or home rule, and it was done without any consultation with the British cabinet, the French or the Czechs themselves.

On the basis of these talks, Chamberlain reported to the cabinet that Hitler's aims were 'strictly limited'. There was more, for apparently Hitler was no longer a lunatic but someone whose opinion was to be valued. Accurately identifying the British Prime Minister's own flaws, Hitler had let it be known that he had liked Chamberlain, whose own account of the Führer's flattery was revealing: 'I have had a conversation with a man, [Hitler] said, and one with whom I can do business and he liked the rapidity with which I had grasped the essentials. In short, I had established a certain confidence, which was my aim, and in spite of the hardness and ruthlessness I thought I saw in his face, I got the impression that here was a man who could be relied upon when he had given his word.' So one might think, if one had not bothered to ascertain that the three hundred dead ethnic Germans Hitler had made theatre from were entirely fictitious.

Moreover, a day after meeting Chamberlain, Hitler authorised the formation of a Sudeten German Freikorps, a paramilitary force consisting of men who had fled conscription into the Czech armed forces. With headquarters at Bayreuth, and officers drawn from the SA, the Freikorps numbered 34,500 men in a fortnight. The funding came from the German military budget. Although they were notionally intended to protect Germans, against what even Goebbels privately conceded was non-existent Czech provocation, their real function was to destabilise Czechoslovakia with incidents on both sides of the border. 'Nothing much being done by Prague. Despite this we'll make a really big meal out of Czech terror. The temperature must be raised to boiling point,' wrote Goebbels in his private diary on 18 September.[62] That meant burning down a Czech customs post, as well as arson attacks on German-owned sawmills and spas. After coming under SS control on 30 September, the Freikorps' remit was extended to abducting exiled German Communists and Czech officials, who were illegally smuggled over the German border.[63]

At the airport Chamberlain bade his German hosts a fond 'au revoir'. On the radio recording of this event, Ribbentrop can be heard uttering an ironic laugh. From across the Atlantic, Roosevelt had a much clearer understanding of what was at stake when he warned Chamberlain: 'If a Chief of Police makes a deal with the leading gangsters and the deal results in no more hold-ups, the Chief of Police will be called a great man; but if the gangsters do not live up to their word, the Chief of Police will go to jail. Some people are, I think, taking very long chances.' A patrician himself, Roosevelt had at least seen a few gangster movies in his day.[64]

A protracted series of Anglo-French follow-up conversations took place at Downing Street on 18 September 1938. Whereas Chamberlain was inclined to believe that Hitler's aims were limited, Daladier had his honest doubts. Despite being from a far more deeply provincial background than Chamberlain, the 'bull of the Vaucluse' had grasped the essence of the Nazi leader: 'He was convinced in his heart that Germany was aiming at something far greater. It was clear from "Mein Kampf" that Herr Hitler did not regard himself in the light of a second Emperor William II, but that he was aiming at dominating Europe as Napoleon had done. He was a popular chief, with something of the religious authority of Mahomet.' Although that was a mixed up way of putting things, it was a great deal more accurate than Chamberlain's petty snobberies about decorators and his fastidious bureaucrat's concern with playing by the rules. The French agreed with the cession of the Sudetenland, but they managed to get the British to guarantee a rump Czechoslovakia.[65]

On 21 September, the British and French governments presented their terms to the Czechs, with the explicit warning that France would not help them if the terms were refused, because in that eventuality the British declined to support them. Although the Czech Prime Minister had asked for an ultimatum to sell these capitulations domestically, the Czechs were taken aback by the brutality with which Anglo-French diplomats roused them from their beds in the early hours to deliver the grim tidings.[66] In Prague, British and French embassy officials pressured Beneš into the early hours to secure his assent. Half a million Czechs listened to the news as it was broadcast from loudspeakers in the trees around Prague's Wenceslas Square. Chamberlain returned to Godesberg to bring Hitler the glad tidings and to wrap up a much broader settlement. Hitler now dealt him a body blow by refusing to claim his winnings in the prescribed manner. He wanted the problem resolved 'one way or another' by 1 October. To dramatise his timetable, Hitler depicted Czechoslovakia as a vast prison from which the German, Hungarian and Polish inmates were straining to escape. Large numbers were bandied around that would not have survived careful audit. Over a hundred thousand Sudeten Germans allegedly had fled to Germany since the present crisis began, leaving depopulated villages where abandoned children wandered about. The frontier had become a lawless zone where there were nightly shooting incidents. In the course of the meeting, Hitler was handed timely intelligence of a further twelve German hostages having been shot in Eger. These were outright lies. Hitler agreed to give Chamberlain an outline of what he wanted: the Czechs had to get out of the Sudetenland by 28 September or he would go to war, commencing mobilisation at 2 p.m.[67]

Hitler's willingness to countenance war perplexed Chamberlain, who was also furious that his patient work in preparing a peaceful solution had been rejected by an interlocutor who had reverted to being a lunatic. He rallied slightly on receiving news of Czech mobilisation and his own cabinet's insistence that enough was enough, a view relayed on unscrambled telephones, which resulted in Hitler staying his hand. In further discussions, Chamberlain forced cosmetic changes, in what they agreed to describe as a memorandum rather than Hitler's original 'proposals'. Hitler scribbled in a few alterations with a pencil to give Chamberlain the impression he had achieved something. Chamberlain agreed to present the memorandum to the Czechs in his capacity as intermediary between Germany and Czechoslovakia.

After bidding Hitler *'auf Wiedersehen'*, Chamberlain flew back to Heston. A waiting BBC reporter was perplexed to find the plane's door jammed shut, so that he could not immediately interview the Prime Minister. When he emerged, Chamberlain said: 'I will only say this, I trust that all concerned will continue their efforts to solve the Czechoslovak problem peacefully because on that turns the peace of Europe in our time.' He hastened to sell the German leader's proposals to his own cabinet, with Runciman on hand to help resolve the technical difficulties of deciding how population densities would determine the cession of a given area. An old man's vanity was sometimes evident. In his presentation to the cabinet on the evening of 24 September, Chamberlain stressed the rapport he had established with Hitler, who he claimed had some respect for him too: 'He thought he had now established an influence over Herr Hitler, and that the latter trusted him and was willing to work with him.' He was inclined to take Hitler at his word when he claimed to be solely interested in 'racial unity' rather than ruling racially undesirable Czechs and Slovaks. Also evident was a certain messianic intent, the lure of one comprehensive settlement of all Europe's woes. The Sudeten issue was subtly marginalised in the interests of a broader Anglo-German understanding, the necessary precondition for a general settlement in Europe.

At a second session of the cabinet on the morning of 25 September, first Hoare and then Halifax, Chamberlain's most reliable colleagues, baulked at the British coercing the Czechs to accept the Godesberg deal. Halifax had been chided by Cadogan the previous night and had lain awake tormented by his High Anglican conscience. He thought that Hitler 'has given us nothing and that he was dictating terms, just as though he had won a war but without having had a fight'. Testy notes were passed along the cabinet table. 'Your complete change of view since I saw you last night is a horrible blow to me,' scribbled the Prime Minister, indicating that he might resign if the French went to war. 'I feel a brute – but I lay awake most of the night tormenting myself, and did not feel I cd. reach any other conclusion at this moment, on the point of coercing Cz' came the reply. 'Night conclusions are seldom taken in the right perspective' flashed back N.C.[68] Nor were the French, who were in Downing Street on the night of 25 September, as ready to renege on their commitments to the Czechs as Chamberlain presumed they were when the discussions were extended to include them.

The French Prime Minister demonstrated a moral conscience, firmity of purpose and realism about where Hitler was heading that was evidently absent from his allied hosts. Daladier questioned whether the prospect of German bombing was as terrible as everyone imagined, pointing out that despite massive Nationalist air superiority Franco was no nearer winning the Civil War. The French Prime Minister was ashamed of what he and

Chamberlain had forced the Czechs to accept already, referring to himself as 'a barbarian'. He had done this because of what he had witnessed as a soldier in the Great War. Showing more guts than any of his British interlocutors, Daladier continued:

It was a different thing to give Herr Hitler the possibility of saying to his people that, without firing a shot, Great Britain and France had handed over to him three and a half million men. This would not suffice for him. M. Daladier asked at what point we would be prepared to stop and how far would we go … The Czechs were, however, human beings. They had their country and had fought at our side. We must ask what they thought of all this. Perhaps formulae of conciliation might be found, although he feared that all conciliation was only preparing the way for the destruction of Western civilisation and of liberty in the world … There was one concession, however, he would never make, and that was that marked on the map, which had for its object the destruction of a country and Herr Hitler's domination of the world and all of that we valued most. France would never accept that, come what might.[69]

The session included the disagreeable spectacle of Sir John Simon, the Chancellor of the Exchequer, followed by Chamberlain, seeking to undermine Daladier's faith in his own country's defence capabilities. Simon imagined he was back in court quizzing a shifty witness rather than speaking to the French Prime Minister. Chamberlain warned of the nightmare of bombs raining down on Paris: 'it would be poor consolation if, in fulfilment of all her obligations, France attempted to come to the assistance of her friend but found herself unable to keep up resistance and collapsed'. He also doubted whether Russian military aid to the Czechs would amount to much. In a final abdication of responsibility, Chamberlain remarked that 'we were not the people to whom the proposals [Hitler's] had been addressed, and we could not therefore accept or reject them. Our role was confined to transmitting them to the Czechoslovak Government as we had done.'[70]

As a result of pressure from within his cabinet and from his French ally, Chamberlain resolved to despatch Sir Horace Wilson to Berlin with an offer of an international commission, and a threat that if France supported Czechoslovakia against a German attack, Britain would go to war. After Hitler rose and launched a tirade at Wilson's first attempt to deliver this message, the envoy had to return a second time, to hear explosions like 'Germany was being treated like niggers; one should not dare treat even the Turks like that.' The Führer added, 'On 1 October I shall have Czechoslovakia where I want her. If France and England decided to strike, let them strike. He did not care a farthing.' As Hitler escorted him out, using 'epithets about Mr Chamberlain and Sir Horace that could not be used in a drawing room', Wilson somewhat weakened the main point by whispering to Hitler, 'I will still try to make those Czechos sensible.' Hitler ordered the preliminaries to full mobilisation once the civil servant had left.[71]

War was becoming a grim, hourly prospect. In France, white-coloured posters went up calling a million reservists to the colours. Gas masks were issued to the British population and the fleet mobilised. In his deservedly famous *Autumn Journal*, the Northern Irish poet Louis MacNeice described the scenes outside his London apartment:

> Hitler yells on the wireless,
> The night is damp and still
> And I hear dull blows on wood outside my window;
> They are cutting down the trees on Primrose Hill ...
> They want the crest of this hill for anti-aircraft,
> The guns will take the view
> And searchlights probe the heavens for bacilli
> With narrow wands of blue.[72]

Cellars were converted into bomb shelters, and ordinary people pondered various DIY solutions to the prospect of massive bombing. Anti-aircraft guns, barrage balloons and searchlights appeared around London landmarks, while local authorities excavated trenches in public parks. Staff at Lambeth's Imperial War Museum, recently ensconced in a former lunatic asylum, drilled with captured Great War German helmets. Feelings in Germany were little different: when Hitler ordered a motorised division to parade through Berlin for three hours, bystanders scowled or scuttled into doorways.

On the evening of 27 September Chamberlain delivered a lachrymose speech on the BBC, about the nightmare of preparations for war because of 'a quarrel in a far-away country between people of whom we know nothing'. He made much of Hitler's feelings of indignation, offering to meet him a third time 'if I thought it would do any good'. Hitler left the door slightly ajar to a last round of talks too when he wrote to Chamberlain that night. The 28 September saw a stream of foreign diplomats bustling into the Reich Chancellery, which resembled a military camp; the Wehrmacht commanders due to invade Czechoslovakia were supposed to be coming to lunch. War was very close that day, so much so that Göring, who knew about war, rebuked the belligerent civilian Ribbentrop for constantly pushing for one, sarcastically offering to take the Foreign Minister up in the first combat plane. In the event, Chamberlain despatched his ambassador Lord Perth to see Mussolini, who at the eleventh hour persuaded Hitler to delay mobilisation for twenty-four hours so that there might be a final conference. This was a request that Hitler could not refuse, especially as the Czechs were excluded and the citizens of the Reich capital seemed so unenthusiastic for war.

Late that afternoon Hitler invited Chamberlain, Daladier and Mussolini to Munich. Uncharacteristically high emotions were on display in the House of Commons when Chamberlain dramatically announced this development, a fortuitous solution to the deflationary ending to his speech that he had planned to deliver. In the public gallery, Queen Mary wept openly, tears filled Baldwin's eyes, but the politician Jan Masaryk and the poet Stefan Zweig were among those who remained stony-faced as they scented betrayal. Churchill commented bitterly: 'And what about Czechoslovakia? Does no one think of asking their opinion?' Churchill stayed seated as the House rose to applaud, although he congratulated Chamberlain afterwards. Enormous gusts of public goodwill accompanied Europe's statesmen on their respective odysseys. Revelling in the attention Mussolini set off by deluxe train; Daladier and Chamberlain took off from Heston and Le Bourget, amid much backslapping from their many admirers.

For experienced statesmen, Chamberlain and Daladier made remarkable errors. They clearly let emotion speed them on their way, instead of seeking to delay their trip to allow calm discussion of alternative possibilities based on a thorough assessment of whether Hitler was in a position to fight a major war at that time. Charismatic diplomacy replaced cold-blooded analysis. They left their respective foreign ministers at home, while Hitler and Mussolini had Ribbentrop and Ciano in attendance. Mussolini spent the night on a train, discoursing to Ciano about the decadence of a people who had cemeteries and hospitals for cats and dogs, before boarding Hitler's train at Kufstein to go over their joint agenda with the aid of models and maps.[73] In contrast, the British and French leaders walked into the conference without having conferred. They did not insist on appointing a chairman – a role Mussolini assumed but did not perform – or agreeing an order of business. They had no briefing books to anchor the discussions in cold fact. They consented to seating arrangements that put Hitler and Mussolini together while separating the French and British.

The conference itself was a chaotic shambles lasting thirteen hours, which suited only the adrenalised Hitler. At Chamberlain's insistence, the Czechs were eventually allowed to station two representatives in an adjoining room. Hitler already had the measure of Chamberlain, so he concentrated his attention on the French leader, professing a long-held desire to see Paris that had been frustrated by the Great War, a theme the French premier warmed to, as he had risen from private to captain in that conflict. Chamberlain's punctilious desire to resolve questions of financial compensation for Czech businessmen or farmers who would forfeit assets in the Sudetenland finally got on Hitler's nerves. The main meeting broke into a series of conversational groups as experts were brought in to resolve technical issues. Mussolini affected a lordly lack of interest in the 'parliamentary' atmosphere of the conference, except whenever he intervened to resolve a difficulty with a flash of genius.

The proposals, drafted by Hitler but presented by Mussolini, were agreed quickly enough, with enough tactical retreats from the Godesberg memorandum to secure assent to a modified form of that deal. The Germans agreed to delay their occupation of the majority German areas of the Sudetenland from 1 to 10 October, while plebiscites would resolve the fate of more ethnically mixed areas. These changes took care of the more sensitive consciences in Whitehall. This fix-up was presented to the waiting Czechs, who were not given the opportunity to demur, as Europe's general peace was at stake. Chamberlain's indifference to the Czechs was on display when he failed to stifle a yawn during their only encounter. With the Czech difficulty resolved with surprising alacrity, Chamberlain sought out Hitler to proffer a document about a wider settlement, ranging from aerial bombing to the war in Spain. He 'warmly appreciated Hitler's words … he thanked Herr Hitler for these assurances … he would not keep Herr Hitler any longer' are some of the casual phrases that reveal where the whip hand lay. After Hitler had expressed an exasperated 'Ja, ja', hardly bothering to glance at the document, they signed the eirenic-sounding communiqué; Chamberlain had not informed the French about this separate venture.[74]

VII 'LES CONS'

As they left Munich, the two Western leaders were impressed by the immense throng of ordinary Germans manifestly relieved at the successful talks. More crowds awaited them at home. At Heston, where Richard Dimbleby was on hand to cover the event for the newsreels, Chamberlain flourished the piece of paper he and Hitler had signed. Echoing Disraeli's words upon returning from the 1878 Congress of Berlin, he claimed to have achieved 'peace with honour', a phrase he instantly regretted using, for honour was something he discovered a bit later after he had ditched the quest for peace. His face broke into toothy smiles as crowds cheered 'Good old Neville' outside Buckingham Palace and along Downing Street, where he 'spoke to the multitudes' from a window, with the BBC in fawning attendance. Duff Cooper thought the crowd was more like a mob.

Daladier was similarly fêted by enthusiastic crowds when he returned to Paris. He is supposed to have muttered, '*les cons* [the polite translation of which is 'the fools'], if they only knew what they were cheering.' Another sceptic was Pope Pius XI. The French ambassador to the Vatican was taken aback when the pontiff declared: 'A very fine thing this peace, botched together at the cost of a weak country that was not even consulted!'[75] Oblivious, Chamberlain took an all-too-apparent delight in gifts that flowed in to the man whose name had become a synonym of peace.

Defenders of Chamberlain argue that at Munich he won a year's grace, during which Britain strengthened its fighter and radar defences. Critics claim that, had he stood firm, Hitler's domestic conservative opponents might have essayed a coup with better chances of success than the one they undertook in 1944, or, more tellingly, that Germany was in a far weaker position in 1938 than in 1939. These are imponderables. What is unambiguous is that the policy of appeasement failed in its wider ambition of a general resolution of European conflicts, proof being that Hitler elected to press ahead with aggression against Poland, now confident that even if the men of Munich stirred, he could defeat them.[76]

And the Czechs, who had lost about 20 per cent of their territory? When the Labour Party's Hugh Dalton rang Masaryk at the height of the crisis to inquire whether Britain and France were being more resolute on the Czechs' behalf, Masaryk exclaimed: 'Firm? About as firm as the erection of an old man of 70!'[77] In Prague people milled around dazed, as if their spirits had been crushed. The Justice Minister broke down and sobbed several times as he tried to talk to the Czechs on the radio about what he referred to as a 'diktat' by his country's allies. The newly appointed Propaganda Minister, Hugo Varecka, the grandfather of future Czech president Václav Havel, said that Poland and Hungary had taken Hitler's side, while Rumania and Yugoslavia had abandoned their Little Entente ally. 'The Russian card was not one to play: both Britain and France would have considered such a war to be a battle between Bolshevism and Europe. Probably all Europe would have turned against Russia. And thus against us too.'[78]

Within a matter of days the Poles, aggressors rather than victims in this context, had realised their own claims on Czechoslovakia. After Beneš's resignation on 5 October, Slovak and Ruthenian separatists proclaimed their own right to self-determination. In November, at Vienna, the Hungarians were granted nearly four thousand square miles of territory, ironically stripped from the newly autonomous Slovak and Ruthenian federal states. An independent Czechoslovakia survived into the New Year, under a government that at Christmas decided to dissolve all political parties, while striking at the Slovak separatists. It also exerted a tighter grip on the state broadcaster, which entered into an agreement with the German Propaganda Ministry to eschew politics. In February, the Czechs signed a deal exchanging radio programmes, in whose fine print the Czechs averred 'we are totally loyal and ... are not employing any non-Aryans', for their government, to appease the Germans, had decided to reduce the number of Jews in public employ.[79]

In the interim, the Nazis had given massive public evidence of their barbarity. Just as the *Anschluss* had resulted in a huge surge of anti-Semitic violence in Vienna, so the incorporation of the Sudetenland saw a number of Jews either murdered or so despairing that they leaped from roofs or turned on the gas taps. Hitler personally gave the Sudeten German Freikorps a three-day period of grace to hunt down Jews and political opponents.[80] In October he wanted to know whether it would be possible to deport the twenty-seven thousand Czech Jews living in Vienna.[81] The policy of forcing German Jews to emigrate by removing their rights had run into the manifest unwillingness of foreign governments to take any more of them.

In Berlin, the chief of police, Graf Helldorf, encouraged his subordinates to turn a blind eye towards those who systematically defaced synagogues and Jewish-owned businesses, while his policemen simultaneously raided cafés and other places where Jewish people still managed to associ-

ate. On 7 November 1938, the fatal wounding in Paris of the German legation official Ernst vom Rath by a seventeen-year-old Polish Jew called
Herschel Grynszpan unfortunately coincided with the highpoint of the
Nazi's ritual calendar in Munich, where they commemorated their own
martyrs from the 1923 Munich Beer Hall putsch attempt. That evening,
Party members and SA men devastated Jewish businesses and a synagogue
in Kassel and other towns in Kurhessen and Magdeburg-Anhalt. Arson
and violence spread to Hessen as a whole the following night. The reason
why this was extended into a nationwide pogrom, to live in infamy as
Kristallnacht, was that Hitler ordered it after he was called, probably by his
personal emergency physician Karl Brandt, whom he had sent to Paris,
and told that Rath had died of his wounds in hospital before Brandt could
save him. That evening Hitler attended his annual reunion with the old
fighters, veterans of the days of bar-room brawls. In the course of the
evening, he instructed Goebbels to allow the 'demonstrations' to run their
course. Goebbels gave a speech later that evening which amounted to
further incitement.

Among those who sprang into action were the nearly forty members of
Julius Schaub's Adolf Hitler Shock Troop, that is men who had acted as
Hitler's bodyguards in 1923 and who had an especially esteemed role in the
Munich ceremonies. They sat very close to the dictator at a comradely meal
that evening, before venturing out wearing their caps with the distinctive
death's-head symbol which the SS had adopted. At around midnight, they
set fire to the Ohel-Jakob and Reichenbachstrasse synagogues in Munich.
Meanwhile, Goebbels telephoned his head of propaganda in the Gau of
Berlin, and ordered him to burn down the imposing synagogue on the
Fasanenstrasse.[82] Werner Wächter replied, 'An honourable task.' As if 91
people murdered and 101 synagogues destroyed were not enough, in the
days following the pogrom the Nazi regime introduced a series of measures which made the Jews collectively responsible for Rath's death, while
excluding them from both economic activity and public places. Without
much exaggeration, on 5 January 1939 Hitler told the Czech Foreign
Minister, 'the Jews are being destroyed,' while inquiring what steps the
Czechs were taking to deal with the Jews themselves.[83]

Throughout the winter months, Chamberlain was desperate for signs
from either Mussolini or Hitler that the Munich Agreement would develop
into a wider peace settlement. In January 1939 'old' Chamberlain, as Ciano
called him, visited Rome for a round of desultory talks with the Italians.
After a session in which 'effective contact had not been made', the Duce

remarked to Ciano: 'These men are not made of the same stuff as the Francis Drakes and the other magnificent adventurers who created the empire. These, after all, are the tired sons of a long line of rich men and they will lose their empire.' There was some truth in that, although it underestimated the eighteen-hour days the sons of rich men were putting in at the Foreign Office and elsewhere in Whitehall. Mussolini defended Germany strongly; Ciano telephoned Ribbentrop to report that the visit had been 'a huge farce'. Chamberlain had tears in his eyes when British expatriates sang 'For he's a jolly good fellow' as his train pulled out of Rome's Termi station. The upper lip, so stiff when disposing of Czechoslovakia, easily succumbed to bathetic sentiment.[84]

The British convinced themselves that a German balance of payments crisis might force Hitler to relax his breakneck rearmament programme in order to put more food on German tables. But the same crisis could, of course, fuel his desire to control Czechoslovakia's industry and gold reserves. In March the Slovak leader, Monsignor Jozef Tiso, fled to Berlin, where Hitler invited him to demand German intervention, warning him that since Germany had no interest in this Carpathian agricultural backwater he might otherwise let the Hungarians gobble it up entirely. He was not finished with the Czechs themselves, despite their manifest willingness to accommodate him in a matter close to his heart. In January they took steps to expel ninety-six thousand German victims of political or racial persecution who had sought shelter in Czechoslovakia. In February they agreed to dismiss all Jews from German schools, preparatory to dismissing Jews from the civil service, and reducing their presence in law and medicine.[85]

On 15 March President Emil Hácha, Beneš's successor, dashed to Berlin to plead his country's case. Hitler kept him waiting until after midnight before receiving him; according to Goebbels, this was a tactic the Allies had used against the Germans at Versailles. Hitler resorted to the extraordinary argument that 'the new regime had not succeeded in making the old one disappear psychologically'. Why did Czechoslovakia need a large army? Since 'the Czechoslovak State no longer had a role in foreign affairs, such an Army had no justification.'[86] As the night wore on and Göring threatened to bomb Prague, the elderly Hácha's health failed. He had to be given emergency medical injections lest anyone think his heart attack was a further example of murder.

This was the reality of politics in central Europe that Chamberlain, Halifax and the rest of them could never grasp. An exultant Hitler announced that 'the machine is on the move, nothing can stop it now' and told Hácha to call Prague and order the Czechs not to resist. At nearly four o'clock in the morning, Hácha signed away Czech independence on a paper Hitler had prepared for him; the order for German troops to move had been given an hour earlier. Advance troops arrived in Prague by 9.15 a.m. A Czech radio reporter, Franta Kocourek, had to report the enormous German victory parade in Wenceslas Square. A Wehrmacht officer stood beside him as he said: 'From somewhere far away, a huge, black crow has flown into Prague. I have seen it spread its wings and sweep down above the square over the searchlights and loudspeakers being paraded here by the German army. It must be surprised at the noise and all that is going on beneath it.'[87] Kocourek was arrested and died in 1942 in Auschwitz. That same night, Hitler slept in Beneš's former bed in Prague's Hradschin Castle, as Hradčany became overnight.

In an annexe to the Munich Agreement, Britain and France had guaranteed 'the new boundaries of the Czechoslovak State against unprovoked aggression'.[88] At a cabinet meeting on 15 March 1939, Chamberlain and Halifax claimed that this German invasion was merely 'symbolic' and that the Anglo-French guarantee of Czechoslovakia was only of an interim nature, and in any event 'was not a guarantee against the exercise of moral pressure' – an odd way of describing German subversion of its neighbour. Rather than admitting the failure of his policy, the British Prime Minister resolved to press on with it, while making half-hearted concessions to the strategies advocated by his critics. That March, even he adopted a different tone, partly because public opinion was so hostile about the 'rape of Prague', partly because representatives of Rumania arrived in London seeking help in resisting Hitler's importunate demands for privileged access to grain and oil, and finally because of the noises Hitler began making about ethnic Germans in Poland.

Having doggedly sought to diminish the number of potential enemies, Chamberlain now, belatedly and fitfully, sought to increase Britain's potential allies, although the priority given to the first endeavour meant a less than wholehearted commitment to the second. For example, the Treasury systematically blocked Polish and Rumanian attempts to secure loans to buy arms, giving them £8 million in export credit guarantees rather than the £24 million they had requested. Nor were effective steps taken to combat steady German economic penetration of the Balkans, whose agrarian produce was not vital to Britain in any case. The net effect of these restrictions was to drive those countries into dependence upon Germany.

Chamberlain proposed a joint declaration by Britain, France, the USSR and Poland that they would consult in the event of further aggression by the dictators. Neither the Poles nor the Soviets were enthusiastic that the other had been invited to the party. Since helping themselves to the coal-rich Teschen district in the dismemberment of Czechoslovakia, Poland's ruling military junta could not decide whether they were Germany's part-ner or its next victim. About all the Poles and Rumanians could agree on was their joint desire to expel the Jews. Mounting German clamour about and from within the Free City enclave of Danzig, and Hitler's personal voyage to Memel, retrieving this German-dominated area from Lithuania, resolved Polish doubts. Instead of the four-power declaration, the Poles asked for a secret understanding with Britain.

On 31 March, Chamberlain announced a British guarantee of Poland's independence – although, like the French, the British aim was to oppose German hegemony rather than to save Poland, a lost cause they were powerless to affect. Alexander Cadogan compared it with putting up a signpost, not to halt Hitler's swift succession of surprises, but as a means of sparing Chamberlain 'the agonising doubts and indecisions' inherent in his own policy.[89] No sooner had this agreement had been announced than *The Times* tried to qualify it, to accommodate further appeasement. It did not guarantee every inch of Poland, which might be the subject of future negotiations, the article grovelled. Nor was it directed against Germany; it was more of 'an appeal to their better nature'. Halifax thought this article 'just right'. Polish objections ensured that Russia was not encouraged to join the guarantee. Consequently, in August 1939 Hitler would complete the encirclement and isolation of Poland by making a deal with Russia.

Chamberlain's belief that Mussolini might soften the impact of this guarantee upon Hitler came to naught in April when the Italian dictator invaded Albania, cynically offering the British Corfu as a consolation prize. Chamberlain was forced to issue further guarantees to Greece and Rumania, in the first case to prevent the Prime Minister General Ioannis Metaxas joining the Axis camp and in the second in an effort to deny Germany oil. Characteristically, he persisted in the belief that Mussolini might restrain Hitler, even though it was now Mussolini who was on the march. Defying calls for an alliance with Russia from the Labour opposi-tion and from Churchill, Chamberlain put forth every objection, enumer-ating the countries this would annoy – not just Germany, or Poland and Rumania, but also Spain and Portugal – even though his own cabinet had come round to the view that such an alliance was necessary. Soviet counter-proposals in April for a triple alliance with Britain and France were treated with dilatory scepticism in London, despite dim awareness that the Russians might seek an alternative alliance with Germany. Having failed to prise apart the dictators or to curb their predations, Chamberlain was instrumental in ensuring that the main alternative policy was never pursued with any vigour. As Anglo-French military talks with Marshal Kliment Voroshilov petered out, Hitler saw his chance – as did Stalin, who had been watching developments with keen interest. Hitler had no moral scruples so an alliance with Stalin was merely an ideological obstacle, but the nature of the Soviet Union raised a large question mark over democratic politicians who would ally with it. Having convinced himself of the righteousness of his war on behalf of the ethnic Germans, Hitler decided that the 'little worms' he had met at Munich would not go to war over something so vacuously intangible as their national honour. In fact that is what the British and French did do, as exhaustion and impatience narrowed down their psychological options to this one conviction. On 25 August war was on, and then suddenly called off; on 1 September Hitler chanced a local war, which on the 3rd Chamberlain and Daladier converted into a European war. 'What now?' a vexed Hitler asked Ribbentrop as they stared out of the Reich Chancellery windows.[90]

CHAPTER 3

Brotherly Enemies

I FAMILY RESEMBLANCES

The advent of the Nazi regime inevitably raised the question of how the Soviet Union should respond to it, especially as Hitler had vowed to secure the Germans' future living space at Russia's expense. If the Western powers offered Hitler membership of the club, in exchange for scaling down his demands to what they regarded as reasonable, how did Stalin respond to the Nazi challenge? Before we can answer that, it may be helpful to examine what these two regimes had in common, for some fundamental identities conditioned how in turn Western leaders regarded the offer of an alliance with Russia.

On 25 January 1937, Winston Churchill addressed the annual dinner of the Chamber of Commerce in Leeds. In a talk devoted to the need for robust rearmament against Germany he touched on what Communism and National Socialism had in common:

> There are those non-God religions, Nazism and Communism. We are urged from the Continent and from different quarters that we must choose which side we are on. I repudiate both, and will have nothing to do with either. As a matter of fact, they are like two peas. Tweedledum and Tweedledee were violently contrasted compared with them. You leave out God and you substitute the devil. You leave out love and you substitute hate. I have made a resolve. I am getting on now in life. I have made a resolve that I will never go to the Arctic or the Antarctic regions in geography or in politics. Give me the temperate zone. Give me London, Paris, or New York. Let us keep to our faith and let us go somewhere and stay there where your breath

is not frozen on your lips by the secret police. Let us not wander away from broad fields of freedom into those gaunt, grim, dismal, gloomy regions.[1]

Within three years Churchill had revised this view, expressing a pragmatic willingness to sup with the Devil in hell to defeat Nazism, a figure of speech that retained his abhorrence for the Soviet system. He had identified some of the key elements which Nazism and Communism had in common: an antipathy towards transcendental religion, the vicious role of the secret police, and ideologies that organised mass hatreds – whether of capitalism, liberal democracy or entire races and social classes. This moral discourse, which out of national necessity Churchill had to put into suspended animation after June 1941, gives us a valuable starting point in considering what Communism and Nazism shared, and where they differed, although a few thoughts need to be aired about comparison itself.[2]

Comparisons should not be confused with equivalence or identity, nor be used to condemn, or exculpate, one historic horror with the aid of the other, especially by insinuating some otherwise tenuous causality. Although the Soviet gulags antedated Nazi concentration camps, Kolyma and Vorkuta did not cause or inspire Dachau, let alone Auschwitz, although the SS were aware of the Arctic gulag and toyed with re-employing it for their own purposes. It is important to emphasise that the history of German anti-Semitism anteceded anti-Bolshevism, for Jews were also blamed for liberalism, democracy and various economic crises, long before Bolshevism came to power.[3]

Time has played a role in distorting posterity's perspectives. Nazi crimes were overwhelmingly committed in 1941–5, and were then examined and judged at Nuremberg by the victors in the Second World War, whereas the crimes of the Bolsheviks came in waves over a twenty-five-year period of violence, and were only fully exposed when Communism itself collapsed in 1991. Most Nazi crimes involved non-German nationals, whereas the majority of victims of Communism were citizens of the multi-ethnic and polyglot Soviet Union. Since many of them were killed because of their nationality, we should dispense with the notion that one regime killed races while the other murdered social classes. On the other hand it is important to note that whereas Nazism expressed an extreme form of ethnic egoism, in which Germans would always be on top, the polyglot Soviet Union was effectively posited on the artificial suppression of the dominant nationality, in fact obliging ethnic Russians, with greater or lesser sincerity, to celebrate the colourful folkways of Tajiks and Uzbeks.[4]

Any decent person should respect the sensitivities of victims, although that is a relatively recent addition to the criteria relevant to writing history. Victims of mass political or religious violence do not appreciate being told that others suffer, any more than the parents of a murdered child derive comfort from being informed that many other children have been killed too. This is particularly so when the victims belong to a national or religious group, rather than a social class, which inherently lacks such intense common feeling and is not a recognised category in international law. The suffering of Chinese, Poles or Jews is more focused and enduring than that of Russian aristocrats, bourgeois or kulaks, a derogatory term for farmers who owned a few cows. But the ineffable uniqueness of suffering can also mutate into its sacralisation, a finite quantum that it is forbidden to subtract from or to diminish through revised totals or lateral comparisons. This is so when the sacral memory of suffering, or in the case of Germany guilt about having perpetrated such horrors, becomes an adjunct to, or a substitute for, transcendental religious identity, or part of a state's legitimacy, as evident in Poland or Ukraine as it is in Israel.

Not all victims are equal either. Europeans and North Americans, living in predominantly urban societies, find it difficult to empathise with victims of state violence if they were anonymous millions of peasants from cultures they do not comprehend, rather than the sort of people who share their own culture and could be living next door. Our eyes have become our primary sense too. The relative dearth of visual evidence of Soviet atrocities, in contrast to the superabundance of film and photographic material from Nazi Germany, has also conditioned how the two regimes are perceived. Although there is no footage, and almost no photographs, from the major Nazi extermination camps, most of us have images of the entrance to Auschwitz printed on our minds in a way that is not true of Kolyma or other Soviet labour camps, which have disappeared rather than being preserved for posterity.[5]

While the motives of Soviet mass murderers have not attracted sophisticated speculative scrutiny, we know much about civilised Nazi killers and their individuated, civilised victims, with whom they shared German high culture. That some loved Schubert is a cliché that masks sadistic violence by men and women who preferred yodel music played on accordions to Beethoven, as well as being an excuse for the arabesques of literary critics, which often strategically distract from what the killers shared with Western society as whole. One might almost imagine that the universe of Nazi cruelty revolves around as precious a figure as the philosopher Martin Heidegger. Hitler is 'our' monster, in a way that Stalin or Mao are for others. Nazi crimes against the Jews drew on an ancient mulch of Christian Judaeophobia that gives the Nazi crimes psychological traction among Western audiences, because its modern mutation of anti-Semitism is part of their more or less conscious heritage. The evocation of Nazi crimes rubs a collective scar in Western societies. No such shared cultural heritage exists for our perception of what was done to Chechens, Chinese, Kazakhs or Koreans, and our common humanity seems too weak to stimulate sustained attention beyond the 'isn't it dreadful?' reaction to starving Africans shown on television. Perhaps we feel we can afford to ignore the fate of Communism's victims, largely because of a guiltless certainty that nothing about us was responsible for it.[6]

The comparison of Communism and Nazism also has political and cultural aspects, which shape historical perceptions of the two regimes. Critics of the concept of totalitarianism invariably contrast the ideals of Communism with the grim practices of National Socialism, to exculpate the former. This is sleight of hand, akin to contrasting the Sermon on the Mount with the depredations of the Emperor Nero in order to calumnify Roman paganism while exalting Christianity.[7] Communism shared the legacy of the Enlightenment and socialism with entire swathes of liberal and socialist opinion in the Western democracies. The ideals of universal equality and fraternity appealed to larger constituencies than the elitist doctrines of Fascist groups, who were the demotic legatees of the anti-Jacobin counter-revolution – even if Fascists and Nazis considered themselves revolutionaries too.

Moreover, for four years the Soviet Union was a major ally of the democratic opponents of Hitler, with the deeds of the Red Army making even inveterate conservatives misty-eyed. Churchill's chief military assistant General Hastings 'Pug' Ismay tells a revealing story about his first trip to Moscow in October 1941. A British soldier, captured at Calais by the Germans, had escaped from a prisoner-of-war camp and made his way to Poland. After fleeing to (then) non-belligerent Russia 'he was accused of being a spy, thrown into solitary confinement on a starvation diet, and beaten almost daily. We took him back to England with us, and he was eventually awarded the Distinguished Conduct Medal. But the citation of the deeds which earned him this distinction was not published. The courageous endurance of devilries perpetrated on a British soldier by an ally of his country could not have been divulged at the time.'[8]

Communism had any number of Western fellow-travellers, most of them individuals who matter little or nothing today, like Sidney and Beatrice Webb or the upper-class traitors who infested Oxbridge and from their vantage points in the Foreign Office or MI6 kept Stalin abreast of sensitive developments. From foreign ambassadors to notable writers and journalists, they came, they saw and they denied everything.[9] It became bad form to denounce Communism in *bien pensant* society, the mark of a Cold War warrior or his rabid progeny, a McCarthyite. All were agreed, except for neo-Nazis and Alan Clark MP, that Nazism was uniquely abhorrent, and by comparison it did not matter that Communism was never equal or universal in practice. Unlike the Nazi *Führerprinzip*, nothing in theoretical Marxism could be construed as justifying quasi-religious personality cults – yet that is what resulted in the cases of Lenin and Stalin, not to speak of Mao or Castro. The *nomenklatura*, or those named to senior appointments, were an unelected elite with another name, from which its members derived enormous benefits and privileges, as did the wider new class of men and women who realised their ambitions through the system. The Oxbridge elite traitors imagined they would have thrived in such a set-up.

The Communist International (Comintern), so successful in recruiting spies among the privileged elites of the West, was not a vehicle of international revolution but a subsidiary instrument of Soviet foreign policy, whose line was set by Moscow. One year social democrats were 'social Fascists', the next they were allies in anti-Fascist Popular Fronts. Self-denial was a Communist virtue, and a number of Western intellectuals, like G. D. H. Cole and Eric Hobsbawm, found a strange fulfilment in suppressing their individuality in its service. All of which is to say that Communism had a network of strategically positioned apologists and supporters in place long after Nazism was vanquished.

II ON POLICE STATES

The cause they served was responsible for the arrest, torture, imprisonment or execution of vast numbers of people because of their class or national origin, with the lucky merely having their lives ruined. Under such a system, class or ethnic origin was a hereditary taint as pernicious, if not as pervasive, as one based on race, although only the Nazis set to work with an exterminatory frenzy. The Soviets preferred to use forced labour to decimate those who were not shot. Although it is vaguely distasteful to compare the ways in which people died, the NKVD secret police constructed special shooting galleries, comparable with those used in Nazi concentration camps, to murder their victims more efficiently; but they did not create industrial-sized gas chambers to kill people in their daily tens of thousands.

Both Communism and Nazism claimed to be scientifically founded ideologies. Since their pretensions to such status had no legitimate foundations, it is customary to refer to them as scientising, meaning that these creeds mimicked the methods and vocabulary of biology, in the way that kitsch mimics art. But this was also linked to visions of their future societies that were of a millenarian utopian variety. In that respect they resembled the dreams of human perfectibility that had inspired the more heretical streams in the Western Christian tradition. Communists thought they were creating a universal Golden Age, for by definition the creed believed in the perfectibility of the masses. Nazis looked forward to a Heroic Age, for their doctrines were more elitist and accorded greater importance to warrior virtues. In both cases this quest for heaven on earth, with which mundane reality never conformed, meant hell for large numbers of people who were deemed to obstruct the road to the brave new world.[10]

That hell is everlastingly associated with concentration camps. These had common origins, but the institutional spectrum was larger in the Soviet case, just as the gulag had a far longer history than its Nazi counterpart. Both the Bolshevik *kontslager* and the Nazi *Konzentrationslager* (KZ) derived their names from the Spanish original, used in Cuba to intern and isolate populations sympathetic to guerrillas, a practice copied by the British during the Boer War. Tsarist Russia also had its forced-labour camps, which at their zenith contained about twenty-six thousand persons, although the imperial regime preferred remote exile for political opponents. Accounts of Stalin's own experience of exile to Siberia, and of the number of times he simply walked away, leaving his indigenous hunter friends behind, suggest this was not life-destroying in the manner of the gulag he created. It also reflected what people had done, rather than who they were, a major distinction between authoritarian systems like Tsarist Russia and the later totalitarian regimes. The young Stalin was a notorious bank robber who fully deserved to be in prison.

Lenin's and Felix Dzerzhinsky's All-Russian Extraordinary Commission for Combating Counter-Revolution and Sabotage (the Cheka, later OGPU and later still the NKVD) was primarily responsible for the Red Terror against political opponents and members of proscribed and persecuted 'former classes' such as the bourgeoisie. The best they could hope for was to be robbed blind, or publicly humiliated through the demeaning tasks akin to the ones the Nazis imposed on middle-class Jews. Most were either shot or sent to a network of concentration camps, which commenced with a former Orthodox monastery on the remote Solovetsky Islands within the Arctic Circle. There an enterprising prisoner called Naftaly Frenkel rose to guard and then commandant, by converting the camp into a unit of production, a transformation enthusiastically adopted by Stalin. As we shall see, collectivisation and hysterical industrialisation generated a host of 'kulaks', 'wreckers' and 'saboteurs', coincident with the regime's need for more labour. The underlying principle in the gulag was brutally simple: fit prisoners who worked hard received more to eat, while the weak were starved to death. A further refinement was to abandon the traditional Tsarist distinction, which the Bolsheviks initially observed by way of fellow feeling, between the treatment of ordinary criminals and honourable political detainees. In fact, as in Nazi Germany, this hierarchy was deliberately and perversely inverted, partly because mere criminals were thought redeemable in ways that class or racial enemies and political opponents were not.

Stalin's Soviet Union contained an immense spectrum of camps, best described by the novelist–survivor Alexander Solzehnitsyn as an archipelago spreading across the country's vastness. People could be spirited away and forgotten. During the early 1930s, huge complexes of satellite camps were established like those around Vorkuta in Komi province or, the most notorious, those studded along the Kolyma river in the remote north-eastern corner of the country. If the three-month journey locked in cattle trucks and the holds of freighters did not kill you, regulations that forbade outside work only when the temperature fell to minus 60 degrees Celsius invariably would. Over the gates of each individual camp was inscribed 'Labour is a matter of honour, courage and heroism', an exhortation with parallels throughout the SS camp system from Dachau onwards whose inmates were enjoined 'Work Sets You Free'.[11]

Yet there were differences that are not trivial. If there was not much to choose between the casual brutalisation and humiliation of the inmates by their guards, the Soviet gulag system was part of the modernisation of remote regions, a process so ambitious that the skills of prisoners simply could not be ignored. The absence of a surrounding society in such inhospitable climes meant that the Soviet regime had to let a hierarchical inmate society evolve, in which those with skills – and some *zeks* or inmates were trained in the camps to occupy skilled and professional positions – assumed non-manual functions. As Solzhenitsyn's *First Circle* showed, there were camps for scientists – working on voice-recognition technology for telephones – which did not resemble Siberian lumber camps, where if the cold did not kill, the mosquitoes and heat of summer would. Nothing like this existed in the early Nazi camps, where in so far as there was work it was of a mindless treadmill variety, like men pointlessly pushing a huge roller up and down Dachau's gravel parade ground, although that too would change.

Nazi camps evolved from the initial wave of *ad hoc* and primitive detention facilities which activist packs of SA men established in barracks and factories so that they could rough up and torture political opponents. The secret police of both the Nazi and the Soviet regimes, it should be emphasised, routinised torture, in contrast to the long-harboured aversion to it of the liberal democracies. The locations of 160 such places are known, but there were many more. An estimated twenty-five thousand people, most of them Communists, were held in these centres in Prussia alone in the spring of 1933 following the Nazi seizure of power. That figure rose by two thousand in the summer as the national and local leadership of other parties were also interned. The historian Robert Gellately estimates that by the end of 1933 one hundred thousand people had spent brief periods in such camps, with a similar number subjected to brutality or harassment without being held in custody. The majority of these camps were soon disbanded, leaving some six to seven thousand detainees throughout Germany. There was even talk of abandoning camps entirely, so thoroughly had opposition been crushed. Many people seem to have believed newspaper reports that the function of these camps was re-educative, with an emphasis upon discipline, hygiene and hard work. Following two amnesties, one at Christmas 1933 and the other the following August, by the end of 1934 there were only three thousand camp inmates in the country.[12]

SS empire-building explained why the camp system was regularised and gradually expanded, part of a prerogative state that placed people beyond the protection – such as it was – of the law. In April 1934 Himmler appointed Theodor Eicke as inspector of concentration camps. Eicke was the commandant of Dachau, a camp in a munitions factory located in a satellite town of Munich. He developed the Dachau regimen for inmates, and for guards drawn from the SS Death's Head brigades, which became paradigmatic for the entire camp system, since all guards were trained at Dachau. Corporal punishment was normal, and prisoners who tried to escape, or who simply displeased the guards in some way, were shot. Eicke reduced the number of camps from seven to four and from April 1936 their costs were assumed by the Reich budget.

Although these camps were supposed to be an improvement on the earlier *ad hoc* arrangements, they were riddled with corruption as incoming inmates were robbed by the guards and every scam operated in the stores and kitchens. Prison labour was routinely used for entirely private ends, such as manufacturing furniture. As ordinary Communist detainees were released, so these camps took increasing numbers of the anti-social or recidivist criminals, together with smaller numbers of Jews convicted of race defilement under the 1935 Nuremberg Laws, which had criminalised miscegenation. By late 1936 there were 4,761 camp inmates, a figure that nearly doubled in early 1938, the year in which three new camps were opened at Buchenwald, Flossenbürg and Mauthausen in the Austrian Ostmark. These were adjuncts to brickworks and stone quarries owned by the SS German Earth and Stone Works, whose major function was to supply monumental building projects. The number of camps expanded again after the outbreak of war, adding Gross-Rosen in Silesia and then Natzweiler in newly reconquered Alsace.

III LIVING GODS

The comparison between Communism and Nazism is not exhausted by the subtle differences that were evident in how both regimes went about the unsubtle business of mass murder, although that is surely what lends them enduring historical significance. It may be fascinating that ordinary Germans and Russians still purchased bread, milk and petrol and slept with each other, but that is not why anyone remains interested in this type of regime. The totalitarian dictators represented a regression to what Churchill called 'one-man power', a form of idol worship alien and odious to Anglo-Saxon civilisation, and more akin to that of the ancient Egyptians and Aztecs with their monumental structures and idols demanding perpetual human sacrifice. Both were based on something that in softer forms perennially threatens liberal societies. They were anti-individualist, with the Nazis' slogan 'the common good before your own good' being as heroically collectivist as anything in Bolshevism. That at least was how the Dresden philologist Victor Klemperer saw things when on 31 December 1933 he wrote in his diary: 'National Socialism and Communism: both are materialistic and tyrannical, both disregard and negate the freedom of spirit and of the individual' – terms one rarely finds in the work of modern historians, for whom freedom, unlike identity, seems to have gone out of fashion.[13]

In Stalin's case, the emergence of a full-blown personality cult was more protracted than in the case of Hitler, whose charismatic dominance of the Nazi movement was established by the mid-1920s, before assuming godlike proportions in the following decade. Both men converted character flaws and social maladroitness into political assets. Hitler made the transition from being an awkward ranting bore into a compelling public orator with a story, indivisible from his own everyman's odyssey, which resonated powerfully with enough of his adoptive countrymen to make his rise irresistible in the view of the elites who jigged him into power. The Nazi Party was nothing without him, and was itself structured around the leadership principle. 'For us the idea is the Führer, and each Party member has only to obey the Führer,' Hitler informed the left-wing Nazi Otto Strasser in 1930.[14] Although Hitler's worldview, as he grandiloquently called it, was a mish-mash of ideas from the anti-Semitic *völkisch* right, his personal synthesis of it was the *fons et origo* of Nazi doctrine. Heterodox tendencies, especially those that sought to elevate issues of class over race, were marginalised along with their exponents at an early stage. Violence was used sparingly against senior comrades, and only when Hitler's power was at stake. The 1934 Röhm purge was not a clash about ideas, but a power struggle between the SA and the army, with Hitler using his SS to destroy the less useful organisation. Commenting on the 'night of the long knives' to his External Trade Commissar Anastas Mikoyan, Stalin exclaimed, 'What a great fellow! How well he pulled this off!' Actually Hitler had not pulled off much more than securing his own position. While he had smashed the German left and his own party militia, until 1944 he never struck at the political right, and came to regard that tactical omission as one of his few failings.

Unlike Hitler, Stalin was not the originator of a doctrine (although there was a theory and practice called Stalinism) and had to work within a vast corpus of Marxist thought, as well as Lenin's adaptations of it to the requirements of the Bolshevik party. He was one of the minor paladins of the Revolution and Civil War, overshadowed by the more charismatic Lenin and Trotsky in the oligarchic leadership. His public persona was modest and stiff, and his oratory ponderous and simple, using mantra-like repetitions and a jabbing forefinger for emphasis. It has been remarked, with justice, that Stalin's real Nazi analogue was the slow and heavy Party bureaucrat Martin Bormann, rather than the more erratic Führer whose aversion to a day's paperwork was notorious. Although Stalin was less assiduous than is often claimed, he was in his element manipulating committees, the preferred format of Bolshevik party-government, while building up a loyal clientele like a latterday boyar. Among these lackeys, he relaxed into a sinister camaraderie, watchful for personal foibles that might emerge during epic drinking sessions.[15] Above all, he was a vengeful man, with an accumulation of resentments for obscure slights. Occasionally he let the mask slip, as when in 1923 he explained his chief pleasure in life to two associates: 'The greatest delight is to pick out one's enemy, prepare all the details of the blow, to slake one's thirst for a cruel revenge and then go home to bed!'[16]

With Lenin's patronage, Stalin became a not especially distinguished member of the Soviet collective leadership, although he had belonged to the Central Committee since 1912. While not without intellectual preten-sions as both poet and theorist, he hated the flashier intellectuals among his comrades, many of them Jews, or men whose role in the Revolution and Civil War was more distinguished then his own.[17] He had the reputa-tion of being a practical man, a pragmatist who supported the partial privatisation of the New Economic Policy (NEP), while eschewing Trotsky's dream of world revolution. The only major area in which he differed from Lenin was his reluctance to accord non-Russian nationalities the degree of autonomy represented by the proclamation of the USSR. Like his colleagues, Stalin undertook a wide variety of roles; so many that in 1922 he had to be instructed to work a four-day week. In that year he was appointed to the relatively insignificant post of general secretary of the Party secretariat. In December that same year, when Lenin contemplated potential successors, he enumerated the flaws of both Trotsky and Stalin in his 'Letter to the Congress' or, as it became known, his Testament. In Stalin he detected a remorseless meanness of spirit beyond the hardness of heart common among the comrades – for Lenin himself had been no shrinking violet in terrorising rivals.

Following Lenin's incapacitating stroke, Stalin made himself indispen-sable to the factions jostling to replace the Bolshevik leader, the Left

Oppositionists and Right Deviationists, factions that differed as to the way forward. He attracted to himself such loyalists as Kaganovich, Kirov, Mikoyan, Molotov, Ordzhonikidze and Voroshilov who became his personal cronies. He used his position on the Orgburo, which controlled Party appointments, to favour supporters with key positions throughout the Communist Party apparat – the 'little Stalins' who, obviously enough, were not without ambitions of their own. Ambitious young fellows like Nikolai Yezhov also knew the value of becoming experts in what is nowadays called HR (human resources) because that was the boss's own expertise. The oligarch-in-chief had dextrously destroyed all rivals by the late 1920s, although at that time it was still not *bon ton* to shoot fellow leaders. What he had achieved was to create a disciplined party of the type that Lenin had aspired to. The inner party debates and discussions, and the factions that resulted, were replaced by an organisation that put discipline above revolutionary idealism, even as the Party's strategic decision-making Politburo itself became the cipher of one man and his immediate cronies, practising a highly informal manner of government.[18]

After a seven-years period of relative grace associated with the NEP, in which Marxist-Leninist dogma was relaxed to enable the economy to recover to its pre-1914 levels, comparison with the advanced Western world, and strategic fear of Britain, France and Japan, led to the fateful decisions in favour of agricultural collectivisation. In Stalin's reasoning, enhanced grain exports from factory-like farms would generate credits for the imported capital plant needed for crash state-planned industrialisation, which in turn would yield enhanced military security. The systematic exploitation of convict labour would also build the symbols of heroic modernity that the regime would present to itself, its people and the outside world in a ferocious drive to catch up with the West in ten years. This endeavour was symbolised by the 140-mile long White Sea Canal, a project begun in September 1931 and completed twenty-one months later, four weeks ahead of schedule. Some 175,000 convicts worked on this project day and night with their bare hands, at a cost of twenty-five thousand of their lives.[19] Finally, the frenzied pace also enabled the regime to remobilise the energies and enthusiasms of the Party itself, as an era of pragmatic compromise gave way to the aggressive resumption of the quest for social utopia. All these things came together to produce mass death on a previously unimaginable scale.[20]

Collectivisation enabled the Party, its secret police and young enthusiastic urban volunteers to penetrate the countryside in depth, making short work of a residual private sector, Orthodox Christianity and the vestiges of several nationalisms. Peasants, with their weather-beaten idiosyncrasy and hidebound superstitious religiosity, were to be remade into muscular adjuncts to machines. Combine harvesters and tractors were to transform the face of the countryside, which would be illuminated with the miracle of electrification that brought light bulbs into the remotest hovels. Force and surprise were used to coerce peasants into new collective farms, where they either worked as labourers employed by the state or had to surrender a proportion of their product from land they rented. An internal passport system in the cities ensured they were not free to migrate there. The kulaks were excluded from this process, and despatched in fulfilment of arrest quotas to remote concentration camps devoted to gold mining or lumbering.

The dragooning of the peasantry encountered resistance in various parts of the empire, notably in the Ukraine, where farmers ceased to deliver grain to meet the exorbitant quotas demanded by the state. It is likely that the hardness of heart Stalin showed towards the Ukraine was also connected to the persistence of nationalist sentiment there. The countryside was reduced to a resentful shambles where starvation threatened. In July 1932 Chairman of the Council of People's Commissars Molotov reported to the Politburo after a visit to the Ukraine: 'We definitely face the spectre of famine, especially in the rich bread areas.' The Politburo, or rather Stalin himself, decided: 'Whatever the cost, the confirmed plan for grain requisition must be fulfilled.' As a direct result of these policies, at least six million people starved to death after their diet had been reduced to bark, berries and rats, while countless others were sentenced to death or terms in the gulag for withholding pitiful quantities of grain.[21]

This heroically irrational attempt to conform reality to an ideology – all dissenting economists were simply shot – was increasingly attributed to the vision of one man who emerged from what had been a collective leadership. Stalin deftly assumed the mantle of the dead Lenin. The loyal mourner, already the authoritative voice at Lenin's funeral, underwent a merger with the myth of the dead leader, the embalmed embodiment of the October revolutionary moment.[22] The Lenin cult included a Red icon corner in many homes, although the zealot who placed a photo of Lenin in his baby's pram to influence its future development was probably overly optimistic. By the late 1920s, Stalin was represented as Lenin's heir. Retroactively his propagandists inflated Stalin's role as Lenin's trusty adviser, gradually giving Stalin greater prominence while Lenin was reduced to a name on the spine of a book Stalin held in his hands. As in the case of Hitler, Stalin's image was omnipresent and the object of hysterical adulation. Such images, especially when children were used for reasons of sentimentality, usefully distracted from the highly dysfunctional nature of both dictators' domestic arrangements, coincidentally involving the suicide of women they had been intimate with, Geli Raubal and Stalin's wife Nadya. Both leaders were bombarded with flattery and gifts from all sides – although in Stalin's case the Red empire was sufficiently vast and multicultural to take this to extremes of Asiatic fawning that even Nazis could not match.

The accidents and setbacks that accompanied crash industrialisation required a search for saboteurs and wreckers, which developed into a much more extensive reckoning with the Bolshevik old guard, and with any individual or category of persons who attracted Stalin's malevolence. Defence was the best form of attack, although this developed into what amounted to a giant blood transfusion within the Party to secure for Stalin more compliant tools than he had. The fortuitous assassination by a jealous husband of the Leningrad Party boss Sergei Kirov in December 1934, a year after there had been rumblings of discontent regarding Stalin's erratic conduct aired at the Seventeenth Party Congress, gave the dictator the opportunity to strike at past and prospective opponents. He did this with documented relish, since at the height of the Terror he personally combed through nearly four hundred albums containing forty-four thousand names, ticking each with his endorsement of Purge Commission boss Yezhov's provisional sentence. His face flickered into view when light flashed into a shadowy recess during show trials whose highpoint was invariably the confession. Bolshevik political culture had assimilated an older peasant mentality of us and them as well as a secularised belief in ambient demons, and the Civil War had acculturated them to colossal violence. In Stalin's own case, and he was manifestly the driving force behind the Great Terror of 1936–8, a vast exercise in purposive paranoia directed at the Communist Party and an early propensity to psychopathic violence, well attested by Simon Sebag Montefiore, was combined with a thoroughly unMarxist admiration for Ivan the Terrible, dark scourge of Moscow's boyars. His iron-fisted henchman Yezhov's maxims for his subordinates were 'beat, destroy, without sorting out' and 'better too far than not enough'.

This political culture ensured that Stalin had many willing executioners, who spoke and thought like thugs and advertised the blood spatters on their shirts after an interrogation. There were also hundreds of thousands of younger cadres who sought to move into the shoes of dead men, although only those who seek some vestige of progress, even in the Terror, regard social mobility as its most salient feature. The chosen instrument was the NKVD, the self-styled 'unsheathed sword of the Revolution', with its Lubyanka headquarters and network of national and regional offices, and the extra-judicial gulag empire of NKVD-controlled concentration camps. Stalin's choice for head of the NKVD at this time was Yezhov, a pint-sized individual he nicknamed 'Blackberry'. Although Yezhov was not a career policeman, he had angled for the post with a stream of indirect criticisms of his predecessor Genrikh Yagoda's professional shortcomings, the oblique manner the Bolsheviks preferred for ousting an enemy or rival.[23]

Lev Kamenev and Grigory Zinoviev were the first targets, arrested and tried for alleged involvement in the killing of Kirov. Conveniently, the assassin, Nikolaev, had already been shot, and a key witness, Kirov's body-guard, had suffered a fatal 'accident' while in police custody. Kamenev and Zinoviev admitted their moral culpability for Kirov's murder and were given five- and ten-year jail sentences. After more arrests had been effected, they and the exiled Trotsky were next accused of collusion with foreign powers, a charge that also leached towards people involved in industrial accidents that were viewed as wilful sabotage. At their show trial in Moscow in the autumn of 1936, they confessed to membership of an Anti-Soviet Trotskyist-Zinovievite Centre that had conspired to kill top Soviet leaders, and were shot the following morning.

Torture and the ensuing faked confessions were used to ramify putative plots endlessly throughout the ranks of the Party. Stalin personally issued instructions to have people beaten to a pulp. By lowering the age of eligibility for execution to twelve-year-olds, it was possible to threaten the accused person's children to secure compliance. This threat was decisive in the case of the revisionist Marxist Nikolai Bukharin, who had fathered a much loved child at an advanced age. Broken men and women humiliated themselves in court, with a few plucking up the courage to recant their confessions, only to reappear more broken and ready to confess again after further sessions with chair legs and iron bars. Judges and prosecutors sneered and vituperated at the defendants, while mob-like meetings were organised to urge the courts to greater rigours.

Bukharin and fellow Right Deviationists were linked to the so-called Trotskyist-Zinoviev Centre, itself linked in turn to foreign intelligence agencies. The web of putative conspiracy spread to include Yagoda and senior NKVD figures, together with Red Army commanders, for the army, military intelligence and secret police had themselves been infiltrated by what was surreally called the Centre of Centres. Yagoda and some 2,273 state security officers were arrested, including many of the commandants of gulags, and accused of corruption and incompetence as well as membership of 'Right-Trotskyist terrorist and sabotage organisations'.[24] Most of them were shot. So were large numbers of political prisoners, and especially Trotskyites, already held in the camps, who were shot with or without the benefit of a perfunctory hearing by an NKVD troika.

Among the false charges against Yagoda was that he had sprayed a mercury-based poison on the windows of his deputy and successor's office. In the real world, at this time Yezhov ordered the killing of Abram Slutsk, the head of the NKVD's own foreign intelligence directorate: he was lured to an appointment, subdued with chloroform and injected with lethal poison in his right arm. The death certificate claimed he had had a heart attack.[25] In July 1937 the focus on high-profile individuals was replaced by blanket categories of suspects. Under the so-called kulak order, 268,500 people were slated for arrest, of whom 75,000 were to be shot and 194,000 sent to camps. By the time Yezhov had finished, 385,000 had been shot and 316,000 sent to the camps. Entire ethnic groups were falsely accused of anti-Soviet activity, to which the only response was a series of 'national operations' that resulted in the murder of 42,000 ethnic Germans and the arrest of 112,000 Poles, of whom half were shot. Even the citizens of Outer Mongolia were not safe, with eleven thousand arrested and six thousand shot.

In early 1938 Bukharin, Alexei Rykov, Yagoda and others were tried and shot, while their families were either murdered too or exiled to the camps, the fate of Yagoda's wife, parents, sisters, nephews and nieces. As Yagoda's example suggests, leadership of the NKVD was a dangerous occupation, giving a new meaning to the metaphor of knowing where the bodies were buried. Despite Yezhov's abject prostration before him, Stalin suspected that his NKVD chief reserved special information for himself. In April 1938 Yezhov was made commissar of water transport, a post Yagoda had also held, as convict-built canals were part of the NKVD's remit. In August one of his key aides in the Far East fled to Japanese-controlled Manchuria. Stalin moved Lavrenty Beria from Georgia to act as Yezhov's deputy, just as Yezhov had been brought in to shadow Yagoda. In a characteristic ploy that Stalin used to distance himself from what he had instigated, the

NKVD was corporately accused of excesses in the previous two years, in which 750,000 people had been shot and buried in mass pits surrounding the big cities. A further 750,000 were deported to the gulags in slow trains that clanked to the frozen peripheries of empire.

Yezhov knew the signs and started drinking more heavily than he habitually did and failing to turn up for duty with his customary zeal. Beria began by arresting Yezhov's subordinates and sent the interrogation protocols to Stalin. Yezhov's second wife Evgenia committed suicide after she had been unsettled by arrests of those near to her. Two days before she killed herself, with Veronal tablets supplied by her husband, she wrote a desperate plea to Stalin, which went unanswered. In November 1938 Yezhov resigned as head of the NKVD. He still entertained hopes of election to the Central Committee when he attended a meeting of party elders in February 1939. When his name was mentioned, Stalin rose and, puffing on his Dunhill pipe, left his corner and summoned Yezhov to the front of the meeting. 'Well, what do you think of yourself?' he asked. Yezhov desperately pleaded his loyalty to Stalin and the Party only to be cut off with sharp questions about his associates, men whom Yezhov had already reported for conspiracy. Stalin again interjected:

> Yes, yes, yes! When you felt you were about to be caught, then you came in a hurry. But what about before that? Were you organising a conspiracy? Did you want to kill Stalin? Top officials of the NKVD are plotting, but you, supposedly, are not involved. You think I don't see anything? Do you remember who sent you on a certain date for duty with Stalin? Who? With revolvers? Why revolvers near Stalin? Why? To kill Stalin? And if I hadn't noticed? What then?[26]

Each sentence interlocked precisely in a relentless steel trap of paranoia from which there was no way out except through the door in response to Stalin's dismissal: 'Well? Go on, get out of here!' Yezhov was arrested in April and interrogated throughout a year of incarceration. His life story was transformed from a Russian Bolshevik with impeccable proletarian and revolutionary credentials into that of a promiscuous Lithuanian bisexual whose factory-worker father had been a brothel keeper before he married Yezhov's mother, a bar-room dancer. At his trial Yezhov struck a defiant note, shouting, 'I have fought honourably against enemies and have exterminated them.' His only sin, he said, was that he had purged too few of them. Yezhov was shot on 2 February 1940.

As an industrial society based on market capitalism with huge nation-alised elements, Nazi Germany underwent no equivalent to Soviet collec-tivisation of agriculture. German farmers were not benighted superstitious illiterates, who had to be dragged screaming into the twentieth century, but rather the nation's finest biological stock with an honourable place in an ideology that mystified soil as well as blood. Whereas Soviet artistic propaganda celebrated the mechanisation of the countryside, machines hardly figure in Nazi-era depictions of farmers, who seemed to belong to a previous age. The law sought to protect family-owned individual farms from the baleful influence of mortgage debt or partible inheritance, although the rate of industrialisation ensured that the secular drift from land to city accelerated. Both regimes extolled the virtues of the industrial worker, whose heroic nobility was celebrated at every opportunity as well as through public art, but neither did much to disturb the boss classes, who in the Nazi economy continued to make private profits for themselves and their shareholders, while Soviet managers were tools of the state, doomed if their businesses underperformed.

IV PARTY MEN

Both Nazi Germany and the Soviet Union were one-party states, with membership being a ticket to privilege and preferment that had no analogue in democratic countries. In Britain, membership of the Labour Party might mean access to a co-operative funeral scheme; for a Conservative admission to a garden fête, but not much more. Much the same applied to Democrats and Republicans in the US, with such local refinements as open primaries. By 1921 the Bolshevik bureaucracy was ten times greater than that of the tsars, employing two and a half million people, or twice the numbers working in industry. For all the differences in ideology, the Nazi Party performed many similar functions to the Communists. Both parties concealed complex personal networks based on patron–client relations that cut across the meritocracy they formally espoused. In theory, members were activist elites that communicated the will of the leadership to the mass of the population, while exercising a vigi-lant tutelage over them.

For both systems, informing on others was a duty at the cellular level, where the Party came really close to life as it was lived. Membership of the

Nazi Party, however, did not entail the remorseless self-scrutiny that was integral to being a Communist, which had more in common with the world of monks and priests. There was no Nazi equivalent to the formal course of study, or the confessional autobiographies that Communists had to prepare for regular Control Commission purges, which served to contract the Party after periods of indiscriminate expansion. After June 1934, when he settled accounts with under a hundred opponents in the night of the long knives, Hitler never undertook anything even approximating to the Great Terror, which as we have seen resulted in the deaths of three-quarters of a million people, the majority of them Communists. By Soviet standards, the Great Terror was not even a major event, if one compares it with the Ukrainian terror-famine, or with what came later.

Corruption was also common to regimes where personal whim became law and the Party stood above normal legal scrutiny. Boorish and delinquent behaviour had been one of the minor forms of Bolshevik subversion of authority under the Tsarist regime. In the 1920s the Bolsheviks advertised their personal asceticism, avoiding jewellery, gold teeth and smart clothes in favour of military boots, crumpled uniforms and scuffed leather jackets. The ideologist Aaron Solts thought it best to look like 'a big slob' such as he was himself. These outward signs betokened proletarian identity, or rather identification with the proletariat, and revolutionary commitment, for the fashion was derived from the Civil War. Bad habits, notably alcoholism, resulted in black marks in a Party that regarded such conduct as symptomatic of the social order it was eradicating. Vodka was like religion in creating a fuzzy worldview. Yet the 'new man' described by Bolshevik moralists and writers was a sober, rational being, with the soullessness of an engineer.[27]

Here again there is a parallel with the generation that came after the founders of Nazism. The founders still paid lip-service to the European values of their parents' and grandparents' generations, from which they represented a sort of grand apostasy. These self-styled revolutionaries were conspirators and buccaneers, who knew enough about great paintings to want to steal them. The next generation, the one that Nazism forged, was described by the exiled Sebastian Haffner in the following terms:

> What inspires and excites them is the vision, already quite undisguised, of the vast, uniform establishment for work, procreation, and recreation to which they will shape the conquered world; the dream of tabula rasa. The intelligent among them read Jünger and Niekisch,

and the saying of Soviet Marshal Tukhachevsky that 'The world must become naked again' draws forth a deep response from them … To them murder, torture, and destruction are no more a voluptuous disorder but 'the New Order'.

Haffner called them 'prize scholars of inhumanity' – or what a contemporary historian calls 'the generation of the unbounded'.[28] There was a similar transition from the old bank-robber Bolshevik generation – epitomised by Stalin himself – to the technicians of power who ran the secret-police empire. In both systems there was a dichotomy between the official public morality and the private squalor beneath it.

Soviet reality did not resemble the ideal image created by such professional moralists as Solts for the benefit of Communist youth or Komsomol members, although Solts did volunteer 'We are the ruling class here, in our country, and life will be constructed according to us,' which proved horribly true.[29] Inequalities between the animals on the farm were as incremental and insidious as George Orwell was to depict them. The senior leadership occupied high-ceilinged apartments in the Kremlin, where they had the benefits of a communal kitchen, domestic servants and a car pool stocked with imported black Cadillacs. The leaders and their families lived in each other's pockets as a tight-knit group. Although until the late 1920s even Stalin could walk unaccompanied to and from his offices, by the end of the decade he had a full complement of OGPU bodyguards and an armoured luxury train for his trips out of the capital. The leadership also shared imposing mansions, built for an oil tycoon, at Zubalovo, about twenty miles from Moscow, which were equipped with libraries, billiard rooms and later a cinema. Holidays grew longer and more luxurious. Instead of taking a week here and there, Stalin and his inner circle took a month or two off in the semi-tropical south, in dacha complexes in the Crimea or around the coast of the Black Sea.

Although Stalin was personally puritanical and mean with money, like Hitler he had an artistic and literary clientele, led by the writer Maxim Gorky, who was given an art deco mansion in Moscow, a country dacha and cash gifts. Other potentates lived extremely well too. The OGPU/NKVD boss Genrikh Yagoda was a notorious sybarite, with an enormous collection of pornographic images, women's lingerie and French wines, distributed around the four houses he used. He spent four million roubles decorating them, and his favourite dacha had two thousand orchids and roses. By the time Yezhov moved into his executed predecessor's Kremlin apartment, leather jackets were a thing of the past. In 1935 Stalin restored the title of marshal for the armed forces, with an equivalent title for the head of the NKVD. Resplendent uniforms came back into fashion, along with lavish parties where the wives of the leadership engaged in competitive display.[30]

Naked self-interest was as evident in Russia as in Nazi Germany. On 29 August 1936, Professor Andrei Vyshinsky, Rector of Moscow University, wrote to the board of the co-operative in which was located the dacha of Leonid Serebryakov, a close friend of Lenin's and head of the Directorate of Roadways. Vyshinsky himself had a modest one-storey house in the same complex, but had long admired Serebryakov's grander establishment. 'You are a lucky man, Leonid Petrovich. Everything you have is wonderful – your life and your dacha.' Serebryakov was arrested on 17 August 1936 and tortured into confessing espionage, wrecking and so forth. As prosecutor-general, rather than professor, Vyshinsky had a very personal interest in the outcome of the trial. By October he had obtained the house, while receiving 38,990 roubles for the one he vacated, together with a 20,000-rouble grant to obliterate every trace of Serebryakov from the new residence. Even as Vyshinsky rose in court to ask of Serebryakov, 'Please tell me when it was that you renewed your anti-Soviet criminal activity,' he was engaged in appropriating, as 'state property', the latter's home, which passed out of the hands of the co-operative thanks to Vyshinsky's lawyerly cunning. The 17,500 roubles which the late Serebryakov had paid for it (he was shot on 30 January 1937) went into Vyshinsky's pockets, although some bold soul deducted 2,574 roubles for eight sets of curtains. Zorya Serebryakov, author of the best-selling *Women of the French Revolution,* was sent to a concentration camp. Vyshinsky had the old house torn down, despite having refurbished it, and then with the aid of 600,000 roubles from the State Treasury, had a new dacha built, which duly acquired a pool, tennis court, volleyball court and a large area of fenced-off private riverside.[31]

Although the Nazis had spent a decade denouncing the snouts-in-the-troughs *Bonzenwirtschaft* ('bossocracy') of the Weimar Republic, they made the maxim *enrichissez-vous* the cardinal rule of political life. Because the Party's last lap en route to power coincided with the Depression, members routinely depicted themselves as hardly-done-by victims of a rotten system, who were entitled to compensation. Although many of them had made themselves unemployed through their extreme activities and opinions, almost to a man they claimed that before 1933 they had been persecuted and victimised. They were unemployed because they had become Nazis rather than, as is often assumed, the other way round. Still, they managed a good living, because those who jangled the ubiquitous collection tins in front of donors to various Nazi causes were entitled to pocket a quarter of the take, a limit respected by few.

The compensation culture swung into high gear after January 1933. A law was passed to waive all fines and penalties imposed on Nazis convicted of assault, theft or vandalism, with the time limit brought forward to August 1934 to cover crimes committed against opponents after Hitler had come to power. An SS man even had his teeth fixed at public expense after he had lost a few brawling with Communists. Nazis who lived in public housing found that the rent was significantly reduced, while there were one-off annual payments to help them celebrate a happy Christmas. Since so many Nazi rank and file were unemployed, strenuous efforts were made to find them decent jobs in either the public or private sectors. The postal service, for example, took on more than thirty thousand 'deserving National Socialists' between 1933 and 1937. Some private firms had to employ so many needy 'old fighters' that they faced bankruptcy. Other firms, with Nazi owners, got the lion's share of publicly awarded contracts, regardless of whether they had put in the most competitive bid. Opportunities for this sort of corruption multiplied with the exponential growth of huge Nazi sectoral formations, such as the German Labour Front or German Womanhood, which in turn awarded lucrative private sector contracts. In addition to the prodigious membership dues these vast organisations accrued, they also benefited from the property and equipment they purloined from prohibited political rivals and trades unions. Many of the benefits they offered ordinary working-class Germans – such as 'Strength through Joy' cruises to Madeira – were disproportionately occupied by Party fat cats and their families.

Meanwhile, the head of the Labour Front's contracts department used bribery to secure building contracts for its construction arm. In 1936–7 he handed out some 580,000 Reichsmarks for this purpose. He went to some lengths to cultivate Sepp Dietrich, the head of SS-Leibstandarte Adolf Hitler, the dictator's personal bodyguards. Dietrich received gold cigarette cases, hunting rifles, paintings, silk shirts and ties, while he and his SS men enjoyed lavish Labour Front hospitality. Each Christmas, Labour Front Chief Robert Ley also gave Dietrich a gratuity of RM 20,000. In 1934 Dietrich received a RM 50,000 loan from the Labour Front's own bank which he used to purchase a villa. Two years later he sold the house back to the bank for twice its purchase price. In return for such generosity, the Labour Front was awarded the contract to remodel Leibstandarte's barracks at Berlin Lichterfelde. The ostentation of these political nouveaux riches, with their Mercedes and fur-coated wives, grated on the moral sense of many ordinary Germans who, doubtless, had frowned at over-dressed Jews. Paradoxically none of this opprobrium attached to the ascetic bachelor Führer, brooding for Germany on his mountain-top eyrie. In fact, he benefited through the widespread belief that 'if only the Führer knew' he would descend on the culprits like Christ among the moneychangers in the Temple.[32]

Jobbing 'old fighters' into posts with the municipal gas or water works was not the only form of political patronage. Starting at the top, Nazi paladins disposed of huge secret funds from which they dispensed largesse to their clients. Although he made much of taking no salary, Hitler's private expenses were defrayed by the state while he had first options at art sales, building up a personal collection of five thousand works. He could also dip into a personal fund, through which the enormous sum of RM 700 million had passed by 1945. This was partly made up of royalties from *Mein Kampf*, a copy of which was presented to every married couple, while revenues from stamps bearing his portrait yielded RM 52 million. Legacies to the Führer from supporters were exempt from inheritance tax. Hitler used this largesse to buy loyalty or reward those he took an interest in. Beneficiaries included senior Wehrmacht commanders such as Wilhelm Keitel (RM 764,000), Leeb (RM 888,000) and the tank expert Heinz Guderian who used RM 1,240,000 to purchase the appropriately named Villa Panzer. Favoured artists, like the actor Emil Jannings or the monumental sculptor Josef Thorak, received country houses. Hitler also paid off senior Nazis who had fallen from grace – Stalin would have shot them.

Such private slush funds were common among senior Nazi figures. Reichsführer-SS Heinrich Himmler had two special accounts with the Dresdner and Stein banks called 'Special Accounts S and R', primarily used to pay off the debts of favoured SS subordinates, or as subventions towards their holidays and house purchases. The accounts were also used to secure larger loans for the SS's own economic enterprises. The weird products of the SS porcelain works – yuletide lights and figurines of SS men – provided the Reichsführer with a range of birthday and seasonal presents for subordinates or such foreign admirers as Lord Londonderry. Command of a concentration-camp empire enabled him to loan Max Amann, the head of the Party's Eher Verlag publishing empire, the services of prisoners as gardeners, bricklayers and roofers. Ilse Hess, wife of the Führer's deputy Rudolf, similarly had Jehovah's Witnesses from the Sachsenhausen and Ravensbrück camps tending her plants and vegetables. Göring was probably the most avaricious. His pseudo-aristocratic lifestyle, involving hunting and collecting paintings, became paradigmatic for the rest, with even a working-class drunk like Labour Front Chief Robert Ley obsessed with filling his walls with Old Masters.

The annual running costs of Göring's magnificent hunting lodge Carinhall at Schorfheide were nearly half a million Reichsmarks, on top of the RM 15 million the complex had already cost the taxpayer. Göring had another hunting establishment at Rominten, a villa in the Air Ministry complex in Berlin, an alpine residence on the Obersalzberg, a castle and five more hunting lodges scattered across Pomerania and throughout East Prussia. Then there was the special train, with its bakery and wagons for ten luxury automobiles. The two residential carriages alone cost the taxpayer RM 1,320,000 per annum. The German car industry threw in a yacht called *Carin II* to complement Carinhall (named after his wife) worth another RM 750,000. His personal art collection, mostly stolen from Jews and others, had 1,375 paintings, 250 sculptures and 168 tapestries worth a total of several hundred million marks. His declared taxable income was RM 15,795, on which he paid RM 190 tax.

Compared to Göring, Propaganda Minister Joseph Goebbels was austere. In 1932 his income as Berlin's Gauleiter was a modest RM 619. A year later he was receiving an annual ministerial salary of RM 38,000, still fairly modest but supplemented by another RM 300,000 in fees for his weekly editorial in *Das Reich*, his own ministry's newspaper. In 1936 he acquired a villa on the exclusive island of Schwanenwerder in the lakeside Wannsee suburb of Berlin. It had been compulsorily purchased for RM 117,500 from a Jewish doctor. In 1939 Goebbels sold it to an industrialist, but continued to live there rent-free. The Berlin municipality also gave him usufruct of a piece of land on Bogensee, where he spent RM 2,200,000 building a splendid house. Later it would gift him a neighbouring 500 acres of woods where he could frolic with his many mistresses.

The Party's regional bosses, the Gauleiters, were supposed to epitomise the genial, populist face of the movement, but were known as 'golden pheasants' or 'pashas'. They created their own foundations, with which they built up major industrial operations and rewarded their clienteles. The initial capital came from the revenue of regional Party newspapers, money diverted from public drives to help the unemployed, or commercial enterprises expropriated from Jews. These 'black accounts', as they were collectively known, were not audited by the Nazi Party's Reich Treasurer, who was powerless to intervene in what was seen as a matter of political patronage. The tax affairs of senior Nazis were also deemed so sensitive that they all had to be centrally filed at an office in Berlin, where all the obvious instances of tax evasion and fraud went unnoticed.[33]

V NEW MORAL BEINGS

It is important to grasp the grubby realities of both the Nazi and the Communist systems, because they claimed to have instituted reigns of public virtue through such slogans as 'healthy popular instinct'. Both dictatorships abandoned traditional moral norms based on transcendental authority or natural law to institute the regimes of hate rather than love that Churchill spoke of. They were contemptuous of what, during the Civil War, Trotsky dismissed as 'papist–Quaker babble about the sanctity of human life', a view he backed up with machine guns pointing at the backs of his own troops.[34] For Marxists, ethics were a branch of metaphysics, superstructural flim-flam that camouflaged an iniquitous social order. Bukharin once wrote that building Communism was akin to a carpenter making a bench, with whatever was expedient being necessary: '"Ethics" transforms itself for the proletariat, step by step, into simple and comprehensible rules of conduct necessary for communism, and, in point of fact, ceases to be ethics'.[35]

Communism and Nazism claimed to be agents of vast historic processes, which served to diminish the individual moral agency of leaders and subordinates. There were a few subtle differences, for Hitler still invoked Providence as his guide and paid lip-service to the Almighty, references which were off-limits for the atheist ex-seminarian Stalin, even if he occasionally referred to a God he thought did not exist and would relicense Orthodoxy when his regime faced defeat in 1941.[36] For Bolshevism, the supreme moral value was represented by the Party as motor force of the class struggle; whatever obstructed or resisted the onward march of progress was, *a priori*, evil. 'Everything is moral that serves the world revolution, and everything is immoral that serves to split the ranks of the proletariat, to disorganise and weaken it.'[37] The concepts of murder and theft were replaced by 'liquidation' and 'expropriation', words that petit-bourgeois apologists continue to use, to show how progressive they are.

Nazism similarly abandoned any notion of a universal morality. It saw the preservation and propagation of the Aryan-Germanic race as the ultimate good, with the operation of allegedly natural laws being evidence of divine inspiration. In this cosmology, the Jews occupied the diabolic role of Satan, as any moral, social or political evil, however improbable, could be blamed on their pernicious influence. To fight the Jew was 'doing the Lord's work' as Hitler put it. While few Germans probably shared the fully developed messianic mania which that statement reflects, anti-Semitism could not have been other than pervasive. Many reasons may explain why Germans disliked Jews – from material envy to provincial resentment of their coruscating urban wit – but they may also have included subconscious resentment towards the moral sobriety even secular Jews espoused, which was why Nazism found such a ready audience for propaganda that generalised on to the group the excesses or misconduct of a few Jews.[38]

In both political creeds, entire categories of people were removed from the orbit of reciprocal moral obligation through the use of egregious stereotypes that converted individuals into members of demonised categories. Both totalitarian parties used zoomorphic imagery to associate their opponents with insects, rats and other vermin, but it was their ability to substitute categories for individuals that was especially pernicious. A man with a Jewish best friend saw him being arrested for deportation by the Gestapo. He recalled that at the time he had not thought 'how terrible they are arresting Jews', but instead 'what a misfortune Heinz is Jewish'.[39]

This reduction of moral universalism, and a gangster-like disdain for sentimental humanitarianism, was accompanied by efforts to curb or eliminate alternative sources of moral authority. Long before Stalin, the Bolsheviks aggressively sought to destroy the Orthodox Church, and not simply because it was one of the major pillars of Tsarism and the old order with its own extensive landholdings. Its monks and priests obstructed the Party's access to the minds of the peasant majority, and provided them with an account of human existence and a moral code that were diametrically opposed to the progressive narrative of Marxism. It is not necessary to rehearse the story of the Church's persecution at the hands of such organisations of fanatics as the League of the Militant Godless.[40] While the Nazis included a generous representation of militant anti-clericals, with an admixture of cranks who subscribed to forms of neo-paganism, in many respects Lutheranism shared their anti-Semitism, nationalism and hatred of the Weimar Republic, and many of its adherents were well disposed towards the Führer as an agent of moral restoration. About a million of them joined the German Christians, a sect that sought to conform Christianity to the tenets of National Socialism. Inevitably, this resulted in schism, as those who refused to go this far broke away to form the Confessing Church. This made it impossible for the Nazis to gather Protestants into a single Reich Church.

Although in history's retrospect totalitarian regimes are associated with millions of people murdered or imprisoned, youthful enthusiasm was their preferred image at the time. Like the German Communists, the Nazis were a conspicuously youthful party, who used the battle cry 'make room you old ones' against the Weimar Republic. The average age of members of Hitler's cabinet was forty, in comparison with fifty-three years of age in Chamberlain's government, and fifty-six in that of the USA. In 1934, Nazi Party members were on average seven years younger than members of other parties, and five years younger than the average age of the German male population.[41] Their politics had something of Peter Pan about them. Hitler said in September 1935: 'I believe the German Volk will not grow older in the next few years, but will create the impression that it remains forever young.'[42] Because of its racial–biological fixations, Nazism was negligent of the interests of the elderly, concentrating instead on transforming young men from beer-swilling students into men 'swift as greyhounds, tough as leather, and hard as Krupp steel' as Hitler had it. All totalitarian societies seek to capture and manipulate children and adolescents, whom they regarded as blank slates or malleable clay to be shaped at will. To control them was to control the future, forging a new type of moral personality with each successive generation, bereft of the Jewish and Christian codes that had inhibited or shamed previous generations. The totalitarian aspirations of both the Bolsheviks and Nazis were remarkably similar. A congress of Bolshevik educational workers announced in 1918:

> We must create out of the younger generation a generation of Communists. We must turn children, who can be shaped like wax, into real, good Communists ... We must remove the children from the crude influence of their families. We must take them over and, to speak frankly, nationalise them. From the first days of their lives, they will be under the healthy influence of Communist children's nurseries and schools. There they will grow up to be real Communists.[43]

Hitler was also concerned to involve the 'little racial comrades' in a succession of Nazi organisations, which culminated in service in the armed forces or police:

> These boys join our organisation at the age of ten and get a breath of fresh air for the first time, then, four years later, they move from the Jungvolk to the Hitler Youth and here we keep them for another four years. And then we are even less prepared to give them back into the hands of those who create our class and status barriers, rather we take them into the SA or into the SS, into the NSKK [the National Socialist Motor Corps] and so on. And if they are there for eighteen months or two years and have not become real National Socialists, then they go into the Labour Service and are polished there for six or seven months, and all of this under a single symbol, the German spade. And if, after six or seven months, there are still remnants of class consciousness or pride in status, then the Wehrmacht will take over the further treatment for two years and when they return … we take them immediately into the SA, SS etc. and they will not be free again for the rest of their lives.[44]

In both cases, existing youth organisations were banned, or subsumed into the new totalitarian arrangements. In Russia, this meant that the imperialist Boy Scouts, whose founder was British, were suppressed to give a monopoly to the Party's Komsomol organisation for fifteen- to twenty-one-year-olds, which in 1922 spawned the Young Pioneers for those aged ten to fifteen.[45] By 1925, a million young men and women were Komsomol members. In Germany the rude arrival of the Hitler Youth for boys, and the League of German Maidens for girls, signified the end of a rich heritage of voluntary associations of young people connected with the Churches and political parties. Those devoted to fresh air and nature were readily subsumed by Nazism.

These organisations were designed to fashion new moral personalities and future Party cadres. The Hitler Youth and the Komsomol undertook anti-religious activities, although only in the Soviet Union were they part of an aggressive campaign of atheism, rather than, as in Germany, a periodic manifestation of anti-clericalism against the despised priests or *Pfaffen* in the absence of any Jews to persecute. Having a Pioneer or Komsomol member in the home exerted a chilling effect on family conversation – perhaps especially on still-religious grandparents – to the point where the older generations fell to whispering when their offspring were about. Anything of a remotely subversive nature was likely to be denounced.[46] Both regimes also experimented, more or less disastrously, with education. Lenin insisted on retaining a traditional system, albeit one in which class-based affirmative action governed access, and such things as religion had been stripped out. Others favoured different types of anti-authoritarian experimental schools, which quickly degenerated into pseudo-democratic shambles. From 1929 onwards a purely vocational approach became more important, with young people sent to work in factories and mines or to run literacy campaigns in the countryside. Later, they became cheap labour for the Five-Year Plan.[47]

Resentment against educational privilege as an obstacle to upward social mobility was evident in Germany too. As in Russia, where every professor of over ten years' standing was simply sacked, venerable German university professors were hounded out by fanatic Nazi students and opportunistic younger faculty members. Jews were peremptorily expelled in line with laws that purged the civil service of political opponents. Both Britain and the US benefited immeasurably from the influx of over a thousand men and women trained in what had been one of the world's most respected higher-education systems. The Nazis endeavoured to circumvent the existing class-based secondary system in favour of a series of experimental institutions such as the Adolf-Hitler Schools, the National-Political Educational Institutions and the pseudo-medieval Ordensburgen. Established by rival factions of the Nazi leadership, these sought to manufacture a new elite to replace those who merely had the benefit of rude experience. The enterprise was doomed to fail, because their emphasis was on physical fitness and a series of subjects corrupted by ideology, taught by a new class of academic hacks. In both Germany and Russia, the content of education was debased with an ideological spin on even neutral subjects like mathematics. A typical Soviet exam question was: 'The proletariat of Paris rose up and seized power on 18 March 1871, and the Paris Commune fell on 27 May of the same year. How long did it exist?' Nazi textbooks invited pupils to calculate the net cost of caring for disabled or psychologically damaged people.[48]

In any free and most merely authoritarian societies, the state stops short of the family, except in egregious cases of abuse or neglect. Life in totalitarian states is different. The Bolsheviks actively subverted the bourgeois family, notably by relaxing divorce laws to the point that it sufficed for one partner to send notification of intent to a registrar to dissolve a marriage.

Chronic housing shortages, and belief that communal living was inherently virtuous, further disrupted the family by forcing strangers into close proximity in apartments with communal kitchens and washrooms. All social classes had to breathe and exude the same smells, while distinctive personal possessions were sold or chopped up as firewood.

The generous representation of emancipated women in the Communist Party meant that Bolshevism at least contemplated liberating lifestyles in ways the male-dominated Nazis never considered, whatever glamour attached to such individuals as the actress and film director Leni Riefenstahl. The first Soviet women's minister, Alexandra Kollontai, was a keen proponent of the view that in a collective society, which explicitly sought to abandon traditional Orthodox morality, sex should be of no greater moment than drinking a glass of water. Both Lenin and Stalin were sufficiently old-fashioned to deplore such views, although Bolsheviks seem to have been more promiscuous than other classes. Of course, this did not mean abandoning selection of partners based on social class, although the bias was now in favour of proletarian partners, in line with the general maxim of *proletarisez-vous*. Marrying a bourgeois had the same stigma as an aristocrat falling for a chambermaid in the pre-revolutionary past. As hard-working activists, Bolshevik parents had a correspondingly greater entitlement to the use of nannies, one of several respects in which they replicated the lifestyle of the former aristocracy they otherwise denounced.[49]

The Nazis did not leave the family as a private sphere either; it was the germ cell of the Aryan-Germanic race and nation. They sought to reverse secular trends towards smaller, or childless, families through policies that penalised bachelors and rewarded those who reverted to the large family of the previous century. Divorce was made easier from 1936 onwards, notably through recognition of the relatively modern concept of irretrievable marital breakdown, which in this case meant encouraging couples who had not reproduced within three years to try their luck elsewhere. Marriage loans, introduced in 1933, were to be amortised through each successful childbirth up to a maximum of four, although a system of medals and other rewards introduced five years later were designed to make four to eight children normative. Such 'child-rich' large families were expected to orientate themselves outwards to Party and state in the sense that working men joined the German Labour Front, women the Nazi Womanhood and children the youth organisations.

These large families were not the same as indiscriminately big 'worthless' families, whose tendency to disorder and delinquency meant that they were categorised as anti-social. They were subjected to the coercions of welfare or, worse, negative eugenic policies that licensed their voluntary and involuntary sterilisation.[50] For selection, based on eugenic and racial criteria, was at the heart of Nazi attempts to control human relations and reproduction to improve the Aryan-Germanic race. Positive eugenic measures would help the racially sound reproduce without secular constraint, while negative steps would curb the rest. Racial laws, backed up by public violence, would prevent intimate relations between Aryan-Germans and Jews. The more advanced-minded Nazis, including Heinrich Himmler and Martin Bormann, regarded polygamy favourably, to enable eugenically exceptional men, including themselves, to breed at an enhanced rate. Their furtive infidelities were as nothing compared with the sexual athleticism of their colleague Joseph Goebbels on the Babelsberg casting couches with would-be starlets.[51]

Both dictatorships lauded the sacrifices of such emblematic youths as Herbert Norkus, killed in a brawl with Communists, or Pavel Morozov, the prototypical Soviet 'enthusiastic nark'. They were key figures in their respective parties' martyrologies, stars on the honour roll of those who sacrificed their lives for ideological ends. The Hitler Youth, from 1931 onwards under Baldur von Schirach, was intended to inculcate unswerving devotion to the man whose name it bore, while training the bodies and minds that Germany needed to wage war. Although membership was liberating, in the sense of enabling young adults to be among themselves, there was no mistaking the military nature of its activities, or the existence of a command structure based on seniority. Camping trips were replete with bugle calls and flag parades, and frequently involved war games with rival units from other regions or towns. Orienteering hikes often led to the borders of countries that Hitler subsequently invaded. Practice with air guns gave way to the use of small-calibre rifles, while specialist courses were available in piloting gliders, sailing, truck driving, Morse code and operating radios. Less athletic types could beat and blast out martial music on drums and trumpets. The attractions of membership were obvious, even to critics.

Parents and schoolteachers were relatively powerless vis-à-vis these children in uniform. Indeed, 'children and young people demand of their parents that they be good Nazis, that they give up Marxism, reaction and contact with Jews'. In this way a little tyrant was introduced to the home hearth, and the little tyrants looked forward to 'the economic paths that have opened up to them due to the persecution of Jews and Marxists', for social mobility was as characteristic of the German dictatorship as it was of Russia.[52] Of course, the formal recitation of Hitler Youth activities does not preclude the bullying and homosexuality that were also part of this world, nor does it deny that many young people were bored by the relentless physical exercise and ideological indoctrination. Even the major attraction, namely 'great times without danger', diminished as Hitler took ever bolder risks. After the introduction of mass conscription, the military connection was made explicit with the appointment in 1937 of Lieutenant Colonel Erwin Rommel, the future field marshal and Desert Fox, as the Wehrmacht's liaison officer to the Hitler Youth.[53]

VI ABROAD IN THE WORLD

If this serves to highlight the similarities and subtle differences between the two totalitarian regimes, their diplomatic relations deserve discussion. Attitudes to time distinguished the ways the two leaders viewed the world. Contrary to popular belief, Stalin did not abandon the goal of World Revolution; he merely realised that such a thing would be a very long time coming and worked accordingly to consolidate its Soviet foundation. History, or the Marxist-Leninist prophetic version of it, would take its course. Hitler had a much more developed sense of his own mortality, being a hypochondriac prone to morbid thoughts, and of his own world-historical uniqueness as a prophet, whereas Stalin was more like a mafia boss dispensing rewards and punishments. Moreover, unlike Stalin, who inherited and completed a long process of violence that pulverised the old social order, Hitler had come to power through accommodation with it, an arrangement that limited what he could undertake in Germany itself. Realpolitik meant that many latent reckonings were deferred. Acts of heroic willpower were also intrinsic to National Socialism, with Hitler setting the pace. While Stalin pursued anything other than a revolutionary foreign policy, Hitler made a series of calculated gambles in the increasing certainty that only he could implement his own vision, and that his time on earth was running out, a feeling that grew more intense after he had turned fifty, the age when the end lap comes into clear view. He brought much the same last-chance mentality to his frenzied attempt to exterminate Europe's Jews.[54]

German–Soviet relations in the 1930s were strained at the public level, where competing ideologies clashed, but diplomatic, economic and military relations were more tortuous in practice. The advent of Hitler led to a sharp deterioration of the rhetorical climate. How could it be otherwise, as his Movement's triumph over a murderous domestic Communist opposition was part of the regime's foundational mythology, something he reverted to time and again as he magnified the numbers of Nazi victims? There was also the matter of what he said about Germany's eastern destiny in *Mein Kampf*, the relevant pages being copied and translated for the Soviet leadership, and his unshakeable belief that Communism was a Jewish-inspired revolt of lesser beings against the Aryan remnant that had ruled Tsarist Russia. German anti-Soviet propagandists merely had to identify Jews all over the place in the Soviet Union; they did not need to demonstrate that the Soviet Union was a nightmare, because Stalin did that for them. There was indeed an ethnic element in the Great Terror, as from late 1934 Stalin began persecuting Germans in the Volga region and Siberia as spies connected to vaster anti-Soviet Fascist–Japanese–Trotskyite conspiracies. In July 1937 some forty-two thousand ethnic Germans were shot by the NKVD in one of several 'national operations' that cost the lives of 247,000 men and women with foreign ancestry.[55] The Germans mounted a Brothers in Need campaign, which duped such people as Cosmo Lang, the Archbishop of Canterbury, and was run by the Anti-Comintern, an organization based in Goebbels's Propaganda and Popular Enlightenment Ministry from 1933. The Anti-Comintern ably publicised the evils of Communism to both domestic and foreign audiences, primarily to incline Western countries towards Germany as the bulwark against world Communism, until 1939, when it was wound up in honour of the German–Soviet Pact.[56]

As for the Soviets, they were tough-minded enough to ignore the Nazis' crushing of their German comrades – many who fled to Moscow were later shot by Stalin as ideological deviants. But in analysing National Socialism the Soviets were hindered rather than helped by Marxism, or what Konrad Heiden memorably called 'a small child's version of world history'. In this, a figure like Fritz Thyssen the steel magnate, who was so stupid that Hitler would not have employed him as a valet, became a monopolist puppet master of sinister proportions. Much of the Soviets' intellectual energy went into identifying which precise faction of monopoly capitalism had engineered Hitler into power, an approach they had applied to his immediate Weimar predecessors. As they also regarded the opposition Social Democrats as 'Social Fascists', they conspicuously failed to identify the irrational mythic elements that made Hitler so dangerous an opponent. But it was what Stalin thought that counted: 'We are far from feeling elated about the Fascist regime in Germany. But what counts here is not fascism, if only because fascism in Italy, for example, has not prevented the USSR from establishing excellent relations with that country.'

Beneath the rhetoric, relations were more complicated. Russia and Germany were historic enemies, but during the 1920s they were drawn together as fellow pariah nations. On 16 April 1922 they concluded a treaty at the Italian town of Rapallo, in which each renounced all territorial and financial claims against the other and agreed to normalise their diplomatic relations and to 'co-operate in a spirit of mutual goodwill in meeting the economic needs of both countries'. A secret annexe signed on 29 July allowed Germany to train its military in Soviet territory, thus violating the terms of the Treaty of Versailles. The leaders of the Red Army, fatally for themselves, sought to maintain cordial relations with the German Reichswehr after Hitler came to power. Even though Hitler closed German bases in Russia in 1934, leaving substantial kit behind, Red Army leaders hoped that they could still send officers for training in Germany, under Reichswehr officers they prized as mentors.[57] Although both sides had proponents of improved economic co-operation, trade between the two countries steadily declined throughout the 1930s until it was almost non-existent by 1938–9. In the mid-1930s there was a minor attempt to translate trade talks into broader political discussions, but Stalin was more focused on the pursuit of collective security – and wiping out his own putative enemies at home – while Hitler's attention was absorbed by rearmament and the Rhineland, and used strident anti-Communism to reassure Germany's western neighbours. In his New Year address in January 1936, Hitler defined Nazi Germany as 'a bulwark of national European discipline and culture against the Bolshevist enemy to mankind'.[58]

Then Stalin struck at the Red Army officer corps, perhaps the single greatest supporters of a rapprochement with Germany. Using documents planted by German intelligence, Yezhov's NKVD claimed that Marshal Tukhachevsky and other senior commanders were engaged in a Trotskyite conspiracy against Soviet authority, financed and instigated by German Fascists and the Reichswehr which had actually been renamed Wehrmacht in 1935. Some 34,301 officers were arrested by the NKVD and 22,705 of them were shot or disappeared.[59] They included 91 of the 101 members of the top military leadership, of whom eighty were shot. Tukhachevsky, who had criticised Stalin during the Russo-Polish War nearly two decades before, was tortured and shot, along with his wife, daughter and other family members. The purges wiped out the main Russian advocates of German–Soviet co-operation, but greatly lessened the potential value of Russia in any military alliance that might be contemplated by Western powers.[60]

Munich transformed the situation. After the dismemberment of Czechoslovakia, Hitler regained the Memelland from Lithuania in March 1939, the last bloodless conquest he made. German military planners turned their attention to Poland, notwithstanding a ten-year non-aggression pact and the complicity of the military regime in Warsaw in the destruction of Czechoslovakia. German rhetoric about the plight of ethnic Germans in Poland was ratcheted up, although Hitler's object was not merely to retrieve Danzig, Posen (Poznań), Upper Silesia and West Prussia, but to liquidate the Polish state for all time. As he said: 'This is not about Danzig.' There was a corresponding shift, at first glacier-like, in the Kremlin. On 10 March 1939 Stalin gave a wide-ranging speech, which reflected his dismay at appeasement. He claimed that Britain and France had adopted a position of neutrality or non-intervention towards Fascist aggression. He said they were encouraging Japanese ambitions in China, and those of Germany and Japan against the Soviet Union. Cautioning them that Germany might turn on the West instead, Stalin used the homely metaphor that they should not seek to 'rake over the fire with someone else's hands', to warn them not to rely on Soviet support. Some historians claim that this speech was a signal to Germany from Stalin that he wanted to talk; if so, few in Berlin noticed. What was about to happen mightily contributed to the notion that beneath the skin the two totalitarian regimes were like twin brothers, lining up for aggression and violence, regardless of their superficial ideological dissimilarities.[61]

On 3 May 1939 Stalin replaced Maxim Litvinov, his Jewish Foreign Minister, with the ethnically Russian Vyacheslav Molotov (a *nom de guerre* meaning 'hammer'), since 1930 the Chairman of the Council of People's Commissars, entrusted by Stalin with the task of 'remov[ing] all the Jews in the Commissariat'. Litvinov was allegedly dismissed for failing to report unauthorised talks held by Ivan Maisky, the Soviet ambassador to Britain, with the Finnish Foreign Minister. Whether the dismissal was part of a decision to downgrade the pursuit of collective security is disputed. Hitler certainly regarded the dismissal of Litvinov as a decisive signal, since he attached such inordinate importance to Jews everywhere. While he continued to inveigh against Russia, his Foreign Minister – who had failed to deliver the Anglo-German alliance during his time in London – used personnel from his private fiefdom, the Dienststelle Ribbentrop, for exploratory talks with Russian diplomats. The latter assured them that ideological 'differences' or 'subtleties' were no obstacle to an eventual rapprochement.

Experts from the German embassy in Moscow were brought to Berchtesgaden to explain to Hitler the significance of this changing of the Kremlin guard. The Germans convinced themselves that the Soviets were fundamentally Russian nationalists, pursuing their interests much like any other great power. A series of meetings designed to clear up the contractual obligations of the Czech Skoda arms works to Russia, which had been affected by the German invasion, mutated into wider exchanges about economic relations in general. At some point in the summer of 1939, the sights were raised towards the prospect of talks about political matters. This seems to have been an initiative of the negotiators themselves, although since both Georgy Astrakov and his German interlocutor Karl Schnurre gave contradictory accounts of who first made the running, it is difficult to decide who was most keen to extend the boundaries of their talks.

At the highest levels, there was intense suspicion. Stalin thought that Germany was exploiting the contacts to induce the Japanese to draw closer to the Axis, while Hitler suspected that Stalin was merely playing him to strike a harder bargain with Britain and France, who were dithering over his Triple Alliance proposals. The chief obstacle was that the Western powers were not prepared to accord Stalin the right to 'protect' the Baltic. This was despite having allowed Hitler to dismantle Czechoslovakia without even consulting the Soviets, who were also allies of the Czechs. Throughout June and most of July it was the Germans who most explicitly revealed their desire for a political settlement. Molotov did not take the bait until 29 July, when he authorised Astrakov to listen to what the Germans were proposing. During the ensuing talks, the negotiators exchanged heady opinions on several subjects, including Stalin's resurrection of Russian nationalism from within the defunct doctrine of World Communist revolution, or the common hostility of Communism and Fascism towards capitalist democracy.[62]

News of these discussions was relayed to Hitler and Ribbentrop, just as the former was having doubts about the strength of Germany's western defences when he toured them near Saarbrücken. His economic experts were also simultaneously reporting that in the event of a British blockade Germany would have no alternative other than to get raw materials from

Russia.[63] Ribbentrop instructed Ambassador Friedrich Graf von der Schulenburg in Moscow to pursue political talks, urging him on in the face of Molotov's apparent reluctance. By contrast, the British and French were almost nonchalant in their approach to talks with the Russians, taking weeks to respond to each communication. One of the reasons was that they were divided; whereas the French were prepared to sacrifice Polish interests to reach a deal with Moscow, the British insisted on respecting Warsaw's acute sensitivities towards Russia. The imminent arrival of an Anglo-French military mission in Moscow added urgency to Hitler's desire for an agreement, for he had already decided to carry out his attack on Poland. In Soviet eyes, the mission was more evidence that the policy of collective security had been destroyed at Munich.

The Anglo-French mission was also not empowered to agree anything without referring back to London or Paris, where further communications had to be made with Rumanians and Poles. General Aimé Doumenc and the improbably named Admiral Reginald Plunkett-Ernle-Erle-Drax left London on 5 August on a slow-moving freighter *The City of Exeter*, which had a top speed of thirteen knots. They arrived in Leningrad on 10 August. In talks a few days later it soon became apparent that the British and French had no co-ordinated military strategy for meeting a German onslaught, which hardly filled the Russians with confidence, any more than did guarded intelligence about the Maginot Line and the tiny force Britain proposed to land on the continent. In addition and as always, Polish Foreign Minister Jósef Beck adamantly refused to countenance the passage of Soviet troops through his country. By contrast the Germans were already talking about secret protocols and expressing a lack of interest in the Baltic States and Bessarabia, provided Stalin would give Germany a free hand in Poland. The term 'German Poland' was employed, clearly implying that there was a 'Russian Poland' up for grabs.

As the talks with the British and French petered out, the Russians indicated that, provided the economic negotiations were satisfactorily concluded, they would proceed to political talks with Germany. Now the Germans began serious importuning, seeking to send Ribbentrop to clinch a deal before their armies moved into Poland. The Russians wanted the terms of the secret protocol copper-bottomed in advance, and insisted that Germany commit to restraining Japan in the Far East. In dictatorships, diplomats are glorified errand boys; gangster types savour reminding these fuddy-duddy survivors of the old order who has the power of command. Knowing the date for his invasion of Poland, Hitler personally wrote to

Stalin to ensure that Ribbentrop would be received earlier than the more leisurely dates Molotov had stipulated. Stalin waited twenty-four hours before responding, but he said that Ribbentrop could come on 23 August. Hitler was jubilant: 'Stalin has agreed ... I have the world in my pocket!', and loaned Ribbentrop his personal Focke-Wulf Condor aircraft for the journey to Moscow.

Ribbentrop arrived with his large entourage at 1 p.m. at a Central Aerodrome decked out with swastikas, hurriedly purloined from the props of anti-Fascist films. At 3 p.m. he and two aides set off for the Kremlin. He was surprised to be welcomed by Stalin in person as well as his Foreign Minister. Stalin's presence ensured the negotiations were both focused and serious. They concluded a ten-year non-aggression pact, from which Stalin personally expunged some flowery verbiage Ribbentrop had included, on the grounds that the two dictatorships had been pouring 'buckets of shit' over each other for years. In a secret protocol they decided to partition Poland along the Narew, San and Vistula rivers, with the final borders to be determined in line with future political developments. Stalin was to retrieve Bessarabia from Rumania with no demur. The only disagreements were over the Baltic States, where Hitler wanted Lithuania, agreed easily enough, but also Courland, the mainly German-speaking part of Latvia. Stalin sought the whole of Latvia, along with Estonia and Finland. Ribbentrop retired to speak with Hitler from the German embassy. After two hours a telegram arrived from Berlin – 'Yes, agreed' – that was relayed to Stalin at 10 p.m.; the Soviet dictator trembled slightly before shaking Ribbentrop's hand on a deal done.

Ribbentrop relaxed into a preposterous estimation of how news of the pact would be greeted by the Italians and Japanese, knowing full well that his old friend Hiroshi Oshima, the Japanese ambassador to Germany, had already resigned over the issue. He assured Stalin that the Anti-Comintern Pact had always been directed against the British. A lavish banquet at which the vodka flowed continued until 2 a.m., although the Germans noted that Stalin drank only water from a hip flask. At that late hour Ribbentrop and Molotov were able to sign the finished documents, including the highly secret protocol carving up eastern Europe in the war they all knew was coming. Ribbentrop telephoned his master at around 4 a.m. The Führer was so ecstatic that he allowed himself a rare glass of champagne, exclaiming, 'Now Europe is mine – the others can have Asia.'

Germany's 'second Bismarck' arrived back to a hero's welcome on 24 August. He told Hitler that, because of the pact, the British and French would not now go to war over Poland, which was due to be attacked on the morning of Saturday the 26th, in less than forty-eight hours. *Pravda* celebrated the agreement as an 'instrument of peace', but one of its key architects, trade negotiator Georgy Astrakov, was recalled from Berlin and died while under arrest. Ribbentrop merely swore his aides to secrecy about what had taken place on that Moscow night. The agreements made the German invasion of Poland inevitable, although strictly speaking by then it had become a joint project.[64]

CHAPTER 4

The Rape of Poland

I BETWEEN A HAMMER AND ANVIL

The Molotov–Ribbentrop Pact confirmed Hitler's calculation that he could conquer Poland with impunity. Britain and France would not dare to fight. Last-minute Italian suggestions of a further conference to dismember Poland diplomatically were not seriously entertained. Hitler and Ribbentropp, however, failed to appreciate that the pact had nullified one of the implicit arguments for Western appeasement, namely the Führer's claim that he was a bulwark against Soviet Communism. They also underestimated the extent to which they had exhausted British willingness to tolerate Hitler, now fully revealed as an insatiable aggressor as well as a liar.

Addressing his armed forces commanders the night before the deal in the Kremlin was struck, Hitler twice expressed fears for his own mortality – 'My existence is therefore a factor of great value. But I can be eliminated at any time by a criminal or a lunatic' and 'no one knows how long I may live. Therefore better a conflict now.' Everything revolved around personalities – his, Mussolini's, Stalin's, even the Spaniard Franco's. There were no personalities, in the sense of Great Men, on the Anglo-French side, merely 'little worms'. He made the object of the forthcoming 'life and death struggle' explicit: 'Annihilation of Poland in foreground. Goal is elimination of vital forces, not the attainment of a specific line.' His mind was locked on war and his staccato peroration was grim: 'Close your hearts to pity. Act brutally. Eighty million people must obtain what is their right. Their existence must be made secure. The stronger man is right. The greatest harshness.' British and French attempts to mediate between Germany and Poland were stymied by outrageous German demands, which the Poles rejected. A last-minute intervention by Mussolini was brushed aside. Jósef Lipski, Poland's ambassador in Berlin, commenced closing down his legation.[1]

German troops moved eastwards from June 1939, ostensibly to participate in defensive manoeuvres, including the strengthening of frontier fortifications they had no intention of using. The Reich Party Day of Peace was used to cover substantially increased domestic rail traffic, although the assembly had been cancelled on 15 August 1939. Two waves of troops were successively put in place so that by the final days of August they were no more than a day's journey from the Polish border. There was no formal declaration of war. At 5.45 a.m. on 1 September, German radio broadcast a proclamation by Hitler to the German armed forces. Ethnic Germans in Poland had been 'persecuted by bloody terror and are being driven from their homesteads … to put an end to this lunacy, there remains no other recourse for me but to meet force with force'.[2]

Hostilities had commenced an hour earlier, with salvoes from a German cruiser stationed off Danzig's Westerplatte, although terrorist and border incidents, notably at Tarnow railway station and the Gleiwitz radio station, had been fabricated by the SS to give substance to Hitler's outrage over alleged Polish violations of German territorial sovereignty. On 28 August, two suitcase bombs planted by German agents exploded in Tarnow railway station, killing twenty-two people and wounding thirty-five more.[3] On the 31st the head of the SS Security Police, Reinhard Heydrich telephoned a code message – 'grandmother has died' – which resulted in SS men disguised in Polish uniforms storming a radio transmission room near the tall larchwood antenna at Gleiwitz four miles inside the German–Polish border. They brought along the war's first casualty, Franciszek Honiok, an ethnic German tractor salesman known for his pro-Polish sympathies who had been abducted the previous day. He was drugged and then shot after the SS had broadcast inflammatory statements in Polish to the accompaniment of their own gunfire. The key line was 'Uwage! Tu Gliwice. Rozglosnia znajduje sie w rekach Polskich!' Or 'Attention! This is Gliwice. The broadcasting station is in Polish hands.' This message was in turn relayed by the BBC, as the Germans hoped it would be, as western decision-makers grappled with the odd idea of Poland attacking Germany.[4]

Elsewhere, more SS men dressed as Poles stormed a German customs post at Hochlinden shouting 'Long live Poland' and 'Down with the Teutons' in Polish. After the gunfire had died down, the frightened customs men stumbled out and tripped over six corpses dressed in Polish uniforms.

They noted their shaven heads, actually acquired in Dachau rather than the Polish army, for these were 'tin cans' as the code dismissively dubbed them, killed to order. The corpses were quickly photographed and then buried. To dramatise these incidents for the world's press, the SS had a model made on which the location of alleged instances of Polish aggression were lit up by touching a button. Heydrich loved this toy, repeatedly pressing the button and exclaiming: 'This is how the war started.'[5] On the morning of the invasion, the Chief of Staff of the Luftwaffe telegraphed the Soviet telecommunications commissariat to request that Radio Minsk punctuate its broadcasts with the call sign 'Richard Wilhelm 1.0' as well as taking every opportunity to announce 'Minsk'. The Soviets refused to broadcast the call sign, but they obliged with the repeated 'Minsks', which were used by German pilots for navigational purposes as they bombed Poland.[6]

At 10 a.m. on 1 September, Hitler was driven through Berlin's sparsely populated streets to the Reichstag, which since being destroyed by fire in 1933 had convened in the Kroll Opera. About one hundred deputies failed to appear because transport was disrupted by troop movements. Their places were taken by unelected Nazi functionaries bussed in by Göring. Someone forgot to install loudspeakers outside and to shut down a noisy construction site, while throughout the capital bars continued to serve customers, with Hitler's broadcast voice competing with bar-room chat and chinking glasses.[7]

Dressed in simple field grey with his lone Iron Cross, Hitler wallowed in the alleged persecutions visited by the Poles upon ethnic Germans, who had allegedly been 'sadistically and bestially tortured only to be murdered in the end'. This was followed by his now standard attempt at damage limitation in the form of assurances to Britain and France that he harboured no aggressive intentions towards the West. Italy was politely informed that its offer of assistance was unnecessary. He said his war aims were modest: to resolve the status of Danzig and the Pomeranian Corridor which separated West from East Prussia, and 'a change of tone in German–Polish relations ... to warrant peaceful coexistence'. This was a lie, as he wished to erase Poland from the map. So too was his expressed desire to limit the damage bombing might inflict on civilians. The night before, twelve hundred Poles had died in a single raid on one town; but still, he threatened that if unlawful weapons like poison gas were used, he would respond in kind. All of this was the prelude to a series of solipsistic remarks that seemed to imply the war was about Hitler himself. 'I am asking of no

German man more than I was ready to do through four years ... I now wish to be nothing other than the first soldier of the German Reich. Therefore I have put on that tunic which has always been the most holy and dear to me. I shall not take it off again until victory is ours, or – I shall not live to see the day!' He mused plangently about a possible successor, and compared himself with Frederick the Great, the warrior Prussian king. Vehement exhortatory slogans ensued. No surrender. No more November 1918s. Iron discipline. Strong will. 'Deutschland – Sieg Heil!'[8]

In London Chamberlain had decided upon the 'arbitrament of war' after the House of Commons had met his last-minute procrastinations with outrage. At 9 a.m. on Sunday 3 September, Henderson went to the German Foreign Ministry and handed over a British ultimatum that would expire two hours later. Hitler's interpreter Paul Schmidt took it to the Chancellery where, after pushing his way through the bustling throng, he reached the calm of Hitler's office. When he had finished translating this communication, he studied the reactions of Hitler and of Ribbentrop. After a long silence during which Hitler stared into space, he asked Ribbentrop, 'What now?' Ribbentrop, who had reassured Hitler that such an outcome was unlikely, replied that a French ultimatum was probably imminent.[9]

Although some call this the outbreak of the last European war, which became global only in 1941, in fact far-flung places were engaged once Britain was involved. It is still moving to recall the process seventy years later. While none of the Dominions had been signatories to the Munich Agreement, nor to the guarantees Britain gave Poland (and Rumania and Greece), in the words of the New Zealand Prime Minister they would 'range ourselves without fear besides Britain. Where she goes, we go. Where she stands, we stand.' The cabinet in Wellington even backdated the declaration of war to coincide with Britain's, symbolically ignoring the time difference. From Canberra the Australians pitched in under the slogan 'one King, one cause, one flag'. So did Ottawa and Pretoria, this last apparently causing Hitler to laugh.[10] In Britain itself, only a few Communist intellectuals like the historian Eric Hobsbawm would go into print supporting the Stalinist line that Anglo-French imperialism was a greater menace than the Fascists who were now allied with Moscow.

II THE FIRST BLITZKRIEG

The German invasion of Poland had land, sea and air superiority underpinning it, and came from almost every point of the compass, with the Soviets invading from the east once the German incursion was a fortnight under way. Case White, the invasion plan, committed sixty German divisions against Poland, or about one and a half million troops, leaving only a token screening force in the west. Although the German army depended heavily on forty thousand horses, the spearhead of the invasion force were five tank divisions, consisting of about three hundred panzers each, with eight more lightly armoured but fully motorised formations. It also used artillery to devastating effect. With fifteen hundred aircraft versus four hundred, the Luftwaffe quickly gained air superiority over Poland's generally obsolete machines, which, contrary to myth, were mainly destroyed in aerial combat rather than on the ground. German aircraft bombed and strafed concentrations of Polish troops, interdicted road and rail transport, and used dive-bombers to terrify the inhabitants of Warsaw and other cities. Two German army groups, under Fedor von Bock and Gerd von Rundstedt, with a stellar supporting cast of generals, fought their way past Polish forces, which for economic and political reasons were massed near the western frontier. Defence in strategic depth would have presumed Soviet co-operation, which the Poles did not have. Moreover, the western regions of Poland were the most industrialised and populous part of the country, which could not be abandoned in case the British and French achieved a ceasefire and forced Poland into a Munich-style settlement with Germany.

Although the Poles fought bravely, mounting various counter-offensives, they were outfought by superior German generals in a series of battles of encirclement. They hoped the West would move against Germany, but this was to hope in vain. Nonetheless, they resisted the German onslaught for only one week less than the combined and well-armed Anglo-French armies were to do the following year. Any hope of tactical retreat eastwards was abandoned when, on 17 September, the Red Army invaded eastern Poland, allegedly to protect ethnic Ruthenians and Ukrainians from the ambient chaos after the collapse of Poland's government, which fled to Rumania the following day. This line had been worked out in repeated discussions between Stalin, Molotov and the German ambassador Schulenburg, negotiations that eventually involved

Ribbentrop in a further flying visit to Moscow. Definitive adjustments to the conquest were made at a Kremlin conference in the last week of September, where the Soviets relinquished the province of Lublin and parts of the province of Warsaw in return for control of Lithuania.[11] In order to avoid a clash between the German and Soviet armies, as the Germans were 125 miles east of the demarcation lines agreed by Molotov and Ribbentrop, the Germans began an orderly withdrawal as the Russians moved in to replace them.

Meanwhile, artillery and air bombardment crushed the last major centres of Polish resistance around Modlin and Warsaw. The capital had been heavily bombed from the first day of the campaign, with seventeen consecutive raids on Sunday 5 September. Soviet Foreign Minister Molotov sent the German government a congratulatory telegram when German forces reached Warsaw's suburbs. Armoured assaults through the suburbs on the 8th were twice repulsed by anti-tank guns, and by such tactics as emptying the stock of a turpentine factory over the streets and igniting it as the tanks crossed. A major counter-thrust, which resulted in the Battle of Burza, also delayed the German advance. From 15 September onwards Warsaw was besieged, with 175,000 German troops ranged against 120,000 Polish defenders. The Germans brought up massive railway-mounted artillery and sent in waves of bombers. The destruction of the city's main water works meant that there was no potable water, nor anything to extinguish the extensive fires caused by German use of incendiary bombs, showered from transport planes as well as bombers. Hospitals and Red Cross stations were also hit, regardless of any identifying symbols. Warsaw capitulated on 27 September.

By the time the fighting stopped in early October 70,000 Polish troops had died, with a further 130,000 wounded. Four hundred thousand were taken prisoner. German losses included about eleven thousand killed, thirty thousand wounded and another three and a half thousand missing in action. Russia suffered seven hundred killed and nineteen hundred wounded.[12] On 5 October, after twelve high-ranking hostages had been held and the streets cleared at gunpoint, Hitler arrived to inspect his troops and to drive through the deserted streets of Warsaw.

Many German officers had a hazy understanding of the rules governing captured enemy troops. In mid-September, General Walter von Brauchitsch issued an order that explicitly associated all Polish POWs with the localised murder of ethnic Germans in Bromberg. This opened the door to systematic mistreatment of prisoners, while the reasoning behind the order set a precedent for the infamous 'Commissar Order' issued two years later in Russia. In a significant number of cases, prisoners were simply not taken. They were shot or herded into barns, which were then torched with pitch and petrol. After an intense fire-fight in a wood near Ciepielów on 8 September, in which a Wehrmacht captain was shot in the head, the monocle-wearing colonel commanding a motorised infantry unit ordered three hundred Polish soldiers to remove their uniforms and then machine-gunned them as insurgents. Prisoners of war were corralled in primitive circumstances, often in fields ringed with barbed wire. Food and sanitation were inadequate. At night the Poles were ordered to remain seated on the ground as their mass was swept with searchlights. Inevitably some stood up, or moved when a fight or panic broke out, which at Zambrów on 11 September resulted in two hundred killed by machine-gun fire and a hundred wounded, who were left untreated. Another violation of the laws of war involved the separation of some fifty thousand Jews from the mass of Polish prisoners of war by means of interrogation, or based on circumcision or names. They were held in separate ghetto POW camps and used for forced labour. By early 1940, half of them, or twenty-five thousand presumably fit young men, had perished.[13]

III NO CIVILISED RESTRAINT

This brief recapitulation of the five-week military campaign does not convey the bestiality of the German assault on Poland, which was accompanied by drunkenness, looting and murder. A joke quickly made the rounds in Warsaw that the Orbis travel agency was offering trips to Berlin under the slogan 'see your furniture again'.[14] The incidence of rape was not high, for the laws on race defilement promulgated at Nuremberg four years earlier were a deterrent. Although the occasional protest by regular soldiers was once used to disguise that fact, the German army was as much to blame for atrocities as the various SS units that accompanied them. For most of the young German soldiers, this was their first experience of a foreign country, where people looked alien and spoke incomprehensible languages, factors which easily inclined men towards violence when, for example, communication was through easily misunderstood hand signals rather than speech. But it was what these troops had in their heads, from their time in the Hitler Youth or in the Reich Labour Service, that partly explains why they disregarded war's important moral aspect, namely not to squander whatever moral capital one's own side possesses through gratuitous violence. Germany lost that intangible battle within five weeks in Poland through indiscriminate aggression that arose from a combination of ideological and situational causes.

The ideological precipitators are easily stated. Prussia-Germany harboured a superiority complex towards the Poles, who were a byword for feckless muddle, or *polnische Wirtschaft* as Germans contemptuously called it. They believed in the existence of a west–east 'cultural gradient', in which the supposedly ideal orderliness of rural Germany itself abruptly tapered off into a chaos of dingy straw-covered hovels, ambient squalor and ill-tended livestock that allegedly characterised the Polish countryside. The only orderly exceptions were places inhabited by ethnic Germans, for *Kultur* had indelibly racist accents. Anything of any value in Poland, from the astronomer Copernicus and the sculptor Veit Stoss onwards, had been the product of German rather than Polish *Kultur*.

Then there were the Jews, who comprised 10 per cent of Poland's population, the first large concentrations of Jews these young troops had ever encountered, as Germany's own diminishing Jewish population constituted half of 1 per cent of eighty millions. Letters written by German soldiers serving in Poland again and again reported that these Jews were worse than even those crudely caricatured in *Der Stürmer*, the most prurient and viciously anti-Semitic Nazi publication, where all the Jewish noses resembled number 6 as they lasciviously ogled innocent-looking blonde Aryan girls. These were Jews unlike the assimilated Jews that German troops may have encountered at home, and readily identifiable as such by dress, names or beards. Their poverty seems to have incited as much animosity as the alleged wealth of the German Jews. These Jews spoke Yiddish, sometimes cravenly shouting 'Chail Chitler', their pronunciation of 'Heil Hitler', as the Germans arrived. These terrified people were subjected to public torments such as having their beards burned, cut or tugged off, scenes captured in countless photos that show them surrounded by jeering German soldiers. In other places Jews were forced to sweep out German billets, or to tow carts filled with their own stolen possessions, or to clean latrines with their bare hands, all actions intended to rub their noses in their allegedly genetic aversion to manual labour. Only the widespread acceptance of anti-Semitism in German society under the Nazis can explain how ordinary young men indulged in such extraordinarily aberrant conduct.

Contempt for the Poles was combined with an exaggerated fear of civilian resistance, which historically the Prussian-German army always met with a mailed fist. Inter-war Poland was home to a number of ultra-nationalist organisations, some of which tried to combat the subversive activities of the ethnic German minority and the Nazi organisations that supported them. The membership of the Polish chauvinist organisations had been carefully monitored by the Reich Main Security Office of the SS, often aided by ethnic German academics who fingered their Polish colleagues for the secret police. As usual, a false or at best a wildly exaggerated threat gave Hitler the pretext he liked to adduce in order to justify what he wanted to do anyway. The intention was not simply to crush any resistance the Germans encountered, or imagined they had encountered, but to wipe out those classes who, from the time of the Partitions (1772–95) until Poland was restored in 1919, had maintained an enduring sense of Polish national identity, which in practice meant landowners, Catholic priests and teachers.[15]

The front-loaded, highly mobile German campaign meant that few military resources were devoted to securing rear areas behind the advancing troops. This partly explains the extraordinary viciousness German troops exhibited towards the civilian population. The invading force moved so swiftly that large numbers of Polish troops were left at large in the Germans' rear, including the usual quotient of deserters and stragglers. Since they sometimes continued or resumed combat, occasionally in civilian clothes, this gave the invaders the feeling that they were being attacked in an underhand way by opponents who had forfeited the right to be treated as regular combatants. Although the Wehrmacht High Command did not issue anything analogous to the murderous orders that preceded the invasion of the Soviet Union, Hitler's intentions were clear enough from what he had said to his generals. During a conference at the Berghof with senior army commanders on 22 August, he assigned the task of pacification and policing behind German lines to the SS. According to some of the generals present, including Bock and Franz Halder, the Chief of the General Staff, Hitler spoke of his desire to depopulate parts of Poland to resettle them with Germans, and expressed his intention of eliminating Poland's elites to make Poland disappear.[16]

NB

IV THE FALSE SS—ARMY DICHOTOMY

The decision to deploy the SS had been taken in April. SS and Gestapo personnel had accompanied German troops into Austria, the Sudetenland and Bohemia-Moravia, under orders restricting them to arresting rather than shooting political opponents during the period before fixed Gestapo posts were established. In May, the head of the SS Security Police, Reinhard Heydrich, was given responsibility for forming four task forces, or Einsatzgruppen, for the Polish campaign, a role he devolved upon Werner Best, a thirty-six-year-old lawyer who was both a senior Security Police and Gestapo officer. Best had to select and deliver two thousand officers and men suited to the tasks Hitler envisaged. All but four of the commanding officers of these task forces, and their thirteen subsidiary Einsatzkommandos, were also graduate lawyers in their thirties. By July these units had grown to seven, augmented by 2,250 Order Police to bring the total available manpower to 4,250. This included a large Special Purpose Task Force under SS-Obergruppenführer Udo von Woyrsch, a Silesian aristocrat who had served on Himmler's personal staff. Three battalions of the SS Death's Head Division, which guarded concentration camps and was utterly wedded to the necessity of annihilating Germany's enemies come what may, along with Hitler's bodyguard, the Leibstandarte-SS, were also deployed to Poland. Their signature approach to pacification was to hang people from lamp-posts.[17] Finally, within a week of the invasion Himmler's adjutant, Ludolf-Hermann von Alvensleben, assumed SS responsibility for *ad hoc* Ethnic German Self-Defence Forces numbering about eighteen thousand men, who it is estimated were responsible for killing between twenty and thirty thousand Polish civilians during this campaign.[18]

Personnel for the SS task forces were selected because of their prior experience of Poland or its border regions, so that they knew the lie of the land and had views about the inhabitants. Many of them were veterans of the ferocious inter-communal strife that had characterised ethnic German–Polish relations in the aftermath of the Great War, when the Poles had risen to overturn the results of a plebiscite in Upper Silesia. While the categories were not mutually exclusive, eleven of the twenty-eight officers were veterans of the Great War, who had sufficient military credibility to interact with the regular army units they were attached to. Lastly, the troopers' SS personnel records testified to their unconditional ideological commitment. Although only Dr Hans Trummler was formally described by his superiors as a 'psychopath', albeit one with the erect bearing of a 'Prussian officer', the common denominator for selection was evidence of involvement in extreme right-wing paramilitary organisations before joining the SS, police or Gestapo, where in turn they had demonstrated ideological soundness and steadiness. These were the missionary elite of National Socialism, with a dualistic view of the world and no vestiges of the Christian upbringing or humanistic education many of them had passed through before acquiring a more compelling and narrower set of values.[19]

In June the leaders of these groups underwent a two-week training period at the SD, or SS Security Service, school at Bernau near Berlin. The instructors included Hauptsturmführer Herbert Hagen, chief of the SD's Jewish Desk, who talked about 'Jewry as a universal political opponent, and its significance in Poland'. At a meeting held at the Berlin Gestapo headquarters on 18 August, these leaders were told that their mission was to combat saboteurs, partisans, Jews and the Polish intelligentsia, and to mete out punishment for the persecution of ethnic Germans. Then there were bonding sessions, usually involving much alcohol, exercise and swimming, as well as group cinema visits. On 27 August they saw a sentimental piece set in Hungary. In this film, a Teutonic wanderer was stabbed in the back by a treacherous Gypsy, and then nursed back to health by simple Hungarian fisher folk. The wanderer then got his revenge on the Gypsy by killing him. A week later, members of that audience shot their first victims – three 'cut-throat-razor heroes' in Lublinitz (as Lubliniec became) in Poland, although for all one knows they may have still been in an imaginary Hungary.[20]

By the end of August, these task forces had been given Special Wanted Persons Lists, which had been compiled jointly by the Security Police and the Abwehr, German military counter-intelligence. These lists consisted of ten ledgers containing over sixty thousand names, who were the targets of Operation Tannenberg – Tannenberg being the name of a famous defeat the Teutonic Knights suffered in 1410 at the hands of the Poles, as well as the location of General Paul von Hindenburg's victory over the Russians in 1914 – for the liquidation of Poland's elites. There was no doubt from where the order came: writing to a colleague, Heydrich said that Hitler had given him the 'extraordinarily radical … order for the liquidation of various circles of the Polish leadership, [killings] that ran into the thousands'.[21]

These particular orders were not shared with the army command, whose view of the role in theatre of these SS formations was confined to rear-area pacification and did not include liquidating Poland's elites or, as it transpired, killing seven thousand Jews before the year was out. Army officers, coming as they did from a culture based on hierarchy, were naturally obsessed with the question of who was in charge. They assumed that the Nazi formations would be under the authority of army field commanders, but in practice they took their orders from Himmler and Heydrich, invariably backed by Hitler in the event of conflict. Judging from their pre-invasion briefings to their troops, the army leadership fully anticipated guerrilla-type resistance from a population they regarded as cruel, hostile and sneaky by nature. German intelligence assumed there were twelve thousand members of Polish paramilitary organisations in the Corridor alone, simply by extrapolating fighters from membership rolls of ultra-nationalist organisations.

Individual army commanders issued orders that were plainly illegal under treaties to which Germany was a signatory. On 4 September, Eighth Army decreed that civilians who were suspected of having shot at German troops, or who were inside buildings from which fire had come, or who had weapons at home, were to be summarily shot without any legal proceedings. Walter von Reichenau, the commander of Tenth Army, issued similar orders the same day, augmented by instructions to shoot three hostages for every German soldier killed. On 10 September Fedor von Bock decreed that, in the event of his troops taking fire from a house, it was to be burned down. If no specific house could be located, then the entire village should be burned down. Further orders lowered the age at which captured resisters could be shot to cover those younger than eighteen, although in practice such orders were academic, as the entire campaign was characterised by massive violence that only firm and repeated intervention by officers at all levels could have stopped.

It was never forthcoming because commanders at the highest level were cowed by the Führer's adamantine views. Military violence is usually kept in check by military policemen, but in Poland the army's own police forces, including the Secret Field Police, were unlikely to prevent atrocities as they were busy carrying them out themselves. A typical incident occurred on 2 September in the village of Wyszanow. The day before, German troops had rounded up a few Polish army stragglers and had taken them away. On the 2nd, newly arriving German troops who had run into desultory sniper fire demanded that the villagers should give up any Polish soldiers they were harbouring. On being told, truthfully, that there were none, they set up firing positions and started shooting into the village, setting part of it aflame. While mopping up, the German troops encountered villagers hiding in cellars. One cellar held twenty-one people, including eight women and thirteen children. Ignoring the sounds of crying children, the soldiers dropped three hand grenades into the cellar, which killed all but three of the villagers. The culprits were not SS men but members of an army motorised pioneer battalion whose motto was 'swift and hard'.[22]

Army commanders had no objections to nipping the operations of active Polish insurgents in the bud by arresting and shooting them, especially when they were caught gun in hand. Although the practice was forbidden by the Hague Laws of Land Warfare, they also resorted to seizing and shooting civilian hostages to deter others, as their predecessors had during the Franco-Prussian War, and in France and Belgium during the Great War whenever civilian resistance had been encountered. By the conclusion of the Polish campaign in early October, the army had summarily executed sixteen thousand Poles, sometimes by firing squad, but more often by less formal executions. Since the hostages were usually selected from local worthies, the practice did part of the SS's work for them in the liquidation of the country's elite.

It may be useful to look a little closer at how specific incidents evolved within the fluid and foggy chaos of battle and its tense aftermath. Some German officers had fought in the Great War, and some troops were veterans of 'inter-racial struggle' (*Volkstumskampf*) against Poles in the early 1920s, but the majority had never been in combat before. Consequently they were extremely jittery, imagining that any noise was gunfire directed at them, even weapons they themselves had discharged. It was rather telling that one German commander ensured that his troops had no ammunition when they marched into the town of Częstochowa, lest they react to some minor event by shooting down curious bystanders. German army training included neither fighting in the dimness of forests and woods – of which there were many in northern Poland – nor, more importantly, close-quarter combat in urban centres where firing could come from any alleyway or window. In addition, the Germans had been told to expect the enemy to use underhand irregular tactics, and so every incident was seen through that conceptual prism, even if the bang they heard was a car backfiring. But there was something more, born of the contempt they felt towards the Poles. Letters from German soldiers revelled in the power to destroy, with almost lyrical accounts of the burning sails of a windmill turning like the 'Germanic sun wheel' in the dark sky.

V BROMBERG

Scenes that were perhaps inevitable in a handful of places where there was bad blood between Poles and ethnic Germans were deliberately generalised and used to legitimise the wholesale commission of atrocities that served a wider agenda. Bromberg, or Bydgoszcz, was a particular flashpoint used for this purpose. Between 1 and 5 September, Polish troops killed about eleven hundred ethnic Germans in the city, figures multiplied fivefold, on Hitler's insistence, before they were published in the German press under the headline 'Bromberg's Bloody Sunday'. As the Polish troops retreated, order was maintained by a Civil Defence Committee consisting of local worthies, while about 2,200 Boy Scouts, labourers, railwaymen and students joined an urban militia, which set up defensive positions at the city hall and in a neighbourhood called Schwedenhöhe. Barricades and firing positions in apartment blocks were set up in anticipation of the German arrival. Gun battles erupted between these militias and soldiers from the 122nd and 123rd Infantry Regiments of the regular army. Superior German firepower soon prevailed and, after the defenders had surrendered, they were kicked and battered with rifle butts. Sporadic sniper fire throughout the city led the local German commander to order searches for weapons, and the arrest of anyone fingered by the ethnic Germans who had attached themselves to the army as local guides. Those found in possession of weapons, even antiquated muskets inoffensively displayed on a sitting-room wall, or accused of killing ethnic Germans, were led away and shot, as were civil servants, lawyers, teachers and priests. When the sniping continued, Fourth Army Command ordered the taking of civilian hostages, who were paraded on the Old Market Square. Four hundred of them were shot in reprisal for an unknown but small number of Germans who may have been hit by by random gunfire.

Meanwhile the free-ranging sub-units of SS Task Force IV had regrouped in the city on 5 September under Helmuth Bischoff. He reported to Berlin that, since many ethnic Germans were unaccounted for, it was likely that 'large numbers of them had been murdered'. This report sent Hitler into a rage, and he ordered Himmler to carry out savage reprisals. Bischoff claimed that what he and his men saw in Bromberg resulted in an 'inner transformation' in which they became 'hard as steel'. They swore 'bloody vengeance' and determined that they would 'radically do away with this riff-raff'. On the 8th, when a bullet fired from the

Copernicus secondary school hit a German army officer, fifty pupils were executed despite the gunman having bravely surrendered himself. Five hundred imprisoned Communists were shot on 9 September, with a further twenty hostages shot on Old Market Square after a further night of gunfire. On the 10th the task force and an army motorised battalion combed a district of Schwedenhöhe favoured by insurgents, or 'bandits' as the task force commander called them, although the resisters had surrendered. Brandishing lurid German newspaper accounts of Bloody Sunday, he told his men to shoot anyone who even looked suspicious. The units went from door to door, driving out the inhabitants and shooting sixty men in the street as they fled. Another nine hundred were taken prisoner and 120 of them, identified as hostile by ethnic German informers, were shot in a field. Those on the Special Wanted Persons Lists were taken away and killed in a forest outside Bromberg. Far from protesting about these massacres, the army helped organise them, and welcomed them as reprisals for crimes committed against ethnic Germans and as part of the general pacification of the city. An Einsatzgruppen report dated 14 November declared that 'There is no longer a Jewish problem in Bromberg, as the town is entirely free of Jews. In the course of the cleansing measures, all those Jews who did not have the foresight to flee have been eliminated.' The Sicherheitspolizei security police, known as Sipo, reported three days later that 'there are no longer any Polish intellectuals present in Bromberg'.[23]

Fierce Polish resistance in the industrial cities of Upper Silesia, which revived memories of fierce inter-communal violence in the early 1920s, resulted in a similar pattern of hostage taking and summary executions. Army commanders suspended the rule under which captured snipers were to be court-martialled; instead they were to be shot on the spot. SS Task Force 1/i arrived to contribute its own higher level of brutality. Splitting up into smaller teams, its members combed Katowice street by street, either killing suspected insurgents on the spot or taking them to a series of courtyards behind factories. A Boy Scout fighter, detained by ethnic Germans as he tried to flee, ended up in a mixed group of prisoners that included women and young girls. He was among forty people separated out and marched to a government building where supposed terrorists such as he were put to one side, away from Polish soldiers with military identification papers. His group were again marched off, kicked and beaten en route before being delivered to an ethnic German paramilitary group, which opened fire on them within a gated courtyard. The boy had the presence of mind to feign death and to lie inert under the corpses that tumbled around him. When more prisoners arrived to be shot, the boy began to shake. The killers noticed movement and shot him in the chest, arm and back. He came round surrounded by about a hundred dead, and slipped away despite his wounds. In that courtyard alone, 250 people were killed, while another 500 were shot into mass graves in the Katowice municipal gardens. None of these incidents prompted any protests from the regular army.

VI BAD FOR MORALE

At least one of the SS task forces was plainly not a happy ship. Sub-unit 3/1 was commanded by Dr Alfred Hasselberg, a thirty-one-year-old graduate lawyer. He had already irritated his subordinates by reserving more comfortable quarters for himself in the weeks before the invasion, and ordering his non-commissioned officers to perform ordinary sentry duty. He made himself more unpopular by regularly commenting that some of his troopers were 'unsuitable for the SS and should be shot'. A large number of them began to plead sickness, usually stress-related stomach disorders. A prime cause of complaint was that Hasselberg insisted that his men should shoot people in the neck, while staying away from the execution pits himself. Others complained about such sadistic practices as forcing a Jewish cantor to sing out the names of people slated for execution, and Hasselberg's mistreatment of a handsome English setter dog he had appropriated. They began to drink heavily, often smashing their glasses after each round. Although Heydrich had recommended Hasselberg as Sipo chief in Cracow, within a few months his staff were sniffing around in SS records in search of a mentally defective Hasselberg forebear, before the problem of his poor leadership was solved by accepting his request for transfer to the regular army.

Although the overall picture was of army and SS co-operation, there were some instances of friction. In Lubliniec, the Secret Field Police handed over nearly two hundred captives to the SS Security Police when they left for another assignment. Before leaving, they reported their opinion that these people would be shot, in defiance of Army Group South's intelligence officers who wished to hold them for questioning. A Major Rudolf Langhäuser had a row with Emanuel Schaefer, the SS task force commander, when he demanded that the prisoners be transferred to

Częstochowa for safekeeping. The reason for his intervention was that eighty of the prisoners were Polish reservists, surrendered to Langhäuser by the town mayor to prevent violence erupting as the Germans entered. Langhäuser had given his word they would be unharmed, but Schaefer referred him to orders from Himmler that insurgents should be shot, although these men had not been insurgents at all. General von Rundstedt, the Group commander, insisted on confirmation that such a directive existed. Senior police figures in Berlin reported to Army High Command that the instructions had come directly from the Führer's campaign train, and Rundstedt pursued the matter no further. All the reservists were shot.

The army also fitfully clashed with the SS task forces over the treatment of Jews, not because the army had any moral qualms but because SS depredations were infectious and threatened to undermine military discipline. By the end of the second week of September, SS policy had become to terrorise the Jews sufficiently to force them to flee, the intention being to drive them across the Narew and San rivers before the German–Soviet demarcation line was consolidated. SS-Hauptsturmführer Adolf Eichmann also seized the opportunity to deport some of the Reich's Jews to the same general area under what was called the Nisko Plan, after a town across the San river. Udo von Woyrsch's special task force was one of the units deputed for the task of terror and expulsion. He used flamethrowers to murder Jews in Będzin before moving on to Przemyśl on 16 September, murdering between five and six hundred Jews within days of his arrival. Some regular soldiers joined in the shootings, but others scorned Woyrsch's men, jeering that they should be fighting at the front rather than massacring old men and women. Next, Woyrsch's unit moved to the Jewish quarters of towns in the Lublin area, to ferret out valuables before their owners were herded eastwards. Brutal scenes followed, with SS men bursting into homes barking 'Your gold or your life!', while carrying out strip searches and cavity inspections of Jewish women, some of whom had their fingers smashed when they refused to surrender wedding rings. The appalled army commander at Chełm protested, and some senior officers tried to get Woyrsch's men withdrawn; but others of equal seniority insisted that Woyrsch was doing a vital job in crushing Polish insurgents. German soldiers were joined by Russian soldiers on the other side in shooting at the Jewish men who were obliged to ford or swim the San river, while their women and children crossed over bridges.[24]

Further north, trouble erupted between General Georg von Küchler, commander of Third Army, and marauding SS units, intent on burning synagogues and murdering helpless and totally unthreatening Jews. A Waffen-SS or militarised SS, artillery regiment ran amok after a member of the Reich Labour Service was shot in Goworowo, killing fifty Jews and herding the rest into a synagogue, which they sprayed with petrol. At that point they were stopped by a passing army officer, who insisted the survivors be released. When reports of such incidents reached Küchler, he protested forcefully to the SS, employing words like beastly, barbaric, dishonourable and wicked. When an SS military court handed down predictably mild sentences, Küchler refused to confirm them in his capacity as theatre commander, and ordered a second court martial under a presiding officer he picked himself. This resulted in a visit from Himmler, who requested the process be stopped. Küchler ignored this intervention. The proceedings were rendered moot after Hitler issued a general amnesty. There was a large element of personal animus in Küchler's stand, for he had been a protégé of General Werner von Fritsch, victim of an SS smear campaign in February 1938, who had been killed in the front line outside Warsaw. Küchler had delivered Fritsch's funeral oration. Yet it was this same General von Küchler who instructed his officers in July 1940 to stop criticising the ethnic struggle being waged in occupied Poland, specifically the 'treatment' of the Polish minority, the Jews 'and church things'. In such a centuries-old conflict between races, Küchler explained, sharp interventions were necessary. Soldiers should not intervene or criticise those organs of state and Party responsible for carrying out these tasks.[25]

VII VESTIGES OF SHAME

Unease about these atrocities in Poland was evident among the German elite. In October 1939, the conservative diplomat Ulrich von Hassell wrote in his diary of:

> the feeling of being led by criminal adventurers; and the disgrace that has sullied the German name through the conduct of the war in Poland; namely, the brutal use of air power and the shocking bestialities of the SS, especially towards the Jews. The cruelties of the Poles against the German minority are a fact, too, but somehow excusable psychologically. When people use their revolvers to shoot down a group of Jews herded into a synagogue one is filled with shame.[26]

Another complainant was the Abwehr supremo, Admiral Wilhelm Canaris, who had returned from Warsaw a shaken man after seeing the shattered city. He relayed the concerns of several generals about SS atrocities to Wilhelm Keitel, the head of the Wehrmacht High Command. Keitel replied that because the army had turned down such tasks, Hitler had decreed that the SS should do them. Ideally, such activities would be postponed until the army had relinquished power in Poland to civil administrators. In the meantime, while military commanders were to be kept informed about such actions, the responsible authorities were Himmler and Heydrich. The army also relinquished the right to hear appeals from SS court-martial proceedings against Polish civilians. A cryptic communication to senior field commanders from the High Command explained that the SS task forces were carrying out special projects for the Führer, which were exclusively the concern of the SS. In other words, the army was fully aware of what Hitler and the SS were doing, but sought to abdicate moral responsibility as rapidly as possible.[27]

On 4 October 1939, Hitler issued a general amnesty for any German army or SS personnel convicted of offences against civilians in Poland. Three days later he recognised Himmler's claim to be the Reich Commissar for the Strengthening of Ethnic Germandom, confirming SS responsibility for the vast processes of expulsion and repatriation that Himmler and Hitler envisaged.[28] On 17 October Hitler decreed that the SS and police were no longer subject to military jurisdiction when engaged in special tasks. The same day he held a conference at which Keitel represented the army, during which the Führer used broad-brush strokes to outline Poland's future. An autonomous rump state was to be ruled by Germans but without being integrated into the administration of the Reich. Unlike any other administration, the object was to retard the country culturally, economically and financially, so that it was merely a source of cheap labour. There were to be no Polish political parties and no independent high culture. Polish 'muddle' was to be encouraged. It was to become a dumping ground for 'Jews and Polacks' from the Reich itself. 'Hard ethnic struggle' would entail 'methods [which] will be incompatible with the principles which we otherwise adhere to', an interesting insight into Hitler's undemanding scale of values. In a parting shot to Keitel, Hitler said the army should welcome offloading the administration of Poland on to others.[29]

CHAPTER 5

Trampling the Remains

I THE KING AND QUEEN OF POLAND

Although formal hostilities with Poland ended on 6 October 1939, there was an increase in violence against civilians in the lawless vacuum between the army's relinquishing of authority and the establishment of civilian administrations in the areas annexed to the Reich – or, worse, in the legal indeterminacy of the General Government, which encompassed what was left. The last three months of 1939 were especially grim.

October proved a bloody month for Poland's elites, as the SS task forces pressed ahead with carrying out their orders to liquidate them. In that month Polish teachers in West Prussian towns were arrested and imprisoned in Deutsch-Krone. It was not necessary to shoot many more priests, since the survivors of the initial massacre of clergy were too cowed to resist. Other shootings took place throughout the wooded lowlands of the newly created Warthegau, where the head of the forestry administration was disturbed to learn that the SS intended to kill all Polish forestry officials. In Königsberg in early November, SS-Brigadeführer Dr Otto Rasch took captive Polish intellectuals out to a wood, where they were shot after signing a paper saying they did not object to their relocation to the General Government. A transit camp at Soldau was also used to concentrate and kill the learned. North of Warsaw in November, a police regiment staged a show trial of Jews for arson, after which 159 Jewish men and 196 women and children were shot. Although the SS task forces did not keep the sort of precise records they would maintain after the invasion of the Soviet Union, it has been estimated that they murdered forty-seven thousand Poles, of whom seven thousand were Polish Jews, before the year ended.[1]

Poland suffered the dual plight of having extensive territories incorpo-rated into the German Reich, while a remnant homeland for Poles and, as it transpired, a transit to eternity for millions of Jews was created in the General Government. On 15 September 1939, Hitler had summoned Hans Frank to his HQ at Gogolin in Silesia, where he appointed him head of a future Polish civil administration, initially subject to Gerd von Rundstedt, the Commander of Army Group South, who would hand over to Frank on 25 October. After selecting future administrative cadres in Berlin, Frank outlined the gist of what Hitler wanted for Poland at a meeting in Posen on 3 October. The country was to be stripped of anything useful to the German war economy. Economically and culturally, Poland was to be 'throttled back' to the bare essentials: 'Poland should be treated like a colony, with the Poles becoming the slaves of the Greater German World Reich.' Labour and plant were to be despatched to Germany, while Poland would be an agricultural tributary, importing manufactured goods from Germany. Following a Hitler-decree on 8 October 1939, the Reichsgau Posen was established in north-central Poland, encompassing far more territory than had belonged to the German-ruled part of Poland before 1918. Frank was not allowed to retain the textile city of Łódź, renamed Litzmannstadt in 1940, which had been in the Russian-ruled part of Poland before the Great War. The city was handed over to Arthur Greiser, Party boss of what became the Warthegau, after the river that was this flat land's principal topographical feature. Other parts of Poland were absorbed into the Reich by expanding existing East Prussia and Silesia, or in the newly forged Gau of Danzig-West Prussia, the fiefdom of Albert Forster. Severally these territories were said to have been 'recovered' for the Reich; they were never described as being occupied.[2]

On 12 October Hitler decreed the creation of a new General Government for the Occupied Polish Territories. The third clause declared that Frank was directly accountable only to Hitler.[3] Frank divided his realm into four districts, based on the cities of Cracow, Radom, Lublin and Warsaw, with Cracow becoming his administrative capital in a further bid to nullify Polish statehood. Hitler would have preferred to erase Warsaw from the map; as it was, over 15 per cent of the buildings were already ruined shells as a result of bombing, including sixty-six thousand homes. The General Government encompassed 37 per cent of pre-war Poland, with around seventeen million inhabitants. In August 1941, following the invasion of the Soviet Union, it acquired a fifth district – Galicia – with three hundred thousand people in the city of Lemberg (Lwów) and a further six million in the surrounding countryside. At its maximum extent, the General Government was roughly the size of Belgium.

These administrative arrangements barely hint at the moral morass they were intended to create in occupied Poland. Hitler elaborated his policy towards Poland at a key meeting on 18 October 1939, after his brief visit there had confirmed his existing prejudices. Poland was to be virtually autonomous (under German rule) and should pay its own way. No attempts were to be made to develop it. The only exception was the transport infrastructure, as Poland was a vital military glacis – a clear indication that he planned to attack the Soviet Union. Its other function was as a refuse bin for the Reich's growing army of unwanted non-persons.[4]

In his initial proclamation to the Polish people, Frank promised a reign of justice, now that the 'adventurous policy of your intellectual ruling elite' had been terminated. This was belied by a second ordinance combating acts of violence, in which the death penalty was specified seven times.[5] Indeed the sheer volume of ordinances banning this or prohibiting that is among the abiding memories of Poles who survived those times, along with the identity cards and permits needed to negotiate their way past every German official or policeman they encountered.

German policy in Poland was based on the aggressive assertion of racial superiority, a view that had to be planted in the minds of even the most modest of 'national comrades'. An October 1939 Propaganda Ministry directive stipulated: 'It must be made clear to even the humblest German dairy maid that "Poledom" is synonymous with sub-humanity, Poles, Jews and Gypsies are situated on the same low rung of human existence ... This view has to be drummed in like a Leitmotif by using such existing concepts as "Polish muddle", "Polish dilapidation" and the like, until every German subconsciously views every Pole, regardless of whether they are a farm hand or intellectual, as vermin.'[6] The Poles were to become Germany's servile class, like the anonymous Blacks and Asians who silently glided about the homes of their colonial masters. Regardless of whether one is talking about the annexed or the rump parts of Poland, the future had a common characteristic: persons of social or intellectual distinction were removed and killed. Their property, along with that of the former Polish state, was expropriated. The Catholic Church was subjected to systematic persecution, including the murder of its bishops and many priests. In so far as Poles of both sexes were not abducted for forced labour in Germany, their incomes and welfare rights were massively reduced, and their restricted movements constantly monitored. Keeping as many Polish

POWs in captivity for as long as possible, while despatching young women to perform farm labour in Germany, served an explicit biological agenda, as it prevented them from breeding.[7]

The physical appearance of Polish cities changed as swastikas appeared on official buildings, together with banners bearing hortatory slogans in pseudo-Gothic script. The Germans took over imposing official buildings such as Warsaw's Palais Brühl, the former Foreign Ministry, which became the seat of Governor Ludwig Fischer. Posters appeared too, adorned with such slogans as 'Jews–Lice–Typhus' or pictures of Chamberlain averting his eyes from a Polish soldier standing amid rubble under the rubric 'England! Your handiwork!' At night the cities fell into an unnatural darkness as streetlights were switched off and people told to block any light escaping from their homes. In Warsaw, only Germans were allowed to venture out at night, on tramcars that were reserved for their exclusive use, to ferry them from their apartments, barracks and hotels into the part of the city centre exclusively reserved for Germans. About sixty thousand German soldiers, policemen and administrators lived in occupied Warsaw, among but separated from the city's 1.3 million native inhabitants.[8]

A series of demeaning regulations affected ordinary life, resembling in their quotidian ugliness those of apartheid. For example, on 3 February 1940 the commissioner for Petrikau decreed that Poles and Polish Jews were to be executed if they had transmitted sexual diseases to Germans. In the incorporated territories, Poles had to salute passing Germans and to remove their caps while vacating the pavement as the master race bustled by. When the Jews obeyed this ordinance, they discovered that Germans responded with blows, so the ordinance had to be changed to exempt Jews even from this obligation.[9] Poles were not allowed to use bicycles, except to go to work, and were banned from buses and trams. They were subject to a nighttime curfew. Regulations that banned Jews in Warsaw from park benches newly designated 'for Germans only' were extended to ethnic Poles in Posen. Economic restrictions also prohibited Poles from being pharmacists, musicians or singers. In the incorporated areas, Poles were allowed to undertake only the most humble administrative roles, whereas in the General Government they continued to occupy middle to lower positions under German supervision, so there were more than eleven thousand blue-uniformed Polish policemen. Positions in the upper echelons of the German administration were taken by Frank's lawyer cronies, with some 22,740 German men and 7,184 German women brought in to occupy all supervisory roles. The main functionaries were the 130 *Kreishauptleute*, the majority law graduates who had gone into public administration. These men were primarily responsible for plundering the produce of Polish farmers, and for compressing Poland's Jews into ever more untenable conditions. In May 1942 one of these men wrote home to Germany: 'unfortunately exterminations are not going as we would like them to, because we have an absolute need for labour'. Such officials were responsible for the steady flow of demeaning ordinances which were so humiliating for Polish people under the occupation. Some of them were deeply implicated in deciding which Jews were handed over to the SS. The five previously roaming SS Einsatzgruppen were converted into stationary police units based in the district capitals, under the overall command of the Higher SS and Police Leader Friedrich Wilhelm Krüger, whose ambition shortly led Frank to call him the 'louse in my fur'.[10]

A specially produced Baedeker guide to the General Government introduced visitors to this parallel world, in which all the good things in life were reserved for the Germans, and in which they always went to the head of the queue or enjoyed reserved hours to do their shopping. All signs displayed by tradesmen and shopkeepers had to be given in German too.[11] Even football was not sacred: when the Warsaw team played the Danzig team on 5 October 1940, neither contained a single Polish player, and the entire crowd consisted of Germans. Apart from those who lived in barracks or hotels, most Germans shared three- or four-bedroom apartments in the more modern inter-war blocks, from which the Poles were evicted, with a domino effect on the Jews who were crammed into ever shrinking, insalubrious conditions. The Germans ate and, notably, drank in large subsidised canteens; an epidemic of intoxication – on and off duty – was the preferred way of coping with living in the eastern 'promised land' that most were only too glad to see the back of on generous periods of home leave in the Reich.

The collective, regimented nature of life of all the occupiers may also have had a role in ensuring that there was little dissent or unease about what they were doing, for even when someone was sound asleep they were liable to be dragged out of bed to continue the incessant party. For those who did not import their wives and families with them, the occupation laid on brothels, where a purely cash relationship with Polish whores circumvented any legal restraints on 'race defilement'. Officers were not allowed to use these facilities, lest it detract from their role-model function, which may explain why in the course of German police raids on the Hotel Bristol in Warsaw in October 1939, thirty-four whores were found in forty rooms reserved for officers. Despite all the high-minded babble about German *Kultur*, the realities of occupation were grimly sordid: drunkenness, inter-service brawling, brutality, rape, graft, extortion and theft being the everyday norm, along with some starving girl hitching her skirts in a dark alley in return for a half-loaf of bread.

Yet there was a moral code of a sort among the occupiers and this was enforced by German courts. The Germans had a mission towards the east as a whole. German honour and prestige had to be protected at all costs; after all this was what distinguished the master race from the surrounding helots. Germans were expected to demonstrate comradeship, discipline and a sense of duty at all times, as well as a racial consciousness that inhibited fraternisation with people whose language the Germans could not speak and never tried to learn. Falling down drunk in public bars, loosing off pistols at street lights or signs, bringing whores to the guardhouse at the Palais Brühl, or taking bribes from Polish businessmen were all punished, sometimes severely. It may be that the maintenance of this partial group morality made it easier for some Germans to behave so abominably to the majority population, who were excluded from their orbit of concern and enjoyed no legal protections. Forbidden by inclination and law from showing pity towards the people they ruled, the Germans felt sorry for themselves, for having to do such things in the name of duty, discipline, racial consciousness and German prestige.[12]

II THE ROYAL COURT

Until 1 November 1939 Frank, his statuesque wife Brigitte and their five children lived in Łódź. On the 7th they moved into Cracow's historic Wawelsburg, the residence of several generations of Polish kings and queens. A string quintet from the Silesian Philharmonic played the Governor in, under the eyes of every conceivable army and SS formation drawn up in the central courtyard. This was to be the Franks' family home until 1943, when Brigitte commenced divorce proceedings, although the unhappy couple also had a large country estate, filched from the Potockis, at Kressendorf, west of the new capital, as well as a villa in Berlin's plush Regerstrasse and a fourth home in Munich. When in Warsaw, Frank availed himself of the Belvedere Palace. He also acquired a villa in the spa resort of Krynica, which he used to conduct love affairs with an old flame called

Lily, and a holiday place in the Tatra Mountains, which he daringly called the Berghof. He could not ski but he enjoyed riding. Sustained bureaucratic work easily bored him.

Instead, he cast himself in the leading role in his own historical pageant. Mimicking royalty, whenever Frank was in residence in his castle the swastika billowed overhead. Pomp and power clearly went to the Nazi lawyer's head. His photograph hung in every room opposite where he sat, and he liked to hand out autographed copies to his guests. For the other walls, he commissioned art thieves to scour Poland and occupied Europe for works by Breughel, Raphael and Rembrandt. He dispensed cigars from luxury humidors on which his castle was depicted. Trumpet blasts greeted his birthday mornings. In addition to dozens of uniforms, adorned with all his insignia and medals, Frank had 120 suits. A red carpet was to be unrolled wherever he trod. There were guards of honour studded around his palace, together with endless receptions where little League of German Maidens formations presented him with bouquets of flowers. Always called 'the castle' rather than 'the Wawel', Frank's palace acquired a castle captain, a castle press, a castle doctor, a castle post office and a castle guard. The Franks' personal staff ran to twenty-five, including cooks, nannies, drivers and personal assistants for the Governor's wife, not counting the Poles and Ukrainians toiling in the gardens. There were Mercedes and Maybachs to chauffeur the royal couple around, be it on official or private business. A luxury railway carriage could be coupled to any train heading to the Reich, although more often than not it was filled with hams, salami and butter, with a couple of trucks for the overflow. Huge sums of cash were quietly salted away in bank accounts in the Reich.

On learning of his appointment in Poland, Frank knelt down before his wife and proclaimed: 'Brigitte, you will be the Queen of Poland.' She took him at his word, inviting several relatives and a former lover to join their court. Frau Frank's long-standing obsession was fur coats, manifest even when she had been a Munich typist who caught Frank's eye. Throughout her sojourn in Poland, she would roll up at furriers in the Jewish ghettos, where, leaving her youngest son to stick his tongue out at starving Jewish children from behind the car window, she would strike very hard bargains with the proprietors.

Inevitably there were blemishes in paradise. Although isolated from general view, the country house at Kressendorf was adjacent to a small town whose population included 570 Jews. From October 1939 onwards these people were subject to the measures that had been introduced in the

Reich – no post, no telephones, no houses – until on 8 July 1942 Kressendorf was pronounced 'free of Jews' and Frank could enjoy his summer idylls undisturbed by their proximity. There was also the matter of Cracow's seventy thousand Polish Jews. In May 1940 Frank told them they had until August to leave the city, which nine thousand did on a voluntary basis. When the deadline came, Frank ordered the compulsory evacuation of 40,000–45,000 more, allowing fifteen thousand Jews to remain in essential occupations. Since none of his district satraps was prepared to take Jews, they quietly slipped back to the city after they had been deported. So, in March 1941, a closed ghetto was established in the neighbourhood of Podgórze. The following year the SS opened their own ghetto in the suburb of Płaszów, the domain of the psychopath Amon Göth. This enabled Frank's propagandists to describe Cracow as a 'purely German town' of 24,800 German citizens, making non-persons of the 275,000 non-Jewish Poles, as well as the ghettoised Jews.[13]

III KULTUR

Frank was what conventionally passed for a cultivated man, whose lawyer's use of Latin quotations irritated the rougher company that gravitated to what even the Nazis called his 'Gangster-Gau'. At official dinners he was wont to push himself back in his throne to hold forth about the radiant future of what was to be the gateway to the Reich from lands further to the east. On such occasions, the sweat on his face resembled a mask of cellophane, wrapping a space consisting of nothing other than ambition. He was a chess enthusiast who in November 1940 instituted both a congress and a chess school under two Ukrainian masters. He inaugurated an annual Dr Frank Prize for German writers and historians, and had a composer write a 'General Governor's March' for ceremonial occasions. He founded a German Theatre in Cracow, with a separate SS and police theatre where off-duty mass murderers could unwind. He also established a Philharmonic Orchestra of the General Government; Rudolf Hindemith was the principal conductor, the brother of the famous composer. In place of the venerable University of Cracow, whose faculty members were deported to Sachsenhausen, Frank founded an Institut für Deutsche Ostarbeit, both to study the German civilising role in the east and to act as a practical ideas institute for the Frank administration. The Institut was one of the hubs that churned out a low-grade mix of romantic legends about the historical role of the Germans in the east, together with more desiccated social scientific materials that directly impacted on people's lives.[14]

This attempt to graft, or resurrect, German cultural life in Poland was accompanied by the elimination of those elite groups which had survived the initial assault by the SS. The largest operation was called the Extraordinary Pacification or AB exercise, which began on 31 March 1940 and extended into July. The victims ranged from politicians who had engaged in resistance to a mass of secondary school teachers. The opportunity was also taken to kill three thousand individuals dubbed career criminals, chiefly to free up prison space for political detainees. Acting in concert with his comrades Bruno Streckenbach and Krüger, Frank declared that it was easier to shoot members of the Polish elites than to imprison them in German concentration camps, which would merely trigger protest letters and campaigns to release them, as had been the case with 180 Cracow professors, on whose behalf the Pope had intervened. Frank also expressed concern for the men detailed to carry out these tasks, claiming that those they shot were to be sentenced by courts martial and insisting that Streckenbach and his officers pay due attention to their psychological health. This was evidently necessary, as Streckenbach himself, when he discussed these sensitive issues with the Berlin police chief, burst into tears and reported that his men were drinking too much.[15] Simultaneously, Frank waived the ultimate right of hearing appeals against capital sentences that he had earlier insisted upon being granted by Hitler as a manifestation of his quasi-regal sovereignty. In the course of these operations, the SS killed 3,500 members of the Polish intelligentsia and upper classes, although this may be an underestimate. By the end of the war, a quarter of the Polish intelligentsia had been killed, including 45 per cent of doctors and dentists; 40 per cent of university professors; 56 per cent of lawyers; 15 per cent of schoolteachers and 18 per cent of the country's Roman Catholic priests. The higher percentages of murdered doctors and lawyers is partly attributable to a large proportion of them being Jews.[16]

Throughout the incorporated territories and the General Government, all higher education was reserved for Germans, with the Polish University of Poznań being superseded by the Reich University of Posen. Education for Poles was reduced to a minimum. Where school buildings were not commandeered for use as barracks or military hospitals, an absence of heating materials meant that they were unable to function throughout winter. In the remaining warmer months – about seven in Poland – instruction took place for only two or three hours a day, in classes of between seventy and a hundred pupils taught by aged teachers, since younger staff – potentially the lynchpins of the resistance – had either been arrested or killed or had fled. Subjects such as geography, history and literature were prohibited and the textbooks confiscated; that left elementary German as the language of obedience, and such necessary evils as arithmetic.[17] All independent Polish newspapers closed; instead there was a range of German-controlled Polish language products, which specialised in anti-Semitism and in deprecating the old order. An array of German-language papers, notably the *Krakauer Zeitung* and glossy monthlies like the *Vistula Illustrated*, catered for German readers.

Polish commentators who had experienced the German occupation of 1915–18 noted the cultural and moral decline of their new masters. The average Pole, they claimed, had more in common with Beethoven or Goethe than did the crude and thuggish characters they encountered after September 1939, as the dross of the German administration was sent to the bureaucratic sin bin in the east, lured by salary supplements and opportunities for graft on a gargantuan scale. In the pre-war Polish capital there were twenty-four professional theatres and two opera houses; yet in the summer of 1940, as German audiences were treated to Sophocles and Calderón, the Slav natives were entertained by the visiting Circus Busch. The same segregation applied to theatre performances – a Pole who visited a German theatre in the annexed areas would be liable to arrest. Low-level smut was encouraged, as long as only Poles partook of it. The Germans encouraged street gambling, as well as establishing a lottery, and opened a Poles-only casino in Warsaw, where shady characters flourished.

While children were reduced to ignorant scavengers, elderly people quietly died, as their new masters stopped paying pensions. Another group of vulnerable people were the mentally handicapped and disturbed. In July 1939 an SS-police reinforcement unit called the Wachsturmbann Eimann had been formed, consisting of five to six hundred members of the SS XXVI Section. On 4 September these men moved into an imposing mental asylum at Conradstein. Starting on the 22nd, they began bussing groups of patients to a wood at Szpegawski, where they were shot and buried while the buses returned to pick up a further batch. Some two thousand patients from Conradstein and neighbouring asylums were murdered in this manner, presumably as a result of a discussion among Gauleiter Forster, Himmler, Hitler, Bormann and the chiefs of the Aktion T-4 euthanasia programme Leonardo Conti, Karl-Rudolf Brandt and Philip Bouhler, who had met at the Casino Hotel in Zoppot a few days before operations commenced. At the instigation of Gauleiter Franz Schwede-Coburg of Pomerelia and Himmler, who wanted to create barracks space for proliferating SS units, a further fourteen hundred psychiatric patients were taken by train to Neustadt, and then bussed about six miles to a wood near Gross-Piasnitz, where they were killed by Eimann's unit. Each victim was led by two SS men to a ditch and shot in the back of the neck by a third. The dozen prisoners from Stutthof who dug the mass graves were then drugged and shot. The Wachsturmbann Eimann members were shown films about Robert Koch and the tuberculosis bacillus to strengthen their resolve.[18]

Cultural superiority was supposed to justify treating the Poles as if they were illegal squatters in their own country, who could be ejected at will. As Frank said: 'It is not the Germans who are aliens in this land but rather the non-Germans.' He continued: 'Polandom, what have you to show from that time, what can you point to from the thousands of years before these epochal events from your period in this territory? What? Where? How? Nothing, nothing!' His tame Nazi academics supplied him with a narrative that nullified anything non-German from pre-history to the present.

IV COLONISATION

A vast programme of population transfer was undertaken to strengthen the meagre German element in occupied Poland, just as even humble places were being transformed – for example, Bogucin into Thorshammer or Krzyszkowo into Friedrichssieg.[19] The driving force behind this megalomaniac project was Himmler, in his freshly minted capacity of Reich Commissar for the Strengthening of Ethnic Germandom. One object was to reverse the historic secular westwards drift of Germans from the relatively backward agrarian provinces of the east. This tide had swelled during the early years of the Weimar Republic, necessitating various covert subventions to keep the German minority in place to sustain political claims.[20]

No thought had been given as to where more Germans were going to come from, beyond occasional mention of repatriating them from the global diaspora, particularly Argentina. The psychological effects of the

Molotov–Ribbentrop Pact on Germans in the Baltic provided what seemed like a gift out of the blue, since on 28 September, and as a result of the fears of terror that preceded him, Stalin agreed to allow ethnic Germans to settle in Germany.[21] Theoretically, the necessary settlers would therefore come from the eastern ethnic German diaspora. To manage this process, a joint German–Soviet Committee was established under the chairmanship of former Foreign Minister Maxim Litvinov and Kurt von Remphohener. The practicalities were to be handled from an office in Łuck by Major Sinicyn of the USSR and SS-Obersturmbannführer Hofmaier, with a number of joint teams based on either side of the inner Polish border.

The first element of Himmler's transfer project, namely mass deportations, was seemingly easy enough, given the regime's total disregard for the rights of Poles and Jews. This was to deport politically active Poles, or civil servants who been rendered unemployed after Germans had taken their jobs. In reality, anybody might be rudely ejected from their homes at twenty minutes' notice and permitted to take only twenty kilograms of essential belongings, as they were obliged to leave cooking utensils, clean dishes and cutlery behind. They were bundled on to trains, each crammed with up to a thousand people and guarded by policemen and ethnic German self-protection squads, and taken on slow journeys to the General Government where they were cast out to fend for themselves.

In West Prussia, Gauleiter Albert Forster drove forty thousand Poles from Gdingen (Polish Gdynia), or Gotenhafen as he renamed it, leaving the port like a ghost town. Forster was obliged to think again about this and about subsequent quick fixes dreamed up by Himmler and his coterie of mad planners. In the Warthegau, his colleague Greiser decided to expel 87,000 Poles in mid-winter, to make way for 128,000 ethnic Germans from the Baltic to settle in a territory where the existing German minority constituted only 10 per cent of a population of over four millions. The entire operation was a shambles that belied the 'Home to the Reich' propaganda visions of happy repatriates debouching from ships to take up their new homes. Most of the Poles who were deported lived in towns, yet the ethnic German repatriates, who were simple country folk, were supposed to receive farms. In other words, Greiser had deported the wrong type of people. The Baltic Germans were soon joined by a further 275,000 ethnic Germans from formerly Rumanian Bessarabia and Bukovina, who, like the Balts, found themselves languishing in transit camps, where they were treated like refugees rather than long-lost family members. Meanwhile, hundreds of thousands of destitute Poles and Jews were arriving in the

General Government, where no provision had been made for them. Some of the deportees froze or starved to death in transit, and even the SS deplored having to unload hundreds of frozen corpses. There was a complete breakdown in co-ordination: of the eleven trains used for the initial deportations, only five chugged back after a week's interval; the rest had disappeared, taken over by the army or the Ostbahn, the railway network in the East. Then the authorities in the General Government issued permits entitling deportees to return home for up to a month to settle their affairs, with the predictable result that they lingered and had confrontations with the ethnic Germans by then ensconced in their homes.[22]

Initially, the authorities in the General Government confined themselves to introducing compulsory labour for Poles who could not prove themselves indispensable. Hundreds of thousands of Poles were forced to work in German industrial plant in the General Government, including 140,000 who worked in arms factories, as well as many more employed in agriculture and construction. In addition, after voluntary recruitment drives to relieve acute labour shortages in the Reich had yielded only 180,000 volunteers, the Germans introduced compulsory labour conscription. The age range affected fell from a minimum of sixteen in 1941 to thirteen years of age in 1942. Göring spoke of needing a minimum of one million Polish labourers, not including the 400,000–480,000 Polish prisoners of war never repatriated. Reports of conditions in Germany did not make it an attractive prospect. From September 1940, Poles in the Reich had to wear a violet P on a yellow square stitched on to their clothing. Hitler personally decreed that even the lowest-paid German was to receive 10 per cent more than any Pole, even though the German might work a maximum of eight hours while the foreign helot put in fourteen or more per day. All sexual, social or religious contacts with Germans were prohibited and transgressions were subjected to draconian penalties. After the number of unemployed Poles scooped off the streets had been exhausted, the Germans resorted to abducting people as they left cinemas, churches and secondary schools. On 13 March 1943, Frank was present at Cracow's main station to reward the millionth departing Polish forced worker with a gold watch, promising that the deportees would return 'fresh and happy' once they had performed their service for the German Reich.

V FINAL SOLUTION IN THE MAKING

Lastly, there was the edifice built on the rancid foundations of the semi-spontaneous violence unleashed by German soldiers and policemen against Polish Jews. The Nazi occupation of Poland meant that 1,901,000 Polish Jews fell into their hands at a time when, as a result of forced emigration, the German-Jewish population of the Reich had declined to 250,000. Warsaw alone, with four hundred thousand Jews, had more Jews than remained in the entire Reich. These numbers, and the fact that war had closed off emigration, led to more drastic measures.

In instructions dated 21 September 1939, which repeatedly stressed the secrecy of (unspecified) final goals, Heydrich ordered the dissolution of all Jewish communities with fewer than five hundred inhabitants and their removal to 'concentration cities' pending ultimate dispositions. These ghettos, located in cities with rail transport links, were to have Councils of Elders to take orders from the German authorities. The only Jews allowed to remain, on licence, were those deemed economically indispensable to the German armed forces, or whom German officials used as *Hausjuden*, that is domestic servants, dentists or hairdressers. The immediate priority for the Germans in the General Government was to get Jews out of areas they used for either administrative or residential purposes. In Cracow and elsewhere this was described as 'improving the city's countenance' in line with German aesthetic criteria. It was quickly extended to spa and ski resorts like Zakopane, which were reserved for Germans.[23]

Long-range policy reflected developing circumstances. The initial notion of a 'final goal' came to hand once the Soviets had relinquished Lublin. This was to establish a Jewish 'Reich ghetto' or 'reservation' in Poland's south-eastern corner. It was to this area, in and around Nisko, that the diligent Adolf Eichmann tried to send Jews from Bohemia-Moravia, Upper Silesia and Vienna, an operation that resulted in total chaos when the Russians proved no less eager to push the Jews back across the San river. Eichmann's over-enthusiastic initiative was halted on 26 October, to be superseded by Himmler's order to expel all Jews from the incorporated territories into the General Government.

It may be that the appointment of the half-Slovenian SS-Brigadeführer Odilo Globocnik as SS- and Police Chief in Lublin district was significant. After an interrupted education in engineering, Globocnik had been a courier on behalf of the underground Nazi organisation in Austria, for which he was rewarded after the *Anschluss* with the post of Gauleiter of Vienna. Chronic financial peculation led to his dismissal after it attracted the scrutiny of the Treasurer of the Nazi Party.[24] Attached to Himmler's staff, in the summer of 1939 Globocnik underwent military training in the SS before taking part as a corporal in the invasion of Poland. Rapidly promoted, he acquired a modernist mansion on Lublin's Wieniawska Street, bringing several Austrian acquaintances to serve as his core staff. Big and brutal, as well as fertile in ideas, Globocnik envisaged himself ruling a Reich ghetto in the remote north-eastern borderlands of his fiefdom. Meanwhile, he deployed Jewish forced labourers, housed in twenty makeshift camps, to construct a huge defensive rampart, 90 miles in length, called the Otto Line, which shadowed the eastern border with the Soviet Union. Those Jews who survived the forced marches in the depths of winter to get there found that conditions in camps like Belzec were atrocious. In his 1941 New Year celebration card illustrating the new order in Lublin district, Globocnik included three little figures digging under armed guard.[25]

Historians of the Final Solution have traditionally moved from the aborted Nisko operation to the next, even more crazed project of deporting millions of Jews to East Africa, an absurd scheme given the oceanic supremacy of the Royal Navy. However, recent archival discoveries point to an intermediate scheme. Russian historians have found a letter dated 9 February 1940 from the Soviet resettlement agency in the Ukraine to Molotov, which refers to two earlier requests from their German analogue. Eichmann, by then promoted to be the Berlin-based Reich evacuation supremo, asked the Soviets whether they would consider taking the Jewish population of Germany, including the Jews in occupied Poland, in addition to the Ruthenians, Ukrainians and White Russians who were also being transported eastwards. For, since the 1920s, the Soviets themselves had been experimenting with Jewish homelands, in the northern Crimea, in the southern Ukraine and on the Amur river, where they sought to create a national entity called Birobidzan. In practice, this idea was based on a very optimistic view of a Soviet regime that had refused to attend the 1938 Evian conference to find an international solution to the plight of German Jews, and which was suffused with paranoia about foreign spies. In the autumn of 1940, Soviet border guards were ordered to treat every Jewish fugitive from Nazi-occupied Poland as a spy. Perhaps it is time more attention was paid to how the Soviets reacted to Hitler's persecution of the Jews.[26]

By early April 1940, plans to resettle the Jews in the north-west of Lublin district had been abandoned, perhaps on the grounds that this fertile region was more appropriate for ethnic German settlers. Instead, the Jews were to be corralled in ghettos by 1 July. The scheme was no sooner started than the fall of France raised the tantalising prospect of transporting between four and six million European Jews to the French colony of Madagascar, off the south-eastern coast of Africa. In its various elaborations, this new scheme involved shipping three thousand Jews per day over a four-year period to the island, which the SS were to run as a vast colonial ghetto. These Jews would be hostages for the good behaviour of their supposedly influential US co-religionists. As Madagascar could barely support its existing inhabitants, many of the deportees would have perished. The Madagascar scheme was briefly entertained by many, including Hans Frank and the Warsaw Jewish leader Adam Czerniaków. The neighbouring German Gaue that had incorporated Alsace and Lorraine seized on the opportunity to deport 6,500 German Jews from Baden and the Palatinate to the south of France, part of the broader, competitive desire of Nazi bosses to cleanse their territory of Jews, which included the efforts of the Viennese Gauleiter Baldur von Schirach to expel sixty thousand Jews to resolve a local housing crisis. As late as July 1941, Hitler still vaguely mentioned Madagascar (joined now by Siberia) as future locations for the Jews, although he knew these options depended on defeating respectively either the British or the Russians.[27] Ironically, he even revealed a certain environmental consciousness when he rejected plans to deport Jews to swamps neighbouring the Bug river, on the grounds that reclaiming them might have upset the climate.

In reality, forthcoming operations in Russia meant that the search for a solution to the Jewish problem refocused on the east, leaving the deportees from Baden and the Palatinate to languish in camps in the Pyrenees as the entirely fantastic Madagascar option receded. If earlier moves to corral the Jews had been carried out in the name of urban aesthetic improvement, now the justification was their alleged morbidity and the risk of typhus spreading to rising concentrations of German troops. Of course, those very same troop build-ups in turn limited the areas available for settling the Jews. The concept of deporting them to the east was retained, even if it was obviously not practical to resettle them in a prospective war zone. These ill-thought-out solutions for problems largely based on ethnic paranoia effectively doomed the Jews, even before the entire climate was further radicalised by the war against the Soviet Union.

In Warsaw, ghettoisation involved moving 138,000 Jews into a one-thousand-acre site ringed by a ten-foot-high brick wall topped with barbed wire. There were twenty-two heavily policed entry and exit points, later reduced to fifteen. With its existing Jewish population, the ghetto had to accommodate over four hundred thousand people in some twenty-seven thousand apartments. The density of occupancy was horrific, with six or seven people crammed into each room.[28] Food rations were reduced to the equivalent of three hundred calories a day, while in most apartments heating was non-existent. The effects of this were soon apparent to outsiders like Stanisław Różycki, who wrote that 'the majority are nightmare figures, ghosts of former human beings, miserable destitutes, pathetic remnants of former humanity … their faces have taken on a skeletal appearance. The prominent bones around their eye sockets, the yellow facial colour, the slack pendulous skin, the alarming emaciation and sickliness. And, in addition, this miserable, frightened, restless, apathetic and resigned expression, like that of a hunted animal.' After an hour moving through children prematurely aged by hunger, and adults reduced to the same 'declassed and degraded' circumstances, Różycki had to avert his eyes.[29]

The ghettos themselves contributed to a more drastic attitude to the Jewish problem for, having created them, the Germans promoted ghetto tourism to show how horrible the Jews really were. The ghettos were also entirely lawless zones where Germans could do what they liked. Horst Goede, the rural commissar in Opole in the district of Puławy between Radom and Lublin, repeatedly raped his seventeen-year-old Jewish chambermaid and frequently appeared drunk in the Opole ghetto, where he randomly beat up or shot passers-by. His demands on the ghetto's Jewish Council were specific: 'forty to sixty bottles of wine, liqueurs, champagne, two pairs of high boots, three men's suits, gentlemen's underwear, ladies' underwear, gloves, slippers, leather goods, tea, coffee, chocolate, cocoa, biscuits, toiletries'.[30] In circumstances where the occupying power routinely practised violence, murder and robbery, how was it possible to prevent individual Germans from taking the same line? Apart from shooting people for the most trivial infractions of the rules, or just for some imagined offence, Germans who could not be bothered to avail themselves of the colossal disparity between their money and the goods available simply helped themselves to what they liked. The ferocious penalties in force also made the ghetto an extortionist's paradise, for who would not pay up to avoid a worse fate? Although regular relationships between Germans and Jews (and non-Jewish Poles) was strictly forbidden, the ghetto provided ample latitude to rapists, since no German court would believe the testimony of a Jewish woman – in any event viewed as having no honour to defend – against that of ethnic Germans or police and SS men, while the drunkenness of the perpetrator, which in other jurisdictions would have been regarded as an aggravating factor, was regarded as a sufficient excuse.[31]

Although in theory unauthorised Germans were forbidden to enter the ghetto, in practice many could pull rank on the perimeter guards or simply talk their way in to satisfy their macabre curiosity. Then there were the German Labour Front coaches that took soldiers through while they were in Warsaw on leave. As time passed, these visitors inevitably saw corpses lying in the streets, waiting to be taken by cart to the cemetery, which was the highpoint of each trip. Accounts of what they saw were included in their letters to friends and relatives in the old Reich or were discussed in long nights on trains, with each atrocity growing in the retelling. Then there were the high-ranking tourists such as Eastern Territories Minister Alfred Rosenberg. In a report on visits to ghettos in Lublin and Warsaw, Rosenberg wrote: 'If there are any people left who still somehow have sympathy with the Jews then they ought to be recommended to have a look at such a ghetto. Seeing this race en masse, which is decaying, decomposing, and rotten to the core, will banish any sentimental humanitarianism.'[32]

On 2 November 1939 Goebbels arrived in Łódź on a trip that included a drive through its Jewish district, for the ghetto had not yet been formed: 'We got out and took a closer look. It is indescribable. These are no longer human beings, they are beasts. It is no longer a humanitarian but rather a surgical problem. One must make incisions here, and definitely radical ones. Otherwise Europe will be ruined by the Jewish sickness.'[33] While scenes of desolation prompted such inhuman responses, there was also a widely perceived gap between what was desired and the means of achieving it. This is evident from a letter written in December 1939 by Eduard Koenekamp to a friend after he had visited several Jewish quarters in Poland:

The extermination of this sub-humanity would be in the interest of the whole world. However, such an extermination is one of the most difficult problems. Shooting would not suffice. Also, one cannot allow the shooting of women and children. Here and there, one expects losses during the deportations: thus in a transport of 1000 Jews from Lublin, 450 perished. All agencies which deal with the Jewish Question are aware of the insufficiency of all these measures. A solution of this complicated problem has not yet been found.[34]

Even in May 1940, in his notorious memorandum on treatment of alien populations in the east, SS leader Himmler had seemed to rule out 'the Bolshevik method of physically exterminating a people as fundamentally unGerman and impossible'.[35] It was interesting that one of the most notorious mass murderers in history could assume the moral high ground vis-à-vis men in whose company he was otherwise happy to be photographed, puffing on a cigar when Molotov visited Berlin in November 1940. The ethics of racial egoism would have to be taken up a notch to make the unGerman very German, combining extreme sentimentalism towards one's own kind with the most callous brutality to others, and making killing a form of racial altruism.

VI SOVIET POLAND

Lest we forget, Poland was invaded and occupied from two directions, and was treated as an experimental laboratory by two totalitarian ideologies. The Germans and Soviets co-operated in establishing their new common frontier, with Stalin personally indulging Ribbentrop's desire for a minor border rectification in the form of deer-hunting facilities in the Carpathians, allegedly also suitable for future secret contacts between the regimes. Ribbentrop also put in a request for more caviar, destined, he claimed, for the sensitive palates of German war-wounded. There were also evidently joint commissions of the NKVD and SS, although neither side had any interest in publicising such contacts.[36]

Initially, many local authorities in eastern Poland welcomed the Soviets' presence, believing they had come to aid Poland against Germany, an impression fostered by the fact that most Red Army troops had no idea where they were or why they were there. The USSR took over seventy-five thousand square miles of Polish territory, inhabited by around thirteen million people. Only a third of them were ethnic Poles; the other two-thirds were Jews – who overwhelmingly lived in small towns of around twenty thousand souls – Ruthenians, Ukrainians in East Galicia and Wolhynia, and various indeterminate ethnicities. Inter-ethnic animosities were rife in this backward and poor region, which explains why Jews and Ukrainians welcomed the Soviets with bread, salt and flowers, together with hugs and kisses. The Ukrainians took the opportunity of the collapse of Polish authority to unfurl their blue and yellow national flags and to turn on so-called Polish military colonists, who had been planted in their midst in the 1920s. The flags were a mistake, since the Soviets hated any manifestations of nationalism. The Jews saw the Soviet invasion as deliverance not only from the existential threat represented by the Germans, but also from the anti-Semitic Polish government, which had also toyed with shipping Jews to Madagascar. 'You wanted a Poland without Jews, now you've got Jews without Poland,' they crowed. Communist Jews eagerly welcomed their Soviet comrades, even though Stalin had liquidated the Polish Party's exiled leadership. So did young Zionists, who asked Jewish Red Army officers when they could leave for Palestine. No need, they were told, because a new Palestine was going to be created there and then. It is doubtful that their elders shared the pro-Soviet enthusiasm of younger Jews.

Like the Germans, the Russians made off with everything moveable. After the currency was changed to the rouble, shops were emptied after freezing prices at pre-war levels. The Soviets did nothing to obstruct anti-Polish ethnic cleansing, which resulted in several thousand deaths, and encouraged expropriation of the rich as a prelude to the imposition of agricultural collectivisation. In October 1939, they organised fraudulent elections to local assemblies in West Ukraine and West White Russia. Candidates were announced at meetings where objectors were compelled to make themselves known. Voters were told by Soviet agents in their apartment blocks to go to the polls, and were accompanied there by Russian soldiers and policemen. They either received a pre-marked ballot paper in a sealed envelope or, if they were allowed to make their own mark, could not fail to notice that their ballot papers bore individual identifying numbers. On 28 October assemblies 'elected' in Białystok and Lemberg voted to unite the territories with the Soviet Union.

While perhaps ten thousand young Jews and Ukrainians enthusiastically threw themselves into the service of the new Soviet regime, the majority of the population was reduced to a common, bleak general level, as Russia's low standard of living leached into eastern Poland. Every chicken or pig was inventoried, and special permission had to be granted by new village committees to slaughter them. It was telling that many Jews soon attempted to escape these conditions by fleeing back into the General Government. The Soviet police apparatus was all too evident, not least in the fivefold increase of the prison population, for which farms, offices and monasteries were expropriated to provide more capacity. In a twenty-one-month period, before the Germans arrived to discover wholesale massacres in twenty-five of these jails, some half a million people were incarcerated, abused and routinely tortured by the NKVD.

The Germans and the Soviets used exactly the same methods to deport huge numbers of people: a few minutes to pack some necessities before being shipped off in cattle wagons to an unknown fate. Before June 1941, when they were invaded themselves, the Soviets deported 1,250,000 Polish citizens, including some tens of thousands of Jews, to the USSR's interior. Deportees left Poland locked in sixty-wagon goods trains, which discarded a trail of frozen corpses in their wake as they ambled over immense distances. At stations Russian policemen periodically opened the doors, holding the corpse of a frozen child under their arm, and asking, 'Are there any frozen children inside?' Half the Polish deportees died during their journey into the Russian vastness. During the same period, the Germans deported around four hundred thousand Poles to the General Government from the incorporated territories. In this respect, at this time, the Soviet record may have been worse, although it is hardly a competition.[37]

Both totalitarian regimes deployed their respective secret policemen, the NKVD and SS, who used similar methods to interrogate, torture and kill not only Poland's elites but any one who resisted them or who expressed strong patriotic opinions. They had a written agreement to 'tolerate in their territories no Polish agitation which affects the territories of the other party. They will suppress in their territories all beginnings of such agitation and inform each other concerning suitable measures for this purpose.'[38] How far that co-operation went remains a moot question, hampered by an absence of available records on what was discussed at joint NKVD–SS meetings. The NKVD certainly handed over to the Gestapo German Communists who had fled to Moscow, as well as forty-three thousand Polish POWs who had been resident in pre-war Western Poland. Significant numbers of Polish POWs were detained by the Soviets, however, and delivered to a network of NKVD-run camps, while other Poles were held in regular prisons in Soviet-occupied Poland.

Three of these, Kozelsk, Ostashkov and Starobelsk, housed a total of 15,570 men, including army officers, police and prison guards, university students and Boy Scouts. Those who revealed unyielding patriotism under interrogation made up the majority of the 14,700 POWs and prisoners whom Beria secured an order to execute, countersigned by Stalin and the Politburo.[39] The fact that five thousand of them were ordinary policemen or prison officers confirms that the primary intention was to eliminate patriots rather than the Polish social elite. Of these men, the majority were shot into trenches at sites hidden in Katyń Forest; others were murdered inside NKVD prisons, where they were held by the arms and shot in the back of the head. The prisoners who left Ostashkov departed in high spirits to the strains of a military band; they were killed in a basement by an NKVD major wearing an apron and elbow-length gloves to spare his tunic splatters of blood.[40] Stalin was to claim that they had gone missing in Manchuria, before German discovery of their remains in 1943 led him to blame the massacres on his erstwhile allies, although, ironically, many Polish officers survived the war in German Oflags, the camps for non-enlisted POWs.[41]

The Catholic Church suffered grievously on both sides of the inner demarcation line, although in contrast to the Nazis the Soviets allowed all levels of Polish-language instruction to continue, despite some changes to the curriculum. They celebrated the national poet Adam Mickiewicz's anniversary; the Nazis took down his statues in Cracow and Posen. There were also differences in how the two regimes behaved towards civilians. Russian occupiers did not systematically treat all Poles as helots, and nor did they have a vicious animus towards Poland's Jews, not least because Jews had played a distinguished part in the Bolshevik movement, had served in the Red Army and NKVD and were a presence in Poland's Communist Party until Stalin disbanded it. By contrast, the Germans issued endless decrees discriminating against both Poles and Jews, and subjected both communities to routine brutality and humiliation.

VII THE FINLAND FACTOR

One of the arguments the Soviets used to justify the slaughter of Poles in NKVD facilities was the need to create extra space for prisoners of war to be taken in the Soviet invasion of Finland, although in the end only a thousand Finns were captured. It may be that exiled General Władysław Sikorski's offer of a Polish contingent to any Anglo-French force destined for Finland may have helped seal the Poles' fate. The Soviets used the concept of 'indirect aggression' to justify their increasingly outrageous demands on the Finnish government, culminating in insistence on a non-aggression pact similar to those that had reduced the Baltic States to helotry. Stalin also demanded the surrender of virtually every element of Finnish defences on the narrow Karelian Isthmus and various islands, in return for which he offered 3,450 square miles of wind-blasted ice in Soviet Karelia. The intention was to create strategic defence in depth for Leningrad.

Even as these talks continued, Stalin ordered preparations for invasion: victory was to coincide with his sixtieth birthday on 21 December, for which Dmitry Shostakovich was commissioned to compose *A Suite on Finnish Themes*.[42] The Soviets used similar tactics to the Nazis to depict themselves as victims of Finnish aggression: on 26 November 1939, half-a-dozen mortar shells, fired from the Soviet side, rained down on Soviet cavalry about a thousand yards from the Finnish border. In line with tactics Lenin had pioneered in Poland in 1919–20, the Finnish Communist leader, Otto Ville Kuusinen, proclaimed a People's Revolutionary Government at Terijoki, which called for the Soviets to liberate Finland from its ruling capitalist–landowning 'clique', from a radio station that only broadcast this message the day after 1.2 million Soviet troops had attacked, supported by three thousand aircraft and fifteen hundred tanks.

Although the Finns only had about two hundred thousand troops, and few aircraft, tanks or artillery with which to meet this Red onslaught, they were fighting on familiar ground, in conditions they were used to. They had a great war leader in Baron Carl Gustav Mannerheim, a sort of Finnish Kemal Atatürk even down to his eye-catching headwear, albeit a white fur hat rather than a fez. Although the Soviet air force bombed Helsinki, hitting workers' houses and the Soviets' own embassy, the limited hours of daylight meant that its operations were restricted and contributed to the loss of eight hundred planes. The Mannerheim Line, a series of defensive positions strung across the Karelian Isthmus to a depth of forty miles, held up the Soviet's southerly front, while troops on skis with sub-machine guns played havoc with Soviet infantry that was ill co-ordinated with the tanks, which were themselves vulnerable to satchel charges and Molotov[e] cocktails, as the Finns spelt it. This last term indicated that the Finns possessed a sense of irony. The deliberate targeting of Soviet mobile field kitchens had a particularly debilitating effect on soldiers who needed huge intakes of calories to survive the cold. The Soviets were also apparently terrified of forests, and ill prepared for the onset of temperatures that fell to minus 38 degrees Celsius. The ubiquity of political officers second-guessing field commanders also contributed to the Soviets' poor performance. After sacking and shooting several commanders, the Soviets suspended the political officers and, as Stalin would do again in 1941, appealed to patriotism with copious reference to military heroes of the Tsarist age like Kutuzov and Suvorov.[43]

In February 1940 the Soviets launched a final assault that broke the Mannerheim Line, while other Soviet forces crossed the frozen wastes of the Gulf of Finland. Since outside assistance was too late to be of any use, the Finns sued for peace. Under the Treaty of Moscow signed on 12 March 1940, the Finns ceded a vast swathe of territory, which included the entire Karelian Isthmus.

The war had certain immediate lessons. Anglo-French responses were hopelessly confused and hampered by the studied neutrality of both Norway and Sweden, which refused all efforts to forge an effective Scandinavian bloc – Mussolini was more sympathetic to the plight of the Finns than they. The delayed Anglo-French reaction became another chapter in the book of Western failure – the stance of the US was even more pathetic – as Finland joined Austria, Czechoslovakia and Poland in the list of abandoned democracies. The Germans noted all the manifold weaknesses of the Red Army in this campaign – which had cost Moscow over two hundred thousand dead – but failed to recognise the dogged capabilities of the average Russian soldier and the rapid way in which the Russians had learned from their mistakes.

CHAPTER 6

Not Losing: Churchill's Britain

I THE CHURCHILL FACTOR

An isolationist US Republican Senator coined the term 'phoney war' to describe the period of relatively inactive Anglo-French and German hostilities that ended in early April 1940, twenty months before the US itself joined the Allied side. Hitler's opening moves in the west triggered a political crisis in Great Britain. It began in Scandinavia, where British attempts to mine the Norwegian coast, to force German ships bearing Swedish iron ore from Narvik further out to sea, where the Royal Navy could intercept them, were overtaken by Hitler's launching of Operation Weserübung. This was the codename for the sequential invasions of Denmark and Norway. Norway's minuscule armed forces were swiftly routed by German airborne troops and by troops landed from fast destroyers, an operation made possible by a refuelling tanker provided by the Soviet Union. However, the swift German victory also contained a major strategic defeat. Norwegian defences in Oslo fjord sank the heavy cruiser *Blücher*, carrying the entire Gestapo contingent of the occupation administration, while the Royal Navy sank ten German destroyers in Narvik fjord, and went on to cripple the battlecruisers *Gneisenau* and *Scharnhorst*, along with a number of other German ships. Thus although the French and British expeditionary forces had to be evacuated – which they would have been anyway when the Germans attacked through Belgium and Holland into France – the German navy had been reduced to one heavy cruiser, two light cruisers and four destroyers. This was to make the German capacity to mount an invasion of Britain entirely dependent on winning air supremacy over the Channel.[1]

Winston Churchill, First Lord of the Admiralty for the second time in his life, put the best construction on the loss of Scandinavia (for Sweden was reduced to a passive German client) in two lengthy speeches, attempting to dazzle the House of Commons with high seas drama and naval science.[2] Few were convinced by his claim that it was Hitler's version of Napoleon's fateful invasion of the Iberian peninsula. Nonetheless, Churchill's record in opposing appeasement since the mid-1930s meant that a Commons debate about the Norwegian fiasco paradoxically passed over its prime mover and instead became a verdict on the record of the Chamberlain government. As Labour leader Clement Attlee crisply observed: 'It is not Norway alone. Norway comes as the culmination of many other discontents. People are saying that those mainly responsible for the conduct of affairs are men who have had an almost uninterrupted career of failure. Norway followed Czechoslovakia and Poland. Everywhere the story is "too late".' The curtain was coming down on Chamberlain's premiership. During the 1940 Norway debate, Tory Leo Amery rose to address the sparsely attended chamber. It filled as he spoke. A seventeenth-century speech he had perused earlier in the day proved lethally serviceable. It came from Oliver Cromwell's dismissal of the Rump Parliament: 'You have sat too long here for any good you have been doing. Depart, I say, and let us have done with you. In the name of God, go.'[3]

The Labour opposition engineered the transformation of a routine adjournment motion into a full-blown vote of censure, although it is important to recall that the Labour leaders were rather keener on Halifax as prime minister than on Churchill.[4] Chamberlain felt moved to summon his 'friends' to his support, providing an opening for a venomous intervention by Lloyd George, which stressed that leadership rather than friendship was what was absent. Although the government won the vote, its majority fell from a nominal 213 to 81, the defectors including forty-two Conservative MPs who had been stalwart supporters of appeasement, many by now in military uniform, and over forty more who abstained. The Prime Minister was stunned and the government Whips vicious in their denunciation of the rebels: Captain David Margesson chided John Profumo: 'I can tell you this, you utterly contemptible little shit. On every morning that you wake up for the rest of your life you will be ashamed of what you did last night.'[5] The following morning, a Thursday, Chamberlain met with Halifax and Churchill and offered the succession first to Halifax, secure in the knowledge that the King and Queen had given Halifax a key to the gardens of Buckingham Palace for his contemplative strolls. Although Halifax knew that as a peer he was constitutionally ill placed for the highest office, he also knew it could be fixed by learned lawyers. But, to give him the benefit of the doubt, he possibly also knew that he lacked Churchill's temperamental steeliness, and declined the offer. With appropriate expressions of modesty, Churchill agreed with alacrity and went on to treat Chamberlain and Halifax with the utmost consideration.[6]

Apart from his outstanding moral courage, past experiences uniquely fitted Churchill for wartime leadership. He was a descendant and the biographer of the Duke of Marlborough, one of the greatest commanders Britain ever produced, although as Attlee once observed he was not a strategist in Marlborough's league or that of Cromwell. As a young army officer and a war correspondent, Churchill experienced combat in India's North West Frontier, Omdurman and South Africa, where his capture by the Boers and his subsequent escape made him famous and permitted him to vault into a political career. He acquired strategic insights as First Lord of the Admiralty in 1914–15, directing the world's largest navy. Both Hitler and Churchill were fascinated by the technical details of weaponry, but Churchill's experience extended far more deeply into the procurement process.[7]

Although, starting with the sight of the brave, slain Mahdists at Omdurman, Churchill was acutely conscious that war was a ghastly business, he was in no doubt that there were worst things for humanity to endure, such as slavery. He was capable of being as ruthless as he was lachrymose and sentimental. When rollicking around various imperial conflicts with this author's rival war-correspondent grandfather, whose memorial committee Churchill chaired in 1914, he had shown an intuitive feel for the the battlefield, coupled with a military historian's ability to conceptualise overall strategy, qualities that were reflected in the voluminous histories he wrote in the inter-war period. As well as his experience as First Lord of the Admiralty, after his resignation in 1915 following the Gallipoli landings fiasco he had briefly commanded an infantry battalion in Flanders, quite near where Hitler was serving as a corporal. In other words he probably had greater experience of warfare, whether at a strategic or combat level, than any other major leader in any war.[8]

Snobs deplored 'crooks and gangsters' like Brendan Bracken and the press magnate Lord Beaverbrook whom Churchill brought into government, but he knew that wars are won by 'sneaks and stinkers' as well as by 'good boys'. In the course of his eventful life he had also come to know outstandingly 'solid' people, like his erstwhile South African opponent Field Marshal Jan Smuts and the New Zealander General Bernard Freyberg, who had won the Victoria Cross in the Great War. Gallipoli had taught him that war was too important to leave to the generals, or more particularly the admirals, who demanded vast resources that did not yield commensurate results. Most crucially, in the informed view of historian Geoffrey Best, Churchill's period as minister of munitions under Lloyd George gave him insights into how war is waged in advanced industrial economies, for example, how to probe the opaque workings of sluggish bureaucracies, or to balance the simultaneous demands for industrial labour and mass armies. The experience also taught him to pare down the numbers attending committees to those whose opinion was worth hearing, while drawing on the informed advice of businessmen and economic and technical experts, an approach that he replicated as wartime prime minister.[9] Churchill insisted on having everything in writing, so as to avoid the ambiguity of remembered conversations. He could process paperwork at high speed, with phenomenal attention to minute detail. Every day (and night) he issued probing memos, the more urgent beginning with 'Pray tell me' this or that, or with the red sticker 'Action this day' leaving no room for delay. His staff chuckled over a spoof memo calling for the creation of temporary office space for the Prime Minister, which specified that there was to be no building noise during 'office hours, that is between 7 a.m. and 3 a.m.', a humorous recognition of Churchill's titanic work-rate.[10] His staff were less amused when in mid-December 1940 he argued that an hour and a half off for divine service would be an adequate Christmas break.[11]

Churchill practised a highly interrogative type of war leadership, taking nothing on faith from his senior military commanders. Since many of these men were veterans of the Great War, they were at a disadvantage vis-à-vis the Prime Minister because he knew that they had dogmatically adhered to strategies which had manifestly failed at enormous human cost. The civilian leadership had been in too much awe of that very British generalissimo Lord Kitchener. Beyond that unhappy precedent, Churchill mistrusted a central feature of all military cultures, namely that the senior officers were surrounded by smiling yes-men on their staffs. As Churchill wrote: 'The whole habit of mind of a military staff is based on subordination of opinion.' Instead, he brought in outside experts who were adept at summarising complex problems or providing him with easy-to-comprehend statistical data about, for example, tonnages of ships lost in the Battle of the Atlantic, a battle where there were no front lines to see on a map. The interrogative method of supreme command could be unpleasant for those on the receiving end, for most people do not take to being humiliated in public.[12]

A dinner on 27 July 1940 at Chequers, attended by Professor Frederick Lindemann, his scientific adviser, Lord Beaverbrook, responsible for aircraft production, General Sir James Marshall-Cornwall, General Hastings 'Pug' Ismay and Chief of the Imperial General Staff Field Marshal Sir John Dill, illustrates this very well. After the champagne, Churchill quizzed Marshall-Cornwall about the readiness of his corps. Everything went well, with Churchill chortling 'Splendid' until the general mentioned that the corps lacked vital equipment. Churchill had a number of statistical tabulations in his pocket that declared otherwise and, in a rage, threw a sheaf of them at Dill, saying, 'CIGS, have those papers checked and returned to me tomorrow.' After 'an awkward silence', Churchill turned to Lindemann: 'Prof! What have *you* to tell me today?' As the frock-coated professor took out a Mills hand grenade, Churchill was exclaiming, 'What's that you've got, Prof, what's that?' Lindeman claimed he had simplified the design and increased its explosive charge. Dill objected that orders were under contract for the existing grenade in the US and it could not be altered, but Churchill ignored him and turned to Beaverbrook: 'Max, what have *you* been up to?' Beaverbrook slipped out for a five-minute phone call, returning to announce dramatically increased production of Hurricane fighters within the last forty-eight hours. Despite the brandy and cigars, the ordeal was not over. Having corralled the generals, Churchill unfurled a map of the Red Sea, jabbed at the port of Massawa and asked Marshall-Cornwall how he would take it. Sensing a trap, the general gave every reason why an attack might fail, to the obvious relief of Dill and Ismay, who knew Churchill might well have ordered Marshall-Cornwall to seize the port had he shown any enthusiasm. 'You soldiers are all alike; you have no imagination,' snorted the Prime Minister, as he rolled up his map.[13] Of course, even amateur painters have imagination in abundance. It has been well said that Churchill approached running a war in the manner of someone painting a picture. He combined a firm sense of the overall composition with a painstaking grasp of detail. Like an artist, he knew the importance of standing back so as to regain a sense of the unfolding whole. Only he had the full picture, which in addition to the fighting, also involved complex international alliances and management of domestic politics and opinion. Of course, his principal opponent was an artist manqué too.

Churchill also appreciated the crucial role of the House of Commons in ensuring that an institution exemplifying hard-won freedoms would not be marginalised by a government which necessarily assumed vast emergency powers, nor by charismatic military chiefs who basked in the celebrity conveyed by a febrile, unelected press, as happened in the USA. He was determined that the dictates of war should not stealthily transform Britain into a simulacrum of its totalitarian opponent, although among his entourage there were youth cultists like Bob Boothby, who were all for doing just this to secure victory. Churchill regularly reported to the House on the war's progress, and submitted himself – often testily – to the nitpicking and grandstanding of members wishing to score points during Prime Minister's Questions.[14] After the death of Chamberlain in November 1940 he accepted the leadership of the Conservative Party to counter his (well-founded) reputation as a political maverick. At times his spirit rebelled against the constraints he had imposed on himself. During the debate following the loss of Crete in June 1941, Churchill noted that Hitler did not have to appear before the Reichstag to explain the loss of the *Bismarck*, or Mussolini the capture of more than two hundred thousand Italian troops and the fall of his African empire. The more puerile sort of MP exasperated him, but he bore it.[15]

When his grandson Winston was christened in 1940, Churchill's family remarked that this was one of the rare occasions on which they had seen him in church. A peculiarly English form of Christianity resonates through many of Churchill's best speeches, in which the more belligerent hymns combined with the gentleness of the Sermon on the Mount. Among Anglican clerics, he favoured the no-nonsense Hensley Henson, in whose sermons there was invariably more (conservative) politics than Christianity. Churchill's religious views were uncomplicated. Exposure to a variety of creeds, and not a few turbaned charlatans, in his youthful pere- grinations through the Empire led him to reject belief in Christ's divinity, a view for which he found intellectual foundation in some of the books he read between polo chukkas in India. Such scepticism was accompanied by fervent belief in some of the secular pieties of the times, such as Darwinism, progress and the civilising mission of the British Empire. But there was something else: 'There was general agreement that if you tried your best to live an honourable life and did your duty and were faithful to friends and not unkind to the weak and poor, it did not matter much what you believed or disbelieved. All would come out right. That is what would nowadays I suppose be called "The Religion of Healthy-Mindedness".'[16] He contrasted this religion of decency with what he vividly called 'a fantastic paganism devised to perpetuate the worship and sustain the tyranny of one abominable creature'.[17]

It is fashionable in some pacifist and US Irish nationalist circles to depict Churchill as a warmonger, eager to rain death on Germans to preserve the British Empire and to involve the innocents of the US in its salvation.[18] The record does not bear this out. One can quote all manner of ethical statements by the quixotic Prime Minister, many of which testify to his fundamental human decency, while others reveal a desire for retaliation and a will to win at any cost. In that Churchill was merely human. Wars are not conducted according to the desiccated deliberations of a philosophy seminar full of pursed-lipped old maids, and the threshold of what could be countenanced evolved over time and under the pressure of circumstances as sensitivities dulled and scruples relaxed. Take Churchill's shifting views on bombing. The legal position was confused, because the pre-war Hague Commission of Jurists, which between December 1922 and February 1923 had discussed bombing cities, had only produced draft rules on aerial warfare which were never ratified and hence were non-binding. However, in June 1938 Chamberlain had issued guidelines to Bomber Command which declared, 'It is against international law to bomb civilians as such and to make deliberate attacks on the civilian population … targets … must be legitimate military objectives.'[19]

In 1917, as minister of munitions, Churchill had expressed scepticism about the impact of bombing on civilian morale, arguing that the Germans were as likely to endure it as the British.[20] In 1940, as prime minister, he expressed ethical objections to attacks on civilians and flatly rejected a suggestion that German pilots descending by parachute should be shot. In October that year, as he sat drinking port in the Commons smoking room, one of the gaggle of admiring MPs called for the unrestricted bombing of Germany, as allegedly favoured by the British public. Churchill eyed him over his glass and said, 'My dear sir, this is a military not a civilian war. You and others may desire to kill women and children. We desire (and have succeeded in our desire) to destroy military objectives. I quite appreciate your point. But my motto is "Business before Pleasure".'[21] This was not a one-off expression of opinion, even though he expressed contrary views on emotionally charged visits to the British victims of German bombing when they called for massive retaliation.

On 8 March 1941, the leader of the Free French Charles de Gaulle, Prime Minister Robert Menzies of Australia and Churchill's daughter Diana and son-in-law Duncan Sandys were among those dining in Downing Street. Sandys was 'bloodthirsty' about the Germans. He wanted to wreck the place, including their libraries, so that 'an illiterate generation might grow up'. Churchill responded by saying that:

> he was in no way moved by Duncan's words. He did not believe in pariah nations, and he saw no alternative to the acceptance of Germany as part of the family of Europe. In the event of invasion he would not even approve of the civilian population murdering the Germans quartered on them. Still less would he condone atrocities against the German civil population if we were in a position to commit them. He cited an incident in Ancient Greece when the Athenians spared a city which had massacred some of their citizens, not because its inhabitants were men, but 'because of the nature of man'.

He later modified his views under the relentless evidence of Nazi barbarity, but it is worth recalling what was his moral starting point.[22]

A case in point was the German tactic of dropping aerial mines on London and other cities from 16 September 1940. Originally designed to be parachuted into the sea to sink ships, they floated down on the suburb of Wandsworth that day, with their 500-kilogram explosive payload causing terrible devastation. Worse, they were triggered by a photo-electric cell which made them almost impossible to defuse safely. Because the wind determined where these devices came to earth, those dropping them could have had no concern with accurate targeting. They were a terror weapon. Churchill's first reaction to these aerial mines was to call for the castration of the Germans and to dismiss talk of a 'just peace' as 'nonsense'.[23] In a more considered memo to 'Pug' Ismay, Churchill ordered preparations to be made for 'equal' and 'proportionate' retaliation with similar devices.[24]

As the American journalist Edward R. Murrow aptly put it, Churchill 'mobilised the English language, and sent it into battle', in speeches which will endure as long as political oratory is valued. He gave the emblematic English lion its roar. Never having been to university, Churchill did not suffer from the slick, and vaguely fake, fluency of undergraduate debaters, counting off clever points and going through standard rhetorical gambits. Instead, he had to overcome both a lisp and a stammer, and laboured over the wording of speeches that took between six and eighteen hours to dictate, to correct and then to rehearse, sometimes with the aid of a mirror. They included written 'stage directions' to refine the use of gesture or the right physical pose. He also drew on his familiarity with both great political oratory – having memorised entire speeches as a young man – and England's enormously rich literary heritage to find phrases which resonated in the collective unconscious of the British people. Yet for all his ability to articulate what would nowadays be called their (Christian) cultural identity, he also spoke from his 'City of Refuge' to much larger audiences in both occupied Europe and the US: 'We are fighting *by* ourselves; but we are not fighting *for* ourselves.' The contrast with Hitler's wars of racial egoism could not have been greater, and did much to win the admiration of even that not inconsiderable number of foreigners who otherwise detested the arrogance and condescension of the British. One could not imagine Hitler broadcasting in French, as Churchill did despite limited fluency and worse pronunciation.[25]

Being sixty-five when he assumed the highest office also helped, in the sense that his oratorical repertory was capacious. Both of these things were evident when he averred, 'Never in the field of human conflict was so much owed, by so many, to so few.' Not only did this echo Shakespeare's Henry V before Agincourt – 'we happy few, we band of brothers' – but it also reworked a speech of 1908 about a new irrigation scheme in Africa: 'Nowhere else in the world could so enormous a mass of water be held up with so little masonry.'[26] A slightly antiquated vocabulary, with words like 'benignant', a low growling delivery, and the long 'a' he pronounced whenever he said 'Nazi' helped to make his speeches instantly identifiable. Although it is less remarked on, since historians seldom understand science, he had a detailed and extensive grasp of the technological aspects of war, his memos littered with comments on highly technical issues in half a dozen fields.

He also knew the value of image in a culture that loved a character, especially one from the top drawer, who was prepared to ham it up as Al Capone brandishing a Tommy-gun. Apart from the ubiquitous cigars and the V for victory sign, there were the black hats that seemed to defy any category known to Jermyn Street hatters, the spotted bowties, uniforms straining at the midriff and a bizarre siren suit that some compared with a baby's night attire. In private he also amused, or amazed, his wartime entourage by continuing important discussions while in the bath or otherwise stark naked, or reclining in bed in red silk dressing gowns decorated with dragons, paying as much attention to 'darling' Nelson the cat as to senior generals. He drank quite a bit, necessary no doubt in his late sixties to pace himself in a job which might have killed a more abstemious or more tautly strung younger man such as Eden. Throughout the day, the night and the early morning, there were snatches of poetry and lines from Shakespeare, together with lewd stories and popular songs, 'Run Rabbit Run' being a favourite.[27] Perhaps the truest observation about him was the most simple. It was written by Robert Menzies: 'Churchill's course is set. There is no defeat in his heart.' That is perhaps the paramount quality for a leader in wartime.[28]

In May 1940, everything seemed to be collapsing as the German army advanced through Belgium and France, routing notionally formidable French forces and trapping the British Expeditionary Force into a contracting coastal pocket. The performance of the RAF's Advanced Air Striking Force was noticeably deficient, partly because orders to bomber crews had to be routed back and forth to Bomber Command outside London rather than decided on the spot according to urgent local need, but also because the defending Messerschmitts had made mincemeat of them. Fighter losses were roughly on a par with those sustained later that summer. The prospect of a Nazi invasion became sufficiently real for Churchill, on his first day in office, to order the round-up of enemy aliens under the Emergency Powers Act. Observing the swift collapse of Holland, the British convinced themselves that Nazi fifth columnists had been at work, the term derived from a comment by Nationalist General Mola concerning the siege of Madrid during the Spanish Civil War. Sundry British Fascists and Communists were interned and two hundred IRA sympathisers were deported to Ireland. In what less fevered retrospect rightly judges to be an absurd overreaction, distinguished German-Jewish refugee scholars were rounded up and sent to Canada.

It was against this dispiriting backdrop that Churchill made his first speech as prime minister, to a House of Commons that gave Chamberlain a more rousing welcome. Churchill invited members to support a new government 'representing the united and inflexible resolve of the nation to prosecute the war with Germany to a victorious conclusion'. After apologising for the 'lack of ceremony' with which he had made his political dispositions, Churchill told the House what he had told his newly appointed cabinet: 'I have nothing to offer but blood, toil, tears and sweat.' There was no 'policy' but rather defiance: 'To wage war, by sea, land and air, with all our might and with all the strength that God can give us; to wage war against a monstrous tyranny, never surpassed in the dark, lamentable catalogue of human crime. That is our policy.' The aim was victory, and he assumed the task 'with buoyancy and hope'. A summary of the speech was broadcast on the BBC that evening, including the 'blood, toil, tears and sweat' line, which Churchill may have adapted from Garibaldi or borrowed from Theodore Roosevelt.[29] Two days later Churchill gave Franklin D. Roosevelt an insight into the direness of the situation when he wrote: 'As you are no doubt aware, the scene has darkened swiftly. If necessary, we shall continue the war alone and we are not afraid of that. But I trust you realise, Mr President, that the voice and the force of a United States may count for nothing if they are withheld too long. You may have a completely subjugated, Nazified Europe established with astonishing swiftness, and the weight may be more than we can bear.'

II HOUR OF DECISION, DAYS OF DESTINY

Two momentous issues loomed as the British gradually realised the scale of the disaster they were facing in the summer of 1940. First, the government had to decide whether to commit more resources to bolster the flagging morale of the French, whose forces, so prodigious on paper, were being so poorly led – while being undermined by Communist subversion – that any additional assistance Britain could have offered would have been militarily wasted. Although the British supplied a few Hurricane squadrons, the head of Fighter Command, Sir Hugh 'Stuffy' Dowding, argued fiercely that no more of the new Vickers Supermarine Spitfires should be sent to France – with reason, since of the 155 lost over France, 65 involved accidents due to pilots' unfamiliarity with the machine. The strategic bomber force, designed for attacks on industrial targets, proved unable to provide tactical support for the British Expeditionary Force as it retreated to Dunkirk. German air superiority, less absolute than the troops believed but significant nonetheless, made the cross-Channel evacuation of British, French and Polish troops from Dunkirk an operation that teetered on the edge of disaster. That it succeeded beyond the most optimistic predictions was due mainly to Hitler's decision to halt his panzers about fifteen miles away. One motive was to preserve German armour for use against the large French forces still in the field; another was that Göring had promised that the Luftwaffe alone could finish the British off. There is no evidence to support Hitler's later claim that he gave the British 'a sporting chance' to persuade them to sue for peace in order to preserve their empire.[30]

Before the British evacuation had assumed any speed, Churchill was faced with a political crisis of equivalent moment. If his patriotic vision consisted of the last Briton fighting to the bitter end, there were those in the War Cabinet who had a much less heroic view of the position and who were concerned with the preservation of the appearance of power within which their vision of an eternal England would endure. On Saturday 25 May, Halifax asked to see the Italian ambassador Giuseppe Bastianini. Although Germany was not expressly mentioned, their discussions about Anglo-Italian relations flowed into talk of a general European settlement, to which the war was apparently no insuperable obstacle. Underlying this was the presumption that Mussolini was as concerned about the impact of Hitler's triumphs on the balance of power in Europe as the British, an assumption left over from the period of appeasement. Implicit was a deal under which Mussolini, after appropriate colonial and Mediterranean concessions, would urge Hitler to conclude a deal that would preserve Britain's independence and overseas interests.

During the War Cabinet on Sunday morning, Halifax raised the conversations he had had with Bastianini in the context of Britain being unable to defeat Germany and therefore anxious 'to safeguard the independence of our own Empire and if possible that of France', which he seems to have written off earlier than the Francophile Churchill. Such a prospect conformed with Hitler's repeated expressions of uninterest in overseas colonies, although experience of his chronic bad faith meant there was no guarantee of his sincerity. When the War Cabinet resumed that afternoon, after dispiriting talks with the French, Halifax asked more pointedly whether Churchill was 'prepared to discuss such terms'. It would be foolish, he said, to ignore proposals that did not jeopardise Britain's independence, and produced a paper entitled 'Suggested Approach to Signor Mussolini'.[31]

Halifax's paper was discussed at the second of three meetings of the War Cabinet held on Monday 27 May, and then again in the afternoon of the following day. The discussions were sometimes so fraught that Churchill had to take Halifax outside into the garden to assure him that his patriotism was not being impugned. Although Churchill certainly had to permit discussion of Halifax's proposal, improving news from Dunkirk helped him to rebut it. He said: 'The essential point was that M. Reynaud [the French Prime Minister] wanted to get us to the Conference-table with Herr Hitler. If we once got to the table, we should then find that the terms offered us touched our independence and integrity. When, at this point, we got up to leave the Conference-table, we should find that all the forces of resolution which were now at our disposal would have vanished.'

The defiant spirit he had conjured up in mid-May would evaporate once Britain was seen to be seeking terms.

In the ensuing discussion, Chamberlain may have recalled Halifax's change of heart in 1938, as well as the kindness Churchill had shown him after his resignation in allowing him and his wife to stay in Downing Street. 'It was right', he said, 'to remember that the alternative to fighting on involved a considerable gamble,' thus portraying Halifax's 'realistic' position as a leap in the dark. He had been to such negotiations, Chamberlain continued, and his fingers had been burned. After bluntly equating Halifax's line with defeatism, Churchill echoed Chamberlain's metaphor by saying that the odds against Hitler offering decent terms were a thousand to one. At 6 p.m. he took a gamble of his own by leaving to meet the larger Outer Group of ministers who were not in the War Cabinet. He told them 'that [Britain] would become a slave state though a British Government which would be Hitler's puppet would be set up'. 'Whatever happens at Dunkirk, we shall fight on,' he concluded, conjuring up the image of the last Briton (meaning himself) lying on the ground choking in his own blood. All twenty-five ministers competed to endorse this defiant spirit. Hugh Dalton suggested that Churchill should secure a recent David Low cartoon to hang in the Cabinet Room. It depicted a very determined Churchill leading an equally pugnacious army of Britons rolling up their sleeves.[32] Thus fortified, Churchill went back to deal with the War Cabinet, where the Labour members, Attlee and Greenwood, were with Chamberlain in opposing Halifax's desire to go down what Churchill called 'a slippery slope'. Halifax signalled a tactical retreat by suggesting an appeal through Roosevelt rather than Mussolini, but Churchill ruled that 'He did not favour making any approach on the subject at the present time.' The following morning, Churchill reported to the War Cabinet that forty thousand men had returned safely from Dunkirk. Two hundred thousand more followed before the end of the week.

Addressing the Commons on 4 June, Churchill used the phrase 'Battle of Britain' to contrast with the lost Battle of France, brilliantly escapsulating what, in the most fundamental sense, the war was about. He identified the arid, pseudo-scientising darkness that the enemy's ideology represented. Britain's colourful riches of history and tradition faced Hitler's ghastly petit-bourgeois modernising vision, while Churchill's use of the word 'perverted' correctly highlighted the unique deviancy of the Nazi project, something that seems to escape those who treat Fascism as simply the opposite of their own preferred totalitarianism:

Upon this battle depends the survival of Christian civilisation. Upon it depends our own British way of life, and the long continuity of our institutions and our Empire. The whole fury and might of the enemy must very soon be turned on us. Hitler knows that he will have to break us in this Island or lose the war. If we can stand up to him, all Europe may be free and the life of the world may move forward into broad, sunlit uplands. But if we fail, then the whole world, including the United States, including all that we have known and cared for, will sink into the abyss of a new Dark Age made more sinister, and perhaps more protracted, by the lights of perverted science.[33]

Relations with the newly installed Pétain regime rapidly deteriorated once it had released to the Germans four hundred captured Luftwaffe pilots whom Reynaud had promised to hand over to the British for safekeeping. The eighth clause of the Franco-German armistice raised the prospect of the French fleet being surrendered, in fighting condition, to German and Italian control. Churchill attached no significance to German protestations that they would not misuse these resources. Convinced Francophile though he was, Churchill took the unenviable decision to seize those ships docked in British ports and to offer those in foreign harbours the choice of joining the British or being sunk. At Alexandria this surrender passed without incident. But after a day-long stand-off on 3 July at Mers-el-Kebir, the naval base adjacent to the Algerian city of Oran, Vice-Admiral James Somerville, commander of Force H based at Gibraltar, who had helped rescue some hundred thousand French troops from Dunkirk, turned his guns on French ships. In a brief but ferocious bombardment, 1,299 French sailors were killed and another 350 wounded. Churchill personally ordered the action, which, though justifiably outraging the French, put the world on notice that Britain was willing to go to extreme lengths to defeat Nazism. Even Ciano, who in a previous chapter we saw lamenting the demise of the old sea dogs, suddenly noted the persistence of the 'aggressive ruthlessness of the captains and pirates of the seventeenth century'.[34] It was in these summer months that Churchill took a number of significant decisions, such as forming the Special Operations Executive, SOE, with a remit to 'set Europe ablaze'; appointing General Alan Brooke commander-in-chief of the Home Forces; and despatching half of Britain's tanks on a long voyage to reinforce the position in Egypt against the Italians in Libya. Interestingly, in a letter on 27 June to his South African colleague Prime Minister Jan Smuts, Churchill relayed his reading of

Hitler's likely intentions: 'Obviously we have first to repulse any attack on Great Britain by invasion and show ourselves able to maintain our development of air power. This can only be settled by trial. [But] if Hitler fails to beat us here, he will probably recoil eastward. Indeed, he may do this even without trying invasion.' Events were to prove him entirely prescient.

The rapidity and success of his campaign in the west left Hitler without a prepared strategy for dealing with the British. There was some awareness in Germany, beneath the clichés about British decadence, effeteness and plutocracy, that this was a really serious opponent with resources on a global scale. Like the Allies themselves a few years later, Hitler knew that a cross-Channel invasion was an extremely hazardous enterprise, all the more so since, as a continental power, Germany had never undertaken such a thing in the past. The Channel was not a wide river, but a potentially rough stretch of sea. Perhaps Hitler's preferred alternative option was indeed a negotiated peace in which he would have been spared the further complication of the collapse of the British Empire and the likely extension of American power in its wake. Given his chip on the shoulder and his vengeful nature, however, it seems highly unlikely that he would have settled for less than the humiliation of Britain.

Still, he was not the prime mover in developing plans to invade England. A desire to catch up with military action dominated by the army and Luftwaffe led the German naval chief, Admiral Erich Raeder, to propose a joint air and sea blockade which would bring Britain to its knees. This was as overly optimistic as the mirror-image British strategy, which relied on a combination of blockade and bombing to tip economic dislocation into open revolt within Germany itself. On 16 July Hitler issued War Directive 16, the general go-ahead for an invasion. This mentioned a broad assault between Ramsgate and the Isle of Wight, plus diversionary attacks as far west as Cornwall. Maps show that the general intention was to arc around London, which even then Churchill was vowing 'could easily devour an entire hostile army'. However, given the parlous state of the German navy, the key precondition to Operation Sea Lion, as the invasion was code-named, was point 2a: 'The English Air Force must be so beaten down in its morale and in fact that it can no longer display any appreciable aggressive force in opposition to the German crossing.'

Even as invasion planning got under way, Hitler concluded a lengthy speech on 19 July, which chronicled his western triumphs, with these 'prophetic' words: 'A great world empire will be destroyed. A world empire which I never had the ambition to destroy or as much as harm ... In this hour I feel compelled, standing before my conscience, to direct yet another appeal to reason in England. I believe I can do this as I am not asking for something as the vanquished, but rather, as the victor, I am speaking in the name of reason. I see no compelling reason which could force the continuation of this war.'[35] The veiled offer was categorically rejected – by Halifax – in a speech broadcast on 22 July. Hitler cannot have been surprised, for he was already thinking his way around the problem of Britain, along the lines of the proverb that there are more ways to skin a cat. Army Chief Halder argued that an emboldened Russia might be contemplating a move against Rumania, one of Germany's main sources of oil, while Hitler himself reasoned that the only explanation for Britain's obduracy must be that it expected help from the Soviet Union. While others handled the planning for Sea Lion, Hitler's own attention turned first to thoughts of a limited pre-emptive strike designed to re-establish the expansive eastern borders achieved at Brest-Litovsk in 1917. By 31 July, the concept had been transformed into a five-month campaign, starting in May 1941, designed to destroy the Soviet state with one blow.[36]

III WAR OVER ENGLAND

The unpredictability of the weather in the English Channel suffused planning for Sea Lion, despite learned investigations of the successful invasions by Julius Caesar, Emperor Claudius and William the Conqueror. The Germans nonetheless pressed on with securing the essential precondition of air supremacy, despite having an air force designed for the tactical support of ground forces. Although the Germans were convinced otherwise, the RAF enjoyed a slight superiority in terms of fighter aircraft, with 1,032 facing the Luftwaffe's 1,011. Furthermore, the British were capable of producing Hurricanes and Spitfires at a phenomenal rate, turning out 4,283 in the decisive year of 1940, although some of these were sent to North Africa. In addition 509 aircraft were imported from Canada and the US in the critical summer and autumn of 1940.[37] German output over the same period was less than half that of the British at 1,870 aircraft, mainly the agile, single-engined Messerschmitt 109 but also the lumbering, twin-engined Messerschmitt 110, although their aircraft had such advantages as armour protection for the pilots and mounted cannon as well as machine guns. Nor did the Germans dispose of a bomber fleet capable of delivering heavy bombloads over long distances, and they had also failed to develop any long-range, torpedo-carrying aircraft capable of interdicting shipping.[38] The British had the advantage of being able to salvage damaged aircraft or to recycle material from those damaged beyond repair over their own land mass, including downed German aircraft which could not make it back across the Channel. Finally, as the battle was fought almost entirely over England, British pilots could return to action after parachuting to safety or being recovered from the sea by the fast boats and seaplanes of the Air Sea Rescue Service, while German pilots who took to their parachutes or crash-landed were lost to the Luftwaffe.

Although the aircraft themselves were a vital element in the battle, trained pilots and the way they were commanded and deployed were no less so. Dowding was an aloof, hard-working commander, who was as modest as he was brilliant.[39] The RAF had made the wise decision to organise its service in terms of functionality, which in this context meant that a unified Fighter Command could focus its efforts against the Luftwaffe's mixed fighter and bomber air fleets. Although the brunt of the fighting took place over three English counties – Kent, Sussex and Surrey – squadrons were rotated in and out from the groups that covered the whole country. A system of thirty thousand observers and twenty-one radar stations relayed information about German attacks to a central command at Stanmore in Middlesex, which in turn directed the counter-attacks of the various groups and subsidiary sectors. Hundreds of young women in the Women's Auxiliary Air Force dealt with the complex flow of information, plotting enemy aircraft movements on huge tables. Time was at a premium, as it took a German fighter only six minutes to cross the Channel, which is why one of the iconic images of the battle is of British pilots running to their aircraft when ordered to scramble. According to Tim Vigors, an Old Etonian Irish pilot who was an exception to Churchill's generalisation that there were no Etonians and Wykehamists in the RAF, the air ace Douglas Bader, who had lost both legs in a training accident but managed to fly again, always propped his artificial legs against the bunks of the pilots – Vigors being one of them – who slept on either side of him when they went to bed. It took two minutes and fifty seconds of combined effort to strap his legs on, and carry him to his plane, and for all three pilots to take off.[40]

The principal area of RAF superiority was in manpower, with a constant average of fourteen or fifteen hundred pilots against eleven or twelve hundred Germans. The ranks of the RAF were swelled by volunteers from the Commonwealth and neutral Ireland, the former pooling their resources in an Empire Air Training Scheme. Notable pilots included the South African aces Albert 'Zulu' Lewis and Adolph 'Sailor' Malan, while a New Zealander, Air Vice Marshal Keith Park, commanded the crucial 11 Group in southern England, and the South African Air Vice Marshal Sir Quintin Brand led 10 Group. There were also refugee pilots from Czechoslovakia, France and Poland. These men were older and had seen aerial combat once or twice before, over Poland or France. This gave them a significant edge. The Polish 303 Kościuszko Squadron notched up the fourth highest kill rate of the RAF's sixty operational fighter squadrons by taking literally one of 'Sailor' Malan's ten combat commandments and not firing until they could see the whites of their enemies' eyes. There were instances of Polish pilots, out of ammunition, flying so close above German aircraft that they forced them to crash. Others were prepared to take off in dense fog, thus rendering themselves unable to land, just to shoot down a single German aircraft. Collectively these were the men whom Churchill praised in a justifiably famous speech on 20 August in the House of Commons – 'Never in the field of human conflict was so much owed by so many to so few' – although interestingly he lavished slightly more praise on the bombers, which every night were thundering towards targets in Germany. He failed to mention the RAF ground crews who worked very long hours ensuring that all types of aircraft were match fit, in particular turning around the fighters to send them back into battle again and again on a single day.[41]

In general the men involved were very young, often growing moustaches to make them look older. Their task demanded constant alertness, a capacity to withstand the G forces of violent combat manoeuvres, and the ability to hit something with guns that ran out of bullets after fourteen seconds of firing.[42] Although some were of a religious bent, killing the enemy does not seem to have prompted much reflection among young men who saw things in less complicated terms, and for whom death was something that happened to someone else. As Vigors put it: 'The way I saw it then was "Poor son of a bitch. He was probably a nice guy and we would probably have got on well had we met. But he was on the wrong side. He shouldn't have signed up with that bastard Hitler."'[43]

Another common denominator, on both sides, was astonishing courage. Many of them lived for the moment and cultivated a devil-may-care attitude, as the cautious tended to get killed more quickly. Sight became the primary sense as they craned their necks around – the reason they wore loose fitting scarves rather than ties – trying to spot specks in the sky before they became larger objects spitting bullets. Often the first sign of trouble was tracer shells streaming past if one was lucky, or destruction and death at the hands of an unseen enemy if one was not. Protective clothing and facewear were primitive, leading to appalling burns when blowtorch-like flames enveloped the cockpit after the engine had been hit. In these circumstances it took enormous presence of mind to escape by parachute. Those who did became the self-styled guinea-pigs of the plastic surgeons at the Queen Victoria Hospital in East Grinstead, where sometimes many years of surgery were required to restore some semblance of mobility and normality to young faces rendered rigid by burns. The psychological effects on handsome men, who on a Friday night had attracted all the girls in the bar but who on Monday were unrecognisable, were as grievous.[44]

By most accounts, the Battle of Britain continued for twelve weeks, longer than any other battle involving Britain except the naval war of attrition that Churchill dubbed the Battle of the Atlantic, or the grinding campaign of Bomber Command. The different phases of the battle can only be defined in terms of relative intensities. Fighter Command was fortunate that the Luftwaffe pursued too many diffuse objectives, such as attacking shipping, before deciding in mid-August to obliterate the fighter bases and radar installations on which the RAF relied, and was perhaps lucky again when the Germans shifted to bombing major cities. Although potentially decisive, the direct attack on Britain's air-defence capability was difficult to undertake successfully. The radar installations were hard to hit and easy to repair, while the existence of satellite airfields meant that RAF squadrons could relocate and remain in action while their home bases and runways were repaired.

Believing they had dealt Fighter Command a crippling blow, the Germans stepped up their bombing of industrial, military and transport targets in and around major British cities in response to a series of pinprick raids by the British. Hitherto the main use of RAF Bomber Command had been to rain down propaganda leaflets on Germany by night.[45] Indeed, that summer the British prided themselves on the morality of their cause. 'We are fighting for a moral issue. We should do nothing unworthy of our cause,' declared the *Daily Mail*. Both sides ostentatiously disavowed any intention of indiscriminately bombing civilians, but the poor bomb-aiming technologies of the time made inadvertent casualties inevitable. The state of navigation was so poor that when in September 1939 the RAF raided Brunsbüttel, two bombs were dropped on Esjberg, 110 miles to the north in neutral Denmark. In May 1940 the first bombs to fall on a German town – Freiburg – were dropped by the Luftwaffe by mistake. Thereafter there was no doubt about who was killing most civilians, inadvertently or otherwise. Luftwaffe bombers killed 258 British civilians in July and 1,075 in August, during which time the RAF launched only two rather ineffectual raids on Berlin.[46]

Although Hitler had decided by mid-September that an invasion of England was not feasible, he ordered the Luftwaffe to step up attacks on industrial and military targets. Given the technological limitations, these inevitably killed civilians by way of collateral casualties long before aerial mines were dropped indiscriminately. The first major raids on the capital commenced on 7 September with an attack by 348 bombers escorted by over six hundred fighters. When on 14 September the Luftwaffe Chief of Staff, General Hans Jeschonnek, requested permission to attack purely residential areas to trigger mass panic, it was Hitler who refused. Such measures would result in reprisals and had greater value as a threat of last resort. Instead, the Führer insisted on focusing attacks on railway stations as well as gas and water works. Leaflets dropped by the Luftwaffe over Britain claimed the moral high ground by blaming the gun-toting 'gangster' Churchill and the air 'pirates' of the RAF for starting a form of warfare which the Germans insisted was a war crime. In fact, in these months the Germans killed around forty thousand people in the capital and other cities. The aim, as various German sources make explicit, was to induce mass panic or, as experts on England in the Foreign Ministry hoped, to provoke a social and political revolution as the deranged poor of London's East End flooded westwards to Mayfair and Knightsbridge, thus forcing a change of government.[47]

London was bombed twenty-four times in September and every night of October, with further raids on industrial cities such as Birmingham, Coventry and Sheffield. Coventry was raided again and again, culminating in a major attack on 14 November which killed 554, injured 863 and destroyed 42,904 houses as well as the cathedral. The British retaliated a month later with an attack on Mannheim which inadvertently hit Ludwigshafen too, killing a total of thirty-four people. When Birmingham was bombed, over a thousand people perished. Although an Air Ministry directive in June 1940 had categorically ruled out indiscriminate attacks on urban areas, pressure from press and public to hit back combined with the impossibility of striking precision targets and a desire to offload bombs before returning home resulted in the *de facto* adoption of such a strategy. This could be rationalised by arguing the complicity of the victims. Arms workers often lived adjacent to arms factories. The fate of their wives and children was passed over in silence. Although Sir Charles Portal, Bomber Command's Commander-in-Chief, clung to the view that the deaths of civilians were a by-product of attacks on primary targets, it was but a short step to regarding them – or rather their morale – as the real target. Any discussion of these issues, if it is to be serious, has to take into account the public mood of the times. At RAF bomber bases, air crews could contemplate photographs of pulverised British cities pinned to the walls together with carefully chosen portraits of teddy-clutching children traumatised by Luftwaffe bombing. The poet and RAF officer John Pudney caught the drama of aerial combat, with blazing aircraft plummeting to earth over London, in a poem he scribbled on the back of an envelope at the height of the Blitz:

> Do not despair
> For Johnny-head-in-air;
> He sleeps as sound
> As Johnny underground.
>
> Fetch out no shroud
> For Johnny-in-the-cloud;
> And keep your tears
> For him in after years.
>
> Better by far
> For Johnny-the-bright-star,
> To keep your head,
> And see his children fed.

The British massively overestimated the number of mortuaries needed, and underestimated nearly two million homeless people. Simultaneous fires also overwhelmed the fire service, whose professionals were bulked out with many more enthusiastic amateurs. In normal circumstances a major fire required thirty pumps to attend it. On 8 September there were nine 100-pump fires blazing at once, with one of them requiring three hundred pumps to control it. At Surrey Commercial Docks, mountains of timber blazed or tumbled into the River Thames, touching off fires in barges which then drifted from their moorings. The most intense fire ever experienced in modern Britain was in the Quebec Yard at Surrey Docks, where rum barrels exploded or sent out streams of fiery liquor, pepper fires reduced eyes to stinging tears, burning rubber made the air thick and black, and blazing paint caused chemical blasts.[48]

Light pollution is so normal in modern cities that it is hard to imagine urban life in the dark, with white rings painted on trees along streets to guide occasional cars that could not use their headlights. Even lighting a cigarette had to be done with cupped hands inside a coat or jacket, on the fanciful grounds that the match flare might be seen by a passing Dornier pilot. The impact of the Blitz on London's population is difficult to assess, not least because of a contemporary fascination with crime and looting, as much by air-raid wardens and auxiliary firemen as by the East End's light-fingered fraternity, for whom pilfering was a normal perk of a job in the docks. The Blitz brought other opportunities, as the need to stay off the streets until the all-clear sounded gave young women an extended opportunity to have their first sexual encounters without worrying about what their parents thought.

A striking number of people seem to have regarded the Blitz as akin to a giant fireworks display. Spectators included Churchill, Dalton and Arthur Harris, 'Bert' to his friends and the later head of Bomber Command, who all headed for the rooftops of official buildings in London to watch the noisy pyrotechnics. Dalton was remarkably prescient when he wrote after witnessing Piccadilly burning: 'Quite like a Götterdämmerung which must make even German pilots brought up on all that Wagner stuff, faintly fearful of their future fate.' Harris agreed, and would soon make that anxiety a German reality.[49] Across the city young boys eagerly collected shrapnel falling from anti-aircraft guns, while crowds gathered to inspect bits of enemy planes, which made the Nazi foe tangible. The Blitz brought massive inconvenience – all chronicled by the likes of George Orwell, at the time a lowly member of the Home Guard. They included sleep deprivation because of the constant alarms between 8 p.m. and 4.30 a.m. when raids usually occurred; electricity, gas, telephone and water supplies disrupted; shops closed and newspapers erratic; public transport halted or subjected to interminable delays; Thames bridges closed for days and entire streets cordoned off because of the threat from delayed-action bombs, with the evicted wandering around with a few possessions in a case, cart or pram.[50] After a visit to Ramsgate during a raid, Churchill forced a compensation scheme for bomb damage on a reluctant Exchequer. Early in the Blitz an instant book suggested that the likelihood of one's house receiving a direct hit was akin to standing on a chair and dropping a handful of salt on a map on which the house was marked with an ink dot. Those without a garden in which to sink an Anderson Shelter had to seek safety among strangers. Extemporised shelters for those bombed out were cramped and uncomfortable (often with no lavatories or washing facilities) and in parts of the East End there were animosities towards 'pushy' Jews who seemed to check in early. The East End became so dangerous that many of the inhabitants decided to camp out in Essex's Epping Forest, or to head up west to spend the nights in the basements of major department stores.

The Blitz reinforced Britain's 'going it alone' sense of itself, although this was in turn relayed to the US by the hundred or so North American correspondents in the capital. It emotionally connected British civilians with the war, because for this period they were in more peril than anyone in the (few) front lines. Some claim it also connected Britain's class-ridden society, especially after Buckingham Palace took a few hits, although typically the British responded with cynicism to what were known as Bomb Bores droning on about how much they had suffered, and to the many who saw a cup of tea as a solution to every crisis, a cliché subsequently worn to death by treasured left-wing dramatist Alan Bennett.

The Battle of Britain was one of the few unambiguous victories in any exclusively aerial conflict, leaving no room for the disputes about effectiveness or morality that surround the later Allied strategic bombing campaign. Even the horrendous civilian casualties of the ensuing Blitz (a 9/11 once a month for a year) pale by comparison with the German death-toll from a mere three nights of Allied bombing over Hamburg three years later. If you are curious about such things, you will find obscure plaques to the dead of the Blitz, under the railway arches south of London Bridge or in Kennington Park where another shelter took a direct hit, killing 104 people. However small the possibility may have been, the battle ensured there would be no Nazi invasion of Britain, nor any prospect of a regime run by a Lloyd George or Edward Duke of Windsor, not to mention the moral compromises which faced ordinary people across Hitler's new order.

IV THE YANKS ARE COMING

The Battle of Britain not only kept the island race in the game, but ensured that it would become a launch platform for the combined resources of the British and US when, nearly a year after the war had commenced, Roosevelt inched away from a stance of benevolent neutrality towards actively aiding Britain. Actual US participation was a year beyond that. It was a very protracted process in which Churchill's written importunities had to be weighed in the President's mind against powerful isolationist sentiments in the US Congress and the country at large. There were also legislative hurdles to overcome, including the Neutrality Act, forbidding sale of war materials to belligerents, and the Johnson Debt-Default Act which banned the extension of dollar credits to those who had defaulted on war loans, the only country to have amortised debts from the Great War being Finland. American travellers were told to avoid using the passenger ships of belligerent nations so that there might be no repetition of the emotional cause that the sinking of the liner *Lusitania* became during the Great War. The first symbolic step, once Britain had exhausted its dollar reserves on cash-and-carry purchases, was to send the British fifty superannuated Great War destroyers – their scrap value being US$5,000 apiece – in return for leases on bases in Bermuda and Newfoundland.[51] The symbolism was almost lost in the prolonged haggling over the details. At one point an exasperated Churchill protested over the telephone, 'Empires just don't bargain,' to which Attorney General Robert Jackson, who had helped bypass Congress by certifying the ships as inessential to national security, shot back: 'Republics do.'[52]

It may seem self-evident that one great democracy should automatically rush to assist another. That was certainly the view of the Committee to Defend America by Aiding the Allies, which had been established in May 1940, and of the influential Century Group which had come up with the destroyers-for-bases deal in the first place. But there were many others who passionately opposed this view. They included pacifists, of whom there were twelve million in the US in the 1930s, many of them college students organised in the No Foreign War Crusade which commenced in 1937. In addition to trying to force the officer-training ROTC off campuses, they founded a spoof Veterans of Future Wars organisation to demand US$1,000 compensation for young men who might be killed in the Republic's future overseas battles. Opponents of involvement in European entanglements also included those who made a realistic appraisal of US security interests, but also inveterate Anglophobes, and in some cases anti-Semites who ideologically sympathised with Nazism.

The organised expression of isolationism was the America First lobby, founded at Yale University Law School in September 1940, before becoming a nationwide association. One of the founders was Gerald Ford, who in 1974 would become US president but was then the university's assistant football coach. America First became more serious when it attracted the support of General Robert Wood, the chairman of Sears, Roebuck, and, still in the windy city, the powerful *Chicago Tribune*. Other luminaries included the anti-Semitic aviator Charles Lindbergh, the actress Lillian Gish, who was promptly blacklisted by Hollywood, and the sensationalist New York journalist John T. Flynn. Supporters covered the entire spectrum of US politics from Republican opponents of the New Deal and Progressives who thought it did not go far enough, to pacifists and socialists who, while deploring Fascism, had no idea how to defeat it. Some suspected that Roosevelt was using the prospect of war to distract from the second 'Roosevelt depression' which hit the US after 1937 to secure an unprecedented third term as president. Many of America First's supporters were isolationists who believed that the world beyond was intractable to American ideals, and that the US should ignore it from the safety of a continent between two oceans. So what if Hitler took over Europe? The realist arguments that Bismarck had once used to justify non-interference in the Balkans were echoed word for word. The whole of Europe was regarded as a belligerent miasma, rife with ancient enmities. As the leading isolationist Senator Robert Nye put it: 'The conflict in Europe is not worthy of the sacrifice of one American mule, much less one American son.' He and his allies did not want the US to play the role of global policeman or, as Herbert Hoover remarked, to embark on a new Children's Crusade against a vast array of totalitarian enemies.

These sentiments were not evenly represented across the Republic. The sole southern state where America First thrived was Florida, for elsewhere the Anglo-Saxon and Scots-Irish warriors of the Deep South were among those most spoiling for a fight and would be heavily represented in US armies, as they have been ever since. It was no accident that America First was especially strong in the Mid-Western states, far beyond the usual Irish-American Democrat-voting suspects in the big cities and the German-Americans of the Great Plains states. There was visceral resentment, especially among farmers, towards the bankers of the East Coast who had used British capital to build railways which depressed farm prices, and who seemed to be urging the nation into war to make yet more money from arms. This view elided with that of the National Legion of Mothers of America which idealised farm life and hated the sort of values promoted by Hollywood, which in their eyes was a synonym for Jews. Others genuinely dreaded war, fearing it might lead to domestic dictatorship, as well as financial ruin and terrible casualties. There were also convinced Anglophobes who thought that the British (and French) colonial empires were morally worse than Hitler's Reich, thereby ignoring the differences between empires which were hesitantly introducing democracy and human rights and those which practised outright slavery. For a significant number of America First supporters, admiration for the Nazis and hatred of the Jews of New York and Hollywood were clearly important motives, notoriously in the case of Lindbergh, although his more intemperate attacks on Jews were firmly smacked down by the Republicans Robert Taft and Wendell Wilkie. As is usually the case, Jews were accused of having dual loyalties, although there was no Israel in the 1930s to animate the large numbers of American anti-Semites and no organised Christian right to trumpet the Jews' cause. Both Lindbergh and the Olympic Games supremo Avery Brundage were dropped by the America First national committee because of their hatred of Jews.[53]

The activities of the Committee to Defend America by Aiding the Allies were no less impressively organised, although they were amplified by FBI moves against isolationists who supported the Axis and by a broadly based propaganda campaign mounted in the US by the British government. This last thrived in fertile soil. A significant majority of Americans liked what they knew of Britain; its sonorous literary culture, its shared common law legal system and its historic role as the mother of parliamentary democracy being among the obvious factors. Due to a felicitously timed royal tour in 1939, the modernising family monarchy was also popular. It was not all as rosy as the country cottages (and castles) Americans imagined most Brits inhabited. Americans reviled Britain's rigid class system, while individual constituencies, including many US Jews, were overtly hostile, in the latter case because of official British concern for the Arabs of Palestine. This was not a unique instance of ethnic loyalties complicating US foreign policy for during the Abyssinian War African-Americans lined up behind the victim while Italian-Americans supported the Fascists. Irish-Americans, and Catholics in general, complicated official responses to the Spanish Civil War since many of them supported Franco.[54]

Key personalities were important in overcoming US obstacles to intervention, although it is important to stress how long this process went on. Despite the obvious iniquity of the Nazis it took a long time for the US to act. Churchill and Roosevelt got to know one another through correspondence, with communications which began in September 1939 and which would number two thousand items by the end of the war. There were also telephone calls: 'Mr President ... Winston here.' Sterling work was done in the US by Lord Lothian, the ambassador to Washington, until his untimely death in December 1940 from a kidney disease that his Christian Scientist principles obliged him to leave untreated. His replacement was the altogether less sympathetic figure of Lord Halifax, the first envoy to arrive on a battleship. A fox-hunting expedition was an accident waiting to happen, while leaving an uneaten hot dog on a seat, as he prematurely left a baseball game, which he adversely compared with cricket, was to court disaster on the publicity front. Fortunately for Anglo-American relations, at roughly this time the defeatist Irish-American Anglophobe Joseph Kennedy was replaced by the Anglophile liberal Republican John Winant as ambassador to the Court of St James's. There was another emissary whose quiet, steely influence is hard to overstate. In early 1941 Roosevelt despatched his close friend and White House permanent guest Harry Hopkins on a fact-finding mission to Britain, partly to assess the country's resilience, partly to establish present and future needs. After prolonged exposure to the natives, including various escapades to Britain's defence installations and twelve dinners in the company of Britain's extraordinary Prime Minister, towards the conclusion of his mission Hopkins rose one night to quote the Book of Ruth: 'Whither thou goest, I will go; and where thou lodgest, I will lodge: thy people shall be my people, and thy God my God.' Then he added: 'Even to the end.' The Prime Minister wept.[55]

Beyond these high-level interactions, the British worked on the sympathies of the ordinary American, wisely preferring to let others do their lobbying for them. One cunning stratagem was simply to allow propaganda films produced by Joseph Goebbels to continue on their way from Bermuda to the US, where triumphalist scenes of Blitzkrieg in Poland, accompanied by stirring male voice choirs, produced the opposite effect from the one intended in Berlin. A British Library of Information, based in New York, briefed journalists and generally sought to propagate positive images of the British way of life by bringing over visiting speakers. Selected speakers addressed such crucial audiences as Christian churches or labour unions. Isaiah Berlin and Chaim Weizmann were brought in to win over the US Jews. Strenuous efforts were also made in Britain itself to assist and hence shape the reporting of hundreds of correspondents who covered the Battle of Britain and the Blitz. Much was made of the US air ace Pilot Officer Billy Fiske, and after January 1941 of the American 71 'Eagle' Squadron of the RAF. US correspondents were given access to London rooftops where they could record stirring radio reports against the background blasts and thuds of bombs and guns. In this way, American reporters became part of the story, to the extent that in 1943 an appreciative Churchill offered Ed Murrow the co-director generalship of the BBC. They were turned into filmic heroes, as in Alfred Hitchcock's *Foreign Correspondent* which concludes with the urgent commentary: 'Hello America. I've been watching a part of the world being blown to pieces. A part of the world as nice as Vermont, Ohio, Virginia, California, and Illinois, lies ripped up and bleeding like a steer in a slaughterhouse. I've seen things that make the history of the savages read like the Pollyanna legend.' Newsreels in the *March of Time* series showed plucky Cockneys cheerfully defiant amid the rubble of the East End. These were the winning human faces of a story that ran from the near death of Dunkirk, via the purgatorial fires of the Blitz, and on to the resurrection of Allied airmen fighting back over Germany, one of the most successful films being *Target for Tonight*, the story of one (real) bomber crew that flew to Germany. The entire crew had been killed before the film had won its Oscar. There were also concerted attempts to depict the Nazis as the murderous thugs they were, whether by publishing atrocity photos taken from captured German airmen or making Hitchcockian thrillers about fifth columnists and secret agents. The Nazi menace to the American near-neighbourhood was brought home by a doctored map of Latin America in a future new world order, in which the states most sympathetic to the Allies – Ecuador, Bolivia, Paraguay and Uruguay – had been swallowed up by their larger neighbours. Dark talk of this 'secret map' found its way into Roosevelt's October 1941 Navy Day address, in which he also mentioned Nazi plans to do away with Christianity within Germany itself, shocking intelligence for America's many religious believers.[56]

British propaganda was not responsible for Roosevelt's decisions to exchange neutrality for gradual belligerency that stopped short of declaring war. It may have moved public opinion, but the cold appreciation of US strategic interests was as operable then as it has been ever since. Roosevelt had powerful advocates of intervention in his administration, notably

Secretary for War Henry Stimson and Frank Knox, the Secretary of the Navy, both Republicans brought in to give his administration a more bipartisan flavour in an election year. In January 1941, after his historic third-term election victory, the President sanctioned secret joint staff talks between British and US military planners, who determined such momentous things as the strategy of taking on Germany first, while waging a war of containment in the Pacific, with defeat of Japan deferred until after that of Germany. Starting close to home, the US pressured Latin American governments to exclude Axis nationals from strategically important positions, so that all the Germans who staffed Pan American Airlines in Colombia were replaced by North Americans.[57]

The next step was regarded by the Axis powers as tantamount to a *de facto* declaration of war: the March 1941 Lend–Lease Act. House Resolution 1776, as it was amusingly called, circumvented Britain's lack of dollar reserves by taking the 'silly, foolish old dollar sign' out of transactions to give war materials in the manner of a man lending a neighbour a hose to extinguish a fire. This homely metaphor concealed the fact that military equipment was unlikely to be returned in one piece, and it did not hint at the colossal sums involved which reached US$50 billion (at wartime values) by the time the war concluded. It was not quite the 'Declaration of Interdependence' hymned by *The Economist* since US negotiators wanted bases and trade agreements in return for US largesse. Aid on this scale (roughly a quarter of all British munitions) required protecting ships crossing the U-boat-infested North Atlantic. In April 1941 Roosevelt moved the US maritime 'security zone' to 25 degrees west longitude, which brought Greenland and the Azores within the area patrolled by the US navy, and then unilaterally extended this to Iceland. This resulted in an undeclared naval war between the US and Nazi Germany, with the freighter *Robin Moor* sunk in June, the destroyer USS *Kearny* torpedoed in October and the USS *Reuben James* sunk in November 1941.[58] These years witnessed the imperceptible transition from hemispheric defence to what came to be called national security interests.

V GUY CROUCHBACK'S WAR

As has been suggested, the British were not idle under the bombs, and this period was more than a parenthetical breathing space before the war became global with Hitler's invasion of the Soviet Union or the US declaration of war sixth months after that, following Pearl Harbor. So much emphasis has been put in recent years on the clash of the totalitarian titans (four out of every five German fatalities occurred on the Eastern Front), not least by British historians of Germany and Russia, that one might imagine the British were not engaged in a shooting war at all.

British strategy was heavily influenced by memories of the carnage on the Western Front during the Great War, in the sense that initially much reliance was put on trying to collapse the Nazi and Fascist regimes with a combination of economic blockade, bombing and subversive operations among the conquered populations of Europe. There were also direct engagements. Germany mounted a counter-blockade, using a few bombers and its small submarine force (at eighteen operational boats they were the real 'few') to devastating effect against merchant ships plying the North Atlantic. In 1940 a thousand ships were sunk totalling four million tons; in 1941 a further 1,299 vessels were sunk, drastically reducing British imports.[59] Although the US decision to extend its maritime zone westwards helped focus British forces against the Germans, there was no mistaking Churchill's anxiety that such losses were unsustainable and would cripple Britain's war economy. Throughout 1941 his correspondence and memos bristled with orders to speed up unloading times, to organise refuelling tankers for warships or to equip convoys with defensive guns as well as destroyer escorts. An urgent technological war also ensued, involving code-breaking, sonic detection and complex methods of keeping a step ahead of the preying U-boats and bombers.

The Italian declaration of war on 10 June 1940 resulted in a disastrous campaign against inferior forces in southern France, but it did achieve the conquest of British Somaliland. This conquest of wind-blown sand whetted Mussolini's appetite to expand Italy's colonies in North Africa and the Horn into a huge littoral empire. Operations were set back after Italian gunners contrived to shoot down an aircraft bearing the designated commander, Marshal Italo Balbo. After much prodding by Mussolini, in September 1940 Balbo's replacement, Marshal Rodolfo Graziani, reluctantly invaded Egypt from Libya. After advancing about sixty miles into Egypt, the Italians decided to halt and defend fortified positions in the vicinity of Sidi Barrani. The British commander in Egypt, General Archibald Wavell, ordered a limited raid, codenamed Operation Compass, against these camps, which, at Churchill's insistence, developed into a much larger offensive. In December British and Indian troops successfully overran these camps, taking thousands of prisoners at minimal loss to themselves. With the Indians redeployed, British forces were augmented by Australians for the next phase of the offensive, which resulted in taking forty-five thousand Italians prisoner at the Battle of Bardia. After further tough fighting, the Australians seized the town of Tobruk, capturing a further twenty-five thousand Italians at a loss to themselves of four hundred dead. By the time the offensive ended, British and Commonwealth forces had advanced 500 miles and had taken 130,000 prisoners. Surveying these men, a Coldstream Guards officer commented: 'We have about five acres of officers and 200 acres of other ranks.' 'Wavell has done well in Africa,' reported his prep-school magazine with some understatement.[60]

Italy's pitiful performance in this theatre was partially due to Mussolini's decision to invade Greece, which activated a hastily issued British guarantee of Greek independence and so obliged the British to redeploy troops from North Africa. This in turn triggered a domino effect that dragged the Germans into both Greece and North Africa, subtracting some of the forces Hitler would need in the invasion destined for southern Russia. It also tempted Churchill to open up a Balkan theatre to further dissipate Axis might, although in practice the force fatally dissipated was Wavell's vast Middle Eastern command, as he was also tasked with dealing with rebellions in Iraq and Persia. Churchill was chiefly concerned that Greece, Turkey and Yugoslavia might all seek solace in the Axis camp if a stand was not made in Greece, a further preoccupation being the way stirring tales from Greece might play among educated philhellenes in the US. Instead, humiliating defeat revealed Churchill's despatch of troops to Greece to have been one of the worst decisions he made during the war, and ended with the evacuation of more than fifty thousand British and Dominion troops and the loss of much of their equipment.[61]

Mussolini was eager to show Hitler that he was capable of lightning strikes too, especially as the triumphant Nazi leader was disposing of occupied Europe with little regard for the sensitivities of the senior Fascist dictator. Churchill's dismissal of the latter as Hitler's 'tattered lackey' clearly stung too. The complete lack of co-ordination between the two Axis predators was striking. Hitler insisted that the Balkans remain quiescent, even as he acknowledged Greece as part of a future Italian sphere of influence. He then appeared to act cavalierly in that region by deploying fifteen thousand German troops to guard Rumania's oil fields, which was the immediate pretext for Mussolini's impulsive invasion of Greece in late October from neighbouring Albania. On a political level the decision was bizarre, as the Greek dictator Metaxas was well disposed towards Italy. The operation was poorly conceived and grievously underestimated the forces at Greek disposal. Without winter clothing, the Italians faced not just the Greeks but their mountainous terrain and cold and wet winter weather.

Within weeks the Greeks had conquered about a quarter of Italian-ruled Albania from whence the invasion had started. Hitler was stupefied by this turn of events in what he regarded as a wholly unnecessary sideshow, as he prepared to take his biggest gamble in Russia. Worse, the Italians' large and modern navy was driven out of the eastern Mediterranean in two major engagements, the attack with air-dropped torpedoes at Taranto in November 1940 – an operation closely studied by Japanese air and naval attachés in Rome – and a fleet engagement off Cape Matapan in March 1941. Meanwhile, following the evacuation of Greece, thirty thousand British and Dominion troops – many without shoes or weapons – redeployed to Crete. After finishing off the Greeks, conquering Yugoslavia in passing, the Germans invaded Crete with airborne forces. Major mistakes were made in the defence of the island, some of them a product of an exaggerated concern to protect the source of highly secret intelligence materials. Some eleven thousand British and Commonwealth troops were captured and many warships damaged or sunk, before the survivors were evacuated from Heraklion.[62] Even as Wavell's forces struck against Italy's East African colonies, taking a further quarter of a million prisoners and conquering Abyssinia, Eritrea and Somalia, the newly arrived German general Erwin Rommel launched a skilful attack that reversed Italian losses in North Africa. In need of a scapegoat and never having warmed to the shy and taciturn Wavell, Churchill decided he was 'tired' and that the Middle East required a fresh eye. Wavell was exchanged with Claude Auchinleck from India, in time for the unfortunate Wavell to preside over the even greater debacle suffered by British arms in the Far East.[63]

CHAPTER 7

Under the Swastika:
Nazi Occupied Europe

I SCANDINAVIA

In modern times, the British have never experienced the moral dilemmas of foreign occupation, nor, the black market apart, the canescent zones in which ordinary life had to be negotiated in the presence of an alien power. Distinctions between such terms as cohabitation, collaboration, collaborationism, opposition and resistance–collaboration, in which both roles were played simultaneously, have little meaning for them. At the time, some of the main terms often meant different things to the French and Germans, and this was true of all the peoples the Germans subjected. *Collaboration* in French was not the same as *Kollaboration* in German – the more apt German translation for the French word was *Zusammenarbeit* which in English, just to confuse things, means the more aseptic 'working together' co-operatively rather than ideological affinity.

One can speculate, endlessly, about how the British might have responded to occupation, in the comfortable knowledge that the most prosaic areas of human conduct have never been subjected to such searing retrospective scrutiny. But such games invariably neglect elites, class and great-power politics, or are focused on such atypical cases as the occupied Channel Islands, from whose micro-experiences unwarranted macro-conclusions are extrapolated. Watching a rich pre-war society hostess – and we can all fill in many names here – the diarist Harold Nicolson asked himself how 'this plump and virulent little bitch [a Mrs Greville of Polesden Lacey] should hold such social power'.[1] One wonders how many plump and virulent little bitches would have entertained the Germans in town or country after an invasion, before speculating how others might have made more slippery compromises for class advantage or a quiet life.

The British were paradoxically omnipresent in Hitler's Europe in disembodied form. With their bombast and lies the Germans rapidly lost what was called *la guerre des ondes*. The BBC's signature of 'This is London calling' and the dot–dot–dot–dash of the Morse code V echoing the opening of Beethoven's Fifth Symphony, proved more compelling than their Nazi equivalents, it being a daring conceit to use a German composer for this purpose. Although Vatican Radio, Radio Moscow and, later, US stations played a limited role, the war was the finest hour of the British Broadcasting Corporation. It had certain advantages. Radio Moscow was inaudible in much of Europe, its contents were heavily focused on the Soviet populations occupied by the Germans and its style tended to appeal only to fellow class-warriors. The US was too distant and lacked the fresh information that helped the British. Most exiled governments were based in London. The British capital was also a clearing house for intelligence derived from Axis-occupied Europe. The BBC moreover had the transmitting power and was geographically well situated to achieve maximum coverage. Above all, the Corporation established almost instantaneous credibility. The fact that Goebbels's broadcasters trumpeted only Axis victories paradoxically meant that the BBC's factual statements and prognoses were more plausible, even though the Germans had much to be triumphalist about.[2]

The BBC did not ignore or lie about Allied reverses. Every night the BBC transmitted 160,000 words in twenty-three different languages, all carefully crafted by a small army of often unorthodox amateurs and with the participation of exiled governments. Each country received its daily exposure, ranging from a quarter of an hour for Albania, an hour and forty-five minutes for Norway and Yugoslavia, two and a quarter hours for Poland, two and half for Holland, and five and a half for France, of which ten minutes consisted of broadcasts by the Free French. The effort the Germans put into confiscating radios, punishing listeners or jamming transmissions confirmed the British impression that these broadcasts were having the desired effect of providing an alternative take on events and an enduring sense of moral values. In an exercise markedly different from the sober tone adopted by the BBC, the Political Warfare Executive ran a number of 'black' transmitters which appeared to be broadcasting from within occupied Europe, but which were really based in the UK. Thanks to outstanding intelligence work, the Polish radio station Swit was able to procure proofs of the main German propaganda paper in Warsaw by 8 a.m., so that even though the paper was not for sale until 1 p.m., its contents could be dissected the same evening on a station that was actually based in England.[3]

The conquest of northern and western Europe happened with disarming alacrity. In the spring of 1940, the Germans undertook a predatory lunge northwards, before invading the Low Countries and France that summer. Denmark surrendered on 9 April 1940, after a campaign that began at 4.30 a.m. and ended an hour and a half later without their navy firing a single shot. Such brevity can be partly attributed to the fact that the week before the invasion senior German officers, including a general, dressed in civilian clothes had simply taken the train to Copenhagen, where proud locals had innocently conducted them around the harbour and its citadel fortifications. To be fair, even the otherwise belligerent Churchill realised that Denmark was too small to resist its huge neighbour.[4]

Since Denmark was a means to further conquests, and had not resisted, Hitler treated it relatively leniently. The Germans did nothing to affect its territorial integrity; indeed it was the British who invaded and occupied Danish Iceland as an essential base for the Battle of the Atlantic. The Germans also ignored ethnic German separatists in northern Schleswig, even though many of them were Nazis. Apart from stationing two infantry divisions in Denmark to guard against the British, the Germans focused on exploiting the country's economy, particularly the thriving agricultural sector. This supplied between 10 and 15 per cent of Germany's needs, notably butter, eggs, beef and pork products. Germany also exploited Danish chemical factories and ship-repair yards. In return the Danes received three million tons of coal a year.

In the Nazi's optic, Scandinavians were unimpeachably Aryan, and most Danes understood German. Instructions issued by the commander of the invading army, General Nikolaus von Falkenhorst, recommended methods of dealing with the Danes. 'Do nothing to offend their national honour! The Dane is self-confident and freedom-loving. He rejects every form of pressure and subjection. He has no feeling for military discipline and authority. Therefore: fewer commands, no shouting … Explain things objectively and convince! More will be achieved by adopting a humorous tone.'[5] In July, the newly appointed Danish Foreign Minister, Erik Scavenius, responded by announcing: 'The Great German victories which have struck the world with astonishment and admiration have begun a new era in Europe, which will bring with it a New Order in political and economic spheres under Germany's leadership. It will be Denmark's task herein to find its place in mutual active co-operation with Greater Germany.'

This conciliatory approach was reflected at the political level, yielding unique circumstances in Nazi-controlled Europe. Until 1943, the Danes were allowed to retain their army and navy. King Christian X, parliament and government continued to rule, with elections in 1943 that must have been genuine, for the Danish Nazis won only 1 per cent of the poll. Bilateral relations with Germany were negotiated by ambassadors, although the German diplomatic representative, Cecil von Renthe-Fink, had the more august title of Plenipotentiary of the German Reich with the Danish Government. This career diplomat also had a staff of about one hundred, which included such undiplomatic departments as SS-Oberführer Paul Kanstein's Gestapo and a twenty-five-strong complement of SD officials with a general watching brief over the Danish police force and representatives in the German consulates throughout the country.[6]

This was a pragmatic arrangement for both sides. By practising what some call state collaboration, the Danish national coalition government of Thorvald Stauning guaranteed the existing social order, while keeping Frits Clausen's tiny German-subsidised Danish Nazis at bay. It was not quite as free as some authors imply by simply remarking on the existence of a parliament under occupation. The Germans were sufficiently powerful to alter the composition of the government if they needed to make a point. When in June 1941 a mass football-match brawl erupted between Danish fans of Copenhagen and German troops supporting the club Admiral Wien, and the Danish police failed to restore order, Plenipotentiary Renthe-Fink prevailed on the Danish government to sack the Justice Minister.[7] Nazi propagandists stationed in the embassy also exerted pressure on the Danish government to force the press to adopt an anti-British and pro-German line.[8] All foreign news came from the press attaché in the German embassy and could not be rewritten. Editors who printed anything 'damaging to Danish foreign interests' (that is, Germany's) faced a year's imprisonment, although ingenious journalists found ways to highlight the conditions under which they worked, like double-spacing printed pages to let readers know material had been censored. In 1941, even informal conversations were criminalised, while those engaged in helping 'enemies of the Occupying Power' faced life imprisonment after being denied their own choice of defence lawyers. After the German invasion of Russia, a thousand volunteers joined a Danish

Freikorps, a branch of the SS, and in November the threat of re-invasion forced the government to reverse its original refusal to join the Anti-Comintern Pact. Anti-government demonstrations in Copenhagen turned into riots that were suppressed with warning shots.

Expectations of similar minimalist arrangements in Norway crumbled after the government resisted the Germans between the 9 April invasion and the eventual capitulation of Norwegian armed forces on 10 June 1940. Considering the disparity of forces, the Norwegians put up a fierce fight whenever the terrain favoured them. A state of war continued to exist between Norway and Germany, with most of Norway's enormous merchant fleet (joint third in the world alongside Japan's) seeking refuge in Allied harbours. Installation of a Fascist government came about through fits and starts after efforts to find local elite collaborators were stymied by the defiance of Norway's brave King Haakon VII. On the day of the invasion, Vidkun Quisling, the Norwegian Nazi Fører, bluffed his way on to the airwaves to proclaim himself prime minister, even though King Haakon and the legitimate government of Johan Nygaardsvold had slipped out of Oslo for Elverum to escape the Germans. While Hitler subsequently backed Quisling's initiative – Quisling had not received advance warning of the invasion for security reasons – he was regarded as a divisive figure not only by most Norwegians, but more importantly by the German special legation in Oslo, which set about establishing an alternative Administrative Council. King Haakon refused to recognise either the Council or Quisling's claims, sticking with the legitimate government as both moved deeper up country before fleeing to England on one of the last warships out of blazing Molde in the far north. These embarrassments inclined Hitler to wash his hands of them all, testily remarking, 'It was a matter of indifference to me who governs up there,' and appointing a German Reich Commissar for the Occupied Norwegian Territories instead.[9]

The appointee was the forty-two-year-old Gauleiter of Essen, Josef Terboven, a former Richthofen Squadron comrade of Göring. After satisfying himself shortly after their first meeting that Quisling was 'stupid to the nth degree', Terboven endeavoured to be rid of him until Hitler recalled Quisling's timely December 1939 warning that the British might invade Norway and forced Quisling back on him. In this manner, the head of a party with fifteen hundred members in a population of three millions became the *de facto* prime minister of a thirteen-member commissary cabinet which liaised with Terboven's imported supervisory administration. Quisling saw the arrangement as a form of probation, hoping that one day his Nasjonal Samling (National Gathering) party would rule an independent Norway within the Greater German Union. Terboven's administration consisted of 364 imported officials. The majority of them, 258 to be precise, were in positions dealing with the economy, most of them drawn from the major trading city of Hamburg or large corporations with existing commercial interests in Norway.[10] There was a separate SS presence in the form of a new Higher SS and Police Leader, a position occupied by Fritz Wetzel, until he was killed in June 1940 by an RAF bomb while on leave in Düsseldorf. He was replaced by Friedrich Wilhelm Rediess who, reversing the power relations of Frank and Krüger in Poland, was eclipsed by the more capably fanatical Terboven. There was also a two-hundred-strong complement of SD and Gestapo officers, successively under Walther Stahlecker and Heinrich Fehlis. The number of these Security Police rose to over a thousand by the end of the occupation.[11]

Terboven's first acts included replacing elected mayors with appointees from Quisling's NS and interfering with judicial appointments, a step which triggered the mass resignation of the Supreme Court. Next he tried to violate the privacy of Lutheran confessionals by compelling pastors to divulge secrets, a step the bishops immediately rejected. Attempts to Nazify Norway's fifty major professional, farming and trades union associations resulted in a joint protest by forty-three of them. Terboven responded by having the Gestapo arrest the main spokesmen while browbeating the rest in a room lined with armed German guards. Attempts to intimidate the powerful shipowners also failed. Efforts to turn the teaching profession into NS propagandists were likewise universally rejected, though some 60 per cent of the police eventually joined the Party.[12] The collaborationist administration increased subsidies to the arts and broadcasting, while simultaneously packing the bureaucracy of its new Ministry of Propaganda and Enlightenment with NS supporters to ensure the Norwegian media's ideological conformity. In September 1940 Terboven proscribed all political parties, except for the NS, to whom he presented the assets, buildings and newspapers of the defunct parties. The confiscated assets of the Socialist *Arbeiderbladet* allowed the NS to increase print runs of its own newspaper, *Fritt Folk*, fivefold. As in the occupied Netherlands, a German monopoly of paper supplies enabled Terboven to constrict papers whose line he did not like, often by cutting the number of days they appeared rather than closing them down.

Although Quisling's name had become synonymous with treachery in Norway and beyond, Nazi experts, with German money, helped him to treble NS membership to a respectable thirty-five thousand. The object was to provide any eventual collaborationist regime with symbolic mass support. The NS was also progressively militarised to conform with other European Fascist movements. Their first, brown uniform made NS members look as if they were coated in chocolate; the second was dark green and made them look like bus drivers. The Fører was also quick to announce an anti-British line and to indicate his willingness to take measures against Norway's 1,350 Jews, whose ancestors had arrived after an early nineteenth-century constitutional ban was lifted. The first Norwegian volunteers departed for service in the SS, which created a specific Nordland regiment for Scandinavians. More joined a Norwegian Legion attached to the Wehrmacht. These troops were deployed in the June 1941 invasion of the Soviet Union.

Unrest mounted in the wake of the invasion of Russia. In August and September 1941, the Germans announced that they would confiscate almost every radio in Norway except those needed by fishermen. The population dutifully handed them in, and the sets were given to Germans who had lost theirs to Allied bombing.[13] When workers went on strike after the regime had stopped the free distribution of milk in factories, Terboven decreed a state of emergency with a number of restrictions on life in the capital. It was against this background that in January 1942 Quisling prevailed on Hitler to let him take over in Norway, although Terboven ensured that the Reich Commissariat continued ruling Norway behind the would-be dictator. On Monday 1 February, Quisling was sworn in as minister president, combining the roles of the exiled King and the proscribed Storting or parliament, bringing together legislative and executive powers. He and his wife moved into the luxury mansion of a former industrialist, eventually renaming it Home of the Gods. One of his first decrees established an NS Youth Movement, compulsory for those aged between ten and eighteen. He also introduced a Teachers' Front to encourage conformity, but this was promptly rejected in writing by twelve thousand out of a national total of fourteen thousand teachers. Quisling's regime responded by mass arrests, despatching the detainees to a rural concentration camp and the most recalcitrant to the holds of a ship located in the Arctic.[14]

One of the tasks of the SD was to deliver regular secret reports on the security situation and manifestations of opposition in occupied Norway. Three substantial volumes testify to an absence of racial comradeship with ordinary Norwegians. In incident after incident Norwegians defaced or ripped down propaganda posters, spat at German troops or struck at them with chairs. On many of these occasions the perpetrators were drunk. They included a twenty-three-year-old woman who, lurching around outside the Café Viking, repeatedly called a passing SS trooper a 'devil' and slapped him in the face. For this she spent four weeks in jail. Another, Hjalmar Olsen, received ten months for drunkenly calling Germany 'the greatest shit and swine country'. A fifty-year-old drunk received three years for telling German officers he encountered in Oslo's Löwenbräukeller that their Führer was 'an idiot', whose hash Stalin and the US would soon settle, and that Quisling would vanish from Norway. Cinema screenings of German newsreels claiming that the RAF bombed civilians while the Luftwaffe hit only military targets in Britain were greeted with demonstrative coughing, derisory laughter and whistling or the singing of patriotic songs. Cinema owners were forced to keep the lights on, so that the SD could identify the culprits, a practice soon adopted in cinemas throughout occupied Europe. An extraordinary range of flysheets were in circulation, reminding Norwegians of their moral duty to shun the Germans and Quisling's traitors. The bravery of those responsible for producing them was evident in the case of a seventy-five-year-old doctor who, having been caught with such materials, slit his wrists in a Gestapo prison shortly after making his confession. The report concluded, 'We must wait and see whether he survives the loss of blood.'[15] Another doctor, forty-year-old Mogens Fraas, could not contain himself at the sight of two local girls chatting with two German NCOs. After drenching them with water from his garden hose he delivered a pre-detention soliloquy: 'You Nazi bandits, fuck off to Germany where you belong where there are only robbers and bandits like you, who come here to Norway and gobble up all the food and send it back to Germany. I hope to see the fine day when the Nazis are chucked out, and I'll have the pleasure of smashing in the heads of NS members. Every girl who goes out with soldiers is merely a harlot. You'll get a visit from the English when they arrive here.'[16]

II LIVING WITH THE ENEMY

The German onslaught in the west, launched on 10 May 1940, was devastating. It took five days to force the Dutch to submit, after slightly more civilians than soldiers had been killed in the initial assault, including eight hundred who were slain in one bombing raid on central Rotterdam. Hundreds of thousands of Dutch people fled, from east to west and then from north to south. Queen Wilhelmina proclaimed London as the seat of the legal Dutch government, instructing the higher civil servants to continue their administration on a provisional basis. The equivalent of British permanent secretaries, these men established a council where they deliberated as if they were ministers, finally free of the vexation of professional politicians. After Hitler's appointment of Artur Seyss-Inquart as Reich Commissar, the five-times conservative premier Hendrik Colijn offered the Germans loyal co-operation while establishing the Nederlandse Unie, largely from the membership of the defunct bourgeois parties. This was intended as the patriotic alternative to the widely detested Dutch Nazis of Anton Mussert's Nationaal-Socialistische Beweging or NSB, and potentially a vehicle for restoring Dutch quasi-autonomy, although Germany would dominate the economy and control foreign policy as the price for the retention of the monarchy.[17]

In France, invasion triggered mass panic and flight. The terrorism involved is often overlooked. The ancient cathedral city of Chartres was repeatedly bombed and by 15 June all but 700–800 of its population of twenty-three thousand had fled. There were unburied bodies everywhere and the city burned until a massive thunderstorm extinguished the flames. German entry into the city was held up by brave Senegalese French colonial troops. At 7 a.m. on 17 June the first Germans arrived, to be met by the mayor, the bishop and the prefect of Eure et Loire, Jean Moulin, at thirty-nine the youngest prefect in France. That evening Moulin was arrested while he was having his supper. The Germans punched and hit him with rifle butts in order to force him to sign a paper falsely asserting that the Senegalese soldiers had raped and murdered a group of French women and children. When asked for proof, the Germans claimed that the massacres 'had the characteristics of crimes committed by negroes', although when Moulin was driven to the hamlet of La Taye to be shown the victims it was obvious they had been blown to pieces by German bombs. Beaten and confined in a small house with a Senegalese soldier, Moulin used broken panes of glass to slash his own throat. The Germans claimed that he had been attacked by his fellow prisoner, one of the few survivors of a massacre the Germans had themselves perpetrated, killing 180 of the Senegalese troops after they had surrendered. The false accusation Moulin refused to sign was intended to spin two atrocities the Germans had committed into an incident they could turn to propagandistic advantage. Moulin survived and went on to be one of the greatest figures in the Gaullist resistance.[18]

As Hitler's armies lanced onward, cascades of refugees turned into a human torrent, with two million Belgians and Dutch swelling the ranks of the six million French people who fled southwards by bicycle, cart, foot, car or bus.[19] The capital took on the deserted air it usually has in August. Supplies in the regions to which the refugees headed quickly evaporated, since the southern agricultural economy produced mainly citrus fruit, olives and wine. Small southern towns had to cope with vast numbers of indigent people who sometimes slept in squares, in parks or on the pavements. Because of its size and world cultural importance, France merits the attention that has been focused on it, although the Greek General Georgios Tsolakoglou was another head of state who signed armistices with the Germans and Italians. There was also a Serbian Pétain, General Milan Nedić, who is considerably less well known than Draža Mihailović, Tito or the Croats' notorious leader Ante Pavelić. In 1943 the Allies stitched up a deal with Marshal Pietro Badoglio, who was Pétain's Italian equivalent.[20]

France seemed to find its man of the hour in Marshal Philippe Pétain, its ambassador to Franco's Spain. Pétain offered France 'the gift of his own person to attenuate its misfortunes'. He was an octogenarian war hero, a noble survivor from the era of mass carnage, ideally suited to the calculated pose of the nation's dignified grandfather. Critics thought him half dead already, although that probably underestimates his cunning. Witty Georges Mandel called him *le conquistador*, both a reference to the Marshal's recent Spanish intermezzo and a contraction of *le con qui se dort* (the cunt/fool who is asleep). Pétain was accorded a sweeping, dubiously legal mandate, by a vote of 569 to 80 in the National Assembly, to revise the constitution of the Third Republic. Thus the professional politicians consented to a policy that, instead of seeking to maintain France's existing republican polity until the war's outcome was decided, anticipated Britain's defeat and sought to take advantage of the opportunity afforded by German hegemony to embark on a programme of radical domestic regeneration.

Pétain formally abolished the Republic, adjourned the Assembly, made himself head of state and designated the ex-Socialist barrister Pierre Laval as his first prime minister. Laval was an anomalous figure, a slippery horse-trader in a regime that affected to despise professional politicians in favour of stiff-backed soldierly types of high morals. Laval calculated that a German defeat of Britain was good for the French, because a negotiated peace between Britain and Germany of the sort aired in the summer of

1940, or Britain struggling on alone, would mean that German exactions would fall exclusively on France. Hence he concluded at a September 1940 press conference: 'From a practical point of view, the only policy is to collaborate with Germany. In terms of our wishes we must hope for a German victory.' Laval pushed this line so far through private dealings with the Germans that in December 1940 Pétain dismissed him and had him arrested.[21]

After the armistice was signed on 22 June 1940, a neutral, semi-sovereign French state with a fleet and an overseas empire, but massively truncated in its metropolitan territory, was established with its capital at the Auvergne spa of Vichy. It had an army, pegged at a hundred thousand men, the same ceiling the Allies had imposed on Germany at Versailles; ironically, the French army would emulate Weimar's strategies to rebuild the Reichswehr covertly. There were also nearly 150,000 soldiers and sailors distributed throughout France's colonial empire, from Algeria via Lebanon, Syria and West and East Africa to a small presence in Indo-China.

Vichy's many hotels were converted into ministries, notoriously including the Hôtel du Parc, where Pétain occupied the third floor. The Vichy government's delegates to the Franco-German armistice commission at Wiesbaden had to absorb such shocks as the transfer of POWs to Germany and daily occupation costs of twenty million francs, which equalled 400 million at the new exchange rate of twenty francs to one Reichsmark. This meant that the Germans were taking 58 per cent of France's gross national revenue, as if the country was occupied by eighteen million soldiers rather than a few hundred thousand.[22] Six lines of division traversed France, although there were potentially others that the Germans might exploit should they decide to play the regional separatist card in Brittany or Provence that the French had used against them in the Rhineland in the 1920s.[23]

A heavily guarded demarcation line, running from Burgundy to Tours and then south parallel with the Atlantic coast to the Spanish border, separated the populous and prosperous Occupied Zone from Vichy France, which consisted of 45 per cent of the whole territory but only a third of the pre-invasion population. Apart from bauxite mines and the refinery of aluminium, the south lacked conspicuous industry. In the east, Alsace and the Moselle department of Lorraine were absorbed into the two adjacent German Gaue, with a view to germanising them and incorporating them in the Reich – the name René was to be made into Reiner. In the north, the strategically crucial departments Nord and Pas-de-Calais were absorbed into a Prohibited Zone governed by the German Military Administration in Brussels. The zone first contained air bases and huge concentrations of German combat troops for an invasion of Britain; three years later it contained most of the million men stationed along the Channel and Atlantic coasts to ward off an Allied invasion. There was also a Reserved Zone running from the Somme to the Swiss border which had its own frontier with the Occupied Zone. Central European (German) time was imposed in the north, so that in winter it was dark until 9 a.m.

Externally, Vichy's position was weakest, although it imagined it was strong. The Vichy authorities took the initiative in trying to win concessions from the Germans, using the prospect of more active participation on Germany's side as a bargaining counter to relax the burdens of occupation, release POWs and restore French national honour. British destruction of the French fleet at Mers-el-Kebir and Anglo-Gaullist military ventures in West Africa tempted the Vichy government to seek improved terms by dangling the prospect of a more active role in Africa, or, as suggested by Laval, the offer of French pilots to participate in the Luftwaffe's assault on Britain. An asymmetric neutrality resulted, one in which French manufacturers provided 1,700 trucks to help Rommel in North Africa, as well as 2,275 aircraft supplied to the Luftwaffe. The degree to which members of the Vichy regime were prepared to collaborate varied from individual to individual. Any dialogue with the Germans was also complicated by the sheer number of rival authorities the French found themselves dealing with, for the complicated skeins of Nazi bureaucracy reached into France, ensuring that Ambassador Otto Abetz was not necessarily what the Americans call the go-to person. Ultimately, Hitler's need to consider Italian and Spanish colonial ambitions meant that such geostrategic overtures came to nothing. Like a judo practitioner, the Vichy authorities sought to make a virtue of weakness against an opponent's brute strength; in reality, time and again, and despite their machinations, they found themselves thrown to the floor.[24]

One of Pétain's expressed objectives was to protect the true French, at least as he defined them, from the burdens of foreign occupation and, over time, to restore the sovereignty of the French state throughout metropolitan France itself. For although Vichy's writ theoretically ran within what remained of France, including Paris, at any time the German military authorities could interdict communications between the occupied and unoccupied regions, prohibiting movement or reducing letters to a printed form indicating by a tick that one was well. In his valediction to the French people in 1944, Pétain claimed, 'If I could not be your sword, I tried to be your shield.' Every decision had allegedly been taken with a Nazi dagger pointed at his throat, perhaps an overly dramatic rendering of life at his court in the Hôtel du Parc. He went on to claim, as Laval had done earlier, that there had been a complementary parity between his efforts to preserve France from within and the external struggle waged by de Gaulle.

Whatever the sincerity of such claims to have been the lesser evil, they harboured a couple of false assumptions that have long been questioned. There was no evidence that the Belgians, Danes, Dutch or Norwegians, under the direct rule of a Nazi plenipotentiary, suffered more than France, nor was it ever Hitler's intention to use the more brutal methods his subordinates employed in what he regarded as a racially inferior Poland or Russia. The Führer admired the architecture of Paris during a fleeting two-and-a-half-hour visit, and his views on the future of France were condescending rather than vicious – he saw it as a future Switzerland writ large, albeit with finer buildings. There was nothing inevitable about Vichy, although its denizens certainly tried to present developments that way. If following de Gaulle into exile with honour intact was not an option for Pétain, he also refused to follow the example of Thiers after the Franco-Prussian War of 1870–1, who called the Germans' bluff by effectively saying 'You wanted it; you govern it.'[25]

The reason was that German hegemony in Europe, which Pétain tacitly accepted, provided an opportunity for him and his supporters to implement a regressive moral, political and social agenda, in which authority and duty would trump liberties and rights. In other words, they sought to use the occupation to their advantage rather than passively enduring it. The France that would emerge within the nascent new order would be a France restored and transformed, anodyne terms for decontaminated or detoxified, words which would have described their policies better. This was a highly ideological and sectarian vision, which, while enjoying no democratic mandate, was thoroughly entrenched in certain reaches of French society. The vision was artfully concealed beneath the Marshal's plangent rhetoric of national unity and self-sacrifice. That he was initially popular is not in doubt. A poster image of the Marshal which asked 'Are you more of a Frenchman than him?' had an inherent plausibility that a poster inviting a Norwegian response to Quisling would have lacked. Quisling was a lightweight; Pétain almost embodied France. There was also the fact that, whereas others talked about abstract rights, Pétain's initial insistence on care for the homeless and refugees, the restoration of employment and relief for prisoners of war were manifestations of national unity in a country that seemed to have disintegrated, and this surely explains some of his appeal.[26]

As an old soldier, Pétain exercised a lachrymose suasion over those touched by war either once or twice in a lifetime: veterans who had served under him in the Great War, when most of the French army was rotated through Verdun, and who remembered his relatively humane role following the mutinies of 1917; and the families of men held captive in Germany after France's defeat in 1940. On his peregrinations through France he endeavoured to win over the peasantry with cloying praise of their 'belles vaches' and 'braves chevaux de chez nous', even though attempts to engineer reverse migration from towns to countryside came to nothing. Virtually every element represented at Vichy had a prehistory. After the carnage of 1914–18 there were plenty of people who believed in peace at any price or in Franco-German reconciliation. Many of the latter belonged to dedicated associations, which would provide both collaborators and their masters, for a striking number of the German occupiers were Francophiles, albeit ones who never lost their faith in German superiority. Pacifists and realists alike were not immune to Pétain's spell, for it seemed absurd that salvation might come from de Gaulle's little band of predominantly conservative military exiles, a mere seven thousand in 1940. Swathes of the majority Catholic population had never been reconciled to the anti-clerical Republic, despite the ameliorative interlude of the wartime Union Sacrée in 1914–18. A significant number of senior clergy were more than ready to pronounce their blessings on France's elderly saviour, even though he was an agnostic divorcee, and what they got in return was only more religious education in state schools and a constantly moralising visibility at public events rather than any fundamental revision of the 1905 separation of Church and state. Although it is easy enough to dredge up compromising statements by clergy who supported the regime, including a blasphemous *Crédo de la France* dedicated to the 'Prestigieux Pilote' at the helm of state, Christian democrats were among the earliest resisters, and of the thousand French priests deported to Germany, one-fifth died. Lastly, there were the pragmatic reformers and technocrats of the dying days of the Third Republic, who believed that a regime of elite experts could clear up the mess created by career politicians. Such figures, including Jean Bichelonne and François Lehideux, were represented at Vichy in strange juxtaposition to the cow and peasant worshippers.[27]

One of Vichy's more dubious acts was to detain and put on trial the leaders of previous governments. They ranged from Léon Blum, leader of the 1936 Popular Front government and a hate figure on the right, to Edouard Daladier, who had set up internment camps for aliens. They were charged with failing to prepare for war, although as a former defence minister responsible for cuts Pétain was arguably as guilty as they. Other French men and women had glimpsed the future in the Popular Front and did not like it, or harboured diffuse resentments towards Communists, freemasons, Jews, parliamentarians and trades unions. They longed for the 'true' France, to be cleansed of the pernicious influence of sundry *métèques* (pejorative term for foreigners). Traditional Catholic animus against freemasons and Jews was much more prominent in this demonology than any animus against Protestants, which had diminished over time. A series of German-sponsored propaganda exhibitions endeavoured to mobilise these ugly sentiments. Such people were nostalgic for an idealised rural society based on community, family, order, hierarchy, religion and stability, an alternative to the atomised and rootless urban cosmopolitanism of the present. A fecund and reinvigorated France would emerge from the sterility of past decadence, symbolised by the aperitif hours. To dismiss them all as Fascists, the catch-all term for whatever is not on the left, would be to ignore the ex-Socialists and anti-Communist trades unionists represented at Vichy, the latter drawn by the regime's promise to transcend the class struggle, giving employers and unions parity of esteem in its new industrial corporations. A more nuanced explanation must also be sought for the freemasons or homosexuals who also occasionally figured in the new order. The diarist Jean Guéhenno, wondering why so many French homosexuals collaborated with the Germans, compared them to the denizens of a small-town brothel after an army regiment had marched in.[28]

How far people were prepared to oblige the Germans was also subject to adjustment, so much so that one could argue that many of the political feuds of the Third Republic were recreated in miniature at Vichy. There was a major ideological fault-line distinguishing Vichy's core conservative supporters from the fanaticised minority of dedicated French Fascists congregated in Paris. Many of the Vichyites were Germanophobic nationalists, unenthused by visions of a federalist Hitlerian new order bound together by transcontinental *Autobahnen* and high-speed rail links. Vichy's supporters were closer to the conservative constituencies that backed such politically demobilising figures as Franco in Spain, Salazar in Portugal and, at a stretch, de Valera in Ireland. Although Vichy's supporters were deeply sectarian in temperament, they were also members of the French elites who thought that they were born to rule. Most collaborationists were socially more marginal, when they were not merely *déclassé* intellectual misfits.[29]

Some of Vichy's supporters were Pétainistes, adherents of the Marshal's personal cult, but others espoused a much wider right-wing platform. In general, unlike many French Fascists, they repudiated intellectuals and felt no need to advertise their hatreds in German-subsidised literary journals. Nor did they need to indulge in the *épater les bourgeois* dinner-table shock tactics of a psychotic genius like the doctor-cum-writer Ferdinand Céline, whose apocalyptic ravings appalled Germans aware of the realities of the policies the Frenchman fantasised about. Vichyites despised political parties so much that they could not contemplate forming one, as Marcel Déat – the former national secretary of the Socialist student association turned Fascist – discovered when he lobbied for a German- or Russian-style totalitarian party at Vichy. After Pétain and Laval had founded a Legion of Veterans instead, Déat returned to Paris, thenceforth the hub of French Fascism, like an ace up the Nazi sleeve should the Germans ever weary of Vichy. Other French nationalists, and even the former Fascist Georges Valois, figured amid the first stirrings of resistance, as did some who refused to give up on the figure of Pétain, such as Gabriel Cochet or Henri Frenay.[30]

After a few years, Vichy had effected only a few cosmetic changes, which masked the failure of, for example, their corporate reorganisation of the economy. Jean Guéhenno paid his first visit to the Unoccupied Zone in June 1942. He wrote of his encounter with 'a strange country, a sort of principality where everyone seems to be in uniform from children of six regimented into "Youth Groups" up to war veterans wearing *francisques* [Pétainist medals] or the insignia of the Legion. Where is France in all this?' It had become a repressive Ruritania with its own rituals and symbols. The regime downplayed the hitherto central value of Revolution in favour of the biologistic theme of Regeneration or Renovation. It retained the *tricoleur* and the Marseillaise, albeit with a different selection of sung verses, as well as Bastille Day, although this was recast as a day of national reflection. As in Germany, May Day became a celebration of work under a regime whose slogan was Work–Family–Nation, while Joan of Arc Day reminded the French of their real hereditary enemy: the English. As in Germany, the American holiday of Mothers Day became a celebration of female fecundity after the decadent and sterile 1930s. There were corresponding campaigns against alcoholism, abortion and prostitution. All advertising for alcoholic drinks was prohibited. While the legal age for consumption of alcohol was fixed at fourteen for the first time in French history, at the other end of the range, occupation reduced the death rate for alcohol-related deaths by 17.5 per cent in the six departments with the highest incidence in the 1930s.[31] As Guéhenno noted, ordinary people joined a range of new uniformed formations, including the Legion and various groups designed exclusively for youth such as the Vichy version of the Boy Scouts, intended to counter the allegedly pernicious influence of left-wing schoolteachers, one of the perennial bugbears of the right. A pre-war charity, the Secours National, was adapted to canalise charity for the needy, with allotments, canteens and a 'national kindness week' to counter the Darwinian shoving in evidence in shops and markets.[32]

Invasion and occupation raised significant moral dilemmas, forcing people to behave in ways that would have been alien if the Germans had not been there. For many the occupation overwhelmingly involved shortages of heat, food and electric light, with those who could alleviate depression in this way taking to their beds to doze through as much of the occupation as possible. Jean Guéhenno ventured out as infrequently as possible, because the deserted winter streets of Paris depressed him. Long hours were spent swaddled in layers of extra clothing waiting in pre-dawn queues for meagre quantities of food, unless one had a grandparent or a paid substitute to keep one's place in line.[33] The 'growling stomach' became the true voice of France, with even carp or goldfish in ornamental ponds no longer safe from ravenous attentions. Pet cats and dogs disappeared, many of them eaten, since they had become too expensive to keep. The five thousand pigeons that thronged in Bordeaux's Square Lafite were reduced to eighty-nine as *pigeon rôti* became a staple.[34] Vast quantities of food (and some 300 million bottles of wine a year) were diverted to Germany, creating chronic shortages for the French. Rationing was introduced in September 1940, together with community canteens for the growing numbers of destitute. Learning how to make weekly or monthly rations last was an art in itself. An average family had to spend 75 per cent of its income simply on food. Basic staples, like butter, became luxury items, while roasted barley or chicory replaced real coffee, which cost 1,000 francs a pound on the black market at a time when the average monthly salary in Paris was 2,500 francs.

The approach to the black market was a gentle slope. The so-called Système-D (*débrouillard,* the French for making do) involved such initia tives as growing radishes or keeping rabbits on an urban balcony as a way of supplementing a diet in which turnips figured all too prominently. The 'grey market' involved regular visits to country cousins, who might charge a modest mark-up for locally produced foodstuffs, assuming they did not barter things (*le truc*) for items available only in the cities. Food shortages engendered colossal resentments against shopkeepers who kept goods back for German clients and against farmers who withheld produce from markets, although urban pilferers who stole produce from the farms were also detested.

Others saw life in more metaphysical terms, as what Guéhenno called a battle between freedom and servitude. Might had triumphed over right, inverting the usual moral order of things. For Christians, resistance could be interpreted in line with teachings on just war, making it their duty to fight. This in turn raised questions of ecclesiastical authority, for if the hierarchy preached obedience to the status quo, then those who resisted were obeying some other law, such as the dictates of individual conscience. Notions of common good were also employed to challenge the legitimacy of Vichy, whether in terms of its failure to ensure basic rights or its disregard for universal human values.[35]

Critics of Vichy rightly saw that fundamental liberties were being negated. The powers of the state were enhanced at the expense of democratically elected communal bodies which were replaced by advisory councils. This was true at a national level, where a National Council consisting of luminaries and worthies replaced elected institutions in the formulation of laws. Towns of over two thousand inhabitants regressed to appointed rather than elected mayors, and the councillors were nominated too. Thirty-five of the eighty-seven prefects (the Napoleonic state's highest plenipotentiary in the regional *départements*) were purged, and most of the rest were rotated to other areas. They all had to swear an oath to Pétain; they were also put into uniform for the first time. Prefectorial autonomy was further constrained by the introduction of regional super-prefects whose writ ran across groups of *départements*. In their post-war testimony at the trials of Pétain and Laval, many prefects of that era depicted themselves as caught between the rival pressures of the Germans, the extreme collaborationists and, from 1941 onwards, the resistance.[36] The general population was controlled by a newly created national police force, including a mobile paramilitary riot formation, and was pinned down more precisely by the introduction of compulsory identity cards. Telephones were tapped and the mail intercepted; delation became a commonplace way of settling more intimate quarrels under an ideological guise. Special Section courts were set up to dispense lethally swift justice against Communists, as a French alternative to the Germans' desire to shoot large numbers of hostages in response to so-called terrorist atrocities. Although internment camps for (mostly anti-Nazi) Germans and Austrians or Republican refugees from Spain predated the war, and Communists were rounded up after the Molotov–Ribbentrop Pact, the Vichy regime filled them with their own opponents.

Pétain himself never mentioned Jews in his public speeches, but his court contained a number of vociferous anti-Semites, including his physician Bernard Ménétrel and the Justice Minister Raphaël Alibert. This probably explains why almost from its inception Vichy legislated for 'a France for the French' without German prompting, although the authorities were clearly informed about the Nazis' burning animus. In July 1940 legislation restricted access to the civil service, medicine and the law to people born to French fathers. This measure did not expressly mention Jews, but its impact on them was nonetheless disproportionate. In late August, Vichy repealed the 1939 Daladier–Marchandeau Law, which had given Jewish people brief respite from the publication of anti-Semitic defamations; thenceforth even blatant calls for violence were legal. In October, the Statute on the Jews used racial criteria to exclude Jews from the top posts in the civil service as well as the officer corps, and sought to break their alleged over-representation in journalism, teaching and the performing arts. This was especially crushing to people who saw themselves as essentially French. In the same month Algerian Jews were denaturalised as a seventy-year-old law granting them French citizenship was revoked.[37]

Meanwhile, in the Occupied Zone, the Germans conducted a census of the Jewish population, stamped 'Jew' in their identity cards and insisted that shops display signs reading 'Entreprise Juive–Judisches Geschäft' in their windows. This measure prompted many French shopkeepers to advertise 'Maison 100% française'. When in October the Germans introduced the registration of Jewish property and nomination of 'temporary administrators' for their business interests, Vichy sensed that aryanisation might entail germanisation, and so set up its own nationwide agency to administer such businesses itself. In March 1941 Vichy established its own General Commissariat for the Jewish Question under Xavier Vallat. A second statute defined Jewishness more expansively than the Nazis had done, and introduced further restrictions on Jews in literature and the arts.

A census of Jews in the Unoccupied Zone broke every French republican canon about the irrelevance of religious criteria in civic life.[38]

Unsolicited encounters with authority are rarely welcome, even when they are the police, social workers or traffic wardens of one's own country, whose powers are well defined and well known. Contemporary experience of Iraq and elsewhere has made us aware of the sheer alien physicality of foreign troops in someone else's country. Apart from their heavy combat garb, they are bigger, fitter and taller than anyone else. So it was with the Germans almost everywhere they ventured in their jackboots and forage caps (only the combat troops or those on guard duties wore the coal-scuttle helmets). The middle-aged art historian Agnès Humbert encountered her first German troops on a train from Limoges to Paris on 6 August 1940. They boarded the train as it halted on the demarcation line at Vierzon in the dead of night:

> I shall never forget the sight of two German soldiers entering our compartment by the dull light of their lamp, punctiliously greeting us with a 'Sieurs, dames', doubtless because they think it is the height of courtesy and terribly French. These are the first German soldiers I have seen. They demand to see my return papers, scrutinize them in minute detail, checking all the dates and stamps before finally waving their lamp in front of my face. Whatever for? My face isn't on any of the documents. My appearance evidently proves inoffensive, and they indicate with a guttural grunt that I am in order. Idiotic though it is, my nerves are strained to breaking point. My teeth are chattering: I hope they can't tell, but I'm terrified the Germans will hear their deafening clatter, like crazy castanets. How sickening it is to have to submit to inspection by these people, when all you want is to go home.[39]

The German occupiers were unevenly distributed throughout France, and were hardly a presence at all in the south until November 1942, when troops rapidly moved into the Unoccupied Zone. Their Italian partners simultaneously carved out a larger role for themselves, without even a dubious right of conquest following their humiliation by the French border garrisons in 1940. The Germans were confident and fit, in contrast to the dishevelled French soldiery they had beaten. Within a year that changed as the young and fit Germans were deployed to die on the Eastern Front and were replaced by older men who bore the usual marks of ageing humanity. Those who were veterans of the Great War often managed to forge bonds with former *poilus* (French infantrymen) they encountered or lodged with.[40]

Initially a hundred thousand German troops were deployed to maintain order in the Occupied Zone, although that figure dropped to sixty thousand in early 1942 as troops were drawn off to reinforce the Eastern Front, before rising again to two hundred thousand men in late 1943. Many of these men were stationed in the capital. The louche delights of Paris must have been seductive for men used to the hearty sportiness of Hitler's Germany, where ideal womanhood hurled a javelin or medicine ball. The Germans were thick on the ground in the smarter western quarters of Paris, with officers dining at Maxim's, Prunier's, the Tour d'Argent and other famous restaurants, while the other ranks ogled semi-naked dancers at the Moulin Rouge or Shéhérazade. High society, including the Beaumonts, Dubonnets, Harcourts, Mumms and Polignacs, easily accommodated the smarter sort of German. Their spiritual kin in the capital's brothels enjoyed their golden years, although afterwards the madames pleaded that it had been merely business or that they had reserved the boss-eyed whores exclusively for the Boches. All but seven thousand cars had been commandeered by the occupiers, leaving the French to take the Métro or travel by bicycle or on foot. Cycle-taxis enhanced the impression of Third World servitude, especially if the passengers were Germans and the driver French. The Métro was where most Parisians came into close physical proximity with the Germans, who took full advantage of being able to travel free to explore the sights. There one got the full martial reek of the conqueror's cheap soap, uniforms and leather, and a close view of the soldiers' short hair and thick muscular necks.

Across official Paris huge swastikas announced that the new order had arrived, lest one fail to notice the sentries in steel helmets and posts festooned with Gothic lettered military signs directing German traffic. A German military parade tramped down the Champs-Elysées every day to remind Parisians who was in charge. Former government buildings and luxury hotels were taken over by German agencies, notably the Hôtel Majestic, which housed the military HQ of Generals Otto and Carl-Heinrich von Stülpnagel, the Prussian cousins who successively ruled occupied France. Life in the Majestic, or the George V and Raphaël, where the Germans hobnobbed with the capital's cultural *gratin*, was very different in tone from the grimmer world of Hitler's field HQ in the east.[41] As conservative 'tin-soldiers' the Stülpnagels recruited a staff in their own image, that is middle-aged and older officers who had little enthusiasm for Nazism, a pose of moral fastidiousness belied by their eagerness to make careers under a grim totalitarian dictatorship.

Fifteen hundred German functionaries as well as businessmen and economists were seconded to Paris, most hand-picked by the former historian turned staff officer Hans Speidel. They liaised with such grand figures as the multi-decorated former cavalry officer Pierre-Charles Taittinger, the founder of the champagne house (and of a small Fascist party), who was chairman of the municipal council of the capital. Shared professional expertise meant that French judicial officials dealt with fellow lawyers, while even those Germans who made off with much of the country's wine were former shippers who knew Bordeaux or Beaune very well. German visitors included Goebbels, Göring and Rosenberg, the lead plunderers in removing a conservatively estimated 21,903 works of art, marshalled from public and private collections into the Jeu de Paume museum. Göring selected Goyas, Rembrandts and Rubens at his leisure, while his wife Edda bustled through Boucheron, Cartier, Dior, Hermès and Lanvin like a provincial shopper from hell.

Diplomatic relations with Vichy were handled by Otto Abetz, a former drawing teacher with a French wife, who had organised the inter-war Sohlberg Circle for Franco-German reconciliation. He returned to Paris to occupy the Hôtel de Beauharnais, now the German embassy. Socially adroit, Abetz was responsible for the largely one-way cultural traffic that was supposed to teach the French the cultural superiority of Germany.[42] A huge German Institute carried out the usual forms of cultural imperialism and subversion that go under the guise of false amity.

The SS, Gestapo and SD were also present, their HQ being in the avenue Foch and at 11 rue de Saussaies. They included Werner Best, deputy head of the Gestapo, who after differences with Heydrich was seconded to run the police and justice branch of the military administration with the rank of an army general. An initial SD complement of just twenty-five men under the thirty-year-old SD officer Helmut Knochen and his colleagues Kurt Lischka, thirty-one, and the Jewish expert Theo Dannecker, twenty-seven, were based at Hôtel Scribe with offices at 72 avenue Foch. Knochen was welcomed by the more mindless sort of society hostess, notably the millionaire Franco-American divorcee Florence Gould. The SS presence mushroomed to five thousand personnel after May 1942 under Knochen's successor, SS-General Karl Oberg. Two prisons were handed over for exclusive German use, including the Cherche-Midi, while the French shared the facilities of the Santé and Fresnes.[43] Fear preceded these men almost everywhere they went, but relations with regular German officers and troops were more complicated, as the latter generally behaved with studied correctness. At any one time there were about forty thousand German troops in Paris. As a world-renowned mecca of high culture and titillating entertainment, the former French capital offered endless possibilities of concerts, exhibitions, restaurants and theatre, as well as bars and nightclubs used for comradely carnivals by troops on leave from fighting fronts.

It is no accident that much of the literature on collaboration focuses on cultural areas, even though the sins of artists, journalists, musicians and writers were objectively negligible compared with those of the relatively anonymous bureaucrats, policemen, bus drivers and railwaymen who arranged the deportation of Jews and others. The recent literature argues that actors, comedians, musicians and writers have political views that should be taken seriously. Most creative artists thought first about their work and personal survival. Was war supposed to intrude into the work of a Bonnard, Braque or Gris? Should we think any the less of their paintings because it invariably did not, particularly when the work of those who did deal with the war was infallibly second or third rate? Were artists obliged to set a moral example or to discount their own professional survival, an expectation we do not routinely have of academics, bank managers, labourers or waiters?[44]

Those who have a highly ethical view of the creative artist's calling will find much to admire in the example of Jean Guéhenno who refused to publish (under his real name) during the occupation. But are we supposed to condemn (in so far as that has any utility) the elderly Matisse because he retreated into his atelier when the Germans moved into his house, to work out lifelong problems of form and colour? Would his work have grown through the inclusion of a few black panels or variations on the swastika? Arguably, ignoring Nazism as some sort of sordid interlude seems more damning. Matisse's younger contemporary Pablo Picasso had one of the most productive – and financially lucrative – periods of his life in occupied Paris, uneasily receiving visiting Germans while insinuating a vaguely oppositional left-wing air that translated into ostentatious postwar Communism. Picasso was protected from Franco by the Germans' fear of his celebrity, but mere celebrity often turned to notoriety as the fortunes of war changed.

Resembling fish out of water, some artistes could not live without the limelight, and were oblivious to the company they kept, like the actor Sacha

Guitry or the singers Maurice Chevalier, Edith Piaf and Charles Trenet. A homosexual southerner, Trenet went to some lengths to disprove malicious collaborationist charges that his surname was an anagram of the Jewish-sounding Netter. This enabled him to continue entertaining audiences that included German officers with lilting songs like 'Douce France', which conveyed a gaily nostalgic view of the country that bore little resemblance to its grim reality in the early 1940s. If that was a matter of taste, Trenet also sang for French prisoners of war in Germany, and hence collaborated in a less ambiguous sense. Those who ostentatiously and repeatedly courted German society, or who went on German-sponsored junkets to Hitler's Reich, crossed an important line. Some of those who did were the pianist Alfred Cortot and the opera singer Germaine Lubin, and the painters Derain, van Dongen and Vlaminck. The latter two, already known to be anti-Semitic and pro-Fascist, were to allege that they were able to negotiate the release of prisoners of war in return for their presence on such trips, although the historical record does not support their claims.

Singers and painters were never guilty of public incitement to, or justification of, crimes against humanity. They did not denounce their enemies or entire categories of people, nor did they call resistance fighters 'terrorists'. That was the lot of the collaborator wordsmiths, who were uniquely vulnerable should fortune's wheel take a further turn. Although one should not construe them as victims, writers, newspaper editors and journalists were especially liable to charges of collaboration, because they left a printed paper trail of their views, which was easy for investigators to compile and use against them after the liberation – although their publishers suffered few consequences for having made their work publicly available. Anyone who writes for publication, however polemically, knows the difference between raving and writing – the point where something that amuses at night is best left unsaid in the cold light of day, usually by consideration of the consequences for oneself or others. They also know, but can rarely do much about, the subsequent intrusions of sub-editors and headline writers who can sensationalise even the most considered utterances. While only Communists blame people for having thoughts, expressing them in a combustible context where they could do mortal harm is morally irresponsible, even when it is not the graver offence of incitement to murderous activity. Since most of these writers, such as Alfred Fabre-Luce and Robert Brasillach, were dedicated ideological Fascists and anti-Semites, they could at least argue consistency. Brasillach was an admirer of the sinister spectacle of Nazism, and used the journal *Je Suis Partout* (I am

Everywhere) to attack other writers, the Jews and the Republic. During the Occupation this escalated to the occasional denunciation of identifiable opponents of the regime and to a notorious statement that seemed to approve of Vichy's deportation of Jewish children.[45]

But collaboration also concerned millions of humdrum civil servants, employers and ordinary working folk, whose attitude was 'We're going to work for the Boches. So what? One has to live.' Was a French worker who sought a threefold wage increase by working for the Todt Organisation constructing Hitler's Atlantic Wall less culpable than a factory owner who took on German contracts to secure raw materials to guarantee the livelihoods of a workforce who would have been deported to Germany if unemployed? Was a wine grower, denied British or US export markets, supposed to let grapes wither on the vine rather than sell the poor vintages (such as 1939) or the sub-standard stuff falsely labelled as premium product, to the Germans who in turn might supply him with copper sulphate, fertiliser or sugar if he co-operated? And then there were the bus drivers who took Jews from Drancy to railheads, and the notoriously left-wing railwaymen who certainly interrupted the flow of forced labour from France to Germany, but did not interdict even one of the eighty-five special trains used to deport Jews. Moreover, throughout the occupation, a large number of ordinary people denounced others for concealing a weapon, hoarding food or being a Jew, mainly for reasons of petty spite within families or between neighbours. Such was the case of a woman and her lover who denounced her prisoner-of-war husband for hiding a gun when he returned after two years, to get him out of the way again. These grubby complicities of the common man (or woman) deserve more attention than is devoted to mere celebrities like Cocteau, Chevalier or Coco Chanel.[46]

Throughout France, the occupied encountered the occupiers with patchy frequency; collaboration was therefore partly a question of geographical or occupational fate. The Germans were unlikely to trouble an isolated farmer, but bar staff, chambermaids, cooks, typists and waitresses in garrison towns would have had frequent dealings with them, as did young primary school teachers, as troops were often billeted in school buildings. As these were largely female occupations, the opportunities for horizontal collaboration increased, especially since so many French men had died in war, were languishing in captivity or were labouring in Germany. Such relationships symbolised the active–passive relationship between the two countries and hence attracted focused opprobrium, especially if the women involved leveraged it to their wider advantage.

From the start, attempts were made to delineate moral boundaries, or rules for casual contact, as had already been elaborated in late 1939 in occupied Poland. An early tract, called *Conseils à l'occupé* written by the Socialist Jean Texcier in July 1940, recommended limited civility in everyday dealings with the Germans. Although busloads of them regularly debouched at the Eiffel Tower or Louvre, Texcier reminded his compatriots that these tourists were armed with more than their Leica cameras. People should affect not to understand German, and politely cut short small talk delivered in halting French. It was all right to respond to a request for a light from a cigarette. Texcier advised people to avoid parades and concerts by military bands in favour of the less corrupting sound of birds singing in the countryside. Others recommended avoidance of direct eye contact, or pretending that these men were not there.

Such manifestations of shunning indifference probably came easily to anyone encountering arrogant or bullying Germans barking out orders or behaving boorishly; but it was more challenging to handle those who knew some French or were Francophone in outlook, or demonstrated humanity and refinement, perhaps by remarking 'La guerre, grosse malheur' and similar eirenic platitudes. Such a personage, a lame young German officer called Werner von Ebrennac, a composer in civilian life, is billeted on an old man (the narrator) and his niece in Jean Bruller's novella *Le Silence de la mer*, which was published under the pseudonym Vercors. The silence refers both to the recommended French response to the organised enthusiasm of the Germans and to the muzzle imposed, or consciously adopted, by those French writers who refused to join the literary collaborationists in the limelight. Ebrennac quickly learns to civilianise himself for his nightly fireside monologues about German culture (genius of) and Franco-German reconciliation. Every night he changes out of uniform into casual civilian clothes. His speeches are delivered with a certain philosophising passion, although they elicit no response whatsoever because the wordy flood is an imperialistic assault in itself, delivered without any regard to the responses or sensitivities of the French couple. The silence becomes as oppressive as lead. The novella also repeats the pattern common to many occupation rumours, of the scales falling from, in this case, a naive German's eyes, although in the rumours it was more often the French who were rapidly disabused about the winning characteristics of the occupier. After hundreds of monologues, Ebrennac appears as a changed man one night, and the old man relents and invites him to sit down for the first time. Ebrennac's anticipations of Franco–German amity have been shattered by fellow Germans, including a poet friend from university days, all stationed in Paris, who severally inform him: 'We have the chance to destroy France, and destroy her we will. Not only her material power: her soul as well. Particularly her soul ... We'll turn it rotten with our smiles and our consideration. We'll make a grovelling bitch of her.' Appalled by their lack of self-awareness, Ebrennac announces to his French hosts that he has volunteered for 'hell' on the Eastern Front, a curious way of expiating barbarity. At the point of his departure, the girl finally utters a faint 'Adieu'.[47]

The occupation of France experienced a minor phoney war of its own, although it is worth recalling that German military courts sentenced ninety-three people to death before May 1941, of whom a third were executed. This relatively peaceful phase ended with the first killing by French civilians of a member of the German armed forces, on 21 August 1941. This was the handiwork of Communists, who after their own period of ideologically determined anti-patriotism in the wake of the Molotov–Ribbentrop Pact smartly rediscovered their anti-Fascism following the German invasion of the Soviet motherland. Alfons Moser, a German naval adjutant, was shot dead by a former member of the anti-Francoist International Brigades in a Paris Métro station. A few hours later, a non-commissioned officer was critically wounded at another station. Even convinced patriots had their doubts about the morality of these random assassinations, which met with reprobation among ordinary people. The method seemed cowardly and German reprisals were likely to fall first on innocent bystanders rather than on the killers, who would have planned their escape. As a result of these shootings the Germans immediately decreed that any prisoners held by them or on their behalf were to be treated as hostages, and that 150 of them would be shot. Upon further reflection the Germans suggested that if French courts would sentence ten notorious Communists to death and execute them, then they would spare the lives of the 150. They gave the Vichy authorities five days to make up their minds to co-operate. Maurice Gabolde, the Justice Minister, left an eloquent account of what happened, it being worth noting that de Gaulle had instructed the judges to remain in place to prevent courts being hijacked by Fascist zealots. The Vichy judicial authorities passed a law setting up Special Sections in courts of appeal which retroactively could sentence certain people to death in connection with terrorist crimes. The Special Section in Paris condemned ten Communists to death, of whom only three were subsequently executed, for the judges were adept at finding mitigating circumstances. Despite this, the judges were also prime candidates for assassination by the resistance, with some gunned down within or on the thresholds of their courtrooms.[48]

The reflex historical response of the German army to violent assault was to shoot hostages detained for that purpose. Although hostage-taking and execution in response to irregular acts of war was legal – under severe constraints – disproportionate, hence illegal, reprisals were mandated by the High Command of the German Wehrmacht. It was a policy of military terrorism that constituted the first, rather than final, response to assassinations and sabotage. Under German military law only senior commanders could take civilian hostages, and only divisional commanders could order their execution. They operated according to a sliding scale, depending on their view of the occupied population's racial value and whether a German soldier had been killed or wounded. Under these codes, for each German killed in Denmark, five Danes would be shot, or two in the case of woundings. In France and Holland these figures increased to ten for one or five for one, depending on whether Germans were killed or injured. In Poland the number of reprisal shootings rose from ten to one (1939) to fifty to one (1940) and to one hundred to one (1941). In the Balkans and occupied Soviet Union it was not uncommon for three hundred people to die in reprisal for the killing of a single German. Between September 1941 and February 1942, some twenty thousand people were shot by way of reprisal in Serbia, one of the worst incidents occurring at Kragujevac, where the Germans murdered 2,300 Jews and Communists after one of their columns was ambushed. Further refinements included public hangings, with the corpses left pendant as an awful warning, or the trans-European 'Night and Fog' operation after December 1941, under which suspected resisters simply disappeared into Nazi concentration camps.[49]

Early on 20 October 1941, two German officers left a café in Nantes and set off for their offices. It was before sunrise. They were stalked by two men, Gilbert Brustlein and Spartaco Guisco, respectively aged twenty-two and thirty-one, who shot only one of the Germans because Spartaco's gun jammed. Lieutenant Colonel Karl Hotz shouted, 'The bastards!' as he toppled over on the pavement, while his lucky comrade Captain Sieger called for medical help. The two assassins fled by tram, while a third conspirator, seventeen-year-old Marcel Boudarias, who had helped them plant bombs on the railway earlier that night, remained in town. The dead man was the local German commander, a sixty-four-year-old who, like many of the occupation personnel, had worked in Nantes before the war, where as a former officer on the 1914–18 Bavarian General Staff he had enjoyed close relations with the local French military aristocracy. A gifted musician, Hotz liked France and was no Nazi. The local French authorities knew they should be worried.

On learning of Hotz's death, Keitel demanded that between 100 and 150 hostages should be shot, while a reward of one million gold francs was posted for information leading to the capture of his killers. Clearly resentful of these edicts from on high, Otto von Stülpnagel decreed that a hundred should be shot, but spared them for three days to allow the assassins to be caught. Later that day Hitler intervened, insisting that fifty die immediately, with another fifty to be shot in forty-eight hours' time. Apart from issues of humanity, the army commander in France thought that such policies would be politically counter-productive, whereas Hitler and Keitel were immersed in eastern campaigns where atrocities and mass murder were the order of the day. They also believed they were facing a pan-European Communist campaign of sabotage and murder.[50] Even when the French authorities tried to spare lives, mitigation of German policy could become mimetic of it. The Interior Minister, Pierre Pucheu, protested that of the first fifty hostages, forty were war veterans. The Germans duly substituted a different list of forty Communists for the forty veterans. Pucheu said nothing, even though he was effectively valuing one Frenchman above another by virtue of their ideology. Further down the scale, the local notables in Nantes tried to moderate the German response, with the mayor and prefect expressing their sincere condolences for Hotz's death. Meanwhile, more radical elements in the German military regime had decided that executing Communists would lack wider social purchase, as many Frenchmen of many political persuasions detested them anyway. Although the Vichy authorities tried to incline them towards Communist internees, the German Abwehr, which made the ultimate call as to who was to be shot, insisted on including a group of middle-aged Nantais war veterans imprisoned for helping French POWs escape. Both the subprefect and local clergy endeavoured to have some of the men released from their fate. They were too late, and on 22 October all of the first group were shot at two different locations, profoundly shocking the local population.

Attention shifted to the second group of fifty hostages, due to be executed on the 24th. Pétain offered to surrender himself at the demarcation line as a symbolic sacrifice, although his ministers rapidly talked him out of this gesture. The desperate efforts of local figures to mitigate human

ABOVE: 'Banzai!' (meaning 'Ten Thousand Years of Imperial Reign') cried Japanese troops from atop the Great Wall of China in March 1933.

BELOW: An idealised vision of Abyssinia a year after the Italians had conquered it, in a poster for an Italian bank in Addis Ababa. Chemical munitions were used to subdue the Abyssinians.

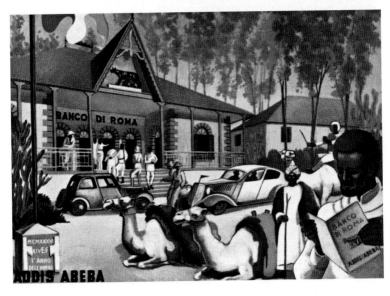

ABOVE: An off-handed Hitler welcomes a stiff Neville Chamberlain to Berchtesgaden in September 1938.

LEFT: Although not as familiar as their counterparts in the Nazi SS, the Soviet NKVD were equally omnipresent in the Soviet Union, including these border guards, routinely engaged in keeping the comrades in, rather than spies out.

RIGHT: A vaguely sickening visualisation of Polish-Soviet amity celebrating the September 1939 Soviet invasion of the eastern half of Poland, after which the NKVD deported and murdered anyone unwilling to conform to their rule.

BELOW: Germans amuse themselves while liquidating the Cracow ghetto in March 1943.

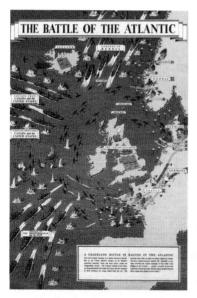

ABOVE: This graphic captures the drama and scope of the naval struggle around Britain, in which so many merchant mariners of all nations, and German submariners, lost their lives.

ABOVE: Comics were an essential means of enthusing boys for future service in the armed forces, as well as a form of escapism for the men who were often little more than boys serving in them.

BELOW: This famous David Low cartoon captured the belligerence of Britain at war under Winston Churchill and his tripartisan cabinet.

ALL BEHIND YOU, WINSTON

ABOVE: Italian mountain troops show affection to a German comrade in Russia (August 1941). Relations between the Axis allies were more complicated, and many of these Italians would perish in combat or captivity.

BELOW: German troops taking a break to eat and smoke amidst a burning town in the Soviet Union during a campaign where the rules of war had been erased or re-written to license genocidal atrocities.

LEFT: Reichsführer-SS Heinrich Himmler consulting two SS cavalry commanders, Hermann Fegelein (rear) and Kurt Knoblauch (front) in Russia. Such informal conversations were at the dark heart of the 'Final Solution' of the 'Jewish Question' in which over six million Jews were murdered.

BELOW: An Einsatzgruppe commander exhorting his staff officers to greater exertions.

BELOW: This photograph of the Japanese Imperial Council illustrates the militarisation of government and the central role of Emperor Hirohito in discussions which were acrimonious, protracted and wide-ranging as Japan sought to realise its Asian destiny.

ABOVE: From 1928 to 1930, Kuribayashi studied in the United States. He wrote copious letters to his wife and children, including this letter to his young son, which featured a car cut out from a magazine to illustrate the vehicle he had recently purchased.

BELOW: 'The Tiger of Malaya', General Yamashita, after whom the doctrine of command responsibility takes its name following his trial and execution for war crimes.

ABOVE: General Tadamichi Kuribayashi, who died defending the island of Iwo Jima.

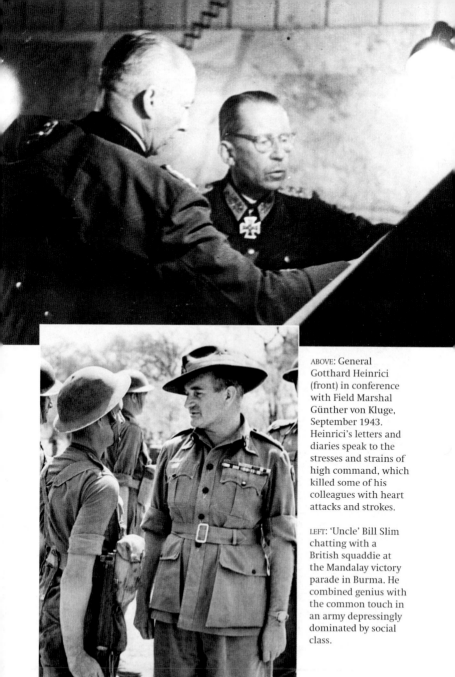

ABOVE: General Gotthard Heinrici (front) in conference with Field Marshal Günther von Kluge, September 1943. Heinrici's letters and diaries speak to the stresses and strains of high command, which killed some of his colleagues with heart attacks and strokes.

LEFT: 'Uncle' Bill Slim chatting with a British squaddie at the Mandalay victory parade in Burma. He combined genius with the common touch in an army depressingly dominated by social class.

· suffering were noteworthy. The mayor of Nantes, the prefect and the local bishop urgently appealed to the better nature of Hotz's replacement, a Catholic aristocrat named Baron von und zu Bodman. Other worthies sought out Vichy's ambassador to the Occupied Zone, warning that the first wave of executions 'has plunged our town into a painful stupor, a sort of moral darkness from which there is no telling what unstoppable emotions may arise if the volleys of a second execution ring out tomorrow'. They also asked a leading literary collaborator to intercede with Abetz. In Nantes, the authorities endeavoured to ensure that Hotz's funeral would be orderly and uneventful, while Bodman sought to place the blame for his predecessor's death on the English. The bishop prevailed upon Cardinal Suhard of Paris to plead with Hitler. Local aristocrats mobilised their local German SS and military contacts to intercede at Hitler's headquarters. Finally, the relatives of the first group of hostages submitted a petition pleading for the lives of the second group.[51]

Perhaps most crucially, Stülpnagel wrote to Hitler, not appealing to his humanity, but outlining the political implications of executing the hostages. He was advised by the Gestapo chief Werner Best, who drew on his experiences of French shooting of German hostages in the occupied Rhineland in the 1920s, which had stiffened resistance. Best counselled that mass executions of hostages would be to play the enemy's own game. Stülpnagel informed Hitler that while Pétain's Deputy Admiral François Darlan had expressed sympathy for such a military response, executions would benefit the British, who were using 'small groups of terrorists' to sow wider bitterness and dissension among the French. He had counselled against the adoption of 'Polish methods' and now felt that his authority was at stake because of the imposition 'from above' of inflexible methods that jeopardised 'a reconciliation of the two peoples'. On 24 October Hitler gave the hostages a seventy-two-hour stay of execution. After that had expired the executions were postponed indefinitely. When the attacks continued, Best recommended a modified response which would minimise public outrage by focusing on a more select group of victims rather than the general population.

On future occasions, a collective fine would be imposed on the Jewish community, while predominantly Jewish detainees would be deported for forced labour in the east. Best hoped that the public would accept this division of French and Jews, thereby implicitly projecting his own hatreds on to the French as a whole. When on 28 November three German soldiers were assassinated, Stülpnagel recommended to the Wehrmacht High

Command that fifty Jewish and Communist hostages, rather than the three hundred Hitler decreed, should be shot, while the Jews of Paris had to rustle up a huge collective fine. He also recommended that a thousand Jews be sent east. When more attacks occurred a few days later, Stülpnagel added another fifty people to those to be executed and a further five hundred Communists to the ranks of deportees. In the event, ninety-five people were executed, of whom fifty-eight were Jews. Only transport difficulties prevented the deportation of fifteen hundred people. Further attacks meant that by early 1942 some 260 people had been executed. Since this did not prevent the attacks, Best extended a mandatory death sentence to anyone found guilty of Communist activity of any kind. Prisoners already convicted of capital offences were to be executed in the wake of any fresh attack. Moreover, with 10,000 Jews and 3,500 Communists in jail, Stülpnagel was experiencing a crisis of prison capacity which made it difficult to carry out any more mass arrests. On 15 January 1942 he wrote to Hitler and Keitel, saying that he could not reconcile further mass shootings of hostages with either his conscience or the judgement of history. He said the only solution to the crisis in the prisons was to deport the internees to the east, but that would have a dramatic political effect. When Hitler and Keitel replied that they wanted more mass shootings as well as deportations, Stülpnagel resigned his command. Policy settled down into an established pattern of strike, reprisal, counter-strike, counter-reprisal. On 18 April twenty-four hostages were shot and a thousand deported east; six days later ten people were shot and five hundred deported. By the end of May, 471 people had been executed and six thousand deported to Auschwitz.[52]

If only minorities collaborated with the Germans, while majorities coped with bleak conditions, during 1941 there were signs that others were prepared to undertake the enormous risks of resistance. Before that can be discussed in a meaningful way, we must follow Hitler's armies into the Soviet Union, the course of events that radicalised and strained the Nazi regime to the point where its exactions did indeed set Europe ablaze, while ensuing events in the Far East made the war truly global.

Effects of Russian campaign — strained & radicalised Nazis

CHAPTER 8

Barbarossa

I 'HAPPY PROSPECTS'

On the morning of Sunday 30 March 1941, a hundred of Germany's top military commanders made their way through Albert Speer's new Reich Chancellery, massed boots echoing on the marble floors. They were the elite among Germany's more than 2,300 active generals. They included Bock, Kluge, Guderian, Leeb, Küchler, Hoepner, Hoth, Manstein, Rundstedt, Reichenau, Schobert and Carl-Heinrich von Stülpnagel: the majority were aristocratic, Prussian Protestants, on average men of fifty-eight years of age, although some, like Rundstedt, were considerably older. (Kleist and Weichs were unavoidably absent, on the frontiers of Greece and Yugoslavia, as was Falkenhorst who sent his apologies from Norway.) The generals entered, via an inner courtyard, passing between two of Arno Breker's sculpted giants, respectively clutching sword and torch. These symbolised the might of the Wehrmacht and the fervour of the Party. Five field marshals and dozens of generals ascended endless flights of stairs, and walked down a long marble gallery, hung with tapestries illustrating the life of Alexander the Great, past the Führer's office.

At 11 a.m. Hitler entered the main auditorium, where he addressed the assembled throng. He spoke for two and a half hours and took no questions, for this was not a meeting of equals. Many of the men sitting before him had benefited from executing his bold strategic gambles in Poland and France: with field marshals' batons and generals' ranks as well as big bonuses to their salaries. Some claim they had been corporately corrupted by the battlefield successes they owed to the dictator's strategic audacity.[1] Skilfully allaying his auditors' historic fears of two-front wars, Hitler dwelled on the strategic and ideological necessity of destroying Bolshevik

Russia before it entered the war on Britain's side. Such an attack would extinguish British hopes of external deliverance, while the Japanese would surely keep the Americans, who were expected to join the British, occupied in the Pacific too. With the resources of the Soviet Union and continental mastery, Germany could hope to win any future war for world domination against the 'Anglo-Saxons'.

The invasion of the USSR, which Hitler announced to this gathering of the commanders chosen to execute it, was intended to destroy the Soviet state, creating protectorates for non-ethnic Russians, while the rest would become a congeries of backward republics. The moral justification was that in the autumn of 1939 Stalin had hoped that Germany would bleed itself to death in the war following the invasion of Poland. Despite the deliveries of grain and raw materials, he had not ceased Communist subversion in Germany. Hitler insinuated that this was to be a preventative war before the Soviets could overwhelm Germany, whereas behind the talk of a racial conflict lay a desperate quest to secure the economic resources needed for a showdown with Britain and a US which was growing ever stronger as it prepared for war.[2] Throughout his address, Hitler made various remarks about the temper of the campaign, which the panzer commander Hermann Hoth noted in attenuated form: 'Russia perpetual source of the anti-social', 'ideological struggle against Bolshevism', '[military] Justice too humane ... protecting them instead of killing them', 'Crimes of the Russian Commissars. Everywhere they appeared, Latvia, Galicia, Baltic wreaked Asiatic havoc', 'Deserve no mercy', 'Not to be handed over to courts martial, instead the troops are to immediately get rid of them', 'Don't relocate them to rear areas'.

This was going to be 'a struggle for our existence', waged not according to the rules observed in the West, but in line with the uncivilised nature of the Bolshevik opponent.[3] As Chief of the General Staff Franz Halder observed in his diary: 'In the east hardness now is mildness for the future'; the assembled generals and their subordinate officers had 'to demand a great sacrifice of themselves in overcoming their reservations'.[4] Two things were clear from this address, with which there was no recorded disagreement. Hitler had decided to murder Soviet commissars, while the civilian population was to be excluded from the heavily restricted ambit of military justice. Another straw in the wind was that Hitler mentioned the SS-Leibstandarte bandmaster who, much against the Führer's own wishes, had been subject to judicial proceedings for killing fifty Jewish hostages in Poland two years earlier, the only oblique reference that morning to the Jews.

Planning for Operation Barbarossa had commenced in a dilatory fashion in the summer of 1940 under General Erich Marcks, with the staff officer Friedrich Paulus designated as the full-time planning co-ordinator only from September onwards. It assumed more urgency in January 1941, while the divisional commanders were admitted into the circle of trust between April and early June. As for ordinary soldiers, the experience of a twenty-year-old corporal, Bernhard Graml, elder brother of a famous German historian, was probably typical. On 30 May 1941 he and other men from the 167th Infantry Division boarded goods trains in the hope that they were going to France. As they clattered eastwards, via Berlin, they were puzzled to be given Polish money: 'nobody thought of an attack on Russia'. What was really afoot did not become clear until 21 June, when their company leader told them that the following morning they were going to cross the River Bug in dinghies, after which thought was drowned out in a flurry of specific orders.[5]

Hitler had mixed views on some of the allies destined to accompany the Germans into Russia. He thought the Finns would fight bravely under an indifferent leadership, whereas the Rumanians were 'cowardly, corrupt and depraved'. The involvement of Slovakian and Hungarian troops was settled only after the German invasion had started, their chief utility being to give Operation Barbarossa the appearance of a pan-European anti-Bolshevik crusade. An Italian army corps would arrive only in July.[6]

The eagerness of Marshal Ion Antonescu to take part in a revanchist anti-Communist holy war meant that a major German military mission arrived in Rumania in October 1940, even before Rumania had formally joined the Axis. The Luftwaffe complement alone consisted of fifty thousand men. The Rumanians were only inducted into the sheer scale of what was afoot at a very late stage. Although Hitler satisfied Antonescu's vanity on 12 June 1941, when he recognised him as commander-in-chief of all forces in Rumania, Rumanian troops were destined to play second fiddle to General Eugen Ritter von Schobert's Eleventh Army as it massed on the Russian frontier.[7]

Since September 1940, the Finnish government had allowed German forces to transit Finland to reach northern Norway for a planned but never realised assault on Murmansk. By December 1940, the Finnish General Staff were vaguely aware of German plans to attack Russia, although Halder had rather presumptuously already factored Finland into German invasion plans. While the Finnish political leadership preferred the public fiction of being sucked into a German–Soviet war after it had started, joint military planning between Germans and Finns commenced in May 1941, with thirty thousand German troops on Finnish territory by mid-June. The Finns hoped their activity would provoke a Soviet response, to which Finland might respond without being seen to be the aggressor. Although the notion of an anti-Communist crusade was popular in Finland, a limited revanchist 'separate war' against the hereditary foe played better internationally, for, after all, the Finnish army had been re-equipped since 1940 not only by the Germans but also by the British and US.[8]

The finalised German invasion plan proved too short-sighted in scope, while the execution revealed the limits of corrective improvisation. A battle of annihilation was blended with a war of political and racial extermination. This involved such absurdities as using scarce railway stock to ship German Jews eastwards to their deaths. There was much wishful thinking about the enemy. The underlying assumption was that the mass of the Red Army would be destroyed on or near the western frontiers of the Soviet Union, which were in a state of flux after the novel circumstances created by the occupation of eastern Poland and the Baltic. While the Stalin Line within the USSR's previous frontier was being dismantled, the Molotov Line two hundred miles further west was under construction. A bonus was that attempts to raise the Red Army's level of alert were thwarted by Stalin's anxiety not to do anything provocative. Planners had to reconcile Hitler's desire to conquer simultaneously the major political and economic conurbations of Leningrad, Moscow and Kiev – or rather his apocalyptic drive to level them to the ground – with Halder's and Brauchitsch's more traditionally minded intention of striking a decisive blow against the mass of the Red Army west of the Dvina–Dnepr rivers. The resulting plans combined these eccentric and concentric approaches, as well as the divided focus on economic, political, racial–ideological and military objectives.

The invasion consisted of three vast army groups, North, Centre and South, although Centre had the lion's share of armour, with two panzer armies to the others' one. Tanks would break through and encircle Russian armies, which would be mopped up by the infantry formations that followed in their wake. From the autumn of 1941, some sixty German divisions would remain in Russia, holding a line from the Volga to Archangel, from beyond which the Soviet air force could never menace the Reich, while the Luftwaffe could destroy the last remaining industrial centres in the Urals. Only these divisions were to be given winter gear, for the mass of the invading army would have been withdrawn before the onset of cold and snow. In the event, because it would have taken 255 trains to move just the clothing for sixty divisions, none of it was supplied on time. The Wehrmacht was to fight into the Russian winter wearing summer denim kit.

This was a struggle between a nation of eighty millions and a polyglot empire of 171 millions, admittedly including many new citizens of countries Stalin had invaded. Germany had a total of 208 divisions in 1941, of which 167 were at full strength; 146 of these were deployed to attack Russia, together with fourteen Rumanian divisions in the south and sixteen Finnish divisions that would push towards Leningrad. This was nothing like the numerical superiority generally regarded as necessary to such an operation, for the Soviets had 186 divisions in the west and a total of 303 potentially available across the Red Empire's vastness. The Soviets had also ramped up their output of weaponry in the years before the war, leading the Germans to underestimate the numbers of tanks and aircraft available to their opponent. The Soviets also had considerable industrial resources and supplies of coal, oil and steel, located far beyond German reach. To match these, the Germans would have had to integrate and exploit the economies of occupied Europe, but when the invasion started there were few signs of that, beyond stealing every lorry in France.[9] Not much thought went into the contingency that a swift battle of annihilation might degenerate into a punishing war of attrition, in physical conditions worse than those of the Great War.

Given that the entire operation depended on using railways to move supplies as far east as possible, where they would be shifted forward on trucks, German planners seriously underestimated the problems of using the broader-gauge Soviet rail network and a Third World road system that alternated between dust, mud and ice. Although the Germans succeeded in converting fourteen thousand miles of track to their own gauge, and brought in six thousand locomotives from their own relatively neglected Reichsbahn, the invading armies suffered chronic logistical problems. The figures are striking. Army Group Centre needed twenty-four train loads of supplies a day, but received only half that amount. Army Group North needed thirty-four train loads a day; instead it was lucky if there were eighteen. Army Group South, which required twenty-four trainloads of supplies a day, got only fourteen. Overall, the number of trains reaching the Eastern Front fell from 2,093 in September 1941 to 1,860 (October), 1,710 (November) and 1,643 (December), and dropped further to 1,420 in January 1942.[10]

Nor were German military dispositions flawless, while military intelligence was definitely the poor relation of bold operational planning. Apart from the general danger that marauding tank formations could easily become detached from the infantry trailing on their flanks or rear, it was clear that only the Centre Group would be able to carry out armoured pincer movements, as the other two groups were like a crab missing a claw, or a hammer its anvil. There were other mistakes born of over-confidence. The operational timetable was for a campaign of eleven to fourteen weeks, including three weeks to refit and recuperate, beginning in May 1941 and ending in September before the onset of winter, although in the event the unexpected diversion caused by the invasion of Greece and Yugoslavia meant that the starting date was postponed by a month. The Germans were so confident of victory that in December 1940 these projections shrank to between eight and eleven weeks, still including the three-week pause. By April, some commanders were predicting victory in four weeks.[11]

This reflected a general hubristic contempt for the enemy, evident in the nineteenth-century cliché that Russia was a 'colossus with feet of clay'. The German generals completely concurred with Hitler's view, although their outward confidence was sometimes accompanied by an underlying anxiety. Stalin had shot many of the capable officers whom at least five of the German commanders remembered fondly from joint exercises in the Weimar era. These men noted that Jews seemed to abound in Bolshevik government offices, although what that was supposed to reveal about military efficiency went unsaid. The Soviet performance in Finland had made the Red Army an international laughing stock; little attention was paid to its contemporaneous victory over the Japanese at Khalkhin Gol. The Germans thought that the Russians were poorly led and badly equipped. The former may have been true, but in purely material terms the Soviets were superior to their enemy. Of course, underestimation of the Russians was common enough elsewhere. Britain's Secret Intelligence Service gave the Russians ten days, Ambassador Stafford Cripps a month, while the Chief of the Imperial General Staff was only slightly more optimistic, predicting six weeks before the Soviets collapsed. Privately, Churchill also thought the Soviets would be defeated, although after the invasion he drily commented: 'If Hitler invaded Hell, [I] would at least make a favourable reference to the Devil.'[12]

While much German mental energy went into murdering political commissars, fear of whom allegedly held this Soviet rabble together, only Rosenberg, who was a Russian-speaking Baltic German, urged that attention be paid to how nationalist resentment against Soviet imperialism might be politically exploited beyond subtracting the wavering non-

Russian nationalities. Oddly enough for a police state, Nazi Germany underrated the extent to which another totalitarian power might militarise and dragoon its own population, and the extent to which defence of Communism's material achievements would be skilfully blended with Russian patriotism and religious Orthodoxy.[13]

It was also conceived as a war of annihilation with no holds barred. The Soviet Union had not signed the Geneva Conventions, although in principle Germany was obliged to observe them unilaterally. Having conceded at least one blatant contravention of the laws of war, the generals readily accepted several more, although retrospectively they were to recall raised eyebrows, red faces and fists clenched impotently in their pockets. On 3 April 1941, the Wehrmacht High Command limited the absolute authority of military commanders to the immediate operational areas at the front, leaving the SS free to carry out special tasks in the vast rear areas that were destined for civilian rule. Although the army had its own Secret Field Police and Field Gendarmerie, the generals concurred in this division of labour, as extended supply lines, and huge numbers of Russian soldiers adrift behind the combat zones, were major vulnerabilities in the invasion plan. As a result of a formal agreement dated 28 April, the SS could deploy SD and Security Police task forces in these areas to destroy any manifestations of resistance that might jeopardise the Germans' logistical tail. It was implicit that these special tasks included the racial–ideological warfare the generals had fitfully objected to in Poland; doubly so since the 'Jewish-Bolshevik' commissars were perceived as more of an active menace than the weedy 'kaftan Jews' of the Polish *shtetl*, who were merely alien rather than malicious.[14] There was an obvious ethical change in the attitudes of senior German commanders between the Polish and Russian campaigns. General Küchler may have protested about SS depredations in Poland in 1939; two years later he told his Eighteenth Army subordinates that 'we shouldn't worry ourselves about their activities'. As we shall see, he was more than prepared to connive in them when it suited his utilitarian calculations. Many of his comrades did not confine themselves to such studied indifference. Nor could the generals pretend that SS activities were a mystery. At a joint conference held in Berlin on 6 June 1941, senior SS figures explained to army chiefs that their remit was to lay the foundations for the final eradication of Bolshevism, by dealing with 'Jews, émigrés and terrorists' with 'the most extreme hardness and sharpness'.[15]

Another flagrant breach of the laws of war involved the army's own logistical arrangements, which were drawn up in anticipation of a total cessation of the grain and meat deliveries that Stalin had been paying as protection money to his fellow gangster. On 23 May 1941, General Georg Thomas issued a series of general guidelines that broadly divided the USSR into a surplus-yielding area and another that depended on it, ideas worked out in conjunction with Herbert Backe, the State Secretary for Agriculture. Thomas cynically remarked that Russians were accustomed to adjusting their consumption to indifferent harvests. In the light of that, agricultural surpluses should be diverted to the German army, or to the Reich itself, regardless of the starvation that was bound to affect those in the non-agricultural northerly regions. For there were 'tens of millions' of surplus Russians who could either emigrate to Siberia or perish.

In a further embrace of criminality, that month Keitel endorsed Hitler's decree on the exercise of military jurisdiction in the area of Operation Barbarossa. This instrument restricted martial law to those German delinquencies that undermined the army's image or military discipline, including running amok, or rape and pillage. It is an odd legal document, as it concluded by exculpating potential criminals: there was no obligation to prosecute offenders, and the contributory role of Bolshevism in Weimar Germany's plight was to be admitted as a mitigating circumstance at courts martial. What the decree licensed with reference to the entire civilian population was even more ominous. It allowed German soldiers summarily to shoot any civilians actively engaged in resistance, although this was ill defined. Officers were to become involved only in the case of shooting persons merely suspected of resisting. Collective reprisals, in the form of burning down entire villages, were legitimised.[16]

The sole concern of the generals who commented on drafts of this decree was with orderly practice, although from the victims' perspective it was academic whether their homes were destroyed by drunken psychotics or by disciplined units acting under orders from their superiors. These stipulations were in breach of the Hague Laws of Land Warfare and of the Manual for General Staff Officers during War issued on 1 August 1939. So too were the Guidelines for the Treatment of Political Commissars issued by the Wehrmacht High Command on 6 June 1941, which set in motion Hitler's plan to kill such people as announced at the 30 March Berlin conference. They were to be shot on apprehension or, following the issuance of further orders during the campaign, after subsequent identification in prisoner-of-war camps. The Commissar Order went in writing to each army group and to individual army headquarters, but it was to be relayed orally further down the chain of command, in itself indirect evidence that it was regarded as illegal by everyone concerned. There is no evidence that any commanders objected to the Commissar Order at the time – indeed some of them, such as Generals Hoepner and Küchler, had already issued identical instructions before they received it.[17]

Finally, the Germans anticipated capturing millions of prisoners within the opening weeks after major battles of encirclement. In theory, those POWs whom the army did not put to work without pay at the front were to be shepherded back through a series of Dulags, or holding camps in the rear areas operated by the relevant section of Army High Command. From there they were to be moved on to Stalags for enlisted men and officers' Oflags in the General Government and East Prussia run under the aegis of the Wehrmacht High Command. In reality, every article of the Geneva Conventions regarding POWs was to be flouted. Germany's limited logistical capacity meant that transporting millions of prisoners to camps in the rear or beyond was going to be a problem. No attempts were made to inform international agencies such as the Red Cross or the Vatican of their capture and condition. Although one's impression is of Soviet prisoners as an undifferentiated mass, in fact the Germans kept individual records, although the majority of them ended up in the archives of the NKVD after the war. Approximately one in eight of the so-called prisoners were not even members of the Red Army, but rather hapless civilians impressed into its employ and then scooped into captivity. Prisoners were not allowed to communicate with their families nor were they allowed their own recognised representatives. So much was clear before a single man had been captured.[18]

II UNDER A BAD STAR

At first the invasion went according to plan. On 22 June three million troops, 3,350 tanks, 7,146 artillery pieces and 2,713 aircraft unleashed a storm of destruction on an opponent whose defences were in total disarray, and whose forces were deployed far forward in line with a doctrinaire belief in immediate counter-attack. Nearly three thousand Soviet aircraft were destroyed within the first couple of weeks, many of them on the ground. For advancing German infantrymen it was extremely hot and dusty, reaching temperatures of 40 degrees Celsius in early July, as they tramped forward with hundreds of thousands of horses conveying their baggage. In moments of recuperation, after marches of twenty miles or more a day, bronzed German soldiers went around bare-chested or cooled down and washed off the dust and sweat in cool streams. High confidence prevailed. On 3 July Halder wrote in his diary that 'it is probably no over-statement to say that the Russian campaign has been won in the space of two weeks'. Hitler concurred, saying that 'to all intents and purposes the Russians have lost the war'. By 11 July, the Wehrmacht had captured 360,000 Russians; by 5 August the number had risen to 774,000. By early August, the invading forces had advanced hundreds of miles and were converging on Leningrad, Moscow and Kiev. All it would take would be one final push. But dark clouds were gathering.

The clear lines of the initial powerful thrusts dissipated into a series of smaller operations as Russian resistance proved more tenacious than it had first appeared to be. This was only partly attributable to the NKVD block-ing divisions stationed behind Russian forces to shoot anyone who fled in panic, or to Stalin's Order 270 in August, under which the families of cowards and deserters would be held responsible too. The contempt the Germans had for their opponent was replaced by the realisation that this was a gigantic, well-equipped army, some of whose commanders knew their trade. They had to, since in some conspicuous cases, for example General Dmitry Pavlov, the failures were arrested and shot. In a letter to his wife, General Georg-Hans Reinhardt recalled the Red Army officers he had studied with in the 1930s: 'Sometimes I almost fear that my fellow class-mates learned too much.'[19] In the frozen Arctic, German troops had performed badly compared with the Finns, who were halted after sustain-ing heavy losses at the hands of the Russians in the vicinity of Lake Lagoda. By the end of 1941, a shocking 17,254 Finns were dead and a further 59,527 wounded. The Social Democrats in the Helsinki coalition government were growing restive about the strains war was putting on such a small economy and population. Hedging their bets, the Finns cunningly described themselves to the Americans as 'co-belligerents' rather than the allies of Germany, while bluntly informing the latter that they were a small nation which had no desire to march as far as Persia.[20]

Army Group South was significantly behind schedule, having encoun-tered dogged resistance in the Ukraine, where the largest Red Army forma-tions were stationed. After the initial battles of encirclement, bold advances by panzer commanders were eschewed in favour of fragmenting and destroying smaller enemy formations, a tactic reminiscent of what Bernard Montgomery would call 'crumbling'. In the first six weeks, the Germans lost 179,500 men. Since there were only three hundred thousand available reserves, this meant that soon there would be an absolute decline in German strength on the battlefield, quite apart from the erosion of fighting power through fatigue. Nearly a third of the vehicles used to move supplies were out of commission either because of enemy action or from wear and tear on what passed for roads, where the summer dust soon turned to autumn's cloying mud. The coal and fuel the Germans looted locally was of a poor standard. The prospect of winter further depressed German spirits; winters in Poland were roughly comparable with those in Munich, but the Russian winter was an entirely different order of coldness. It was not only feet and toes that numbed; in his remarkable account of the Russian campaign, the young infantry soldier Peter Reese describes a man using an axe to hack off the lower legs of Cossack corpses to get their prized felt boots. Since the half-legs were frozen solid, the German soldier then popped them in an oven along with the unit's baked potatoes, to thaw them out and remove the boots. No one present around the stove found this remarkable.[21] An arrogantly racist attitude towards the Russians was replaced by a greater realism. In mid-August Halder wrote: 'In the general situation what stands out is that we have underestimated the Russian colossus, which has consciously prepared for war with all the effort that a totalitarian state can muster ... At the start of the war we counted on about 200 enemy divisions. We have now counted 360. These divisions are not as well armed or equipped as ours, they are often poorly led. But they are there. And if we knock out a dozen of them, then the Russian puts up another dozen.'[22]

Meanwhile, as the weeks slipped by, and the weather deteriorated, there was no decision about whether to concentrate forces for a big push against Moscow or, as Hitler wanted, to focus on Leningrad in the north and the industry, grain and oil of the Ukraine and Caucasus regions in the south. The Führer underestimated Moscow's vital importance as an industrial centre and as a major rail hub. A decision that should have been made when the invasion was being planned was only taken on 21 August 1941, when Hitler got his way. While the Germans went on the defensive between Smolensk and Moscow, a major offensive in the south resulted in the capture of a further 665,000 prisoners as well as 884 tanks and 3,436 artillery pieces in a great battle of encirclement around Kiev. By 8 September, Leningrad was effectively encircled too, although Army Group North commanders resented being denied the opportunity to conquer the city on the Neva. Instead, they were ordered to reduce it by starving its

inhabitants to death and by indiscriminate artillery and aerial bombard-
ments. The Einsatzgruppen commanders were also frustrated, as they
wanted to get started on killing the city's Jews. Satisfied with these results,
Hitler then allowed Halder and Brauchitsch to resume the advance on
Moscow, redeploying the forces subtracted for use against Leningrad and
Kiev. The generals in the field – who included such luminaries as Bock,
Leeb and Rundstedt – exercised strikingly little influence on an operation
they knew relied on troops at the limits of their physical and mental
endurance. Operation Typhoon, the offensive against Moscow,
commenced on 2 October 1941, with a further 673,000 prisoners scooped
up at Vyazma and Bryansk, as well as 1,277 tanks and 5,387 artillery pieces,
one of the greatest German victories of the war. The volume of prisoners
led Hitler to the misleading conclusion that 'No army in the world, including the Russian, can recover from that.'[23]

Although the intention had been to concentrate all forces against
Moscow, which seemed ripe for the taking, the Army High Command
began redeploying troops from Army Group Centre to bolster those in the
North and South. Instead of facing facts and making preparations to sit out
the winter before resuming operations in the spring of 1942, Halder saw a
window of opportunity in the hard frosts of November, before the onset
of December snow made forward movement impossible. It is important to
note that Halder, rather than Hitler, was responsible for a series of catastrophic decisions. On 13 November Halder arrived in Orsha near
Smolensk to outline fantastic plans for comprehensive attacks on all fronts,
taking Army Group South to Stalingrad on the Volga and Army Group
North to Vologda, while Army Group Centre was supposed to encircle the
Soviet capital. This was a step too far. After encountering resistance from
Bock and others, Army Group Centre's objectives were scaled down to a
frontal assault on the western approaches to Moscow. In the south,
Rundstedt also baulked at operations that were supposed to take his Army
Group to the Volga. Instead there was a limited push to Rostov-on-Don,
which was repulsed by a Soviet counter-offensive. Only at that point did
Hitler intervene, flying to Poltava to boost morale, after replacing
Rundstedt – the most senior commander on the entire Eastern Front –
with Walther von Reichenau, then belatedly realising that Rundstedt's decision to retreat had been correct. This intervention, the first of its kind in
this campaign, was symptomatic of what was developing into a three-way
struggle between Hitler, the Army High Command – which was largely
responsible for the shambles that was unfolding – and the senior

commanders in the field, who were the least empowered in the decision-making triangle. They were riven by professional rivalry and personal animosity, and were collectively ill-represented by prodigious numbers of military bureaucrats at the three army group headquarters.

On 15 November, Army Group Centre resumed its offensive against Moscow. The Germans had to cross countryside where the Russians had burned everything before retreating, and then ran into successive defensive lines manned by NKVD troops. Exhausted German infantrymen could make little headway, while the heavily depleted panzer forces ground to a halt. As their troops battled to conquer a few more miles of frozen ground in conditions that plummeted to minus 40 degrees Celsius on 1 December, the generals began to blame each other. On the 5th, German soldiers were ordered to dig in as best as they could, wherever they found themselves.

No sooner was the halt order given than the Germans were hit by a ferocious Soviet counter-offensive, its build-up undetected by German military intelligence. The counter-attack included ninety-nine fresh Soviet divisions, many of them drawn from Manchuria, where the Soviets knew the Japanese would not attack thanks to intelligence supplied by the brilliant spy Richard Sorge in Tokyo. Ironically, the Germans were fortunate that they had not entered Moscow (from which much of the government apparatus had been evacuated), for they would have been drawn into a grinding battle of attrition and could well have been encircled by the Soviet counter-attack, directed by some of the most able commanders in the Red Army, including Ivan Konev, Konstantin Rokossovsky and Georgy Zhukov, who used the most ruthless measures to drive their men onwards. From being able to see the Kremlin through field glasses, the Germans were rolled back 50–100 miles, managing to stabilise the front only after ferocious fighting that reminded commanders of what they had experienced as junior officers at Verdun or the Somme, and of the disaster that had befallen Napoleon on the same ground. Like Army Group North outside Leningrad, Army Group Centre would never get any closer to taking Moscow.

In these circumstances, many generals turned to Hitler as their saviour, hoping that this military genius would intervene to reverse the disasters that Halder and Brauchitsch had inflicted upon them. Perhaps he could repeat the magic that had carried the Wehrmacht to Warsaw or Paris in a matter of weeks? On 16 December Hitler relieved Brauchitsch of the army command, assuming the position himself. This brought the latent danger that the individual who had to maintain an eagle-eyed view of global strategy might end up micro-managing the most important theatre. His first orders were to forbid any further retreat, partly because this would have meant abandoning heavier weaponry to the enemy, but also because no adequate defensive positions had been prepared further west. The distinguished tank commander Heinz Guderian visited Hitler to demand greater tactical flexibility. He was undermined by Halder and Army Group Centre commander Günther von Kluge, who had replaced Bock, and Hitler brushed him off with the remark 'Believe me, one sees these things more clearly from a distance.' After Guderian had persisted in conducting tactical retreats, Kluge advised Hitler to remove him from his command. Hitler's mantra was to fight to the penultimate man until the reserves flowed in from the west, but these were not going to compensate for the rate of attrition. Between 1 December 1941 and 31 March 1942, a fresh 180,400 reserves reached the Eastern Front; over the same period, the Wehrmacht suffered 436,900 casualties. As more commanders objected to being denied operational flexibility, Hitler raved and ranted, denouncing the Army High Command for having 'parliamentarised' the army. When the brilliant panzer commander Erich Hoepner unilaterally withdrew his XX Army Corps, he was summarily dismissed from the army 'with all legal consequences', although no further steps were taken.

The Soviets were just as punished by the atrocious weather conditions as their opponents. The exhaustion of the Russians, who suffered enormous losses against a dogged German defence, explains why the position eventually stabilised. Only in the far south did the Germans continue to notch up spectacular victories, as Erich von Manstein succeeded in taking Eleventh Army into the Crimea, a peninsula roughly the size of Sicily. Soviet seaborne counter-attacks were defeated after heavy fighting, while the naval base of Sebastopol was pounded into submission. Hitler claimed that he had snatched victory from the jaws of defeat, because he alone had kept his nerve. The German generals, most reduced to sleepless wrecks when they were not ailing from acute heart or stomach troubles, readily concurred. Throughout the higher echelons of the invading army, commanders had forfeited any operational flexibility; henceforth they were in post to execute 'faithfully', 'fanatically' and above all 'ruthlessly' the orders of the dictator. Some outside observers did not find these men impressive. After attending a conference of Army Group Centre leaders in April 1942, the very able Luftwaffe General Wolfram Freiherr von Richthofen wrote: 'What a lot of small minds in grand positions. Shocking! The level of a schoolteachers' meeting.' The real cost of stopping the

Russian winter offensive was paid by the 1,073,066 men who were counted as killed, wounded or missing by March 1942. A third of the original invasion force had been lost in eight months, even as more and more Russians kept on coming.

In a sense, the first Soviet offensive in the first five months of 1942 made the same error that Hitler and his generals had made in the summer of 1941: too great an expenditure of effort across too broad a front. The aim was to roll the Germans back whence they had come. That was manifestly not achieved, for in early 1942 the Germans still occupied many of the positions they had reached in December 1941. German losses were also a seventh of Soviet ones, and indeed dropped off during the spring. But stasis, however economical of men, was not an option for an army whose ethos was based on hitting hard while moving fast. In June 1942, the Germans launched Operation Blue, a limited southerly offensive, consisting of four successive phases. Its elaborate choreography went wrong when Soviet forces melted away, rather than obliging the German armies bent on encircling them by fighting stubbornly in place, so the haul of prisoners was modest by recent German standards. By late July it became obvious that the first stages of Blue had misfired badly, a series of blows into empty air.

An alternative plan was rapidly improvised, with Army Group South split in two and Operation Edelweiss involving Army Group A and Operation Heron involving Army Group B. After three months, Hitler became so frustrated that he personally assumed command of Army Group A, which had shadowed the Caucasus mountains in a lunge towards the oil fields of the south-east. His fixation with secondary objectives gave the Soviets time to sabotage systematically the oil wells that were the whole point of the operation. German troops ventured ever further south, in conditions of 100 degree heat, before being chopped to pieces in freezing mountain ambushes.[24] Hitler also allowed the ancillary objective of Stalingrad – which had scarcely been mentioned in planning – to become the sole focus of Army Group B, whose actual remit was to provide a roof over the lunge into the Caucasus while mopping up Soviet forces in the bend of the Don river. Even the German army's superiority in radio communications became a liability, as commanders habituated to acting with considerable individual latitude were bombarded with hourly orders from Hitler's field HQ. Both army groups had to operate at the end of vastly extended supply lines, and tank crews had to spend as much time nervously eyeing their fuel gauges as looking for the enemy, while the wounded died in field ambulances as they bumped agonising distances along what passed for roads.

The trap fortuitously escaped by Army Group Centre at Moscow in December 1941 snapped shut on Paulus's Sixth Army at Stalingrad, bogged down fighting the sort of attritional battle German army doctrine sought to avoid. The Soviets launched Operations Little Saturn and Uranus to smash through the Axis forces holding the long flank of the Stalingrad salient and surrounded the city. Although the Luftwaffe had repeatedly bombed Stalingrad, thereby creating more defensible rubble, it proved incapable of supplying Sixth Army from the air. As winter enveloped them, German troops took on the appearance of hungry vagrants, wrapped in anything that might keep out the cold. Their commander reported scenes where soldiers were begging him for bits of bread, or fell eagerly on the corpse of a horse, smashing open its head to eat the raw brains. Others who tired of eating horsemeat discovered that cat meat did not taste bad. Three and a half thousand Soviet prisoners held by the Germans got nothing and starved to death, their deaths excluded from the sentimentalising pathos devoted to the Wehrmacht.[25]

Hitler construed the suddenly inverted siege of Stalingrad in terms of a clash of wills.[26] Stalin did too, issuing Order 227, which effectively mimicked Hitler's order forbidding retreat the previous winter. Hitler's angry inflexibility ran into an opponent who was mastering deception and high mobility. Not only did Hitler refuse Paulus permission to break out of Stalingrad, but he hurled more German forces against the cleverly deployed Soviet armies encircling the city. Paulus eventually surrendered, although Sixth Army held out long enough to permit Army Group A to beat a hasty retreat from the Caucasus, having failed to reach the main oil fields at Baku and Grozny. Exotic photographs and views from mountain peaks are all that remain of this epic adventure. The 327,000 men Germany lost in the winter of 1942–3 were irreplaceable, and Hitler would not be able to mount an offensive on this scale again.[27]

III 'A HEALTHY FEELING OF HATRED'

A certain type of sacralising Holocaust literature has almost extrapolated the genocide against the Jews from its wartime context. European Russia consists of over two million square miles and could have easily accommodated imperial India; beyond the Urals lay the six million square miles of Russia's empire in Asia. The European quarter includes forests, swamps and major rivers, with human settlement much less dense than in western Europe – perhaps fifty rather than five hundred inhabitants per square mile. The sheer space seemed eerily oppressive, or *Unheimlich* as German has it, while as the invaders ventured far into the south-east, the population became ever more alien. The Germans found themselves in a vast inhospitable landscape, fighting a war that reminded the more historically literate of the Thirty Years War in terms of brutality and indiscriminate destructiveness: a nightmare of burning settlements and corpses hanging in public places.

Born in Prussian Gumbinnen in 1886, the son of a Protestant pastor, infantry General Gotthard Heinrici commanded XLIII Army Corps on the central front. He was not an ambitious political fanatic like Walther von Reichenau; more a steady pair of hands who had crept up the military hierarchy through diligence. Heinrici wrote three parallel accounts of the campaign: a semi-official war diary, monthly typed reports derived from this which he sent to his family, and handwritten personal letters to his wife, which he did not trust to the field post but sent via colleagues on leave. The general was palpably glad to leave Polish Siedlce: 'Not very nice here, bad cold weather, there is no spring. Flies and lice crawl around everywhere, as well as ghastly Jews with Stars of David on their arms.'[28] Russia was no improvement as successive letters revealed: there were more Jews and flies that attacked like Stuka formations. 'Lord God,' wrote Heinrici to his wife on 6 July 1941, 'this is a dark country, north of the Pripet Marshes, forests, everywhere forests, interspersed with kilometres of wide swamps, where one sinks up to the knees in mud.'[29] A week later, in stifling 40-degree heat, his corps reached a town called Kopyl, the 'real Russia' as he called this 'nest'. The place was in a state of advanced ruination, with only the most primitive facilities, and a cast concrete statue of Stalin as the town's focal point. The inhabitants had been impoverished by Communism and seemed too frightened to talk; in any event no one could understand what they said.[30] On 1 August, Heinrici wrote of 'this horrible forest and swamp terrain, miserable roads and the exhaustion of the troops, and on top of that the unimaginable distances'.[31] On 8 October: 'Bolshevism has fundamentally destroyed anything of beauty in this so very unlovely country. Whatever little remains has finally been wrecked by the war.'[32]

By the 23 October, XLIII Corps had waded through mud as far as Kaluga in the valley of the River Oka. Heinrici reflected: 'This people can't be measured according to our standards. I believe one can only do it justice, not by advancing into it on foot as we are doing, but as if we were arriving by ship in some alien part of the world, and as we embarked from our shores, mentally severed every connection with what we are used to at home.'[33] After the autumn rains and mud came the cold. On 19 November Heinrici typed one of his regular monthly reports to his family:

> −10, −15, −19 degrees cold. These are the temperatures we've been labouring and fighting under since 8 November. The range varies between these two extreme figures. Their effects only differ according to whether the wind is totally still, or there is suddenly an icy north or north-easterly wind. The moment that commences, it's almost impossible to stay outside. It pricks your face like needles and blasts through both gloves and protective head gear. Your eyes weep, to the point you can no longer see … Only about half of our men have head gear and gloves, and all of them are wearing our German coats and thin old trousers … For the last eight to ten days we haven't had any tea or coffee, no cigarettes or cigars, not to speak of alcohol, frequently no bread either. Ammunition is so sparse that in some places it's run out. It's amazing that we've only had 180 cases of frostbite, which had to be taken to casualty stations.[34]

By early December, he noticed that his breath froze, while crystallising on his scarves; indeed breathing had become painful in itself. Writing to his wife on 12 December, Heinrici said, 'in every respect this country is immeasurable: in its size, its woods, its climate, the masses of people. In two positions we've had outbreaks of typhus because of lice. There is everything here that is hateful and ugly.'[35]

Despite the bombast, the war crimes of the Wehrmacht were not discovered by German (or US) left-wing historians in the 1990s; they had been known since the Nuremberg Trials, and were written about by several eminent historians over the next thirty years. About eighteen million men served in the Wehrmacht during the Nazi era; while the victorious Allies held some of the senior commanders responsible for war crimes, they never condemned the armed forces as criminal organisations, as they did the SS. Scholarly estimates of the number of soldiers who committed such crimes range from less than five per cent to between 60 and 80 per cent of those who fought on the Eastern Front. This latter figure seems absurdly high, not least because the majority of soldiers deployed on the Eastern

Front fought the Red Army in zones from which potential civilian victims had fled or been evacuated.[36]

Between these combat zones and the former German or Polish territory they had started from in June lay vastnesses across which every piece of food, ammunition and replacement equipment had to be transported, along roads which were either rivers of mud or frozen ribbons on which horses and vehicles slipped and slid. The rear area of Army Group Centre was the size of Bavaria, Baden-Württemberg, Rhineland-Palatinate and Hessen together. Individual armies were responsible for territories the size of Mecklenburg or Schleswig-Holstein; the Caucasus was the size of Germany in its pre-1938 borders. The entire rear area of the whole Eastern Front was policed by one hundred thousand troops from military Security Divisions, together with Order Police, Waffen-SS Brigades and units from the SS Security Police and SD, although the latter's definition of police work – that killing people should be construed as *Arbeit* – was as unorthodox as it was predictable.

The sheer speed of the German advance meant that hundreds of thousands of Soviet troops were marooned behind German lines. Some were deserters, others were lost. According to Heinrici, the latter sometimes asked the Germans for directions to the nearest POW camp. Some were still uniformed and under command; others switched into civilian clothing to flee homewards. Many were armed; others were not. The Germans encountered them out in the open, or skulking in woods and farm buildings. Inevitably these men had to support themselves by plundering. Under these circumstances it was difficult to determine who was a regular combatant and who had migrated into the partisan campaign Stalin had ordered in July. In addition to the risk of being shot by the Germans, all these displaced Russian soldiers were liable to be executed as deserters and traitors should they manage to reach their own lines. Theirs was an unenviable fate.

The rules of engagement outlined by Hitler were reflected in exhortations from field commanders, and in the propaganda designed for the common soldier. General von Manstein decreed: 'This struggle against the Soviet army will not be solely fought according to the customary European laws of war.'[37] The humble *Landser* – the German equivalent of GI or squaddie – was told: 'This is about wiping out Red sub-humanity which is incarnated in those who rule in Moscow. The German people stand before the greatest task in their history. The world will witness how this task is ruthlessly performed.'[38] That was evident everywhere from the start, although whether atrocities can be solely attributed to 'criminal orders' and ideology – let alone national character – seems doubtful. Neither satisfactorily explains why, for example, Hungarian troops sometimes relegated their German allies to second place in such grim stakes, or why the sanguinary depredations of the Rumanians appalled even the Einsatzgruppen.[39] Indiscriminate murder became commonplace, grim evidence of it being captured on the cheap Leica cameras soldiers took along to show the folk at home what this war was really like, or to tantalise each other with their acts of barbarity. To be on the safe side, the Germans shot anyone in civilian clothing with so much as a razor stuffed inside their boot, a crude rule of thumb being that anyone with shorn hair had to be a Red Army soldier. Red Army soldiers of Asiatic origin were always killed, as they fitted pervasive German stereotypes about a cruel and devious oriental opponent often dubbed 'the Red beast'. Any female Red Army soldiers captured were immediately shot, since armed women flew in the face of German notions of military propriety, and because many of them were snipers, who were invariably shot regardless of sex. Only five hundred of two thousand Soviet women snipers survived the war.

The Germans were not wrong to imagine that Red Army soldiers were being forced forward by pistol-wielding commissars who shot them if they deserted or retreated, for that did indeed happen. They executed between two and three thousand captured commissars, although a more common practice is illustrated by the case of the 3rd Battalion of the 490th Infantry Division, which in the early morning of 25 July stormed a slightly elevated Soviet position near Kulotino and Kreni in the Baltic. The attackers took fire from two Soviet tanks, which were put out of commission after three-quarters of an hour, when they found a wounded man in one of the tanks. The man was a political officer, who crawled out after they dropped in a grenade. Forty-one-year-old Major Günther Drange, a veteran of the Great War turned bank employee in civilian life, perhaps with something to prove, although exactly why we will never know, shot him dead.[40] More Soviet political personnel were weeded out from POW camps and killed by the SD. They were identified by the gold star and hammer-and-sickle badge on their caps, and by the fact that their hair was longer than that of shaven-headed private soldiers. Unfortunately for them, Russian army bandmasters and war correspondents all bore the same badge, while all Russian officers had longer hair than the shorn conscripts.[41]

Then there was an interconnected spiral of atrocities, driven by grim fact and inflated by rumour, which included the massacres of political prisoners by the NKVD troops before they abandoned their Galician, Ukrainian and Baltic prisons to the Germans. The victims had routinely been subjected to torture in the months of captivity, ranging from having their fingers and hands smashed in slammed doors to being beaten senseless with cables or lengths of timber. In Lemberg, the Germans were shown half a dozen prisons where the NKVD had slaughtered 3,500 people. The post-war Christian Social Union leader and West German Defence Minister Franz Josef Strauss was among the German soldiers who were importuned by desperate Polish or Ukrainian women with photos of relatives imprisoned by the Soviets, many recently shot as truck motors drowned out the noise. German pathology reports on corpses exhumed from the courtyard of the jail on Lacki-Street said:

> In general all of the victims revealed heavy multiple wounds from blunt instruments. Women were often multiply mutilated, for example their breasts cut off. Male sexual organs were also the object of Bolshevik perversity. From the contorted faces of the dead, and their torn clothing, as well as other traces of evidence, it was evident that the detainees had undergone a considerable ordeal. Most of them had literally been beaten to death, according to the doctors, and there were signs that some had suffocated under the mounds of corpses.[42]

Such shocking sights, which did not need to be fabricated, were filmed by German propagandists and used by the Einsatzgruppen on Heydrich's orders to incite the surrounding population against the Jews, who were alleged to be disproportionately represented in the local NKVD, it being left unsaid that they also figured prominently among the victims. In Lemberg four thousand Jews were killed by militiamen from the Organisation of Ukrainian Nationalists (OUN). In Łuck, German troops discovered a further 2,800 victims of the NKVD. The NKVD used machine guns and grenades to kill them; 'blood flowed in streams and body parts flew through the air'. The wounded were finished off with pistol shots. Such scenes were repeated in dozens of prisons as the NKVD retreated, the number of Ukrainian victims being estimated at up to thirty thousand.[43]

When, on 2 July, they found the bodies of ten German soldiers, Order Police immediately killed 1,160 Jews. Further atrocities against German prisoners were often revealed whenever German forces swept past Russian positions, as the Soviets had usually killed any captured German soldiers in their hasty retreat, along with any Luftwaffe pilots who had been shot down. Although the 226 German dossiers on crimes committed against the Wehrmacht in Russia are far from complete – most of the evidential photos disappeared into the US archives – German army legal investigators put together a three-volume selection, two of which contain depositions, autopsy reports and photographs. On 9 July investigators from the 4th Mountain Division were shown the bodies of seventeen of their comrades who had been captured by the Soviets. Six revealed signs of mutilation:

> two of the fallen had their hands bound behind their backs. One of them had his right eye cut out, while his face was smashed in with brutal blows, probably from a rifle butt. In the second case, his tongue had been cut off, and his throat had been cut high on his neck. The other four had also been mutilated. One had had his right hand and right elbow hacked off, so that the hand and forearm lay separately. Another's right arm had been repeatedly punctured either with a side arm or some sort of knife, so that it resembled a sieve. The corpses of two other soldiers had stab wounds all over them. All six had been robbed, so that they had no pay books or other means of identification.[44]

In another massacre, discovered in a turnip field near Jemtschita in August 1941, twenty-four German prisoners of war had been killed. Two had had their genitals cut off. Another had been disembowelled, and a third had had his eyes poked out. One had his throat cut and another his head cut off. From the agonised expressions on their faces and the positions of their arms, these acts had been carried out while they were still alive.[45] There were also well-publicised instances of Russian mutilation of German corpses. There were cases of Red Army soldiers surrendering and then massacring their guards, and others of Russians pretending to be dead in order to shoot Germans in the back as they passed by. Finally, German commanders such as Reichenau informed their troops that Stalin had given orders for the Russians to take no prisoners, which, although not an accurate rendering of what Stalin had said, encouraged the Germans to do the same, and hence stiffened the resolve of Russian soldiers never to be captured.[46]

Heinrici's letters afford grim insights into the unparalleled ferocity of this campaign. 'In places, no quarter is being given. The Russian conducts himself bestially towards our wounded. Now our people beat and shoot dead everything running around in a brown uniform,' wrote Heinrici to his wife on 6 July 1941.[47] His interpreter, an ethnic German Ukrainian from Odessa called Lieutenant Beutelsbacher, proved especially zealous in tracking down partisans, whom he then hanged. Beutelsbacher's father and brother had been killed by the Bolsheviks, and his mother and sister sent to Siberia to build roads. Heinrici had to order him not to hang anyone within a hundred metres of his own quarters, as the general found the sight disagreeable as he breakfasted in the mornings. A literary-minded subordinate told him that Goethe had spent three weeks living in the shadows of gallows in Jena.[48] On 21 November Heinrici and his men 'experienced' the death of a commissar in Grajasnowo, shot as he tried to flee from one of the Field Gendarmes; 'not nice for our people' commented the general.[49]

In a sense it was academic how they died, for those Russians who were taken prisoner were largely doomed as a matter of policy, with scarcely any of the kind of attention that has been, enormously, devoted to the Holocaust. By 1 February 1942, the Germans had captured 3,350,000 men. Of these, 1,400,000 died between June and November 1941, and a further 600,000 in the winter months of December and January. By the end of the war, some 3,300,000 Red Army prisoners were dead, the majority before the spring of 1942. The equivalent death toll for Germans in Soviet camps has been estimated at between 350,000 and 800,000 men, which pales only by comparison. In contrast, 8,348 British and US prisoners died in German captivity throughout the war – or roughly the same number as Russians who perished in camps in Poland in just two days. The ultimate responsibility lay with the senior quartermaster generals, although there were lesser culprits all down the line, for it was not generals who shadowed these men along their lines of march or guarded them in camps.

Assuming they were not simply mown down at the point of capture, the initial ordeal was the march to the first stockades. On Hitler's express instructions, prisoners were robbed of any serviceable winter kit such as fur hats, scarves, gloves and felt boots, with which the Russians were generally well equipped. If they were lucky, they might be marched through fields that had not been picked clean by German troops or harvested for the Reich, where food from Russia was regarded as essential to maintaining popular morale. Drinking water was what rain could be captured in some improvised device or one's bare hands. Those who fell exhausted by the wayside were routinely shot by their guards, as there was no medical provision. The shooting was done by regular German troops seconded to guard them. For example, the 113th Infantry Division guarded two hundred thousand prisoners during a march to the rear in October 1941 and shot one thousand of them en route. The 137th Infantry Division left Vyazma for Smolensk with nine thousand prisoners, and arrived with only 3,480, having shot the rest along the way.[50] Those who were transported by rail fared no better, as the freight wagons were sometimes uncovered and always unheated so that, after a journey of three weeks in sub-zero temperatures, between 25 and 70 per cent of each rail transport might have perished.

In the camps, daily rations of 150–200 grams of bread ensured staggering death rates of up to 2 per cent a day, with hundreds of corpses dumped into hastily excavated mass graves each morning. Even the permanent camps in Austria or the General Government merely consisted of fenced-off areas situated on former military training grounds. The POWs were expected to build their own huts, but in practice they dug holes in the ground, since they were given no building materials. They were also liable to be shot for the most trivial reasons; Lieutenant General Reinecke, head of the Wehrmacht camp system, ordered guards to shoot at the first sign of 'mutiny', an interpretation sometimes placed on the desperate rush to the meagre food flung out to the ravenous mob. The Wehrmacht camp administrators also rapidly arranged for the Security Police to comb the camp population for political officers, who were then shot by the Einsatzgruppen. For the reasons stated earlier, many of those combed out were army officers, of whom only 30–35 per cent survived captivity. And of course the Security Police were given access to the camps to identify Jews among the prisoners, who were also shot by the Einsatzgruppen, often after being identified as such by fellow prisoners. Although sixty to eighty thousand Jewish Red Army prisoners were taken, by April 1942 there were only sixty-eight alive in German captivity. Many ethnic Georgians were shot because they allegedly looked Jewish and were usually circumcised. Anyone of Asiatic appearance was also liable to be murdered in the camps, until the decision to recruit ethnic legions for the SS brought a change of policy, with Heydrich warning his men to be more discriminating in selecting their victims. Any prisoner too ill to work, which included those maimed in battle, was also shot or else simply left outside to freeze to death. After army commanders at the front had decided belatedly to set amputees free to beg in the streets, in September 1942 Keitel arranged with Himmler to have them shot on the grounds that, crippled or not, they might help the partisans. In so far as the army objected to SS activity in its domain, it was to tell the Security Police not to kill prisoners near the camps.[51]

Not every German commander agreed with this wholesale murder of captured Russian soldiers. Some, such as Maximilian Freiherr von Weichs regarded the brutality of guards as incompatible with German military honour. More pragmatically, Weichs knew that murdering Russian prisoners negated the leaflets the Luftwaffe was raining down urging their comrades to surrender. Others cited international law. Among the first to protest was the Abwehr chief, Admiral Wilhelm Canaris, who in September 1941 wrote to Keitel reminding him of international legal obligations to treat POWs correctly. Apart from the brutalising effects on the Germans' own troops, Canaris spoke of the likelihood that the Russians might reciprocate atrocity for atrocity. Keitel brushed off such outmoded concerns which smacked of 'chivalric warfare'. In Russia they were fighting 'to destroy a worldview'. General Rudolf Schmidt of Second Panzer Army was another who reminded his men on 3 March 1942, 'Prisoners who have committed no offence against international law should be treated in accordance with international law.' A few camp commandants, notably Major Wittmer at Dulag 185 in Mogilev, refused to allow Einsatzkommandos access to their charges. In a complaint to the Higher SS and Police Leader Central Russia, the EK commander complained that Wittmer sought to bolster his 'eccentric point of view' with a punctilious use of the military rule book. Specifically, he claimed there were no orders that allowed him to hand over Jews for execution. To the extent that treatment of Russian prisoners did improve, it was solely due to a pragmatic realisation that they were a useful source of labour, although that often meant they were worked to death instead.[52]

Such officers were very much the exception. Orders issued by some of the most able and charismatic German generals were very different in tone, although the fact that they felt obliged to issue them may indicate that spontaneous fanaticism was not what they thought it should be, or that they felt obliged to demonstrate their ideological conformity to the Commander-in-Chief. The wiry, grey-haired Hermann Hoth was the son of a Prussian army medical officer. Hoth had won the highest decorations in the German army for his service during the Great War and commanded the 3rd Panzer Group until October 1941, when he took command of Seventeenth Army. On 17 November 1941 he issued a decree on the conduct of German troops. It is worth looking at in some detail.

This was a war between two irreconcilable outlooks, Hoth declared, between 'German honour and sense of race, centuries-old German soldiering against an Asiatic mentality and the primitive instincts whipped up by a tiny number of mostly Jewish intellectuals – fear of the knout, disrespect for moral values, levelling down to the lowest denominator, throwing away one's own worthless life. We clearly recognise that our mission is to rescue European civilisation from the advance of Asiatic barbarism. This struggle can only end with the extermination of one or the other; there is no compromise.'[53] Hoth's tone was unambiguous:

> pity and gentleness towards the population is totally out of order ... every manifestation of active or passive resistance or any machinations by Bolshevik-Jewish agitators is to be pitilessly exterminated. The necessity for hard measures against racially alien elements must be understood by the troops. These circles are the intellectual props of Bolshevism, the bearers of this murderous organisation, the partisans' supporters. It is the same Jewish class of people, whose racially and culturally subversive activities did so much harm to our fatherland, and who today foster so many anti-German tendencies throughout the world, and who will be the executants of revenge. Their extermination is a dictate of self-preservation. Whichever soldier is critical of these measures has no understanding of the earlier, decades-long subversive and treasonable activities of this Jewish-Marxist element among our own people.

Hoth concluded with revealing comments on the relationship between officers and other ranks in an army that historically prided itself on discipline and intelligent leadership: 'The simple trooper often has a harder, tougher view of the enemy than the officer. The officer needs to reorientate himself to this viewpoint. A healthy feeling of hatred and the rejection of pre-existing circumstances should not be repressed, but rather should be encouraged. But brutality, slave-driving and torture are unworthy of a "lord".'[54] Hoth's criticism of officers receives confirmation from an entry in the diary of Major Rudolf-Christoph Freiherr von Gersdorff of Army Group Centre in December 1941. In the course of lengthy conversations, his fellow officers had brought up the mass shootings of Jews, commissars and prisoners of war. They thought the killing of commissars was counter-productive, as it dishonoured the German officer corps and stiffened Soviet resistance. They were concerned about questions of responsibility. Gersdorff didn't record their thoughts on killing Jews, although he would become involved in a notorious argument with the SS about them.[55]

Soviet Jews felt the full force of Nazi hatred. While the mainly tatterdemalion Jews of Poland had merely elicited a sort of murderous contempt, prompting some German commanders to question why it was necessary to kill such supine figures, there was real fear regarding the well-educated and highly assimilated Jews of Russia proper, who were functionaries, secret policemen, academics, white-collar employees and industrial workers. Hitler and many of his senior commanders believed that the extermination of the Jewish-Bolshevik intelligentsia was a necessity in order to hasten the collapse of the Soviet Union, an apocalyptic mentality that led to the Führer's decision to bring about a final reckoning with this cosmic foe, the source of all evil in the world as he had long understood it.

Although Jews had not been expressly mentioned in the April 1941 army–SS agreement about SS activity during the campaign, they were specifically identified in meetings between the SS and Army High Command in June. On the 8th of that month a senior army commander anticipated the arrival of the Einsatzgruppen who would be 'carrying out fundamental special measures against the Jews'.[56] The Einsatzgruppen alone numbered 3,500 men, and in addition there were thirty thousand from the three Waffen-SS brigades of Himmler's Commando Staff Reichsführer-SS, the police battalions of the new Higher SS and Police Leaders, and nine Order Police battalions which arrived as supplementary forces. One part of their remit was clear enough, which was violently to suppress any resistance behind German lines; it may have been widely assumed that Jews – or rather the Jewish-Bolshevik intelligentsia – figured prominently within that limited context.

In areas from which the Soviet occupiers were expelled such as Western Ukraine, Lithuania and Bessarabia, the Einsatzgruppen endeavoured to spark pogroms among local nationalists who crept out of the woodwork as soon as the NKVD and Red Army had departed. German soldiers sometimes either participated in these examples of what Heydrich dubbed 'self-purification' or, more often than not, stood around as enthusiastic spectators with their Leica cameras, a practice the army discouraged. Sixteenth Army reached Kovno (Kaunas), the Lithuanian capital, on 24 June. A pogrom erupted which went on for five nights. Two to three thousand Jews were killed on a petrol-station forecourt, and houses and synagogues burned. The forecourt was a hundred yards from the HQ of Sixteenth Army, whose chief, General Ernst Busch, remarked, 'this is a political dispute that doesn't interest us; that is, it does concern us, but we can't do anything; what should we do then?'[57] Walter Stahlecker's

Einsatzgruppe A arrived on the 25th to take over local security. Incorporating the militias who had carried out the pogrom, they obliged the army by not killing Jews under their noses; instead they were taken to the city's Fort VII where they were shot, bringing the total for Kovno to 7,800, a fraction of the 230,000 Jews Stahlecker and his men would murder before January 1942.

In the interim, the Commander-in-Chief of Army Group North, Field Marshal Wilhelm Ritter von Leeb, had established his HQ in the city, joining Busch's Sixteenth Army HQ. On 3 July Hitler's chief adjutant, Colonel Rudolf Schmundt, arrived too and was questioned about the events in Kovno. He left to put in a call to Berlin before replying by telephone that 'soldiers should not be burdened with these political questions; it has to do with a necessary racial cleansing'. On 8 July, Leeb and Busch received General Franz von Roques, head of the Army Group North's rear area. They talked about the pogroms and shootings which Roques clearly disapproved of. In his diary, the Catholic Leeb wrote: 'we have no influence over these measures. All that remains is to keep oneself away from them. Roques remarked very accurately that the Jewish question would not be solved in this fashion. Leeb volunteered that it would be more surely solved by sterilising all the male Jews.'[58]

After commencing with killing Jewish men, between mid-August and early October 1941 the net widened to murdering women and children, who most certainly were not part of any putative Jewish-Bolshevik intelligentsia. The few surviving documents which concerned co-operation between the Einsatzgruppen (principally Groups B and D) and senior army officers reveal that the former invariably enjoyed a free hand and needed to use no circumlocutions when reporting their activities. Thus Arthur Nebe, head of Einsatzgruppe B, quite openly reported to Army Group Centre that his task force had 'liquidated' 1,330 people between 9 and 16 July. Those who received this report included Major von Gersdorff and Lieutenant Colonel Henning von Tresckow, who like Nebe himself would later become part of the conspiracy to kill Hitler.[59] Co-operation between the Einsatzgruppen and the army did not consist merely of the former keeping the latter informed by way of professional courtesy. There was considerable social interaction, and not just with the army intelligence officers the Einsatzgruppen were obliged to deal with. The Einsatzgruppen received broad logistical support from the Secret Field Police and other types of military policemen, who also helped select victims and provided perimeter security around SS killing grounds.

They in turn were often more than eager to help out at the front, for it was not just soldiers who sought campaign medals. This undermined the initial attempt to delineate respective spheres of command and activities. In September 1941, Army Group South called in Sonderkommando 4b, a mobile sub-unit of Otto Rasch's Einsatzgruppe C. There had been three instances of military cables being sabotaged in the vicinity of Kremenchug. On their first day in town, these men massacred 1,600 Jews there, surely a lot of people to cut a cable or two. Elsewhere, in Army Group Centre, Generals Weichs and Erwin von Witzleben specifically requested more SD units to deal with security problems in rear areas. After an SS Cavalry Brigade had successfully eradicated 'partisans' in the Pripet swamps – in other words shot or drowned 13,788 mainly Jewish people in a few feet of water – General Max von Schenckendorff invited the senior SS commanders to a two-day 'exchange of experiences' conference at Army Group Centre's HQ in Mogilev. The striking maxim this meeting resolved upon was 'Where there are partisans, there are Jews, and where the Jew is there is the partisan too.'

There was nothing the Einsatzgruppen would not turn their hands to when asked by senior army officers. The following examples come from Army Group North. In November 1941, General Georg von Küchler, commander of Eighteenth Army, decided to resolve the problem of a thousand starving patients in the Kascenko Clinic in Nikolskoe – which the army sought as a field hospital – by calling in Stahlecker to 'remove' them elsewhere. They were killed with lethal injections and buried in an anti-tank ditch. This was not a one-off affair. On 26 December Küchler decided that a sanatorium in the former monastery at Makarevskaya Pustin would be useful accommodation for his soldiers. To that end he called in the Security Police, who shot the 230 to 240 mentally ill women cared for there. At his post-war trial he claimed that this was in line with the euthanasia policies being pursued in the Reich. No wonder that when, at the major military conference at Orsha in mid-November 1941, Chief of Staff Halder had inquired, 'What are Himmler's people actually doing?', he was told: 'These people are worth their weight in gold to us, they are securing the rear-area communications and spare us having to deploy troops for the task.' They had done that, but they had also slaughtered half a million people by the end of 1941, and would slaughter many more as they worked their way back to round up the Jews they had missed in the initial sweep.

In so far as there was a discernible pattern in these events, initially large numbers of male Jews were killed in 'hot' affect-laden pogroms involving indigenous anti-Semites, although the majority were murdered by the

Einsatzgruppen, who generally acted coldly and deliberately rather than in a drunken or emotional rage, although any Jew resisting tended to be beaten to death rather than shot. Justifications based on the Jews being responsible for NKVD atrocities, or as constituting a generalised security threat, represented the entry level for mass murder; thereafter they were a superfluous burden on resources, or rather their disappearance was one way of sparing some food for the civilian population after the army had taken the lion's share. More imagination was required to construe even infants as a future source of revenge so that one might usefully brain them against a wall. The levels of violence ratcheted up in August 1941 as German forces entered places with large Jewish populations that had not managed to flee eastwards. Kamenetz-Podolsk had twenty-six thousand Jews, ten thousand of them having been expelled there by the Hungarians from the Carpatho-Ukraine. With the agreement of Field Marshal Gerd von Rundstedt, the local German commandant requested the services of the Higher SS and Police Leader Friedrich Jeckeln. Jeckeln's men spent three days in late August shooting 23,600 Jews in Kamenetz-Podolsk. Many of the mass murders of Jews in the Ukraine were carried out by Paul Blobel's Sonderkommando 4a. This unit closely followed the fighting troops and liaised with their commanders. Thus after the local army commander at Zitomir had reported that the Jews were 'impudent', Blobel's men shot 3,145 of them.

Blobel and his men entered Kiev along with the vanguard of Sixth Army on 19 September. They were joined later by Jeckeln, Rasch and the staff of Einsatzgruppe C and various Order Police battalions. The army's role is worth highlighting, although few records of it survive. Much of the city was ablaze. Initially, the army ordered all male Jews to be interned; they were detained by men from the 99th and 299th Infantry Divisions. On 24 September, NKVD saboteurs remotely detonated mines in several buildings in central Kiev, including those used by the German military. On the 26th and 27th, the SS officers met with General Kurt Eberhard, the city's commandant, to discuss security issues, including the evacuation of the Jews. Obersturmbannführer August Häfner recalled the general's parting injunction: 'You must shoot them!'[60] An army propaganda company put up two thousand posters telling all male Jews to assemble at 8 a.m. on 29 September; any who failed to appear were to be shot on sight. The army also supplied a hundred thousand rounds for sub-machine pistols. A total of 33,771 Jews were taken to ravines in a municipal park at Babi Yar and shot over a two-day period, after which engineers from the army Pioneer

Battalion 113 blew in the sides of the ravines. Thousands more were ferreted out in the town and killed too, so that by 1 April 1942 there were only twenty Jews left in Kiev. The army requisitioned the Jews' vacant homes.[61]

It was shortly after this that Field Marshal von Reichenau issued his notorious tirade, explaining that the object of the campaign 'against the Jewish-Bolshevik system was the total defeat of its power and the eradication of its Asiatic influence in the European circle of culture'. The German soldier was not just a fighter 'according to the rules of war' but 'the bearer of an implacable racial ideal and the avenger of all the bestialities committed against German and racially cognate peoples'. That primarily meant understanding the need for 'legitimate atonement' on the part of Jewish sub-humanity, which was also, he mentioned in ancillary fashion, responsible for 'uprisings' in the army's rear. He wanted to counteract evidence of 'stupid German goodwill'. Field Marshal von Rundstedt readily concurred and sent this document to all the commanders in Army Group South. After Hitler pronounced it an 'exemplary order', it went to every commander on the Eastern Front. Manstein issued his own version of it, retaining the essence, but adding that his men should maintain 'soldierly honour' and treat the non-Bolshevik population properly.[62]

Another major bloodbath occurred in Kharkov, the fourth largest city in the Soviet Union. After entering the city the Germans endeavoured to expel as many women and children towards the east as possible, to reduce the number of non-working mouths to feed. Aware of what had happened in Kiev, and in Odessa where Rumanian troops had carried out the largest single massacre of Jews of the war, the Germans in Kharkov first locked Jews into public buildings, the idea being that they or their relatives would reveal if the buildings were mined. The tactic failed and on 14 November delayed-action mines exploded under the HQ of the 60th Infantry Division, killing the general commanding 68th Infantry Division. Fifty Jews and Communist Party members were publicly hanged and a thousand more people interned as hostages in the International Hotel, which was converted into an *ad hoc* concentration camp. An advance unit of Security Police shot 305 Jews. Since the Soviets had made off with most available supplies, hunger set in very quickly among Kharkov's citizens. The army also faced a chronic shortage of beds for the wounded. To resolve these problems, it decided that the 'Jewish Question' had to be solved. The local population played its own part in identifying Jews to the Germans.

Meanwhile, the army commandant urged Sonderkommando 4a to find additional manpower. On 5 December 1941 a company of Order Police

Battalion 314 arrived, fresh from murdering the Jews of Dnepropetrovsk. After the army commandant and the SK leader had conferred, posters went up on the 14th telling the city's Jews to assemble; they were herded by Order Police units into a tractor factory. Between 26 December 1941 and 7 January 1942, SK4a and Police Battalion 314 shot fifteen thousand Jews, although a mobile gassing van was also used on women and children.[63] Far to the south, Otto Ohlendorf's Einsatzgruppe D also received sterling help from the newly minted Field Marshal von Manstein (born Fritz Erich von Lewinski) and his Eleventh Army, even as Manstein's Iago-like admirer Heinrich Himmler was seeking to establish the field marshal's Jewish ancestry – for behind a Lewinski must lie a Levi.

Since Ohlendorf's unit had only six hundred men, it was reliant on the army to help kill the twenty-eight thousand Jews it murdered by April 1942. The army ghettoised the Jews and ordered them to wear identifying Stars of David. Its intermediate officers were inextricably involved in acts of mass murder, and recommended the SD murderers for medals after the event. In December 1941, at Simferopol, the capital of the Crimea, the army supplied trucks, ammunition and 2,320 soldiers, fifty-five Gendarmes and twenty Secret Field Police to help Dr Braune's small Sonderkommando 11b kill thirteen thousand Jews, not least because food resources in Simferopol, where the army had its logistics base, were tight. The army also carried out successive raids to winkle out Jews who had escaped the first massacre. There is no way that their commander, Manstein, did not know what his officers and men were doing.[64] Ohlendorf's men also killed a few hundred Gypsies and 1,500 ethnically mixed Krimtschaken, who were Tartar-Jews. In a telling slip of the pen, the army commandant in Kertsch corrected one word in a report: 'The ~~liquidation~~ evacuation of the Jews, approximately 2,500 in number, was carried out on 1, 2 and 3 December. One anticipates subsequent executions, since part of the Jewish population has fled, and is in hiding, and will first have to be captured.'[65] Ohlendorf threw a winter-solstice party for his men and senior army guests, with Order Police acting as waiters. Although the evening was agreeable, Ohlendorf grumbled that 'it was much harder to have to shoot a Jew from a distance of two metres than to shoot at entire suburbs with artillery'. Manstein's staff officers gratefully received Ohlendorf's gift of 120 watches, and the promise of fifty more that needed repair – presumably damaged when their owners were manhandled before execution. In fact, Manstein himself had asked for them.[66]

CHAPTER 9

Global War

Hitler's invasion of the Soviet Union forced his existing opponents – Britain and its Dominions – to recalculate how they saw the war developing. Churchill's belief that the US would soon declare war on Germany was undermined by Roosevelt's public avowal, after they met at Placentia Bay in Newfoundland in August 1941, that the US entry to war was no closer, despite Lend–Lease, the Atlantic Charter and singing 'Onward Christian Soldiers' on the deck of the battleship *Prince of Wales*, which was to be sunk off the coast of Malaya within days of the Japanese attack on Pearl Harbor that finally forced the US into the war.

On the Sunday of Barbarossa, 20 June 1941, Churchill worked all day on a radio broadcast in which he contrasted the humble, home-loving helots of the Soviet Union with 'clanking, heel-clicking, dandified Prussian officers … [and their] dull, docile, brutish masses of Hun soldiery plodding along like a swarm of crawling locusts', not the most elegant example of the Prime Minister's fabled oratory, and hardly an adequate description of what secret British radio intercepts were revealing from Einsatzgruppen reports to Berlin.[1]

As US intervention proved a false dawn, so Churchill had to overcome a lifelong aversion to Communism in order to aid the Russian people, for he had few illusions about Stalin and his cronies, once having stopped foreign secretary Eden visiting Moscow lest the comrades murder him. But necessity led to some unpleasant choices. In August 1941, Britain and Russia jointly ordered the ruler of Persia, Reza Shah Pahlavi, to expel several thousand German advisers and technicians in his country. 'Taking a leaf out of Hitler's book', as Churchill privately put it, he and Stalin despatched their *persia*

forces into Persia to secure oil supplies and warm-water supply routes into Russia, forcing the Shah to abdicate the Peacock Throne and obliging his young son, Mohammed Reza Pahlavi, to expel the Axis nationals. This was all in breach of international law, as Churchill acknowledged when he said, 'we had been doing something for which we had justification but no right'. Involvement with Stalin also meant some further unpalatable decisions. Britain had guaranteed Rumanian independence in early 1939, although it had done nothing to aid it when the Soviets invaded and seized Bessarabia and Northern Bukovina. Now, Britain duly declared war on its former ally and victim of Soviet aggression. It helped that Rumania was another authoritarian dictatorship. However, only a year earlier Britain had praised (and armed) the democratically elected Finnish government in its fight against the Red Army. Churchill hoped to avoid a complete volte face, supported by a Labour Party leadership strongly hostile to the Soviets, but in December Eden got his way, and Britain declared war on 'heroic little Finland'.[2]

The British also sent aircraft and tanks, and agreed to the diversion of US Lend–Lease aid from Britain to the Soviets, via Murmansk. Some of the problems of supping with the devil without a long spoon quickly became apparent as many of the moral dilemmas that had dogged appeasement repeated themselves, albeit with a change of cast. Four days after the Japanese attack on Pearl Harbor on 7 December 1941, Hitler declared war on the US and later that month, while Churchill went to Washington to ensure that the US would not focus exclusively on the Pacific, Eden travelled via Murmansk to Moscow, for high-level deliberations with the Soviets. The British delegation had ample time during the circuitous train journey to the Soviet capital to enjoy the rime on the trees and the rapid transitions from sunrise to sunset with hardly any intervening daylight, although the compressed caviar was not up to scratch and the fellow-travelling diplomat Oliver Harvey kept up a running commentary on the necessity for gulags. In the Kremlin, permanent under-secretary Sir Alexander Cadogan encountered Stalin for the first time: 'with his little twinkly eyes and his stiff hair brushed back he is rather like a porcupine. Very restrained and quiet.' There was little restraint during seven-hour boozing sessions, during one of which a paralytic Voroshilov collapsed on to Stalin's lap. Observing that he was interested in 'practical arithmetic' rather than high-flown 'algebra', Stalin airily discounted the German armies outside Moscow and demanded that the Allies recognise the Soviet frontiers that existed in June 1941, in return for which he would not press them to open a second European front.

Wholeheartedly converted to the policy of appeasement against which he had resigned in protest before Munich, Eden tried to get Churchill to persuade the Americans of the need for 'stark realism'. From Washington Churchill despatched a withering retort:

> We have never recognized the 1941 frontiers of Russia except de facto. They were acquired by acts of aggression in shameful collusion with Hitler. The transfer of the peoples of the Baltic States to Soviet Russia against their will would be contrary to all the principles for which we are fighting this war and would dishonour our own cause. This also applies to Bessarabia and Northern Bukovina and in a lesser degree to Finland, which I gather it is not intended wholly to subjugate and absorb.

Back in London, Churchill had been partly persuaded by the objections of prominent churchmen to reject a deal which would have surrendered the Balts to the Soviets, with far less justification than Chamberlain had had in the case of the Sudeten Germans. The Bishop of Gloucester was especially graphic in his account of a Latvian police chief who had been driven mad and a Riga cabinet minister who had had needles pushed under his fingernails. He told Churchill that forty-nine thousand Latvian men and boys had been murdered or deported to the Soviet interior.[3]

The geostrategic picture was about to become more immediately threatening, although much more optimistic than it had been in the longer term, when the Japanese wild card was played. Germany's defeat of the French and Dutch imperial metropolises, and the likelihood that Britain would follow, emboldened the Japanese to strike once they were relieved of fear of Soviet attack by the April 1941 Neutrality Pact with Moscow. Having moved into northern Indo-China in September 1940 under an agreement with Vichy, the Japanese entered the south of the country with forty thousand troops and established multiple air and naval bases from which they could menace the Dutch East Indies, Malaya and the Philippines. The Japanese also secured transit rights for their troops across Thailand by appearing to support Thai irredentist claims against French Indo-China, whose integrity they had promised to respect, making Burma vulnerable to attack.[4] In response to Japan's virtual occupation of Indo-China, the US froze Japanese assets and imposed an oil embargo, which the British and the exiled Dutch government in London were compelled to follow. The ban was clumsily implemented. While it was intended to cover only high-octane fuels, it turned off 80 per cent of Japan's oil imports. The Japanese consumed twelve thousand tons of oil a day, with only 8 per cent of their supply derived from synthetic sources.[5] Further provocations arose from Roosevelt's desire to jerk the noose he had arranged around Japan's neck. In the summer of 1941 the US extended Lend–Lease aid to China, where Major General Claire Chennault had been training Chiang Kai-shek's air force and would shortly go on to recruit an American Volunteer Group to protect the Nationalists' overland supply routes from Burma.

Until July 1941, Japanese politicians were divided over whether to strike north at Russia or to move south where they would encounter the flagging might of the European colonial empires and the US, an enemy they reduced to the acronym ABCD, meaning the Americans, British and Dutch, with the Chinese tacked on. Although victory in China was its main priority, the army also inclined towards a southward swoop since it had been badly mauled fighting the Soviets at Khalkhin Gol in 1939, where the Japanese lost eighteen thousand men in battle with Zhukov's armies. Although in July the army conducted exercises involving fourteen divisions in Manchuria in preparation for a possible invasion of Russia, the Japanese cabinet emphatically vetoed such an operation. The die was now cast for the direction of attack, although the timing of it still depended on diplomacy.

Those in the Japanese government who sought peace, notably Prime Minister Prince Fumimaro Konoe and Foreign Minister Teijiro Toyoda, tried the unusual gambit of seeking a face-to-face meeting with Roosevelt to resolve outstanding issues. The general idea was to deal by telegram with Emperor Hirohito to bypass the more belligerent members of the Tokyo cabinet. Personalised diplomacy was risky, as it might have entailed the peace party's pre-emptive assassination by enraged nationalists. In the event, such talks never happened. Influenced by Churchill at their Placentia Bay meeting, Roosevelt opted to string the Japanese along instead.

The path to war reflected the fortunes of the various factions that made up the Japanese ruling elites, whose protracted decision-making processes were quite different from the more impulsive spirit of Berlin or Rome. By tradition, the Emperor was supposed not to intervene as decisions percolated up to him, while convention dictated that superiors should never contradict inferiors, which gave the latter a surprising amount of latitude compared with other systems of government. Meetings of up to seventeen hours were not uncommon, with occasional resort to poems to express a point. While Japanese diplomats endeavoured to negotiate an honourable exit from China, the Japanese army drew up plans for a rapid swoop southwards, to secure the raw materials, especially of the Dutch East Indies, with which to prosecute the war in China to a victorious conclusion. Singapore was also a target, because its rich and well-organised Chinese diaspora gave significant financial support to Chiang Kai-shek. The navy worked on parallel plans to gain a temporary tactical advantage by knocking out the US Pacific fleet at Pearl Harbor, enabling the Japanese to consolidate their land conquests before the US managed to bring its awesome resources into play.[6] It is worth emphasising that the Naval Chief of Staff, Admiral Osami Nagano, recommended war with the US on 21 July, five days before the imposition of the US oil embargo.[7]

The alternative to war with the ABCD powers was increasingly perceived in existential terms. Japan would be reliant on strategic oil reserves totalling 9.4 million tons, which would run out within a year, bringing the entire country and its far-flung forces to a halt. The Dutch East Indies were – wishfully – thought to produce 7.9 million tons, or precisely what Japan needed to wage war on the ABCD powers. Peace meant reversion to being a relatively poor peasant country, a 'Little Japan' that was of no account on the world stage. The army especially stressed the blood sacrifices that had been made in China; it would be dishonourable to abandon the ghosts of so many valiant dead. Since the majority of its fifty-one divisions were tied down in China or stationed to protect Manchuria against any Soviet incursion, this meant that the Japanese had only eleven divisions available to strike southwards. They did, however, have considerable airpower, and a navy whose carriers would enable them to project force far from the home islands.

In a key discussion on 5 September 1941, Hirohito accurately identified the weakness of the war that was envisaged, although he did nothing to avert it. He asked about the probability of victory. The Army Chief of Staff, General Hajime Sugiyama, assured him it would come. The exchanges, which involved Admiral Nagano at a crucial point, deserve to be cited at length.

> Emperor: At the time of the China Incident, the army told me that we could achieve peace immediately after dealing them one blow with three divisions. Sugiyama, you were army minister at the time …

Sugiyama: China is a vast area with many ways in and many ways out, and we met unexpectedly big difficulties ...

Emperor: Didn't I caution you each time about those matters? Sugiyama, are you lying to me?

Nagano: If your Majesty will grant me permission, I would like to make a statement.

Emperor: Go ahead.

Nagano: There is no 100 per cent probability of victory for the troops stationed there ... Assume, however, there is a sick person and we leave him alone; he will definitely die. But if the doctor's diagnosis offers a seventy per cent chance of survival, provided the patient is operated on, then don't you think one must try surgery? And if, after the surgery, the patient dies, one must say that was meant to be. This indeed is the situation we face today ... if we waste time. Let the days pass, and are forced to fight after it is too late to fight, then we won't be able to do a thing about it.

Emperor: All right, I understand.

Konoe: Shall I make changes in tomorrow's agenda? How would you like me to go about it?

Emperor: There is no need to change anything.[8]   (βικ)

General Hideki Tojo put the rather slender moral case for war: 'As to what our moral basis for going to war should be, there is some merit in making it clear that Great Britain and the US represent a strong threat to Japan's self-preservation. Also, if we are fair in governing the occupied areas, attitudes toward us would probably relax. America will be enraged for a while, but later she will come to understand [why we did what we did].'[9]

Heady talk of liberating the oppressed peoples of the European colonial empires, who would then flourish under the tutelage of the Japanese Greater East Asian Co-Prosperity Sphere, became the antipode to Churchill and Roosevelt's Atlantic Charter. While this did not explicitly mention Japan, its reaffirmation of Wilsonianism self-determination and a reversion to a collective-security regime in East Asia that had ill-served Japan was seen as a national slight.

In a successful attempt to box in the diplomats, the Japanese war party elected to give negotiations a further six weeks, after which they would start the countdown to war. They mobilised and moved in order to collapse the negotiations indirectly through the ambient momentum towards war. Despite fitful support from the Emperor, who during one conference recited a poem by his grandfather which asked 'why do the waves rage, the winds roar', the peace party nonetheless acquiesced in this impossibly tight schedule, persuaded by the do-or-die arguments advanced by Admiral Nagano. Negotiations with the US broke down as the Japanese refused to reduce their presence in China to what they had possessed before 1931. The Japanese cabinet was increasingly cowed by the Army Minister Tojo, who in mid-October sarcastically declared: 'Of course, if we want to go back to the little Japan of pre-Manchurian Incident days, there's nothing else to be said, is there?'[10]

Following Konoe's resignation after the US had formally declined the offer of a summit, Tojo became prime minister. Although he was obliged to go along with the diplomacy the Emperor had sanctioned, Tojo manifestly regarded this as camouflage for Japan's war preparations. In a private contretemps with Konoe, he had exclaimed: 'There are times when we must have the courage to do extraordinary things – like jumping, with eyes closed, off the veranda of the Kiyomizu Temple,' a famous shrine perched on the edge of a cliff.[11] Suicide was an odd basis for national policy, as US diplomat Stanley Hornbeck remarked when he said, 'Name one country in history which ever went to war in desperation.' Actually, many come to mind.[12] Although the Japanese were aware of their strategic weaknesses, arguments based on the blood and treasure expended in China and on national honour, and a mentality that combined reckless gambling with noble fatalism meant that plans for war became more concrete as a diplomatic solution slipped into the realm of illusions. Like Imperial Germany before the Great War, the Japanese feared encirclement, even though their policies had largely brought this predicament about. On 5 November, the cabinet resolved that if a final round of negotiations failed, the Japanese would simultaneously conquer British and Dutch colonial possessions, while the imperial navy would strike the US Pacific fleet at Pearl Harbor in a brief window of opportunity when Japan's navy had 70 per cent of US strength.

The Emperor was briefed on the final war plans in mid-November. Rather like Operation Barbarossa, the initial 120-day offensive was comprehensible enough, but such factors as enemy air and submarine interdiction of supplies and the pivotal role of Australia, and whether the ABCD powers would ever accept such a fait accompli, were never given sufficient thought. A few months into the attack, the future Vietnamese independence leader Ho Chi Minh identified what was wrong with it: 'In war the one who is most consistent and durable in strength will win … the longer the war lasts, the more it will benefit Britain and America and harm Japan. Japan's victories are preliminary, like a straw catching fire – it burns quickly, and is quickly extinguished.' Ho was right about the first issue, even though it would take three and a half years before Japan itself was engulfed in fire.[13]

Japan's attempts to prolong talks with Washington were subverted by the Americans' ability to read their diplomatic ciphers, which were not speaking the language of peace. US intelligence did not detect the battle fleet that slipped out of the Kurile Islands heading for Hawaii on 26 November. It included six carriers with 432 aircraft, nine destroyers and a light cruiser, two fast battleships and two heavy cruisers, and three submarines. After delivery of US Secretary of State Cordell Hull's steely response to Japanese proposals, which left it ambiguous whether the withdrawal from China that the US was demanding included Manchuria, on 1 December Hirohito assented to war with a series of nods in response to Tojo's promise that victory would 'set his Majesty's mind at ease'. The following day Hirohito sanctioned the imminent attack at Pearl Harbor which was to commence on 8 December Japanese time with the coded signal 'Climb Mount Niitaka'. Hoisting the flag flown by Admiral Togo at the Battle of Tsushima in 1905, Admiral Chuichi Nagumo's fleet struck at Pearl Harbor, to devastating effect, early on what in Hawaii was Sunday 7 December 1941. An hour before the Japanese ambassador to Washington managed to complete the deciphering and translation of the lengthy declaration of war, the waves of aircraft struck after receiving the codeword 'Tiger, tiger, tiger'. They used air-launched torpedoes brilliantly, as the British had done against the Italian navy at Taranto the previous year. The two-hour assault, in which 3,700 Americans were killed or wounded, really should not have come as such a surprise since, to general Western acclaim, the Japanese had used just such a pre-emptive attack in 1905 against the Russian fleet at Port Arthur. Although Pearl Harbor was an apparently devastating outrage, in fact only one battleship, the *Arizona*, was a total write-off, and the three US Pacific Fleet carriers were absent and unscathed.

II HITLER UNBOUND

Pearl Harbor also surprised Hitler, who first heard about it via the BBC on the evening of the attack. He was elated by a move whose cunning audacity reminded him of his old self. He took a purely instrumental view of the Japanese, who would divert the US and British. The Japanese took an equally dispassionate view of Germany, hoping it would preoccupy the British and US sufficiently for Japan to secure its Asian colonial empire before the US could mobilise its enormous resources.[14]

It is no mystery why Hitler declared war on 11 December, even though a Japanese attack on the US did not oblige him to do so under the Tripartite Alliance. He did not warm to the Japanese and found the thought of Asians ordering around white men uncongenial, while the Japanese did not exempt a special category called 'Germans' from their overall racial disdain for 'whites'. Racist weirdness combined with severely practical considerations to make a decision that was very much Hitler's own. Initially an admirer of the energy of the predominantly Nordic immigrants who had slaughtered the Native Americans, during the 1930s his view of the US became coloured by loathing of the Jews who he believed pulled Roosevelt's strings like malign puppeteers. Not for the last time, a tiny minority was held responsible for the policy decisions of that vast and powerful country, and in Hitler's mind the Jews became synonymous with America.

There were also more immediate reasons for declaring war. The US had been waging an undeclared war in the North Atlantic and was sustaining Britain, and increasingly the Russians, with Lend–Lease deliveries. Since the writing was on the wall, any self-respecting dictator was obliged to take the initiative and strip away the pretence of peace. Hitler hoped that war between Japan and the US would mean a dwindling of Lend–Lease supplies to Britain and Russia, while diverting future US military efforts away from Europe. War with the US would also enable him to remove restraints on the submarines endeavouring to sever Britain's Atlantic lifelines, while the Japanese pilfered its imperial wealth in Asia. A global war clarified another issue and on 12 December 1941 he repeated what he had said in January 1939, vowing that its outbreak would signal the annihilation of the Jews in Europe and beyond. It was a completely crazy decision, bringing down on Germany's head the greatest economic power on earth.

III ARROW'S FLIGHT

Pearl Harbor was only part of more ambitious operations that had begun several hours earlier at Kota Bahru. Thirty-five thousand Japanese troops, under the brilliant General Tomoyuki Yamashita, took ten weeks to conquer Malaya and Singapore, which were defended by three divisions, one Australian and two Indian, and then reinforced by another that was solely British. The inadequacy of these forces reflected Churchill's belief in the overriding strategic importance of the Middle East and Mediterranean. The Japanese had used their large diaspora community to ascertain the lie of the land well before hostilities commenced. Each division brought six thousand bicycles, which lent momentum to their attacks up and down the Malay peninsula. They also brought 150 tanks against an opponent with none, which struck terror into colonial forces that had never encountered them. Manuals which addressed how to deal with tanks were never distributed.[15] The Japanese army air force ranged freely, raining bombs on urban centres and strafing the roads, outclassing the RAF's little contingent of obsolete aeroplanes, the best having been reserved for the European and North African theatres. Dominion and Indian troops ended up protecting forward air bases long after the RAF's planes had been annihilated.[16]

Second-eleven British generals were clueless about an opponent who was brilliant in surprise offensives. Experienced Japanese troops smashed their way through improvised defences in northern Johore, whose multi-ethnic armies suffered from social and cultural tensions. There was also some irony in the British attempting to stoke the martial spirits of colonial peoples such as the Malays, whom they had spent decades pacifying with the aid of Punjabi troops imported from India's North West Frontier. Troops newly arrived from Britain had no time even to correct their shipboard lurch or otherwise acclimatise themselves. There were tensions between military and civilian rulers in Singapore, and between the three services, whose headquarters were absurdly far apart. A further complication for a regime with too many chiefs was the visit of the bumptiously ignorant Duff Cooper as Churchill's emissary. In late January, British forces fell back on Singapore island and blew a seventy-foot gap in the causeway. The tall, buck-toothed General Arthur Percival, a weak, over-promoted staff officer with no operational experience, dithered under the weight of stupid suggestions from, among others, the Australian General Gordon

Bennett, and refused to order his troops to dig in because of its supposedly adverse effect on civilian morale.[17] Meanwhile, from a sort of glass conning tower atop the palace of the Sultan of Johore, General Yamashita had a bird's-eye view of the entire battlefield as his men crossed the narrow waterway from the mainland.

The vague intention had always been to hold Singapore until reinforcements arrived from the Middle East. Swathed in noxious oil fires, Singapore itself descended into chaos, its huge guns lacking shells for land bombardment. The gin-fuelled bravado of the expatriates at Raffles Hotel crumbled into mass panic, which spread to troops already demoralised by the rout on the northern peninsula. There were desperate battles on the successive lines of defence on the island, but in mid-February 1942 Percival surrendered sixty-two thousand men to Yamashita, who became known as the Tiger of Malaya. A few days before, Churchill had signalled Field Marshal Wavell, the Far Eastern Commander-in-Chief based in India: 'There must be at this stage no thought of saving the troops or sparing the population. The battle must be fought to the bitter end and at all costs ... Commanders and senior officers should die with their troops. The honour of the British Empire and the British Army is at stake.' He reacted furiously to the capitulation, although ironically it was during Churchill's spell as chancellor of the exchequer in 1924–9 that Singapore's defences had been most neglected for budgetary reasons. He had also insisted on despatching the new battleship *Prince of Wales* and the old battlecruiser *Repulse* without the aircraft carrier supposed to have accompanied them, left behind after running aground during trials off Jamaica. *Prince of Wales* – which had fought the *Bismarck* and had conveyed Churchill to Placentia Bay – and *Repulse* were sunk by waves of high-level and torpedo bombers.[18] The diarist Harold Nicolson captured the deeper implications of the fall of Singapore: 'It is dread that we are only half hearted in fighting the whole-hearted. It is even more than that. We intellectuals must feel that in all these years we have derided the principles of force upon which our Empire is built.'[19]

To protect their Malayan operation, and to secure the Dutch East Indies oil fields, the Japanese landed in British Borneo, taking the entire island by early March. Meanwhile, Japanese bombers based on Taiwan pulverised the US air force in the Philippines, prior to invading the archipelago. US and Filipino forces fell back to the strongholds of the Bataan peninsula and Corregidor island, where they held out until, respectively, April and May, after which eleven thousand of the emaciated survivors died during a sixty-five-mile march to the POW camp at San Fernando. Three separate seaborne Japanese forces converged on the islands of the Dutch East Indies; Sumatra, Java, Sulawesi and Timor all fell, and, while some oil fields went up in flames, Japanese use of paratroops took the Dutch defenders by surprise. To complete the rout, Dutch Admiral Karel Doorman went down with his flagship when the small ABCD fleet he commanded was destroyed.

Worse was to come. Operations originally intended as a limited strike to protect the flank of their advance into Malaya developed into the Japanese conquest of Burma, a potential invasion route into British India. The occupation of Burma also cut the road route used to supply Nationalist China, which henceforth had to go by air over the 'Hump' of the Himalayas. Burma was the same size as France and Belgium combined, with deep jungle, few roads and major rivers. The Japanese endured the same adversities of jungle fighting as their opponents and, despite having their food rations reduced to a bare minimum, were required to carry an artillery shell each, and to make bayonet charges to save ammunition.[20] Since more Japanese understood English than vice versa, they took advantage of sloppy British radio security. They also had air superiority in Burma, as they had in Malaya. Their commanders regularly infiltrated troops around their opponents, sowing panic in British Empire troops who believed – with some justification – that they were being surrounded.[21] This was despite the fact that their pre-war belief in the 'effeminacy' of the Burmese meant that the British depended upon more warlike Punjabis, Gurkhas and Sikhs. A Nationalist Chinese force under the seconded US General 'Vinegar Joe' Stilwell distinguished itself, while the British finally managed to disengage and retreat to Imphal as the Japanese advance flagged under the impact of exhaustion, over-extended supply lines and the monsoon. If General Winter saved the Soviet Union, so General Rain, and wind-driven horizontal rain at that, saved British India.[22]

Although Yamashita would be hanged for war crimes committed on the Philippines two years later, his forces also carried out acts of barbarity in Singapore. Ironically, he had expressly forbidden arson, looting and rape, writing in his diary on 19 December 1941: 'I want my troops to behave with dignity; but most of them do not seem to have the ability to do so. This is very important now that Japan is taking her place in the world. These men must be educated up to their new role in foreign countries.'[23] His soldiers were issued with manuals on how to conduct themselves without giving offence, for example in mosques, although there were darker warnings about the perfidy of the Chinese diaspora vaguely reminiscent of what equivalent German instructions said about the Jews.[24] Despite their commander's orders, upon entering Singapore after ten weeks of hard fighting the Japanese soldiers indulged in the widespread rape and slaughter that had characterised their behaviour in China. At the Alexandra Hospital, a British lieutenant showing a white flag was bayoneted, as were a number of patients, including those on operating tables. The rest of the patients and the medical staff were marched off to a primitive lockup. Those who survived the night were bayoneted the following morning. Yamashita executed the officer responsible. He also executed three soldiers who committed rape in Penang, and had their officer, a major, put under close arrest for thirty days. On the other hand, he authorised what the Chinese call 'purification through elimination' or the Sook Ching massacre.

Yamashita was never prosecuted for what happened in Singapore, although the issue of command responsibility would figure in his subsequent conviction and execution for war crimes in the Philippines. The Yamashita Standard, as it was called, made commanders responsible for a sort of criminal negligence in omitting to control their troops; in Singapore, Yamashita was undoubtedly guilty of far more than negligence. Men under his command, and acting in line with his order to 'purify through elimination', terrorised the large ethnic Chinese population. They included supporters of the China Relief Fund, rich men in general, civil servants and former soldiers, or anyone wearing spectacles – which indicated academic intelligence – or decorated with tattoos, or scars acquired in removing them with acid – which indicated triad membership. The army provided manpower to enable the Kempeitai secret police, under Colonel Masayuki Oishi, to set up screening points to examine Chinese males aged between eighteen and fifty. Those who received a triangular stamp on their arms or clothing were taken away in trucks to beaches and golf courses to be bayoneted or machine-gunned. The practice was extended to the rest of Malaya, and was especially murderous in Penang before it was halted in March 1942, by which time anywhere between twenty-five and fifty thousand Chinese had been killed – the Singaporean Chinese claim there were one hundred thousand victims. A second wave of screenings was averted only when the Chinese community agreed to come up with a collective ransom of 50 million Straits dollars, delivered to Yamashita as a cheque inside a casket, with apologies for having been 'running dogs' of the British.[25]

Pan-Asianism became popular in Japan in the 1930s. In theory, the Japanese conceived of their conquests in terms of a large family of peoples, who would adopt the ethically superior Japanese view of the world without deranging its patriarchal hierarchy. In what became Indonesia they used slogans based on the three As: *Asia tjahaja, Asia pelindoeng* and *Asia pemimpin*, or 'Japan the light of Asia, the protector of Asia and the leader of Asia'.[26] Despite the heady rhetoric of the Greater East Asia Co-Prosperity Sphere that did the rounds in Tokyo think-tanks and Konoe's government before the invasions of 1941–2, the Japanese had devoted little thought to how talk of liberation would be reconciled with the desire to reap the material fruits of empire, or with military rule in conquered territories that sometimes already had the rudiments of constitutional government, and always the rule of law, under European colonisers. After all, pan-Asian rhetoric had not won the hearts and minds of the Chinese or Koreans, who had a closer cultural affinity to the Japanese than Malays, Indonesians or Filipinos.[27]

The Japanese endeavoured to sell the war to their domestic population and to the peoples of occupied Asia in terms of liberating the latter from decadent and drunken colonial rulers, who had treated them like helots. As their radio broadcasts said: 'You English gentlemen, how do you like our bombing? Isn't it better tonic than your whisky soda?'[28] As their troops emerged exhausted from various battlefields, they were delighted by the luxury hotels and golf courses, and the shiny modernity of Singapore which they renamed Syonan, or 'light of the South'. The rhetoric of liberation was not credible, coming as it did from people who believed they were the God-sent master race of Asia, and who ruled with the lash. Until March 1945, they left the Vichy French ruling client monarchies in Vietnam, Cambodia and Laos, kept the Malay sultans in place and initially, as we shall see, hoped to maintain the Dutch administration *in situ* across the Indonesian archipelago. Long before the invasions, the Japanese also sought to exploit anti-colonial national liberation movements, notably in Burma, where an ineffectual Burmese Independence Army arrived in their slipstream. They found willing local clients, and in August 1943 allowed Burma to become the first independent country in their empire, although its government was kept on a very tight leash. Other would-be collaborators were rudely disappointed. Indonesian nationalists were ignored when they volunteered their services. When the nationalist Union of Malay Youth organisation demanded independence, its leader was told, 'Let the Japanese be the father. Malays, Chinese and Indians live like a family.

However, if the Malay child is thin, and needs more milk, we will give him more milk.'[29] The Union was proscribed shortly afterwards.

One aspect of Japanese culture proved particularly repellent, namely the reflexive resort to slaps in the face, a grave insult in this part of the world, whenever Japanese encountered anything they construed as dissent. In mitigation it is worth remarking that one Japanese soldier recalled being beaten 264 times during his service, and that the legendary brutality of recruits from Korea or Formosa may have been some sort of compensation for their own much slapped, lowly status. The Japanese also harboured their own racial clichés about most of the populations they ruled over, which echoed the usual British, Dutch or French plaints about feckless, lazy and perfidious natives. Imperial rule under extreme wartime conditions meant co-opting local elites to keep the masses sufficiently docile to supply the extortionate demands of the Japanese economy. A South Sea islander may have caught the practical differences when, after the war, he said: 'We feared the Germans, but did not obey them. We feared the Japanese, and them we obeyed. The Americans we neither feared nor obeyed.'[30]

In the Dutch East Indies, the Japanese initially planned to rule through the existing administration, a plan which broke down after the Dutch civil servants refused to swear oaths of loyalty. As a last resort, the Japanese turned to local elites, anti-Dutch nationalists and the Muslim imams. But while they encouraged campaigns of mass mobilisation around such slogans as 'Movement for the Concentration of the People's Total Energy' or 'Movement to Destroy the Americans and English', they simultaneously banned the word 'Indonesia', together with the nationalist anthem and flag. The Japanese may have indirectly paved the way for independent state formation in this part of the world, but their contribution was the largely negative one of smashing the colonial powers beyond resuscitation.

CHAPTER 10

The Resistance

For a brave minority in Europe there was a seamless transition from angry rejection of occupation, a desire to thwart the Germans, or to escape the dead time of internment and imprisonment, in to what became known as the Resistance, although this assumed varying degrees of virulence. The term 'resistance' only gradually became generic to describe whatever actively challenged the Nazi new order, rather than behaviour that was of purely symbolic significance. For some people, just glimpsing armed Germans in their streets was enough, although the disappointing way in which fellow citizens reacted was often important too. The Lyons journalist Yves Farge recalled:

> The trolley-bus from Tassin stopped to let a German motorized column pass, and some type on the bus dared to say in a loud voice 'The French are at last going to learn what order really is.' I nearly hit him. Then in front of the Grand Hotel there were women waiting to see the German officers emerge. To one of them I said 'Too old for prostitution.' It all began in ways like that.[1]

Individuals from a variety of backgrounds and creeds – ranging from Socialists to the clerical, anti-Semitic and Germanophobic extreme right, an alliance which one resister recalling Stendhal wittily called 'les Rouges et les Noirs' – felt so strongly about the conditions imposed on them that they undertook activities that could result in arrest, torture, execution or, from 1941 onwards, deportation to an uncertain fate.

Exactly why only a minority of individuals embarked on this course – albeit over time rather than all together from the start – is unclear, or at least it is impossible to generalise. Material factors, such as food shortages, seem to have played no part in decisions that involved mind and spirit, or witness in the case of committed Christians. If hunger created resistance then it would have been a mass movement rather than the minority affair it was, with only a quarter of a million officially recognised resisters in France after the war.

Perhaps an insistent individualism and a capacity to hold on to essential moral truths were the common characteristics linking colourful adventurers such as Emmanuel d'Astier de la Vigerie, a man of the south, with a steely-minded civil servant like Jean Moulin, or Catholics with Protestants, Jews and atheists, monarchists with republicans, conservatives with Socialists. As a disillusioned Communist astutely said, resistance was primarily a question of 'character' or 'nature' rather than of conscious deliberation. A significant number of resisters seem to have decided that Nazism was inherently evil, again a word that historians – as opposed to say clerics or judges – affect not to use nowadays.[2]

Although patriotism is another unfashionable word, many of these people were patriots who rejected Nazism, the Munich Agreement and the policies which had led to France's defeat. Because of the line stipulated by Moscow, and their class-based analysis of events, the French Communist Party adopted what was tantamount to neutrality between 'imperialist' Germany and Britain, until the invasion of the Soviet Union in June 1941 dictated another line.[3] Other than the Communists, patriotism was evident at all levels of society and was beyond the monopoly of any existing political party, especially as these were universally blamed for France's defeat. A conservative landowning farmer called Louis de la Bardonnie, who founded the group Confrérie Notre Dame in the Dordogne, singled out the role of humble people, even quoting the Socialist leader Jean Jaurès' dictum 'The fatherland is the only wealth of the poor,' but he was referring to those who indirectly supported the active resisters. These were, initially, overwhelmingly urban and middle class.

A willingness to seek friends outside class or ideological encampments also helped, although more often than not, since it relied so heavily on trust, resistance developed among groups of the like-minded. As Bardonnie recalled: 'The members of our group were mostly friends from childhood, all orientated to the political Right.'[4] Similar bonds had already coalesced among supporters of Republican Spain. As a civil servant in Pierre Cot's Air Ministry, Jean Moulin had been engaged in secretly shipping aircraft to Spain's Republicans in the mid-1930s, despite the official embargo on supplying arms. Other groups were a veritable social melting pot, which seems to have been one of their major attractions. The army officer Henri Frenay altered his views under the influence of Berty Albrecht, a Swiss-born woman who had left her English husband to return to France, and who introduced Frenay to exiled German Jews and Spanish Republican refugees. Moreover, in a clandestine war, women were as important as men, particularly because they could exploit their feminity or maternity to evade close scrutiny by policemen. Many foreigners – including exiled Germans, Poles and Spanish Republicans – also figured alongside indigenous elements.[5] In the earlier years resistance was very much an urban phenomenon centred on Paris, Lyons and Marseilles, but from 1943 the geography of revolt shifted towards the remoter countryside with the growth of the *maquis*, armed bands which took their generic name from the scrublands of Corsica. Each region, or sub-region, brought its own micro-conditions to resistance – so that the Protestant Cévennes showed more solidarity to *maquisards* and Jews than did the Catholic north of the Lozère.

Another common denominator among resisters was their willingness to court risks, represented by the hand on the elbow, the screech of police cars or a pre-dawn pounding on the front door. They had enormous courage, acting in the knowledge of their potential fate. The memoirs of leading resistance figures, such as Henri Frenay, are punctuated by the visceral shock caused by the loss of valued comrades. One such was the lawyer Jacques Renouvin, a former supporter of the ultra-conservative Action Français, who was one of the main advocates of violence against collaborators: 'My legs crumpled, my voice deserted me. Renouvin, my old friend, in the hands of the Gestapo. If they identified him, he was done for. Once again I had that sensation that always seized me when I heard of the arrest of some dear friend: a constriction in my throat verging on nausea, deep inner dejection, outward distress.'[6] The alternative to torture included throwing oneself out of a Gestapo building window – the fate of the northern resistance leader Pierre Brossolette in February 1944 – or swallowing a cyanide capsule, which Jacques Bingen elected to do three months later.

There was enormous stress involved in living under multiple identities, constantly moving between safe houses and subjecting oneself to the demands of a meticulous tradecraft that left no room for error. Did the initials in a shirt or hat correspond to those of the wearer's papers, and did his or her place of residence correspond to a laundry mark in an item of clothing? Every journey involved trusting guides whom one had never met, or using public transport where German and Vichy policemen would carefully inspect forged papers, comparing them with the genuine article. Had the forger retained, or corrected, the single deliberate spelling mistake the authorities had included to trap the unwary? Some put their infants in foundlings' homes for the unknown duration, to avoid the added risks a baby entailed for anyone who might have to move, silently, at a moment's notice, although the teacher Lucie Aubrac and her Jewish husband Raymond combined looking after their young son Jean-Pierre with activity in the Lyons resistance, while another leading resister had eight children. Aubrac's memoirs combine the sights and smells of a normal family life with episodes of extreme danger, as when she twice ventured into the office of Klaus Barbie, the infamous Lyons Gestapo chief, to ascertain the whereabouts of Raymond, who had been arrested.[7] Other accounts convey the psychological troughs resisters experienced. As he sat writing organisational papers, even such a dedicated resister as Frenay asked himself whether the loneliness was worth it, as armies, airmen and sailors clashed on vast foreign battlefields. In a rare moment of despair, he called it his 'antlike struggle'.[8]

The division of France meant that in the north resisters primarily confronted the Germans, while in the Unoccupied Zone they had to deal with Vichy. This represented an insidious challenge to many conservative or Catholic resisters, since Vichy's regressive National Revolution encompassed values they also espoused, up to and including the desire to find a local French solution to what they concurred was a 'Jewish problem' involving an overly dominant elite minority. Many southern resisters, especially those with backgrounds in the military, took some time to relinquish their loyalty to Pétain, a process that became definitive only after he brought Pierre Laval back into office in April 1942. By then Vichy's claim to be playing a complex *double-jeu* seemed hollow. Vichy's attitudes to those who solely opposed Germans rather than Vichy itself was also ambiguous. Since Vichy itself did not recognise the legality of the physical division of France, it was complicit with resisters who slipped back and forth across the demarcation line. As they surveyed the see-saw of Allied and Axis fortunes, the more sinuous Vichy ministers also dabbled in localised truces with the resistance – with Henri Frenay meeting the Interior Minister Pierre Pucheu on two controversial occasions. Vichy officials also tested which way the wind blew; the most striking example was future Socialist President François Mitterrand, as he smoothly migrated from Pétain, who awarded him a medal, via General Georges Giraud in Algeria to de Gaulle, who treated him with unsurpassed frostiness.[9]

Resisters could be involved in clandestine networks, closely connected to, or indeed established by, the secret services of the Allies and their own exiled governments; or they might be part of self-proclaimed movements which sought to dispel the passivity which the occupiers hoped would spread among the subject population in the absence of mass Fascist mobilisation. They operated in a sort of fog, for they inevitably had complex dealings with a host of agencies they sought to subvert, including the Vichy police, since the boundaries between resistance and collaboration were dynamic, as collaborators made their own complex calculations of self-interest with the rise and fall of Axis fortunes. In other words, resisters were often interlaced with the world they simultaneously fought.

Unfortunately resisters are often synonymous in people's minds with scruffy partisans bedecked with bandoliers of cartridges, a view which reflects left-wing romanticisation of bandits and guerrillas everywhere. Nothing could be further from the truth, at least before the outbreak of the insurgencies associated with the *maquisards* in 1943–4. In several places, predominantly conservative Catholic army officers decided to ignore the Armistice by hiding rather than surrendering caches of weapons, which proved useful when resistance took on an armed aspect. Others, such as Frenay, decided to escape from German captivity. The army's own intelligence service – the Deuxième Bureau – became another hub of resistance, although it combined spying on the Germans with monitoring both Communists and Gaullists, who were deemed 'anti-national forces'. In such circles it took time to lose old habits of hierarchy and obedience, and loyalty to Pétain took longer to dispel. Another group represented in the resistance were Christian democrats, regular clergy and intellectuals, who also combined opposition to the Nazis with support for Pétain. Often drawn from the ranks of Dominicans and Jesuits, who had no parochial duties to interfere with sustained reflection, these people had already grasped the pseudo-religious essence of Nazism in the 1930s, something also evident in the case of Frenay, who in a lecture to reservists in September 1938 had remarked: 'The German Army is imbued with a mystique which has potentially dangerous consequences. Tomorrow this army will set out, not on a "lovely war" but on a holy war, its chieftains and its soldiers inflamed with a quasi-religious faith.' Journalists and academics, evinced a touching regard for the truth in a world of circum-ambient lies.[10]

The first signs of organised resistance often involved statements of principle and right conduct under German occupation that would appal a modern moral relativist. An air force general called Cochet issued one whose drift was 'watch, resist, unite'. The art historian Agnès Humbert, who was a leading light of a resistance group that formed in the ethnological museum in Paris, gave an eloquent account of the psychological state of those who embarked on resistance in August 1940:

> I find [the art critic and poet Jean] Cassou in his office ... Suddenly I blurt out why I have come to see him, telling him that I feel I will go mad, literally, if I don't do something, if I don't react somehow. Cassou confides that he feels the same, that he shares my fears. The only remedy is for us to act together, to form a group of ten like-minded comrades, no more. To meet on agreed days to exchange news, to write and distribute pamphlets and tracts, and to share summaries of French radio broadcasts from London. I don't harbour any illusions about the practical effects of our actions, but simply keeping our sanity will be success of a kind. The ten of us will stick together, trying between us to get to grips with the situation. Basically, it will be a way of keeping our spirits up.[11]

Such tracts were laboriously copied using carbon paper and manual typewriters, long before anyone acquired mimeographs or a willing printer, the indispensable condition for mass production. The censorship, and the ideological distortion of news, meant that some of the earliest manifestations of resistance took the form of an alternative clandestine press, its historic exemplars being the clandestine papers of occupied Belgium during the Great War or the partisan press of the Dreyfus era. Much of the content derived from broadcasts by the BBC and Swiss or Vatican radios, the only sources of news uncorrupted by enemy propaganda. The most noteworthy French papers included *Défense de la France*, *Libre France*, *Libération*, *Le Franc-Tireur*, *Combat*, *Valmy* and *Résistance*. A group of Lyons-based Jesuits who helped escaping Jews issued their own *Cahiers du Témoinage Chrétien*.[12] Those who issued these papers invariably claimed they were the organs of shadowy groups, whose grandiloquent names belied the fact that they had very few members. In this respect they resembled most revolutionaries everywhere, going back to the Carbonari conspiracies of the early nineteenth century.[13]

These papers might be followed with booklets of slogans to be chalked or daubed on prominent walls, a spectacular example being the black-lettered 'THE RESISTANCE GROUP COMBAT PUNISHES TRAITORS' which appeared on the aqueduct at Montpellier, but it was often just a Cross of Lorraine (the symbol adopted by de Gaulle's Free French) or a V for Victory echoing the signature signal of the BBC. German or Vichy posters were defaced or torn down too. The newspaper distribution networks drew in recruits, maintaining their activist commitment and forging group solidarities, while giving those involved experience of the rudiments of clandestine activity. Tracts had to be left on public transport, or slipped into clothing displayed in shops and department stores, or covertly put in mail boxes by brave concierges. The readers of underground papers developed a sense of being a complicit group, with the newspaper or pamphlet taking the place of public meetings, which were prohibited. In other words, the papers were the sinews of a broader movement which for reasons of security operated as distinct cells. From there it required more grit, and a higher level of resolution, to destroy the competition. This was the task of the *corps francs*, which Jacques Renouvin organised from his base in Montpellier, to deter collaborators. A newsstand owner selling German illustrated magazines such as *Signal* would receive an anonymous appeal to his patriotism. Next would come an unfriendly warning, accompanied by an explosion or fire in the newsstand if he ignored it. A circular would explain to other businesses why this had happened. Further attacks hit the offices of Fascist parties or the recruitment offices for the labour-prisoner of war substitution programme known as the *relève* which exchanged French workers in greater numbers for returned POWs. Such attacks initially amounted to stunts when compared with the assassinations and bombings being perpetrated by the Communists – occasioning the sanguinary German reprisals we saw in an earlier chapter.[14]

In most occupied countries, organisation of disparate resistance groups was the precondition for sustained fighting. In France concerted attempts to unite the highly fissiparous and localised resistance movements resulted from Jean Moulin's visit to London in September 1941, during which he met de Gaulle. In so far as either man was capable of much human emotion, they liked what they saw. Although Moulin was not entitled to speak on behalf of the internal resistance, de Gaulle empowered him as his official Delegate of the French National Committee to the Unoccupied Zone, with his written commission in the form of a microfilm strip concealed in a matchbox. While many resisters regarded the authoritarian de Gaulle as a Fascist, Moulin had one major asset, namely the money and arms he was promised from London, which tended to concentrate minds. One should not underestimate the difficulties he faced in making large egos co-operate with one another, especially since Frenay's Combat was much bigger than the rival organisations in the south, notwithstanding the larger-than-life personality of d'Astier. There was also the parallel problem of dealing with the Communists, who sought to monopolise all resistance by forming so-called national fronts, which they could covertly control.

Moulin discovered that indirect, practical co-operation was the most effective route to unity, founding a joint Press and Information Bureau and a General Study Committee to mull over long-term issues. Unity at the activist base that was derived from joint participation in demonstrations also put pressure on the leaders at the top. A single southern resistance movement called the United Movements of the Resistance (MUR) emerged only in January 1943. Although the idea of obeying orders from London was often anathema to them, the three southern military wings coalesced into a Secret Army under a regular army officer, General Charles Delestraint. This was a mixed blessing, as it meant the subordination of armed resisters to de Gaulle's strategy of linking any substantive action to an Allied invasion. How did one maintain group cohesion and effectiveness for a fight that seemed to be indefinitely postponed?

By this time, de Gaulle's own hard-won position had been complicated by the emergence of Admiral Darlan and then General Giraud in North Africa, in whom US President Roosevelt saw an alternative French leadership with serious armed forces at their disposal. The domestic resistance also had to consider how to respond when in the spring of 1943, following the introduction of compulsory labour service in Germany, thousands of young men decided to take to the hills. Further difficulties arose when de Gaulle decided to incorporate the old political parties into the resistance, to prove his democratic credentials, with the establishment of a new Resistance Council. There was concerted opposition to this development, not only among the movements of the Occupied Zone, but also among some of those in the south who despised the 'greasy pot-bellied politicians' of the Third Republic. Representatives of eight resistance movements and five political groupings (there was no representative conservative presence) met in a Parisian apartment on 27 May 1943.

Despite Roosevelt's animus, de Gaulle demonstrated greater political skills and managed to exclude Giraud from the National Committee of

French Liberation, the provisional government founded in Algiers which he headed. The murky circumstances surrounding the capture of Jean Moulin at Caluires on 21 June 1943, and de Gaulle's preoccupation with events in North Africa, meant that much of the work done by Moulin to centralise – or, as his critics averred, 'bureaucratise and sterilise' – the resistance was undone after his demise. What had begun with the printing of pamphlets and newspapers was increasingly dominated by the bomb and gun, especially when at this late stage the Communist Sharpshooters and Partisans (FTP) set the tone among resisters. In the first nine months of 1943 there were 3,800 acts of sabotage, and an increasing number of assassinations of collaborators and members of the newly founded paramilitary Milice, a rag-bag militia of delinquents, fantasists and Fascists. Even movements which had refrained from violence for religious reasons now found themselves employing a rabid tone. Witness the following from a Catholic resistance movement called Défense de la France:

> Kill the German to purify our country, kill him because he kills our people … Kill those who denounce, those who have aided the enemy … Kill the policeman who has in any way contributed to the arrest of patriots … Kill the *miliciens*, exterminate them … strike them down like mad dogs … destroy them as you would vermin.[15]

One major consequence of this mentality was that resistance mutated into an outright civil war between resisters and collaborators, notably members of the Milice. It was no longer only the Germans who carried out reprisal killings against innocent civilians. Already in 1943 the Communist underground paper *Franc-Tireur* warned: 'For each new murder that they commit, the *milicien* and the PPF, or Fascist French Popular Party must expect immediate and merciless reprisals … the French Resistance sends a warning – "For an eye, both eyes; for a tooth, the whole jaw!" This principle could affect many more than individuals directly responsible for atrocities. Thus in April 1944 the resistance assassinated the Milice chief Ernest Jourdan in Voiron near Grenoble. But they also killed his wife, his octogenarian mother, his ten-year-old son and his fifteen-month-old daughter.[16]

Inevitably, in such a vicious struggle, it was not only the Germans, or supporters of Vichy, who bent the rules of war. The SOE agent Harry Peulevé was an exceedingly brave man who organised and equipped *maquisard* forces in the Corrèze. This meant leaving pocket torches containing bombs in the coats of German soldiers in bars and cafés, which blew off their right hand when they switched them on; sabotaging arms dumps, factories and railways; and eventually organising ambushes of German convoys on open roads. The effect was to subtract large parts of the region from Vichy control. The *maquis* did not take prisoners and shot the wounded, as they had no facilities to treat them. Savage German reprisals against civilians were discounted by Peulevé himself:

> For every German we killed, they would kill twenty or thirty hostages, taken at random from the villages through which they passed, but we never let up on them. They were haunted day and night by us, the ghosts in the woods who swooped down on them at every opportunity. This was my revenge for the years when unequal odds and circumstances had put me in the humiliating position of a fleeing coward … Their reply to this treatment was the coward's way out. They took revenge on the women, children and old men … But they could not get us out of the woods.

Suspected spies were treated ruthlessly. On one occasion, Peulevé surmised that the young British airman he was exfiltrating to Spain was a German plant. The 'pilot' made the mistake of being overly familiar with a Cambridgeshire pub Peulevé had invented. Eventually, Peulevé ran a small quantity of plastic explosive around a sapling tree which was instantly cut in half when detonated. He then wrapped a similar charge around the 'pilot's' right shoulder and lit the fuse. The German agent confessed and was shot. Although Peulevé endeavoured to have him decently buried, his *maquisard* comrades dug the man up and sent the corpse in a crate to the Gestapo HQ in Paris, courtesy of the 'British Intelligence Service'.[17]

The New Zealander Bill Jordan, who subsequently became a Catholic priest, was an SOE agent attached to resisters in the Lozère in 1944 after a protracted mission in Greece. His comrades included former policemen attached to the Deuxième Bureau, whose remit included interrogating suspected traitors and captured Germans. To this end they savagely beat them before getting to work with irons heated in a small forge, sometimes by inserting these implements into the suspect's rectum or pressing them into the back and stomach simultaneously to simulate disembowelling. The victims were invariably shot after their ordeal. Jordan was uneasy about the entire process, especially when inflicted on women or girls. When he pointed out that the person operating the forge seemed to be enjoying his work, he was told that the man's entire family had been killed by the Germans after his role in the resistance had been betrayed. It seems unlikely that torture was any more effective than other forms of interrogation. In this case, were it not for the overwhelming evidence of Nazi murderousness, it might have damaged the resistance's claims to moral superiority. In the event, it would take the presence of multi-decorated veterans of the resistance among the military and police torturers unleashed in colonial Algeria in the 1950s and 1960s to do that, although the opprobrium has never become totally retrospective.[18]

It was not only Communists who courted German or Vichy reprisals for their multiplier effect in recruiting more sympathisers to the cause. However, the Communists were certainly those who took the most cold-bloodedly instrumental view of the casualties of this sort of dirty war. Blood spilled in resistance became a form of stake wagered on the board of post-war politics, a blood sacrifice whether to restore the nation's honour or as part of a class war, for the Communists took to referring to themselves as the 'party of the executed' or of 'the 75,000 dead' to give it a round number – a sacrifice justifying their bid for power or a moral debt that others would owe. After the Allies had invaded France, many non-Communist resisters elected to liberate their own nation before the Anglo-Americans arrived, subtracting ever larger areas from either German or Vichy control, although that sacrifice was for France rather than in the interests of the Soviet Union. This conjunction of abstract sacrifices brought multiple human tragedies in its wake.

Saint-Amand-Montrond was a small town of about ten thousand people in the Limousin's sub-region of Cher-Sud. Despite the fact that it was suicidal to try to liberate such a place in rural central France with German troops still in neighbouring towns, the Communist-led resistance in Limoges gave the order to seize it, even though the Limoges Communists would not take part in the action. Closer to the ground, young resistance leaders, spoiling for a fight after years of distributing leaflets, ignored wiser counsels and decided to act. In days rife with unfounded rumours, they imagined simultaneous uprisings would occur in neighbouring towns. They were wrong.[19]

At six in the evening on 6 June 1944 about seventy resistance fighters attacked Saint-Amand. They were welcomed by the sub-prefect, the mayor and the local chief of police, who all sympathised with the resistance. The only fatalities were two hapless members of the Milice who drove into their midst and were captured and shot. The attackers laid desultory siege to the local Milice outpost, which after a perfunctory exchange of inaccurate gunfire and a grenade decided to surrender. An honourable resistance leader thwarted the general desire of his comrades to shoot the eight prisoners, who included a woman with a child of three and another of six months, apparently suffering from bronchitis. They also captured the woman's mother-in-law, with whom the family was lodging. The young mother's name was Simone Bout de l'An, but this meant nothing to them. Inside the base, the resistance fighters found files with the names and addresses of many more *miliciens* in the region – orders went out to detain them too. The prisoners, including Simone, but not her children or mother-in-law who were sent to the local hospital, were removed to the town hall to serve as hostages. Simone's husband was alerted to the fate of his family after one of the Milice men escaped through a window. Soon her captors would learn it too. He was Francis Bout de l'An, the thirty-four-year-old Assistant Secretary General of the Milice throughout France, the organisation's national chief since its titular head, Joseph Darnand, had assumed general responsibility for the Interior Ministry. Bout de l'An, a professor by vocation, left Vichy with thirty *miliciens* while German spotter planes circled Saint-Amand. There, a party spirit erupted among the liberated inhabitants, while young men who had missed the war rushed to volunteer at a sort of *maquis* recruitment fair at the Rex cinema.

Many more citizens presciently realised that there had been no general uprising and fled. Grasping their predicament, the resisters put up posters warning that their thirty-six hostages, including Simone, would be shot if there were any attempt to free them. They also decided to move the hostages elsewhere, releasing a few of them as ordinary people indicated that they had been falsely arrested and had never belonged to the Milice. They drove to a neighbouring town, with one of the women hostages miscarrying in a truck as it bumped along a rural route where the signs had been obscured with tar.

At dawn on the 8th, German troops with their faces blackened and wearing helmets camouflaged with foliage entered the town with armoured cars and light tanks. People they encountered were randomly shot in the street, while about two hundred others arbitrarily identified as sympathisers of the resistance were herded into the sub-prefecture building. In the afternoon, they separated eight of those easily identified as resisters by armbands and the like and shot them in a garden. When one of their Milice associates accidentally fired his weapon, the Germans used flamethrowers and incendiary grenades to burn down several houses. After the arrival of Francis Bout de l'An, who liberated his mother and his two children from the town hospital, the surviving Milice in Saint-Amand set about their own man hunt, arresting sixty persons whom they took to be resisters or their relatives and sympathisers. In other words, the resisters' gambit of taking hostages to prevent reprisals had backfired – they now had their own hostage crisis involving their own friends and relatives and other innocent people.

While young men with guns postured on either side, more reflective individuals acted to prevent multiple tragedies. The town mayor, a sixty-year-old wine grower called René Sandrin, sought out Bout de l'An's deputy, successfully interceding for the release of about twenty of the hostages who he claimed had no connection with the resistance. They were rearrested once Bout de l'An heard of this development. Moreover, he told his deputy to announce that if his wife was not freed in forty-eight hours he would shoot all the hostages and destroy the town. As a demonstration of earnestness, he sacked his errant deputy, replacing him with a notorious Jew-hater called Joseph Lécussan, an alcoholic with a reputation for extortion and murder of elderly Jews. In the time before his arrival, Mayor Sandrin struck a deal with the outgoing deputy. If he could find and return Simone Bout de l'An, both the hostages and town would be spared destruction. Together with two brave volunteers he set off, with only the vaguest idea of where the resisters and their hostages might be. The day ended with no success in making contact, even as Bout de l'An ordered the arrest of more hostages that night. Moreover the newly arrived Lécussan was contemptuous of the deal Sandrin had arranged, despatching the hostages to Vichy the following morning.

Meanwhile, after receiving a tip that the resistance was holding its hostages in a nearby château, Sandrin and his colleagues set off in their car, bedecked with the white sheets of those seeking to parley. In addition to negotiating multiple checkpoints, they were frequently halted by herds of cattle or flocks of sheep. In the end, although a rendezvous with the *maquis* was set up, they waited on the wrong road. At Vichy, Francis Bout de l'An greeted the sixty hostages sent by Lécussan by informing them that men and women would be shot in batches of ten starting at 10 a.m. the next day, and that the whole of Saint-Amand town would be erased if Simone was not released by that deadline. All the male hostages were repeatedly assaulted throughout the night and underwent terrifying mock executions.

Among the rival groups of hostage-takers confusion reigned, for over the radio the Free French Forces commander, General Pierre Koenig, demanded that the resistance refrain from large-scale insurrectionary activity, largely because of the Allies' problems of resupplying them with arms. On finally learning of Mayor Sandrin's attempts to contact them, her captors dictated a letter for Simone Bout de l'An to write, pleading with her husband to spare the lives of the hostages he held. This was delivered by a circuitous route to Bout de l'An in Vichy. He agreed to delay the executions by a further forty-eight hours. Contact with the men holding Simone and the Milice hostages proved hard to establish, since they had fled into the Creuse, where the hostages were being held in the chapel of a remote castle. Both Sandrin and the Archbishop of Bourges offered themselves as substitute hostages, a gesture Francis Bout de l'An rejected in one of many telephone conversations with the major. The archbishop was more effective. After pleading Christian charity, the archbishop argued that if Bout de l'An shot the hostages he would never see his wife again. Bout de l'An saw reason and postponed the decision to shoot them while negotiations continued. However, he also warned that he would cut off Saint-Amand's utilities and deprive its children of milk by way of piling pressure on the partisans.

Gradually, the terms of a potential trade-off came into view, at least among those engaged in saving lives rather than posturing. Bout de l'An was interested only in the release of the women hostages. He had written off the Milice men on the grounds that they should have put up a better fight to defend his wife. For his part, he was prepared to release all his hostages provided they had not been caught bearing arms. He backed this up with a warning that if Simone was not freed, he would turn the town over to the Germans and have his hostages shot, regardless of the outcome of any trial. The fate of Oradour-sur-Glane, where the SS had massacred nearly a thousand people on 10 June, hung over the dinner arranged by Bout de l'An and Lécussan for the Saint-Amand negotiators, for this was still France. The negotiators even managed to extract a 'proof of life' visit to see Bout de l'An's female captives, held with the others at a racecourse.

After further adventures on dangerous roads, the negotiators (no longer including Sandrin, who had hurt his foot) eventually met a senior resistance figure, who struck the tough postures he thought synonymous with guerrilla leadership and claimed to be leader of the group holding Simone Bout de l'An and the Milice members. Actually he was not, which meant that the ensuing talks with him represented a loss of valuable time. In a striking echo of Bout de l'An's indifference to his cowardly militiamen, this partisan leader – François being his nom de guerre – was uninterested in the male hostages Bout de l'An was holding, on the grounds that if these men had had any guts they would have joined the partisans already. Nor did he want to be seen to acquiesce in a deal whose terms were seemingly dictated by Bout de l'An, with whom he was engaged in a remote battle of masculine wills. However, he would be prepared to release 'his' hostages if the Germans would free an important resister they had captured, although that was to overestimate Bout de l'An's influence. Finally telling the negotiators that he would hang them if he encountered them again, the *maquis* leader handed them a letter to give to Darnand – on the erroneous assumption that Simone Bout de l'An was the latter's mistress. The gist of this missive was that if Bout de l'An harmed any of his hostages, the resistance would cut Simone Bout de l'An into pieces and mail her to her 'lover' in Vichy. While Bout de l'An improved the condition of his own hostages, he also arrested the wives of three men whom he had misidentified as running the resistance organisation responsible for his wife's abduction, again to multiply the pressure.

Meanwhile, the tough Lécussan had grown impatient with the perpetual motions of the negotiators, whom he regarded with as much disdain as the partisan François had shown. He announced that that he was going to start shooting hostages, and summoned German troops, who took up positions near the town, decisions he took while fortified by drink. The negotiators made a final effort and succeeded in meeting the group actually holding Simone Bout de l'An and the Milice hostages, men it transpired who were themselves from Saint-Amand. These resisters in turn had to seek authorisation from the same François who already been so implacable with the negotiators. 'Do what you want,' he replied. On 23 June the negotiators took custody of five women, including Simone Bout de l'An, who were dropped off blindfolded at a remote junction. Simone's favourable view of her captors irritated Lécussan, who had wept tears of inebriate joy on seeing her. Two days later, Bout de l'An kept his word by releasing the hostages and the wives of resisters.

The resistance still held about twenty male Milice hostages, as well as a baker's daughter who had elected to stay with the partisans rather than face the wrath of her father for dating a Milice member, and another mysterious woman known only as 'the Jewess'. As German forces converged on the area, the partisans split into smaller units; the group that had taken over Saint-Amand was surprised by Ukrainians serving in the German army. Nine men were killed and sixty-two captured after a ferocious firefight in a wood. The wounded were shot dead. The captives were handed over to the SS and in August deported to concentration camps in Germany. The group holding what had become thirteen Milice captives kept themselves just ahead of the pursuing Germans, their speed restricted by heavy equipment and the exhausted hostages. As matters became more desperate, it was decided to kill them, since they could easily alert the Germans who were within earshot. This was a difficult decision, because over the previous six weeks the partisans and their prisoners had bonded; after all they were all mainly from Saint-Amand. As the noise of gunfire would have attracted the Germans, the partisans used parachute cord slung over branches to hang the thirteen Milice men, holding them up to create a sufficient drop to break their necks. On learning of these deaths, Lécussan decided to unleash his wrath against the 'real' culprits, as he conceived of them – the two hundred Jews in Saint-Amand, the remnant of two earlier waves of deportation. A combined force of Milice, German soldiers and the Gestapo descended on Saint-Amand. After a celebratory dinner, they detained nearly eighty Jews, ranging in age from a fifteen-month-old infant to war veterans in their seventies, in the Rex cinema.

The majority of these people were moved to a Gestapo prison in Bourges the following day. Since the Allies' interdiction of rail transport made it impossible to ship the Jews to the places of death that had consumed millions, the Gestapo decided to liquidate the twenty-six men on the spot, for the prison was overcrowded. This had to be done surreptitiously given that the Allies had landed in France. After a lengthy search for a suitable site, during which the victims sweltered inside a truck, the Germans (and some of their French associates) alighted upon a disused farm with three deep wells littered with abandoned building materials. The Jews were split into groups of six. Each man was told to pick up a heavy stone or sack of spoiled cement before being thrown down one of the wells. They either died as they hit the side walls or were asphyxiated under corpses and bags of cement. Only one man managed to escape, and was hidden by local farmers. The Jewish women, who had been spared execution, turned out not to be safe. After the *maquis* had boldly assassinated the Milice chief in Bourges, eight of the women without children, and a man the Gestapo had also held back, were taken to the wells and killed too.

The weeks before and following the Allied invasion of France witnessed an upsurge of acts of sabotage which were met with a sanguinary response. Although a rosy hue surrounds the deeds of the partisans, for many people they were not only thieves who issued dubious promissory notes for the food they took, but a dangerous liability that brought indiscriminate German reprisals in their wake. Ascq was a small town near Lille in the region of north-east France incorporated into occupied Belgium. On Saturday 1 April 1944 a small charge exploded on a track near the town's railway station, halting a troop train carrying the SS Panzer Division Hitlerjugend to the Normandy coast. These men were mainly recently recruited members of the Hitler Youth, but most of the officers, who were scarcely older, had served on the Eastern Front. Although the train suffered minimal damage and no one was injured, it was stuck in an area apparently alive with partisans and with Allied aircraft searching for targets of opportunity such as the stationary SS convoy now presented. Unsurprisingly the troops were agitated and jumpy, always a recipe for someone getting killed.

All German forces in the west had been issued with fresh orders on 3 February regarding how to respond to 'terrorist' attacks such as this. They were to seize civilians from the immediate surrounds, burning down any houses from which they took fire. That was not exactly what these SS had undergone at Ascq, yet acting on orders from twenty-six-year-old SS-Obersturmführer Walter Hauck, the SS troopers raided the town, dragging together all adult males and shooting anyone who resisted or tried to flee. The men they captured were shot in batches at the crossing near where the train had halted, a process that took about an hour. In total some eighty-six innocent civilians were either massacred in their homes or by the railway, including the town's curate who had been giving the last rites to the dying in the street. This action adversely affected the good relations which had existed between the local German authorities, the regional prefect and the Catholic Church. Cardinal Liénart, a notorious Pétainiste, was moved to protest about the killing of one of his clerics. He was not satisfied when the Germans shortly tracked down and executed six railwaymen, whom they held responsible for the bomb blast. He also dismissed German claims that before their deaths these men had identified thirty resisters among the Ascq citizens slain. The cardinal also dismissed Hauck's claims that the convoy had come under fire after the explosion.[20]

As part of attempts to divert German forces from Normandy, the Free French planned Operation Alligator, which involved the large-scale mobilisation of *maquisards* on the Massif Central. Although the plan was subsequently abandoned, after consulting the SOE agent Maurice Southgate, the local Auvergnat resistance leader Emile Coulaudon went ahead regardless of the absence of orders from London or Algiers. A large group of *maquisards* converged on the area of Mont Mouchet, many of them factory workers or students from Clermont Ferrand and Montluçon, in other words men wholly lacking combat experience. After a strong German force had counter-attacked, the partisans divided into smaller groups and dispersed. En route to this engagement, German troops – who seem to have included many Azerbaijanis – ran into small-arms fire in various villages along their route. At Ruines they machine-gunned twenty-five of the inhabitants; at Clavières they killed nine people and burned the village down. Meanwhile, at Murat, where the *maquis* assassinated the Vichy Gestapo chief, twenty-five local people were summarily court-martialled and shot. Subsequently a further 115 people were deported to concentration camps.

The perils of precipitate action by the resistance were also evident in the unremarkable town of Tulle. Throughout March and April 1944, both an SD and Sipo commando unit and a heterogeneous force called the Brehmer Division, largely consisting of Georgians, attempted to suppress the *maquis* in this part of the Corrèze, although most of the fifty-five people they shot had nothing to do with it. Tulle itself was garrisoned with seven hundred German troops, with a similar number of Garde Mobiles and Milice stationed in the town, although local partisans miscalculated the total enemy force at 250 Germans and 400 Garde Mobiles. Local Communists decided to attack the Germans in Tulle, despite this course of action having been vetoed by the resistance leadership in the parallel case of the Limousin's capital of Limoges.

At 5 a.m. on 7 June forces from the Communist Franc-Tireur et Partisans irregular riflemen under the charismatic schoolteacher Jean-Jacques Chapou, or 'Kléber' to use his nom de guerre, infiltrated the town and attacked the German garrison. The Garde Mobiles force asked to leave town under a flag of truce which was granted. Throughout the day the Germans – mainly older men, albeit with military training – kept up a withering fire from the Ecole Supérieure. This took its toll on the *maquis* who began to run out of ammunition or did not know how to operate more sophisticated weapons such as bazookas. One group of Germans eventually surrendered and Tulle's citizens gradually came out into the evening light to celebrate their liberation. No steps had been taken to create obstacles to slow down a relief force. The rumble of tracks and the noise of engines was audible and coming nearer. The partisans retreated as a reconnaissance unit of the SS 'Das Reich' 2nd Panzer Division probed the town, establishing that a group of frightened German soldiers were still resisting from the school. Throughout the night, heavily armed and camouflaged SS troops retook control of Tulle, but not before nine captured members of the Gestapo had been shot in addition to the 139 men killed in the day's action. Despite seeing that wounded Germans had been treated in the town hospital, the SS affected horror at the 'mutilation' of some of the German fatalities, who had in reality been torn apart by grenades. The core of the 'Das Reich' Division were SS veterans of the Eastern Front, who were well acquainted with every sort of depredation against civilians.[21]

In line with orders issued by their commander, General Heinz Lammerding, the SS rounded up every male aged between sixteen and sixty, corralling about three thousand of them in the town's arms factory, where many worked. All but five hundred were gradually released after various French notables had assured the Germans of their indispensability to the smooth running of the arms plant and Tulle itself. One of the survivors of the attack on the German garrison, a Sipo–SD officer called Walter Schmald, whose closest comrade had shot himself rather than surrender to the partisans, then selected a group of 120 men from the detainee pool, his criteria being that their muddy boots or dirty and unshaven faces indicated they were *maquisards*. By the afternoon it became evident that the SS intended publicly to hang this group, with the five hundred men from the larger surviving group forced to watch. When the mayor protested against the method of execution, he was told that it was 'nothing for us', as the division had hanged 'a hundred thousand' people in Kiev and Kharkov in the Ukraine. The SS set up *ad hoc* gallows on trees and lamp-posts or the balconies of apartments. While the executions took place, other SS personnel loitered, listening to gramophone music in the Café Tivoli. Eventually after hanging ninety-nine men, they called it a day and reprieved twenty-one. Of the larger surviving group of detainees, 149 were subsequently deported to Dachau, from which only forty-eight returned alive, while the rest were released.[22]

CHAPTER 11

Moral Calculus

I THE CROWN'S TERRORISTS?

Britain was the main external sponsor of resistance in Nazi-occupied Europe, whether in setting up its own networks of agents or in subsidising the networks and movements led by each country's own nationals. The chosen instrument was the Special Operations Executive (SOE) formed in July 1940 – an historical example of irregular violence much favoured by moral relativists seeking to excuse contemporary terrorist movements. SOE's organisational sinews went back to the immediate pre-war years, when the foreign intelligence service, SIS, formed a sabotage department (D) which merged with a smaller research department in the War Office (GS R) and a propaganda unit named Elektra House (or EH) after its building in the Foreign Office. Its early personnel set about writing the rules of guerrilla warfare from scratch, drawing upon the history of the Boer War and, in many cases, their own experiences in Ireland. The activities of IRA terrorists were to become paradigmatic for the SIS officers and City businessmen who made up SOE's initial recruits, although this should not be sensationalised, as they undertook many other kinds of activity, and the IRA of the 1920s was not the same indiscriminately murderous beast as the Provisionals of 1970s and 1980s. It may have shot people in the back, but it did not blow up women and children.

In seeking to explain the precipitate collapse of France, Belgium or the Netherlands, many people suspected that the Germans had used fifth columns within those countries; the British decided to create their own, to reverse-engineer their own reconquest of the continent. SOE's mission was partly determined by the outlook of its first political master, who put a very ideological slant on Churchill's romantic injunction to 'set Europe ablaze'. Since Tory ministers Lord Halifax and Sir John Anderson were in charge respectively of SIS and the domestic security service MI5, it was thought politically desirable to appoint a Labour minister to run SOE, the choice falling on Hugh Dalton, the Minister of Economic Warfare until February 1942, who, having established an effective naval blockade, was at something of a loose end. A London School of Economics lecturer turned politician, Dalton idolised Churchill, although the feeling was not mutual: Churchill detested Dalton's 'booming voice and shifty eyes'.[1] In a letter to Attlee, Dalton reasoned that this sort of warfare was best left to civilians, for 'regular soldiers are not men to stir up revolution, to create social chaos or to use all those ungentlemanly means of winning the war which come so easily to the Nazis'.[2] His preferred metaphor for how SOE would operate was 'body-line bowling against the Hun', a (then) unsporting practice in cricket where the bowler aims the ball straight at the batsman's body. SOE's initial remit was to cause popular uprisings. Dalton spelled out what this unorthodox style of warfare entailed:

> We have got to organize movements in enemy-occupied territory comparable to the Sinn Fein movement in Ireland, to the Chinese Guerrillas now operating against Japan, to the Spanish Irregulars who played a notable part in Wellington's campaign or – one might as well admit it – to the organizations which the Nazis themselves have developed so remarkably in almost every country in the world. This 'democratic international' must use many different methods, including industrial and military sabotage, labour agitation and strikes, continuous propaganda, *terrorist acts against traitors and German leaders* [italics added] boycotts and riots.[3]

Although some have highlighted the terrorist side of SOE operations to remove some of the opprobrium of terrorism from post-war practitioners, it is worth noting that this was merely an aspect of SOE activities (and one focused on German functionaries and collaborators) rather than a campaign of politically motivated indiscriminate violence designed to terrorise civilians for its own sake. SOE, and more importantly the exiled governments it liaised with to recruit native-speaking agents, was highly conscious of the need to protect civilians, even as this form of warfare necessarily blurred the distinction between them and uniformed combatants, virtually courting German reprisals against entirely blameless groups of people.

The name for this new organisation was chosen by Neville Chamberlain, who spent the summer before his death that November working out how SOE could be meshed into the wartime bureaucracy and financed without close parliamentary scrutiny. Under its first chief, the former Tory MP and spy Sir Frank Nelson, and his deputy, the Anglo-Danish banker Sir Charles Hambro, SOE spread out in office space in and around London's Baker Street. Unsurprisingly it was hard to contact, while its senior personnel went around in regular service uniforms well below their actual rank within the clandestine organisation. Since the Political Warfare Executive gained responsibility for subversive propaganda, of the 'Who is sleeping with your wife while you are serving on a U-boat' variety, SOE was free to concentrate on clandestine warfare more narrowly conceived. Once it became apparent that there was not going to be a continent-wide rising against the Germans, SOE settled for the strategy of establishing secret armies which would spring into action, if and when there was an Allied return to the mainland. The model here was the underground armies of occupied Poland, which SOE intended to generalise and detonate like a series of well-laid mines. Ironically, the one country not to receive substantial British support prefatory to such a rising was Poland, which some policy-makers may already have mentally consigned to the sphere of influence of Russia.

SOE was regarded with suspicion in and beyond Whitehall. The armed forces did not care for its call on their resources or its ungentlemanly methods. RAF Bomber Command resented having to divert precious aircraft to drop SOE agents by parachute, once it became clear that seaborne infiltrations were unfeasible. Eventually a squadron dedicated to SOE and SIS service, called 100 Group, was established at Newmarket. When SOE proposed Operation Savannah, which involved dropping agents into France to kill German pathfinder-bomber pilots being bussed to their base near Vannes, Air Chief Marshal Portal strenuously objected: he thought that 'the dropping of men dressed in civilian clothes for the purpose of attempting to kill members of the opposing forces is not an operation with which the Royal Air Force should be associated ... I think you will agree that there is a vast difference, in ethics, between the time honoured operation of the dropping of a spy from the air and this entirely new scheme of dropping what one can only call assassins.'[4]

Both the Foreign Office and SIS were concerned that SOE's conspicuously loud operations might interfere with delicate diplomatic gambits or with the stealthy insertion of secret agents into enemy territory to gather intelligence. For example, if British policy was to bribe high-ranking Spanish generals to keep Spain from joining the Axis, there was little point in talking up the potential use of left-wing Spanish Republicans as resistance fighters after a hypothetical German invasion. Likewise, murky diplomacy with the Vichy authorities meant that until November 1942, when the Germans occupied Vichy too, SOE was forbidden to carry out any major acts of sabotage in the Unoccupied Zone of France. Romantically convinced that should the Nazis invade Britain it would be men like his Durham miner constituents who would conduct the fight back, Dalton believed that socialists and trades union members would be the backbone of resistance to the Nazis in occupied Europe, a view not shared by many of SOE's stock conservative operators, or by SIS, which ironically was riddled with upper-class Communists.[5] Such fantasies of general revolution anyway did not coincide with the political complexion of most of the exiled governments represented in London. Those exiled governments also quickly exercised a veto over violent direct action of the sort favoured by the Communists, once Russia had been invaded, who had to make a complex calculation between seeming to do something and triggering savage German reprisals against innocent people, never much of a concern in Communist circles. The Russians, it has been said by SOE historian David Stafford, were prepared to fight to the last European. But then again, Europeans were just as keen to fight to the last Russian. British government policy was to support the status quo ante rather than to embark on the revolutionary transformation of Europe. They airily envisaged patriotic risings, until the activation of occupied Europe's Communist parties immensely complicated matters to the point of triggering what amounted to civil wars within resistance forces, which left SOE supporting all those reactionary forces which appalled Dalton.

SOE had no agents in France until the first was dropped by parachute in May 1941, so the agency's energies were initially focused on the Balkans, seeking to interdict German supplies of oil from Rumania and shipping along the Danube. Neither operation was successful. British efforts to create a firewall of anti-German governments in the Balkans, notably through an SOE-backed coup in Yugoslavia in March 1941, also came to naught as the Germans rolled into the region in early April. Throughout 1941 SOE concentrated on building up resistance movements in France and Yugoslavia, once de Gaulle and the Royalist Chetnik leader Draža Mihailović had created a semblance of resistance unity in their respective countries. However, instead of becoming an independent 'fourth arm' of

Britain's war effort, SOE was destined to be subordinate to Allied grand strategy, co-ordinating resistance activities with the wider conduct of warfare. This, from June 1941, involved taking into consideration the aspirations and sensitivities of the USSR, which went from being the ideological enemy but military ally of Hitler to being Britain's best hope of eventual victory over Nazi Germany.

SOE consisted of a singular group of men and women, ranging from burglars to City bankers, from pimps to princesses, their mission to organise intelligence and subversive networks while harnessing them to Britain's wider strategic interests. It is impossible to generalise about the motives of so many courageous individualists, beyond such common denominators as bilingualism, extensive time abroad either as a child or on business, or possession of such indispensable skills as radio electronics. There were probably as many former pacifists among them as adventurers in the mould of characters created by John Buchan and Dornford Yates, who were rightly regarded as a liability. Some of them were embarrassed by the swift collapse of their countries to the Germans; others were former soldiers who quickly tired of kicking their heels after Dunkirk, at a time when British civilians were in the war's real front line. The agent Violette Szabó may have been motivated by a desire to avenge the loss of her husband, a Foreign Legion officer killed in North Africa; her colleague, Christine Granville, loved Britain as much as her native Poland and freedom most of all, being the epitome of the cosmopolitan restless spirit that SOE attracted.[6]

Specialist SOE training included sessions with Jasper Maskelyne, a music-hall conjuror who taught agents how to hide gold sovereigns or silk maps on or in their bodies at SOE's base in Cairo, or Eric Sykes, a figure one could have mistaken for a seedy bishop, but who had learned unarmed combat as a policeman serving on the waterfronts of Shanghai in the 1930s. A Norwegian recruit remembered Sykes's guiding philosophy: 'Never give a man a chance. If you've got him down, then kick him to death.' In the field, this Norwegian turned out to be an uncommonly moral man. As well as painstaking tradecraft, agents had to learn how to handle explosives for sabotage or to survive night parachute drops from as little as 500 feet.[7] Theirs was very risky work. According to SOE's leading historian, half the agents sent to Holland, a third of those to Belgium and a quarter of the large number dropped into France did not survive the war.[8]

The term 'terrorism' can be used too casually in connection with SOE's activities, whose remit, as defined by Hugh Dalton, included boycotts, demonstrations and strikes, and industrial and military sabotage, as well as the assassination of German leaders and traitors. Most of these actions would not be considered terrorism by most reputable experts on the subject, unless, in the case of assassination, a bomb or gun attack caused indiscriminate civilian casualties. Nor did Dalton's list of tactics include the deliberate use of political violence to create public fear and panic – feelings already well catered for by the Germans, their ideological confederates and some of the authoritarian regimes that nestled under the Nazi eagle's wings. Yet matters were never that morally transparent, for a war waged by secret agents in occupied Europe inevitably blurred the notion of non-combatant immunity, making civilians liable to indiscriminate reprisals. On occasion, SOE also deliberately encouraged the Germans to act terroristically in the few places where they were not already doing so.

II IN THE SHADOWS

A case in point was the relatively benign and hands-off regime the Germans imposed on Denmark. The first cases of sabotage took place in the summer and autumn of 1942, a period that coincided with the death of Prime Minister Thorvald Stauning. SOE had a number of setbacks in building a Danish network. Too many of the agents were ill-educated seamen who lacked quick wits in tricky situations. A more capable doctor whom SOE carefully trained was killed when his parachute failed to open on his first home mission. Another agent talked too much and on orders from Baker Street had to be shot by his own comrades.[9] German overestimation of the extent of sabotage, and King Christian X's curt response to a seventy-second-birthday telegram from Hitler, inclined the Führer to impose a harsher regime in Copenhagen. This was symbolised by the appointment of a new army commander, Lieutenant General Hermann Hanneken, and a fresh SS supremo Werner Best, who, since we last encountered him, had moved from occupied Paris to the Foreign Ministry.

The Germans were reluctant to dispose of the legally constituted government, however, especially as the former Foreign Minister Erik Scavenius proved more accommodating than Stauning. In March 1943 the Danes were even allowed to hold elections, primarily in the interests of German propaganda and to keep the butter and milk flowing. The four main collaborationist parties won 95 per cent of the poll, while the Danish

Nazis got 3 per cent and a small anti-collaborationist party 2 per cent. In a report to Berlin, Best boasted that it took only 85 German bureaucrats and a further 130 clerical personnel to extract what Germany needed from four million Danes. In contrast, there were three thousand German administrators in Norway, with its much smaller population of 2.8 millions. An RAF raid on a Copenhagen shipyard which produced diesel engines for German submarines gave the Danes a necessary incentive to carry out sabotage, as several workers had been killed in the raid. Sabotage became the lesser evil, its incidence climbing from sixteen attacks in January 1943 to seventy-eight in April and 220 in August. In addition there were industrial strikes which spread to fifteen cities, including Odense, where a German officer was grievously assaulted. Government appeals for calm were ignored and few volunteered to act as factory 'sabotage guards'.

After ruefully acknowledging the failure of his softly-softly policy on a visit to Berlin, Best returned to present the Danish government with ultimata designed to force it to take a tougher line. With the exception of Scavenius the cabinet refused, although eventually even the Prime Minister discovered his backbone. On 29 August the Germans imposed a state of emergency, with a curfew, the interdiction of communications and courts martial for saboteurs and strikers. Denmark had ceased to be the anomaly in Nazi occupied Europe. Thereafter, SOE played a major role in encouraging the two rival wings of the Danish resistance to co-operate: the Communists, under Professor Mogens Fog, and members of the radical right, Dansk Samling. SOE agents Flemming Muus and Ole Lippmann encouraged them to unite under a Freedom Council, and then dextrously encouraged a process of 'regionalisation' to prevent the growth of antagonistic party political armies. A few hundred resisters in 1943 became ten thousand in 1944, and some fifty thousand by the end of the war.[10]

All SOE actions in the Balkans and Greece, which the Allies used as a diversion from their major operations in the Mediterranean, were undertaken under the shadow of indiscriminate reprisals in which hundreds of people were shot in return for each German casualty. SOE shared the playbook of many terrorist movements by forcing a regime (one that needed little encouragement) to reveal its true terrorist face, but it was not itself a terrorist organisation, however much its 'ungentlemanly' manner of warfare sometimes discomfited more conventionally minded soldiers.

But there is a further moral twist, evident in the case of Denmark, which is sometimes overlooked in discussions of SOE activities. The alternative to sabotage of a tyre factory or railway marshalling complex – in which agents placed charges in well-chosen positions and then left with all blame attached to British 'parachutists' – was to flatten them with RAF bombing raids. These, as everyone knew, were rarely precise and tended to hit the surrounding residential areas, killing many innocents. For example, an RAF raid in July 1943 on the Peugeot works at Montbéliard resulted in 160 French casualties and little substantive damage to the plant. The SOE agent Harry Ree – a former conscientious objector – decided to blow up the factory's transformers and turbo compressors, winning the co-operation of its owner, Rodolph Peugeot, who did not want to see sixty thousand people out of work. Ree and his team of locally recruited saboteurs blew up the transformers and turbos on 5 November, reducing the factory's output of tank tracks and engines by three quarters for a whole six months while the machinery was repaired in Germany.[11]

Dalton's (and Churchill's) assessment of SOE's potential reflected a romantic belief that the occupied peoples of Europe would rise up to overthrow Nazi oppressors already reeling from British bombing and enfeebled by naval blockade: 'Nazidom will be a dark pall over all Europe, but, after only a few months, it may dissolve like the snow in spring.' A romantic leftist attachment to the myths of revolution – reflected in Richard Crossman and Kingsley Martin's 1940 tract *A Hundred Million Allies if You Choose* – fused with the naivety of a country that had itself never been invaded and occupied in modern times to exaggerate the prospects of local resistance. As the Joint Planning Staff looked into 'The Distant Future' in June 1941, there were creeping signs of realism about SOE, even as the document envisaged a ten-division armoured force and free Allied contingents supplementing mass patriotic uprisings against depleted German forces.[12]

The initial, romantic conception of SOE withered under a combination of pressures. Propaganda activities were hived off to the Political Warfare Executive. SIS (MI6) and the Foreign Office did not want delicate diplomatic or intelligence gambits sabotaged by the attention that spectacular acts of resistance inevitably attracted. The Chief of the Air Staff, Portal, was sceptical about the impact of minor pinpricks compared with the damage done by RAF bombing. As he bluntly told Dalton: 'Your work is a gamble which may give us a valuable dividend or may produce nothing. It is anybody's guess. My bombing offensive is not a gamble. Its dividend is certain; it is a gilt-edged investment. I cannot divert aircraft from a certainty to a gamble which may be a gold mine or may be completely worthless.' The views of the RAF, as the major element of British strategy, counted for a great deal. Moreover, with the entry of the Soviet Union and the US into the war came the sobering realisation that it was going to be won not by detonating a series of mass uprisings, but by the enormous industrial and military might that these powers would bring to bear on Germany. Then there were the officially recognised exiled governments based in London, concerned – especially after the Soviet Union's entry into the war – lest SOE should back their domestic ideological opponents. Grand strategy towards the Soviets also meant that the interests of the Poles were never treated as urgently as they deserved – notably when they asked for arms which the British feared they might use to halt the advancing Soviets to force them into acknowledging a democratic Poland. The overwhelming desire to pummel the Nazis into submission meant turning a deaf ear to the entreaties of a country Britain had gone to war over, and whose dismemberment by the Molotov–Ribbentrop Pact it became inconvenient to remember.

The exiled governments also acted as a brake on SOE in a further sense. As compatriots of the internal resistance, they were acutely sensitive of the need to avoid anything that would result in horrendous Nazi reprisals – although, in fairness, that was also a dominant consideration in SOE's operational planning. While this concern could not paralyse all aggressive activity, it had to be constantly borne in mind. As the head of SOE's Norwegian section explained to the War Cabinet: 'The use by the enemy of reprisals as a weapon demands that the utmost care be taken in the preparation and planning of every operation that is undertaken, particularly the thorough training of all personnel.'[13] One group of resisters who took a more utilitarian view of reprisal shootings were the Communists. Their attitude was reminiscent of the early Christian martyrs: 'The blood which stains our paving stones is the seed of future harvests.' As devotees of an allegedly scientific doctrine, they were contemptuous of ethical considerations, while their view of themselves as an elite made them indifferent to the petty concerns of lesser unenlightened mortals. Lenin and Stalin had shown the way: history was on their side, its iron laws indifferent to mere individuals. Certainly, some individual Communists agonised over the sacrifices their ideology demanded; but the homely but intrinsically genocidal mantra about breaking eggs to making omelettes usually prevailed. As a Paris-based Communist colonel put it: 'Even at the price of this precious blood of hostages, France could not afford to be presented to the world as a passive prostrate country without will to resist and react ... The price had to be paid ... bitter as it was.'[14] As we shall see, the political necessity of advertising a country's active resistance sometimes outweighed the terrible reprisals it provoked, as well as the security crackdowns that adversely affected patiently constructed resistance networks. The founder of the southern-zone Combat network, Henri Frenay, articulated his reasons for rejecting the Communist approach very well, even though there was also grudging admiration for their implacability:

> We were familiar with the Communist belief that, since war inevitably involves the death of innocent persons, the execution of hostages had an essentially positive effect in that it aroused the hatred of the people against the enemy. They insisted that ten volunteers would rise up to replace every hostage that was shot. Though I understood this viewpoint, I could not share it ... that I, of my own free will, should sign what would in effect be somebody else's death warrant, for the sole reason that it might instil a greater combative ardour in the people (and this without any serious damage to the enemy) – no, I could never have consented to such a policy. Between the Communists who held this 'utilitarian' point of view, and those who thought as I did, the quarrel was of a philosophical or religious nature and hence without any practical solution. And yet their cold determination compelled my respect, for it never flinched, even when the hostages themselves were party members.[15]

As this indicates, resistance movements consisted of groups with manifold political outlooks, in the French case ranging from Marxist-Leninist-Stalinists to several former supporters of the extreme right, up to and including, it was rumoured, senior members of de Gaulle's inner circle.

For SOE, several knotty problems arose in the general area where organising resistance inevitably overlapped with domestic politics or desired long-term political outcomes. The smoothness we have seen in Denmark was often not replicated elsewhere. Relations with the exiled Belgians were so poor that the Foreign Minister Paul-Henri Spaak could not bring himself to communicate with SOE for months on end. While the Greek exiled government was devoted to King George II, the two main internal resistance movements were the conservatives (EDES) and Communist (ELAS) who detested one another. SOE's Cairo HQ, which was responsible for the Balkans, lied to each about its dealings with the other. For two years SOE backed Draža Mihailović's Yugoslav Chetniks, despite their collaborating with the occupying Italians to defeat their Communist rivals under Tito, believed at first by SOE agents to be an organisational acronym rather than the nom de guerre of a real person. In the course of 1943, the greater success of Tito's Communists in killing Germans eventually tilted material support in their direction, even though a Communist Yugoslavia was not a desirable outcome for the British. Since Greek and Yugoslav resistance movements were tying down far larger numbers of German troops, twenty-four divisions in Yugoslavia alone, their interests in turn overrode those of the resistance movements in neighbouring Albania where Hitler had a mere two divisions.

The enthusiasms of SOE agents on the spot were not invariably shared by its Balkan HQ in Cairo, or by the Foreign Office in London. In the Albanian case, opinion was divided about whether to back royalist supporters of King Zog, ensconced in London's Ritz Hotel with bodyguards armed with sawn-off shotguns, or the Communist Enver Hoxha, whose post-war regime was an offence to humanity. Matters were further complicated by Greek claims on southern Albania and Yugoslav Serbian claims on Kosovo, which the Germans had cunningly reunited with Albania.[16] Away from the Balkans with their inter-ethnic hatreds, SOE's desire to keep former Vichy supporters on side, to win French North Africa without great bloodshed, collided with the refusal of de Gaulle in London to collaborate with these potential rivals. De Gaulle's desire to gather the reins of resistance in his own hands had in turn to be balanced with SOE's interest in the 60 per cent of French resisters who were not Gaullist sympathisers, one of the reasons for SOE having separate F and RF sections, the latter exclusively dealing with French Republic Gaullists. Relations between SOE and the Poles and Czechs were conditioned by the fact that they were only partially within the maximum range of 100 Group's base in East Anglia, which meant there was little SOE could do to supply the resistance organisations in those countries. SOE dropped only sixty-five tons of supplies to the Poles between February 1941 and October 1943, a spit in the bucket compared with airlifts to France.

The fruits of SOE's activities initially seemed paltry. Gross operational negligence sent dozens of agents and supplies into a trap in the Netherlands, the *Englandspiel* run by the Abwehr, which, once revealed, gave SOE's critics – RAF Bomber Command in the forefront – ammunition to use against it.[17] In a second Joint Planning Staff report in August 1941 it was admitted that SOE's performance was unimpressive. Sabotage should be confined to the smaller sort of targets that were impossible for bombers to hit – rather an ironic conclusion given the RAF's inability on occasion even to find major cities. The decision was taken to devote all efforts to creating and maintaining resistance networks for what would be a single opportunity to strike in conjunction with a large-scale Allied invasion. Acts of sabotage would help maintain morale, for a resistance movement merely waiting for action was one that was doomed to atrophy.[18] This scaled-down version of SOE was reflected in the replacement of the abrasive Dalton by Lord Selbourne, a Tory supporter of Churchill, which signified the end of the so-called detonator phase, in which SOE hoped to encourage mass risings, and the onset of SOE's deployment as an integral element in overall Allied military strategy. The first evidence of this was the destruction of the Gorgopolous viaduct, a vital communications link for German forces in Greece, and the first action by SOE to have a major strategic impact.

Throughout 1941 a British desire to achieve symbolic successes resulted in such SOE operations as the hijacking of the Italian cargo liner *Duchessa d'Aosta* from the neutral Spanish port of Fernando Po, but there were also ventures which had serious consequences for civilians in enemy occupied territory. Immediately after the German invasion of Norway, former soldiers created an underground resistance organisation called Milorg, designed to recruit and train resisters for the eventuality of liberation by the Allies. Meanwhile, a handful of other Norwegians slipped away to Britain and joined SOE. In March 1941, these men were accompanied by 450 Combined Operations commandos for a raid on the lightly defended Lofoten Islands off Narvik. They blew up six German and Norwegian ships and four fish-oil factories. They left, taking 213 German prisoners with them, as well as a few Nasjonal Samling supporters. Three hundred and fourteen islanders also elected to go to London to swell the ranks of exiled Norwegian fighters, although there was as yet no Norwegian SOE section. Apart from leaving the islanders without a livelihood, the Lofoten raid resulted in heavy German sanctions. A hundred homes were burned to the ground and several hostages were executed. Seventy people were taken to the Grini concentration camp outside Oslo and held as hostages to discourage future raids. Milorg wrote to King Haakon in London protesting about the raids which had deprived fishermen of their trawlers and the fish-oil factory workers of a job. The letter was intercepted by SOE in the Shetlands, whose officers referred disparagingly to this 'military Sunday school' organisation. Eventually SOE and representatives of Milorg and the Norwegian government patched up a compromise to avoid the repetition of such a tragedy. Despite these arrangements, at Christmas 1941 two large parties of commandos revisited the Lofoten Islands and the ports of Maloy and Vagsoy. The latter operation went like clockwork, with 150 Germans killed and extensive damage to coastal gun batteries and fish-processing factories. On the Lofotens, where the intention was to hold a northerly base for several months, a robust German counter-attack meant that the islanders' mood quickly changed from welcoming to contempt as the British hurriedly pulled out. The SS arrested and imprisoned any islanders whose relatives had left with the British – a policy subsequently widened to include the parents of any Norwegian who opted for the 'Shetland bus' of fishing boats that took fugitives on the perilous route through stormy seas and minefields to Britain.[19]

One of the favoured exit points to the Shetlands was Televåg, a small fishing village south of Bergen. Loose talk and the presence of police spies resulted in two Norwegian SOE agents being trapped in a barn by German troops. Two German officers and one of the agents died in a firefight, while the surviving agent was wounded and captured. On Reich Commissar Terboven's orders three hundred houses were burned down, the livestock were killed and all the village's fishing boats sunk. The entire male population was deported to German concentration camps, while women, children and old men were interned elsewhere in Norway. A further eighteen young men – who had no connection with Televåg – were shot in Ålesund, while a wave of arrests scooped up virtually the entire Milorg operation throughout southern Norway. These events were commemorated in a great poem *Aust Vågøy* by the Communist writer Inger Hagerup. SOE attempts to build a resistance movement in northern Norway were quickly stymied by the Germans, although Hitler's fears about what Churchill might be planning for the frozen north did ensure that he retained huge numbers of troops, and a prodigious naval presence, in the country.

III CONSEQUENCES

One SOE operation highlighted many of the moral dilemmas of secret warfare. Pre-war Norway was more advanced than Germany in the production of deuterium-enriched heavy water, thought to be indispensable to the production of an atomic bomb. After the invasion of Norway, the Germans took control of the Norsk Hydro Works, situated on a thousand-feet-high rock outcrop at Vemork, near the small town of Rjukan, which lay shrouded in winter darkness at the foot of a gorge rising to four thousand feet. They immediately increased production of heavy water. A very brave engineer called Einar Skinnarland shuttled back and forth to London to bring the bad tidings to the British. They ruled out a bombing raid as too lethal for the surrounding civilian population. In response to a directive from the War Cabinet, SOE opted for a double-punch attack, in which a four-man Norwegian team codenamed Swallow would prepare a landing site for glider-borne British commandos who would shoot their way into Vemork and blow up the equipment that made heavy water. Even had they pulled off their mission, it was unlikely that British soldiers would then survive for very long in a country where all strangers are conspicuous and where the climate requires survival skills of an exceptional order. In the event, survival never came into it. In November 1941 two Halifax bombers towing gliders took off from Scotland for the four-hundred-mile flight to Norway. One crashed into a Norwegian mountainside, killing the bomber crew and all but fourteen of the troops in the glider. The survivors were taken to Egersund and shot as saboteurs before they had been thoroughly interrogated. Four who were critically injured were quietly poisoned by the German doctor who treated them, their bodies dumped in a fjord. Three more survivors, who were picked up later, were tortured until they revealed their target destination, confirmed by maps they had failed to destroy, and were then shot. The second bomber–glider combination returned homeward after failing to locate the landing site, and the men in the glider died when the tow rope snapped over the North Sea.

The four Norwegians of the Swallow team, who were supposed to handle the landings, survived to fight another day through the atrocious conditions of a Norwegian winter. They lived off moss until they shot a reindeer shortly before Christmas 1941. The commander recalled, 'In all I think we shot fourteen reindeer, which was our main source of food. We used the contents of the stomach as a vegetable. The reindeer did the preliminary cooking for us so we just mixed it with blood and used it with the meat. We used everything from the animal, everything except the skin and feet.'[20] The Germans appear to have believed that the catastrophic outcome of the raid was insurance against a repetition, and failed to reinforce the guard at Norsk Hydro, although they laid mines around the plant to discourage the locals.

With RAF bombing still ruled out, SOE assumed sole responsibility for destroying the plant. In February 1943 Operation Gunnerside involved a six-man team of Norwegian saboteurs who linked up with the Swallow team. Along the way they encountered a Norwegian poacher whom they captured and used to drag sledges. The group had to decide whether or not to kill him to preserve the mission's secrecy, a discussion they had in the bright snowy silence of a beautiful day, standing in a circle in their soiled and lice-ridden clothes. Eventually they decided to make the poacher sign a confession of his illicit activities which they warned would find its way to the Germans if anything happened to them.[21] After reaching their target, the team climbed down waist-deep snow on the side of a gorge, crossed the icy Maan river and then ascended the other side – all laden with heavy equipment – to creep into Norsk Hydro at around midnight. High winds and the hum of the plant's machinery muffled any noise they made. For the final assault, the SOE men wore British uniforms to minimise reprisals against civilians and deliberately left a gun marked 'Made in Britain' as they left. Without firing a shot, the team laid explosive charges, which demolished the cylinders of heavy water as they made their escape, spilling two thousand pounds of heavy water into drains. Remarkably, the entire operation was bloodless, as it had been designed to be to minimise the possibility of German reprisals against the local civilian population. The Gestapo wished to shoot ten local hostages anyway, but were overruled by the German commander in Norway, General Nikolaus von Falkenhorst, who blamed British commandos. After a three-hundred-mile journey on skis the SOE team reached neutral Sweden, where they celebrated by going to the opera, pinching themselves to make sure they were not dreaming.

This most celebrated SOE mission of the war seemed to be nullified within a month, as the Germans quickly repaired the plant and resumed production of heavy water at an increased rate. At this point, the head of the US atomic bomb Manhattan Project prevailed upon the Army Chief of Staff, General George C. Marshall, to bomb the plant, regardless of civilian casualties. On 16 November 1943, US Flying Fortresses dropped seven hundred 500-pound bombs on the plant, and another hundred on the neighbouring town of Rjukan, where most of its technicians lived. Twenty-two Norwegian civilians died. The exiled Norwegian government protested to both the British and US, and was ignored. Although the raid failed to disable the plant, the Germans decided to move their stocks of heavy water back to the Reich. In February 1944 fourteen tons of heavy water were put into thirty-nine huge drums for a journey that included a passage across Lake Tinnsjø on the ferry *Hydro*, a squat-looking flat ship with two funnels. There were two possible lines of attack. An assault on the train to the ferry was ruled out because there were SS troopers stationed at every tenth railway sleeper and a passenger carriage full of Norwegians was included in the train. The Germans also took forty hostages to ensure that the train reached the point of embarkation. That left a mine on the *Hydro*, preferably to be detonated as it crossed the lake's deepest waters. Without telling the Norwegians, SOE put two back-up plans in place, to derail the train that would transport the heavy water to southern Norway after crossing the lake, and, failing that, to launch an RAF raid on the ship that would take it to Germany.[22]

There is much elegant academic disquisition about just-war theory, but it is rare to see it practised with such extraordinary scrupulousness in the most stressful circumstances imaginable. The SOE agent who led the operation to sink the *Hydro* was a tough hunter called Knut Haukelid who had commanded the earlier incursion into Norsk Hydro. He was a morally scrupulous as well as a remarkably courageous man. He already had the fate of two Norwegian guards at the Vemork plant on his conscience, sent to a concentration camp after the first raid. In general terms he reflected:

> It is always hard to take a decision about actions which involve the loss of human lives. An officer often has to make such decisions in war-time, but in regular warfare it is easier; for then the officer is a small part of an organised apparatus, and his decisions as a rule have consequences only for soldiers, or at most for an enemy population. In this case an act of war was to be carried out which must endanger the lives of a number of our own people – who were not soldiers.[23]

First, Haukelid assured himself that the British regarded the mission as absolutely vital, even if it resulted in civilian casualties or reprisals. Few would gainsay that. Even though the Germans were barking up the wrong scientific tree, there is no doubt that a desperate Hitler would have used an atomic bomb. Secondly, Haukelid and an engineer in the plant delayed the train's departure by prolonging the siphoning of heavy water so that the consignment could connect only with the earliest ferry on a Sunday morning, when there would be few passengers and no children going to school. Extraordinary precautions were taken to protect the engineer – surely the first port of call for the Gestapo; he was admitted to hospital to have a perfectly sound appendix removed by way of an alibi. In addition the plant's chief engineer, who knew nothing of the attack, was sent to neutral

Sweden both to spare him interrogation and to make the Germans believe he had planned the operation. The night before, Haukelid and a comrade boarded the ferry, telling the nightwatchman that they were fleeing from the Gestapo and persuading him to let them remain on board. They placed charges shaped like a ring of sausages, enough to blow a hole eleven feet square, below the bilge waters in the bow – for if the ship went down by the bow, the captain would be unable to use the propellers to run the crippled ship aground. The explosives were connected to detonators wired to two alarm clocks set for 10.45 on Sunday morning. The explosion tilted the *Hydro* so that the railway carriages broke loose, plunging the drums into fourteen hundred feet of water. The ship sank very rapidly, taking down twenty-six crew and passengers including two young brothers. Haukelid was especially troubled that the friendly nightwatchman also drowned.[24]

The occupied populations of Europe were generally prepared to support sabotage as a means of warfare because they understood the practical effects. They were also largely sympathetic to the assassination of collaborators, especially when, as was the case with the Polish underground, they were found guilty by three-man secret tribunals, which included one who acted as a defence lawyer. If it seemed to be the outcome of a semblance of legal procedure, then it was more acceptable. All understood that collaborators enabled the occupiers to operate effectively in countries they scarcely knew and whose languages they did not speak. Except in those areas where partisans turned every ambush into an assassination, resistance movements tended to reject the deliberate targeting of occupation personnel, largely because it brought unwanted attention upon underground networks as well as savage reprisals. Shortly after the German reprisals in Nantes in October 1941, de Gaulle in a radio broadcast to France explicitly prohibited assassinations: 'War must be conducted by those entrusted with the task ... for the moment my orders to those in occupied territory are NOT to kill Germans there openly. This is for one reason only: at present, it is too easy for the enemy to retaliate by massacring our fighters, who are for the time being disarmed.' Resistance movements also realised that the Germans would probably replace the individual assassinated with someone of an even more vicious disposition. This was less of a consideration in the Balkans or Russia, where all Germans seemed to be afflicted with a collective murderous psychosis, whether attacked by the resistance or not.

That reasoning could be reversed in cases where the most radically minded Nazi leaders demonstrated political sinuosity as well as brutality.

The killing of SS security chief Reinhard Heydrich was a case in point, although his assassination was the product of cold political calculation on the part of the Czech exiled government, supported by SOE, which facilitated the attack.[25] Following the Slovak declaration of independence and the German occupation of Prague, the Czech remnant became the Protectorate of Bohemia-Moravia. After the former president, Edvard Beneš, went into British exile, a Czech government under President Emil Hácha and Prime Minister Alois Eliáš notionally retained control of domestic policy. Real power lay with Konstantin von Neurath, the Reich Protector, a silky career diplomat, although some lay with the more abrasive and plebeian Sudeten-German SS chief, Karl Hermann Frank. Hácha was a poet and former chief justice, who declared that patriotism overrode political and moral concerns. Before the German invasion, he and his colleagues had already dismantled Czech democracy, banned trades unions and introduced discriminatory measures against Jews. After the occupation, Hácha founded a National Solidarity Movement, which most males joined, while suppressing anti-Semitic hooliganism by Czech Fascists. All appointments and laws made by Hácha's regime were vetted by Neurath, while some ten thousand seconded German bureaucrats kept a close eye on four hundred thousand Czech civil servants.[26]

In so far as there was resistance, it took the form of patriotic demonstrations, including one to commemorate a student shot by the Germans in which Karl Hermann Frank's chauffeur was roughed up. The bruised chauffeur was flown to Berlin and shown to Hitler, who ordered draconian measures. The universities were closed, nine students were shot and twelve hundred more deported to concentration camps. As in occupied Poland, repression disproportionately affected the patriotic middle-class intelligentsia rather than the working classes, who had to be kept placated to maintain Czechoslovakia's arms industry, the seventh largest in the world. The German invasion of the Soviet Union galvanised Czech resistance, not least because it put pressure on basic food supplies, which were diverted east. Communists took the lead in sabotaging the railways and telephone lines, while industrial output fell by a third. In September 1941 there was a mass boycott of newspapers run by Czech collaborators, which hit circulations in the capital by 70 per cent.

Hitler reacted by sacking Reich Protector Neurath and replacing him with Reinhard Heydrich. Heydrich dramatically increased the number of executions as well as deportations to Mauthausen concentration camp. The Gestapo effectively destroyed the patriotic resistance movement and even made inroads into the steelier Communists. Heydrich also arrested Prime Minister Eliáš, who had clandestine contacts with Beneš, sparing his life to ensure the total compliance of Hácha's cabinet. At the same time Heydrich endeavoured to keep the workers quiescent with increased rations, free shoes and benefits drawn from confiscated black-market supplies. Attempts were made to divert them with cinema, circuses, concerts and sport. On a flying visit to report to Hitler at his Rastenburg headquarters, Heydrich said that the Czech workers had reacted calmly to the elimination of the resistance, being more concerned about the shortage of edible fats. Ever fertile in ideas, he introduced mobile X-ray scanning units for tuberculosis as cover for the racial inspection of the entire Czech population. In an expansive speech, he stated that those who could not be Germanised were to serve as guards in the Arctic labour camps taken from the Soviets, which were to be used to accommodate eleven million deported Jews.

Czech resistance activity was sneered at by the Polish exiles and generally discounted in London and Moscow, which had a humiliating effect on the exiled Czech government. If Beneš was to have any hope of restoring an independent Czechoslovakia within its pre-Munich Agreement borders, then he had to give his allies a sure sign that the Czechs were resisting the Germans as much as their Polish neighbour. To that end, a plan emerged to assassinate Heydrich, although the precise authorship of what was code-named Operation Anthropoid remains a mystery. One key player was the former Czech intelligence chief, Colonel František Moravec, who acknowledged what he called 'an abominable calculation, without doubt, [as] we weighed up for a long time the immense propaganda advantages abroad of such an action against the obvious suffering that would ensue for the Czech population'. Exiled Czech soldiers underwent months of training at SOE bases near Glasgow and Dorking. Several SOE-trained parachutists were dropped into the Protectorate, some to carry out sabotage, others to establish radio links with London. The Anthropoid team included warrant officers Josef Gabčik and Jan Kubiš, who spent five months hiding in safe houses in Prague. Virtually every family who hid them would perish in Mauthausen after Heydrich's assassination. Other parachute teams codenamed Silver A and Silver B were responsible for radio communications.

The nature of the Anthropoid mission gradually dawned on the leaders of the domestic Czech resistance. On two occasions its leaders warned Beneš that killing Heydrich would be a catastrophe:

The assassination would not be of least value to the Allies, and for our nation it would have unforeseeable consequences. It would threaten not only hostages and political prisoners, but also thousands of other lives. The nation would be the subject of unheard-of reprisals. At the same time it would wipe out the last remainders of any resistance organisation. It would then be impossible for resistance to be useful to the Allies. Therefore we beg you to give the order through Silver A for the assassination not to take place. Danger in delay; give the order at once.

In his reply, Beneš ignored the major issue at hand, highlighting instead his fears that the Germans might seek a negotiated peace and that Czechoslovakia might prove expendable. Where national salvation was at stake, 'even great sacrifices would be worth it'.[27]

Ignoring the pleas of their underground helpers, Gabčik and Kubiš decided to proceed with the assassination of Heydrich. The night before the attack, Heydrich attended a performance by the Arthur Bonhardt String Quartet, which included the Piano Concerto in C minor by Bruno Heydrich, the Reich Protector's musician father. He was ambushed when his Mercedes with the SS-3 number plate slowed on a bend as he was driven to work on the morning of 27 May 1942. Gabčik tried to shoot him with a Sten gun that jammed; Kubiš hurled a modified anti-tank grenade, which exploded under the car and drove a seat spring into Heydrich's spleen. Heydrich got out and staggered along the road, shooting at his fleeing assailants, before turning back and collapsing. A passing motorist stopped and took him to hospital. On learning the news, Hitler ordered the execution of ten thousand Czechs. Martial law was imposed and people over sixteen were given twenty-four hours to get newly issued identity papers, without which they were liable to be shot. Karl Hermann Frank hastened to Berlin to urge his Führer to rescind his order for being too indiscriminate. Heydrich died in agony on 4 June and received two state funerals, in Prague and Berlin. During the latter, Himmler reported feeling a little queasy at holding the hands of Heydrich's 'mongol' sons. Heydrich's replacement was another powerful SS figure, Kurt Daluege.

Hitler did reduce the scale of the reprisals, but ordered the burning of the village of Lidice and the murder of its male population, because it was believed to have had some connection with the parachutists on the basis of a letter sent to a girl working in a pocket-torch factory by her boyfriend in Lidice, who boasted falsely that many enemy parachutists were holed up there. She talked to the factory owner, who duly told the Czech police, who passed the information on to the Gestapo, including Heinz Pannwitz, the officer who in 1959 wrote a detailed account of the Heydrich investigation.[28] As a result of interventions by Pannwitz's ambitious superior, 173 men were shot in the village by Security Police; the killers included men drawn from Heydrich's birthplace at Halle on the Saale, while the Gestapo traced a further eleven who were working in a local factory and a miner recovering from a broken leg in hospital. They were all shot too. All the women were sent to Ravensbrück. Four who were in hospital waiting to give birth were deported after their babies had been delivered. The village children were not spared either, as in the summer of 1942 eighty-two of them were gassed in the Chelmno extermination camp. Lidice consisted of smouldering ruins that were blown up by army engineers and the Reich Labour Service. The tombstones in the cemetery were taken away to use as building materials, while the village pond was filled in with rubble and the trees felled. With the Germans threatening further mass reprisals – which people feared would encompass every tenth Czech – a Czech parachutist called Karel Čurda surrendered to the Gestapo and gave the names of the underground network protecting the assassins. After further arrests, their location was betrayed, leading seven hundred German troops to the St Cyril and Methodius Orthodox church in Prague. After a six-hour gun battle, the seven Czech parachutists either committed suicide or were killed.

Beneš was exultant about the assassination. 'What the Germans are doing is horrible, but from the political point of view they gave us one certainty: under no circumstances can anyone doubt Czechoslovakia's national integrity and her right to independence,' Beneš signalled a resistance leader killed soon afterwards in a gunfight with the Gestapo. In the village where that leader had hidden his transmitter and where Silver A had been active, all the adult inhabitants were shot. The entire democratic and Communist underground was rolled up, with 3,188 arrests and 1,357 people sentenced to death. On 24 October, 257 people who had been arrested on suspicion of helping the assassins were shot in the back of the head during a day-long execution session in Mauthausen, with a further thirty-one shot the following January. The Orthodox bishop and clergy who had hid the assassins were tried and executed and the Orthodox Church proscribed as a 'treasonable' organisation. However, in two major respects Beneš's assessment was correct. Firstly, in the autumn of 1942 the British formally repudiated the Munich Agreement, meaning that an independent post-war Czechoslovakia would regain the Sudetenland, increasing the likelihood – already being discussed – that its ethnic German population would be expelled. Secondly, the fate of Lidice became synonymous with Nazi barbarism. As the US Navy Secretary Frank Knox remarked on 13 June 1942: 'If future generations ask us what we were fighting for in this war, we shall tell them the story of Lidice.'[29]

After the Germans advertised what they had done at Lidice, miners in Stoke-on-Trent established a Lidice Shall Live fund, and towns in Brazil and Mexico were renamed after the vanished Czech village. Cecil Day Lewis wrote an elegy about it and Humphrey Jennings made a film to commemorate the village. That Heydrich, the key figure in the implementation of Hitler's Final Solution, needed killing was stressed in two notable movies dealing with his death: *Hitler's Madman* directed by Douglas Sirk in 1942, and *Hangmen Also Die* by Fritz Lang and Bertolt Brecht.[30] Those who say that Lidice was almost trivial in the scales of Nazi barbarism towards the Jews or other civilians in the occupied Soviet Union protest too much. It gave a poignant example on a comprehensible scale of things the human imagination could not otherwise easily accommodate. In that sense, although the scale of the reprisals effectively destroyed Czech resistance for the rest of the war, Operation Anthropoid was a justified act that swelled the Allies' moral capital, however much those responsible may have regretted the deaths of around five thousand innocent people – casualties they cannot have failed to anticipate.

Sinister calculations may have been at work behind the bomb attack on a detachment of German Order Police as they marched along Rome's via Rasella towards their quarters in the Quirinale Palace at around 3.30 p.m. on 23 March 1944. A twelve-kilogram bomb packed with scrap iron and hidden in a dust cart had been positioned by Rosario 'Paolo' Bentivegna. After priming his homemade bomb, Paolo was supposed to meet twenty-two-year-old Carla Capponi, who would hand him a raincoat to disguise the workman's overalls he was wearing. While waiting longer than she anticipated, Carla shooed away some children playing football in the neighbouring garden of the Palazzo Barberini. When the bomb exploded it killed thirty-three men from the 11th Company of the 3rd Battalion of the Police Regiment Bozen. Two more later died from their injuries and forty-five of them were so badly wounded that they were granted medical discharges. These were middle-aged policemen, nearly half of them married with children, who had been recruited from South Tyrol, the disputed frontier area known as Bolzano in Italian, and their officers were

Reich Germans. Although they were not like the SS torturers in the Gestapo's Villa Tasso headquarters, the previous October these policemen had participated in the round-ups and deportations of Jews in Rome. The bomb also killed ten Italian civilians, including six children whom Carla Capponi had not been able to drive away.[31]

Their killers were mainly young students who belonged to the Communist Groups for Patriotic Action resistance movement, known as Gappists, short for Gruppe di Azione Patriottica. They had warned some passers-by to give the street a wide berth, but it was not possible to warn them all. More seriously, the Gappists were aware that German policy in newly occupied Italy was to carry out extensive reprisals, even though since 14 August 1943 Rome had been declared an open city. Since late January 1943, the Germans had responded to Gappist attacks by shooting ten hostages for every German killed by the resistance. The Gappists may have calculated that the inevitable reprisals would be beneficial to their faction, as the resistance hostages consisted largely of Trotskyites from the Bandiera Rossa, or members of the another resistance group, the Fronte Clandestino Militare. Their given reason was the hope of provoking a general popular uprising, a delusion condemned by the entire spectrum of resistance opinion, from the Catholics and monarchists to the Trotskyites.

The Germans' response was drastic. They made no attempt to get the partisans to surrender in order to preclude reprisals, and undertook no operations to capture those responsible for the bombing. The city's military commandant, General Kurt Mälzer, inspected the carnage, and, habitually drunk as he was, threatened to blow up an entire quarter of the city, a view endorsed by Hitler who wanted to destroy three or four. The SD commander, Herbert Kappler, dissuaded Mälzer from that course of action, while arranging with General Eberhard von Mackensen to shoot ten people already condemned to death for every dead German, in line with orders from theatre commander Field Marshal Albert Kesselring, who claimed quite falsely after the war that the SS were a law unto themselves rather than subject to his command. However, the Gestapo established that only three such candidates were available in prisons. Instead, 154 people held in the Gestapo's prison, including five Italian generals and eleven other senior officers, forty-three held in Wehrmacht prisons, fifty people handed over by the Italian police, a number of residents of via Rasella picked up at random and seventy-five Jews were hurriedly assembled to make up the final number of 335 persons. These unfortunates were taken to the Ardeatine Caves on the outskirts of Rome where, their hands bound, they were shot in groups of five in tunnels dimly illuminated by flaming torches. One SS officer, Hauptsturmführer Reinhold Wetjen, found the whole process so disagreeable that he refused to participate, until Kappler reminded him of the impact such a refusal to carry out orders would have on group discipline. He and Kappler then shot the next five together. When locals converted the caves into an impromptu shrine, German engineers blew up the entrances.[32]

This was not the largest reprisal massacre carried out by the Germans on Kesselring's direct orders in Italy, which from late July 1944 onwards were specified in writing. Point 3ii stated that 'If German soldiers fall victims to attacks by civilians, up to 10 able-bodied Italians will be shot for each German killed.'[33] In August 1944, men from an SS armoured division shot 362 civilians at Forte dei Marmi, and the following month 770 more were shot at Marzabotto near Bologna. The victims included a priest and three elderly parishioners who were shot in their church, while the rest were machine-gunned in the cemetery. But the via Rasella bomb attack provoked the most condemnation, from the Vatican as well as from all sections of resistance opinion, obviously excepting the Gappists themselves. It was not, however, out of line with the wishes of General Harold Alexander, commanding Allied forces in Italy, who on three occasions used the BBC to enjoin partisans to attack German troops.

The threat of reprisals did influence partisan operations. The 8th Garibaldi Brigade was a formidable band, numbering about fourteen hundred people, including escaped Allied POWs, which operated in the mountains around Forlì in the Romagna. In July 1944 Kesselring created a counter-partisan force of 3,500 German and Italian troops to secure the rear of the Gothic/Green Line, running across Italy from Pisa to Pesaro. Unable to bring the partisans to battle, this force routinely shot civilian hostages or left them strung up while their homes burned. The Garibaldi Brigade leader Bruno Vailati – or Italo Morandi, to give him his real name – ordered his men to stop attacking the Germans, who were responsible for the most savage reprisals. Instead they would blow up roads and bridges, while confining their lethal operations to Fascist militiamen and collaborators, whom the Germans would not bother to avenge.[34]

CHAPTER 12

Beneath the Mask of Command

I DIALOGUES OF THE DEAF

Deserved attention has been devoted to the relationships between the Allied big three, Churchill, Roosevelt and Stalin, and between their senior military commanders such as Marshall and Sir Alan Brooke, Chief of the Imperial General Staff. With reason, there are many more studies comparing Hitler and Stalin than those which pair Hitler with Mussolini, or with the leaders of Japan or the other Axis and satellite nations. This disparity of historical interest reflects the role of summit leadership in the Axis and Allied camps. The Germans convened rare one- or two-day conferences, often at Schloss Klessheim near Salzburg, but in the interpolated military briefings all bad news was filtered out, while Hitler hogged proceedings, regarding such summits purely as a propaganda vehicle to Europeanise his crusade against Bolshevism. Any Axis leader, such as King Boris of Bulgaria, who really wanted to know the state of war, had to find a German officer willing to whisper the grim truth.[1]

There was virtually no summit-level co-ordination of Axis strategy among Germany, Italy and Japan. Germany and Japan fought parallel wars and the Italians tried to do the same, with no combined operations. Relations were exiguous on every level. Allied domination of the oceans played a major part: whereas hundreds of millions of tons of war materials worth US$50 billion flowed from the US to Britain and the Soviet Union, Japan supplied Germany with 112,000 tons of raw materials and food, while Germany sent around 59,000 tons of strategic raw materials and technologies to Japan – *throughout four years of war*. Moreover, the Japanese did nothing to interdict the flow of Lend–Lease materials heading to Vladivostok so as not to contravene their neutrality pact with the

Soviets. The annihilation of Japanese merchant ships sailing to occupied Europe led to a switch to submarines, which carried only 2–3 per cent of the load of a single cargo ship.[2]

There was no German–Italian–Japanese equivalent to the bi- or tri-lateral conferences which Churchill, Roosevelt and Stalin held during the war. When Hitler and Mussolini met during wartime it was not to co-ordinate grand strategy, which was always Hitler's sole preserve. Mussolini bitterly resented the way these meetings were arranged: 'I am sick and tired of being summoned by the bell.' A 'wake-up call' told him of the invasion of Russia. 'Even I don't dare to disturb my servants at night,' said the Duce, 'but the Germans make me jump out of bed at any hour without the slightest consideration.' Mussolini favoured the Japanese because he resented the 'ugly' Germans so much: 'The Japanese are not a people with whom the Germans can take liberties such as getting the Emperor or the Prime Minister out of bed at two o'clock in the morning in order to announce decisions that have already been made and carried out.'[3]

There was nothing on the Axis side approximating to the enormous diplomatic and military presences which the British and Americans established in Washington and London. True, Vice-Admiral Paul Wenneker and General Alfred Kretschmer were despatched to Toyko, while Admiral Naokuni Nomura and General Ichiro Banzai were stationed in Berlin. But relations were not helped when a Japanese naval captain posed the question, in a Tokyo newspaper, how it was that the Japanese could conduct combined operations two thousand miles from home, while the Germans seemed incapable of crossing the twenty-mile English Channel.[4] From December 1940 to June 1941, General Yamashita, the future Tiger of Malaya, was head of the Japanese mission to Germany and Italy, from which vantage point he was able to study the power of German combined operations in the west. Tipped off about Barbarossa, he was somewhere in the Soviet Union on a train heading for the Far East when news filtered through of the attack.[5]

There were no formal high-level contacts between the Germans or Italians either; neither Keitel nor his deputy Alfred Jodl visited Italy before the collapse of the Fascist regime, although Göring often visited in his self-appointed capacity as the expert on Italy. Only the upgrading of the Luftwaffe theatre chief based at Frascati, General Albert Kesselring, to overall German commander in the Mediterranean ensured some regularity, as he met with Mussolini almost every day. Otherwise, communications ran through the military attachés in the embassies in Berlin and Rome. The respective ambassadors, Dino Alfieri and Baron Hans Georg von Mackensen, quickly realised that they had to deal with the profusion of agencies and personal fiefdoms which were normative under nominally totalitarian systems.[6]

The contrast with the densely meshed British and American joint war effort was glaring. Some nine thousand British personnel were seconded to Washington during the war, including Field Marshal Sir John Dill as a permanent member of the Combined Chiefs of Staff, as well as the former Foreign Secretary Lord Halifax as British ambassador to the US.[7] The US supreme commander in Europe, Dwight Eisenhower, had an enormous military establishment based on his HQ at Norfolk House in St James's Square. Wartime London was also host to a polyglot army of foreign exiles, with their Dutch, French or Polish officers' clubs in Knightsbridge and beyond. Despite the secretive, untrusting nature of the Soviets, who rejected combined operations and refused to share intelligence, it is important to recall that the US ambassador Averell Harriman met with Stalin once a month. Apart from permanent embassies, only four hundred Japanese visited Nazi Germany, while a mere nineteen Germans made the long – and dangerous – journey to Tokyo during the entire war.

Hitler admired certain personality traits among his confederates. Mussolini was the world's first Fascist dictator, although the erstwhile senior partner became a junior liability as the war progressed. Hitler respected the Finn Mannersheim as an old soldier, and Rumania's Ion Antonescu because of a 'breadth of vision' which included a visceral hatred of Jews approximating to his own. His sole meeting with the cunning Spanish Caudillo was so disagreeable that Hitler famously compared it with visiting a dentist. This stereotypical stuff was unlike the complex and subtle relations that existed between Churchill and Roosevelt, or indeed between these men and the human enigma in the Kremlin. Hitler did not have to waste much time on what his partners were thinking, since none of them was very important to him, whereas Churchill, as the weaker party in a Big Three that became the Big Two and a Half, had to study the thought processes of Roosevelt and Stalin very carefully. Stalin studied his with the aid of secret intelligence derived from upper-class Oxbridge traitors who had graduated to MI5, MI6 and Whitehall. In Hitler's mind, Germany was the only power that mattered – his allies existed to play bit parts in his nation's unique drama, their spoils of war being akin to scraps thrown from the table to obedient dogs. Among the cannier of them was Croatia's Ante Pavelić, who started claiming that the Croats were descendants of the ancient Goths, a gambit which may have pleased Hitler, but which infuriated Mussolini who regarded Croatia as falling within Italy's sphere of influence.[8] Axis leaders undertook major operations without informing one another. For example, when Mussolini invaded Greece, part of his motivation was that 'Hitler always confronts me with a fait accompli. This time I'll pay him back with his own coin: he'll learn from the newspapers that I've occupied Greece.' This was his way of getting back at Germans, who dismissively referred to him as 'our Gauleiter for Italy'.[9]

II THE NICE PEOPLE AND THEIR ALLY

German–Italian combined operations were fitful and characterised by mutual resentments. The Italians found the Germans haughty but hugely efficient; the Germans thought the Italians were lackadaisical and ludicrous in their plumed helmets and jaunty caps. Mussolini rejected Hitler's suggestion that Italian troops should invade France through Burgundy, and also initially declined the Führer's offer of an armoured division to fight in North Africa. However, two hundred aircraft from the Regia Aeronautica joined the Luftwaffe over Britain, while some Italian submarines operated in the North Atlantic out of Bordeaux. Wherever Mussolini ventured alone, disaster usually followed. He could not even conquer a third-rate power like Greece on his own. German troops had to be sent into Greece to bail out the Italians – whose commander Rodolfo Graziani suffered a mental breakdown – while Rommel was despatched to North Africa to salvage something from the disaster the British had inflicted on the Italians in Cyrenaica. In the beginning Hitler allowed his ally to carve out Italy's own *spazio vitale* (*Lebensraum*) in Albania, coastal Croatia, Hellenic Greece (the Bulgarians occupied Macedonia and Thrace), Slovenia and the south-east corner of France from near Geneva down to Toulon. As Italy's fortunes waned, the erstwhile ally was downgraded to the status of satellite, symbolised by Hitler's Instruction of 28 December 1942, which subordinated the Italian army to General Alexander Löhr, the Wehrmacht Commander-in-Chief in south-east Europe.[10]

The Italians had become what are known as dependent imperialists, although there was one theatre where they had to be handled as valued partners. In July 1941 Mussolini despatched the Corpo di Spedizione

Italiano in Russia (CSIR) to the Soviet Union. This was commanded successively by Generals Francesco Zingales and Giovanni Messe. Mussolini
hoped that strident anti-Communist rhetoric would mask a naked desire to
gain raw materials, while ensuring that Hitler would have to acknowledge
Italy in any final division of the overall spoils.[11] Efforts were made to give
this sixty-two-thousand-strong motorised expeditionary corps an air of
modernity. One of its concealed functions, evident from the fact that it was
positioned between them, was to stop the Hungarian and Rumanian allies
from killing each other rather than the Soviets. Another irony was that
although the Italians were part of Army Group South, battling towards the
Crimea, Hitler ultimately intended to settle the peninsula with South
Tyroleans, to be extracted from northern Italy in defiance of Mussolini's
wishes. After the losses in Russia in late 1941, Mussolini despatched more
reinforcements eastwards so that the Italian Eighth Army eventually
numbered around 230,000 men under Italo Gariboldi.[12]

Relations between German and Italian troops were mixed. Staged
events, such as international football matches or the doling out of medals,
went well enough, but they could not mask the fact that the Germans,
knowing themselves to be the finest soldiers in the world, regarded their
allies as slovenly, their boots disintegrating for lack of care and obsessed
with chasing Russian or Ukrainian girls. This reflected a wider problem,
namely that Italy's mainly peasant soldiers had no racist animus against the
Russians and Ukrainians. The latter were also instructed by Soviet propaganda to be accommodating to the Italians so as to foment divisions within
the Axis.[13] As the Germans and their allies reeled from Soviet counter-
attacks they sought to blame each other.

Apart from problems of communication, there were differences of
temperament. The Italians thought the Germans were cold and stiff, always
butting in with unwanted military advice even with more senior Italian
commanders, while the Germans thought the Italians were chaotic and
overly emotional. Kesselring, for one, pronounced the *abbracci* (embraces)
and *bacci* (kisses) showered upon him by Marshal Ugo Cavallero, the
Italian Chief of the General Staff, 'a form of greeting new to me'.[14] One
obvious difference, in Russia, was that German soldiers had local helots –
usually civilians or POWs – to perform any manual work, whereas the
Italians did not. A German NCO who tried to turf Colonel Mario Bianchi
out of his quarters – only to be repulsed at gunpoint by this much decorated war hero – was an extreme example of this German superiority
complex.[15]

Italian military sources chronicled any number of incidents in which their self-esteem was rudely offended by their ally. Lieutenant Giuseppe Mononeri sustained a broken arm as a German lorry tried to run him over by way of a jest, a fate that Private Idrio Citrino suffered later in the same column. A German officer abused an Italian driver whose truck had run out of fuel, eventually pulling a gun and telling him to 'fuck off', probably so that he could loot the lorry's load. When German soldiers wanted a table Italians had already taken in the railway station buffet in Dnepropetrovsk, one of them lifted up an Italian and his chair above head height before letting him drop, amid raucous laughter from the other German diners. An Italian soldier who tried to find a bed in a Russian house after a twenty-five-mile march, was rudely shoved outside by a German soldier who said, in Italian: 'Hitler and Mussolini are comrades, Germans and Italians are comrades at the front – but not here.' Italians trying to hitch a ride on German trucks were booted off or had their hands smashed with rifle butts, while on trains even Italian officers were directed to cattle trucks. Italian troops went in to battle shouting 'Savoia!' in honour of their royal house, which the Germans turned into the jibe 'Avanti Savoia, cikai!' – *cikai* being the Russian for flight.[16] While the troops often fought bravely, once their officers were killed they tended to succumb to panic. By the time the CSIR was recalled to Italy in early 1943, it had lost 42 per cent of its officers and 37 per cent of its NCOs and private soldiers. An estimated 25,000 died in combat, while of the 70,000 prisoners of war, 22,000 died en route to camps, and a further 38,000 perished in Soviet captivity. Only ten thousand Italians made it home from Russia long after the war.[17]

German and Italian troops also met one another in the occupied territories. On Crete, an Italian recalled initial Axis contacts with a sense of embarrassment: 'On the outskirts of town we encountered the first German soldiers, who gazed down at us from their gigantic Panzers with curiosity and amusement as we shuffled past. Our grand allies must have found the sight of our expeditionary corps, with its train of donkeys like a gypsy caravan, irresistibly comic.'[18] Italian troops envied the lavish equipment of their allies, while they went around in wooden clogs because their boots had worn out, or donned a colourful array of local clothing rather than wear their tattered uniforms. At the most senior levels of the Italian army, officers viewed the Germans as arrogant bullies who were taking over Italy's colonial possessions by stealth, the fate of the Balkans which slipped from one Axis partner to the other as if by osmosis.

Kesselring, who respected the Italians more than most, identified some of the problems in an Italian army which, individual acts of extraordinary heroism apart, was more suited to display than combat. Its generals were aged between sixty and eighty and the officers' keen sense of dignity prevented interaction with their semi-literate peasant subordinates. There were no common field messes, and the quality of rations increased according to rank, so that Kesselring ate better in an Italian officers' mess than he did in his own staff canteen. Not least, the Italian troops were invariably paid late.[19]

Italian officers did indeed pride themselves on their immaculate appearance and gentlemanly manners, in marked contrast to the black-shirted Fascist *uomo nuovo* as well as to the Wehrmacht's ideological soldiers. Like those British military personnel and commentators involved in today's wars who console themselves for their material and numerical inferiority by believing they understand Afghans or Iraqis better than the Americans, the Italians thought they understood Croats or Greeks better than the Germans. The Germans did offend puritanical Greek sensibilities by wandering around towns and villages in their underwear to get a tan when off duty, but their attitude was not in essence any different to the Italians' own pronounced racism towards the Balkan peoples, notably the Greeks, whom they regarded as little better than savages.[20]

Considerations of national prestige and pride largely account for the refusal of the Italians to emulate the racial policies of the Germans and their Croat and Vichy French allies towards the Jews. If the Italians disliked being bullied by the Germans, they were certainly not going to behave like the conquered Croats and French. 'The thing is out of the question … I naturally oppose it with a flat refusal' was the response of the commander of Second Army in Yugoslavia, General Mario Roatta, to Croatian demands that the Italians should hand over the Jews sheltering in the Dalmatian coastal strip annexed by Italy.[21] Well-meaning books like *Captain Corelli's Mandolin* have presented a rather saccharine view of wartime Italian soldiers. The attitude of the Italian military to the persecution of the Jews is often ascribed to the Italian self-image as 'nice people' (*brave gente*). This 'niceness' is difficult to reconcile with the internment camps run and the reprisals decreed by the same General Roatta, or the murderous policies pursued in Abyssinia or Libya. The Italians were as capable of mowing down a group of hostages as the Germans – they just did not share their allies' psychosis about the Jews.

The Regio Esercito was not as permeated by Fascism as the Wehrmacht was by Nazism. Many of the elderly senior officers were liberals and freemasons, their views proscribed by the regime in the country at large. Mussolini was constrained by the monarchy and the Vatican, powers that Hitler either did not have to deal with or crushed. Despite its own history of anti-Judaism, the Church raised awkward questions about the fate of the Jews. Italian anti-Semitism was more genteel, or at least less endemic or virulent than that of Nazi Germany. Fascism did not believe that Italy's future greatness depended on killing the Jews, whereas the Nazis saw the Jews as an existential threat. Far from it: a German geographer was horrified to see Italian officers lounging around with Jewish women in Dubrovnik's Café Grodska, and was appalled that the same men had delivered Mostar's Jews from the waiting hatchets of the Croatian Fascist Ustaše.[22] There had been several distinguished Jewish officers in the Italian army, while, according to Alexander Stille, before the 1938 racial laws one in three adult Italian Jews had been card-carrying Fascists themselves. In the Balkans, the civil and military authorities tended to regard Italian Jews as influential agents of Italian economic or political goals rather than as the pariahs the Germans made of them.

But there were other differences that we should not pass over. The Italians were good at dressing up hard-nosed realism in the language of honour and moral outrage, which has sometimes been viewed too indulgently by Italophile foreign historians, writing without the benefit of the embargoed war crimes files in the Italian Ministry of Defence. On the whole, nations do not like to admit to the combination of calculation, cowardice and kindness that may have more accurately reflected the mood of the time. Certainly it is possible to find Italian soldiers who took an overtly moral stance. After learning that non-Italian Jews were to be handed to the murderous Ustaše, in autumn 1942 the chief of staff of Second Army, General Clemente Primieri, exclaimed: 'It's a violation of our word which we gave them [the Jews] and will have terrible repercussions on our relations with all the others who have fairly put their trust in us. They will be afraid that we will abandon them from one moment to the next. Our prestige will be greatly reduced.' A commander of a machine-gun unit wrote to a friend: 'The Italian army should not dirty its hands in this business.' Such men would presumably have concurred with the statement of the Foreign Ministry official Luca Pietromachi that 'there is no corner of Europe that has not witnessed the Germans' innate, ineradicable wickedness. And these are bringers of Kultur and the artificers of the New Order!'[23] Of course, attitudes accompanied a dynamic policy environment, and it is these which reveal the calculations of national advantage and personal salvation that accompanied the moral stance.

The Italian government knew from BBC broadcasts in June 1942 that up to that date an estimated seven hundred thousand Polish Jews had been killed, many with poison gas. On 18 October, the number two in the German embassy in Rome, Otto von Bismarck, grandson of the first German Chancellor, formally requested Italian co-operation with the 'measures' being taken by the Croats and Germans for mass deportations of Croatian Jews. Bismarck also informed the Italians, in total breach of extreme secrecy, that this would 'almost certainly involve the definitive elimination of the Jewish groups in question'. Apart from the considerations of honour and prestige that made the Italians baulk at co-operating with the Croats, the way the war developed in the following six months also inclined them to non-co-operation with the Germans. Many members of the army and even of the regime realised the game was up for Italy, a view increasingly monitored in public opinion. In October 1942, representatives of the regime opened clandestine talks in Lisbon with British SOE agents about a separate peace. In December 1942 the Allies had issued clear warnings about future war crimes trials, another reason for the Italians to distance themselves from German genocide. They might get a better deal for switching sides if they were not morally tainted, and they certainly did not wish to be hanged alongside the Germans.[24]

III TROUBLE AT THE TOP

If there was no meaningful strategic interaction between the Axis dictators, and no love lost between their soldiers, nor did they have wise counsellors, for the Führer and the Duce were the depositories of all wisdom. Roosevelt's closest confidant, Harry Hopkins, moved into the White House after his wife died. Roosevelt deferred to Marshall in military matters, and the indefatigable British Prime Minister found his wilder strategic flights brought down to earth by the strong men with whom he surrounded himself, knowing he needed their discipline, notably the stubborn military bureaucrat Alan Brooke. Even so, the only person who could cut short Churchill's late-night sessions and tell him to go to bed was the massively self-confident South African Field Marshal Jan Smuts. Hitler brooked no opposition and surrounded himself with yes-men; after hours he liked to relax in the company of sycophants like Albert Speer, or his 'chauffeureska', a coterie of glorified servants whose British and American counterparts would not have had access to either Churchill or Roosevelt. Hitler's entourage had to fight off sleep as he droned on about arcana such as what soup the Spartans drank, for none of them would have dared to stop the Führer in full flood. Disagreement caused Hitler to fly into towering rages, until everyone else acquiesced in his way of seeing things. They learned to avoid these outbursts by filtering out anything the dictator did not want to hear, at a time when Churchill's spirits often sank under the weight of unvarnished bad news.[25]

We know the story of Churchill and his commanders from both sides, whereas we only know of Hitler's relations with his generals from their selective recollections. The Wehrmacht's marriage of convenience with Hitler broke down, albeit in relation to only a few generals, as the fortunes of war tilted against the Axis. The post-war memoirs of those belatedly disenchanted are as reliable a guide to their relationship with Hitler as an account by the surviving partner of a sour divorce that ended in the suicide of the other partner. Like most memoirs, they are light on the authors' less creditable concerns such as rivalries with colleagues, their desire for decorations, promotions and the country estates and covert bonuses which flowed from the Führer's slush funds, choosing instead to portray themselves in a heroic or tragic light.

The formal structures can be easily outlined. In 1938 Hitler abolished the War Ministry after Blomberg's dismissal and made himself Führer and supreme commander, while Keitel and Jodl became the key figures in the new Armed Forces High Command (Oberkommando der Wehrmacht, or OKW). Hitler was the sole begetter of grand strategy, a mystery he liked to reserve for himself. As he told Army Chief of Staff Halder, 'My true intentions you will never know. Even those in my closest circle who feel quite sure they know my intentions will not know about them.' As the principal service, the army had its Oberkommando des Heeres (OKH) under Werner von Brauchitsch, until December 1941 when Hitler assumed the post himself under circumstances we have already described.[26]

Since there was no cabinet, there was also no institutional mechanism for overall direction of the German war effort, and no powerful military commanders analogous to Brooke or Marshall on the Allied side. Brooke could generally save Churchill from mistakes of his own making; there was no one of similar stature in the German camp capable of deflecting or defusing Hitler's enthusiasms. Not for nothing did Keitel's name pun with the German word for 'lackey' or 'Lakeitel'. When he was appointed, Blomberg remarked that it was Keitel who ran his office. 'That's exactly the man I'm looking for,' Hitler replied, for he would treat the heads of OKW like a Dictaphone.[27] Churchill knew he lacked higher military training and ultimately deferred to the professionals, however much he corporately despised them for their lack of initiative and their desire to have everything in place before going on the offensive. In Hitler's Germany there was no co-ordination of the three services, which vied for Hitler's favour, nor between them and the civilian ministries responsible for other aspects of the German war effort. The dictator's erratic habits did not help, for like Churchill he was a night owl, given to rising in the late morning. He also liked to exchange the fetid atmosphere of his command complex at Rastenburg in East Prussia, or at Vinnitsa in the Ukraine, for the airy heights of his Berghof eyrie in the Bavarian Alps. While this meant that he was not in personal contact with the army top brass, who remained in East Prussia, he often bypassed them entirely by summoning individual field commanders.[28]

Some professional soldiers were sceptical about Hitler's qualifications as a warlord, although Keitel, for one, genuinely believed him to be a military genius. Hitler imagined that his experiences as a corporal in the Great War afforded him greater insights into waging war than contemporaries who had commanded units in that conflict, and who were graduates of one of the most demanding officer and staff educations of the age. He took every opportunity to venture down memory lane even when there were more pressing matters: 'I just thought of something, because people are always complaining that they get the replacements too late. We marched off for the second offensive in 1918 on the evening of the 25th. On the 26th we spent the night in a forest and on the morning of the 27th we lined up. We marched off at 5 o'clock. One day before, in the afternoon, we received the replacements for the big offensive on the Chemin des Dames.'[29]

He seethed with class resentments towards middle- and upper-class generals, regarding the purple stripe down their trouser legs as akin to a yellow streak down their backs. Hitler came to regard them as the last surviving freemasons, members of an exclusive club to which he did not belong, and he dismissed their expertise as skill at war games conducted in a sandbox, or as manoeuvres on a parade ground. His favoured means of attack was to use his own worm's-eye experience of soldiering against them, or to overwhelm them with technical details, usually about weapons. During a discussion about flamethrowers, he produced an entirely apocryphal account of the loss of Fort Douaumont, whose capture by the Germans at one point seemed to presage victory at Verdun:

> In 1939 I fought for the flame throwers, but the idea was rejected by the general in charge of the engineers – this genius was called Förster – with the claim that they hadn't proven useful during the Great War. I said, 'How can you say such a thing? The flame thrower was one of the most effective weapons used during the Great War.' I participated in that mess myself, but the general hadn't. He said, 'You could see at Douaumont that it was dangerous for our own people but not for the enemy.' Now, of course, Douaumont blew up because a couple of people tried to make coffee with a hand grenade. One went off, which set fire to the munitions, and that set off 1,600 litres of flame thrower oil. Douaumont burned down because of that, of course. That could happen anywhere. With the same right you could say: ammunition is something completely obsolete; did you hear that a munitions train blew up again? That was the general who distinguished himself at Rzhev again. I shunted him aside back then.[30]

Efforts to blind the generals with science generally worked, but the more perceptive saw through this smokescreen. The war operations planner, General Walter Warlimont identified several fundamental flaws:

> A man like Hitler could not be expected to grasp the full import of the job which he had taken over; quite apart from the fact that in many respects he was ignorant of the basic principles of the exercise of command, he was overloaded with other responsibilities, and finally it was not in his nature. As regards intelligence of the enemy he only accepted what suited him and often refused even to listen to unpalatable information. As before, time and space were for him only vague ideas which should not be allowed to affect the determination of a man who knew where he was going. As a soldier of the First World War, he felt himself better qualified than any of his advisers to judge the capacity of the troops, and this was the subject of inter- minable and repetitive dissertations … He had already shown that strategically he did not understand the principle of concentrating forces at the decisive point; now he proved incapable of applying it tactically also, so nervous was he of exposing himself to attack anywhere … he showed he lacked the most important quality of a

military leader, knowledge of men and the understanding and mutual confidence which spring therefrom.[31]

Hitler increasingly drew upon the capital of past glories, or used an apodictic rhetoric that masked brute facts. During a military conference in late 1944 he claimed: 'Brilliance is just a phantom if it isn't supported by persistence and fanatical toughness. That's the most important thing in all of human life … You can only write world history if – behind intelligent reason, a lively conscience and eternal alertness – there is a fanatical persistence, a strength of will, that makes a man an inner warrior.'[32]

Decisions were made for non-military reasons, with resources devoted to mere territorial acquisition and retention. Stripped of individual initiative, generals were told to fight to the last man, by a supreme commander scrutinising the positions of armies on maps that were invariably out of date. Instead of cool appraisal of the situation, there were endless neurotic telephone calls, which merely served to confuse the picture further. Dissent triggered tirades, with hard malevolent stares for those whose warnings were proved right by events. Halder recalled that Hitler would listen to a counter-argument and then revert to his original stance as if the rebuttal had never been made. Very few generals had the nerve to stand up to him. One was Walter Model, in January 1942 the newly appointed commander of Ninth Army. Hitler liked Model, remarking after a meeting, 'Did you see that eye?' The dictator added: 'I trust that man to do it, but I wouldn't want to serve under him.' In Hitler's view Model exemplified the qualities he sought in generals: 'Generals must be tough, pitiless men, as crabbed as mastiffs – cross-grained men, such as I have in the Party.'[33] Almost immediately Hitler unilaterally decided to divide and hence weaken Model's first offensive. The general flew to Rastenburg in driving rain and during an interview with Hitler brusquely asked, 'My Führer, who commands Ninth Army, you or I?' After trying to change the subject, Hitler finally conceded, 'Good, Model. You do as you please, but it will be your head at risk.'

None of Hitler's declamatory bombast and social chippiness did his generals justice. How did one become a German general? Most of them came from military families, although Model's father, for example, was a master in a girls' school. From the age of ten or twelve, they attended one of the cadet academies, such as Lichterfelde in Berlin, before joining a regiment as an officer candidate, prior to selection for the ten Prussian war schools or their Bavarian analogue. This led to the slow peacetime ascent from regimental lieutenant to captain and major, although the Great War speeded up the promotion process by creating sudden vacancies, as happened to Model, who rose rapidly to serve on the General Staff during the Ludendorff offensive of spring 1918. The best and brightest were in turn selected for the 160 places at the Prussian War Academy, where they received three years' intensive training as future staff officers. Only a third became probationary General Staff officers, while only a sixth of each cohort were actually appointed to the ultimate honour of shadowing field commanders. Hitler's generals survived a total war in which every fourth active officer had perished, with most of them winning the Iron Cross First Class or the Prussian Knight's Cross for bravery. Two generals esteemed by Hitler, Ernst Busch and Eugen Ritter von Schobert, had gone one further by winning the highest honours, the Pour le Mérite or its Bavarian equivalent. They also survived defeat, revolution and hyperinflation which wiped out family wealth, as well as the reduction of the officer corps to one-tenth of its wartime complement. Although the Weimar Republic was inventive in finding ways to circumvent the limits on the armed forces imposed at Versailles, the hard core of the professional Wehrmacht welcomed the Republic's demise, and the advent of a regime that ignored Versailles and gave them the resources to wage the all-hands-to-the-pump style of total warfare they advocated.

Hitler's price for granting the officers their wish list was to make himself their master, the figure to whom they swore a personal oath of loyalty. The longer-term cost was the sacrifice of their individual initiative. As the Russian campaign drew on, generals who had regarded themselves as independent warlords were steadily reduced to little more than military functionaries. Long before Hitler took to directing individual divisions via radio links from his field HQ, the operational independence of commanders had been curtailed by the military bureaucrats of OKW and OKH, whose functions overlapped in an awkward way. As we have seen, it was the Chief of the General Staff Halder, rather than Hitler, who decided against taking Leningrad, and refused Army Group Centre permission to bypass Moscow. OKH also took over direct command of panzer corps, subverting the generals commanding army groups, and became itself subject to the operational whims of Hitler, who took to directing armies and even divisions himself. While he had a good grasp of how to manoeuvre a division, the Führer's lack of General Staff training showed in his poor handling of corps and armies. Above all, he was irrationally opposed to flexibility in the face of enemy counter-attacks, regarding a mobile defence as tantamount to cowardly retreat.[34]

In the summer heat of his forward command centre at Vinnitsa, open rows broke out. Field Marshal von Kluge stormed out of one meeting saying, 'You, my Führer, therefore assume responsibility for this,' only to be accused of ruining the operation a fortnight later because of dispositions Hitler had made himself. In August 1942 Hitler insulted Halder personally, screaming at him, 'I expect commanders to be as tough as the fighting troops.' Halder replied: 'I am tough enough, my Führer. But out there brave men and young officers are falling in thousands simply because their commanders are not allowed to make the only reasonable decision and have their hands tied behind their backs.' This response drew another tirade: 'Colonel General Halder, how dare you use language like that to me! Do you think you can teach me what the man at the front is thinking? What do you know about what goes on at the front? Where were you in the First World War? And you try to pretend to me that I don't understand what it's like at the front. I won't stand that! It's outrageous!'[35] The surrender of Paulus at Stalingrad allowed Hitler to give full vent to his view of the value of human life, amid his evocations of the Roman General Varus ordering his slaves to kill him: 'What does that mean, "Life"? Life ... people; the individual indeed has to die. What remains alive beyond the individual is the people. But how one can fear this moment – through which he [can free] himself from misery – [if] duty [doesn't] hold him back in this valley of suffering?'[36]

While Hitler's physician kept him going with injected cocktails of strange stimulants, his generals bore the real stresses of command. In Allied captivity after being released from Flossenbürg concentration camp, Halder described a typical working week as army chief of staff:

> During my last year, in 1942, I averaged three or four hours' sleep per night and once or twice a week I worked through the night without any sleep. The reason for this was that during the day we received all troop information from the front. After that came conferences with the various fourteen section chiefs. Then I had to have a few hours daily to work by myself – this could only be done around midnight. In between times the telephone rang continuously. You had to know how to work in a place like that without wearing yourself out completely.[37]

The stress experienced by field commanders was intense. On 6 February 1942 Gotthard Heinrici wrote to his wife: 'My mind is exclusively devoted to military matters. Everything else simply goes by the board. In any event, I simply can't busy myself with other matters, since inner calm is wholly lacking.' Things were so parlous that his thoughts turned to God, as only He could 'intervene at the last minute'. Aged fifty-six, General Heinrici was exhausted from lack of sleep, chain-smoking and swilling cognac to keep going. Such comforts as a bath, a flush lavatory or cut flowers seemed impossible luxuries, at least until he savoured them during a brief spell of home leave. But he was determined to stick it out, although all of the generals commanding adjacent fronts had 'suddenly disappeared, having posted themselves sick'. The strains of command took their toll: sixty-year-old Field Marshal Walter von Brauchitsch suffered a heart attack in December 1941 and his semi-successor, fifty-eight-year-old Field Marshal Walter von Reichenau, died of a stroke in 1942.[38] Nor were generals immune to the dangers of combat: in North Africa, Rommel's deputy General Ludwig Crüwell was captured by the British, while Rommel's replacement, General Georg Stumme, died of a heart attack as he clung to the side of his staff car when it came under enemy fire.[39]

Ninety per cent of the historical record left by senior German commanders concerned tactical or operational questions, with less attention devoted to logistics, occupation regimens or broader strategic considerations. Their writings reveal an overriding preoccupation with causing the enemy the maximum damage at minimal cost to their own troops. This was a constant spiritual burden, the 'powerful invisible weight' that Ernst Jünger felt as he watched General von Kleist poring over his charts at his field HQ in the Caucasus in January 1943. Though they failed to exercise command responsibility towards civilians or prisoners of war, virtually all of them had a keen sense of obligation towards their own troops, which General Hoepner considered even greater than his responsibilities to his own superiors. Reminders of what each decision on a map entailed were not hard to see. Field Marshal Wilhelm Ritter von Leeb described his sense of responsibility not only to the fatherland, but also to 'the hundreds of thousands of mothers' of the young men he commanded. General Georg-Hans Reinhardt described to his wife in August 1941 being 'deeply and painfully moved when the evening before yesterday I passed along long rows of graves and saw how the newly fallen were being buried'. He also wrote of the heavy weight of responsibility when he looked into the pale, hollow-eyed faces of 'my people' whom he expected to perform superhumanly.[40]

Of course, some generals were oblivious to losses. As the 'fireman' parachuted in to revivify Ninth Army, Model prided himself on knowing his troops, to whom he paid endless surprise visits during which he was usually brusque with the junior officers but solicitous of his men. However, he had a very different attitude towards the elite operational reserve divisions, which were supposed to act as shock troops. He saw that even if they took high casualties, such units would be withdrawn, replenished and despatched elsewhere. Ignoring the Grossdeutschland Division's desire to fight as a single formation, Model immediately detached almost half of it for assignment to Ninth Army formations, while pushing the division's infantry into bloody battles with the Soviets. This use of its resources was bitterly resented by the Ninth's equally seasoned commanders. With reason, since after the army had entered the Rzhev salient with eighteen thousand men in September 1942, by January ten thousand of them had been killed or wounded.[41]

These officers subscribed to the doctrine of adapting orders to tactical realities (*Auftragstaktik*) rather than the 'corpse-like obedience' that the Prussian army had modelled on the monastic Teutonic Knights of the Middle Ages. The *Auftragstaktik* tradition led many officers to disobey out-of-date or unrealistic orders in the field, and prompted some to dispute increasingly crazy commands from their hierarchical superiors at Hitler's HQ. A keen sense of duty kept the best at their posts, refusing the easy options of taking sick leave or resigning their commands. Reinhardt captured this sense of obligation when he wrote after repeated clashes with Kluge: 'Either I am "the Führer", in which case I should be left alone to lead, or if they don't like my attitudes, then they should choose someone better, or get themselves a puppet who would eat out of their hands. I didn't want to report myself sick and simply go home. In my eyes that would be desertion of the colours, which none of us must do, especially not in the present difficult circumstances.' While fiery individuals like Guderian were prepared to confront their superiors, anything resembling a collective démarche was out of the question to men with keen memories of the breakdown of discipline in the army in the last stages of the Great War.

Many German commanders also realised that the colonial, as opposed to liberationist, approach to conquered peoples was entirely counter-productive, turning potential allies against Bolshevism into diehard foes. Populations which had welcomed the Germans as liberators from the murderous collectivism of Stalinism became sullen and resentful under the reality of German occupation. Several of these officers not only forbade indiscriminate looting, but wrote insightful memos on the wider theme, memos which were ignored by a dogmatic political leadership that preferred to view all Ukrainians as 'Negroes', thereby ignoring the powerful nationalist sentiment in western Ukraine. Indeed, the rejection of such pragmatic occupation strategies, rather than any pangs of conscience about the Jews, may explain why so many members of Army Group Centre were to figure in the military plots to assassinate Hitler.[42]

IV JAPANESE WARRIORS

While German generals have become almost household names to a certain sort of war buff, it is important not to forget others who were not just commanders of genius, but human beings who afford unique insights into the welter of emotions that men in high command were subject to. Japanese generals tended to have as formulaic a career trajectory as their Prussian-German equivalents – indeed, the Prussian system was the model for the modern Japanese army, which was also permeated by the cult of the samurai, the feudal warrior caste outlawed in 1873 in Japan, and its code of bushido. Most future generals had attended Military Preparatory Schools before going to the Military Academy and then the Army War College, followed by the General Staff College. We have already encountered General Yamashita, the commander who conquered Malaya and Singapore. He was the son of a country doctor who passed out sixth from a General Staff College class of fifty-six and then spent three long stints in Berne, Vienna and Berlin. By 1934 he had risen to the rank of major general, despite his indifference to the political machinations of many of his colleagues. He held a succession of field commands in Korea and Manchukuo and was famously unimpressed by the aristocrats who commanded the Imperial Guards divisions. Large for a Japanese, at five foot ten and a bulky fourteen stone, Yamashita was an austere, silent, reflective man in his fifties who had thought deeply about modern warfare. Ironically, he favoured ending the war in China to avoid conflict with Britain and the United States.

Yamashita was chosen to command the invasion of Malaya and the capture of Singapore, alongside Masaharu Homma (Philippines), Hitoshi Imamura (Dutch East Indies) and Shojiro Iida (Burma). Based in Saigon, he used research and intelligence derived from a special investigative unit on Formosa, and consular spies in Kuala Lumpur and Singapore, to modify an existing invasion plan, which involved landing in Thailand and then hurtling down the Malayan peninsula to seize Singapore across the Straits of Johore. At the end of November 1941 he moved to his HQ at Hainan Island off the coast of China. Perhaps his greatest achievement was to overcome the rancorous inter-service animosities which dogged relations between the army and navy, so that the landings in southern Thailand went off perfectly, while also thoroughly integrating his air resources with the three divisions he used to invade Malaya. The fact that he denied himself the use of a fourth division to minimise the logistical drag on the 'driving charge' he had in mind says a lot about Yamashita's qualities of generalship.

A force of some thirty-five thousand men, closely supported by over six hundred aircraft, smashed its way through poorly led and demoralised British, Australian and Indian defenders, at a cost of about five thousand men. The Japanese went straight down roads on their bicycles, darting into the jungle only when they needed to outflank hastily erected roadblocks. Seaborne troops were also landed on Malaya's west coast to add to the panic air raids were causing. In Singapore, the British commander Arthur Percival imagined that his 109,000 men were being decimated by a force of 150,000, whereas by the time Yamashita launched his attack across the Straits of Johore he was down to 30,000. In the course of a lightning advance, which took them 680 miles from their starting point, the Japanese used supplies and trucks abandoned by their fleeing opponents, either repairing some 250 blown bridges or bicycling across improvised log bridges propped up by the shoulders of engineers standing in the water below. When a railway needed repair, an entire division did the work and finished it in a week. Reflecting on what his men had achieved after reaching Singapore, Yamashita said, 'On average our troops had fought two battles, repaired four or five bridges, and advanced twenty-five kilometres every day. Our small boats, without armaments, had manoeuvred and carried out landings up to six hundred and fifty kilometres behind the enemy's lines on the western coast.'[43] His successful crossing to Singapore was partly the result of a brilliant piece of strategic deception, confirming Percival's overestimate of the forces facing him, by ordering his limited number of trucks to drive continuously around a loop of road in view of Singapore island with their lights on. The military aristocrats had their petty revenge on him after his brilliant victory by posting him immediately to a command in Manchukuo, denying him the customary honour of an audience with the Emperor.

One psychological burden which British, German and Japanese commanders shared, but which the Americans were spared, was the bombing which put their families on the front line. This consideration was uppermost in the mind of General Tadamichi Kuribayashi, who was responsible for one of the most lethal engagements ever fought by the US Marines. Thanks to the researches of Kumiko Kakehashi, the general's home thoughts from abroad have immortalised him. Anyone still labouring under residual prejudices about the Japanese should read the thoughts of a loving father and kind man who was also a remarkable soldier. Although the circumstances on Iwo Jima, which he defended to the death, made it impossible for him to commit the war crimes that doomed other Japanese generals to the gallows, one feels he would not have done so if things had been different.

The Marines' assault on Iwo Jima, a small volcanically active island where Japanese territory technically started in deep Pacific, was supposed to take five days; it went on for thirty-six, costing the sixty thousand Marines who landed 28,686 casualties, nearly seven thousand of them fatal, while virtually all the twenty-two thousand Japanese defenders perished, including their commander. Much was at stake here. Iwo Jima would put fleets of US B-29 bombers within range of Tokyo, since they could use the island's three airfields to make emergency landings on the way back to the Marianas. Fully aware of what their huge payloads of incendiary bombs would do to the city's ancient wooden houses, where his own family lived, Kuribayashi was determined to delay the inevitable. Having evacuated the island's small civilian population, he and his men excavated a warren of tunnels, despite having to work in baking heat and amid choking sulphurous gases. The island's only source of drinking water was rainfall, and all food had to be flown in. Many soldiers suffered from malnutrition while being afflicted with dysentery. Kuribayashi was adamantly opposed to suicidal banzai charges and to defending the beaches, where his troops would be exposed to pulverising air and naval bombardment. His plan was to let the Marines come ashore and then wipe them out from well-concealed artillery and machine-gun emplacements. Every one of these positions had to be taken, with tanks, flamethrowers or grenades, in one of the most ferocious engagements of the war. At the end, Kuribayashi led his last nine hundred men on a dawn assault, while in the tunnels those wounded who could not walk blew themselves up with hand grenades.

Kuribayashi was the scion of an old landed-gentry family. Unusually, he had attended middle school where he learned English, rather than the

German favoured at Military Preparatory School. He briefly toyed with the idea of being a foreign correspondent before joining the army, passing from the Military Academy into the cavalry. Leaving behind his thirteen-years-younger wife Yoshii and their small son Taro, he spent two years in the US, attending classes at Harvard and the University of Michigan. He clearly admired America, on one occasion driving eight hundred miles from Kansas to Washington DC in his new Chevrolet. He made many friends in the US 1st Cavalry Division, marvelling at such egalitarian novelties as married women with their own bank accounts or girls who could repair his car. From the letters he wrote home, the thirty-six-year-old Captain seems an attractive man, who felt sufficiently sorry for the paperboy to invite him in for dinner, or who handed out money to two barefoot Mexican waifs whose drunken father did not even feed them. His letters to Taro were illustrated with charming drawings: 'This is an American child at play. Here tricycles are all the rage. And when your daddy sees children playing that way I always stand rooted to the spot a while and look at them thinking: I wonder if little Taro is having fun like this, see?'

After taking part in the conquest of Hong Kong, Kuribayashi spent most of the war as commander of the home army division charged with defending Tokyo. His domestic life seems to have been happy – he insisted the maid ate with the family and he helped out drying the dishes. His main pleasure was home improvements; the day before he flew out to Iwo Jima, he was making shelves for the kitchen. Even on Iwo Jima, Kuribayashi advised his wife how she might repair a draughty floorboard, and included a detailed sketch of the work he had meant to finish. Kuribayashi was fifty-two years old when he took command of Iwo Jima, his son Taro was nineteen and he also had two daughters: Yoko, aged fifteen and the apple of his eye, and nine-year-old Takako, whose favourite game was to ride 'Mister Horsey' on her father's back. In Tokyo, every morning while he waited for his driver, she would dance for her father in the hall.

A realist in whose correspondence neither politics nor hyper-patriotism intruded, Kuribayashi knew exactly what was at stake on Iwo Jima. His letters home constantly advise his family how to cope with the air raids he knew would intensify if he did not turn the island into a death trap for the Americans. He had vivid dreams about his wife and youngest daughter. In his letters home, there are constant intimations of death. 'These days', he wrote to Yoshii on 25 August 1944, 'I am enjoying every day I am alive, one day at a time. I have made up my mind to think of my life as something I have today, but will not have tomorrow. I want so badly for all of you to be able to live long and happy lives. I feel sorriest for Takako because she's the youngest.' When he left for the Iwo Jima command, his parting words to his wife were: 'This time even my dead bones won't be sent back home.' She thought he was joking.

One month after reaching Iwo Jima, he mailed home those personal possessions he no longer needed. His innermost concerns were evident in the letter that accompanied them: 'I want to say something to the children. Always do what your mother tells you. After I have gone, I want you to help your mother, treat her as the centre of the family, and help each other so you can all lead vigorous, positive lives. With you in particular Taro, I pray with all my heart that you become the kind of strong, tough-minded young man that your mother and your younger sisters can depend on. Yoko, you are pretty robust, so I'm confident about you. I feel sorry for your mummy because maybe she hasn't got that strength of character. I do regret that I had so little time to love you, Tako-chan. Please grow up to be big and strong for me.'[44]

Kuribayashi immediately purged any officers he thought were not up to the coming battle. His solicitude for his men was constant. He drank no more than the single canteen of water they received each day, and washed and shaved in a cup of water. He sought to extend this frugality to the family, advising them how spinning a basin in a bath would collect the scum, enabling them to reuse the water. He distributed any extra food (or whisky) either sent by his family or brought by visiting naval personnel. The general ordered his troops to try to grow vegetables and had a go at breeding chickens. He paced the entire island, lying down to establish the best lines of fire by using his cane as a rifle surrogate, and lending a hand with the incessant digging of the geothermal rock that melted the rubber soles of his men's shoes. Like his men, Kuribayashi discovered that the whole place was infested with cockroaches and alive with ants.

These became minor worries on 8 December, when the Americans began a seventy-four-day aerial bombardment in which 6,800 tons of bombs were dropped, while there were also five massive naval bombardments. Given that the island consists of only eight and a half square miles of land, this was equivalent to wrapping it – Christo-style – with a yard-thick layer of steel. Almost every blade of grass as well as every tree was blasted into nothingness in this holocaust of steel. After savagely resisting the landings, the garrison was slowly forced back as the Marines inched their way across the island. When all hope was gone, Kuribayashi at last ordered the final death charge. He had been right to predict that his remains would never come home: all officers had removed insignias of rank before the final assault, and there was no way of knowing which of the thousands of corpses was his, as opposed to belonging to one of the men he had commanded so skilfully in life.

CHAPTER 13

Antagonistic Allies

Churchill

Of all the war leaders, the most anecdotes adhere to Churchill, who uttered epigrams and witticisms in the way that others blink or breathe. His erratic interventions in strategy are well known, but it is less often remarked that he created a remarkably effective system for direction of Britain's war effort, for which he was ultimately accountable to parliament. Following the fall of Tobruk in June 1942, he faced a vote of no confidence, an embarrassment never faced by Hitler, Roosevelt or Stalin.

Any visitor to the Cabinet War Rooms off Whitehall can see that the British meant business, whatever their national propensity for muddle and making-do, or the contrived self-deprecation that underplays their own efforts and sacrifices. Churchill's experiences in the Great War, of political turmoil and generals running their own shows, led him to combine political and military power in his own hands as both prime minister and minister of defence. He had what the medieval monarchs called *plena potestas*, with the solid backing of a coalition War Cabinet that seldom questioned his conduct of the war. Apart from the coterie around former premier Lloyd George who were positioning themselves to take power when, as seemed inevitable, Britain sued for peace, it was not until the immediate peril of defeat had passed that Churchill faced any challenge to his leadership. The limitless conceit of Stafford Cripps led him, alone, to conceive of himself as an alternative war leader, but in general opposition took the form of opportunistic, when not Soviet-inspired, sniping by leftists like Aneurin Bevan, more concerned with the class war in Britain than the national struggle for survival. The almost treacherous behaviour of the Lloyd George clique, and the demands of such as Bevan for a – certainly catastrophic – invasion of Europe as early as 1943, which would have cost many thousands of British lives and could only have served Soviet interests, has never been subjected to the intense forensic scrutiny lavished on the pre-war appeasers.

Much of the machinery of war was inherited from the Chamberlain government, although galvanised into a more urgent tempo by the new Prime Minister. Churchill inserted himself into its structures, creating two defence committees for supply and operations, the second chaired by himself and directly linked to the Chiefs of Staff Committee (CSC). The successive Chiefs of the Imperial General Staff (CIGS) were Field Marshals Edmund Ironside, John Dill and, most successfully, Alan Brooke. The CSC spawned two parallel sub-hierarchies, responsible for planning and intelligence, and would also accommodate a new Chief for Combined Operations, eventually led by Lord Louis 'Dickie' Mountbatten. But that is enough of acronyms and structures. It is easy to forget that the only two rooms Brooke claimed to visit in the War Office were his office and the lavatory.

Eschewing anything as ponderous as today's Ministry of Defence, Churchill relied on a tight office under General Hastings 'Pug' Ismay, who also belonged to the CSC as Churchill's eyes and ears. Churchill detached the Statistical Service from the Admiralty, placing it under Professor Frederick Lindemann, who monopolised the area of technical innovations too, using it to form an accurate picture of developments and trends across the whole war effort. *Ad hoc* committees were formed to deal with emergency situations such as the Battle of the Atlantic or problems of supply. Labour politicians such as Clement Attlee, Ernest Bevin and Herbert Morrison were generously represented in the cabinet, and Churchill also imported such unappealing cronies as Brendan Bracken and Lord Beaverbrook to force things along according to business practices rather than the glacial creep of the civil service.[1] Churchill also had to deal diplomatically with problems that Hitler and Stalin would have solved with firing squads. The absurd Cripps was fobbed off with the harmless job of leader of the House of Commons, while Attlee was made deputy prime minister to help contain the vanity of the highly strung Eden, who at one point schemed to strip Churchill of the defence portfolio.[2]

Churchill's main contribution to the running of the British war effort was to light a fire under the far from pressurised boilers of the government and military bureaucracies, while maintaining popular morale under extraordinarily strained circumstances. If some of his strategic

interventions unfortunately reflected the mere dash of a Victorian caval-
ryman – notably his enthusiasm for commando raids on enemy territory
– in mitigation it could be said that he appreciated his people's need for
drama and theatre at a time when Britain was hardly engaged at all.[3] He
had a rare ability to grasp a complex brief, working through his morning
load of papers while propped up in bed, where he was occasionally
diverted by Nelson the cat. Although better known for his cigars and
whisky, other companions included a device he called 'Klop' to punch
holes in papers, and the stashes of red labels marked 'Action this day'
which he attached to urgent inquiries. It was not unusual for secretaries
to be taking dictation at 4.30 in the morning. Nothing escaped his beady
eye, especially leaden language. He had the Local Defence Volunteers
rechristened Home Guard after taking a dislike to the letters LDF on their
armbands; when the Ministry of Food tried to introduce Communal
Feeding Centres he decided that this smacked of Communism and had
them renamed British Restaurants. The striking names for British military
operations derived from his conviction that mothers would not appreciate their sons having been killed during Operation Bunny Hug.[4]

It was arguably Churchill's ability to ask searching questions and
marshal the relevant facts that injected vigour into the torpid negativity of
the British bureaucracy. Gone were the endless tea-and-chat breaks, along
with the 9-to-5 mentality, for Churchill expected everyone to match the
punishing schedule he kept himself, which routinely meant going to bed
somewhere between 1 and 3 in the morning. To some of his cabinet
colleagues and military chiefs the late-night sessions seemed like an old
man's excuse to revisit past glories and to ramble, but they enabled him to
get to know them better and, in some cases, to win them over. The working week devoured weekends, which merely brought a change of venue to
Chequers or Ditchley Park, a low-visibility Oxfordshire country house
made available to the Prime Minister. There were no holidays and generals got used to seeing more of Churchill in his bath than their own children. In addition to his domestic movements around Britain, bringing his
special magic to a city devastated by bombing or to a remote RAF bomber
base, it has been estimated that during his wartime premiership Churchill
travelled more than 105,000 miles, often at considerable personal risk. The
stress on a man in his late sixties was enormous – he had two heart attacks
and a bout of pneumonia that almost killed him. He was a steady but not
a heavy drinker, and although alcohol took its toll in later years, it kept
him going at a pace that wore out many younger and sober men.[5]

Churchill and many of his age and class group went in for shows of manly emotion inherited from their days at boarding schools, although their speech was littered with endearments that sound camp to modern ears. As we have seen in our earlier encounters with him, Churchill combined ruthlessness with sentimentality, many commenting on the tears streaming down his chubby face when he visited survivors of bombing raids or saw soldiers about to go into battle. Like anyone else he was liable to dark thoughts of vengeance – whether 'drenching' invading Germans with mustard gas on British beaches or shooting the most senior Nazis on capture after summary courts martial. Yet he retained a sense of humanity and proportion. At a dinner on 8 March 1941, where de Gaulle and the Australian Prime Minister Robert Menzies were the main guests, Churchill's son-in-law Duncan Sandys vehemently expressed a desire to lay Germany waste, burning its towns and factories. Even the libraries were to be destroyed to create a future generation of illiterates. It is worth citing what Churchill's private secretary John Colville recorded about the Prime Minister's reply:

> He did not believe in pariah nations, and he saw no alternative to the acceptance of Germany as part of the family of Europe. In the event of an invasion he would not even approve of the civil population murdering the Germans quartered on them. Still less would he condone atrocities against the German civil population if we were in a position to commit them.[6]

It is not entirely correct to say that religion was unimportant to him, as he liked a rousing sermon – Hensley Henson was his favourite – or a martial hymn, and regarded the Sermon on the Mount as a good guide in life.[7] Churchill's attitude to the rules of war was based on common sense and a keen grasp of good and evil rather than on a lawyer's desiccated objectivity or a philosopher's leisurely reflection. Facing an enemy that had abrogated the rule of law and that murdered innocent people by the millions, he was prepared to discard international law when it suited him, notably the rights of smaller neutral states. He put this very well in late 1939: 'The letter of the law must not in supreme emergency obstruct those who are charged with its protection and enforcement. It would not be right or rational that the Aggressor Power should gain one set of advantages by tearing up all laws, and another set by sheltering behind the innate respect for law of its opponents. Humanity, rather than legality, must be our guide.'[8]

On the Allied side, Churchill's conception of war strategy is easiest to outline; he wanted to hit back at the Nazis (and Japanese) as quickly as possible. The audacious raid appealed to the late-Victorian imperialist in him; he was less enamoured of the slow build-up of overwhelming force and never grasped that modern armies require a huge logistical tail, something he tended to regarded as akin to the finery of a peacock. He loathed inaction, whether in a sluggish bureaucracy or large armies apparently doing nothing in important theatres, notably the Middle East where hundreds of thousands of Dominion troops seemed just to atrophy in the heat under over-cautious theatre commanders who lounged about amid the fleshpots of Cairo.[9] Once the danger of an invasion had passed, his mind turned from Sten guns defending Whitehall and poison-gas clouds choking Nazis on British beaches to bold counter-attacks, for neither the naval blockade of the continent nor the attrition of German military and civilian morale by bombing offered the prospect of quick results. On the other hand, a key reason why he favoured a peripheral Mediterranean and Balkan strategy was that the alternative – the American determination to kick in the front door through a seaborne invasion of northern France – reminded him of the Gallipoli disaster and the carnage of the Western Front in the First World War. The Mediterranean was a more manageable theatre, where Britain's military resources were more evenly matched with the Italians and the small Afrika Korps than they would be locked in combat with the cream of the German army in Europe. 'Action this day' was best served by low-cost pinpricks like the derring-do of commando raids and the doings of SOE. Some argue that this reflected Churchill's realistic appraisal of the limited capabilities of Britain's army, as opposed to its air force and navy.[10]

Churchill's relations with 'his' generals (who were actually the King's) could never be smooth, for he was a demanding taskmaster. Ismay believed there was an unbridgeable cultural gulf between politicians and soldiers. Among politicians, style usually triumphs over substance and, after vicious knockabouts in the Commons, they can retire to have a friendly drink together.[11] They routinely attack each other's proposals regardless of their merits, demonstrating the utmost bad faith. Military commanders are insulated from such testing by an entourage of admiringly loyal staff officers, resulting in a relative lack of mental nimbleness, which can make them appear irresolute and unimaginative when they are merely inarticulate, the failing that most irritated Churchill.[12] The cerebral General Wavell's taciturnity seems to have doomed him from his first encounter

Brooke

with the voluble Prime Minister.[13] Wavell handled his complicated Middle Eastern command with great skill until Churchill spread his forces too thin for them to be decisive in either of the major theatres to which they were committed. When disaster followed Wavell's faithful attempt to obey the orders he had received from London, he was made the scapegoat. It was a dishonourable and deeply resented action, not least because of a well-founded belief that Churchill had been motivated by personal dislike. Churchill's tendency to meddle down the chain of command was halted by Brooke, who insisted that he countersign any communication by Churchill to subordinate officers.[14]

On the day he was appointed CIGS in November 1941, Alan Brooke wrote:

> I suppose I ought to be very grateful and happy at reaching the top of the ladder. I can't say that I do. I feel a heavy depression at Dill going after the close contacts I have had with him ever since the war started. I had never hoped or aspired at reaching these dizzy heights and now that I am stepping up onto the plateau land of my military career the landscape looks cold, black and lonely, with a ghastly responsibility hanging as a black thunder cloud over me.[15]

From one of Ulster's largest landowning families, twenty-six Brookes served in the First World War and twenty-seven in the Second; twelve were killed. Brooke had a successful Great War, being one of the pioneers of the creeping artillery barrage. He was a tough-minded career army officer, who had lost his first wife in a car accident in 1925; he had been driving and blamed himself.[16] His diaries go to the heart of command at the highest level, revealing emotions that he otherwise repressed. The night he was offered the top job by Churchill at Chequers, Brooke knelt and prayed to God for guidance. It is worth noting what this 'not highly religious individual' had to say, looking back at the ethical principles that had shaped his war on the day it ended in Europe:

> I am ... convinced there is a God all powerful looking after the destiny of this world. I had little doubt about this before the war started, but this war has convinced me more than ever of this truth. Again and again during the last 6 years I have seen his guiding hand controlling and guiding the destiny of this world toward that final and definite destiny which He has ordained. The suffering and agony

of war in my mind must exist to gradually educate us to the fundamental law of 'loving our neighbour as ourselves'... humanity in this
world is still young, there are still many millions of years to run
during which high perfection will be attained.[17]

In the course of the war, Brooke was exposed to constant strain that left his
brain numbed by the end. It was not simply a matter of despatching
millions of men into battle. Anyone working in London during the war
had to run the gauntlet of German bombing, or, in the latter part of the
war, unguided missiles. On 18 June a V1 flying bomb hit the Guards Chapel
at Wellington Barracks, killing sixty people during a Sunday Service.
Brooke had a letter on his desk from one of the victims, an old friend inviting him to lunch the same week.[18] His much trusted flatmate in London
was also killed in an air accident. Brooke the man was the sort of uncomplicated Briton who has amusing sayings hanging in his bathroom: 'Life
consists of Monday to Saturday, not Saturday to Monday' being one to
ponder. Rare moments of relief came from ornithology – he liked to
slip away from his office to spend the afternoons browsing books on birds
and buying the equipment he filmed them with – as well as fishing and
shooting.

First there was the problem of dealing with Churchill, who behaved like
a petulant prima donna, no matter how much Brooke otherwise respected
him. Brooke said he was like a child persistently playing with a toy he was
told would burn or cut his fingers.[19] At a meeting with the Americans,
Brooke's homologue George Marshall remarked that he was lucky if he
saw Roosevelt once every six weeks. Brooke thought, 'I was fortunate if I
did not see Winston for 6 hours.'[20] He felt he had no choice, since to be
physically separated from him was to run the risk that Churchill might
embark on some mad escapade.[21] Exasperated though he was by
Churchill's flights of fancy, a deep sense of loyalty inhibited any public
disagreement.[22] Early on, Brooke learned how to put up a metaphorical
umbrella under which he sat silently, although sometimes Churchill
seemed to lose it completely. On 27 April 1941 at Chequers he had a row
with his Director of Military Operations at the War Office, General Sir
John Kennedy, who had intimated that the British might lose Egypt:
'Churchill flushed at this and lost his temper. His eyes flashed and he
shouted, "Wavell has 400,000 men. If they lose Egypt, blood will flow. I
will have firing parties to shoot the generals."' According to Kennedy, no
one took the threat seriously, however often Churchill repeated it.[23] Again

according to Kennedy, Brooke used to strike out nine-tenths of any draft minute for Churchill on the grounds that 'The more you tell that man about the war, the more you hinder the winning of it.'[24] On 28 February 1944, Brooke recorded: '[Churchill] was in an impossible mood, with nothing but abuse about everything the Army was doing! Every commander from Jumbo Wilson (the Commander-in-Chief, Middle East) to the least company commander was useless, the organisation was useless, the Americans hopeless etc. It was all I could do to contain my temper.'[25] The essential problem was that 'In all his plans he lives from hand to mouth. He can never grasp a whole plan, either in its width (ie all fronts) or its depth (long term projects). His method is entirely opportunist, gathering one flower here another there! My God how tired I am of working for him!'[26]

Sometimes Churchill brought cabinet ministers to meetings with the generals; 'fresh ideas' according to him, reinforcements for some madcap scheme according to Brooke. At a meeting on 8 March 1944 to discuss Pacific strategy, Brooke spent two and a half hours patiently demolishing one bad idea after another, until well after midnight. 'The arguments [of the four ministers] were so puerile that it made me ashamed to think they were Cabinet ministers ... [they] had only been brought along to support Winston!'[27] Some of Brooke's defensiveness arose from his awareness that the Great War had destroyed the cream of his military generation.[28] On 23 October 1941 he wrote: 'The dearth of suitable higher commanders is lamentable. I cannot quite make out to what it can be attributable. The only thing I feel can account for it is the fact that the flower of our manhood was wiped out some 20 years ago and it is just some of those that we lost then that we require now.'[29] Of course, in that war the Germans sustained similar losses of officers, but without equivalent effects. Brooke noted that the First Sea Lord, Admiral Dudley Pound, was 'an old dodderer' who was asleep '75% of the time he should be working'.[30] He also had to smooth not only egos ruffled by Churchill's basilisk stare and sharp tongue, but also those involved in rancorous rivalries within the army: 'Running a war seems to consist in making plans and then ensuring that all those destined to carry it out don't quarrel with each other instead of the enemy.'[31] He was fortunate that the explosive possibilities of Anglo-American rivalry could usually be contained by dismissing the squabbling staff officers and having an off-the-record meeting with Marshall, accompanied only by Dill, the Chief of the British Joint Staff Mission – whom the Americans esteemed so highly that they honoured him with burial in Arlington, under one of only two equestrian monuments in the whole cemetery – and Roosevelt's Chief of Staff Admiral William Leahy.[32]

As the authority who shaped campaigns, chose commanders and allocated resources, Brooke was at the heart of the British war effort, reluctantly eschewing major field commands in the knowledge that only he could contain Churchill. The toughest challenge, Brooke felt, was to maintain the mask of command: 'The hardest part of bearing such responsibility is pretending that you are absolutely confident of success when you are really torn to shreds with doubts and misgivings! But when once decisions are taken the time for doubts is gone, and what is required is to breathe the confidence of success into all those around.'[33] Brooke took a sober view of ordering men into battle. Late in the war he feared that the New Zealand government was influencing General Freyberg to fight over-cautiously. Paraphrasing Stalin, Brooke commented that 'Unfortunately it is hard in war to make omelettes without breaking eggs, and it is often in trying to do so that we break most eggs!'[34] Very lengthy discussions preceded the bombing campaign against French railways in the run-up to D-Day. Churchill opposed using heavy bombers on these targets: 'he does not think the results to be achieved will be much and secondly owing to the casualties amongst French civilians which must result from it'.[35] There was a further long discussion of the same subject at cabinet on 2 May, 'more waffling about and vacillating politicians unable to accept the consequences of war', wrote Brooke.[36]

British generals do not have the dark charisma of a Manstein or Model, but many of them had enough charisma at the time. Like Hitler's generals, most of their British equivalents were born between 1880 and 1891 and were in their fifties and early sixties when they achieved high command. In Britain, social class tended to play its usual anti-meritocratic role, although it was a career more open to talent than many, following in the minimally researched footsteps of Alan Clarke's history *The Donkeys*, are prepared to admit. Senior commanders tended to come from roughly similar social backgrounds, but Montgomery's father was vicar of St Mark's in Kennington before becoming bishop of Tasmania, while William Slim was the son of a Birmingham iron merchant. Many were products of private schools with a strong military tradition that catered to lower-middle-class students, before attending either the Royal Military College at Sandhurst, the Royal Artillery School at Woolwich or the Indian Army Staff College at Quetta in what is now Pakistan. For the chosen few there was the Staff College at Camberley and the Imperial Defence College in London. Little of their training could compare with the precise Clausewitzian *Wissenschaft* that their German contemporaries had to acquire.

Like their German peers, British generals had been decorated junior officers in the Great War. Some had been wounded, including Montgomery, who was shot in the chest and survived by sheltering behind a dead comrade's body from further sniper fire. Many of them had continuous combat experience in the inter-war period, fighting low-level imperial insurgencies that taught them little of use in a major war. Uniquely, the debonair Ulsterman Harold Alexander had commanded German Freikorps troops in post-war Latvia and so spoke German. Only a few were what might be called intellectuals, although several had cultivated interests beyond horses, hunting and polo. In truth, some of them, as Brooke knew, merely looked the part or cut the sort of dash that Churchill found so impressive in Alexander, a classic case of style over substance.[37] After Dunkirk, Brooke lamented, 'How poor we are in Army and Corps commanders. We ought to remove several but heaven knows where we shall find anything very much better.'

It was a very big problem indeed. On a visit to North Africa, Brooke talked to an exhausted General William 'Strafer' Gott, who said: 'I think what is required here is some new blood. I have tried most of my ideas on the Boche. We want someone with new ideas and plenty of confidence in them.' Despite Brooke's objections, Churchill appointed Gott head of Eighth Army. Only after he was killed when German fighters ambushed his plane did Brooke get his original choice of commander: Montgomery. The Rommel 'Desert Fox' legend had adversely affected the morale of British and Dominion soldiers, and Montgomery set about rebuilding confidence in typically brusque style. On his first day in command, he bluntly asked Brigadier Freddie de Guingand: 'Well, Freddie, my lad, you chaps seem to have got things into a bit of mess here. Tell me all about it.' Montgomery's virtues included the fact that, as Lord Gort had it, 'he was not quite a gentleman'. Montgomery purged any officers who seemed defeatist or uninspired, while issuing a general warning that 'bellyaching' would no longer be tolerated.[38] He felt obliged to do the same when he took command of 21st Army Group in preparation for the invasion of France. The class-conscious lamented that 'The Gentlemen are out and the Players in,' although any one making such a remark was surely not to any manor born.[39]

Monty's only rival in the uncrowded pantheon of successful British Second World War generals was Bill Slim, whom many believe to have been the greater commander. Slim turned around a badly beaten multi-ethnic army in South-east Asia and, with a fraction of the resources Montgomery enjoyed, led it to victory against a tenacious enemy and some of the worst terrain and climate conditions in the world. Both took a keen interest in their soldiers' fitness and welfare, and went to great lengths to explain what was expected of them in personal visits and in leaflets which explained objectives in simple language. They exuded self-confidence even if they did not feel it, to excess in Montgomery's case. But there was no doubt that Monty had his soldiers' interests at heart. He once asked a young soldier what his most valued possession was. 'My rifle, Sir,' came the dutiful reply. 'No it isn't. It's your life, and I'm going to save it for you.'[40] Significantly, both Monty and Slim were well regarded by generally sceptical American soldiers. A young British corporal described hearing Slim speak to his unit. The general appeared, 'large, heavily built, grim-faced with that hard mouth and bulldog chin'. His speaking manner was blunt and matter of fact, with a thumb hooked in his rifle sling:

> [He] talked about how we had caught the Jap off-balance and were going to annihilate him in the open; there was no exhortation or ringing clichés, no jokes or self-conscious use of barrack-room slang – when he called the Japs 'bastards' it was casual and without heat. He was telling us informally what would be, in the reflective way of intimate conversation. And we believed every word – and it all came true. I think it was the sense of being close to us, as though he were chatting offhand to an understanding nephew (not for nothing was he 'Uncle Bill') that was his great gift … You knew, when he talked of smashing the Jap, that to him it meant not only arrows on a map but clearing bunkers and going in under shell-fire; that he had the head of a general with the heart of a private soldier.[41]

II REDS

General Sir John Kennedy spoke Russian and knew the country well from his time with Anton Denikin's White Russians fighting against Semyon Budenny's Reds in the Civil War of 1919–21. The winning Reds were a rough lot. At a dinner in the Soviet embassy in London in September 1941, Kennedy noted that one of his Russian colleagues ate caviar off a knife, while others had a two-handed grip on pieces of bread which they ripped off with their teeth.[42] They were also brutal field commanders, with an indifference to the lives of their troops that bears comparison only with the Japanese.

On what might be dubbed Barbarossa+2 in June 1941, Stalin established what was to become the Stavka of the Supreme High Command, with himself presiding over Chief of the General Staff Georgy Zhukov, Foreign Minister Vyacheslav Molotov, the Navy's Admiral Nikolai Kuznetsov and the Civil War veteran Marshals Kliment Voroshilov and Budenny. In July, they were joined by Marshal Boris Shaposhnikov. Zukhov's talents lay more in battlefield command, and he was eventually replaced by the brilliant planner General Alexei Antonov.[43] Stalin also formed a small war cabinet, called the People's Commissariat of Defence, consisting of himself, Molotov, Voroshilov, Secret Police Chief Beria and Georgy Malenkov, Stalin's personal secretary since 1925. This body took over the political-strategic direction of the war, including industrial mobilisation, while the Stavka was responsible for military operations as advised by the subordinate General Staff. Because of the total confusion that reigned after the initial German three-pronged thrust, which in two weeks saw Army Group Centre advance three hundred miles into Soviet territory, Stavka created three Strategic Directions, under Budenny, Semyon Timoshenko and Voroshilov, to impose its will on the country's disintegrating western forces. By 8 August when the prospect of total defeat had ebbed, Stalin assumed the role of supreme commander, confident that the moment for a Politburo challenge to his supremacy had passed.

Although 'only' 22,705 out of 142,000 army commanders and commissars were murdered, Soviet military leadership was seriously undermined by the purge in the Red Army of 1936–37. The most senior figure in the surviving armed forces was Voroshilov, People's Commissar for Defence from 1925 to 1940 and a member of the Politburo. This alcoholic political crony of 'the Boss' was eventually sacked in April 1942 after prevaricating about taking command of the Volkov front during a telephone conversation with Stalin.[44]

Stalin's incessant requests for information resembled Churchill's, although real menace backed them up. Harry Hopkins noted that whenever the Russian dictator could not recall a fact, an aide would glide in, remind him of it and then noiselessly depart. Like Churchill, Stalin set up a number of committees. When he created a Military Transport Committee, his first words to the assembled top brass and heads of the railways were, 'I propose Comrade Stalin as head of the Committee' to which there was no demur. Unlike Churchill, Stalin could motivate committee members by reminding them that the price of failure was a military tribunal – that is, they would be shot. The Transport Commissar, Ivan Kovalev, recalled the terrors of dealing with the Boss, who reduced lesser mortals to trembling white sheets. He required two-hourly updates on the movements of a single train. When Kovalev appeared to have lost its location, Stalin burst out: 'If you don't find it, General, you'll be going to the front as a private.' Kovalev said that Stalin was always incredibly cold, merely acknowledging his presence with a curt nod, while telephone conversations with him consisted of a few questioning sentences 'Don't you know? What are you doing then?' before the line went dead with no goodbye.[45]

A chainsmoker, Stalin's habit was to pace up and down his offices, with his hands behind his back, keeping his words to the minimum. His sense of humour was sadistic. In the course of a well-watered Kremlin dinner to honour Churchill in 1944, Stalin spotted his London ambassador Fyodor Gusev somewhat the worse for wear among the throng. 'There are all sorts of people in this world,' he said. 'Take Gusev: it is said he never smiles. But I believe he can. Come on, Gusev, let us see you smile.' The rapidly sobering ambassador to the Court of St James's rose unsteadily to his feet and 'a sickly grin appeared on his face'.[46] At boozing sessions in the Kremlin, Stalin had the sinister habit of encouraging everyone else to down heroic quantities of vodka while he sipped water or Georgian wine from a vodka glass.[47]

His coldness extended even to those trapped in the most terrible dilemmas. The German besiegers of Leningrad adopted the entirely criminal practice of advancing behind screens of women, children and old men towards the Soviet lines. These hostages screamed, 'Don't shoot! We're your own people!', causing confusion among the Red Army defenders. Stalin resolved the matter on 21 September 1941 by defining the hostages as 'unwilling enemies' and decreed: 'if there are such people among the Bolsheviks [that is, soldiers who refused to shoot innocent compatriots] then they should be destroyed first, because they are more dangerous than the Fascists. My advice is, don't be sentimental, smash the enemy and his willing accomplices in the teeth. Hit the Germans and their delegates, whoever they might be, with everything you've got, cut the enemy down, never mind if they are willing or unwilling enemies.'[48]

Soviet generals suffered greater attrition than those of any other country during the war. The opening of Barbarossa claimed several, such as

Major General Mikhailin, assistant commander of Western Special Military District, who was killed in a surprise German air strike on Volkovysk on 23 June 1941. At 5 a.m. the following day, Major General of Tank Forces Puganov was killed by German shrapnel as his 22nd Tank Division was annihilated near Kobrin. A further 426 Red Army generals died in combat, a figure that does not include those who died of illness or suicide, nor the nineteen or more whom Stalin had shot. Those listed as missing in action included General Gol'tsev of Soviet armoured forces within Eighth Army. He allegedly went missing in 1941. In fact, he had been arrested by the NKVD that October and was shot on 13 February 1942. In October 1941 General Kachalov was tried *in absentia* and sentenced to death for having surrendered voluntarily; his family thenceforth bore the stigma of traitor to the motherland, even though in fact Kachalov had been killed by a German shell on 4 August 1941.[49]

The Red Army generals were representative of the upheavals that had ravaged their country during and after the Revolution. Some were survivors of the imperial army, like General Alexander Bobrov, who had studied at the Kazan Military Academy and served in the Great War, then switched to the Red Army to become adjutant at the prestigious Frunze Academy in Moscow after the Civil War. Named in honour of Mikhail Frunze (whom Stalin may have had poisoned during a surgical operation), this was the Soviet equivalent of Camberley or Fort Leavenworth, until it was superseded by a Voroshilov Academy for Staff Officers. By the end of the war there were nineteen military academies training men for high command, as well as some three hundred specialist military schools for artillery, infantry and engineers. There were other changes, like the reintroduction of epaulettes and other signs of high rank derived from the Tsarist era, while Russia's generals basked in the reflected glory of past patriotic heroes like Bagration or Suvorov.

It was advisable under this system for all commanders to emphasise a rough pedigree. Writing an autobiographical sketch in 1938, General P. I. Vorob'ev stressed that although his father had been a farmer with 4.5 hectares of land, he had had to support twelve people, and 'was always forced to do the work himself and find jobs with local landowners as a worker, a forest watchman, a worker in a match factory'. The father had acquired a horse only in 1907, while the future general had left home at sixteen after working on the farm too. One can almost visualise his shaking horny hands. Vorob'ev had joined the Tsar's army, switching to the Reds at the start of the Civil War. He was sent on the Course to Improve the Red Army Command (KUVNAS) preparatory to becoming a general in 1937. He was not quite home and dry: he had to explain a mix-up about his patronymic to the NKVD, to quell suspicions that he had forged official documents; people were tortured and shot for a lot less in 1937. Some of those with impeccable Bolshevik credentials, like General Z. Iu. Kutlin, an instructor at the Frunze Academy, spent the year 1938–9 in NKVD jails until no offence could be established. In 1940 one of the ablest Soviet commanders, the Russified Pole Konstantin Rokossovsky, went straight from an NKVD torture chamber to command a Soviet army. Having endured three mock executions, the pulling of his finger-nails, three broken ribs and nine teeth knocked out, he had to recuper-ate at Sochi before assuming his command. Yet this was the man who, as Poland's defence minister, sent tanks against demonstrating workers in 1956.[50]

Stalin's strategic interventions were inept, for like Hitler he was completely out of his depth with complex operations. However he had an encyclopaedic grasp of the names of army, corps and divisional command-ers, whom he removed or shuffled laterally, often with no apparent logic. Old Civil War cavalry lags were kept at the top until, as in the case of Voroshilov and Budenny, their incompetence proved undeniable. Stalin's memory for names and where they fitted in the organisation had already served him well in ordering the Party *nomenklatura* to his entire satisfac-tion. Military leadership skill was secondary to whether or not Stalin was sure of a given officer's loyalty: he kept hundreds of proven combat commanders in NKVD prisons in Moscow while regiments at the front were commanded by inexperienced lieutenants. He also ordered the forced evacuation and in some cases imprisonment in the gulag of entire nation-alities he did not trust.[51]

Stalin's dabbling in strategy led to the refusal to evacuate Kiev, despite the advice of field commanders, and hence the loss of over half a million prisoners in September 1941. After Order 270 of 16 August 1941, all captured Red Army officers were to be regarded as 'malicious deserters', while the families of rank-and-file POWs were to forfeit rations, which meant condemning them to starvation. The order also authorised the deploy-ment of blocking detachments to prevent retreat. Henceforward Russian troops faced German guns with NKVD tommy guns behind them, while their officers had guns pointed at their heads in the event of failure. Signs of panic were repressed in the most brutal way. In September 1941, the newly formed 2nd Guards Rifle Division found itself defending three villages in the Glukhov district from Guderian's 2nd Panzer Group. Red Army soldiers in one of these villages, Chernevo, were pounded by German dive-bombers before taking artillery fire. The commander, Major General A. Kh. Babadzhanian – who would become a Soviet marshal – described in his memoirs the following telephone conversation with Colonel A. Z. Akimenko, whose rifle regiment was down to a hundred active men: 'They informed me that you intend to withdraw to the east of the river at nightfall. Not a step back. Stand to the death,' said Babadzhanian. 'That is clear, comrade general,' said Akimenko. 'I have no other requests.' The 395th Rifle Regiment was trapped by seventy to eighty German tanks and about nine hundred new Soviet replacement troops from Kursk surrendered. Observing this, Akimenko ordered his two artillery battalions to open fire on them – 'A traitor is a traitor, and he deserved immediate punishment on the spot.'[52] After Order 227 in August 1942 decreed 'not a step back', General Vasily Chuikov, defending Stalingrad, shot an estimated 13,500 of his own men to stiffen morale.[53]

According to former General Dmitry Volkogonov, Stalin learned how to combine general exhortations – such as not allowing the Germans to draw breath – with adding a few final touches to detailed operational plans drawn up by General Staff officers, and then he would claim authorship of victory as his own. Rokossovsky was one of the few senior commanders to dispute Stalin's strategic recommendations successfully – during the planning for the 1944 Operation Bagration which cleared the Germans from Byelorussia – without losing his job or his life. By that time Stalin had gone through seven Chiefs of Staff and was comfortable with Antonov, limiting himself to signing the directives that Antonov drafted for him.[54]

The Grand Alliance afforded Stalin his first high-level contacts with foreigners since his dealings with Ribbentrop in August 1939. In September 1941 General Ismay was part of an Anglo-American delegation to Moscow. He found the Soviet military too scared to share even basic details such as the number of anti-tank guns per Russian division. His first encounter with the source of their fear was at a reception in the Kremlin, when he was surprised by the Soviet leader's diminutive stature:

> He moved stealthily like a wild animal in search of prey, and his eyes were shrewd and full of cunning. He never looked one in the face. But he had great dignity and his personality was dominating. As he entered the room, every Russian froze into silence, and the hunted look in the eyes of the Generals showed all too plainly the constant

> fear in which they lived. It was nauseating to see brave men reduced to such abject servility ... There was too much food, too much vodka, too many speeches, and too much artificial bonhomie.[55]

Arguably, Stalin's greatest contribution to Soviet victory, during and after the war, was to make Churchill and Roosevelt compete for his goodwill while using his people's sacrifices as a form of blackmail. He tried to bully Churchill, whom he admired, every time they met and constantly belittled Britain's war effort, while flattering Roosevelt, whom he despised, into thinking that his patrician charm could work on a man who probably killed more millions of his own people before the war than the Nazis did during it. He used the blood sacrifices of the Red Army, sneeringly contrasted with the Allies' delayed invasion of Europe, as moral leverage to demand ever more supplies of war materials and weapons, taking whatever they offered without a word of thanks. He also exploited Western fears that he might do a separate deal with Hitler, helped by Anglo-American differences concerning the correct way to handle his despotic regime, differences arising mainly from the large number of Soviet agents among the technocrats in the Roosevelt administration, who found it relatively easy to manipulate the affluent amateurs who mirrored Roosevelt's vanity in the conduct of foreign policy.

In the US State Department, under the long-serving and eminently forgettable Cordell Hull, Soviet experts in the Eastern Division were sidelined in favour of the more pro-Soviet European Division.[56] Those who demanded proof of Soviet reciprocity in such fields as intelligence, such as George Kennan, George Kelly or Charles 'Chip' Bohlen, found themselves at a disadvantage vis-à-vis the pernicious influence of Joseph E. Davies, a wealthy Democrat lawyer who had contributed enough to Roosevelt's re-election to become ambassador to Moscow from 1937 to 1942, before becoming the President's main adviser on Russia. He had succeeded the much more sceptical William Bullitt just in time to become an apologist for Stalin's purges. Davies's art-collecting mania was a weak point Stalin exploited by giving him export licences available to no one else, although the ambassador's decision to become a cheerleader for the regime was not entirely venal.

Stalin also knew exactly how to play the visiting American dignitaries (none of them professional diplomats), the surrogates upon whom Roosevelt offloaded much of his foreign policy at the expense of the State Department. Harry Hopkins, Roosevelt's infirm emissary, breathlessly reported the following:

Mr Stalin spoke of the necessity of there being a minimum moral standard between all nations and without such a minimum moral standard nations could not co-exist. He stated that the present leaders of Germany knew no such minimum moral standard and that, therefore, they represented an anti-social force in the present world. The Germans were a people, he said, who without a second's thought would sign a treaty today, break it tomorrow and sign a second one the following day. Nations must fulfil their treaty obligations, he said, or international security could not exist.

This hypocritical guff was the prelude to a highly technical session on the USSR's armaments requirements, in which Stalin revealed a sure grasp of aluminium and armour plate.[57] Others to follow Hopkins's indulgence of a totalitarian monster were the plutocrat Averell Harriman, who had successfully washed off the dirt of a dynasty of robber barons with art and racehorses before his appointment as ambassador to Moscow, and the liberal Republican corporate lawyer Wendell Willkie, who used a ten-day visit to the USSR in 1942 as a way of reviving his domestic political fortunes through aggressive advocacy in support of Stalin's desire for a second front.[58] US military men were less tantalised by Stalin, with General Henry 'Hap' Arnold noting, 'He was a tough SOB who made his way by murder and everything else and should be talked to that way.'

In late November 1943, Roosevelt had his first encounter with the Soviet leader, travelling six thousand miles to reach Tehran while Stalin anxiously flew six hundred miles south escorted by three fighter squadrons. Prior to this meeting, Roosevelt had prevented Churchill from shaping the terms of discussion by inviting Chiang Kai-shek (and his diverting wife) to join them in a meeting he reluctantly agreed to in Cairo. He made sure he saw much of Chiang and less of Churchill.[59] In Tehran, where he lodged in the Soviet legation to get away from the rumbustious Englishman, Roosevelt overruled Churchill's desire to postpone the planned Sledgehammer/Overlord cross-Channel operation, and joined Stalin in facetious banter at the British Prime Minister's expense, while privately intimating that the British and French empires were destined for the wall, in what he knew would be a two-power carve-up of the post-war world. As for the Red Empire, although it was never called that, this was given the green light to re-expand back to its pre-1941 outer borders. There was a row over dinner when Churchill angrily rejected Stalin's suggestion that after the war fifty thousand German officers should be shot. Roosevelt mocked Churchill's indignation by quipping that maybe forty-nine thousand would be more appropriate. After Churchill had walked out, Stalin and Molotov followed him, explaining that it was all a joke. Since Stalin had shot more than twenty-two thousand Red Army officers before the war, there was no reason for either Churchill or Roosevelt to doubt the seriousness of the suggestion; it was a depressing performance by the president of a country that believed itself to be 'the shining city on a hill'.[60]

Churchill's anger was also fuelled by the knowledge that the man Roosevelt and the British press referred to as 'Uncle Joe' had murdered all the Polish officers captured by the Red Army after its stab-in-the-back invasion of Poland in 1939. On 5 April 1943, the Nazi *Völkischer Beobachter* published a report that German troops had uncovered ten thousand corpses in mass graves in the Katyń Forest, north-west of Smolensk. Pathologists established that these were the Polish officers killed in 1940, as we have seen, long before the German invasion. The Polish exiled government in London asked the International Red Cross to investigate. An expert IRC delegation would eventually join German and Polish Red Cross pathologists at the site of the massacres, all their findings eagerly lapped up by Goebbels, who on this occasion told the unvarnished truth.

Churchill was in no doubt of it and remarked to the Polish ambassador in London: 'The Bolsheviks can be very cruel.' There was, however, nothing he could do about it. The Soviets were indispensable as an ally against Nazism, and it seemed increasingly likely that sooner rather than later Europe would lie at their feet. Ten days later Churchill wrote to Stalin saying that he had counselled against the Poles making 'charges of an insulting character against the Soviet Government [which] seem to countenance the atrocious Nazi propaganda'. He had urged the London Poles to withdraw their request for an IRC investigation, hoping to prevent Stalin from revoking recognition of the Polish government in exile – a vain hope, as Stalin always intended to create an alternative government in exile of Communist stooges. In May, Eden drew the attention of the House of Commons 'to the cynicism which permits Nazi murderers of hundreds of thousands of innocent Poles and Russians to make use of a story of mass murder, in an attempt to disturb the unity of the Allies'. This bent the truth in a sinuous way. Others felt pangs of conscience about using 'the good name of England like the murderers used the little conifers to cover up a massacre'. Alexander Cadogan had the disturbing thought that 'we may eventually, by agreement and in collaboration with the Russians, proceed to the trial and perhaps execution of Axis "war criminals" while condoning this atrocity. I confess that I shall find this extremely difficult to swallow.'[61]

Marshall

III ALL THE PRESIDENT'S MEN

While Churchill and Stalin remained actively engaged in the conduct of the military campaign, the late-arriving Roosevelt ceded control of the armed forces to a masterly military bureaucrat and technician. George C. Marshall was a graduate of Virginia Military Institute in the Shenandoah Valley town of Lexington. Clement Attlee thought that Marshall was like a southern Cincinnatus, the Roman general who retired to his farm. There was much in that comparison.[62]

A man of rigorous self-discipline, he was at his desk by 7.45 a.m. and then home shortly after 5 p.m. No one, he claimed, had an original idea after that hour, for he had firm convictions about matters large and small. Only Roosevelt or Henry Stimson, Secretary of War, could telephone him at home, where after an evening ride he retired to bed at nine o'clock. Neither man called him George, a habit Marshall discouraged to insulate himself further against the President's easy patrician charm. He once remarked, 'I have no feelings except for Mrs Marshall.' That was not quite true: he was distressed by the death of a stepson, killed in his tank turret by a German sniper, as well as by the many letters of condolence he wrote personally before the number became overwhelming.[63]

Aloof to the point of rudeness, Marshall was capable of flashes of anger, as he had shown in 1917 when, as a humble operations officer to the 1st Division, he laid hands on General 'Black Jack' Pershing, the commander of the US Expeditionary Force, in the course of a row. From 1927 to 1932 Marshall was assistant commandant of the infantry school at Fort Benning, Georgia, where his students included two hundred of the twelve hundred US Second World War generals. The tactics instructor at Fort Benning was Omar Bradley, who joined Stilwell, Patton, Ridgway, Bedell 'Beetle' Smith and Eisenhower in Marshall's little black book of talented protégés. Not all went on to fulfil their mentor's expectations: one of those he noted was the hapless Lloyd Fredendall, who as we shall see fell at the first fence. He was, however, fiercely opposed to political nepotism, once slamming down the phone on a senator seeking a promotion for one of his clients.[64] His approach to high command can be summed up in the remark: 'Gentlemen, don't fight the problem. Solve it!' In common with all Great War veterans, Marshall's overriding goal was to avoid a repetition of the bloody stalemate of trench warfare by emphasising the importance of movement.[65]

Some of the structures Marshall put in place to run the army were copied from British exemplars. He presided over a powerful Joint Board, renamed the Joint Chiefs of Staff (JCS) in February 1942, which was akin to the British Chiefs of Staff Committee (CSC). The original members of the JCS were Marshall, Admirals Harold Stark and Ernest King, and the US Army Air Force (USAAF) commander General 'Hap' Arnold. The chairman of the JCS was Roosevelt's appointee Admiral William Leahy, as Ismay was Churchill's man in the CSC. The US chiefs were directly answerable to Roosevelt as commander-in-chief rather than to the septuagenarian Henry Stimson, who it was said took care of the armed forces' civilian housekeeping. Even before Pearl Harbor the JCS and CSC had established co-ordinating mechanisms, which developed into the Washington-based Combined Chiefs of Staff Committee, presided over by Marshall. The Combined Chiefs had several sub-committees that dealt with intelligence, planning, munitions and transport. It met some two hundred times throughout the war, or roughly once a week, and eighty-nine of its sessions were held in conjunction with the major wartime summit conferences.

Marshall brutally centralised and simplified the power structure within the army, eliminating the competing satrapies of the infantry, cavalry, artillery and so on, and cutting the number of people with direct access to his private office from sixty-one to six, and merely indicating yes or no after letting supplicants make their case. After his experiences in 1917, where he had seen the terrible effects of sending an ill-trained army into battle against experienced German troops, Marshall's first task was to implement combat training programmes under General Lesley McNair, who in Normandy on 25 July 1944 was to become the most senior Allied officer killed in action, by USAAF bombs. Vast manoeuvres were conducted in Louisiana, Tennessee and the Carolinas. 'I want the mistakes made down there in Louisiana, not over in Europe,' said Marshall, 'and the only way to do this thing is to try it out, and if it doesn't work, find out what we need to make it work.' These exercises were also a way of identifying and firing old, over-promoted and unfit officers. At the same time General Brehon Somervell organised the even larger numbers of servicemen and women engaged in engineering, transport, logistics and the medical corps. After May 1942, some ninety thousand women joined the new Women's Army Corps under Colonel Oveta Culp Hobby. The Operations Division eventually directed eleven US armies, totalling ninety divisions, all around the world, and all of them were regularly visited by Marshall and other top brass in a punishing travel schedule.

The rapid expansion of US forces deserves the overused Americanism 'awesome'. The army went from 190,000 personnel in 1939 to eight millions in 1944, growing at the rate of three hundred thousand men and women a month even in 1941, with the cost rising by $160 billions before the first year was out. A telling anecdote concerns a visit by General Leslie Groves to ask Marshall for US$100 billion for the development of the atom bomb by the Manhattan Project; Marshall authorised the money and remarked, 'It may interest you to know what I was doing. I was writing the check for US$3.52 for grass seed for my lawn.'[66] The USAAF began the war with seventeen bases; by 1943 there were 345, its manpower rising from twenty thousand to nearly two millions. Over the same period the number of aircraft rose from 2,470 to nearly 80,000. The 1,000 ships in the US Navy in 1940 had become 67,000, with 75,000 aircraft, by the end of the war. The US marines went from 28,000 men in 1940 to 485,000 when the war ended, with 100,000 more in the separate Marine Aviation Corps.

Marshall required the skills of a diplomat in handling a global alliance which included a democratic Old World empire as well as a sanguinary totalitarian dictatorship. His experiences of US intra- or inner-service rivalries stood him in good stead, as did his awareness that 'in battle no division ever admits that the divisions on its right and left kept abreast of it'. These rivalries became more serious when different nationalities were involved. For his part, Marshall wrote: 'the thing to watch in the international aspect is whether or not our leaders, meaning me for example, are not sufficiently broadminded in their approach to these problems and also not naïve in dealing with the most experienced and astute diplomatists in the world today. We must be tough enough in representing our national interests, while not contesting every little point in a small-minded or too suspicious manner.'[67] Early in the war he issued a memorandum to eradicate expressions of ill-will towards the British, which he rightly sensed was being exploited by German propaganda to foster animosities between the Allies.[68] Although some US generals (and admirals) were Anglophobic, any open expression had grave consequences. Ismay once confidentially told Eisenhower – who regarded the alliance 'almost as a religion' – of an American officer who disparaged the British when drunk. Eisenhower went white with rage and barked to an aide that he wanted to see the

Eisenhower

offender, growling, 'I'll make the son-of-a-bitch swim back to America.'[69] He also had to ensure that the hard-bitten attitude that won battles did not tip over into brutality – most notoriously when he had to discipline George Patton for drawing a gun and verbally abusing shell-shocked US soldiers.

When Eisenhower took charge as commander of US troops in the European theatre, he was aware that they had not been blooded, as the fox-hunting metaphor employed by the more experienced British officers put it. Reporting to Marshall on his first inspection in Britain, Eisenhower said his men lacked 'punch'. He banned officers from wearing civilian clothes at weekends and told them: 'We're here to fight, not to be wined and dined.'[70] His first major challenge was Operation Torch. On 8 November 1942 117,000 Allied troops – most of them Americans – landed at three beachheads in Vichy-controlled North Africa. Waiting anxiously on Gibraltar, Eisenhower had time to reflect on 'Worries of a Commander', which included maintaining absolute confidence in public: 'My manner-isms and speech in public would always reflect the cheerful certainty of victory – that any pessimism and discouragement that I might ever feel would be reserved for my pillow.'[71] By this stage his cigarette consumption had risen to between three and four packs a day, with a pot of coffee consumed every hour. Complicated dealings with the French meant delays in attaining the real goal, which was to trap the Axis forces in Tunisia. Brooke acidly observed that Eisenhower 'allowed himself to be absorbed in the political situation at the expense of the tactical', setting the tone of incomprehension for Eisenhower's alliance-management skill, the quality that led Marshall to promote him over the heads of several hundred senior officers, which was to colour British assessment of him throughout the war and well beyond. Nonetheless, it is true that Allied delay in Algeria gave the Germans in Tunisia time to redeploy their forces to painful effect, although in the end this meant that they were to lose more men and matériel in Tunisia than in the near-simultaneous Battle of Stalingrad.[72]

Hindsight may find a silver lining, but at the time British fears that the US troops were exuberantly over-confident as well as green were proved correct. Had the Americans' wish to proceed directly to a landing in north-ern France in 1943 prevailed, they would have been massacred. As it was, their learning curve climbed steeply as the planned six-week campaign in Tunisia dragged on for six months, a school of hard knocks administered by the German–Italian Army of Africa. Not the least of the underlying problems was that Eisenhower partially delegated theatre command to

Lieutenant General Kenneth Anderson, commanding British First Army, who proved unable to command the respect he could not inspire. Both US II Corps' General Lloyd Fredendall and Free French XIX Corps' General Alphonse Juin bridled at serving under Anderson, who in turn held them in low esteem. Poor communications across a two-hundred-mile front added to the recipe for disaster, which duly came when Rommel launched a successful offensive against Allied forces, driving back the leading French and US forces in Tunisia. This was followed by an armoured thrust through the Kasserine Pass, which resulted in the rout of Fredendall's command. Fredendall himself simply collapsed, whistling disconsolately while muttering, 'If I were back home, I'd go out and paint the garage doors. There's a lot of pleasure in painting a garage door.'[73]

Eisenhower was badly shaken by the reverse, and revealed his feelings in a letter to his wife Mamie:

> Loneliness is the inescapable lot of a man holding such a job. Subordinates can advise, urge, help, and pray – but only one man in his own mind and heart can decide, 'Do we, or do we not?' The stakes are always high, and the penalties are expressed in terms of loss of life or major and minor disasters to the nation. No man can always be right. So the struggle is to do one's best, to keep the brain and conscience clear; never to be swayed by unworthy motives or inconsequential reasons, but … to do one's duty. It is not always easy.[74]

With the blame game in full swing, Eisenhower moved swiftly to resolve the problem of divided command that had contributed to the setback. He appointed General Sir Harold Alexander, already in overall command of the British forces in the Middle East, including Montgomery's Eighth Army, to command a unified 18th Army Group, whose job it was to co-ordinate converging attacks on Tunisia from Libya and Algeria. Fredendall was sent home and replaced by the dynamic General Patton. Anderson remained in place, but Patton answered directly to Alexander. Not for the last time, the British underestimated how rapidly the Americans learned from experience, and some of them, including Alexander, acquired a low opinion of their allies' fighting abilities that they never lost. In May 1943, some 240,000 Axis soldiers surrendered in Tunisia after a series of battles during which Patton did much to restore US pride. Drawing a sober line under the campaign, Eisenhower reported to Marshall: 'Our people from the very highest [that is, himself] to the lowest have learned that this is not a child's game.'

Not unnaturally, military history tends to favour the colourful hard-charging commanders such as General Patton. Such types were not uncommon in other US services, for example Admiral William 'Bull' Halsey, whose sobriquet indicates his penchant for hot pursuit in the Pacific. As it happened, a fluke skin ailment in May 1942 prevented Halsey from commanding one of the most significant naval engagements of the Second World War in the Pacific. In June 1942, the Japanese despatched two huge fleets towards the tiny US outpost at Midway, the backstop to Hawaii, their aim being to draw the US Pacific fleet based at Pearl Harbor into a decisive battle, after which they could menace the US West Coast with impunity. This would have been an earth-shattering turn of events, since with cities like San Diego, San Francisco and Seattle under direct threat, the US might have been forced to rethink its Germany First strategy, with knock-on implications for the British and Russians as the Americans subtracted resources.

Thanks to the brilliance of US naval code-breakers, the US navy knew when and where the Japanese carrier force under Admiral Chuichi Nagumo planned to strike, although they were not aware that this was a trap designed to lure any counter-attacking force into the path of a much larger formation under Fleet Admiral Isoruko Yamamoto. With Halsey ill, the US response was commanded by Admirals Jack Fletcher and Raymond Spruance. Spruance had never commanded a carrier. Worse, he was a very cautious operator, although his sensitive face betrayed a keen intelligence. Nagumo duly carried out massive bombing raids on the two interlinked atolls that comprised Midway. The Americans responded with ground-based bomber sorties which entirely missed their targets, although they would claim that they had sunk the Japanese fleet. Meanwhile, Spruance decided to engage the Japanese, launching torpedo-laden planes, which burned off more and more fuel as their pilots anxiously waited for their full complement to assemble aloft. Admiral Fletcher, whose own force comprised one arm of the V converging on the Japanese off Midway, attacked as well. This rather ragged formation headed out in search of the Japanese, which involved flying to the limits of their range. Requiring a long low steady run for their attacks, these torpedo planes were decimated by the Japanese Zero fighters which routinely protected any Japanese fleet. This was not a kamikaze attack by the Americans, but one in which the odds were massively stacked against them. At best, if they lived, they would run out of fuel, and find themselves bobbing about on inflatable dinghies amid twenty-five million square miles of ocean.

The annihilation of most of the US torpedo planes led Nagumo to take his eye off the ball. Should he send his own planes back to bomb Midway, or should he rearm them for his own torpedo runs on the US fleet? He had half his force returning from its attack, and the other half on board ready to be armed. Nagumo equivocated, first arming his 108 reserve planes with torpedoes, only to switch to bombs, and then back to torpedoes, even as the first strike force to bomb Midway was coming in to land back on the carriers. The result was that his carrier decks were covered with fuel drums, pipes and munitions when, unopposed by Zeros, US dive-bombers swooped from the sky. Four Japanese carriers were either sunk, scuttled or damaged beyond repair. Several officers elected to go down with their ships.

Learning of this debacle, Admiral Yamamoto presumed that any fleet commanded by Halsey would aggressively seek out the remnants of Nagumo's formation, leaving it vulnerable to colossal stand-off bombardment at night by his own forces. This would probably have been the case since the Americans were unaware of the existence of Yamamoto's fleet. By this time, Fletcher had handed over command to Spruance after Fletcher's carrier *Yorktown* was badly hit.

To the astonishment of his staff officers, Admiral Spruance concluded that his main objective had been accomplished – namely preventing the Japanese landing on Midway – so he decided not to pursue the remnants of Nagumo's forces. He said: 'We have done just about all the damage we are going to do. Let's get out of here.' Yamamoto kept searching for Spruance's forces, but they had withdrawn to defensive positions around Midway. Despite the urgings of his staff officers, Spruance refused to take an unnecessary gamble, which might have afforded Yamamoto the victory he sought to snatch from the jaws of Nagumo's defeat. Spruance's kind of moral courage was as admirable as that of the torpedo bomber pilots who, by distracting the Japanese fighters, gave the US dive-bombers an even chance of doing their job. He was also sensible of the fact that all commanders of ships have hundreds (or thousands) of lives at stake, men with little or no possibility of escape from engine rooms and gun turrets.[75]

CHAPTER 14

'We were Savages': Combat Soldiers

Paci 18 support for each combat soldier

I THE CULTURE OF COMBAT

Only some of the men who served in Second World War armies were directly involved in killing other human beings. In most cases they were not. Behind every US combat soldier in the Pacific theatre there were eighteen in support and an average of eight to one in all other Western armies. Only the Japanese claimed that for every combat soldier there was a single support soldier, but then logistics were one of their weakest points.[1] However, airpower, artillery and the mechanised nature of modern warfare meant that the rear echelons could easily find themselves swept up in war fighting. As to the danger of death or horrifying injury, on the Western fronts not many front-line soldiers were exposed for more than a few days to the risks run for weeks and months on end by the civilian crews of the ships, and in particular the ammunition ships and fuel tankers, without which the armies could not function. Death was often a matter of sliding unconscious into an icy darkness while covered in spilled oil after a merchantman had been found by a prowling enemy submarine.[2]

If armies were more functionally stratified in the Second World War than in the Great War, where a higher proportion of soldiers had fought as ordinary infantrymen, much of the fighting still revolved around overcoming the natural advantages of defence over attack. Nothing in the Great War resembled the epic tank battle at Kursk in summer 1943, but it was still line after line of stubbornly defended infantry and artillery positions that blunted the German armoured thrusts before the Soviet tanks launched their counter-attacks. Airpower simply extended the range of artillery (Japanese bombers at Pearl Harbor dropped naval shells with fins attached), and the massed bombardments that preceded attacks in the

Second World War came as no surprise to veterans of the Great War. Denied mobility at the topographical bottleneck of El Alamein 150 miles west of Cairo, Rommel commented that the battle would go to whomever could bring down the heaviest weight of fire, gloomily acknowledging that it would not be he. The fighting in Italy in 1943–5 was some of the grimmest in either war, with topography working heavily against the Allied armies. Yet a German soldier at Girofano judged that the Allied bombardment was worse than anything he had endured at Stalingrad.[3]

Where a soldier fights influenced *how* he fought. The vast featureless spaces of the North African deserts resulted in a different war from the mud and rain of Tunisia, while the jungles of the Pacific required a different response from the tall bocage hedgerows of Normandy. In purely physical terms, Italy may have been the hardest going, with the addition of a harsh winter climate that came as a shocking disappointment to those dreaming of sunny Italy. Mechanised armies could not advance across steep mountains, the passes between them were easily made into death-traps and even the coastal plains were criss-crossed with rivers, and studded with olive groves and terraced vineyards that channelled tanks into killing grounds, while stone-built peasant cottages with deep cellars made ideal defensive strongpoints.

The war in Russia was uniquely savage for the many reasons we have reviewed, including the existential clash of rival totalitarian ideologies, racism and a relentless spiral of retaliatory violence. The existence of large numbers of partisans, who sometimes fought one another, further blurred the distinction between combatants and civilians, with horrendous consequences. One becomes insensible by the catalogue of horrors, the victims to a degree dehumanised by the sheer numbers involved. It may be because they are more emotionally accessible that we are perhaps more shocked by the limited number of occasions when people in western Europe were exposed to behaviour that was the norm in the east. We have noted the depredations of the SS 'Das Reich' armoured division as it moved from southern France towards Normandy in June 1944, yet the massed hangings at Tulle and the destruction of Oradour-sur-Glane were all in a day's work for the SS in the Ukraine or Russia.[4] After the SS had shot American POWs at Bullingen, Honsfeld and Malmedy during the 1944 Ardennes offensive, US troops were markedly less inclined to accept surrenders, shooting all SS prisoners out of hand, and also enemy tank crews because they wore black uniforms, which ironically Waffen-SS combat troops wore only on ceremonial duties. The deadly spiral of atrocity and counter-atrocity was not absent from the western theatre: it was simply considerably less endemic. It is not remarkable that many find it difficult to speak about their wartime experiences.[5]

Most soldiers in Western armies remained civilians in spirit and came from societies that had not encouraged them to hate, although like anyone else they could enjoy the adventure, the thrills, the tourism, as well as the release from civilisation's constraints. Anyone who has fired a high-velocity rifle will know that it is rather like unleashing a crack of lightning, for weapons extend a man's power, cancelling out mere physical strength. Many veterans on all sides also remarked that modern battle had an aesthetic beauty, a pyrotechnic symphony of dust, coloured fire and dense smoke. It had a unique smell too, of cordite, petrol fumes, coppery-scented blood and the sickeningly sweet odour of newly killed human flesh. Men raised in the country had probably killed small animals, or something much larger if they were hunters; now, in total contravention of received laws and moral codes, they had to kill a stranger resembling themselves. Although the effects were the same, the act of homicide involved widely different degrees of psychological engagement.

Distance was a crucial part of a soldier's capacity to kill without psychological disturbance. For bomber crews and fighter pilots, or men firing artillery and mortars, killing was at such a range that those destroyed were the de-individualised targets of the technology they served. Of course these were not risk-free activities for any of those involved, whether from enemy flak or fighters in the air, or from counter-battery fire on the ground. Mid-range killing with small arms was akin to firing on a range, the anonymous target identified only by a different-coloured uniform or the distinctive shape of a helmet. Most of those killed by bullets fell to machine-gunners or to the essentially random fire of riflemen, giving rise to the quip that the bullet with your name on it did not exist: the one that got you would be addressed 'to whom it may concern'. Hand grenades were also a relatively remote way to kill people, unless you chose to examine the effects. At the narrowest end of this spectrum was close-quarter or hand-to-hand combat, shooting at a range when you could be splashed by blood, or stabbing, clubbing or strangling a struggling human being during a frantic life-or-death physical struggle. In these cases, with the antisepsis of distance removed, the psychological scars could be permanent.[6]

However much men may have tried to imagine the act of killing, the reality was often surreal, combining fear, curiosity and excitement. When Günther Koschorrek, a young German machine-gunner, caught sight of his first Soviet troops in November 1942, he recalled that the 'brown huddled figures remind me somehow of a great herd of sheep moving over a snow-covered field' as they separated and then recoalesced under German fire. As he fired controlled bursts at the Russians he wrote, 'my mind goes blank. I only see the advancing stream of enemy soldiers coming directly at us. I again fire straight into it. Only fear is there – fear of this dirty brown heap of destruction constantly moving closer, which wants to kill me and everyone around me. I do not even feel the burning pain on the inner surface of my right hand, which I have caught on the hot metal while changing barrels seconds after getting a jam.'[7]

Fear was ever present on the battlefields, although soldiers learned to control it lest it become paralysing. 'I went where I was told to go, and I did what I was told to do, but no more. I was scared shitless just about all the time,' said James Jones of his combat experience.[8] In many armies shouting helped stiffen the sinews, with the Japanese 'Banzai!' more famous than the Russians massed 'Ura!' There were also more idiosyncratic battle cries. Lieutenant Gerry Maufe (the humble Yorkshire Muff family had metamorphosed into the posh Maufes after making a bit of money) of the King's Royal Rifle Corps, won a Military Cross for using a Bren gun to kill Germans on either side of a 600-yard stretch of track as he sped to relieve a trapped unit at Mezzano in Italy. Maufe liked to shout 'Aren't we having a lovely time?' as he hurtled into action.[9] Combat often led to an automaton-like state in which much of the conscious mind closed itself down and instinct took over: 'everything concerning an individual in battle is immediate, both in time and space, and one's mind reacts instantaneously,' wrote a Seaforth Highlander lieutenant. In the chaos of Kursk, Lev Levovich found that orders brought a welcome structure: 'to aim for this bank or trench, to focus on this oak tree, aim three fingers' width toward the left ... That sort of thing helps very much.'[10]

The Red Army had its own way of dealing with the fear that led so many of its troops to be captured or desert under the initial German onslaught. Crack NKVD paramilitary police and blocking detachments of regular troops were used to kill any would-be deserters or those who deliberately mutilated themselves to avoid combat. They were stripped before they were shot so that their uniforms and boots could be recycled. The number of those formally sanctioned in this way was in the region of two hundred thousand men, a figure which does not include those casually bumped off by the wayside.[11] At Stalingrad, 13,500 men were shot in a week, only slightly fewer than the number the Germans executed for similar offences in the entire war. Anyone who had a bullet wound in their left hand was liable to be executed, since this was a favourite of self-mutilators seeking to escape combat. Some 990,000 Soviet troops were condemned to punishment in the war, of whom 420,000 were despatched to punitive battalions to carry out near-suicidal tasks, with casualty rates between three and six times higher than were suffered in the regular army.[12]

Most men could not recall a coherent mental image of a battle. Instead it became 'fucking rough ... really tough', words that reflected the impossibility of spinning a finished product from wildly disparate inputs not even remembered consecutively, often interspersed with vivid memories of incongruous moments of farce. The reality of death often dawned after the event when soldiers had mental space to reflect. 'That could be me,' thought a US Marine as his first sighting of a dead Japanese soldier on Guadalcanal reminded him that he was 'not playing Cowboys and Indians'. Shortly after landing on the Pacific island of Peleliu, another Marine, Eugene Sledge, came across his first dead enemy, a medical orderly and the two men he had gone to treat:

> His medical chest lay open beside him, and the various bandages and medicines were arranged neatly in compartments. The corpsman [the US term for medical personnel] was on his back, his abdominal cavity laid bare. I stared in horror, shocked at the glistening viscera bespecked with fine coral dust. This can't have been a human being, I agonized. It looked more like the guts of one of the many rabbits or squirrels I had cleaned on hunting trips as a boy. I felt sick as I stared at the corpses.

He was further shocked when a couple of veteran Marines blithely stripped the Japanese dead of flags, spectacles and leather holsters, something Sledge himself would soon do without second thoughts.[13]

Such an occasion presented itself after he had taken part in storming a concrete Japanese bunker, from which the Japanese occupants repeatedly threw out the grenades the Marines dropped in, until it was eventually silenced with the aid of a flamethrower and a 75mm gun firing at point-blank range. His team moved around the Japanese dead with Apache-like expertise, checking helmets, packs and pockets for souvenirs. Sledge noticed a comrade dragging along what he assumed was another corpse. However, the Japanese was not dead but wounded in the back and unable to move his arms. Sledge watched as the Marine used a large combat knife, striking the butt so that the point would smash out a gold tooth. Since the Japanese wriggled and writhed, the knife sank into his mouth. The Marine slashed the man's face open and used his foot on the man's jaw in order to get the tooth. By this time blood was everywhere. Sledge was relieved when another Marine shot the Japanese in the head, enabling the tooth to be prised out.[14] In so far as Sledge could explain this conduct it was with reference to an incident where he happened upon Marine dead, one of whom had been decapitated and had his hands cut off at the wrist – his head was posed on his chest – while his penis had been cut off and stuffed in his mouth. Another man had been 'butchered' into neat pieces. 'From that moment on I never felt the least pity or compassion for [the Japanese] no matter what the circumstances.'[15] The only American conduct that offended Sledge was that of a Marine officer who routinely urinated into the mouths of dead Japanese, or who had a thing about pulling down the trousers and shooting the penises off their corpses. Sledge felt this was what some immature college boy might do without regard for the dignity of dead enemies.[16]

Fun and games with corpses was also a standard feature of the conflict in Russia, as the war correspondent Vasily Grossmann vividly described:

> Practical jokers put the frozen Germans on their feet, or on their hands and knees, making intricate, fanciful sculpture groups. Frozen Germans stand with their fists raised, or with their fingers spread wide. Some of them look as if they are running, their heads pulled into the shoulders. They are wearing torn boots, thin greatcoats, paper undershirts that don't hold the warmth. At night the fields of snow seem blue under the bright moon, and the dark bodies of frozen German soldiers stand in the blue snows, placed there by jokers.[17]

Such incidents raise a broader and often unremarked moral aspect of the intensity of small-unit comradeship which all soldiers in every army experienced in the war. These were the 'bands of brothers' who sustained each other's morale, and whose members were never left behind to die alone. Even in the Red Army, where the casualty rate saw off most infantrymen in under three months, intense friendships briefly flourished: 'It's enough for a person to be with you for two to seven days and you will know his qualities, all his feelings, the things it takes years to know in civvy street.' Naturally, in that army you would not want to share too much with a stranger, since the eyes and ears of political officers and their spies were ubiquitous.[18] The basic units were a surrogate family, although, as in families, close proximity to someone they disliked, or the dominant black humour, bonhomie and constant profanities, could be wearing for more delicate or solitary souls. Even so, immersing oneself in the minutiae of another life could also be beneficially distracting, as when a unit became emotionally involved in the letters a comrade received from a girlfriend, down to the 'Dear John' that announced she had found another. In all armies, men at the front groused about the lives of luxury lived by men at the rear, or worried that their wives and girlfriends at home were cheating on them. Men in the field hardly lived monastic lives, however, and both German and Soviet officers acquired what were almost harems on either side of the Eastern Front.[19] All armies had high instances of sexually transmitted diseases as the voluntary or involuntary comfort of strangers indicated how war deranged more traditional mores. Abandoned children of the German occupiers and their girlfriends were one more problem for post-war reconstruction in previously occupied countries, and the Germans would have to deal with the consequences of mass Soviet rape.

But there was a darker side to relationships that are often served up by film makers in overly sentimentalised form. One function of comradeship was to reinforce the new killing self, whenever it was involuntarily subverted by the reappearance of the pacific civilian self within, for only about 2 per cent of combat soldiers are reckoned to have positively revelled in lethal violence. If small groups of soldiers are, as John Keegan claims, like gangs, often grouped around one charismatic larger-than-life individual, then like gangs they developed a group moral code in a similar way to the way a street gang rationalises why 'x had it coming to him'. In most armies a small group of warriors did most of the serious fighting.[20] As a lieutenant in the US 7th Armoured Division put it: 'A few guys carry your attack, and the rest of the people sort of participate and arrive on the objective shortly after everybody else.' The less eager had another use, of course, which was to draw the enemy's fire away from the more determined elements.[21]

The group could make anything morally palatable. An American infantryman called Sidney Stewart once leaped into a bomb crater on Bataan, landing face to face with a Japanese soldier who had done the same thing. Stewart covered the Japanese with his .45 before the enemy could raise his rifle: 'He didn't look as I had expected Nips to look, like the faces of the dead ones I had seen. His face was clean and clear cut. Sort of simple, and his eyes were wide and brown and somehow honest. Yet there was a hopeless look in them … I knew I had to move on. I knew I couldn't take him prisoner. We didn't have time … He said something in Japanese … I knew it was surrender … He didn't cringe or sneer, nor did he show any hatred. Why, I don't hate this guy. I can't hate him … This man was like a friend.' Ordered to move out, Stewart ignored the prayer board the Japanese was tugging from his pocket and shot him. The memory of it haunted him for days afterwards until a comrade said: 'Sid, you shouldn't let that thing worry you. You shouldn't think about it all the time. After all, boy, this is war, and that's just one of the things of war … As long as men are men, and countries made up of individuals, we'll have wars.' Thoughts of the dead Japanese soon faded.[22]

Training was essential in building peak physical fitness or making groups of men act in a co-ordinated manner under command. In the pre-war Soviet army, it was not helped by shortages of kit and weapons, or the redeployment of conscripts to perform agricultural labour. In their bleak training camps, many learned little more than to wash, how to bind their foot cloths properly, how to dig a hole, with hours of tedium spent listening to earnest political officers droning on about Marxist-Leninism. Only later in the war would Soviet training improve, with more emphasis on creating specialists and integrating the different elements of modern battle. One notable lesson was to make men sit in trenches while tanks churned above them, something done to overcome *Panzerschreck* or fear of German tanks. In such ways a horde army, whose earlier emphasis on mere mass resembled that of the Tsar's peasant helots, was refashioned, in part at least, into a quality modern army.[23]

Training also emphasised that the recruit was going to kill someone. It unwound the values of a clean fight which most boys had learned at home or school. As one of Sledge's Marine instructors had it: 'Don't hesitate to fight the Japs dirty. Most Americans, from the time they are kids, are taught not to hit below the belt. It's not sportsmanlike. Well, nobody has taught the Japs that, and war ain't sport. Kick him in the balls before he kicks you in yours.'[24] Unfortunately for the Americans, their opponents received excellent training in skills of moving stealthily that were more suited to a cat burglar or poacher. This was essential if they were city boys, unused to the blackness of open country at night, which it usually took about an hour to adjust to. They learned that opponents were most torpid between three and six in the morning, which explains the Japanese preference for pre-dawn attack. They learned to crawl forward using their elbows, hips and toes, that looking at something from an angle was better than staring at it because the rods useful for night vision are towards the edges of the retina.[25] In striking contrast, US troops posted to Queensland for eighteen months 'jungle training' only once went out on a mock patrol at night and paid the price when they encountered Japanese on New Guinea.

gear

The different mobility of the two armies was largely due to the fact that whereas a US infantryman carried about 132 pounds of kit, his Japanese opponent bore less than half as much weight, including his weaponry. How soldiers reached the battlegrounds varied from theatre to theatre. In amphibious operations, they were densely packed below decks in ships, assaulted by tobacco fumes, body odours, the smell of engine oil and of vomit induced by motion sickness. Trains were not much better, as we learn from the account by Peter Reese, a twenty-three-year-old German, of interminable train journeys through the vastnesses of Russia, wedged into any available space, journeys he used for keeping a diary and writing a large number of letters to friends and family. Occasionally he alighted into the blur of activity at major marshalling yards, before at journey's end the long march to the front began, either in intense summer heat or in unbearable cold, where dirt, flies and lice, as well as stomach upsets and frostbite, awaited him.[26]

No training, however realistic, prepared troops for the confusion and intensity of battle, with its weird effects on the body's higher senses, or the lower functions that sometimes slipped from control. A fifth of one US army sample freely admitted soiling themselves, and it is a certainty that many more chose not to be so frank. Men aged rapidly, with hair turning prematurely grey under the strain of the combat experience, and eyes developing the notorious thousand-yard stare.[27] Deep battle induced deep tiredness: 'My men are tired. Their eyes are bloodshot. Some of them are so tired they literally cannot see. Two men coming into this area yesterday walked right into trees. Two days ago, two other men, sound asleep on their feet during a march, walked right off a road and out into a field. Another man had to go after them, wake them up, and get them back into line.'[28] After an intense firefight with the Russians, in which he was wounded in the back by a piece of shrapnel, Peter Reese took a breather by a stream. He could not drink the water as there were Russian corpses half lying in it, but he and his comrades could wash in it. He looked in a mirror 'and was shocked. Three deep steep folds were on my forehead, and sharp lines ran from my nostrils downwards, my lips were pale and bloodless, tensed together. I had seen death and survived. Perhaps I am marked out for life.'[29]

Under these stresses, some senses switched off, while others went on to a higher state of alert, with ears attuned to catch every breaking twig or sound of moving tall grass. There was something feral about being a combat soldier: focused on eating, sleeping, evasion and pursuit, with perceptions of terrain, sound and movement all acute. It was unlike hunting in the sense that the prey had the equal advantages that animals lost long ago vis-à-vis weapons-making mankind. Peter Reese wrote: 'The primitive being in us awoke. Instinct replaced mind and feelings, and a transcendent vitality took over.'[30] One of the Sherwood Foresters at the Anzio beachhead wrote: 'It was every night, every night everybody hunting Germans, everybody was out to kill anybody ... we was insane ... We did become like animals in the end ... Yes, just like rats ... It was far worse than in the desert.'[31] It was possible to smell the proximity of the enemy, for different clothing, diets or soaps created a distinctive odour; Soviet soldiers exuded a strong stale tobacco smoke that the Germans could smell in advance, while Japanese officers sometimes doused themselves in perfume to give their troops something to follow along pitch-black jungle trails. In the jungle there were also unfamiliar noises as trees cracked and fell, or the sounds made by every creature from land crabs to exotic species of birds. Modern life's complex needs were reduced to a dry billet, water and food as refuel, together with weapons that worked. Not for nothing was a dual-purpose entrenching tool known as the Infantryman's Friend, since being able to excavate a hollow, whether with this implement or an upturned helmet, to avoid murderous fire might save one's life. Compared with Western troops, the Japanese carried the minimum of kit, usually so that they could transport more shells and ammunition, and expected to live on the 'Churchill rations' their enemies abandoned. Quality of kit knew no national boundaries. The British admired the rubber-soled boots of the Americans, and the well-designed 'Jerry can' water containers of the Germans which leaked less than their own primitive tins. Russians admired the soft leather coats some Germans wore, although as the campaign ground on they were bemused to see that the enemy even donned women's bloomers or shawls to keep out the cold.

A German soldier, Helmut Pabst, once wrote, 'The bullet you hear is already past.' If you didn't hear it, that was because you were likely to be dead or wounded.[32] Death came quite randomly, its selections capricious and mysterious: 'Five days ago in our firing position ... I sat together with our intelligence chief and talked of Würzburg with him. He then fetched his shorts, drying fifteen metres away and waved to me. There a piece of

J cannibaление

shrapnel hit him in the head. Today I am ... at his grave.'[33] Battle consisted of deafening noise, although soldiers learned to distinguish between the degrees of lethality of hot metal rushing through air, interspersed with shouts and the screams of the wounded. The worst experience was sustained bombardment, which ripped up the world around one and flung it back in the form of earth and rubble, not to speak of sharp shards of coral or rock. It also did weird things to atmospheric pressures, giving air a solidity it otherwise lacks. In Russia, Peter Reese found himself repeatedly buried alive as shells ploughed up the snow and earth around his foxhole, until his comrades dug his unconscious weight out of it.[34] John Steinbeck described how 'under extended bombardment or bombing the nerve ends are literally beaten. The ear drums are tortured by blast and the eyes ache from the constant hammering ... At first your ears hurt, but then they become dull and all your other senses become dull, too ... In the dullness all kinds of emphases change ... The whole world becomes unreal ... [Later] you try to remember what it was like, and you can't quite manage it.' The Allied gunners fired 206,929 rounds – four thousand tons of metal – in a two-day bombardment of Monte Camino in December 1944. Under this weight of fire, even elite German soldiers cracked up or lost their will to fight.[35] The German dual-purpose, high-velocity 88mm gun was the nemesis of Allied tank crews. If a tank took a direct hit, the crew had only seconds to get out before they were burned alive in an all-metal oven, assuming that the hatch opened, and that the concussed and wounded could force their way past the inert dead. Sometimes tank commanders were literally blown out of the hatches like corks exploding out of a bottle. Of the 403,272 Red Army tank personnel, a shocking 310,000 were killed.[36]

Close-quarter combat was not as it was taught even by experienced instructors. Bayoneting a straw dummy was one thing; struggling with twelve stones of resisting muscle with teeth that bite was another, as an Australian corporal found when a Japanese bit a 'large piece of flesh' from his face during a close engagement on New Guinea.[37] Although the Australian corporal's comrades regarded this as a bit of a joke, especially on an island where the indigenous peoples had abandoned cannibalism only a couple of decades before, they were enraged to discover that elsewhere starving Japanese soldiers had used razors to carve out strips of buttock or leg flesh from dead Australians to have something to eat after it had been dried inside leaves to make 'white pork' sushi. Firing at target circles (cut-out collapsible men were a post-war consequence of poor Second World War marksmanship) was not the same as seeing a man's expressions through rifle sights before blowing half his face away. The British poet and tank commander Captain Keith Douglas died in Normandy a year after writing 'How to Kill':

> Now in my dial of glass appears
> the soldier who is going to die.
> He smiles, and moves about in ways
> his mother knows, habits of his.
> The wires touch his face; I cry
> NOW. Death, like a familiar, hears
>
> and look, has made a man of dust
> of a man of flesh. This sorcery
> I do. Being damned, I am amused
> to see the centre of love diffused
> and the wave of love travel into vacancy.
> How easy it is to make a ghost.[38]

At Stalingrad, Grossman interviewed a Soviet sniper called Anatoly Ivanovich Chechov, a twenty-year-old from Kazan who as a boy had never so much as held a slingshot. He became one of the most accomplished snipers at Stalingrad: 'When I first got a rifle, I couldn't bring myself to kill a living being: one German was standing there for about four minutes, talking, and I let him go. When I killed my first one, he fell at once. Another one ran out and stooped over the killed one, and I knocked him down too … When I first killed, I was shaking all over: the man was only walking to get some water!… I felt scared: I'd killed a person! Then I remembered our people and started killing them without mercy.'[39] Often identifiable by their heavily bruised right shoulders and cuts on their eyebrows, left by the recoil of telescopic sights, snipers were invariably killed when captured, largely because they had made death highly personal rather than random.

One way of dealing with battle was to assimilate it to the known, namely the world of work. Some claim that was all that was left after honour and patriotism had been rendered unfashionable in the 1920s by war poets and novelists who repudiated the stockyard slaughter of the trenches even as they naively celebrated the new Communist type of hero in 1930s Spain.[40] But one wonders whether this sort of intellectual cynicism had become general. Men in overalls can be patriotic too. The German-Jewish survivor Victor Klemperer expressed snobbish surprise that US troops looked like workmen in 'overalls', not at all like the starched Prussian officers who had helped murder most of Klemperer's race. Those who have studied combat to greatest effect, such as John Ellis or Richard Holmes, argue that patriotism was not an especially salient motivator of men who killed the enemy because they were the enemy rather because they were Germans, although they felt differently about the Japanese. A GI explained this: 'Ask any dogface [infantryman] on the line. You're fighting for your skin on the line. When I enlisted I was as patriotic as hell. There's no patriotism on the line. A boy up there 60 days on the line is in danger every minute. He ain't fighting for patriotism.'[41]

Certainly there was no dearth of patriotism when men joined up, although it was not of the hurrah variety commonplace in all the late nineteenth-century European empires. Nor was patriotism absent from the Frenchmen and Poles who fought at the successive battles of Cassino, which Ellis himself has described so movingly. The Poles fought with suicidal abandon, partly because they hated Germans and wanted to kill them, but partly in the vain hope of making the Western Allies acknowledge a debt of honour to their prostrate nation. There was also the matter of lineage; those whose fathers and grandfathers had been soldiers or sailors were likely to feel a higher sense of obligation than others. Fighting was in their blood. Men also took immense pride in belonging to elite divisions and regiments, where they were constantly reminded that 'as descendants of the men who gained such splendid victories in so many battles from 1702 onwards we are simply unable to be cowardly. We've got to win our battle, whatever the cost, so that people will say "They were worthy descendants of the 32nd,"' as one British officer put it.[42] In a novel Evelyn Waugh caught the ancient regimental lore explaining why his Honourable Company of Free Halberdiers were known as 'The Copper Heels' and 'Applejacks' – the last after they had repelled French troops at Malplaquet in 1709 by throwing apples.[43] The British army had many proud traditions, like the red hackle 'vulture's feather' adorning the Black Watch bonnet. Their motto 'Let no one provoke me with impunity' was also useful on Glasgow streets, for the Scots (and Ulstermen) had a sort of belligerence that made them natural fighters, like their kinsmen the southern Scots-Irish across the Atlantic. Soldiers felt proud to wear specific uniforms which advertised their prowess, such as Scottish kilts or the green or maroon caps worn by respectively commandos and paratroops.

Airborne troops also quickly developed a reputation for ferocity – the basic leap from a plane requires courage even before the fighting has commenced – in all armies. The 1st Parachute Division was probably the single best fighting force in the German army. These paratroops were quite distinctive in their rimless saucepan-shaped helmets and baggy combat overalls. While they did not do much jumping after heavy losses on Crete, they were used as firefighting troops, making an ordeal of every yard of territory the Allies fought for in Italy. The US 101st Airborne were made conscious that though they lacked history they had a rendezvous with destiny, as the Screaming Eagles portrayed on their division badge. The equally fêted 82nd Airborne were known as the All-Americans because recruits came from every US state; they adopted the nickname 'devils in baggy pants', the description that figured in the diary of a dead German officer who fought them.

Seeking to add to the 'war is hell' literature of the Great War, academics have distorted the average reaction to combat. Many men enjoyed combat as a chance to prove themselves and to put their training into action, and it also gave them the biggest rush of adrenaline they were ever likely to experience. While some people, in later years, regretted having killed, others never gave it another thought, and merged effortlessly back into civilian existence. A few actively courted anachronistically honourable death, like Colonel 'Mad Jack' Churchill, a legendary commando leader who went into action in a kilt, with a dirk and bow and arrows, having been a champion archer in civilian life.[44]

At the combat coalface, killing became a job of work, a routine with a higher purpose based on a set of skills that could be acquired. Some of these skills were taught in training, such as always keeping one's head down, or learning that platoons should disperse rather than presenting a consolidated target, even though time and again men instinctively clung together under fire. But what really counted could not be learned in training any more than school or university prepares anyone for real life.[45] Begrimed combat veterans instructed fresh-faced new arrivals in the lore of the battlefield, rather like master craftsmen instructing apprentices. Young Germans learned to call their NCOs *Kumpel* or mate, rather than 'comrade', since, as the NCOs sourly remarked, all the ideologically motivated *Kameraden* tended to get killed. During the gruelling Italian campaign, a German veteran noted that 'It was vicious fighting. These young soldiers had been so anxious to get to the front and to fight man against man, but they had no experience. Once again, the older men were left and the younger men died. It's more than experience. It's a kind of sixth sense. When there was danger, I could smell it. The older ones were the same.'[46] Old in this context meant being thirty rather than nineteen.

Of course, not all the old-timers were as benevolent as this suggests. They sometimes shunned replacement troops, knowing that they had death hovering over them. An American sergeant at Anzio received eight replacement troops in his platoon. The old guys sent these naives out on the next exploratory raid, knowing full well that they would not be coming back. That was how the old guys survived Africa, Sicily, Salerno and Anzio.[47] Even the ingrained dirt on hands and faces was instructive, for together with oil it helped keep out cold, as did the layers of clothing that bulked them out like vagrants. In the frozen wastes of Russia, German soldiers learned to pee on their hands to warm them. Everywhere troops learned to keep their mouths open during heavy aerial bombardment, for otherwise their eardrums would burst and blood trickle from their noses. Jungle warfare brought its own terrors, for the Japanese as well as Western troops, because there are no jungles in Japan, nor for that matter in Korea or China. A common saying among Japanese generals was 'I've upset Tojo, I'll probably end up in Burma,' the equivalent of a German fearing transfer to the Eastern Front.[48] The Japanese learned such tricks as breaking a piece of bamboo to simulate the crack of rifle fire, to reveal the location of enemy positions when they shot back. Western troops assimilated these skills too, as well as learning, for example, to cut out the crotch of their trousers to deal with dysentery without having to undress.

Australian troops discovered that beards were useful camouflage in dense jungle, where a pale face might fatally attract a bullet out of the gloom. Their officers learned to remove insignia of rank, and to wear their pistols slung round their backs rather than in a side holster, since Japanese snipers, often concealed in trees, were trained to kill the officers first. Much the same lesson was learned by Allied officers in Normandy, who stopped carrying binoculars and map cases.[49] Veterans learned how to discriminate between incoming ordnance, so that they could seek shelter in time, or carry on in the knowledge that a shell was going to miss. In situations where one could not see the enemy, the danger of friendly fire was constant and it was important to distinguish between the *tatatatat* of a US machine gun and the *bubububub* of the Japanese equivalent. Anyone engaged in house-to-house fighting in northern Europe learned that it was better to blow holes in party walls to work one's way along rather than entering by the front doors, and that attackers had an advantage in clearing each building from the upper floors downwards.[50] In dense jungle, night was a more palpable version of the gloom of day, so dense that an Australian soldier laying mines at night felt the hand of a Japanese brush past his face. In the jungle soldiers fought within hailing distance of each other: 'Johnny you die tonight!' being a Japanese favourite. 'Fuck Roosevelt' ... 'Fuck Tojo' ... 'Fuck Eleanor' ... 'No you fuck her yourself' being typical of exchanges on Guadalcanal. The surprising discovery that some Japanese had rudimentary English led Australian troops who had been in North Africa to use combat codewords based on pigeon Arabic, or to choose words like 'Woolloomooloo' (in Sydney harbour), since Japanese found the 'l's unpronounceable.[51]

Soldiers also made prudential calculations that did not figure in basic training. According to historian and veteran Paul Fussell, 'it took up to six weeks for a unit to learn to stay alive by abandoning most of the tactical knowledge instilled by [seventeen weeks of] basic Stateside training'.[52] American soldiers who jumped into holes and found them occupied by Germans might decide that sharing cigarettes with them was the better part of valour.[53] Sometimes officers unilaterally decided to ignore suicidal orders, simply by pretending that they could not hear their commanders on a poor radio link, or removing connectors to make sure they could not. At other times troops threw away their guns in the middle of a battle and sat down refusing to fight, as in the case of the Mid-West Urbana Force guardsmen posted to New Guinea.[54] Textbook armies might march on full stomachs, but empty guts were less likely to contaminate an abdominal wound. Soldiers and combat medics learned not to clean maggots from wounds, as the maggots favoured gangrenous flesh, and practised a basic triage of treating survivable wounds and simply making those with fatal wounds as comfortable as possible. In some armies, medics carried pistols to put dying soldiers out of their misery, although possession infringed their non-combatant status and made them liable to be shot. The always extreme Japanese went into battle without morphine and regarded any illness as a personal failing. They shot their own wounded if they were too incapacitated to kill themselves, rather than leaving them to dishonourable capture. That was fully in line with the expectations of their relatives back home, for whom having a POW in the family brought unfathomable social disgrace, regardless of how their relative had been captured.

Battle meant getting used to the sight and prospect of death at an age when most people have hardly begun to think about life's unavoidable outcome, because as young adults they are poised between the generations and can scarcely comprehend the finality of the future. That sense of immortality is one reason why young men make better soldiers than their more cautious seniors. Dealing with dead bodies became routine for Peter Reese out in his frozen hell-hole in Russia: 'one of our unit took a direct hit. We collected together his limbs from the blood-drenched snow, scraping together the mass of flesh and bone and throwing earth over brains and blood. We wrapped the lighter bits in a sheet of tent and buried him, as if this matériel battle had made us into soulless automata.'[55]

Most soldiers sought supernatural protection, striking what amounted to bargains with God, reinforcing this with lucky charms or preparatory rituals. The Red Army was officially atheist, but a large number of men wore metal crosses, and crossed themselves before going into battle. Others swore that it was bad luck to touch one's genitals the night before, to swear while loading a gun or to don a stranger's greatcoat.[56] The cockpits of some Allied bombers must have resembled the huts of witch doctors, so full were they of talismans and charms, seeking some element of personal control in an objectively random environment. Other calculations are familiar to any risk-taker: sudden death was something that happened to someone else, or as the Great War song had it, 'The Bells of Hell go ting-a-ling-a-ling For you but not for me.'[57] A variant of this was that fatalities already bore an invisible number, and when your luck or number was up, you were dead. Belief in the random inexplicability of death – whose obverse was the artillery round that failed to explode or the bullet that hit a pocket Bible – made it easier to cope with the fact that there were other resourceful men bent on doing you lethal harm. Such tricks of the mind enabled men to overcome exhaustion and fear for months on end, often unaware of other costs to themselves. So did the general climate of each theatre, for in some the possibility of capture or surrender brought few terrors, while in others fear of what would happen meant that troops fought to the bitter end, knowing they could expect no mercy. The Commonwealth troops might have fought better at Singapore if they had known what captivity had in store for them. There were also entire units that felt jinxed by bad fortune. The US 36th 'Texan' Infantry Division had such bad luck that other units feared it might be contagious. As the Texans set out to cross the icy-cold Rapido river in Italy, a company commander knew something was amiss when he noticed his regimental commander in tears before the action had even commenced. By the time the crossing had failed, the company commander had seventeen men alive after starting with 184.[58]

II THE 'CLEAN' WAR

In North Africa, highly mobile forces fought over sparsely populated terrain, which a war poet memorably compared with a shabby lion pelt. As a German general remarked, it was a tactician's paradise and a quartermaster's nightmare. The British and Italian leaderships thought much was at stake, respectively Suez and the route to India, while Mussolini dreamed of turning the Mediterranean into *mare nostrum*. By contrast, Hitler regarded North Africa as a sideshow, something forced on him by Mussolini, which distracted from his ideological showdown with the Soviets. The importance of Russia to Hitler in turn led Mussolini to divert manpower and vehicles to the Eastern Front, which weakened the Italian effort in North Africa. Many US commanders shared Hitler's view of North Africa, wondering why they had to make a lengthy detour to prop up the British Empire rather than striking direct at the industrial heart of Nazi Germany. The British, rightly, doubted that their allies knew what they were facing, something the Kasserine debacle did much to confirm.[59] In this theatre of disputed significance, which the war poet Sidney Keyes called a 'sullen gritty land' (he died there in 1943), there was sand and more sand, with winds and storms altering the topography daily. Burned-out machinery lay everywhere, interspersed with corpses on which clouds of flies settled along with the maquillage of fine sand. There was no relief from the heat of the day or from the freezing nights, especially for the Italian soldiers in wool uniforms suited to neither extreme of temperature.[60] It was one of the most boring environments on earth, hence the inordinate importance of the daily rituals of making tea and trying to invest some variety in a diet of tinned bully beef and hard tack biscuits. Eating was always a one-handed activity, since the spare hand had to beat off the flies which zeroed in on any food.[61]

This featureless environment, in which all participants had sore eyes and sand-caked faces, was conducive to a relatively clean war, although to the classically educated its mechanised nature jarred – as a poet put it, 'Oh glory that was Tetrarch's might, Oh drabness that is Ford', a Tetrarch being a British tank. The terrain afforded relatively few opportunities for booby-traps, snipers and all the factors which in more developed (or primordial) environments triggered spirals of retaliatory violence. Huge swathes of anti-tank mines lay partly exposed by the shifting sands and the armies could see one another more often here than in any other theatre.[62] The seesawing tempo of mechanised battles meant that today's POWs could become tomorrow's captive-takers, so that prudence contributed to the relatively gentlemanly manner in which the desert war was fought. What the Afrika Korps may or may not have done to the Jews of the Yeshuv had they not been stopped by British, Dominion and US troops is largely irrelevant to that analysis of desert warfare. The British evidently did not think they were fighting criminals, but rather other professionals who in most respects were like themselves. Montgomery invited the captured General Ritter von Thoma to dinner, joking that he had 'enjoyed the battle very much'. Thoma gave a sickly smile. Despite having lost 150 men in a battle with German paratroops, Colonel John Frost of the British 2nd Parachute Battalion insisted that his men share out a rum ration with German and Italian prisoners, finishing up with a joint singsong: 'We had met no cases of "Hunnish frightfulness", and on the whole they were a chivalrous foe,' commented Frost. After Harold Harper's field dressing station had been overrun by the Germans, he was surprised to see that the officer who jumped down from a tank to ask a British medic about his charges' welfare was none other than Rommel. When in May 1945 Lieutenant Maufe managed to persuade an SS panzer officer to surrender, he did it by commenting on the man's Afrika Korps campaign medal.[63]

These rules of the game seem to have evolved, rather than being decreed from on high, and had to be imposed on newcomers, who included officers eager to make a reputation for themselves. Elsewhere, one always machine-gunned the survivors who baled out of a burning armoured vehicle; in the desert, sometimes one did not. Eighth Army took its manners with it. When Maufe drew a bead on a limping German straggler in Italy, one of his riflemen jogged his arm saying, 'Give him a chance, guv, the poor sod's wounded.' The Red Cross markings of field stations were generally respected, whether by opponents on the ground or in the air, and atrocities tended to be attributed to the more exotic participants. They included Moroccan tribesmen serving with the French, known as Goumiers from a corruption of *qum*, the word for group, who collected severed heads and would rape thousands of women in Italy. Gurkhas and Maoris spread terror by slitting the throats of sleeping enemy soldiers during silent night raids, leaving a few to wake up to the ghastly sight, evidence of a grim sense of humour but hardly a war crime.

A British poet contemplating a war grave wrote: 'Not British and not German now he's dead, He breeds no grasses from his rot. The coast road and the Arab pass his bed, And waste no time brooding on his lot.'[64] In

wogs

fact, it was the local Bedouin who were more often the targets of wanton cruelty, partly because their nomadism raised suspicions that they were spies. Universally known to the British and Americans as 'wogs', they were sometimes used for target practice, 'like you're shooting gophers'. In Le Tarf, a village in northern Algeria, drunken US engineers gang-raped six middle-aged Arab women. Of course, some of these 'wogs' – Algerians and Moroccans – would fight superbly under French command in Italy, where they advanced over mountain terrain that defeated the British and Americans. Italian mountain-dwellers were not so enthusiastic after the Goumiers passed through, raping their daughters and sons, saying that one night with them in the house was worse than having Germans lodged with them for several years.

While the desert war was never what Rommel's propagandists dubbed a 'war without hate', hate took some encouragement, at least in the years before the Battle of the Kasserine Pass had blooded the Americans. This was not exclusively their problem. In 1942, the British had to introduce hate training, by spreading slaughterhouse blood around their assault courses as well as giving lectures which emphasised German brutality. The fact that the US army HQ in Algiers had to issue a memo enjoining commanders to 'teach their men to hate the enemy – to want to kill by any means' indicated that in this theatre there was a problem.[65] Some units needed little urging. At Alamein, members of the Seaforth Highlanders passed trenches in which Germans were cowering under their blankets. When a private asked a sergeant what to do about this problem, he was told to use the unit's anti-tank grenades to kill them. But generally it took some conspicuous deviation from the rules of the game for a unit to abandon its own norms. During the assault on Longstop Hill in Tunisia in April 1943, a captured German drew a concealed pistol and shot several of his Argyll and Sutherland Highlander captors. The latter were 'roused to a state of berserk fury – We just had a hate – at the Germans, the hill, and everything.' For a few days they accepted no surrenders, but by the time they had stormed the hill, losing a third of their own men in the action, they had taken three hundred prisoners.[66]

III HIM OR US

This already gives us a few clues to why soldiers might abandon the rules of war for reasons other than bloodlust and sadism, for which there is plenty of scope on battlefields. Anything that seemed sneaky, such as snipers, booby-traps and unmarked anti-personnel mines, which all armies deployed, and also attacks on medical personnel and field stations, were liable to elicit a vicious response. Men from the US 180th Infantry Regiment under the command of Patton came under sniper fire in the environs of Biscari in Sicily. At one point they captured forty-six prisoners, including three Germans. A major identified nine youngsters whom he wanted interrogated, handing over the whole group to a thirty-three-year-old sergeant called West. This man, a cook in civilian life, marched the men towards some olive trees. There he separated out the nine interrogatees, asked for a sub-machine gun with extra clips 'to shoot the sons of bitches', and gunned down the other thirty-seven prisoners, including three who tried to run, and then methodically shot those who still showed signs of life. 'This is orders' was his sole comment. That afternoon the same unit captured another thirty-six Italians. A firing squad was formed and all of them were shot dead as alleged snipers. An army chaplain happened on the corpses of these men and some soldiers loitering near by told him they were ashamed of their fellow countrymen and were fighting 'against that sort of thing'. The chaplain complained to the divisional commander, Omar Bradley, who went to see Patton. So did two war correspondents who had also seen the bodies. Knowing the cat was out of the bag, Patton reported the incident to Marshall, alleging that the victims were snipers and that 'in my opinion these killings have been thoroughly justified'. Bradley disagreed and Patton was forced to issue the order, 'Try the bastards.' The officer who had ordered the firing squad in the second case was eventually charged and court-martialled. He simply cited Patton's own order 'kill devastatingly' and was quickly acquitted. The prosecution failed to examine him. Sergeant West, who also cited Patton, was sentenced to life imprisonment. In fact, he was jailed (in North Africa) for a year and then, reduced to the ranks, returned to active duty.[67]

At the further end of the scale was anyone feigning surrender to kill their captors, followed by the mutilation or killing of prisoners – evidence of which we have already seen from both sides on the Eastern Front. Bitter experience led to pre-emptive violence. Koschorrek, the young German soldier we encountered earlier, was appalled when an NCO ordered his unit to shoot apparently dead Russians strewn around a bombed-out dugout. After detecting a certain reluctance to do this, the NCO calmly shot the Russians in the back of the head with his sub-machine gun. Pausing to give one a hard kick in the stomach, he said, 'This one too is alive,' before shooting him in the forehead. Asked why he was not taking them prisoner, the NCO angrily replied: 'Then just try to get them up when they are playing dead! The swine think we won't realise they're alive and will cut us down from behind. I've seen it before.' He added, 'Him or us!'[68] Another reason for killing prisoners was equally pragmatic, even though it was in violation of the Geneva Conventions. Canadian troops routinely killed German captives after D-Day, partly because there had been instances of atrocities, but mainly because they were viewed as an encumbrance to advancing troops.[69] That then developed into a grudge match between the Canadians and the Waffen-SS Panzer Division Hitlerjugend, whose commander Meyer was found to have murdered 134 Canadians.

Common sense suggests that one should distinguish between hot-blooded and cold-blooded atrocities. In the Normandy bocage, both sides found themselves fighting intensely in an environment where the enemy was liable to pop up out of nowhere. Men had split seconds to react, and sometimes did not notice, or care to notice, that the enemy was in fact surrendering. It was also difficult to make everyone cease fire at the same time. A member of the East Yorkshire Regiment reported: 'Some Germans were trying to surrender but in the excitement we fired on them before they had any chance to put their hands up … Some people still kept firing, but I don't think our lads were saying, well, I don't care if that man wants to surrender or doesn't want to surrender. I'm going to shoot him anyway. I don't think that was in anyone's mind. I think it was the excitement of constantly stuffing fresh ammunition into magazines and blazing away.' Only the most hair-splitting lawyerly mind would call that a war crime.[70]

Jungle combat provided the ultimate environment for sneaky warfare, and there was certainly nothing nationally exclusive about such practices. The Australians perfected an ambush technique of strewing tins of bully beef in order to machine-gun the starving Japanese who eagerly fell upon them. 'Tell me, corporal,' asked a visiting British officer learning jungle tactics, 'how close do you let them get?' 'About six feet, Sir. Any closer and the bastards'll fall on top of you,' replied Corporal Brian 'Bluey' Malone. Racial animosity towards 'little yellow buck-teethed bastards' was a given, but it hardened into hatred as certain aspects of Japanese martial conduct

*PNG + Aussies victory, vs. MacA claim
credit*
+US historiography of Triumphalism
atrocities, → racism

became notorious during the New Guinea campaign, the first reverse on land the Japanese experienced. It is little known because it coincided with the crucial naval engagements of the Coral Sea and Midway, but also because the involvement of US troops was belated and shameful, and the telling of the Pacific war has been dominated by US triumphalism. The massive ego of General Douglas MacArthur led him to claim that he had directed the campaign, but even US historians have baulked at that, with the result that a stunning victory won by Australians is hardly known beyond their shores.

In July 1942, elite Japanese troops from the Special Naval Landing Party and the South Seas Detachment landed on the northern shores of New Guinea and drove inexperienced Australian militiamen back along the Kokoda Track. This was a 150-mile trail running over the Owen Stanley mountain range to Port Moresby on the south coast, which combined the elements of jungle and mountain warfare in an extreme form. The Australian militia were known disparagingly as Chocos (short for Chocolate soldiers), gangs of mates who had signed up with nothing more arduous in mind than support duties. The Australians had no reason to doubt that Port Moresby would be the springboard for an invasion of their homeland, when most of their regular troops were away fighting in North Africa or had fallen into Japanese hands at Singapore. To buy time for some of their men to return from North Africa, the Chocos conducted a grim fighting retreat, while the Japanese over-extended their supply lines. Once reinforcements arrived, the Australians drove the starving Japanese back to their starting point. Of the twenty thousand Japanese troops who invaded New Guinea, maybe a hundred survived.[71]

The Japanese felt no shame about their brutality. A war diary recorded, '13 August: Natives brought Australian prisoners – five men, three women and a child. 14 August: About 8am decapitated or shot the nine prisoners.' As they pursued the Japanese, the Australians encountered countless examples of sadism: the body of a native boy, his head incinerated with a flamethrower and a bayonet protruding from his anus; a woman whose left breast had been cut off before she died; the body of a militiaman tied to a tree with bayonet wounds in both arms and the bayonet left rammed into his stomach. By the time the Australians found evidence of cannibalism, they had come to regard the enemy as something other than human. As their commander, General Thomas Blamey, told them: 'You know that we have to exterminate these vermin if we and our families are to live. We must go on to the end if civilisation is to survive. We must exterminate the

Japanese.' In an interview, Blamey observed that 'Fighting Japs is not like fighting normal human beings. The Jap is a little barbarian … We are not dealing with humans as we know them. We are dealing with something primitive. Our troops have the right view of the Japs. They regard them as vermin.' There was also the practical consideration that Japanese wounded often had concealed hand grenades and orders to try and take an enemy soldier with them, while the Australians simply lacked the resources to treat or evacuate the few genuinely helpless Japanese wounded who fell into their hands as well as their own wounded. Even so, by the end Australian loathing ebbed away when they saw the emaciated, disease-wracked state of the few Japanese survivors.[72]

Initially, Western troops facing the Japanese suffered a violent disloca-tion of expectations. Pre-war contempt for them as myopic little yellow men was rapidly replaced by a no less exaggerated fear that they were supermen capable of amazing military prowess. To some extent, this revised opinion was justified. The Japanese were extraordinarily brave and stoical. Notwithstanding outrage about Pearl Harbor, official US reports from Corregidor in the Philippines said that the Americans did not 'have much honest hate for the Jap until some of his comrades have been killed by the enemy'. While they knew about well-publicised Japanese atrocities in China, not a few in the West shared Japanese views about the value of Chinese lives. Allied commanders also knew that the Japanese had treated Russian POWs humanely, not only in the war of 1904–5, but as recently as the August 1939 clash at Khalkhin Gol. The Japanese had signed the 1907 Hague Convention on Land War, and in 1942 their government promised to respect the 1929 Geneva Convention. Yamashita spoke of the 'spirit of Japanese chivalry' when urging the hapless Percival to surrender Singapore. But they also practised extremely brutal internal military discipline, and officers were sometimes indifferent to their own wounded. This was only partially ameliorated, at least in the realm of human sentiment, by exam-ples of individual Japanese soldiers who felt deeply about their dying comrades, or occasionally expressed what they called 'humanitarian' feel-ings towards dying opponents. In March 1942 a Major Misao Sato wrote about a wounded British sniper whom his men captured in Burma:

> I went to see him lying in the shade of a tree. He was young-looking, about 18 years old, a handsome British soldier. He was treated by our doctor Kikuchi. A bullet had gone through his abdomen, and the doctor told me there was no hope of survival. I asked him in my

broken English, 'Where are your father and mother?' He said just a word, but clearly, 'England,' and as I asked 'Painful?' he again said a word, 'No.' I knew he must be suffering great pain ... As I looked at him closely I saw a thin stream of tears coming from his eyes. I understood that he was enduring his pain with all his might, his young, pale face contorted. Ah! His attitude was really dignified. He was doing his best to maintain the pride of the Great British Empire while his life was ending. Unconsciously I cried and held his hands. I would never forget the last minutes of that young British soldier![73]

Evidently, while the Japanese regarded their own capture as a form of social death which would taint their families, for whom they became non-persons, they were capable of acting humanely when confronted by brave opponents, in stark contrast to how they regarded any demoralised rabble that fell into their hands. The situation was reversed in Europe, where nothing irritated Allied troops who captured Germans more than their haughty arrogance. When a German officer reluctantly surrendered to a US sergeant in a Normandy barn, he handed over a reversed eighteen-inch knife with an ivory handle, only to have the sergeant plunge it into him. 'He had a very startled look on his face,' said the sergeant.[74]

IV RACISM

One charge which requires careful discussion is the now devalued (through overuse) slur of racism, for the Japanese did not regard other peoples in quite the same light as the Blameys of this world regarded them. Any enemy who fell into their hands was potentially in trouble, but none more than ethnic Chinese, who were indubitably of the same Asian race as the Japanese. What for want of a better word we call Japanese racism was more concerned with the ethnic and cultural superiority of the Japanese themselves than with crudely asserting that this or that colour of skin was inferior – although, like many Asians, they looked down on those with black skins, even as their propaganda deplored the way Afro-Americans were treated in the USA. The Japanese could hardly despise whites for, like high-caste Brahmins in India, lightness of skin was highly prized among upper-class Japanese, while 'white' had deep connotations of purity in a language that can merge colours and values in a single ideogram. Darkness indicated regular exposure to the sun and hence lowly occupations, while the Japanese attitude towards primitive peoples like the tribesmen of New Guinea was akin to regarding them as a different species. In this they were not unique: Australian 'black-birding' of Pacific islanders, a slave trade by another name, persisted well into the twentieth century.

Although the Japanese admired many aspects of Western modernity, a much older fear of foreigners as brutish devils proved more visceral. Their Anglo-Saxon opponents were invariably depicted either as devils in human guise or in the more modern (American) image as gangsters, a bifurcation that underlines a wider Japanese ambivalence towards modernity. Whereas in 1904–5 the Japanese were keen to advertise their Western credentials – including a civilised attitude towards POWs – from the 1930s onwards the country's international posture was based on defiance of Westerners, who they felt posed an existential threat to the survival of Japan's civilisation and a way of life based on extreme filial piety and emperor worship.[75] The Japanese government also bombarded the population with evidence of Anglo-American atrocities. Some of these were fanciful, like using tanks to crush POWS; others were not, for Allied trophy-hunters did indeed collect gold teeth and ears from Japanese corpses, or use the skulls as ashtrays and candleholders, a notorious instance being published on the cover of *Life* magazine. Although the Japanese said they would respect the Geneva Convention, neither officers nor other ranks were instructed in its stipulations. In a culture which vested all authority in the divine Emperor, there was no transcendent moral code to check savage behaviour generated within the armed forces, in which, as in Nazi Germany, humanitarianism came to be seen as weak sentimentality. At least the Japanese had the genuine excuse that they lacked an external frame of moral reference, whereas most Germans still nominally subscribed to a common set of Christian values.[76]

Like the German army's war crimes investigation unit, the Japanese organised war crimes trials, notably when they condemned eight captive US pilots to death following the April 1942 Doolittle Raid on Japanese cities, named after Lieutenant Colonel James 'Jimmy' Doolittle, who led these first strikes on the home islands. It did not occur to the Japanese to equate the American raid with their own devastating bombardment of defenceless Chinese cities – an attack on the sacred soil of Japan was akin to blasphemy. Even when they took prisoners, the Japanese systematically mistreated them, although as part of their post-war denial mechanism they alleged that the sadistic POW camp guards were Koreans. While only 4 per cent of Anglo-American prisoners – or 9,348 men – died in German captivity, the figure for POWs of the Japanese was 35,756, or 27 per cent of those captured. Death rates among Indian, Malayan and Burmese soldiers serving in the Commonwealth armies were far higher. While not in the same league as the millions of Soviet and German soldiers who died in captivity, it was still a shockingly large number, particularly as a high proportion of POWs who died in Japanese captivity were the victims of sadistic violence. Few were shot: bullets were expensive. The lucky were beheaded with swords or bayoneted, the latter weapon being the ordinary trooper's surrogate sword. More died as the result of revolting torture, and many more from lack of adequate nutrition and medical attention, often in situations where the guards themselves had nearly as little. Still, some Japanese were capable of acting considerately and humanely towards both POWs and civilian internees, which militates against the widely held notion that cruelty was innate in the Japanese character.[77]

US Marines on Iwo Jima went into combat with 'Rodent Exterminator' stencilled on their helmets. Whereas killing every German soldier was not viewed as essential to the defeat of Nazi Germany, the Allies certainly adopted that radical approach in fighting the Japanese. From top to bottom the view was the same. General Joe Stilwell opined that 'the only way to defeat this enemy was to kill him', while a Marine sergeant briefed his men before the Peleliu landings: 'We'll have to kill every little yellow bastard there.'[78] The belief that the only good —— was a dead —— was far less universally held for Germans than it was for the Japanese. Whereas German Nazi or Italian Fascist sympathisers in the US were never rounded up, all 110,000 Japanese-Americans were interned under appalling conditions, notwithstanding considerable evidence of their loyalty to their adopted country. American attitudes towards the Japanese were not far distant from the Nazi view of the Jews. In the anti-Semitic film *The Eternal Jew*, the Nazis depicted the inmates of Polish ghettos as rushing vermin; at around the same time, the US comic *Leatherneck* discovered 'Louseous Japanicus', an insect with slanted eyes and buck teeth that would not have looked out of place in *Der Stürmer*. Flamethrowers and phosphorus grenades were recommended as the best means of 'extermination', although 'before a complete cure may be effected the origin of the plague, the breeding grounds around the Tokyo area, must be completely annihilated'. Even when the Japanese were accorded some degree of humanity, they were regarded as 'half devil and half child', the white man's burden described in Rudyard Kipling's 1899 poem welcoming the US to the ranks of the imperialists when it acquired the Philippines. Not that the Americans needed Kipling to coin the phrase: they had used the same rhetoric to justify their dispossession of the Native Americans. A twist was added by opportunistic academic anthropologists, who drivelled about the 'situational' character of Japanese ethics in terms of over-rigorous potty training, so that in situations where there were no prescribed behavioural rituals the Japanese went crazy.[79]

V THE WEIGHT OF SHEER NUMBERS

The Soviets started turning the Great Patriotic War into history and myth as early as March 1943, when they opened a museum that was the first step towards the triumphal granite giants who were to brandish huge swords over the post-war landscape.[80] The sheer numbers of dead on the Eastern Front could create the impression that no one else was fighting the Germans. The statistics are certainly telling. Four out of every five German soldiers killed in the Second World War died on the Eastern Front, but they killed many times their number of Red Army troops. The Soviet army destroyed in the summer of 1941 had to be reconstructed again and again throughout this gigantic war of attrition, steadily gaining in professionalism. The breakneck output of the tank and aircraft factories and the arrival of enormous numbers of jeeps and trucks from the West meant that it became more modern and mobile. The destruction of the entire pre-war hierarchy between 1937 and 1941 made way for vigorous new commanders, who quickly learned how to co-ordinate armour and tactical airpower in huge operations that relentlessly ground down the once all-conquering Nazi war machine. Considering how comparably repugnant the two totalitarian regimes were, one might muse that it was a pity both could not lose. But one of them had to win, and few would dispute that it was the lesser of two monstrous evils that did so.

Elite Guards armoured and rifle divisions were created to bolster attacks and to set an example to lesser mortals. They were often named in honour of notable victories, such as the 3rd Guards 'Stalingrad' Mechanised Corps. Although the policy was never explicit, the elite formations were overwhelmingly ethnic Russian in composition, partly because Stalin did not trust many of the seventy other Soviet nationalities represented in his legions. Throughout the army, there was a new emphasis upon spit and polish. Cleaning and repairing boots became obligatory. The less than helpful profile of political officers was reduced, while the status of the officer corps was collectively boosted, even though the term 'officer', as opposed to 'command staff', was formally reintroduced only in January 1943. As talismans of class privilege, shoulder epaulettes had been ostentatiously ripped off in Eisenstein's 1920s class-hate films; they were restored along with a very officer-like range of high-peaked hats. Officers received the services of batmen and orderlies in a further reversion to the civilities of the imperial past, to the delight of generals who were the sons of cobblers and peasants. Medals proliferated, often with names reflecting Tsarist Russia's military heroes, with some eleven million decorations awarded during the war through vetting mechanisms that were more lax than in any other wartime army. These decorations also brought rewards for the families of the servicemen so honoured, and would further privilege them in the long post-war era.[81]

Although some Red Army soldiers undoubtedly felt motivated to fight by the radiant tomorrow that Communism promised, for many more a desire to expel a cruel invader from their homelands dovetailed with Stalin's exploitation of a denatured version of Russian nationalism. It was denatured because even before the war Russian national identity had been selectively subsumed and refashioned into a new Soviet-Russian identity. This also reflected Stalin's view, expressed in 1934, that Soviet history texts had substituted 'sociology for history'; instead of a succession of economic epochs, children needed facts, names and 'content'. The result was the inclusion of a few deracinated remnants of Russia's rich history so that a spurious continuity would seem to underlie the brave new Soviet reality. The Great Patriotic War accelerated these trends. The internationalist slogan 'Proletarians of all lands, unite' was dropped in favour of narrower sympathies towards the ethnic Russian motherland, not least because beyond the Russian Soviet Federative Socialist Republic, ethnic Russians were the cadres, graduates, teachers and technicians who represented the Soviet idea among the benighted peoples.[82] The generic enemy of Fascism was supplanted by more exclusive concentration on 'the Germans', notably in the wartime hack journalism of Ilya Ehrenburg. The Germans helped this process. Russian troops captured a German tank crew in July 1941. One wrote in his diary: 'what naïve philanthropists we were! In our interrogation we tried to get them to express class solidarity. We thought talking to us would make them see the light, and they would shout "Red Front!" ... But they guzzled our kasha porridge from our mess-tins, had a smoke from our freely offered tobacco pouches, then looked at us insolently and belched in our faces "Heil Hitler!"[83]

Although the newfound tolerance of Orthodox Christianity was certainly cynical and was accompanied by a process of subversion designed to turn the priesthood into a branch of the NKVD, the restoration of pre-revolutionary symbols and traditions represented a continuation of Stalin's qualified admiration for the state-building achievements of the tsars, already evident in the late 1930s. Russia's history also yielded any number of inspirational military exemplars, heroes who had led the Russian people against invaders, from Alexander Nevsky and Dmitry Donskoy to Alexander Suvorov and Mikhail Kutuzov.[84] But the most powerful motivators of men were the old-fashioned concepts of *Rodina* (Homeland), family and loved ones, the latter plangently epitomised in Konstantin Simonov's poem 'Wait for Me and I Will Return'.[85]

Western conscripts tended to be shocked by their initial induction into military life, whether having to live with strangers or being shouted at. That transition was much smoother for young Germans who from the age of fourteen had undergone ideological and military conditioning, as well as compulsory Labour Service. 'Today we have Germany, but tomorrow the whole world will belong to us,' sang the Hitler Youth, who were taught how to rough it in outdoor camps, and experienced hiking, orienteering and any number of specialist training schemes, from gliding to mechanics, as well as a special police unit for future members of the SS. They also learned comradeship and obedience to leadership, again based on merit rather than class superiority.[86] They believed in Hitler and in Nazism's claim to be building a national racial community which combined egalitarianism with meritocracy, and which was responsible for Germany's economic recovery and rebirth as a great military power. German basic military training was also tough and realistic, with many exercises involving live ammunition, which killed a small percentage of the men involved. It included clambering on board moving tanks to place mines on the collar between hull and turret, as well as digging a trench in which they had to shelter when it was run over by a tank. Men were trained to make a cradle of their arms to carry a notionally wounded comrade over long distances. Common soldiers in the German army received more comprehensive training than British or US officers until the very end of the war, while their NCOs and officers were the product of a process of selection and training that no other army even tried to match.[87]

E

The Germans fought as well in defence and withdrawal as they did on the advance, their special forte being aggressive counter-attacks to regain a position. They were brilliant at reassembling Humpty-Dumpty from the fragments of shattered units. When the British investigated 377 prisoners taken at Velletri near Rome, they were surprised to find that they were drawn from fifty different companies belonging to several regiments and even divisions. Field Marshal Alexander knew his enemy's virtues all too well: '[he] is quicker than we are: quicker at regrouping his forces, quicker at thinning out on a defensive front to provide troops to close the gaps at decisive points, quicker in effecting reliefs, quicker at mounting attacks and counter-attacks, and above all quicker at reaching decisions on the battlefield. By comparison, our methods are often slow and cumbersome, and this applies to all our troops, both British and American.'[88]

It was not simply a matter of better training; the Germans felt they had something to fight against, and something to fight for. Although racial arrogance was part of this, it was not the whole. They thought they represented the superior society, or at any rate one that had improved the prospects of the ordinary working man by curbing and domesticating the plutocrats and expelling the Jews. The British were cynical, decadent colonialists perched on the back of the global everyman from India to Ireland; their French sidekick barely warranted a mention, although in Italy the Germans developed a newfound respect for the Free French forces they had defeated so easily in 1940. Cultural snobbery towards the land of chewing gum, and more racism towards African-Americans and Jews, neutralised the obvious democratic modernity of the GI foe. In Poland and then in the Soviet Union the Germans found plenty of evidence of backwardness in each miserable run-down hovel. In the Soviet Paradise, they encountered deprivation that had long ceased to exist in Germany. As the contemporary Berlin joke put it: 'The first Communists were Adam and Eve. They had no clothes to wear, had to steal apples for food, could not escape the place in which they lived and still thought that they were in paradise.' This German soldier noted, 'The reality of the situation is that in twenty-two years of Communism a salted fish occasionally is for this family the height of luxury.'[89]

Even as the Germans were murdering millions they argued that they were saving German or European civilisation from the godless bloodthirsty hordes that were animated by humanity's ultimate enemy: 'The battle against these subhumans, who've been whipped up into a frenzy by the

Jews, was not only necessary but came in the nick of time. Our Führer has saved Europe from certain chaos. You at home must always keep in mind what would have happened if these hordes had overrun our fatherland. The horror of this is unthinkable,' admonished one soldier. When the Prussian snobs tried to kill Hitler in June 1944, the ordinary soldiers were outraged by this final gasp of a class system they thought Nazism had eradicated. If many British soldiers thought they were fighting for a democratic tomorrow, with better healthcare, education and housing, the Germans believed they had already achieved it under National Socialism.[90]

This is not to argue that German troops were the galvanised machine-men that Ernst Jünger had fantasised about during and after the Great War, although philosophising mumbo-jumbo akin to Jünger's was evident in many diaries and letters. The Germans were no less human than their opponents, although they managed to inflict 50 per cent more casualties on their enemies than they suffered themselves, under all circumstances – in attack or retreat, with or without local numerical, artillery and air superiority. They did this although many of them, particularly on the Eastern Front, reverted to sheer animal survival in the frozen dugouts or urban ruins that were their lot when they settled into defensive winter positions. As Peter Reese put it, for the men freezing in a lonely, snowbound dugout surrounded by trees smashed into jagged stumps, 'Our ideals were oneself, tobacco, food, sleep and the whores of France.'[91] Other consolations included alcohol or the billions of items of field post that flowed back and forth to the *Heimat*, or home. The mail was not an unmixed blessing. For German troops, the relentless Allied bombing of Germany meant that home was no longer an oasis of peace; rather it was a fighting front almost as terrifying as the one they inhabited. In a reversal of the norm, soldiers were instructed to write cheerful letters to families who were enduring one of the most sustained bombing campaigns in modern history.[92]

Not all German soldiers evinced the tenacity for which they were famous. In army rear areas in Russia, some units simply subtracted themselves from the larger picture, settling down as 'slippered soldiers', who ducked and dived while war raged elsewhere, striking deals with the partisans to plunder villages in alternation.[93] By 1943 some of the bronzed, confident men who had tramped through the heat into Russia in June 1941 had become vagrants, dirty and unshaven, desperately trying to keep out the cold with layers of ragged clothing purloined from dead or captured Russians. Only half jokingly the novelist and veteran Heinrich Böll once wrote that lice had cost the German army the war. Soldiers took a keen interest in the insects, discovering that a fresh bandage tied around the neck acted as a magnet for them, as did clean underwear. These men were also plagued by boils and tormented by the blackened flesh that frostbite entails. Had they not unleashed barbarism on an entire continent, one might almost sympathise with them.

War entailed not just violent death but also the nightmare of being seriously wounded. One might dream of just the right sort of wound – the *Heimatschuss* that got one sent home – but the reality was juddering along in a slow Red Cross train, while the stump of a leg turned gangrenous or life bled out through a stomach wound, surrounded by men rendered comatose by head injuries or flailing around in blindness. The horrific casualties on the Eastern Front also meant that that army consisted of a constant churn of relative strangers through regiments disembodied in all but name and heavily populated by ghosts. These may still have borne illustrious regional identities, but the men passing through them were a mixture of raw recruits and the gathered-up survivors of formations that had been annihilated. Thus while there was still an 18th Panzer Division in December 1941, it actually consisted of only four battalions, roughly four thousand men rather than a notional eighteen thousand.[94] Given the desperate circumstances of the average *Landser*, it might seem surprising that more did not just throw in the towel, but there were powerful reasons why they did not. Some fifteen thousand soldiers were executed for various offences, mainly desertion, and many more were incarcerated in the Wehrmacht's jail at Torgau-Fort Zinna and its satellite prisons, or in the bleak penal camps on the moors around Emden. Some twenty-seven thousand men from military jails were also impressed into the '500' penal battalions which were used to clear minefields or to shift enemy corpses.[95]

That desertion was infrequent, despite front-line broadcasts by German deserters and Communists designed to encourage it, was due to well-founded fear of the 'Asiatic' enemy, and the knowledge of how the Germans themselves treated Soviet deserters. There was also a guilty awareness that they deserved no mercy, and that if they gave way the Mongol Swarm of Nazi propaganda would slaughter and rape its way into their *Heimat*. The mild-looking Peter Reese almost casually recorded how his colleagues had used rifle butts to smash in the head of a farmer who tried to resist the theft of bread, eggs and honey, and had then shot his wife and burned down his house.[96] According to Omer Bartov, not a few fought on because of their near-religious faith in the wonder-working Führer, who might save the day at any moment, a faith bolstered by the imposition of the death penalty on those who so much as murmured criticism of the political leadership in the hearing of a stranger in his unit, placed there as the only way of detecting such sentiments.[97]

CHAPTER 15

Massacring the Innocents

I COMMAND STAFF REICHSFÜHRER-SS

When the 8th Company of the 8th SS Infantry Regiment entered a village in Russia in 1941, an SS platoon leader called Alois Knäbel was informed by the village head man of the existence of a Jewish cobbler and his wife, a young couple in their mid-twenties with a three-year-old child. Knäbel had the pair brought to him by his troopers, and told them to wash and scrub the company's quarters. As they did so, he frequently knocked them down with a wooden club. After they had finished cleaning, Knäbel and two or three of his men escorted the couple to the edge of the village, where he shot them both in the back of the neck. He was holding their child by the hand at the time. When the child started screaming, Knäbel picked it up, and stroked the child's hair, uttering soothing words. He used his free hand to shoot the child in the neck, as his left hand cradled it to his chest. One of the SS spectators said, 'Look and see, how finely Knäbel did that, how he first calmed the child down and then shot it.'[1]

Knäbel's unit was one of the Waffen-SS regiments which comprised the Command Staff Reichsführer-SS. We have seen some of its constituent elements, notably units from the Death's Head (Totenkopf) Formation, operating in Poland after the September 1939 invasion, where they and others were responsible for murdering tens of thousands of Polish Christians and Jews. The Command Staff itself was established by Himmler in April 1941 and consisted of around 18,500 men who operated as motorised infantry and two cavalry formations. Their commander was a highly decorated Great War colonel called Kurt Knoblauch, a short stocky fellow aged forty-five in 1941, with the demeanour of a pastry cook who enjoyed his own product. Most of his officers were middle-class, middle-aged National Socialists, many of them veterans of the imperial army or the inter-war Freikorps, where they got their first taste of killing civilians. One had participated in Hitler's 1923 putsch, while another had joined the Nazi Party a year earlier. The other ranks were men aged between twenty-six and thirty, with similar levels of long-standing ideological commitment, as reflected in membership of the SS Verfügungstruppe or the Death's Head Formation, guard units stationed near the major concentration camps. Four of them had committed arson or murder in the course of the November 1938 pogrom known as *Kristallnacht*.[2]

The four mobile Einsatzgruppen A, B, C and D, bulked out by men from Reserve Police Battalions 9 and 3, had murdered adult Jewish males (who comprised 90 per cent of their victims) since the start of the Russian campaign. The additional deployment of the Command Staff Reichsführer-SS, as well as further battalions of Order Police and indigenous Baltic or Ukrainian militia units, was needed once it had been decided to kill women and children too. It is not hard to discern ultimate authorship of this infernal project from a flurry of movement and meetings, none recorded on paper, even as the executants of the orders were allowed much creative leeway. Himmler visited these units in early July 1941, telling the 1st Cavalry Regiment that they would be riding as far as the Urals in this campaign. On the 8th he conferred with Knoblauch in Białystok, even as three thousand Jewish men were being shot on the town's periphery by Police Battalions 316 and 322.

On 10 July Himmler formally attached his Command Staff troops to the Higher SS and Police Leaders (Russia), who had a closer understanding of local conditions. These were Friedrich Jeckeln, Hans-Adolf Prützmann and Erich von dem Bach-Zelewski. From then on they would be the competing pace-setters in mass murder. A meeting Hitler held on 16 July 1941 with Bormann, Göring, Keitel, Reich Chancellery chief Hans Lammers and Rosenberg was notably frank in tone, even by their standards, since the Führer remarked that the war against partisans 'had its advantages, it affords us the possibility of exterminating anything that opposes us'. Himmler had lunch with Lammers and Rosenberg the following day, deciding shortly afterwards to deploy the Command Staff troops in the fight against partisans. Just before their deployment in the Pripet Marshes, Himmler flew into Baranowicze to emphasise the need for 'unbending hardness, harsh intervention, and adherence to the great thoughts of the Führer'. As they entered the marshes the men were reminded of alleged attacks by Jews on German military ambulances or the mutilation of downed Luftwaffe pilots, while being informed that the intention was to liquidate the Jews.[3]

The Waffen-SS Cavalry Brigade consisted of two regiments, mainly recruited from the Death's Head Formation mounted units. The brigade commander was Hermann Fegelein. The 1st SS Cavalry Regiment, led by Gustav Lombard, aged forty-six at the time, traced a more northerly route than the mounted section of the 2nd SS Cavalry, under the former wartime cavalry trooper and peacetime riding-school instructor Franz Magill.

Lombard had an unusual background for a man who looked so comfortable in his SS uniform. He had been born on a country estate in eastern Germany to well-to-do parents. In 1913 he was sent to the US to meet his American relatives. He spent the war at a high school, before reading modern languages at the University of Maryland. After dropping out for lack of funds, he then trained as a banker. After returning to Germany he worked for American Express and Chrysler, before setting up in Berlin as a car salesman in 1931. He married an opera singer, with whom he had a son. Lombard joined the Nazi Party and SS after Hitler had come to power, fabricating a history of political persecution – he falsely claimed to have been interned in the US – which enabled him to rise fast in the organisation despite having missed 'the time of struggle'. That he had opinions on Jews can be gauged from his insistence that his men attend screenings of Veit Harlan's nasty film *Jud Süss*. Otherwise 'Papa' Lombard, as they called him, was no martinet. The younger Magill also had a reputation for being rather slack.[4]

Under Lombard's command the 1st Cavalry Regiment killed two thousand Jews in Chomsk in Byelorussia on 2 August, by machine-gunning them into prepared graves. In Motole, which they reached next, the Jews made the mistake of laughing at Germans they thought were fleeing a Russian offensive. However, they were just the advance guard of Lombard's unit, who in their camouflage uniforms did not have the demeanour of defeat. Eight hundred male Jews were herded in to the market place while 2,200 women and children were confined in a synagogue and neighbouring school. Thirty fit young men were selected to dig ditches in a nearby wood and then shot. The eight hundred men were also shot, some of them having had their hiding places betrayed by Christian children to whom the SS cavalrymen gave sweets. After a night's rest, the SS turned their attention to the women and children. They were marched out of town, ordered to undress and then mowed down with machine guns hidden in bushes. The SS went back to Motole to winkle out any hidden survivors, whom they killed; they then left, but not before sitting down to lunch. Bach-Zelewski, or von dem Bach as he preferred to be known, to obliterate the Slavic element of his name, flew in by Fieseler Storch to hear what Lombard had done and to urge him to continue.

Bach-Zelewski was a scion of an old Prussian gentry family, who aged fifteen had volunteered to serve in the imperial army. In 1915 he was wounded in the shoulder, and three years later he was badly gassed; he won the Iron Cross 1st and 2nd Class and continued in the post-war army as a lieutenant. After re-entering civilian life in 1924, he founded a successful taxi business, which four years later enabled him to purchase a substantial country estate, where he lived with his wife and six children. Having joined the SS, he was directly responsible for murdering two jailed Communists in 1933 and for helping two of his SS men to flee after they had murdered an imprisoned Social Democratic Party official. After the Nazi seizure of power, when he was elected to the Reichstag as a Nazi deputy, Bach-Zelewski organised the abduction, torture and murder of two brothers who had knifed a member of the Hitler Youth in a brawl. As a practised political murderer, he used the 1934 Röhm revolt, as it was styled, to kill Rittmeister Anton von Hohberg und Buchwald, 'the best showjumper east of the Elbe', because despite his SS membership the Rittmeister had been offended when at a conference an SS officer had said the SS would fight the army if ordered. After General von Reichenau had rebuked Himmler in the sharpest manner, Hohberg's card was marked; two of Bach-Zelewski's men shot him dead outside his country house. Bach-Zelewski, who remained a Reichstag deputy until 1945, was well accustomed to murder long before he got down to slaughtering Jews.[5]

After a few days during which Lombard's men roamed around shooting small groups of Jews wherever they found them, at dawn on 5 August they surrounded a small town called Telechany. As they ordered the Jews to assemble, the SS burned the town library, while forcing Jews to sing and dance in time with a piano they had dragged on to the street. The SS spent the rest of the day shooting all two thousand Jews in a nearby wood. Over the following days the cavalrymen shot several hundred Jews in smaller places before alighting upon Hancewicze, where they murdered another 2,500 Jews. In his concluding report, Lombard spoke of heavy fighting, although miraculously only one of his troopers had sustained a minor injury, in what Lombard alleged were engagements that had left 411 Red Army soldiers dead. He probably meant men who had tried to surrender and been shot. His maths was not good either, since he claimed his men had killed 6,504 Jews in the preceding fortnight, whereas the real number was more like nine thousand. Probably his roaming squads simply lost count, or did not bother to report their progress on their notoriously erratic radios.

Meanwhile, Franz Magill was in the dog-house and would be removed from his command. Something had gone wrong the moment his regiment split into roving squadrons, for Magill received a radio message: 'Express order from the Reichsführer-SS. All Jews to be shot. Jewish females to be driven into the swamps.' The modest numbers of Jews they reported caught, shot or drowned seemed to indicate a lack of enthusiasm for the task – something Magill's SS superiors had already noted on his personnel file in 1940. These allegedly unenthusiastic murderers rounded up and shot five hundred Jewish men in Janów, before riding into Borobice and Lohiszyn for further massacres. On reaching Pinsk, which had a large Jewish population, they put up posters requiring Jewish men aged between sixteen and sixty to report for labour duties. They locked up two hundred hostages to ensure the men appeared. The thousands of Jews who did muster the following day came with packages of sandwiches. They were marched out of Pinsk in columns (the SS cavalry rode down and shot fugitives) and shot in batches of twenty into ditches. In his obligatory midday radio report, Magill said they had shot 2,461 men so far. Bach-Zelewski flew in for a briefing. By the time Magill had made his evening report, another 2,300 Jews had been shot. Unfortunately for his career, this was inaccurately recorded as the day's final tally, as the earlier figure reported was not included. In the following days Magill's men combed through Pinsk, this time looking for boys under sixteen and men over sixty, as well as any mature men who had eluded their grasp. This meant another 2,400 male Jews were shot. After leaving Pinsk, the cavalrymen carried out further massacres in six small towns they passed through; in Dawidgorodek they shot a further two thousand men, while local Christians drove Jewish women from the town. In his final report on his unit's mission, Magill said that he had tried to drown Jewish women and children but that the swamps they were driven in to were too shallow for this purpose. It was his failure to kill women and children that was the real black mark against him, although poor accounting and communications gave his 2nd Regiment a recorded tally of only 6,450 rather than the fourteen thousand men they had actually murdered.[6]

Lombard had demonstrated that it was possible to kill women and children as well as male Jews. He was even asked to lecture senior army officers on the theme 'Fighting Partisans', during which he remarked, 'It is superfluous even to say a further word about the Jews,' which was too true in his case. For such actors these murders were career opportunities. As a mark of favour, Lombard was invited to a very special lunch on 14 August in Baranowicze. The other guests included Hermann Fegelein, the senior SS cavalry commander, the army's General Max von Schenckendorff, Bach-Zelewski and Himmler, who flew in with his chief of staff Karl Wolff and Hans-Adolf Prützmann, his Higher SS and Police leader in Latvia, for the occasion. Lombard was promoted shortly afterwards.

After the lunch Himmler set off for Minsk, stopping on the way at Lachowicze to be warmly greeted by the SS cavalry brigade stationed there. A German army pioneer had allowed an SS sergeant to sit writing a letter to his wife on a sunny balcony, while a hundred Jews toiled in the summer heat below. The SS man noted the arrival of a fleet of limousines and hastened outside to watch. Himmler spent about half an hour conferring with his SS subordinates and talking to the men who gathered around him. The SS man returned to the pioneer's quarters in a state of high excitement: 'Now things are getting going, the Jews are really going to have their arses torn out.' The SS man told the army man that Himmler had been instructed by Hitler to exterminate all Jews, so as not to make the same mistake as in Poland where the ghettos the Germans had established were a breeding ground for diseases.

That night Himmler reached Minsk and conferred with senior SS officers. He had a photographer in his entourage and the following morning men from Einsatzkommando 8 organised a demonstration shooting of a hundred 'partisans', actually Jewish men and two women. Contemplating their mass grave, Himmler noticed movement and said 'Lieutenant, shoot that one!' Afterwards he addressed the men of the Einsatzkommando, expressing understanding for the emotional burden they bore and confirming that all Jews were to be exterminated. In the afternoon he visited a POW camp and went for a drive through the Minsk ghetto. His final port of call was a psychiatric hospital, where, five weeks later, a police unit gassed the 120 patients. It may be that the untidiness of the shootings he had observed led him to order the use of other methods. On 16 August he flew to Hitler's HQ at Rastenburg, where over lunch the following day he reported on the progress of the project.[7]

On 12 August Himmler had rebuked Friedrich Jeckeln for his unit's less than impressive performance, and told him to put his foot down harder on the accelerator, for what has come to be called the Holocaust was like a journey with a choice of speeds.[8] The West Ukrainian town of Kamenetz-Podolsk had a large indigenous Jewish population swollen by Jewish refugees driven out of the Carpatho-Ukraine by the Hungarians. This doubling of the town's Jewish population, to about thirty thousand, severely strained the logistic arrangements of the local army authorities, ultimately a problem for General Karl von Roques, head of the Army Group South rear area and younger brother of (General) Franz von Roques. He and Jeckeln had much in common, and indeed had lunch together every day. Roques had been a captain in the Great War and had won the Iron Cross 1st and 2nd Class; Jeckeln had been a lieutenant and won the Iron Cross 2nd Class.[9]

After the Great War, Jeckeln married well, although he fell out with his father-in-law whose country estate he administered, and messily divorced his wife. The man was called Hirsch. Although he was not Jewish, from this point on Jeckeln conceived a violent animosity towards Hirsch's 'typically' Jewish characteristic of extracting the alimony his daughter and their three children were entitled to. Charlotte Hirsch-Jeckeln's complaints to all and sundry did not impede her ex-husband's SS career: in 1933 he became head of the police in Brunswick, five years later Higher SS and Police Leader Central Germany.[10]

Between 26 and 28 August, Jeckeln and what he grandiosely called his own Command Staff murdered most of the Jews in Kamenetz-Podolsk. He used fifty or sixty men from his own SS guard, as well as well as novices from Order Police Battalion 320, which consisted of career and volunteer policemen. Every single shooter was a volunteer – although he did not question the operation, police Captain Scharway said he could not order anyone to shoot. One policeman said that what was planned contravened the Hague Protocols on Land Warfare and that he could not reconcile killing defenceless people with his conscience. He was told to report sick. Many of the shooters vomited, either because of the blood and brains flying around or because they had consumed too much schnapps. Jeckeln, by contrast, was in his element. He made a Jew wave a red flag over the site of a massacre before personally shooting him in the head, and told his men, 'That is a typical Jew, whom we must exterminate so that we Germans can survive.' He developed a new technique of packing down layers of victims to make the best use of the excavated space. By the final day they had murdered 23,600 people.[11] In October 1941 Himmler swapped Jeckeln with Prützmann as Higher SS and Police Leader in Northern Russia and within a month of his arrival Jeckeln had liquidated twenty-eight thousand people from the Riga ghetto in woods near Rumbuli station.

II 'PUTATIVE EMERGENCY'

In this manner 2.9 million Jews were killed by men standing a few feet away from them, for there was nothing 'factory-like' or 'industrial' about how these people were killed. Nor were the killers exclusively German, whether Reich, Austrian or ethnic. Many others were involved, notably Letts, Estonians, Lithuanians, Rumanians and Ukrainians. About thirty or forty thousand Ukrainians participated, most of them auxiliary policemen, but also the so-called Trawniki (named after their training camp) who manned the main extermination camps. While this militates against the idea of a uniquely murderous German anti-Semitism, Daniel Goldhagen was surely right to reject the overly bloodless, sociological manner in which a generation of academics wrote about these crimes, attributing them to 'modernity' or structural dynamics that minimised individual human agency or malice.[12] There is not a single recorded instance of any German mass murderer being sanctioned in any formal sense for refusing to participate in what were voluntary activities. Witnesses in post-war German trials who testified that SS or policemen were executed or sent to concentration camps for refusing to obey orders were all subsequently shown to have committed perjury.

Lawyers for the minority of SS men and policemen who faced post-war prosecution more usually invoked the defence of putative emergency. This meant that their clients had *imagined* something untoward *might* happen to them if they refused orders, although nothing ever did, at least as far as every trial conducted by the Allies or the Germans has revealed in the last sixty years and more. The purpose of the putative-emergency argument was to shift the emphasis away from the massive evidence of willed criminality and sadism on the part of the perpetrators. Nobody gave any orders at any time to rob and rape the victims, nor did they tell anyone to brain an infant against a tree or wall rather than shooting it. Men did that because they felt like it.[13] The following story gives the flavour of that time and place, where the absence of a legal framework had created what many dubbed 'the Wild East'. On the night of 28 April 1942, Heinrich Hamann, head of the Security Police detachment in the

West Galician town of Neu-Sandez, organised a party to celebrate the killing that day of three hundred 'Jewish Communists'. After several beers, Hamann came up with the idea of continuing their rave-up (*Remmi-Demmi* in German) with a visit to the Jewish ghetto. There, in pitch darkness, Hamann and his police associates killed twenty people, many of them women and children asleep in their beds. In the process Hamaan also shot dead his own deputy, but he evaded any disciplinary consequences by claiming that in the dark he thought the man was a fleeing Jew.[14]

The truth of the matter was that the overriding concern with operational smoothness meant that anyone who did not want to kill did not have to do so, although obviously there were times when changes of personnel were made to suit circumstances where the wishes of an individual were not considered. It is specious to distinguish between supposedly hardened ideologues in the SD Einsatzgruppen and the 'ordinary men' of mobile police battalions. The former units were bulked out with many ordinary policemen, and besides, policemen in a police state were far from ordinary. They would already have accustomed themselves to blameless members of the public being cast outside the ambit of the law, while through ideological instruction and image the police had been gradually refashioned in the universally belligerent mould of the SS. Many of them belonged to the SS and wore its runes on their tunics and helmets.[15]

A former member of Police Battalion 322, which shot some eleven thousand people before May 1942, recalled that he was able to ask his NCOs if he could be put on guard duty rather than shoot people. After a couple of similar requests the NCOs tacitly agreed that he would not participate directly, although guard duty, like carrying ammunition or the tea urn, also enabled the operation to run smoothly. The only negative consequences for this man were that he had to work longer hours.[16] There were also instances of men having some sort of nervous collapse under the strain of killing people, such as Martin Mundschütz, a member of Einsatzkommando 12, which with others murdered five thousand Jews in Nikolajew in September 1941. It became too much for Mundschütz, who got the unit medic to declare him unfit for duty. Depressed at being called 'an Austrian layabout' by his colleagues, he sought a meeting with Einsatzgruppe D's commander, Otto Ohlendorf, to discuss a transfer home, and wrote a letter before their meeting to set out all his reasons. He was having horrible delusions day and night, he wrote, which resulted in constant weeping. Although he had been reassigned to requisitioning provisions, he did not believe it helpful to have a crying soldier hiding in alleys and doorways to avoid his comrades. He wanted a rest, from which he promised to return to duty fully restored. In the event, he was sent to the SS psychiatric clinic in Munich, after which he rejoined the Criminal Police in Innsbruck in his Austrian homeland.[17] Even the top police commanders were not immune to breakdowns. In February 1942 Bach-Zelewski underwent an intestinal operation in Karlsbad which did not heal. This brought on a depression during which he was plagued by nightmarish visions of the killings of Jews in the east.[18]

The problem of dissent hardly ever arose, because, as a member of the 8th SS Infantry Regiment testified: 'there were always enough volunteers'. When a company leader from a related unit asked for men to shoot Jews, all but one took a step forward. The worst that happened to him was that a few people avoided him and the company leader called him 'an old sod'. In some units, the older men tended to volunteer, in an inversion of what we have seen in the case of most combat units. How many claimed sickness on the day or contrived to busy themselves doing something else, like one SS man who broke the bolt-action mechanism in his rifle, we cannot know. But these were exceptions and the great majority willingly stepped forward. Why? Both deep-seated eliminatory anti-Semitism in German society and group psychological dynamics, potentially applicable to all societies, have been used to explain what happened. While there is evidence of both aplenty – often drawn from rival readings of the same sources – there is perhaps another way of looking at it.[19]

III HEINOUSLY MORAL ACTS

The great historian of the Holocaust Raul Hilberg once said that if the Final Solution had depended on orders it would never have happened, by which he meant that the full-blown phenomenon evolved from impulses and creative initiatives interacting from above and below, combining both Berlin centre, Hitler's or Himmler's field HQ and special trains, and the far-flung peripheries of the Nazi empire. It also consisted of waves of murderous aggression, so that after the initial sweep eastwards, the Jews who had been placed in ghettos or retained as labour were in turn murdered by locally based security police and dedicated mobile units, or in the industrialised facilities of Chelmno and the three Aktion Reinhard death camps of Belzec, Sobibor and Treblinka. Death moved back and forth like the action of a weaving machine or scythe, tightening the density of the detail and cutting a bit lower to the ground. For example, long after the initial forward sweeps of the Einsatzgruppen, the Command Staff Reichsführer-SS and the independent Order Police battalions, between May and October 1942 around seven hundred thousand Jews were killed in a more detailed operation in East Galicia, West Volhynia and Podolia.[20]

While there were notorious haters of Jews, or *Juden-Fresser*, who often set the tone in these units, the role of anti-Semitism was not as straightforward as it sometimes seems to Jews. The crimes often involved individuals spotting opportunities to 'go shopping with a pistol' as one policeman put it, perhaps for a fur coat for a girlfriend at home, or to rape Jewish girls whose parents they had shot and who would be murdered themselves to get rid of the evidence. Anti-Semitism defined the victim group, but it also provided a pretext to cover acts of murder that were ancillary to robbery or rape. Anti-Semitism does not explain the equally matter-of-fact way in which these men killed non-Jews, like the elderly Polish Catholics shot by Reserve Battalion 101 after a rumour circulated that a policeman had been killed. After shooting the old people, the unit burned their homes and then returned to the cinema in Opole where their R&R had been interrupted. Reserve Battalion 101 included fourteen Luxemburgers and relied on Ukrainian farm boys to do the really dirty work for them. The anti-Semitic depredations of non-German collaborators have since become notorious.[21]

It is important to situate what these men thought they were doing. Murdering Jews was neither legal nor a crime, but something beyond both; it was a historic deed, mission or task, to be recorded on buried tablets of iron. That is why one SS-Scharführer insisted that his participation in murder (he called them executions) be recorded in his paybook and personnel file, while another claimed that the high body count he had achieved justified the award of the Kriegsverdienstkreuz, one of Germany's highest military medals.[22] The grim reality of this was apparent to the German labour official who encountered a very drunk member of the Gestapo as he entered one of the recreational German House bars in Nowy Targ, or Neumarkt as it had become. He had a beer mat attached to his tunic, on which he had scrawled '1,000' in red ink. He announced in a drunken slur: 'Man, I'm celebrating the thousandth shot in the neck.' 'Charming' said the official. The drunk wandered past, remarking that he'd shoot his own father if he was ordered to.[23]

The drunken-murderer incident raises an important issue. The notion of a moral crime is superficially tautological. It becomes clearer if one recalls post-war prosecutors asking these men whether, if ordered, they would also have shot their own children, to which the response was indignantly negative. Since that suggests they retained a sense of crime and wrongdoing, how did they reconcile this with their own heinous actions?

If the killing of the Jews could be entirely independent of orders, it utterly depended on the perpetrators *retaining a sense of morality*, however perverse that might seem. This morality was based on a pseudo-scientific belief in the absolute inequality of the human races, which accorded the higher race (the Germans) the absolute right to rule lesser races, and to eliminate the Jewish race which they believed posed an existential threat. Killing the Jews was a mission with which this generation was burdened, on behalf of future Germans as yet unborn. Like a crime, the deed had to be kept secret and referred to in euphemistic terms, not because it was a crime but because the general population was not at a sufficiently advanced stage of consciousness to comprehend the necessity for what evidently lacked the sanction of law. It was as if the killers found themselves participating in something detached from everyday reality, like a movie, except that it ran for months and years. The fact that these men laughed when the German press denounced the NKVD 'crimes' discovered at Katyń suggests that they knew they were living in a world apart. Once it seemed certain that Germany would lose the war, the prospect of retribution dispersed their sense of apartness, and with it the illusion that the revolting crimes they had committed were high-minded historic deeds.[24]

After participating in shooting two hundred Jews, including Germans whom he knew, one perpetrator remarked: 'Man alive, damn it, a generation has to go through this, so that things will be better for our children.'[25] Thus post-conventional morality helped the individual killer deal with any manifestations of weakness in his own character, weakness largely derived from the traditional, universal morality that Nazism had transcended. This separation of personal feelings was akin to that of a surgeon, with the major difference that these surgeons were operating on the human race. Provided that central new moral fact was understood, the individual could accommodate as much conventional morality as he (or she) liked.[26] This helped rationalise what were no longer acts of murder. Hence, the emphasis on the retention of decency and respectability (or *Anständigkeit* in German), despite the horrors, which recurred in several of Himmler's addresses to his senior commanders. From top to bottom *the perpetrators became victims.*

'*I was deeply shocked*', Himmler confided in early 1943, 'by this order, [which clears up several issues] since it burdened the most loyal of the Führer's supporters with a historical mortgage of monstrous proportions … I suffered a lot under this order and know, no matter what comes, what it signifies for the SS.'[27] Killing was an emotional and moral test which the killers had to overcome: 'we're making great strides, without pangs of conscience', said one policeman. In other addresses, Himmler insisted that his men would not steal a single cigarette from the victims. Retention of a sense of right and wrong was important to men who prided themselves on not being murderers; they also knew the meaning of honour, since the SS men had 'my honour is loyalty' inscribed on their belt buckles. A regimental clerk in Lombard's 1st Cavalry Regiment disapproved of a corporal who each week asked for stamps to post five or six packets home, unlike his fellows who only sent a maximum of two. He decided to open one of the packets and found gold rings and earrings stolen from Jews the corporal had shot.[28] Heinz Seetzen, the head of Einsatzkommando 10a, was a fanatic philatelist, who spent his spare time breaking into Russian post offices and private houses to expand his collection. His obsession was taken up by his men, who began to steal and swap stamps too. This led to a lengthy SS disciplinary investigation in Berlin, at which Seetzen was reprimanded; the mitigating circumstances cited were the conditions of service in the east.[29]

This moral logic was capable of far greater contortions than that of thieves who claimed that the Jews they killed had been looters. Whenever Germans were thin on the gound, they preferred to foist the job of killing children on Ukrainian auxiliary policemen.[30] Where killing children was unavoidable, some bizarre justifications emerged. A thirty-five-year-old member of Order Police Battalion 101 specialised in shooting children, next to a colleague who always shot their mothers, on the grounds that it was not right to leave the children alone in this world: 'To a certain extent it salved my conscience to release children who would be unable to live without their mothers.'[31] In two infamous speeches to senior SS and army figures later in the war, Himmler claimed that the children had to be killed, for otherwise they might grow up and take revenge on the Germans. When a Jewish woman offered Erwin Denker gold and jewellery to spare her life, he regretfully 'tried to make clear to the Jewess [Denker's phrase] that I couldn't help her. In such a case I had to reckon with a lot of bother.' In the last chapter we noticed how the collective moral mind of US combat troops could make cutting off the ears of Japanese dead seem normal. Something like that happened here, but often in reverse. What German lawyers call 'excess perpetrators', meaning drunk Ukrainian militiamen who threw babies in the air as clay pigeons and Herbert Kindl who sat down on the back of a naked, dead Jewish woman to enjoy his lunch, were morally and psychologically useful to the average shooter, by allowing him the illusion that at least he had retained a vestigial decency by merely going about his tasks in a conscientious workmanlike manner.[32]

The cliques that formed within these units (which could number between five hundred and a thousand men) were also useful, for everyone could find their temperamental niche, and the various niches, for the cynics, laggards or fanatics, enabled the whole to function. A unit consisting solely of psychopaths and sadists would not be efficient. That was apparent to the Highest SS and Police Court, which convicted one Obersturmbannführer in 1943 for murdering hundreds of Jews – by then the SS had killed millions – because he was responsible for 'such an evil brutalisation of his men ... that they conducted themselves like a wild horde. The men's discipline was so badly put at risk by the accused that it is almost impossible to imagine.' After a period serving in Einsatzgruppe D, Lothar Heimbach succumbed to post-traumatic stress. The former member of the Dortmund Gestapo had got a little above himself in the east. One day in 1944 he got incredibly drunk, lurching through the streets of Białystok raving at passing soldiers and civilians 'that he was Lord of life and death ... if he was ordered to shoot three hundred children, he'd shoot 150 of them himself'. He was sentenced to ten months' imprisonment for damaging the image of the SS, which was converted into transfer to the front.[33]

One way of retaining a veneer of apparent decency was to kill in an apparently orderly military fashion. This gave these various types of policemen the illusion that they were soldiers. Initially, some of the Einsatzgruppen attempted to give murder a patina of legality by pronouncing sentences no court had delivered. A day after the invasion of Russia, men from the Tilsit Gestapo post shot two hundred Jews and Communists in Gardsen in Lithuania. The group leader took out his sabre and announced, 'You are to be shot by order of the Führer for offences against the German armed forces.' After six days the unit gave up the pretence. More typically they now told Jews to dig their graves more quickly: 'Get on with it, Isidor, you'll soon be with your God.'[34] They started

Babi Yar

by lining up their victims in front of the graves in the manner of firing squads, but in too many cases this required the SS officers to deliver the *coup de grâce* with their pistols. Next, they tried shooting standing victims from close behind, only to find that brains, blood and bits of skull flew back into their faces. After technical discussions in earshot of the next line of victims, it was deemed easier to shoot people kneeling or lying down within the graves, which minimised the first difficulty while making for a tidier body disposal. Reserve Battalion 101's doctor actually traced an outline of a torso on the ground and then explained how to use the bayonet attached to a rifle to measure the right distance to shoot someone in the neck.[35] Shooting people in a trench also prevented victims from leaping in and feigning death, a problem that had occurred with the firing-squad technique. Killing children raised the dilemma of whether to shoot the child or mother first, generally resolved in favour of killing the child first, since the traumatised mothers would be less trouble than a hysterical child and might even be relieved that their child did not have to see them die.

In other words, killing people became a job of work in which the killer could take a craftsman's pride. This shortened the moral distance, and enabled killing to become routine. Problems with defective equipment were as common as in the army. For example, because the barrels of German sub-machine guns overheated too quickly and were hard to handle, many shooters preferred to use the more reliable Russian version. Like any working day, there were necessary intervals for rest and recuperation. One Einsatzkommando had tea breaks, while their victims shuddered in anticipation, although this unit thought it poor taste that the tea was accompanied by canned blood sausage. Another welcome distraction, especially for operations like Babi Yar which took days to accomplish, was the arrival of the mobile field kitchen with warm food and special rations of schnapps for the shooters. Babi Yar was like a vast open-air amphitheatre, with good viewing points for the sort of people who like to slow down to look at car accidents. Army onlookers dressed in shorts or watching from a distance with binoculars were welcome, since this further contributed to the perpetrators' sense of moral normality, although taking photographs was rapidly discouraged. A Reserve Battalion 101 officer who took his pregnant new bride along to his workplace was widely thought to have gone too far. Comradely get-togethers and excursions were laid on to maintain group spirit. At one of these sessions on 10 January 1942 a Berlin policeman recited to his colleagues in Reserve Police Battalion 9, attached to Einsatzgruppe D, a lengthy piece of doggerel which charted the group's progress to the Crimea where: 'From Yalta to Sevastopol / and round about to Simferopol / we wreaked havoc like the Titans / really powerful. And finally the partisans really got it nicely / right in their big arseholes / And the Jews and Krimshacks quickly learned nut-cracking too. / So the fight raged on every front / we were omnipresent / gladly showing what we could do / and no one fired to miss.'[36]

The public nature of these spectacles, news of which filtered back to Germany as rumour or in letters the killers wrote to colleagues, friends and relatives, combined with the psychological stresses on the perpetrators to ensure that new methods had to be found before the larger project of killing all European Jews could be realised. The impetus came from Hitler who on 22 July 1941 confided in his soul-mate the Croatian Marshal Slavko Kvaternik: 'if even just one state for whatever reasons tolerates one Jewish family in it, then this will become the bacillus source for a new decomposition. If there were no more Jews in Europe, then the unity of the European states would no longer be destroyed. Where one will send the Jews, to Siberia or Madagascar, is all the same. He [Hitler] would approach each state with this demand.'[37] A warped epidemiology combined with a utopian vision of harmony: the world's problems would disappear if the Jews vanished.

Hitler had been confident that the destruction of the Soviet Union could be accomplished very rapidly. Once that confidence proved misplace, his expressed thoughts about the Jews became more primitively vengeful, although among historians no consensus reigns about when, or if, he took a single decision to murder them all.[38] On the evening of 25 October 1941 he told Himmler and Heydrich:

From the rostrum of the Reichstag I prophesied to Jewry that, in the event of war's proving inevitable, the Jew would disappear from Europe. That race of criminals has on its conscience the two million dead of the First World War, and now already hundreds of thousands more. Let nobody tell me that all the same we can't park them in the marshy parts of Russia! Who's worrying about our troops? It's not a bad idea, by the way, that public rumour attributes to us a plan to exterminate the Jews. Terror is a salutary thing.[39]

Translation seldom conveys the wandering, raving nature of his utterances as well as this.

Hitler was perhaps the most extreme but by no means the only exponent of the dualistic view that divides mankind into good and evil, that reduces individuals to culpable groups, and that sees the solution to the problems of mankind in their extermination. Robespierre, Stalin, Mao Tsetung, Pol Pot and Bin Laden are just the most famous of his fellow psychotics – thousands, perhaps millions more who thankfully never have the power to influence history console themselves for their personal inadequacies, or seek to explain the failure of their ideologies, by reference to some omnipresent evil force. In Hitler's case, dualism led him to ascribe to the Jews the fact that, thanks to his own errors, he was no longer in control of events. As we saw with the Einsatzgruppen, a multiplier effect developed from the desire of occupation regimes in the German east to make their satrapies free of Jews, a view enthusiastically shared by the Gauleiters in the Reich itself who competed to make their districts *Judenrein*.

IV THE DREGS OF HUMANITY

A key element in any genocidal regime is the empowerment of frustrated, cowardly individuals who in the normal course of events might have committed smaller-scale crimes or none at all, the blackness of their souls hidden from the rest of humanity. The executants of the next stage of mass murder were those sort of people. In the few photographs that exist of them they look shabby in their ill-fitting uniforms, although some – such as Christian Wirth or Kurt Franz – exude a palpable raging violence. These men positively relished beating Jews to death, releasing all their pent-up rage in outbursts that left them as spent as if they had enjoyed coitus. Wirth came from the T-4 euthanasia programme, which had begun in September 1939 and which had shown how a small number of expert and dedicated personnel could kill large numbers of people without most of the demoralising effects that police shooters had experienced. Some T-4 people may have grumbled about their 'shit work', but given that their job was to kill people with mental problems, nervous breakdowns would have been inadvisable. While a modified euthanasia programme called Aktion 14f13 had been extended to the concentration camps, to liquidate sick prisoners, once T-4's initial target of adult psychiatric patients to be killed had been achieved by August 1941 many personnel were available for other assignments. The programme had also developed criminal deception into a

ABOVE: US troops try to make themselves small in an assault boat crossing the Rhine in March 1945. The Americans may have joined the war late, but their troops often displayed outstanding bravery.

BELOW: British combat engineers at a field canteen as they build a bridge over the Rhine in 1945. Such men could easily find themselves under fire in modern warfare.

ABOVE: A 1944 painting by an Australian war artist captures the intractable hell of the Kokoda Track (New Guinea), where they achieved the first major reverse of invading Japanese forces in the Pacific theatre. Dominion troops also fought in several other theatres in a moving demonstration of residual loyalty to the motherland.

ABOVE: German troops savour the fleshpots of occupied Paris, where their presence meant innumerable dilemmas for the locals.

ABOVE: Zarah Leander, the German forces sweetheart, entertaining wounded soldiers.

ABOVE: The comedian and singer Danny Kaye entertains US enlisted men (officers seem to have been banned by popular demand). Tastes were quirky, with Bob Hope or John Wayne being more popular than movie tough-guy Humphrey Bogart.

RIGHT: George Formby, with his cheek and ukulele, was highly popular among British soldiers.

THIS PAGE: German paratroops descending on Crete in 1941. They included some of the toughest troops deployed in the entire war, requiring the efforts of two superpowers (and two European empires) to defeat them.

ABOVE: SS officers and guards from Auschwitz on an R&R trip which was more earthy than listening to Schubert. Commandant Rudolf Höss is the leaning figure in the front row.

LEFT: Staff from the Belzec extermination camp. The gas chambers were dubbed 'the Hackenholt Foundation' in honour of Lorenz Hackenholt (front right), who operated them.

RIGHT: Elderly Jewish men (one has had his beard shaved or torn off) photographed shortly before dying in the Birkenau gas chambers, a fate they shared with babies and infants.

ABOVE: An exhibition of goods produced by captive Jews in the Łódź ghetto, although most of the output consisted of kit for the German armed forces as well as German consumers.

RIGHT: A graphic produced by Nazi economists with 'before and after' views of a Polish economy rationalised by the removal of Jewish middlemen. In fact, the Germans discovered that the Jews were highly productive, although this did not inhibit them from murdering them.

Die Originalbildunterschriften lauten: «In der früher unregulierten Marktordnung stand der Jude als Vermittler der landwirtschaftlichen Erzeugnisse.»

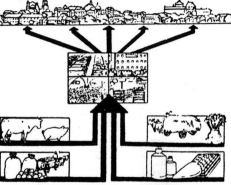

«Jetzt sorgt eine geregelte Marktordnung für die Erfassung und Verteilung der Produktionsgüter.»

LEFT: Arthur Harris, the commander in chief of Bomber Command, in a rare moment of repose with his wife and daughter, providing relief from dread responsibilities which involved a major battle every night of the week. Seventy years too late, a monument is about to be erected to the men of his command, over 55,000 of whom perished in the war.

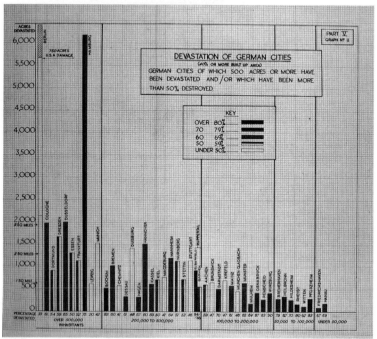

ABOVE: The industrial nature of modern warfare lent itself to cold-blooded statistical extrapolation, which could become an end in itself.

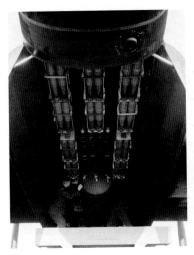

ABOVE: Armourers loading an assortment of high explosive and incendiary ordnance into an Avro Lancaster. The Hanseatic port of Bremen was on the receiving end of this payload in September 1942.

BELOW: Victims of Allied bombing laid out in a school gymnasium at Christmas 1943, hence the incongruous rows of fir trees in the background.

ABOVE: Like Harris, the USAAF's General Curtis LeMay was one of the tougher-minded warriors in the global conflict, responsible for laying waste Tokyo and for the planes which dropped two atom bombs on Hiroshima and Nagasaki. Like Harris, too, LeMay was more complicated than the caricatures of him suggest.

ABOVE: The Vemork hydroelectric plant at Rjukan in Norway, where the Germans produced heavy water for their atomic bomb researches.

BELOW: German and Italian troops arrest civilians in the aftermath of the 13 March 1944 bomb attack on German policemen in Rome's via Rasella. The Germans exacted horrendous reprisals against innocent civilians.

LEFT: Knut Haukelid was one of the Norwegian SOE agents who destroyed the heavy water in an operation that was as daring as it was morally scrupulous of civilian casualties.

higher art, which again would come in useful.[40] The camp model itself would guarantee greater secrecy, especially if the camps were dedicated to extermination and located in remote places in the east where the local authorities were in any case demanding that their Jews disappear.[41] Finally, SS resettlement experts had their own fund of experience in how to uproot and move entire populations.[42]

Late autumn 1941 saw a series of significant technical initiatives which, in hindsight, were conducive to murder on a vaster scale than had been committed already. Experiments with carbon monoxide gas were initially undertaken at the behest of the Einsatzgruppen, after failed experiments such as trying to blow up groups of victims with explosives. Albert Widmann, the chemist who had developed the technology used in the euthanasia programme, joined forces with the chief mechanic in the Security Police motor pool in Berlin to develop a vehicle resembling a furniture-removal truck, into whose air-tight interior exhaust gases could be fed. Meanwhile, at Auschwitz, the commandant experimented on Russian POWs with the pesticide gas Zyklon B, and began the construction of new crematoria which for the first time included purpose-built gas chambers. He also began work on a large camp at Birkenau, initially intended to hold a hundred thousand Russian POWs. The first working gas chamber and crematoria complex, known as Bunker 1, was completed in early 1942. It had originally been intended for Mogilev, to receive Jews deported from the Reich, but the SS scrapped the project because of transport problems in Russia.[43] Bunker 1 could kill eight hundred people at a time, but between June 1942 and June 1943 much larger installations increased the killing capacity to twelve thousand people at a time. In eastern Poland, Odilo Globocnik had the expert services of T-4 veteran Christian Wirth in building experimental gassing facilities at Belzec, although the first effort was not built near a railhead. This was rectified in November 1941. While the work was done by Polish builders, the maintenance of such camps and their personnel was carried out by a small number of Jews, who lived under appalling abuse, before they were also killed.

In the Warthegau, the roving SS euthanasia killer Herbert Lange, who had murdered over five thousand psychiatric patients in northern Poland by shooting or using a gas van bearing the logo Kaisers Kaffee Geschäft, set up at a remote village called Chelmno, whose small baroque manor house was converted into another killing centre. Many of the indigenous Polish inhabitants of the village were expelled and replaced by ethnic Germans.

The Reich Main Security Office in Berlin supplied Lange with three of the modified gassing vans that Widmann had developed. SS surveyors, including the buildings expert Richard Thomalla, selected the small railhead at Sobibor as a suitable location for an extermination camp, although building work did not start until March 1942. Thomalla was also construction chief at Treblinka, the camp designated to murder the occupants of the Warsaw ghetto, throughout July of that year. Clearly, something major was being prepared in several locations.[44]

The January 1942 Wannsee Conference, where the SS initiated a wider pool of senior bureaucrats into its continent-wide project, took an existing killing operation – camps where eventually twenty thousand Jews died while working on Transit Route IV in Galicia – and then generalised it as vague road-building projects on which most Jews would be worked to death, while the biologically tougher survivors would be 'dealt with accordingly', since by natural selection they would otherwise 'form a germ cell from which the Jewish race could regenerate itself (that is the lesson of history)'. There was also passing reference to taking over Soviet Arctic gulags for similar purposes; but the real death camps were situated in Poland, the choice of sites determined by Poland's incredibly fine-meshed rail system that served some very remote locations. This had everything to do with location, including that of Polish Jews, and nothing to do with how pervasive anti-Semitism was in Polish society.[45]

Although less well known than the three other Aktion Reinhard camps, Chelmno was the first to become operational, a demonstration project to show that extermination on such a vast scale was technically feasible. The first killings at Chelmno involved people from the Kolo ghetto, which was only six miles distant. The date was 8 December 1941, the day originally scheduled for the Wannsee Conference, which was postponed to 20 January 1942, and coincidentally the day after the Japanese attack on Pearl Harbor. Kolo's Jews were told to assemble for labour duties and were then driven in trucks to Chelmno. Inside the manorial courtyard, an affable SS officer explained that they were being sent to labour camps in Germany, and that after the squalor of the ghetto they needed to wash and their clothing required disinfection. Leaving their luggage behind, they entered the building, placing valuables in baskets after the name of their owner had been recorded in a ledger. They were shepherded further inside, past signs saying 'to the showers', encouraged to undress, and then herded towards a rear exit where a steep wooden ramp led into the back of a van. After the doors closed, the driver, Gustav Laabs, attached a pipe which fed the exhaust gas into the back of the truck. The engines ran for about fifteen minutes before the truck drove off. After two and a half miles the truck pulled into a series of clearings where there were mass graves and small parties of Jews who had to empty the trucks. These men were shackled at the ankles to prevent flight, and they were shot and replaced each week.[46]

In early January 1942 the first major inroads were made on the 163,000 inmates of the Łódź ghetto, ten thousand of whom were taken to a remote railhead near Chelmno and gassed. We shall follow their journey to that point in the following chapter. A further ten thousand were killed between 22 and 28 February, by which time Lange had been replaced as commandant by Hans Bothmann. In March 24,687 more disappeared, leaving behind those who had frozen to death waiting for the trains at the city's Radogoszcz station. By April nearly forty-five thousand persons had been murdered. In order to deceive future victims, a senior Gestapo officer informed the Łódź Jewish Council that he was the commandant of a giant labour camp near Wartebrücken (Kolo) where a hundred thousand Jews had allegedly been resettled. In May it was the turn of eleven thousand German, Austrian and Czech Jews who in the interim had been deported to Łódź. Over these five months 9,500 people died inside the ghetto from hunger, disease and cold. In conjunction with these major operations, all the Warthegau's smaller ghettos were liquidated except for a residuum of 18,500 Jews, who were temporarily reprieved as slave labour in the main ghetto in Łódź, for the demands of the war economy had not yet been overridden by the Final Solution.

Since the only Jews to remain in Łódź were those who toiled in German factories, anyone superfluous to requirements could go next. In September, the hospitals were emptied, with children thrown out of windows to save time in escorting them downstairs to the waiting trucks. Next the Germans demanded the assembly of all children under ten and adults of retirement age, the total to be twenty-five thousand willy-nilly. Since the fate of those who had been deported was clear to everyone, the Germans could not rely on the Jewish Council to make their selection. Instead they imposed a total curfew and then in combination with Jewish Order Police and even the Jewish fire brigade (all of whose relatives had been placed in safety) raided each apartment block to drag the victims away. The Germans provided the lethal firepower against anyone who fled or offered resistance. Anyone found hiding was shot on the spot. Although Chelmno was used to kill these people, men from an SS unit called Aktion 1005 moved in to disinter and burn the tens of thousands of corpses. Auschwitz Commandant

Rudolf Höss also visited the complex to see how this work was done, and shortly afterwards put in an order to Schriever & Co. of Hanover for a crushing mill for unspecified 'substances'. By March 1943 Himmler decided to close Chelmno and the key facilities were destroyed, although the cellars were left intact. Before their redeployment to Croatia as field policemen attached to the SS Prinz Eugen Division, the Sonderkommando Lange murderers were given a lavish dinner by Gauleiter Artur Greiser in the Riga Restaurant in Kolo. The bill came to RM 237.89, which Greiser readily paid for the men who had made the Warthegau *Judenrein*.

In the following months the German civilian authorities in Łódź – backed by Greiser – conducted a complex dispute with Himmler's SS. While the Łódź officials wished to exploit the labour of the remaining eighty-nine thousand Jews in munitions factories, the SS economic administration sought to transfer them to their own factories, so that the ghetto could be deemed liquidated and an SS concentration camp established there. In the event, Greiser and Hans Biebow, the official responsible for the ghetto, put up a tenacious defence of their local interests and compromise prevailed. The ghetto population would be reduced to the barest minimum needed for the munitions industry, while Bothmann's unit would be brought back from Croatia to murder the rest. There would be no concentration camp. Since his men had wrecked Chelmno before their transfer to Croatia, Bothmann turned to the clearings where the dead had originally been buried. The materials for what he had in mind and the manpower to build it came from the Łódź ghetto. He built two brick crematoria, and wooden barracks, about sixty feet long by thirty wide, where people would undress (hooks were provided for their clothes) before following signs 'to the showers' until driven into the gassing vans.

Some of the Jews used to build the camp were made to write postcards saying what a fine time they were having in Cologne or Düsseldorf, before they were shot in the head. The ruse was designed to counter the forebodings in the Łódź ghetto. Between 23 June and 14 July 1944, some 7,100 Jews were killed in the new extermination centre. In August, with the Red Army sixty miles away, the remaining seventy-one thousand Łódź Jews were deported to Auschwitz, where they were mostly killed on arrival. The Germans remained at Chelmno until the third week of January 1945, when they murdered the remaining prisoner work details who had been engaged in removing yellow Stars of David from the mountains of clothing the camp had accumulated. Two SS men were killed when they entered the barn where these prisoners were confined. Faced with Jews who fought back, Bothmann had the barn burned down rather than risk any more of his men. Two work-detail Jews survived, but the two SS men were the sole German fatalities in a place where at least 150,000 Jews had been murdered.

V EICHMANN'S WORLD

Mass murder was grim work, although those in charge, such as Rudolf Höss at Auschwitz, found it less disturbing than the beatings they had witnessed as junior camp guards in Dachau, scenes so shocking that a public hanging seemed humane by comparison. As the men in charge, they could dull themselves with cognac after each day's labour, as Franz Stangl claimed to do at Sobibor and Treblinka in his revealing prison interviews with Gita Sereny.[47] From time to time the men running these extermination centres had to put on a show when the bosses of mass murder came to call in a flurry of self-importance. The bosses wanted to see method amid the madness, a zealous steadiness of purpose rather than the sadistic excesses that had resulted in the removal of Stangl's predecessors. Stangl would have his white jacket pressed and his riding boots polished – by Jews, for in his world, where he was lord of all he surveyed, enough Jews were kept alive to ensure that the place was spick and span, including landscape gardening around gas chambers. In addition to creating an appearance that belied the camps' function, Stangl was a stickler about proper accounting for money or valuables taken from the Jews, yet another effort to retain vestiges of moral normalcy.[48]

The cliché 'banality of evil' was coined by Hannah Arendt, a US Jewish intellectual who covered the 1961 trial of Adolf Eichmann in Jerusalem.[49] Unfortunately she had little detailed knowledge of how millions of her people had been exterminated, otherwise she might have chosen her words more carefully. While it is true that Eichmann himself worked far from the stench of burning human flesh, surrounded by the familiar smell of offices everywhere, the suggestion that many of those involved in the Final Solution were simply unimaginative clerks has been one of the more persistent alibis used to minimise their whole-hearted participation in the revolting enterprise.

On paper the bosses were hidden behind a welter of acronyms – RMdI, Gestapo, RSHA, RuSHA, RFKDV, WVHA, VoMi, EWZ, HSSPF, SiPo and SD – each sub-divided into anonymous smaller departments such as the

SD's II-112 which mutated into the Reich Main Security Office's (RSHA) desk IV D 4 in early 1940. Letters were cluttered with these markings, along with runes and swastikas, and stamps for 'Top Secret'. The anodyne Desk II-112 was commanded by Eichmann, whose career in despoiling and deporting Jews started with the forced-emigration programme in Vienna, where he and his team set up shop in a palace once owned by the Rothschilds on Prinz-Eugen-Strasse. Their conduct was more malicious than banal as anxious Jews were made to loiter around until they passed through a series of counters, whose effects were exactly like a press squeezing juice out of grapes. There was much verbal abuse. 'What are you?' To which the only answer that did not involve a slap in the face was 'I am a Jewish fraudster, a crook.' 'Very good, very good' came the reply.[50]

After impressing his bosses with the Jews he had 'externally resettled' from Vienna, Eichmann was promoted to head the Reich Main Security Office's desk IV D 4 in Berlin. This was responsible for the external resettlement (*Auswanderung* rather than *Umsiedlung*) of Jews within the much larger ethnic reordering of central Europe that the SS embarked on at the time. It became the nerve centre of the deportation of Europe's Jews to their deaths, handling everything from train scheduling – there was a giant map of Europe's rail network on the wall – to ordering the 'special treatment' of Jews in regular concentration camps, rather than extermination centres. Its offices were in a building formerly used by a Jewish charitable organisation at 115/116 Kurfürstenstrasse in Berlin. It's a nice address – I lived in that street for eighteen months while doing research for my PhD in the late 1970s. Eichmann's office was on the second floor overlooking the rear courtyards. It was big at 2,400 square feet with a desk that was approached across a wide expanse of parquet flooring. All the other floors were occupied by his subordinates, though there was also a communal recreation room and a small library given over to II-112's collection of reference books on Judaica and the Jews. One of the key subordinates was Franz Nowak, who was responsible for liaising with the German railways so that the death trains ran on time. From the very top, via the operations directorate in Warsaw and down to the stationmasters and conductors en route to the death camps, railwaymen knew about what they sometimes called 'soap allocations'.[51]

The Berlin building was quiet except for ringing telephones and the clack-clack and sliding sounds of typewriters. Young women served as secretaries, taking down dictation. They rapidly realised that there were an awfully large number of cases of heart failure or pneumonia among those slated for 'special treatment', for the deception used in the T-4 euthanasia programme was carried over into the murder of Jews. Any initial caution collapsed in the familiarity of the office. 'Well, there goes another one,' remarked one of the SS officers to his secretary of another 'heart failure' case. Another woman listened as a group of men talked about extracting teeth in Auschwitz: 'Look, they don't need those teeth any more, they're dead' was one of the comments. While one SD officer had a momentary lapse into humanity, saying, 'Anyone who's got kids of their own can't do that to someone else's children,' before resuming his dictation deporting them, others were prone to rabid outbursts of bitter anti-Semitic abuse.[52]

Around the headquarters, maintenance work was done by Jews with Aryan partners who were conscripted into service; they glided about while assuming the invisibility of ghosts to avoid abuse and violence. If they encountered any of the SS personnel, they had to face the wall while they passed, or address them from a regulation distance of no less than nine feet. If they did not, Eichmann was wont to scream, 'Pig, stand against the wall when you address me.' Along with the terror within, the desk officers of IV D 4 often sallied out to decimate the ranks of Jews employed at Berlin's Jewish Community self-administration in Oranienburgstrasse. On 26 October 1942 they stormed through the building, with Eichmann's deputy Rolf Günther shouting, 'The time has come to clean out this nest of rats,' a turn of phrase difficult to reconcile with the term 'banality'. They were also a regular bullying presence at the city's Jewish Hospital, where they tried to tug off the Jews' yellow stars in order to create an infraction warranting deportation. The merest glimpse of those approaching SS uniforms (and they chose not to wear civilian suits) spread waves of panic and terror.

They brought death to the Jews of Europe either in person or by telephone. On 13 September 1941 Eichmann was irritated to be interrupted when dealing with the Jews of Łódź by a call from the Foreign Ministry regarding eight thousand Jews in Serbia, whose transfer to Russia he had not yet aranged. 'Shoot them yourselves,' he recommended before terminating the call. Eichmann's men were responsible for roving across Europe, organising the business end of deportations which had been calculated down to the last detail in their Berlin HQ. Their zealotry was as evident as cruelty and greed. Josef Weiszl, taking a rare evening stroll through Vienna's Schonbrünn Park with his wife, found the energy to upbraid a Jewish woman who worked for his wife, spotted sitting on a bench without her yellow star. Threatening the woman with deportation, Weiszl had her imprisoned for six weeks and then delivered to an assembly camp. In faraway Salonika, a dozen SD officers under Alois Brunner were enjoying the winter sun and the Turkish baths, which, in a jaunty letter to a Gestapo comrade in Vienna, Brunner recommended as a way of relaxing wives before sex. This was a revealing communication, since normally letters were official, with the barest hint of human personality at work. But this was a personal communication, asking his friend whether he could provide a set of cutlery, presumably seized from Jews, for Brunner's sister.

Brunner and his team established a sort of Ali Baba's cave in a comfortable villa from which to direct the deportation of Salonika's Jews. The tables were piled high with gold watches, diamond rings and bundles of US and Canadian dollars, pounds sterling and Swiss francs; the floor was covered with laundry baskets overflowing with antiques as well as rolled-up oriental carpets. When Brunner flew out in May 1943, after despatching forty thousand Greek Jews to Auschwitz, he had difficulty lugging suitcases of cash and valuables on to the plane. In June 1944 his colleague Anton Burger came back for two thousand Jews on Corfu and the hundred more they found on Kos. All died in Auschwitz. These desk-bound perpetrators savoured their power over life and death. On one of the last deportation trains from Vienna to Riga, which he accompanied, Brunner tortured and shot an elderly banker called Siegmund Bosel. When a Greek Orthodox priest offered a Jewish man a cigarette during the deportations from Lefkadas, Burger shot the deportee in the head. Such men had many attributes, but banality was not one of them. The fertility of their cruelty and malice rippled out to any number of actors in Germany and beyond. How did they react as the enormity of these events unfolded?

CHAPTER 16

Journeys through Night

I CHOOSING DEATHS

The Jews affected by Nazi crimes operated in an even denser fog of uncertainty, generated by Nazi lies and disinformation. Throughout the occupied east, the SS ordered the formation of ghettos, which were intended to be interim warehousing pending ultimate resolution of how to remove the Jews from Europe, and it instituted Councils of Jewish Elders by a decree promulgated on 21 September 1939. These Councils were intended to relay German orders, rather in the way that terrorists use hostages to coerce governments, to people denied direct contact with authority. It was a crushing responsibility. As the Councils endeavoured to maintain civilised existence, senior German policemen speculated about dumping Jews on the Soviet border, shipping them to Madagascar or utilising the Soviet Arctic gulags, until other more overtly murderous solutions were adopted, camouflaged with conceptual elements of plans long abandoned.

The Councils were at the lethal interface of direct contact with representatives of the master race. If the Elders impeded or sabotaged German orders, they and their families were killed and replaced. The Germans went to any lengths to secure the compliance of the Jewish leadership. In Lechatov, they executed eight successive Jewish Councils until the ninth they appointed decided to do their bidding. As we shall see below, in Łódź the Gestapo killed and replaced the entire Council, leaving only the chairman-designate alive. In Mlana every member of the Council was hanged for non-compliance with an order.[1] While the members of the eight successive Lechatov councils were incredibly brave in refusing to co-operate, as a whole Councils of Jewish Elders were merely a convenience rather than a necessity for the Germans. In the conquered parts of the Soviet Union, the Einsatzgruppen, Waffen-SS and Order Police murderers did not need Councils: indeed there was no formal Jewish community leadership, as the Soviet regime had abolished it along with all other associational life that might have stood in their way.

It is difficult to speculate about alternative outcomes, but the Elders generally believed that the same results would have been virtually certain, and might have been implemented with far more indiscriminate bloodshed, without the mediation of the Jewish Councils. The Elders lacked our wisdom of hindsight and so we need to be exceptionally careful in assessing moral choices which invariably involved such lesser evils as sacrificing a part to maintain the whole. The Councils have sometimes been denounced by those like Hannah Arendt or Raul Hilberg who were spared the awful choices forced upon European Jews by the Nazis, and who have been too ready to credit the contemptuous line of such as Eichmann or Stangl that the Jews went to their deaths like lemmings. At the end, most of them did: but by that stage they were physical and mental shadows of what they had been, and were driven to their deaths with overwhelmingly brutal force. Nobody else could or would have resisted either under such circumstances.

The Council members were not collaborating with the Nazis, if that term means actions and words based on ideological congruity, for there was no evidence of that anywhere in Nazi-occupied Europe. Different Jews wanted different things; none of them wanted Nazi victory. Instead, the Councils of Elders obeyed and propitiated the Nazis, who enjoyed absolute power over them. They sought to gain collective time, using the argument that the Jews were essential to the German war effort. Like British appeasers, they thought they were dealing with rational people rather than psychopaths. They also exploited such divisions of policy as they could identify among different German agencies, while hoping the Allies would win the war. This meant discerning German intentions from the casual remarks or facial expressions of the individuals they dealt with. The diarist and member of the Kovno Ghetto Council, Avraham Tory, described the Germans rather well on 12 February 1942:

> They do not tell you things clearly, except when they curse you and scream at you. It is therefore imperative to assess their mood properly before they open their mouths. You must understand that, from their point of view, our situation must always remain unclear; we are

not to be allowed to understand anything, even if our lives are at stake. Anything that happens to us must occur like a bolt from the blue. We are to remain always in a state of anticipation, without understanding what is going on around us.

There was no way of predicting, least of all among the victims, what the final evolution of anti-Semitic ideology and policy would be, since that was a process rather than a single identifiable master decision, and the Jews were not privy to such exalted circles where the decisions were taken.[2]

Council members cannot be described as volunteers, although Jews are no more immune to self-importance and vanity than the rest of humanity. In the occupied territories, German-speakers were preferred, as well as the few who had municipal-government experience. This favoured middle-class, assimilated Jews, who might be unable to communicate fluently with the Yiddish-speaking majority. There were other hazards. In some places intellectuals and professionals were told to report for duty as councillors, only to be shot under the 1940 AB (Extraordinary Pacification) Aktion designed to liquidate intellectuals; in Kovno five hundred educated people were told to report for archival work and then killed. Elsewhere, the Germans arbitrarily stopped some middle-aged or older person on the street and ordered them to select a Council. In Warsaw, Einsatzgruppe IV alighted upon Adam Czerniaków, a German-speaking engineer and minor municipal politician, after the original leader of the Jewish community had fled. At the first Council meeting, Czerniaków grimly showed his colleagues the key to a desk drawer containing twenty-four tablets of cyanide he had horded. Similar circumstances accounted for the rise of Mordechai Chaim Rumkowski in Łódź, perhaps simply because he had flowing grey hair. He was a failed businessman whose subsequent career running Zionist agricultural projects for young people resulted in rumours of child abuse. After the community leader Leib Minzberg had fled, the Germans chose Rumkowski to lead the newly established Jewish Council, whose thirty-one members he then selected after all members of the first Council had been 'disappeared'.

In his early sixties, Rumkowski may have looked the part, but he was ill educated, abrasive and impulsive, with wandering hands whenever young women were about. One wonders what possessed him to put his own portrait on the ghetto stamps and scrip notes, or to be driven around in a horse-drawn carriage, or to wear a white Panama hat and white gloves for his only audience with Himmler when he swept into the ghetto in June

1941. Unfortunately, men who utterly lacked Rumkowski's character flaws often made precisely the same decisions as he did.[3]

We have followed the Jews into the hell of Chelmno. Now it is time to see the hell they came from. Ghettos were often deliberately established in the most insalubrious quarters of cities to associate Jews with filth and vermin, a line that sometimes played well with the surrounding Gentile Poles. In Łódź, which the Germans rapidly rechristened Litzmannstadt after a famous nineteenth-century Prussian general, some 167,000 Jews were crammed into the Baluty, Old Town and semi-rural Marysin areas in the north-eastern peripheries of this Polish Manchester. The Łódź ghetto was the second largest after Warsaw and consisted of about one and a half square miles physically isolated from the rest of the German (and Polish) city with barbed wire and police guards at fifty-yard intervals.[4] The quarantining of the Jews meant a sevenfold rise in population density in a tiny area that lacked a modern sewage system and in which 98 per cent of the tenements lacked indoor sanitation. Between October and November 1941, the SS decided that the already severely burdened ghetto economy could support an influx of twenty-five thousand Jews from Austria, thus exerting greater pressure on housing. Five thousand Austrian Gypsies were also shipped in, but were temporarily confined in a special mini-camp inside the ghetto until they could be killed.

The ghetto was controlled by what one might call the flow-chart men of the relevant sub-section of the Main Office of Food and Economy. This sub-section was led by an ambitious thirty-seven-year-old coffee importer from Bremen called Hans Biebow, who worked under the Main Office's Johann Moldenhauer, himself an appointee of Karl Marder, the mayor of German Litzmannstadt. Marder's vision was to refashion Łódź as a modern German city, akin to Hamburg, which would involve rationalising the squalid Jewish parts out of existence. A managerial, streamlining mentality was characteristic of their peculiar depredations, although it may well have been how they rationalised more intense hatreds and squalid motives. The German officials disagreed about how to achieve their goals. Alexander Palfinger did not believe that the Jews had relinquished all their hidden wealth and proposed to use starvation to force the last złoty from them. He was explicitly genocidal: 'A rapid dying out of the Jews is for us a matter of total indifference, if not to say desirable, as long as the concomitant effects leave the public interest of the German people untouched.' By contrast, Biebow argued that the ghetto had to be made economically self-sufficient by ensuring that Jewish labour became more productive. After Biebow had won the argument at a meeting on 18 October 1940, Palfinger left Łódź for Warsaw, where his arguments were similarly defeated following the intervention of bigger players.[5] However, Biebow accompanied the Gestapo on a visit to the extermination centre at Chelmno in early 1942, indicating that his plan to make the ghetto more productive included the extermination of the unproductive.[6]

Biebow was responsible for lending the ghetto investment capital from the sums that the Germans had extorted from the Jews in the first place. This arrangement bridged short-term uncertainties about the ghetto's ultimate future, once it became clear that the General Government was unwilling to take Jews from the neighbouring Warthegau. The Łódź ghetto was also the focus of a parallel police bureaucracy consisting of the uniformed officers who guarded the perimeter, the intelligence-gathering Gestapo under Otto Bradfisch, and the Criminal Police whose main task was to prevent smuggling and to uncover hidden valuables. Council leader Rumkowski also disposed of five hundred Jewish policemen to maintain order on his side of the wire, although the Criminal Police opened a small torture centre themselves inside the ghetto, while the Gestapo ran its own network of paid Jewish informers. The Gestapo also liaised with the ghouls at Chelmno from the Sonderkommando Lange.[7]

In all ghettos people were uprooted from their homes, deprived of their habitual employment and denied every welfare benefit including pensions. Any educational or cultural activities also had to be created from scratch.[8] This meant that the Councils quickly developed bureaucracies to administer essential services – the Warsaw ghetto alone had to provide for four hundred thousand people, all destitute with the exception of the racketeers and spivs who thrived amid so much death and destruction. Accordingly the number of people employed by the Councils' ramifying sub-departments rose to 12,880 in Łódź and 6,000 in Warsaw. These were coveted posts because they brought access to increased rations, and their holders did not have to work twelve hours a day in hard manufacturing tasks. Possession of one of a burgeoning range of official Council service armbands meant the difference between life and death.[9]

In his New Year address in 1942, Rumkowski stressed the theme 'The plan is work, work, and more work!' He proudly opened a small exhibition of such items as ladies' brassieres, beneath a banner inscribed in Yiddish with 'Work is our Only Path'.[10] Work was a necessity in the sense of providing destitute Jews with just enough money to purchase the meagre rations the Germans allocated to them, rations which were supposed to match those given to German prison inmates, but which always fell below that level. Much of the food the Germans allocated to the ghetto was spoiled: off-colour meat, rancid butter, weevil-infested flour. Potato peelings became a desirable source of nourishment. Deliveries of heating fuel consisted of bags of coal dust, and to avoid dying of hypothermia Jews had to chop up fences, floorboards and furniture for firewood.[11]

Most of the output of the larger ghettos served the German war economy, with orders coming mainly from the Wehrmacht, and much of the profit stuck to the fingers of the local German managers. In 1941 an embroidery department made 1,053,000 earmuffs while a tailor's workshop struggled to produce fifty thousand white camouflage suits, all destined for soldiers on the Eastern Front. Other items included belts, hats, helmets, badges and epaulettes. Łódź also churned out quality lingerie and dresses destined for the German domestic market, as well as clogs and rag shoes destined for concentration-camp inmates. Individual German firms supplied specialist machinery, enabling, for example, Łódź Jews to manufacture corsets for Spieshauer & Braun of Haubach. Łódź became the most industrialised ghetto partly because of the city's past, but also because most Jews had worked in craft workshops or light industry before the occupation. Rumkowski ordered the surrender of seven thousand sewing machines to provide equipment for the reworking of tons of old clothing into uniforms and civilian garments. Cobblers and carpenters were similarly ordered to relinquish their tools to collective workshops. By 1943, a total of 73,782 of the inmates of the Łódź ghetto worked in 117 factories and workshops. Apart from clothing and footwear, these factories produced huge quantities of cooking utensils, carpets, furniture and such toys as dolls' houses, where the small fingers of Jewish children came in handy in making the miniature furniture.[12] Anyone who caused Rumkowski trouble, such as carters, butchers and fishmongers, would find themselves assigned to an external work party, which meant one of the construction or irrigation sites that dotted the Warthegau. Captured escapees were publicly hanged by the Germans in the ghetto.[13]

The pride the Council Elders took in these feats of productivity was understandable in the light of the prevailing German slur that the Jews were parasites who lived on the backs of others. Rumkowksi also ensured that Jews looked like modern workers, banning from his factories anyone with a beard or wearing a traditional kaftan.[14] Work kept people alive in circumstances where, in Łódź, during August 1942 alone, 1,736 people died of disease or malnutrition. However, this mentality could lead to the internalisation of German attitudes, so that those who worked (including those in the Councils' own swollen bureaucracies) were rewarded with increased rations and better quarters than the unproductive, expendable residue. A sort of food pyramid evolved, based on differential rations, as well as exclusive canteens where essential personnel received decent meals. Once the Germans had started to demand quotas of deportees, it was a short step from this extreme utilitarian approach to the decision to relinquish children, criminals, the unemployed, the elderly and sick, on the grounds that the better elements in the community, as defined by the ghetto leaderships, would at least survive the war.

This raises the more delicate matter of how the Council Elders dealt with implacable German interlocutors who met the slightest dissent with verbal abuse or physical violence, as Rumkowski discovered in June 1943 when Biebow put him in hospital, in an assault so furious that he managed to smash his fist through a window. Any significant dissent, let alone resistance, would result in a bullet in the head. Even the most managerially objective-seeming Germans could quickly turn into raging beasts in circumstances where they were under no restraint. Initially, the Jews reverted to the way they might have dealt with the nineteenth-century tsars, by adopting the posture of humble petitioners seeking the righting of a wrong. In themselves such supplications rarely worked, unless accompanied by a bribe, for German venality was endemic. It was so pervasive that the Gestapo had the intelligence officers working in Łódź's branch of the Aviation Ministry tap Biebow's telephone, presumably after policy rifts opened up between the SS and the ghetto administration. For the Council Elders this meant maintaining special repositories of alcohol, fur coats, jewellery, watches and so on, which could be used to moderate but never deflect overall German policy.

A more efficacious approach was to exploit perceived divisions of opinion among different German agencies about the ultimate fate of the Jews. Some ghetto administrators, such as Biebow, were so wedded to economic rationality, as well as to their own cupidity, that it was logical to exploit the economic utility of the Jews in a strategy known as 'rescue through work'. Surely, they reasoned, those Germans who lauded *Arbeit* as a marker of racial worth would not do away with those Jews who toiled so hard at a pivotal moment in the war effort? Rumkowski became messianic in his desire to 'productivise' his 'gold mine', and megalomaniac in imagining growing German dependence *on him*. In that sense he was like a pathetic copy of the redemptive religoid politics espoused by the dictators, especially since all the democratic or oligarchic features of Jewish life succumbed to what amounted to an autocracy. At one point Rumkowski reflected:

> When I moved into the ghetto on 6 April 1940, I told the mayor that I was moving in the belief that this was a gold mine. When he, astonished, asked for an explanation, I told him: 'I have forty thousand hands for work in the ghetto and this is my gold mine.' As I began successfully to organise work, the authorities gradually began to deal with me and to count on me more and more ... Today there are 52 factories in the ghetto testifying to my success in creating places of employment. These factories have been visited by the highest representatives of the authorities on many occasions, and they have been amazed. They repeatedly have told me that up to now they have known only one type of Jew – the merchant or middleman – and have never realised that Jews were capable of productive work.[15]

It was all here, the self-importance and the willingness to be deceived by the 'highest representatives'. In the event, in late 1942, Rumkowski was told to select twenty thousand ghetto inmates for deportation; after successfully halving this total, he managed to have the task devolved on his own five-man Resettlement Commission. Among its members were a lawyer, Naftalin, a judge, Jakobson, the head of the Jewish Order Police, Rozenblat, and Hercberg, the director of the central prison. The Commission decided who should be deported in a 'collegial' spirit without 'subjectivity'.[16] Ghetto runners hand-delivered warrants telling people to report to an assembly point where they were issued with such things as winter gloves and earmuffs, as well as bread and sausage for their journey. Those chosen to go were selected primarily because of their marginality: they were either new arrivals from the provinces or previously convicted criminals and prostitutes, as well as anyone remotely associated with them. This meant that the poorest of the poor were deported first, many of them women. Judging from written appeals to be left off the lists, the selection paid no regard to such things as separating fit adults from elderly or sick family members. Jewish Order Police were despatched to track down anyone who tried to elude deportation. The Jewish underground resistance in Warsaw refused to regard all of these policemen as collaborators, rejecting the German notion of collective responsibility, and their ranks included men who bravely tried to help Jews escape the round-ups they were conducting.[17]

Rumkowski tried to convince the ghetto dwellers that the deportees were being resettled in the countryside. 'They will not be behind wire, and they will work on farms,' he said. That he at least suspected the truth is revealed by his insistence that only 'connivers and cheats' would be deported, since 'they deserved it', and by the obvious point that bedridden invalids who had to be stretchered to the assembly points would not be working anywhere. In fairness, Rumkowski and other Council leaders elsewhere depended on German officials who dismissed increasingly pervasive Jewish desperation with the line that their fears were unfounded rumours or that they themselves were not privy to any further information. Among the more pernicious lies was the one that accompanied an order for the manufacture of fifty thousand children's beds, which a Gestapo agent explained 'will be made for the little Jewish children who are in a special, large camp not far from Lublin'. It took time for the only two survivors of the Chelmno work detail to bring the intelligence, initially to Warsaw, that the deported Łódź Jews were being killed, but their account was harder to believe than German disinformation that the deportees were happily farming in the neighbourhood of Kolo. The tale the Chelmno survivors told was too extraordinary to be believed, since there was no precedent in modern European history for people being murdered in such a clinical, systematic fashion. Even if they did suspect the worst, the staggered, episodic way in which deportations were conducted – a strategy largely determined by the capacity of gas chambers – lent plausibility to claims that each would be the last. Among many Jews a resigned fatalism was combined with a readiness to clutch at the straw of divine deliverance, although many also vented their fury against the Councils and the Jewish policemen, or struggled to prevent their children being wrenched from them. The Gestapo chief Günther Fuchs shot a woman who refused to let go of her five-year-old daughter's hand and then shot the girl as well.[18]

Some Councils made the decision to preserve the better elements who would form the future of their communities with the air of Moses leading his people out of Egypt. Some, knowing their own intellectual limitations, drew upon the advice of rabbis as well as representatives of the learned professions when they made their grim choices. In Kovno, where in October 1941 the Germans told the Council to assemble the entire ghetto population to announce who would be 'resettled', and where it was known that mass graves were being excavated at nearby Fort IX, the Council consulted a wise old rabbi the night before, who sat up all night poring over books. Maybe overcome with the burden, or having a hesitantly meticulous mind, he failed to produce an opinion until the time for the decision had passed. He had considered, and then rejected, Jewish traditions derived from the age of Maimonides, who had ruled that Jews should never sacrifice individuals for the sake of the community. The old rabbi said the resettlement decree had to be published. Other rabbis immediately took issue with him, perfectly normal in rabbinical circles but wholly inappropriate at such a desperate time. In the event, before dawn on 28 October 1941, all thirty thousand Kovno ghetto inmates were assembled. A Gestapo master-sergeant called Helmut Rauca used hand gestures to select ten thousand people from this mass, steering the fated group to the Small Ghetto, whose inmates had been 'deported' earlier. At great personal risk, Jewish policemen enabled some of those selected for the Small Ghetto to join those left behind, while the Council leader, a physician called Elkhanan Elkes, intervened to save the lives of one hundred who were already in the Small Ghetto, even though at one point Lithuanian militiamen clubbed him to the ground. The Germans were interested only in the overall number rather than individuals. All ten thousand confined in the Small Ghetto were marched up to Fort IX and shot into mass graves.[19]

Lacking useful guidance from the professionally wise, Council leaders adopted the posture of generals faced with sacrificing troops to save an army. Elkes compared himself with the captain of a battered ship trying to steer through a perpetual storm.[20] Moshe Merin, head of a Council that represented several smaller ghettos in East Upper Silesia, rehearsed some of these arguments even as he vividly described the alternative to co-operation with the authorities:

> I have saved 25,000 people from resettlement. Blood would have flowed in the streets. I have information from very reliable sources that the resettlement would have engulfed 50,000 people, and our entire district would have been crushed, so that no might in the whole world would have been able to rebuild it. It is easy to imagine what the lot of the remaining ones would have been. Nobody will deny that, as a general, I have won a great victory. If I have lost only 25 per cent when I could have lost all, who can wish better results? Diaspora has made an asocial people of the Jews. Only we could have adopted the teaching of Maimonides, who ordained that the entire community be sacrificed for the sake of one man. We shall all be

condemned to extinction if we do not change our mentality in this respect.

These decisions were made by men who were drained and crushed by the burden of responsibility, often with tears rolling down their distraught faces. Many Council members simply refused to co-operate in making such life-and-death decisions, either committing suicide, like Adam Czerniaków on 24 July 1942, or being shot by the Germans after they had registered their dissent. A number of Council members simply removed their official armbands and silently joined the deportees. The obverse of this was that some Council members took part in searching for Jews to deport, or did whatever was necessary to save their own skins. So did the Jewish Police, the firemen and the warehousemen, who co-operated in return for bread and sausage when the Germans needed extra manpower to comb Łódź's hospitals and houses after they had imposed a week-long curfew in September 1942. They also dragged away every child under ten, including those whose mothers had deliberately lowered their children's age to receive increased milk allocations. In early September, the Jewish Police came for the 850 orphans in the Marysin colony; a photograph shows a column of wide-eyed waifs aged about four to six being escorted to their deaths. These devastating culls reflected ongoing arguments between the SS, who periodically arrived to insist that the ghetto was uneconomic, and local defenders of the Gau-Ghetto, led by Gauleiter Artur Greiser and Biebow's civilian ghetto administration. The SS wanted to obliterate the ghetto after removing anyone capable of labour to Otto Globocnik's camp complex in Lublin. Greiser and Biebow used the needs of the army and Speer's Ministry of Production to justify their own local rackets, which in Biebow's case spared him and his two hundred staff the prospect of being conscripted for military service. In the end Greiser and Biebow won the argument, partly because the SS murdered the inmates of the Lublin labour camps in the course of the November 1943 Operation Harvest Festival.[21]

One interim solution satisfying all relevant parties was that non-productive elements were successfully deported, leaving some seventy-eight thousand persons alive in the Łódź ghetto by the summer of 1944. By mid-August, with the Russians already inside Poland, the Germans decided to liquidate the remaining ghetto population. Knowing that the Jews understood what deportation meant, both Bradfisch and Biebow employed almost pleading tones to get the worker Jews to go voluntarily to the Reich, since the Russians would regard them as collaborators with German industry. Faced with the refusal of the Jews to report for deportation, the Germans had no alternative other than to cordon off apartment blocks and then go in with their Jewish Order Police auxiliaries, assisted by the firemen and chimney sweeps. Among those to leave Radogoszcz station for Auschwitz was Chairman Rumkowski, whose last exchanges included the statement: 'What are you telling me about Jewish history? I am myself a piece of Jewish history.'

II BENEATH THE SMOKE

The vast majority of victims of the Holocaust were ousted from their homes and more or less immediately murdered, either in the killing fields of the occupied east and the Balkans or via the mass transports which debouched into dedicated death camps. They arrived at the camps, and after a brief blur of baying dogs and screaming men, disappeared into the blackness of gas chambers. Some of them sang or marched erect to their fate, in a desperate attempt to reassert their human dignity. The ensuing smoke of their remains was watched by those spared this ultimate ordeal.

Huge numbers of others were processed into concentration camps, some of which doubled as extermination centres, the most ominous being at Auschwitz-Birkenau. On entering this mephitic world, sometimes the first thing one saw were neat beds of geraniums or monkeys and peacocks in mini-zoos, before the ominous reality dawned behind these Potemkin façades. Some people broke down under the shock, others tried to make the best of it with black humour, shrugging off fate as it belched and burned from tall chimneys. That moral norms were totally inverted became horribly obvious as SS doctors directed most arrivals to their deaths and the others to a stay of execution in a purgatory that was in fact hell. Those whom civilised societies accord the most care – infants, the sick and the elderly – were usually killed immediately, in the most striking signal that moral norms were no longer operative. The biggest favour one could grant a woman with a baby was to squeeze its nose gently until it suffocated, because it was destined to join its mother in the gas chambers.

A host of people, separated by age, gender, nationality, occupation, politics and religion, entered these hellish environments, whose sole function was to strip them of their complex humanity and to derange their morality so that they became the equivalent of an animal herd. Outward signs of individual self-worth such as hair or civilian clothing were removed so as to reduce the inmates to a shorn and uniformed mass. Authority imposed its grim imprint on them by diminishing their identity to that of an ascriptive group: anti-social, Gypsy, homosexual, Jew and political to name but a few of the possibilities. They were also deprived of any personal privacy and the dignity that accompanies it. Beds consisted of multiple-occupancy roosts with straw mattresses, which along with a blanket that had to be precisely shaped each new day. All ablutions were communal. Feeding time was supposed to degrade human beings to the level of animals, fighting to stick their snouts in the trough first by dint of strength or size. In an ultimate denial of individual autonomy, prisoners were not allowed to kill themselves, despite being in places geared up for mass murder. A woman about to be hanged infuriated the SS by slashing her arteries before they could get a noose around her neck. When Filip Müller, a member of the Auschwitz inmate 'special commando' which dealt with corpses and their effects, tried to walk into a gas chamber, he was dragged out by an SS man who shouted, 'You bloody shit! Get it into your stupid head: we decide how long you stay alive and when you die, and not you.'[22]

Entrance into this alien environment also meant realising that reason itself was suspended; as Primo Levi was told, 'there was no "why" in Auschwitz'. That meant that the normal relationship between crime and punishment had been dispensed with. In the vast majority of cases, inmates were being held not because of what they had done, but because of who they were, by the dismal lights of this regime's reasoning. They were slave labour, with an average life expectancy of around three months, after which even their dental fillings and hair would become material in the Nazi productive process, along with their rags and clogs. For while evil and cruelty have always been with us, only the compartmentalised, techonological imagination could have been responsible for this.

The German Communist Margarete Buber-Neumann, who spent two years in the Karaganda gulag before being extradited to Nazi Germany and imprisoned in Ravensbrück, once wisely observed that 'you're never so badly off in a concentration camp that it can't get worse'. The rules existed not to ensure smooth running of the camps, but rather to keep the inmates in a state of dread tension, their days and nights punctuated with head counts and roll calls. At night no dream could entirely suppress dread at the coming day. In addition to any formal rules, all derived from the Dachau exemplar where SS commandants and guards were mostly trained, each guard simply invented his or her own. In Ravensbrück, one female SS guard was constantly on the lookout for curls, tearing off an inmate's cap and bashing her face every time she found one during roll-call. The offenders were reshorn and had to parade around with a placard reading 'I broke camp discipline and curled my hair'. While some guards may have been the sort of jobsworths one finds in any penal institution, seeking to avoid service on the fighting fronts, many were ideological fanatics who were able to fulfil each and every fantasy about brutalising other people. This could be motivated by some overtly deviant sadistic urge, as displayed by SS-Unterscharführer Binder with whom Margarete Buber-Neumann had to negotiate in a sewing workshop: 'His cheeks would puff out and his face go purple from the shrieking, and then, with a maniacal look on his face, he would seize his victim, bang her head against the machine, drag her off her seat and punch her until blood poured from her nose. The man was a sadist; he had to see blood every night. Then he would let his victim fall in a heap on the floor and stand over her gloating.'[23] Violence was often a matter of malicious humour or the relief of boredom, as when guards threw prisoners' caps over the trip wires so as to see how expertly their colleagues in the watch towers could shoot them. Those falling foul of a guard could expect to be beaten, punched and kicked until they were dead. Any dissent meant being shot.[24]

Anyone made conspicuous by education or bearing was liable to attract the most ferociously resentful attentions; survival meant disappearing quickly into the anonymous mass. People learned that it was far better to be indistinguishable at roll calls inside a huge formation than to be within range of eye contact with the SS or the trusty kapos carrying out the head count.[25] In the camps past wealth and social position meant nothing. A rich person, used to a comfortable life, would be less likely than a humble worker to withstand manual labour, which was the lot of most inmates for more than twelve hours a day. People accustomed to work on their own – which included peasants as well as academics and intellectuals – were less likely to survive than urbanised workers who were used to co-operating with one another and managing collective tasks. Although the SS were especially abusive to anyone who looked like an intellectual, they also needed prisoners with such skills as engineers, medical doctors and artisans, who thus had opportunities to survive by making themselves useful. In fact, one survivor of Auschwitz has written that the best preparation for surviving such an experience would be to do a medical degree. Attaching oneself to where the power lay was one route to survival. As in most penal institutions, the volume of inmates made control in detail difficult; the SS co-opted those prisoners distinguishable by their coarseness and brutality into an informal hierarchy, a practice which also performed the function of divide and rule familiar in the Soviet camps. These camp administrators and barracks leaders accepted the permanency of the camps and chose to play the game according to SS rules, often surpassing the latter in terms of sheer brutality. A sprinkling of the SS's power rubbed off on them, and many of them exploited it to the full so as to be exempt from physical labour or to win more food or sexual favours. As Paul Steinberg recalled of his time as a seventeen-year-old in Auschwitz, homosexuality was rife in the camp.

There was no hard-and-fast rule for surviving the camp experience. One could wrap oneself in moral armour, maintaining a solid core of prin-ciples, or rely on a combination of cunning and luck. The former approach, invariably refracted through Primo Levi's grave reflections, tends to get most attention from moral philosophers, since his words are most seductively amenable to their type of analysis. But then Levi was a middle-class, middle-aged man with certain certainties; younger people were not so preformed, and many less fortunate people had long learned that aspects of conventional morality were entirely flexible when it was a matter of duping authority or putting food on a tin plate. In fact, some like Paul Steinberg also survived by combining the talents 'of a lion-tamer, tight-rope walker and even magician', or, to put things less picaresquely, by exhibiting the wheedling charm of a conman or the allure of a prosti-tute in the case of women. Steinberg 'concluded that each one of these monsters [he meant the kapos] had a flaw, a weakness, which it was up to me to find: this one needed flattering, that one had a repressed paternal instinct or the need to confide in someone who seemed to take an interest in him'.[26] Most prisoners came armed with whatever morality had guided them through civilian life, albeit often in conditions of wartime occupa-tion where peacetime norms were already modified. Steinberg thought it best to assume that 'nothing else had ever existed. I have no feelings of anguish, no more than I have questions. It all goes without saying. I'm at the age where one adjusts, and I economize on everything by getting rid of moral suffering, emotions, memories – and regrets as well, a crucial imper-ative.'[27]

The capacity to work largely explained why an inmate was still alive in the first place. Work did not liberate; either it helped prisoners survive or it killed them. Given the harshness of central European winters, manual work outside was lethal, except when it involved some small-scale indoor project supervised by one or two guards whose residual humanity could be worked on. In Ravensbrück a posting to the camp greenhouses was valued, not least because the SS supervisor turned a blind eye to inmates eating cucumbers and tomatoes, whereas unloading bricks from a barge meant abrasions and sunburn in summer or frostbite in winter.[28] Factory work was slightly preferable, although the urgency of production meant pitfalls for anyone unused to working at speed with sensitive equipment like sewing machines which can easily run out of an inexperienced operator's control. Work in an office or similar environment may have brought close proximity to the SS and other Germans, but familiarity could mean discovering a shared humanity, provided any evidence of indispensability did not tip over into a fatal air of superiority over the German. Margarete Buber-Neumann closely observed one wardress who was a bundle of nerves, and who had conflicting feelings about a system she thought was a distortion of what Hitler and Himmler allegedly envisaged. Buber-Neumann was able to help several inmates by mislaying crucial files and persuading this individual not to exercise the arbitrary power she disposed of. Others were less subtle in finding some fatal flaw in those with power over them. Camp hospitals had a terrible ambiguity. On the one hand they were a relatively safe space, where the sick could be ministered to by prisoner doctors, giving the former respite from indiscriminate daily terrors; on the other hand, these medical stations were the first place the SS looked to when they decided to cull a given number of prisoners to make way for fresher arrivals. Beyond the range of sick inmates who had a brief time to recover their health was the generic camp underclass of *Musulmänner*, or those who by dint of physical and mental exhaustion simply gave up and died.[29]

Most inmates did not work in SS offices or hospitals and laboratories. That meant it was vital to attach oneself to, or to form, a group of prisoners who recognised that in order to survive people had to act and think together. Recognising the strengths and weaknesses of the individual members, the group established its own working pace to moderate the impact of labour that was designed to kill everyone slowly. The group also learned to read the minds of individual guards, establishing who could be corrupted by alcohol, goods or sexual favours, or who was to be strenuously avoided. Within such groups individuals cared for one another – possibly the major reason why some people survived the camps. As Tzvetan Todorov has shown, heroism revealed both virtues and limitations.

Nationality, politics or religious persuasion sometimes enabled small groups to create larger solidarities and to act as cohesive groups. That was how resistance managed to develop, even within such an unpropitious context as a concentration camp, where the sanctions included horrific torture before execution. Of course, such solidarities were not quite as admirable as they are often held to be.

Jehovah's Witnesses opted to remain in the camps, regardless of their families outside, rather than renounce their faith, and were notoriously indifferent to the sufferings of anyone outside their own elect group. Likewise, national solidarity could mean indifference or hostility to anyone not of the group and the perpetuation of inter-ethnic prejudices. In many camps, Stalinists were notoriously tricky towards other socialists. If they managed to get a lock on the camp administration, that could mean assigning Trotskyites and the like to lethal labour details. Buber-Neumann nearly died of blood poisoning because Czech Communists found her eyewitness accounts of Stalin's concentration camps inexpedient.[30]

We now have a few clues to how some people survived concentration camps. What is called survivor guilt often fuels the wider suspicion that people must have done anything to survive. It helped not to be a Jew since Jews were all slated to die, as well as attracting the full-on malice of their guards. Essential skills were immensely important, whether those of doctors, electricians and carpenters or of the jewellers who refashioned gold into rings and the like, whereas academics and lawyers found they had no purpose. Membership of a group helped too, whether a national or political underground, or a smaller surrogate family of people who cared for one another. For it has been well said that if evil is banal, so is good, including those unforced acts of simple kindness without which survival would have been impossible. That helped, but so did a strong measure of cunning and luck. As Steinberg wrote, shortly before his death in 1999, a survivor needed 'an inordinate appetite for life – and the flexibility of a contortionist'.[31]

III AMONG THE GERMANS

As the numbers of women held in wartime Ravensbrück expanded, the SS ran out of female guards. They went to civilian factories and recruited ordinary workers keen to escape the factory grind by working in 'rehabilitation centres'. After a week in the camp, half of these women were so shocked that they asked to return to the factories. Those who remained were told to stifle any human sympathies and were given hardened wardresses as escorts. After a short time, and with the addition of jack-boots and forage caps, 'these young working women were soon every bit as bad as the old hands'.[32] That mixed response may be said to exemplify the wider question of how the Germans reacted to the crimes we have been considering.

The deportation of Reich Jews began in mid-September 1941, the same month in which the Jews were visually identified with yellow stars of David to stigmatise them openly and deepen their social isolation. The prospect of deportation led many Jews to commit suicide. On one day, 15 October 1941, nineteen Viennese Jews killed themselves by drowning, hanging, gassing, leaping from a building or taking pills. Within three weeks another eighty-four had followed. In Berlin, 243 Jews committed suicide in the last three months of 1941. Sometimes the Aryan partner decided to die with the Jewish spouse, as did the actor Joachim Gottschalk, who died with his Jewish wife and their child.[33]

The Jews were told to gather on a specific date at assembly points, after which they were marched or driven to railway stations.[34] This was often done in broad daylight. The population was intensely curious rather than indifferent.[35] In some places, like the university city of Göttingen, the local Nazi Party office received applications to take over the Jews' vacant homes even before they had been deported. In the small Swabian village of Baisingen, a man contacted the treasury because he already had an eye on a fine mattress owned by his neighbour 'the Jewess Stern [German allows that gender distinction] who was going to be leaving there in the middle of the month'. In Hamburg, the Gauleiter Karl Kaufmann had lobbied Hitler to remove the Jews to provide emergency housing for the victims of RAF bombing. The Jews were marshalled in front of the city's Logenhaus, which enabled those on the trams that passed every few minutes to gawp at them. The departure of the Jews was enthusiastically followed by groups of children and young people; in Bad Neustadt on the Saale they contin-ued to jeer as the trains pulled away from the station, trains on which insulting slogans had been scrawled.[36] In several places, Münster for exam-ple, which had been heavily damaged by the RAF, the local populace regarded the deportation of the Jews as a useful solution to an acute local housing shortage. There were more humane reactions; in some towns and villages older people and those who still practised their Christian faith were appalled by the callous uprooting of elderly neighbours, and by the jocular baiting by young people that accompanied it. In little Baisingen, some deplored the public auctioning of the effects of their former neighbours, either regarding the goods as irredeemably cursed or already intimating that such evil deeds would not go unpunished.[37]

Since the Jews were allowed to depart with only fifty kilograms of personal effects, their homes, furniture and possessions were up for grabs. Even the pitiful allotments of personal effects were stolen, as the Jews of Düsseldorf and Königsberg discovered when the freight wagons containing them were decoupled before their trains departed. The head of the German Red Cross, Kurt von Behr, was put in charge of distributing the Jews' personal effects – bed and table linen, porcelain, dishes, silverware, furniture and household appliances – to the victims of British bombing. Nasty inter-municipal spats, for example between heavily bombed Cologne and untouched Trier, were resolved by the incoming shipments of possessions stolen from the Jews of Belgium or France. By the end of 1943 a million cubic metres of furniture had been removed from France, requiring twenty-four thousand railway freight cars to shift it. Most of this was distributed to bombed-out Germans, except for the entire wagons earmarked for the politically well-connected.[38]

As for the ultimate fate of the Jews, the observant could make a few simple calculations. For example on 15 December 1941, a Berlin schoolteacher wrote in his diary: 'The few remaining Jews in Germany are being taken away, to the east, as they say. And doing that now, in winter! It is clear as day that this means their destruction. They are being deposited in depopulated, devastated Russia, where they'll be left to freeze and starve. Whoever is dead doesn't talk any more.'[39] It required a considerable effort of denial for Germans not to be aware of what was going on. The steady drip of information from multiple sources was cumulatively compelling.

Karl Dürkefälden was a technician in a machine-tool factory in Celle. He made the following notes throughout 1942. In late February he noted a piece in his local Lower Saxon newspaper under the heading 'The Jews will be Eradicated'. This reported Hitler's latest repetition of the exterminatory prophecy he had first uttered in January 1939. A few days before, Karl had jotted down a remark made by a soldier on a train: 'Such mass exterminations did not happen in the last war.' In June, his brother-in-law returned from a construction job in the Ukraine. He told Karl about the mass shootings of Jews by German policemen that he had directly witnessed: 'There are no more Jews in the Ukraine, what hadn't fled, was shot. Jews and commissars who were captured were shot.' More soldiers told him that in Poland in the previous year thousands of Jews had been murdered, after first being forced to dig their own graves. On 20 June, his boss, who had a son serving in Białystok, told Karl that entire villages had been wiped out, including women and children. In August 1942, his stepmother reported that in the course of distributing cake to wounded German soldiers one of them had said: 'In Russia we've bumped off ten thousand Jews.' In October a colleague remarked: 'The poor Jews. My brother-in-law was on vacation in the Caucasus. All the Jews there have been mown down, regardless of whether they were pregnant women, children or infants.' At the same time Karl tuned in to BBC broadcasts which talked of the 'destruction of the Jews' and gave the first intimations that the Jews of Warsaw had been murdered by gassing. In December 1942 he jotted down the figures of massacres which the BBC had broadcast, adding that 'Poland has become a vast abattoir.' In January 1943 a former colleague who was by then serving in Vilna (Vilnius) told him that only 10 per cent of the Jewish population was still alive, and 'he added that Jews from France and other countries are being taken to Poland and partly gassed, partly shot there'. Dürkefälden had no high-level contacts and he never went anywhere near an extermination camp, having spent the war in Celle. What he recorded came from newspapers, the BBC and conversations with relatives, colleagues and strangers on the train.[40]

Such systematic notation of so many discrete clues to build an overall picture was unusual, and historians still struggle to achieve it, even with the benefit of documentary evidence and hindsight. The episodic, decentralised ways in which the murder of Europe's Jews evolved meant that people were discussing parts rather than the whole. The Allies were in much the same boat, with their intercepts of police radio traffic, until the Russian advance revealed the full ghastly truth. But they also had another source which has recently come to light in British archives. Captured German generals were held by the Combined Services Detailed Interrogation Centre houses at Latimer House and Wilton Park in Buckinghamshire and at Trent House in Middlesex. The atmosphere was relatively relaxed, and hidden microphones recorded their unguarded conversations.

Most of the generals, such as Wilhelm Ritter von Thoma, Ludwig Crüwell and Hans-Jürgen von Arnim, had been captured in North Africa and Tunisia, to be joined a year later by comrades who had fallen into

Allied hands in Normandy. British transcribers routinely capitalised place names with which they were unfamiliar. The transcript for 10 July 1943 includes the following from General Georg Neuffer to General Gerhard Bassenge:

> What will they say when they find our graves in Poland? The [Soviet] OGPU couldn't have done any worse. I myself saw a train in LUDOWICE?, near Minsk. I must say straight away that it was revolting, a horrible sight. There were trucks full of men, women and children – really small children. That is really a shock, this sight. The women, the small children, who were naturally totally unaware of what was happening. Naturally I didn't watch how they were then murdered. There were German policemen with machine pistols all around, and you know who they had with them? Lithuanians, or something like that, in brown uniforms, who did it.

On 19 December Colonels Reimann and Köhnke discussed atrocities in Russia:

> **Reimann:** This time it's true. Tell me, in 1914–18 did you really believe in your bones that a German soldier could do this?

> **Köhnke:** Never.

> **Reimann:** Never – now do you believe it today?

> **Köhnke:** I've been told so much about this, I have to believe it. I wasn't there myself, so I can't judge.

> **Reimann:** One day on the train a senior police officer told me that in Berdichev and Zhitomir thousands of Jews and women and children were shot dead – he told me that himself, without my asking him about it, and he described it so gruesomely and vividly that I reached up into my bag and took a bottle of vodka out. Eventually the conversation switched on to other subjects and we both got drunk. I've heard similar things from others. He talked about it all with the businesslike calm of a professional murderer.[41]

In Germany, rumours of what was happening in the east were so pervasive that it posed a dilemma for police and public prosecutors. Some vigorously prosecuted those who spread 'malicious rumours' or 'horror lies'. Thus a Munich woman received a three-year jail sentence for having said to her neighbour's mother: 'Do you think then that nobody listens to the foreign broadcasts? They have loaded Jewish women and children into a wagon, driven them out of the town, and exterminated them with gas.'[42] That was unusual, since rumours of mass gassings were much less frequent than those regarding open-air shootings, if only because the extermination centres were well hidden and involved far fewer perpetrators, who tended to keep to themselves. Other prosecutors, who knew that the rumours may have been true, thought better of having these subjects aired in open court. A Stuttgart Special Court decided in 1943 not to proceed against a forthright chimney sweep who had said, 'In Poland they've shot piles of Jews.' The senior prosecutor wrote on the case file, 'what was said about the treatment of the Jews is not suitable for public discussion'. However, it was the subject of much private discussion, possibly along the lines of what Walter Laqueur once memorably described as the belief that while the Jews were no longer alive, 'the Germans did not necessarily believe they were dead', an illogic all too common in wartime.

How Germans reconciled this information with their consciences partly depended on the wider course of the war, for it is incorrect to argue that the war forced people back into the private sphere with their horizons limited to personal survival. Moral lessons were drawn from the course of the fighting, which people followed intensely for their fathers, husbands and sons were involved. El Alamein and Stalingrad raised the distinct prospect that Germany might lose the war. Rumours abounded that the Soviets had shot all the German prisoners taken at Stalingrad. There were also Allied war crimes, from the discovery of mass graves at Katyń – which Goebbels rightly blamed on the NKVD – to increasingly devastating Allied bombing raids, which were regarded as a form of terrorism. Among the captured German generals in England, there was an acute consciousness of scale. General Neuffer could not understand the fuss Germany made over Katyń, 'Because that is almost a minor detail compared with what we've achieved'. A few days later Neuffer remarked that the Russians 'haven't yet reached the sites where the big mass murders happened'. For with defeat there was no more talk of 'evacuation' or 'special treatment'. Asked whether these murders were so vast, he replied: 'Yes, against the Russian Jews, and also the Polish ones. That was what I told you about before, that they bumped them off with all the possible evil side-effects. Compared with that, Katyń is next to nothing.'[43] This response to Katyń was also evident inside Germany, where religious circles were outraged by propaganda attempts to ramp up outrage over what the Russians had done, for 'in the east the SS have used similar forms of butchery in the fight against the Jews'. These crimes fully deserved God's punishment: 'The German people have burdened themselves with such a debt of blood that they cannot reckon on mercy and forgiveness. Everything revenges itself bitterly on this Earth. Because of these barbaric methods it is no longer possible for our enemies to conduct war humanely.'[44]

bombing

The Allied bombing raids were increasingly coupled by the German people with the fate of the Jews in ways that suggest public consciousness that a colossal crime had been committed. A Hamburg businessman, after the massive August 1943 RAF raids on his city, wrote that many local people were privately saying that 'this was revenge for the way we had treated the Jews'. Some imagined that the RAF was deliberately targeting churches in revenge for the destruction of synagogues in 1938, although the RAF was certainly never that accurate. To those who rhetorically asked what the Germans had done to deserve this treatment, some increasingly replied, 'because we've knocked off the Jews', an answer which resulted in a four-year prison sentence for the Berliner who uttered it in November 1943. This cause-and-effect logic became so commonplace that the Protestant bishop Theophil Wurm used it in his December 1943 appeal to Lammers, the head of the Reich Chancellery, linking the 'policy of destroying the Jews' with the carnage the Allies were raining down on Germans.

There were also dedicated anti-Semites who claimed the bombing was 'the Jews' revenge' and argued that it had been a tactical mistake to deport the Jews, who should have been kept as hostages in Germany. The RAF allegedly would never have bombed German cities if it knew it ran the risk of hitting ghettos. Another response was to project forward to the time when the community of the guilty would face collective punishment. The regime's leaders had their Macbeth moment of realising that they had waded so deep in blood that there was no way back for them, the common reason for so many suicides in 1945. Before that final accounting, they tried to turn a consensus of guilt into what lawyers call common cause. They insinuated multiple complicities that bound them to the German population, notably on 26 May 1944, when Hitler coupled his 'brutal' measures against the Jews with the benefits that had resulted for the Aryan majority. There had been hundreds of thousands of new jobs for the 'more able children of the *Volk*', jobs which peasant and proletarian children could aspire to which otherwise had been monopolised by the 'alien body' he had removed from their midst.

CHAPTER 17

Observing an Avalanche

Beyond the existential agonies of the ghettos, and the belated angst of the perpetrator nation, intermittently the fate of the Jews attracted the non-Jewish world's notice and sympathy. Isolated indications of what was abroad gradually became known, although this did not transcribe into knowledge of a general conspiracy to murder the Jews of Europe. Activists who drew attention to the plight of the Jews found that liberal democracies are adept at frustrating calls for inconvenient action, kicking them into touch by setting up committees to discuss them. In fairness, there were also major epistemological issues. There was an important gulf between being presented with discrete facts, being able to collate and verify them, and, finally, emotionally and intellectually grasping that a modern state in a civilised European country had reverted, with the aid of modern technologies, to practices dimly recalled from when the Mongols had assembled pyramids of skulls from conquered populations. That defied the pervasive post-Enlightenment belief in human progress. Those responsible for interpreting the significance of fragments of testimony that pointed to the systematic extermination of the Jews had a far harder task than would be the case nowadays, when television reporters convey vivid images of contemporary atrocities to back up the reports from NGOs – although Western equivocation over the genocides in Bosnia and Rwanda indicates that the will to ignore the inconvenient can ride over any amount of evidence.

More recent episodes of Western amorality are far more contemptible than the choices made by wartime Allied governments, whose primary concern was their own existential struggle against a Nazi state bent on their destruction, and which had killed many thousands of the Allies' own civilian populations. It is also easy to forget that policies about which so much

Nazis burned written orders (cf. Japan Aug '45-)

P 552

444 · MORAL COMBAT

is now known were once camouflaged with euphemisms and shrouded in secrecy. At the highest level, even today, one is compelled to infer certain things from Himmler's appointment book and telephone logs about conversations he had with Hitler. Himmler himself travelled incessantly because he wanted to communicate the most lethally sensitive orders by word of mouth. In August 1941, Heydrich insisted that all written orders to the Einsatzgruppen be burned or returned once their contents had been divulged.

Nonetheless, units operating in the field made regular reports of their murderous activities, usually by radio because secure telephone and telegram links were almost non-existent. Different SS agencies used a variety of equipment, frequencies and encryption methods to communicate from the field to headquarters. The Order Police used a code called Double Transposition until September 1941, when they began switching to Double Playfair. This involved a single codeword, for example 'magnet', followed by twenty-five of the letters of the alphabet (with j appearing as ii) arranged in a square, either in alphabetical order or jumbled out of sequence. Under this system, m would be a, g turned into c and so forth.[1] This was not a difficult code to break. From September 1939, British crypt-analysts at Bletchley Park were able to read Order Police communications on any given day, although after the invasion of the Soviet Union the Germans doubled the number of key pads employed and switched them every day. Given that British experts were only capable of decoding between half and a quarter of the messages they intercepted, they inevitably could not grasp the whole picture of what the Germans were doing, although they could and did draw inferences. After learning that Erich von dem Bach-Zelewski had killed more than thirty thousand people by 7 August, the cryptanalysts wrote that 'the leaders of the three sectors (meaning the four Einsatzgruppen) stand somewhat in competition with each other as to their "scores"'.[2]

There were other problems in analysing such material. The intelligence decrypts themselves necessarily replicated the deliberately vague way in which the originals referred to Bolsheviks, plunderers, partisans and so forth. While there was plenty of evidence of massacres, they did not add up to a deliberate policy of genocide, especially since the Jews of western Europe were not included at that time. British intelligence cannot be blamed for failing to see the wood for the trees, not least because most historians agree that the crucial decisions affecting all Europe's Jews had not been taken and involved a complex dialectic between centre and periphery. A fraction of this material was presented once a month to Churchill as part of his daily intelligence briefings. In a rare lapse from his usual caution about revealing intelligence sources and methods, on 24 August 1941 he said in a broadcast, 'As his [Hitler's] armies advance, whole districts are being exterminated. Scores of thousands – literally scores of thousands – of executions in cold blood are being perpetrated by German police-troops upon Russian patriots who defend Russian soil.' As a result of Churchill's overly specific reference to 'police-troops', on 13 September the head of the Order Police, Kurt Daluege, forbade his units to communicate 'Secret Reich Matters' by radio, namely anything relating to killing Jews which thenceforth was referred to in blander terms.

In addition to radio intercepts, the British secret service also managed covertly to open the diplomatic pouches of, for example, the Mexican ambassador to Portugal or the Chilean consul in Prague. In his reports the Mexican referred to disapproving stories in Italian newspapers about mass shootings in Russia. The Chilean, Gonzalo Montt Rivas, was much more approving of the fact that 'The German triumph will leave Europe freed of Semites,' although he feared that the Jews might seek asylum in Latin America. The British SIS sent such reports to their newly founded US equivalent, the Office of Strategic Services (OSS), which could do nothing at a time when the only apparent interest of the US government was to block Nazi-induced Jewish immigration.[3]

It is also easy to decontextualise these killings from a particularly desperate time in the Allied war effort. Many Jewish historians are exercised by the fact that in this broadcast Churchill did not specifically mention that most of the Nazis victims were Jews, or that in the midst of a global war in which the fate of Britain hung in the balance his attention to the dire circumstances of foreign Jews was intermittent. The broadcast had multiple agendas. It was a celebration of the unity of the English-speaking peoples, one alone (the US) being still at peace, while Canada, Australia, South Africa and New Zealand were at war, and it was an effort to rally British support for the Soviet Union, which itself did not regard the Jews as exceptionally victimised amid the murderous Nazi onslaught. The object of his broadcast was essentially political, directed at the Soviet Union as much as the British people, at a time when the latter were enduring a nightly rain of German bombs while the former were facing annihilation at the hands of the Wehrmacht. It seems doubtful whether the Soviets would have appreciated hearing that the Jews were the principal victims of Nazism when they were losing millions of soldiers. Churchill also mentioned every country in Nazi-occupied Europe, hoping to stimulate resistance.[4]

Jewish historians have also argued that Allied reactions to the murder of the Jews reflected not only indifference (and baser calculations and motives), but a universalist liberalism hostile to Jewish assertions of particularity. They may be right, although their views have gained no traction outside their own community. Criticism focuses on Britain's allegedly pro-Arab Foreign and Colonial Offices, although elsewhere in government the Labour Party's Home Secretary, Herbert Morrison, was repeatedly insisting that an influx of Jewish refugees would increase popular British anti-Semitism, an assertion never tested by polling, nor posed in terms of whether the British people would have opposed Jewish immigration if they knew the alternative facing the refugees was death. On virtually every occasion when the subject of rescuing Jewish refugees emerged, Morrison narrowly construed in terms of immigration what should have been within the country's generous traditions of asylum. The British did have legitimate anxieties lest the Nazis infiltrate spies among the refugees, and there were also geostrategic issues in the Middle East that trumped a more humanitarian response, before and during the war.

Ministers in the Colonial and Foreign Offices, notably Oliver Stanley and Anthony Eden, feared that at a time when the Afrika Korps was poised to break into Egypt any increase in Jewish immigration to Palestine would further antagonise not only the Palestinian Arabs but the Muslim world more generally at a time when more Muslims lived under British rule than any other. Increased Jewish immigration would bolster Zionist claims to the mandate and would upset the status quo the British had botched together, a settlement threatened by both a Palestinian Arab revolt and the mounting anti-British and anti-Arab terrorism of the Stern Gang. Having fixed Jewish immigration in 1939 to seventy-five thousand until March 1944, the British were niggardly in using such quotas to help European Jews evade the Nazis. The endemic problems of Palestine also had strategic implications. The Arab revolt had required stationing huge numbers of British troops there. Anything that avoided stoking up the Arabs would enable Britain to withdraw them for home defence or offensive operations. Moreover, the British also had to consider the fact that most of the best troops in the Indian Army, who would also be shipped over to fight in North Africa, happened to be Pashtun and Punjabi Muslims.[5] With Home Secretary Morrison barring the door to Jewish refugees, the Colonial Office was loath to admit them to other Crown colonies such as Kenya, and the

Dominions reported that their far-flung inns were full too. The logistics of wholesale rescue were another problem. Shortages of shipping, and the fact that ships were vulnerable to bombardment and submarines, also played their part. Once the Axis forces were expelled from North Africa, it was the US military that was most reluctant to give Jews a haven there, for in this respect US policy was as grudging as the British, despite the importance of Jewish-Americans in the Democratic Party, and President Roosevelt's appointment of a significant number of Jews in his administration. Jewish officials themselves tried to play down specifically Jewish issues, alive to the fact that in official Washington Jews were seen as 'screamers' and complainers. The US military was also keenly sensitive to avoid anything that might suggest that Gentile soldiers were dying to save Jewish lives. When an NCO reporter tried to publish a story about Auschwitz in the servicemen's magazine *Yank*, the editors told him the piece was too Jewish and to go away and find other victims of Nazi atrocities.[6]

There is no point denying that British politicians like Foreign Secretary Eden were biased in favour of Arabs over Jews, despite the Arabs being at best neutral towards the Allied cause or actively hostile in the case of the Mufti of Jerusalem, to whom Hitler had confided his murderous intentions. The region contained crucial oil resources and was also vital for communications to India, so it is not necessary to attribute the attitude of the Colonial and Foreign Offices to anti-Semitism, or to the belief, still prevalent, that it stemmed from a homosexual penchant for Arab boys. The ranks of Britons who tried to help the Jews included the upper-class homosexual anti-Semite Nigel Nicolson, which rather qualifies that line of argument. Maybe homosexuality inclined them to sympathy with other 'ambivalent' peoples?[7] There are better explanations regarding the conduct of entire bureaucracies, which applied just as much to the US as they did to Britain. Civil servants were acculturated to inter-government relations, rather than to dealing with individuals or lobby groups of indeterminate status. Jewish groups generally claimed to speak for Jews in general, although Britain itself had a historic Board of Deputies which performed such a function. The secular messianism of Zionism posed a threat to British interests akin to the Mufti of Jerusalem, although Jewish nationalists were perfectly correct in perceiving that their lack of statehood was a serious disadvantage in dealing with state bureaucrats of all descriptions in the Allied capitals. Jewish or pro-Jewish historians have been concerned mainly with magnifying the moral debt owed the people of Israel by

Western powers and naturally do not place their wartime demands in the context of many other peoples with no less legitimate national agendas. Working fifteen hours a day and seven days a week does not improve anyone's temper, and all wartime bureaucrats were chronically tired and emotionally ragged. If British officials sometimes spoke privately in a rebarbative way about Jews, they also spoke in similar terms about exiled Czechs and Poles, who likewise doggedly pursued what the officials saw as sectarian interests. It really should be noted that when one exasperated, and much quoted, Foreign Office official wrote of 'wailing Jews' a more senior colleague rebuked him by writing that the Jews 'had been given cause to wail by their sufferings under the Nazi regime'.[8]

Overall Allied government policy reflected the absolute priority, and agreed strategy, of defeating Nazi Germany and its allies. As Robert Reams, the US State Department's refugee specialist, baldly put it in December 1942, after receiving the first concrete reports about co-ordinated Nazi exterminatory policy: 'Whether the number of dead amounts to tens of thousands, or, as these reports state, to millions is not material to the main problem ... Our main purpose is the winning of the war and other considerations must be subordinate thereto.'[9] Nothing was to be done to relax the economic strangulation of the enemy represented by the Allied naval blockade. On one of the two occasions, in 1941, when under US pressure the British relaxed the blockade to ship 800,000 tons of wheat to France, Vichy's Admiral Darlan promptly turned the whole shipment over to the Germans. Relief for Greece followed for geopolitical reasons, which in turn triggered supplications from Belgium and Norway.[10] Once the doctrine of unconditional surrender had been adopted, there were to be no separate negotiations by the individual members of the alliance, even if such negotiations – in the notorious case of Eichmann's offer to trade Hungarian Jews for trucks – were ostensibly designed to rescue victims of Nazi persecution. The Soviets flatly opposed the scheme because those trucks would be deployed against them on the Eastern Front at a time when, thanks to Lend–Lease, the Russians enjoyed a considerable advantage in motorised transport over the Germans. That this offer was also, transparently, an attempt to drive a wedge between the Western Allies and Russia, and involved at least one Jewish double agent, Andor 'Bandi' Gross, who worked for the Gestapo, explains why no one, from Churchill downwards, was prepared to take it seriously. Finally, none of the Allies wished to collude with Hitler in his goal of making Europe *Judenrein*; the Allies wanted the Jews to remain in Europe, paradoxically despite mounting evidence that the Nazis were killing them. This last point is a distinction that needs more emphasis, if only to counteract the insinuation that the Allies were colluding with Hitler because of an allegedly pervasive anti-Semitism, an insinuation first made by David Ben Gurion, Israel's first prime minister.[11]

In addition to intelligence intercepts, another trickling stream of information about the plight of the Jews came from Richard Lichtheim of the Jewish Agency, the executive branch of the World Zionist Organisation, and from Gerhart Riegner of the World Jewish Congress, established in 1936 to combat Nazi persecution, both men based in neutral Switzerland. They were the tenuous bridge between the persecuted Jews of occupied Europe and Jewish organisations that had decamped to Jerusalem or New York. Chronically under-funded, they collated rumours and reports from across Nazi-occupied Europe and then relayed this information to Jewish and Zionist organisations in Jerusalem, London and New York in the hope it would be conveyed to Allied governments. For example on 4 March 1942 Lichtheim reported to Jerusalem that seventy thousand Jews were being expelled from Bohemia-Moravia and 'will be slowly starved as in the ghettoes of Warsaw and Łódź'. Later that month he reported the deportation of tens of thousands of Slovak Jews to 'a ghetto near the Polish border'; in fact they were being shipped to Auschwitz, although the gas chambers did not start operations until a few months later. Further information reached the Polish exiled government in London in May 1942 from the underground Jewish Socialist Bund inside Poland. Its report included details of how the Jews were being killed, as well as an approximate total of three hundred thousand dead for the region around Vilna. The report mentioned Chelmno: 'A special automobile (a gas chamber) was used. Ninety persons were loaded each time. The victims were buried in special graves, in an opening in the Lubard Woods. The victims had to dig their own graves before being killed.' The report calculated that forty thousand people had been murdered at the rate of a thousand a day, the majority from the Łódź ghetto. These were part of the seven hundred thousand the report claimed had been killed throughout Poland between June 1941 and April 1942.[12]

This report went to the National Council of the Polish exiled government. Its two Jewish members, the Bundist Szmul Zygelbojm and the Zionist Ignacy Schwarzbart, helped the exiled Polish leader General Władisław Sikorski make a highly specific BBC broadcast, which was then summarised in the BBC's daily news directive. Zygelbojm also published an article on 25 June 1942 in the *Daily Telegraph*, under the headline 'GERMANS MURDER 700,000 JEWS IN POLAND'. This was the first article on German mass murders of Jews to appear in any British newspaper. A few days later the story was picked up by the *Daily Mail* – 'GREATEST POGROM – ONE MILLION JEWS DIE' – as well as *The Times* and the *Manchester Guardian*. The Prime Minister's powerful special adviser Brendan Bracken attended a Polish National Council press conference in early July to publicise the report, which was given further attention in a broadcast by the Catholic Cardinal Arthur Hinsley.

By July 1942 there was testimony that these killings were being centrally orchestrated by the German authorities. Riegner in Geneva had indirectly received reports from the dissident German industrialist Eduard Schulte that the Nazis intended to kill all the Jews in Europe. It took him two days 'to take it in, to grasp it', even though he 'was of German origin ... [and] knew the real character of the Nazi movement. I knew they were capable of doing such things.' Riegner managed to get the British and US consulates to telegraph this intelligence to London and Washington. After receiving no response, he spent weeks gathering further information, which was transmitted in turn. Perhaps because Riegner said that these plans were 'under consideration', the Allies were dilatory in passing this information to either Stephen Wise of the World Jewish Congress or even to the MP Sydney Silverman, who would have relayed it to Wise.

Throughout the second half of 1942 more details flowed in. In November, a hundred or so Palestinian Jews from throughout Europe were exchanged for Germans interned by the Allies, one of a number of small exchanges that happened throughout the war. Their testimony lent substance to the continent-wide scale of Nazi atrocities, which militated against any illusions that these crimes were the work of rogue elements. That month too, one of the bravest men of the war, the Polish underground courier Jan Karski, journeyed across an occupied continent, literally rendered speechless by contrived dental problems and with a precious key in his pocket. Welded inside the key was microfilmed testimony about Nazi murderousness towards the Jews. Karski had not only smuggled himself into occupied Warsaw to talk to Jewish leaders who came out of the ghetto to meet him, but, more tellingly, had donned a Ukrainian uniform to get himself into Izbica Lubelska, a satellite camp of Belzec. One of the Jewish leaders in Warsaw told him, 'Witold [Karski's cover name], I know the English. When you describe to them what is happening to the Jews, they will probably not believe you.' Karski saw the Nazis robbing Jews of their valuables and then holding them in the satellite camp until the Belzec gas chambers caught up with the backlog, when they were re-entrained for their last journey. His eyewitness testimony, which included references to Sobibor and Treblinka as well as Belzec, was given to the Polish government in exile, and to leading British civil servants and politicians including Eden. They did believe him, but seemed more interested in the details of his odyssey – Eden even moved him into better light, the better to see a real hero – and in what value his information might have for SOE operations in Poland.[13]

These several sources of information led to the Allied declaration on 17 December 1942 condemning Nazi atrocities that had claimed the lives of 'hundreds of thousands' of Jews and which spoke of practical measures to visit retribution on the perpetrators. By that time two million rather than hundreds of thousands of Jews were dead. So far there was no reference to Auschwitz, regarded erroneously as exclusively a concentration camp for Christian Poles, although from early 1944 burgeoning industrial activities at the nearby IG Farben plant at Monowitz also began to attract Allied notice. The largest extermination centre for Europe's Jews therefore eluded Allied notice for a long time. But no matter how much intelligence about the extermination of Jews accumulated, it was not apparent what might best be done about something to which the word 'genocide' – let alone 'Holocaust' – had yet to be applied.

Before Karski left Warsaw in the direction of Belzec, the two Jewish underground leaders he contacted made various suggestions as to what the Allies might do. They should incorporate stopping the killing of the Jews into their war aims. They might 'name and shame' culpable German officials. They should appeal to the German people over the heads of their rulers, while warning that they would be held collectively responsible for such policies. The RAF had leafleted Germany in 1940 regarding the euthanasia programme, thereby forging a connection between German government criminality and Allied bombing. If this did not stop the exterminations, then the Allies should bomb targets selected for cultural significance, while executing any self-proclaimed Nazis they held in captivity. Karski responded by saying that 'It is against international law. I know the British. They will not do it.' He meant that to their credit.

The reprisal massacre of Czechs at Lidice, whose scale made it easier to comprehend, independently prompted British calls for retaliatory bombing of Germany. A Conservative MP made the fatuous suggestion that for every innocent person murdered by the Nazis, a German town or village should be subjected to low-level bombing, to which Churchill acidly replied that there 'would not be enough German villages to go round'. He might have added that it was no business of the British to sink as low as their opponents. Such raids would also have diverted the RAF from attacks on targets of major strategic significance. When in January 1943 Chief of the Air Staff Sir Charles Portal was asked his opinion about reprisal bombing operations against German targets in Poland, he raised a number of objections. It is worth noting that the appeal to him came from the Polish leader Sikorski, and therefore service chiefs were obliged to take it more seriously than such a plea from civilians. The extreme range meant that bombers would be able to deliver only a token payload, since the option of landing and refuelling in Soviet-held territory was not available. In addition it would be an extremely dangerous mission and, although civilians may not always appreciate it, service chiefs are honourably concerned with balancing the risks they ask their men to take against the likely benefits to the overall war effort. If the retaliatory purpose of these missions was announced through broadcasts or leaflets, the Germans would execute any downed pilots as war criminals. Portal warned that such operations would delegitimise and criminalise the bombing campaign as a whole. Surely, he argued, such attacks would also confirm the Nazis' own insistence that the Allies were waging war at the behest of the Jews? It was not in Britain's national interest to reinforce the paranoid imaginings of Nazi propaganda.[14]

Another suggestion was to take reprisals against German prisoners of war. This would have been a violation of international laws to which Britain subscribed. The great majority of German prisoners were held by the Soviets rather than the British, and Hitler had declined the International Red Cross's offer to aid these captives on a reciprocal basis with Soviet POWs held by the Germans – not surprisingly, given that most of the Soviet POWs had already died in German captivity. Stalin regarded all Red Army prisoners as cowards and traitors, and Hitler set no value on his own captured soldiers either. Lastly, the Nazis would certainly take reprisals against Allied prisoners if the British ignored their own civilised values and began to treat as hostages the Germans captured in North Africa, who many British combatants thought had waged a decent war.[15]

All that was left were increasingly threatening warnings of condign retribution for the perpetrators. Again, the Foreign Office was most sceptical about war crimes trials, largely because attempts to get the Turks or the Germans to prosecute their own nationals after the Great War had proved a farce. In the current conflict, pressure to prosecute the Germans had come from Allied governments, culminating in the April 1940 Anglo-French-Polish declaration on war crimes committed by the Nazis in Poland. Nine Allied governments also signed the St James's Palace Declaration of January 1942, which made war crimes trials a principal war aim. The War Cabinet discussed 'Treatment of War Criminals' in late July the same year, sending a request to Washington that the surrender of such persons be included in any eventual armistice with Germany. That October, the British won US assent to the creation of a United Nations Commission for the Investigation of War Crimes. The Russians refused to participate, partly because they had not been a party to the deliberations, but mainly because they wanted to embark on war crimes trials immediately. The British were concerned that the Germans might respond by treating their POWs more harshly, a consideration of no importance to the Russians.[16] In November the Allied foreign ministers issued the Moscow Declaration, which undertook to repatriate war criminals to the locations of their crimes in liberated Europe. Crimes committed inside Germany against German nationals were excluded because of difficulties stemming from the fact that they had legal sanction.[17] Finally, in December, an Anglo-American–Soviet declaration condemned the 'bestial, cold-blooded extermination' of the Jews and vowed retribution.

In March 1944 Eden rose in the House of Commons to express the British people's 'detestation of Germany's crimes and their determination that all those guilty of them would be brought to justice'. In July, Churchill instructed Eden that anyone associated with such murders should be tracked down, tried and executed. The British leader also acknowledged that 'this is probably the greatest and most horrible single crime ever committed in the whole history of the world'. The governments of Axis satellite states were warned that they would be held liable if they collaborated with Nazi exterminism, with the added warning that Allied bombing would be extended to them. Meanwhile, following the escape of Rudolf Vrba and Alfréd Wetzler from Auschwitz in early April 1944, first-hand testimony of what was being done there began its tortuous journey to Switzerland and the West. Every day that elapsed meant that another twelve thousand people were murdered and burned at Auschwitz. The report that finally reached Washington in June and London in July calculated that between April 1942 and April 1944 between 1.5 million and 1.75 million Jews had been killed in Auschwitz-Birkenau, by methods the report described in accurate terms.

A mini-literature has been devoted to why the (Western) Allies failed to bomb Nazi extermination camps once escapees like Vrba and Wetzler had provided the Allies with sketch maps that roughly indicated where the most lethal areas of Auschwitz were situated. This debate focuses on Auschwitz because Chelmno and the Aktion Reinhard camps were incredibly small, and had been decommissioned and dismantled anyway by the time any such raids were technically feasible. Armchair moralists have condemned the Allies for inaction, usually by isolating the desperate plight of the Jews from the entire global Allied war effort. The practical difficulties and extremely remote prospect of success have been forcefully demonstrated by distinguished historians of the air war like Tammi Biddle, James Kitchen and Williamson Murray, who know a thing or two about flight times, bombloads and aerial reconnaissance.

The workings of the (military) bureaucratic mind are important in considering this subject dispassionately. In December 1940 Count Stefan Zamoyski, aide to General Sikorski, wrote to Air Marshal Sir Richard Peirse, then head of RAF Bomber Command, requesting him to bomb the concentration camp at Oświęcim. At the time the camp housed ten thousand Polish political prisoners, of whom around twenty were Jews. There were indications, however, that the camp was being expanded. The response of the RAF High Command was instructive. Sir Charles Portal acknowledged that there might be political considerations which would make such a raid desirable, but he rejected such an operation primarily because it was a diversion from planned strikes against oil-related targets. He also argued that at such distances planes flying from English bases could not hope to deliver a sufficiently decisive payload, since more fuel meant fewer bombs. Peirse was also sceptical whether bombs would sufficiently damage the camp's perimeter wire to enable prisoners to escape, and worried that the RAF might contrive to kill them all by way of collateral damage. (In the context we should anticipate the Butt Report in the summer of 1941, which showed that only one in five British bombers dropped their bombs within five miles of their designated targets.) As is crushingly normal in all bureaucracies, once that line had been adopted it became difficult to reverse. It categorically had nothing to do with anti-Semitism, and everything to do with Allied priorities for winning the war.[18]

The issue of bombing Auschwitz recurred in the context of the Nazis' decision in 1944 to murder the Jews of Hungary. It is important to establish the wider strategic context of Allied decision-making before presuming to second-guess the men making these decisions. Before D-Day, vast aerial resources were devoted to wrecking the entire rail network of northern France, to prevent the Germans from reinforcing the troops facing the Allied beachheads in Normandy. The planned invasion was the largest amphibious operation in history, in which the consequences of failure were unthinkably great. The Western Allies simply had to get into the continental land battle to match the effort of the Soviets. After the invasion, massive bomber forces were still needed to blast a way out of Normandy for the Allied armies, which were held up by tenacious German defence. After the break-out, Allied progress was so rapid that it outran logistical support, requiring the bombers to airlift supplies to the advancing armies. Other bombers were also at work in Italy as well as over the Reich in a punishing cycle of round-the-clock destruction. RAF Bomber Command's supremo, Arthur Harris, was sceptical towards what he called 'diversionists', even those who demanded he send his bombers to destroy the launch sites for the V1 flying bombs and V2 ballistic missiles that were raining down on London.

Harris also had to comply with a joint directive committing the RAF and the USAAF to mount precision raids against German oil installations, ball-bearing plants and other critical targets. This approach seemed to pay off when Allied intelligence noted the Germans' concerns that they were running out of aviation fuel and were dipping deeply into strategic reserves. Training flying hours for Luftwaffe pilots were curtailed to economise on aviation fuel. However, it was also the case that, like the railways, the Germans were adept at repairing these plants, so that while aviation-fuel production fell by 98 per cent in July 1944, by August it had risen to 64 per cent capacity, before falling again to 30 per cent in September. In other words, the Allies had to return time and again to ensure that the Germans could not restore production. The only mission that could be compared to a notional raid on Auschwitz came when the Allies attempted to resupply the Polish underground fighters in their Warsaw uprising, where most of the drops fell into the hands of the Germans and the Soviets permitted only a limited number of bombers to refuel at their Poltava air base.[19]

The Allied air forces had developed a limited capacity to carry out pinpoint raids on vital targets. Ironically, the much vaunted Norden bombsight of the USAAF could not 'drop a bomb in a pickle barrel' as advertised, and it was the RAF that delivered the really accurate attacks. Even then, the drain on resources was significant. The famous attack on the Ruhr dams required the development of specialist 'bouncing bombs', took a squadron of the most experienced crews in Bomber Command out of the front line for weeks of intensive training and cost many of them their lives. By early 1944 the RAF had developed expertise in low-level attacks using the astonishing Mosquito multi-purpose aircraft. In February, one such raid was mounted at the request of the French resistance to smash the walls of the Gestapo prison at Amiens, where many resistance fighters were awaiting execution. One hundred prisoners were killed during the raid, and the majority of the 250 who escaped were recaptured and shot. The target consisted of a single identifiable building – as was the case in a subsequent raid on the Gestapo offices in Copenhagen, where a Mosquito crashed into a children's school – and the flying distance from Britain was not great. It is much less certain that a Mosquito force could have undertaken such an operation against Auschwitz-Birkenau, although some argue that this would have been morally or symbolically important even if it had not succeeded. The air crew who would have died might beg to differ.[20]

The campaign against German oil facilities took heavy Allied bomber formations into the general proximity of the death-camp complex at Auschwitz, although this was 650 miles distant from the air base at Foggia in southern Italy, across the Alps and Carpathian mountains. The oil installations were a highly dispersed set of targets that included oil refineries at Trzebinia, thirteen miles away from Auschwitz-Birkenau, and, two and a half miles from the camp complex, the IG Farben synthetic-petroleum plant Buna with an adjacent concentration camp called Monowitz or Auschwitz III. This was the satellite slave-labour camp where the chemist Primo Levi had been a prisoner. Commencing with a South African reconnaissance flight on 4 April, the complex was photographed from high altitude with cameras which recorded each frame on nine-inch-square plates. Back at the analysis unit at RAF Medmenham in Buckinghamshire, experts had lenses which magnified these images four times, or to a maximum of seven with more specialist equipment. These photos were among the twenty-five thousand negatives and sixty-thousand prints the analysts received each day, images that covered a host of targets from factories and fortifications and warships to rocket launch sites. The analysts used manuals of earlier images as keys to help them interpret the new photographs. If the object was to disable a synthetic-fuel plant, then they sought to identify crucial choke points whose destruction might bring the whole complex to a halt. None of these key manuals had any sections marked crematoria or gas chambers; the death complex was marked as 'hutted camps', which might have been anything from a barracks to construction sites.[21] Further flights in May, June and September surveyed the entire complex of camps, including Auschwitz I and Birkenau, to assess the effects of USAAF raids that struck Buna-Monowitz for the first time on 20 August. A second wave of photography on 25 August included images of what have been identified, with modern technology, as gas chambers and crematoria. That level of magnification was not, however, available to photo-analysts in 1944.[22] Ironically a bombing photo taken during the raid on 13 September shows a prematurely released stick of bombs falling towards Auschwitz-Birkenau. In sum, the photo-analysts' focus was on destroying a synthetic-fuel plant. They did not see a chemical plant at either Auschwitz I, the old main camp, or among the barracks at Birkenau, therefore they had no reason to examine them any further, and turned to the thousands of other images awaiting their attention.

There is one more point worth making if we are to lay to rest the vexed question of bombing Auschwitz: the proposal came up in the context of the project to exchange Jews for trucks, which the Allies could never seriously consider. Aiding and abetting the SS, who made the initial proposition, would have infuriated the Soviets, who were always on the look-out for evidence that their Western allies might make a separate peace.[23] The way in which Jewish representatives posed the matter of bombing Auschwitz is also instructive, for it hardly suggested it was among their priorities, while the manner of its presentation would have been off-putting for anyone listening to them. When one reads the relevant documents, the limited importance they attached to bombing vis-à-vis other matters is also instructive. On 6 July 1944 Foreign Secretary Eden received a visit from Chaim Weizmann and Moshe Shertok, the senior Jewish Agency representatives in London, whose agenda was dominated by attempts to reactivate the exchange, originally proposed by Eichmann, of trucks for the Hungarian Jews. In the aide-memoire they left with Eden, items 3a-c, 4 and 5 concern the trucks-for-Jews proposal. Only in the final point 6e did the Jewish Agency request that the British bomb the railway line connecting Budapest and Birkenau.[24] Before that, one had to figure out such involutions as the following items 4 and 5:

> Since the submission of these proposals, one of our friends in Istanbul, a Palestinian, has received a message from the Jewish centre in Budapest urging him to come to Budapest for a discussion, and informing him that his safe return would be guaranteed. While fully

realising the risks involved, we would submit that he should be allowed to proceed, preferably together with Joel Brand.

...

That any Gestapo offer to release Jews must have ulterior motives – avowed or hidden – is fully appreciated. It is not, however, improbable that in the false hope of achieving these ends, they would be prepared to let out a certain number of Jews – large or small. The whole thing may boil down to a question of money, and we believe that the ransom should be paid.

Eden relayed the memo's contents to Churchill, adding, 'I am in favour of acting on both suggestions.' On 7 July Churchill categorically rejected the Brand mission as tantamount to giving succour to the enemy, but ordered Eden: 'Get anything out of the Air Force you can, and invoke me if necessary.' That was easier said than done. A week after Eden had despatched his inquiries, with no suggestion of urgency, the Secretary for Air Sir Archibald Sinclair replied, pointing to the enormous force required to disrupt the railway system of northern France before D-Day – which, it is as well to recall, had been launched the previous month and was the focus of Allied attention, along with finding and destroying the launch sites of the V1 flying bombs that were causing panic in London. Interdicting a railway line was not as easy as it sounds, since track could be rapidly replaced. Sinclair did not rule out a raid on the camps, although he recalled the technical difficulties of February's attack on Amiens jail. He was unsure whether such attacks would help the victims, to which Eden acidly remarked, 'He wasn't asked his opinion of this; he was asked to act.' Sinclair also suggested seeing what the Americans felt before acting further, perhaps secure in the knowledge that in late June both the Operations Division of the US War Department and Assistant Secretary of War John McCloy had categorically rejected such operations in favour of whatever was deemed decisive to the Allied defeat of Germany. When similar requests were repeated in November 1944, McCloy again rejected them.[25]

The prospect of the Allies killing camp inmates was real enough. When, on 24 August, the USAAF bombed a V1 rocket-guidance plant next to Buchenwald, releasing over three hundred bombs in near-perfect conditions, they killed 315 inmates and badly wounded 525 more, with a further nine hundred minor casualties. Given that Auschwitz functioned as a dual-purpose slave labour and death camp, it is not the case that the Allies would have killed people destined to die anyway. They would have been killing people who, according to the huge literature on survival were desperate to stay alive. It was a hard call to make, especially since one can all too well imagine modern lawyers retroactively accusing the bomber crews of murder. In an attempt to globalise guilt for the Holocaust – including a 1990 pseudo-legal condemnation of the USAAF by an Israeli entity for failure to save the lives of thousands of Jews – the Allies have been taken to task for what are not merely alleged sins of omission. Coolness to the plight of Jewish refugees in the pre-war period, which there was, is carried over to insinuate culpable neglect during the war itself, all designed to show that the Gentile world was indifferent to the Jews. The only way it can be portrayed as such is if every other human or strategic consideration which decision-makers confronted is ignored.[26]

There is another omission from this story that seems curious. In September 1944 the British Board of Deputies asked the Soviets to bomb the extermination camps. They received no acknowledgement or answer to what was a reasonable request, given the proximity of the Red Army to these targets. The Soviets were the first to commence trials of captured German war criminals, starting with the public show trials at Krasnodar in July 1943. The Soviets contrived not to mention the ethnicity of the seven thousand people who had been slain there in 'murder vans'. Further evidence of mass murder emerged at a Soviet trial of three Germans and a Russian collaborator watched by six thousand people in the theatre of newly liberated Kharkov in December of the same year. The London *Times* account of the trial followed Soviet practice of never mentioning that the horrendous number of people killed by the accused were Jews. Some grainy film footage shows the four guilty men swinging at a public hanging attended by forty thousand spectators.[27] Every study of the Allies' response to the Holocaust either omits the Soviet Union entirely or appends the Soviets as an afterthought, even though 1.5 to 2 million of the USSR's five million Jews perished at Nazi hands. Some of this bias possibly reflects wartime solidarity with the undoubtedly heroic Red Army. It is also the case that many historians of Nazi Germany tend to be on the political left and hence disinclined to consider the moral equivalence of Soviet crimes. The Soviet Union was the only state to accord the Holocaust no heightened significance after the war, and *Pravda* reported the 1961 Jerusalem Eichmann trial without once using the word 'Jew'. But the most likely reason why the Allies have been accused of culpable negligence for not performing an operation that would almost certainly have ended in disaster, whereas the Soviets have received a pass for their failure to make the slightest effort to destroy the gas chambers when they were within easy reach of their highly effective fighter-bombers, may be the different susceptibilities of the two sides to guilt, a crucial element in the establishment and survival of the Jewish state.

So let us try to apportion blame, if we must, according to the facts. The Soviets certainly knew about concentration camps, since they operated the largest camp system in the world at the time and had the equivalent of major urban populations behind barbed wire. They were also familiar with deporting entire ethnic groups, as the Chechens, Crimean Tartars, Poles and Volga Germans discovered. They also persecuted people for their religious beliefs as well as for their class or nationality. The Holocaust would not have caused Stalin and his associates any difficulties of comprehension. They tortured and murdered people all the time. Although Jews of an internationalist and proletarian outlook were certainly welcomed into the Communist Party, it was adamantine in its opposition to Orthodox Jews and Zionists, who emphasised Jewish apartness. Stalin had also risen to supreme power by defeating enemies like Trotsky, Zinoviev and Kamenev who were all of Jewish origin. Although the Hungarian Jew Arnold Paucker, who commanded his security detail, shaved him every morning, one day in 1937 Stalin had him arrested and shot for no given reason. Stalin verbally disparaged the 'Yids', even though his circle of cronies included several Jews who had a rare dispensation from being expected to get blind drunk. One of his first instructions to Molotov on appointing him foreign minister to replace the Jewish Maxim Litvinov, who was sacked to appease the Nazis, was to 'Clean out the synagogue,' meaning the Jews employed in his ministry.[28] A year later he vowed to Ribbentrop that 'as soon as he had adequate cadres of Gentiles he would remove all Jews from leading positions'.[29] During the two years of the Molotov–Ribbentrop Pact, and NKVD liaison with the SS along the joint border, all references to Nazi persecution of the Jews disappeared from official Soviet media. In line with the Marxist-Leninist interpretation of history, the Soviets declared that Fascism was the most extreme variant of monopoly capitalism, an evident imbecility. The tactical and ideological downplaying of the centrality of Jew-hating to the Nazi regime meant that no attempts were made to warn the Jews to vacate areas menaced by the invaders, although large numbers of Jews did flee, or enjoyed the mixed blessing of being deported to Siberia after the Soviets invaded eastern Poland and suppressed all Jewish communal or religious life. When the poet Zelig Akselrod protested against Soviet closure of

Yiddish newspapers and Jewish schools in Vilna, he was arrested and shot by the NKVD.

The Soviet Union's need for Western support explains why Stalin quickly appointed the disgraced Litvinov as ambassador to Washington, while Stalin licensed five sectoral anti-Fascist committees representing women, youth, scientists, Slavs and Jews, all under the umbrella of the Soviet Information Bureau. The Jewish Anti-Fascist Committee was chaired by the actor and theatre director Solomon Mikhoels. Two Polish Bundist Socialists temporarily released by the NKVD had other ideas about how this might be organised. They were rearrested in 1942; one committed suicide in his cell, the other was shot. The Committee sought to raise money from wealthy Jews in the US through tours where they were fêted by the likes of Albert Einstein and Paul Robeson. Another object of the Committee was to document and publicise Nazi crimes against Soviet Jews. At the instigation of Einstein, and under the leadership of the prominent Soviet-Jewish war correspondent Ilya Ehrenburg, two dozen writers, including Vasily Grossman of the paper *Red Star*, were invited to investigate and write about Nazi mass murders, which in Grossman's case had claimed his own mother in Berdichev. Grossman wrote devastating accounts of what he saw in Majdanek and Treblinka after the Soviets rolled over these camps.[30] In 1943 Ehrenburg and Grossman began collecting materials for a *Black Book of Soviet Jewry*. Thousands of Jewish survivors wrote in with poignant personal testimony. Sixty-five reports were to be incorporated into a vast twelve-hundred-page monument to the Jewish dead. Grossman knew on which side his bread was buttered; while fawning on the 'genius liberator', he omitted the extensive evidence of indigenous, Baltic, Russian and Ukrainian collaboration with the Nazis in murdering Jews.

Once the war was over, everything changed. Even before the *Black Book* was published, it had fallen into official disfavour, in line with a general hostility to Jewish particularism, especially in the armed forces after Grossman and Ehrenburg had emphasised the feats of Jews in the Red Army. As early as 1941 the novelist Mikhail Sholokov had turned on Ehrenburg, saying: 'You are fighting, but Abraham is doing business in Tashkent.' Jews were often also disparaged as 'Tashkent partisans' for hiding out in that remote place while Russians did the fighting, despite the fact that Jews were over-represented among Soviet servicemen.[31] In 1943 Ehrenburg's daughter was sacked from the paper *We Will Destroy the Enemy* by a Red Army colonel who screamed, 'Is this [editorial office] a synagogue?' After the *Black Book* was printed in 1946, not a single copy found its way into bookstores or public libraries, and the warehoused books and type blocks were destroyed two years later.[32] In that year, Solomon Mikhoels was murdered by the NKVD in Minsk, a killing dressed up as a car accident. Fifteen members of the Committee were arrested, including a man under sedation in hospital, and tortured. Thirteen of them were executed. Grossman's epic war novel *Life and Fate* was also consigned to what the authorities thought was oblivion.[33]

To summarize the blame game: although an inordinate amount of criticism has been focused on the Western Allies for not bombing extermination camps, or for failing to air-drop arms to the imprisoned Jews, no one seems to ask why the Soviets did not use their huge air force for similar raids – the flight time from Poltava, where RAF and USAAF bombers refuelled, was a great deal shorter than from Foggia in south Italy or Lincolnshire – nor why they failed to drop paratroops who would have made short work of the SS men who ran the death camps. Nor have the Russians ever admitted to what the NKVD did in occupied Poland. The reason for this blatant bias may well lie in the geopolitical and ideological considerations already suggested, although total lack of access to the wartime archives of the NKVD also helps to explain the remarkable dearth of books about the Soviets (inaction of) and the Holocaust. About that there is no debate.

CHAPTER 18

Tenuous Altruism

I RESCUERS

In 1942 the West Galician town of Przemyśl was an important transport hub for supplying the southern section of the Eastern Front. About a third of the town's sixty thousand inhabitants were Jews, all confined in a ghetto separated from the town by the River San. The first wave of deportations hit Przemyśl in late July 1942, when the SS began preparations to transport Jews to Belzec, leaving only a smaller number of those aged sixteen to thirty-five alive as forced labour. On the night of 26 July, a few Jews managed to slip out of the ghetto, pleading with one of the city's army administrators, Lieutenant Albert Battel, to save them. He persuaded his fellow officers of the necessity of such a course of action, and then enlisted the support of Major Max Liedtke, the city's military commandant. Liedtke intervened with the SS on behalf of what were called 'armed forces Jews', people needed to keep the logistics flowing. Battel then warned the SS that the army was taking control of the bridge over the San, which gave access to the ghetto, and that they were closing it to all civilians, including the police. When the SS tried to cross the bridge, they found themselves staring into army machine guns.

The SS in Cracow quickly agreed to respect the papers the army issued to the Jews it sought to protect. Although Battel and Liedtke did not ultimately stop the SS carrying out their raids on the ghetto, Battel did shelter ninety Jews and their families inside his own HQ. He sent two trucks to rescue 250 more, warning the SS who tried to stop him that he would impose martial law. The Jews Battel saved were then fed from the military canteen. Although Battel did not stop the deportations, he issued permits for a further 2,500 Jews, which spared their lives. The SS did not like being impeded and complained all the way up to Himmler about Battel and Liedtke. They discovered that Battel was a former lawyer and Nazi Party member from Breslau, against whom there had been earlier complaints of his being friendly to or helping Jews. In 1933 he had helped his sister-in-law and her Jewish husband to escape to Switzerland. Nothing happened to Battel for the almost singular offence of threatening the SS with force; in fact, in August 1942, he was promoted to captain. After the war he was imprisoned by the Allies after lawyer colleagues in Breslau denounced him as a fervent Nazi who had profited from Nazi Aryanisation measures. Liedtke was not so lucky. He was a former editor of a conservative nationalist newspaper in Greifswald. Maybe he hoped to resume that career after the war. In 1946 he was detained by the Soviet security police in Denmark and tried for war crimes: among other charges he had allegedly executed a thousand hostages. He died in a camp hospital near Sverdlovsk in 1955.[1]

It might be argued that these two German officers were primarily concerned to retain Jewish workers for what was a major railway hub. That seems unlikely, although rescuing people in any numbers certainly depended upon being in a position to conceal or protect them. Battel had a record of philo-Semitic activity, and was the first port of call when danger threatened Przemyśl's Jews. More significantly, both men were in a position to act altruistically, since they could use the argument of military necessity to trump the SS and had the railway yards to employ the Jews they saved.

Although threats to use force were almost unique, other German soldiers also risked much to help the Jews, including their own lives. Reinhold Lofy was a young soldier from a Catholic background. Having refused to join the Hitler Youth, this former altar boy was badly assaulted when such a Nazi gang ran into him in his Boy Scout's uniform. Called up in October 1941 he was posted to Woronesch, where one day he refused a corporal's order to shoot an elderly Jew on the grounds it was incompatible with his faith. Three years later, as a newly minted lieutenant, he refused to send his men out on suicidal missions. Remarks he made about the Nazi Party and the war on the Jews resulted in his being denounced. Lofy was sentenced to six years in a penal battalion.

Corporal Anton Schmidt was a tall, quiet, middle-aged soldier stationed in Vilna, in a unit whose task it was to reassemble shattered German army formations. He was no intellectual and never opened a book or a newspaper. He ran a truck-repair yard near the city's main railway station. For six months in late 1941, he forged false papers which he used to spirit three hundred Jews out of Vilna, depositing them in the smaller towns of Lithuania where they seemed safer. Once a week he hid them behind logs and drove them to their new homes. He also employed 140 Jews and their families inside his truck park as maintenance workers. Taking incredible risks, he made contact with the Jewish underground resistance in Vilna, driving their leaders to Warsaw for meetings with their opposite numbers in the former capital. Members of the Vilna resistance met in his quarters, where on New Year's Eve 1941 the leaders of the newly formed partisan movement gathered at his invitation. He was arrested by the Gestapo in January 1942 after they noticed that many of the Jews in Lida originated in Vilna. Under torture they revealed who had brought them there. Schmidt was sentenced to death by firing squad and executed on 13 April. He left a letter to his wife and daughter Gerta. To get past censors he said that he had seen Lithuanian militiamen, rather than Germans, shoot two to three thousand Jews in a meadow. Children had clutched at tree trunks on their way to their deaths. At his workplace Jews begged him to save them. 'You know what I'm like, with my soft heart. I couldn't think, and then helped them, which was bad from the court's viewpoint,' he wrote. 'My beloved Steffi and Gerta, please consider that although this is a hard blow for us, please forgive me nonetheless. I only acted as a human being, and never wanted to harm anyone. By the time you, my beloved ones, have this letter in your hands, I'll be gone from this world … rest assured that we'll see one another again in a better world with our beloved God.'[2]

A dictionary defines altruism as behaviour 'carried out to benefit another without anticipation of rewards from external sources'. In the eyes of Auguste Comte, who coined the term, it is the opposite of egoism, a faculty Comte knew well, as he founded his own religion as well as sociology. Some biologists and geneticists think altruism is innate in the human race, although circumstances have to trigger it. Religious people believe it is a divine presence, albeit in human hearts which are also subject to the competing temptations of evil. Acts of rescue were usually the product of a momentary wave of human feeling, as when confronted by some lice-ridden, scabrous child. Altruists saw a fellow human being in distress rather than the Jew the Nazis meant them to see. Of course this was not like helping an injured bird, cat or dog. To pursue that analogy, one would have to imagine the creature in question surrounded by a triangulating pack of wolves, maybe adding in a few deadly snakes crawling around too. Then think about saving the bird, cat or dog again, substituting informers for the snakes and uniformed policemen for the wolves.

But rescue could also be the more emotionally detached actions of those with a professional or religious vocation to serve other people. One would not have much confidence in a dentist saying, 'This is hurting me as much as you.' Professionals were not usually swayed by sudden bursts of feeling, since they often needed to suppress such emotional responses to carry out their vocation, decade in, decade out. The sociology of rescuers is uninteresting. Businessmen, peasants, monks, nuns and priests did a great deal more rescuing than academic philosophers, of whom history has recorded not a single example of altruism in this era, although they do a lot of writing on these subjects. Rescuers acted for myriad motives which can be crudely rehearsed, for good is a lot harder to fathom than evil. Some acted to please an external authority, whether God, Jesus or a notably ethical parent, recalling a father who 'taught me to respect all human beings'. Others were driven by a patriotic hatred of the Nazis, thereby combining what many regard as evil with good. Rescue was often an act of defiance rather than focused on Jews as such, something which may also apply to the individualists and mavericks who relished defying convention. There were also religious believers with their own experiences of being a hunted minority, like the Huguenots who saved five thousand Jews at La Chambon, or groups like the Hungarian Mennonites, Ukrainian Baptists and members of the Dutch Reformed Church, who accorded the biblical Jews special religious meaning. Dutch Reformed Church members were only 8 per cent of the Dutch population, yet they were a quarter of all known rescuers in that country.[3]

Around thirteen thousand people have been formally recognised by Israel's Yad Vashem Holocaust memorial as righteous Gentiles, although the official responsible for awarding such an honour reckons the real figure should be ten times that, allowing for the deaths of both the rescuers and the Jews who might have nominated them. Although the act of rescue was often the spontaneous choice of individuals, it also reflected conditions that were beyond individual control. This is why a few German businessmen and industrialists are justifiably celebrated, including Friedrich Graebe and Franz Fritzsch, and the Austrians Julius Madritsch and Raimund Titsch. The Sudeten German Oskar Schindler rescued fifteen hundred Jews by employing them in his enamelware factory in Cracow, partly by bribing and manipulating the SS officers with whom he remained on genuinely cordial terms. It was a dangerous path this human enigma elected to tread. Schindler was very quick-witted, as he demonstrated when he scribbled his own factory as the destination on a bill of lading for a truckload of a hundred Jews freezing to death on a railway siding. That propensity to act spontaneously for the good of a human being in distress was the common characteristic of rescuers. Rational deliberation, carefully weighing up the pros and cons, would have meant delay and death for many, including the rescuers. Entirely prosaic by background and future life, rescuers were people who in a brief moment made certain choices which humanity rightly admires.

It is important to outline certain objective circumstances which contributed to national disparities in the numbers of Jews who survived the war. The margin for manoeuvre was much wider in countries where the Germans ruled indirectly, since collaborating native officials might be simultaneously susceptible to the rival calls of patriotism to hedge their future bets. How the Nazis viewed a given population was also relevant. They actively sought collaborators among racially cognate Danes, Dutch and Norwegians, while in the case of Poles their racial doctrines made any institutionalised collaboration impossible, although there were many Poles who blackmailed and betrayed Jews or responded with alacrity when the cry went up 'Catch the Jew.'[4] Physical geography also played a part, since there were fewer places for Jews to hide in densely populated Holland than in the Italian Apennines or the remote uplands of central France. The size and degree of assimilation of the Jewish communities had bearings on rescue efforts. It was easier to help the small Danish Jewish community, a mere seven thousand persons and fifteen hundred refugees (the Danish authorities had refused sanctuary to many more), than the three million Jews of Poland. Denmark had a functioning government and parliament until late 1943, and only the two-miles-wide Øresund channel separated Denmark from neutral Sweden, which, once it realised how the war was likely to end, had abandoned its earlier restrictive refugee policy. Most Danish Jews were physically and linguistically indistinguishable from their fellow Danes. Last but not least, the Nazi plenipotentiary to Denmark, Werner Best, decided that rocking the Danish domestic political boat was too high a price to pay for deporting a few thousand Jews, especially as they were not easily identifiable. Whether or not Best allowed the Jews to escape remains highly controversial, but he had technically made Denmark *Judenfrei*. None of which should detract from those Danes who took Jews across the Sound, whether or not for a fee, but this exceptional rescue effort was clearly the result of very specific constellations rather than more romantic notions of national character.[5]

High levels of assimilation, and the low resonance of anti-Semitism also meant that many Italian Jews survived, although it helped that Italy had a dense network of ecclesiastical sanctuaries amenable to the instructions of Pope Pius XII, who, recent research shows, intervened to help the Jews with a familiar clerical combination of caution and kindness that hardly justifies the Communist-inspired attempts to demonise him in the post-war years.[6] While such sanctuary very occasionally involved attempts to convert Jewish children to Christianity, it should be recalled that the Franciscan friars who sheltered two hundred Jews at Assisi actually provided them with kosher meals, which suggests that conversion was not among their priorities. Rather it reflected the religious virtues of charity and hospitality.[7]

Poland was sandwiched between Nazi Germany and the occupied territories in Russia, with more German-occupied countries to the south. It was subject to the most brutal regime in occupied Europe, which in the course of the war murdered three million Christian Poles as well as 90 per cent of the country's Jews. Before the war, many Polish Jews, whether for reasons of religious orthodoxy or Zionist ideology, rejected assimilation and sought to preserve an autonomous Jewish culture in a country that was anxious about its ethno-religious homogeneity as well as about its totalitarian neighbours. Nearly 80 per cent of the Jewish population spoke Yiddish rather than Polish, with many of these eastern Jews further identifiable through physical appearance, diet and occupational profile. The Polish word *Zyd* also had many of the offensive resonances of the English 'Yid' rather than the term 'Jew' into which it should be translated.

There was another unique difference. Unlike the rest of Europe, where overt anti-Semitism was restricted to small groups of pro-Nazi Fascist collaborators, in Poland, anti-Semitism was part of the patriotic consensus and was politically represented in both the underground and the exiled democratic governing parties. Many Polish patriots found it possible to hate both Germans and Jews, linked linguistically anyway by German-sounding Yiddish. The Nazi plans to remove the Jews to Madagascar were based on Polish government feasibility studies completed in the late 1930s. Anti-Semitism was especially, but not exclusively, evident on the Catholic conservative right, reflecting a long-harboured desire to mitigate what such circles regarded as a Jewish problem, as well as opposition to Soviet occupation, towards which many Jews had been sympathetic.[8] Poles and Jews regarded each other with suspicion, while Gentile Poles were divided into those who deplored German treatment of the Jews and those who sneakily admired its radicality. Only a small Fascist minority openly celebrated the removal of the Jews, although large numbers of Poles benefited from the expropriation of the Jews, or from the employment opportunities and social mobility that their removal afforded. When Zofia Kossak, a famous writer who belonged to a Liberal Catholic opposition group, condemned the Nazis' barbarous treatment of the Jews, and the Pilate-like response of many Poles, she added the rider that 'our feelings towards the Jews have not undergone a change. We have not stopped regarding them as the political, economic and ideological enemies of Poland. What is more, we are well aware that they hate us more than the Germans, that they hold us responsible for their misfortune.'[9]

Despite being primarily focused on helping the Allies win the war, in the air or at Cassino and Arnhem, while dealing with the existential matter of Poland's future eastern borders, the exiled Polish government did publicise Nazi crimes against the Jews, which it condemned in a number of forceful statements. One should not underrate the perils of saving Jews in Poland. Jews were physically isolated from Gentile Poles – who faced the death penalty, not only for helping Jews cross over from the ghettos to the Gentile world, but even for giving Jews a cup of water or selling them an egg.[10] It was only in late 1942, by which time many Polish Jews were dead, that the underground ruling body – the Delegatura – licensed the Żegota organisation, which equipped Jews with false documents and funded a few thousand families living in hiding. Zofia Kossak was a leading light of this Council for Assistance to the Jews, personally hiding Jews in her apartment. This meant concealing people under the floorboards or in alcoves hidden by armoires and cupboards. If the person could pass for Aryan, it meant schooling them in their false identity and their newfound Roman Catholicism. Perhaps forty thousand Jews were assisted in this way, although between 160,000 and 240,000 Polish Gentiles are estimated to have been involved in rescuing Jews overall. While some of these people had pre-war relations with the Jews they helped, like the peasant woman who was allowed not to pay a small bill in full, the majority were simply spontaneously touched by the sight of human suffering, in the way that certain people will instinctively respond to a distressed animal or a lost child. They ranged from poor peasants who shared their food with Jews who spent a couple of years lying in a hideout underneath a dog kennel or a hen house to surgeons who used plastic-surgical techniques to reverse circumcisions.

Not all these relationships were plain sailing, since while one rescuer might have been motivated by compassion, another might have resented

Jews or have helped them only until their money ran out. It was also easier to rescue pre-verbal infants, people who did not look Jewish or fit adults rather than elderly people requiring medical care that was not available. Having capacious buildings also helped, though, as we have seen, some very poor people did not mind having another couple of bodies arranged around the stove or tucked up in the rafters. Religious orders took in children even when German troops were also quartered in their buildings. Those caught doing this were executed, some nine hundred monks and nuns joining the fifth of all Polish Catholic priests who perished in the war. Some Catholic clerical rescuers maintained their belief that Jews were being punished for having killed Christ, even as they saved the lives of individuals. Father Stanisław Falkowski was a twenty-four-year-old Polish priest, with conventional views on the Jews, who nonetheless took in a fifteen-year-old Jewish boy who had escaped from a death transport to Treblinka. He saved the youth's life, despite his theologically grounded animosity towards the collective.[11]

Poland had the largest and most effective armed underground in occupied Europe; the Home Army alone numbered 350,000 fighters and activists. Early in 1943 it began assassinating those Poles who made a dirty living by blackmailing or informing on hidden Jews. Not all the blackmailers were Gentiles, as Jews in one precarious hideout sometimes threatened to denounce Gentiles concealing other Jews in more secure circumstances.[12] The Home Army would not, however, liaise with the significant numbers of Jewish partisans, whom its leadership regarded as either a bandit rabble or agents of future Communist influence. Nor did it provide significant assistance to the Warsaw Ghetto Uprising, less because of prejudice, more because it regarded this rising as premature, preferring to wait for a more strategic turning point in the war.

II JEW-HUNTING

Ending this account of responses to the Final Solution with individual instances of moral greatness might have had a necessary civic or pedagogic purpose, but it distorts a history in which there was no happy ending. The fact of the matter is that rescue was statistically insignificant in a story of catastrophic bleakness, from which there is no redemptive message. Gentiles, and some Jews, may derive consolation from the British spy Frank

Foley, an Oskar Schindler or a Raoul Wallenberg, but human goodness really did not triumph in the end.

In total, some 102,000 Dutch Jews were murdered by the Nazis, 34,294 at Sobibor, the rest at Auschwitz once it had disposed of the Jews of Greece. They came from a camp at Westerbork – originally built to house German-Jewish refugees – which held a pool of Jews, constantly emptied and replenished, according to the capacity of the central German authorities to exterminate them. The Jews of the Netherlands were murdered with a thoroughness in detail that was matched only in Germany and Poland, for only 9 per cent of the pre-war population survived.

Although a far higher proportion of French Jews survived the war, the Netherlands has never attracted the sort of intense scrutiny devoted to Vichy France. The reasons may reflect the fact that its exiled government was replaced by a German administration, which then ruled through the professionally anonymous Dutch civil service, whereas part of France nominally ruled itself under Pétain at Vichy. Moreover, although the Dutch pride themselves on their tolerance, they never ostentatiously promoted the universal rights of man as the French did, making France's derogation from its own standards correspondingly more striking. France was also a European great power, the Netherlands a minor one, and Dutch culture has attracted very little interest from the rest of the world, whereas Western universities still devote considerable attention to French culture. French collaborators include international names like Coco Chanel, Maurice Chevalier and Charles Trenet, but I doubt any reader of this book could name a Dutch intellectual or singer from the 1940s, collaborator or not – the author certainly cannot. As in post-war France, a relatively minor resistance movement was exalted to camouflage a multitude of sins, including twenty-five thousand volunteers in the Waffen-SS 'Westland' Division, the largest contingent of recruits from any of the so-called Germanic nations.

The Germans concentrated most Dutch Jews in Amsterdam, whose historic indigenous Jewish population had once served as biblical-era models for Rembrandt. An old Sephardic elite had been joined in early modern times by German and Polish Ashkenazim, who together comprised one of the groups into which Dutch society was segmented, alongside Catholics, Protestants, Liberals and Socialists. Figuratively speaking, Netherlands society resembled the segments of an orange, so that everyone could consider themselves part of a minority. At less than 2 per cent of the population, the Jews had no Jewish *zuil* or pillar, for the richer

Jews were Liberals and the poor were Socialists. The monarchy, and distinctive Dutch values, lent the Netherlands overall cohesion, although there were perils in how each group dealt separately with the authorities in a society where there was much trust in government and the civil service. The officials endeavoured to retain control of their compatriots' destinies by keeping one step ahead of the Germans, often by anticipating their perceived wishes. Dutch civil servants duly registered the Jews' names and addresses, as well as calculating the total Jewish population at 160,820 souls. Because of the ways in which existing Jewish residential streets shaded into areas inhabited by Gentiles, the Germans decided not to create a sealed ghetto of the kind they had established in Poland and further east. They had to move carefully after a huge raid in early 1942 in search of hostages, following Jewish defence unit clashes with Dutch NSB Fascists, resulted in Europe's only mass protest strikes on behalf of the Jews, in the course of which the Waffen-SS shot nine people and then executed twenty of the trades unionists who had organised it.

The Germans established a Dutch Jewish Council, consisting of fifteen notables from the Jewish community. It was led by an academic ancient historian and a wealthy diamond dealer, who had little in common with the majority of Amsterdam's Jews, in the main poor manual workers, craftsmen or semi-indigent pedlars. A combination of altruism and nepotism led to the Council's bureaucracy being deliberately inflated to some 17,500 employees, who had temporary exemptions from deportation stamped in their papers. The Council acted as a conduit for German orders, while controlling any information the Jews received through its official newspaper. If it did not collude with German demands for deportees, then the SS and Dutch policemen would round up Jews indiscriminately and violently. The German authorities in the Netherlands were themselves subject to relentless pressure from Berlin to deliver their assigned quotas of Jews for the two trains a week which left for the east. Having deported refugee German and Polish refugee Jews first, to create the initial pool at Westerbork with the least friction, the Germans ordered the Jewish Council to provide men and women aged sixteen to forty for what they called forced labour under police supervision. By the close of 1942 some forty thousand Dutch Jews had disappeared eastwards, as the age range of those encompassed rose to fifty. Anyone who imagined that the deportees were performing labour service in Germany alongside four hundred Gentile Dutch compatriots was disabused in January 1943 when eight thousand old and sick Jews, as well as patients in the Het Apeldoornse psychiatric asylum, were bundled on to trucks and taken away. Eventually some 75 per cent of Dutch Jews were deported, including the Jewish Council employees, of whom all but fifteen hundred were killed, half those who lived having survived the concentration camps.[13]

The impetus to deport the Jews came from the Reich Commissar, Artur Seyss-Inquart, and his fellow Austrian, Hanns Albin Rauter. Because of Seyss-Inquart's SS membership and common Austrian background, their relationship was marred by none of the friction that characterised dealings between Hans Frank and Friedrich Wilhelm Krüger in Cracow. Rauter was a big man, six foot four inches tall, with scars on his face from a student duelling fraternity and the three sets of wounds he acquired in the Great War. He saw himself as more of a bold warlord than a policeman. One of his five children had Himmler as her godfather, for relations with the boss were close. It was ominous in the extreme that Rauter's deputies were Erich Naumann, the former commander of Einsatzgruppe B in Russia, and Karl Eberhard Schöngarth, the former Sipo chief in the General Government, a participant in the Wannsee Conference and former senior lecturer at an SD training centre in Poland for mass murder. Willi Zöpf and Ferdinand Hugo Aus der Fünten attached to Eichmann's department IV B 4 were the main movers of the deportations in the Netherlands.[14]

The head of Sipo and SD in Amsterdam once remarked that 'The main support of the German forces in the police sector and beyond was the Dutch police ... it would have been practically impossible to seize even 10 per cent of Dutch Jewry without them.' The paramilitary Dutch Maréchaussée were especially useful. As Rauter informed Himmler: 'The new Dutch police squadrons are performing splendidly as regards the Jewish question and are arresting Jews in the hundreds day and night.'[15] The local constabulary was drawn in too, dutifully and sometimes reluctantly escorting individual Jews living on streets they knew to the assembly points. In various towns, including Apeldoorn, Rotterdam and Utrecht, Dutch detectives were charged with ferreting out handfuls of Jews. Sometimes the cells were so filled with Jews that there was no room for criminals. In Amsterdam, the new police chief was a former lieutenant colonel in the Royal Dutch East Indies Army called Sybren Tulp, one of a number of former colonial officials who figured in the occupation administration in the Netherlands. Young Dutch police officers both delivered warrants informing Jews of their impending deportation and took part in dragging them out of their homes if they failed to comply. Judging from an anonymous letter sent by a policeman to the chief state prosecutor in September 1942, these policemen were often deeply disturbed by having to do this: 'many of us consider the assignment to carry out this work as an insult to our Dutch force'. However, an inspector called van der Oever, encouraged by his wife to refuse to take part, was sacked, and in northerly Groningen fourteen policemen were sent to a concentration camp for refusing to round up Jews.[16] The vast majority continued to help with the deportations, with Tulp omnipresent to ensure that his men did their duty, until he fell ill and died.[17] To bolster the men at his disposal, Rauter also formed members of the Dutch SS and the NSB's paramilitary Storm Detachments into a two-thousand-strong squad of voluntary auxiliary policemen, which also engaged in Jew-hunting.

As the deportation trains from Westerbork rattled eastwards, the Germans embarked on systematic robbery of their Jewish victims. They alighted upon the bank Lippmann, Rosenthal & Co., which they divided into two sections, all under German oversight. One would continue to function as a normal commercial bank; the other, known as the *roofbank* (or plunder bank), was to act as a depository for the Jews' valuables, which were then sold, although the depositors could withdraw small amounts of money for their everyday necessities. With twenty-nine thousand empty properties in the city, 666 barges and a hundred railway cars were used to ship furniture and the like to Germany, where it was given to victims of Allied bombing. A removal company, Abraham Puls & Co., moved the goods from homes to canal sides for the voyage to the Ruhr. Before anything could be touched, it had to be inventorised by an Office for the Registration of Household Effects. This had four sub-sections known as *Colonne* in Dutch, one of which was tasked with finding anything the Jews might have squirrelled away. Most of its employees had come from the municipal unemployment office and were also members of the NSB, a coincidence suggestive of blighted prospects under the old oligarchic liberal democracy. After scandals involving embezzlement by his predecessor, a thirty-one-year-old Dutchman of German parentage called Wim Henneicke, who had run an unsuccessful illegal taxi firm, was promoted to run this section. He received 270 guilders a month, quite a step up from the 60 a month he had received the year before, while on the dole, a benefit he continued to claim for a month after he was employed by the Germans.

About fifty-four Dutchmen, mainly members of the NSB and from the strata where workers and criminals overlapped, joined this section. The

Colonne Henneicke's role changed. By March 1943 the Germans were concerned that some twenty-five thousand Jews had never registered and were in hiding. The Security Police offered 7.50 guilders head money or *kopgeld* for every Jew this unit could bring in. Because the work involved unsocial hours and extensive travel, bounty-hunting for Jews also meant generous overtime and expenses. There was also rent to pay on the Dutch Theatre, where adult Jews were held, and on a small nursery opposite where the under-thirteens were housed, until families could be deported together. There were some outgoings in the form of payments to informers for tips about the location of hidden Jews, although threats usually sufficed in the case of Jews who betrayed many fellow Jews to save their own skins. All these sums were defrayed by Lippmann, Rosenthal & Co., from funds that as we have seen were embezzled from the Jews themselves.[18]

Over the following eighteen months the Colonne Henneicke tracked down around 8,500 Jews. Frederick Cool boasted that one day he simply walked up to a Jewish-looking woman, thinking 'If I pick up a Jew today, that's a quick fifteen guilders for me' – double the bounty because her papers were fake, and if a Jew was guilty of any offence, no matter how minor, the bounty automatically doubled. To avoid the opprobrium of dragging out the non-ambulatory old and frail, they were picked up in municipal ambulances. In August 1943 two bounty-hunters made a day trip to a small town called Zuilen, to pick up two-and-a-half-year-old Andre Ossendrijver from the Schoonderwoerds, a couple who had taken him in the year before. After the foster mother claimed he was their child, one of the bounty-hunters said: 'You mean that little Jew, I suppose … Are you trying to tell me this isn't a Jew?' The following exchange ensued:

Schipper (the bounty-hunter): I guess you'd prefer to have a police van outside your door.

Mrs Schoonderwoerd (the foster mother): It's no disgrace.

Schipper: It breaks my heart too, to have to do this.

Mrs Schoonderwoerd: No, it doesn't, otherwise you wouldn't be doing it.

Schipper: It's still a baby Jew, but a baby Jew turns into a Jew boy and then a full-grown Jew.

After Mr Schoonderwoerd had arrived home and had similarly protested, he and his wife were escorted to the police station in Zuilen where the child was dumped on the lap of a Jewish couple whom Schipper had arrested earlier. 'Please take good care of him,' pleaded Mrs Schoonderwoerd as she was ushered out. Bizarrely, the Jewish couple and Andre were driven off on a police motorbike and sidecar. None of them was ever seen again.[19] The bounty-hunters relied on a constant flow of anonymous tips, some from professional informers, but many from people with a grudge or acting out of need, including people in mixed families or other Jews. One thirty-seven-year-old Jewish shop assistant, Ans van Dijk, betrayed a hundred people. Most Jews who betrayed people did so after being threatened or beaten up by the bounty-hunters, such as the man whose teeth they knocked out before he revealed the whereabouts of his own hidden children.

Informers seeking personal advantage were not confined to the Netherlands. In Denmark a young woman betrayed over a hundred Jews to have her German soldier lover posted back to Denmark, thereby giving a whole new meaning to the notion of a crime of passion. Similarly grim scenarios were enacted daily across the whole of occupied Europe. Most of the blackmailers, bounty-hunters, informers and policemen scuttled back into the woodwork once they realised the war had turned against the Nazis. After huge protest strikes in May 1943 over the decision to conscript former prisoners of war for labour in Germany, the Dutch police began to reconsider their options, with some joining the underground resistance, which created a fresh set of moral ambiguities. There is a larger point here. If, as experts claim, some two hundred thousand Reich Germans were actively involved in the Final Solution, at least double the number of non-Germans (or Austrians) were also perpetrators. Indeed, that is likely to be an underestimate, since they included a hundred thousand auxiliary police in the Ukraine and fifty thousand militiamen in Byelorussia. In the death camps, Ukrainians outnumbered the SS by between fifteen and twenty to one.[20]

We would have to multiply even the lower number of four hundred thousand many times over to accommodate all those foreign bureaucrats and policemen who were merely complicit in these crimes. Like ripples, complicity moved outwards to encompass opportunistic Gentile businessmen who absorbed firms expropriated from Jews, not to speak of more humble beneficiaries of the Final Solution who got a better apartment or furniture as a result of the removal and dispossession of the Jews. The tiny gleams of light provided by the stirring human-interest dramas of such as Schindler or Wallenberg are lost in the vast areas of human darkness, shading from pitch black to generalised grey, that defined the moral behaviour of the time.

CHAPTER 19

'The King's Thunderbolts are Righteous': RAF Bomber Command

I LUCK AND EXPERIENCE

Airmen say that you start with a full pot of luck and an empty one of experience, and hope that the latter fills up before the former has run out. The title of this chapter was the motto of the 44th (Rhodesia) Squadron of the RAF's 5 Bomber Group, a component of RAF Bomber Command whose own motto was 'Strike Hard, Strike Sure'. The 44th was the first squadron to fly the new Avro Lancaster aircraft, the one which suffered the largest Lancaster losses in the group. That gave it the dubious distinction of third-equal placing for losses in the whole of Bomber Command. The Lancaster was not the only bomber deployed by the RAF, but it was the most famous, after various failed planes were belatedly retired from service. Over 7,300 were built during the war.

Understanding the aircraft is important to any dispassionate analysis of the ethical issues raised by the policy of area bombing. A Lancaster was about 70 feet long from nose to tail with a 100-foot wing span. It had fifty thousand separate parts, not including those inside the four engines. Fully loaded, the aircraft weighed 65,000 pounds, which included 2,154 gallons of aviation spirit distributed in four tanks along the wings, as well as up to 22,000 pounds of bombs. The Lancaster had an operational ceiling of over 24,000 feet and a range of more than 1,600 miles. A round trip from a base in East Anglia or Lincolnshire to Berlin took over eight hours. Disastrous early experience with daylight raids meant that the British habitually bombed at night. The moment the aircraft passed the coast of Hitler's Europe it was liable to attack, whether from anti-aircraft guns with searchlights that transfixed the aircraft in a cone of light or from German night fighters that struck out of the darkness.[1]

Air crews habitually rose late, for their nightly work ended with a debriefing at four or five in the morning. As the evening approached, they would be assembled for briefings on where they were going that night: maybe 'Happy Valley' in the Ruhr, or the 'Big City' as Berlin was known. Intelligence officers would take the stage to emphasise the military value of the target, followed by meteorologists to predict the likely weather conditions the airmen would encounter. Take-off time for distant Berlin was usually 4.30 p.m., before which they had to conduct a short test flight to identify any mechanical faults. The guns were normally test-fired during the initial stage of the mission. Northern European weather conditions meant that take-off times often slipped back into the night, or that the mission was scrubbed entirely. Such a pause brought only temporary relief for the crews and their targets, because the Allied strategic-bombing campaign was relentless.

All aircraft rely on the dedication of ground crews, which in this case included the WAAF women who packed parachutes, the men who electrically fired up the engines, and the armourers who spent an hour cranking mixed ordnance into the plane's 33-foot bomb bay with the aid of manual winches. The bombs could be a single device, such as a Tallboy weighing 12,000 pounds, but more usually mixed loads that included a 4,000-pound Cookie, some 250-pound or 500-pound general-purpose bombs, and canisters containing dozens of thin stick incendiaries, about the length of a garden cane. In the final months of the war, specially adapted Lancasters carried 22,000-pound Grand Slam bombs, which, like the Tallboy, were designed to bore deep into the ground before exploding to create an earthquake effect. Maintenance work went on in all weather and was usually done outside. Cases of men dying from pneumonia and the like were not unknown.

The seven crew members had specific tasks, which they had mastered in about two hundred hours of training flights before they were even allowed on to this remarkable aircraft. Each man cost £10,000 to train, in Britain or further afield in Canada or South Africa. The pilot and flight engineer monitored twenty-eight instruments, including separate dials for each engine, and the hydraulics which powered the controls, the bomb bay and the rotating gun turrets. In pre-computerised aircraft there was a lot of sheer physical effort, especially if the plane had to undertake evasive manoeuvres. A relatively large number of bomber pilots won posthumous decorations, chiefly because in order to enable the crew to bale out they had to stay at the controls until the aircraft burst into flames or crashed. After Bomber Command abolished the post of co-pilot, the flight engineer was notionally the only person capable of flying the plane if the pilot was incapacitated or killed.[2] The navigator had a duplicate set of the main instruments to help him plot the aircraft's course. In the early years of the strategic-bombing campaign, navigation involved nothing more sophisticated than a sextant to plot a course by the stars. The navigator was also responsible for keeping the aircraft in line with the pulse beats sent by the Gee or Oboe radio-guidance systems, although neither system was effective much beyond 280 miles. From early 1943, Lancasters were equipped with a ground radar device called H2S, which gave the navigator the ability to distinguish major ground features such as coastlines and lakes regardless of cloud cover. The limitations of Gee, Oboe and H2S explain why ports like Bremen, Hamburg and Rostock were bombed so much more effectively than sprawling Berlin, where the Germans used giant floats to disguise or conceal the city's huge lakes.

A fourth man was responsible for communications and electronic warfare, as well as maintaining the aircraft's survival equipment, from a dinghy to fire extinguishers. Down in a Perspex bubble under the nose lay the bombardier, who effectively controlled the aircraft over the target. If he got his work wrong, then the aircraft would have to turn and repeat the bomb run, something all crew members dreaded. Other than over the target, the bomb aimer operated the twin 0.303 Browning machine guns in the forward gun turret. The .303 round was the standard infantryman's bullet, effective up to a thousand yards, but hopeless in this aerial context. The mid-upper gunner, with the best all-round vision, also operated two guns; he seldom used the guns, his principal function being to scan the blind spot above and behind the pilot. These guns were underpowered and could have been replaced with the cannon from defunct fighters. Happily an earlier scheme to have aerial mines dangling on a long cable, which the bomber pilot was supposed to wiggle into the path of an incoming fighter, was not pursued. Nobody covered the blind spot below the aircraft, but the Tail-end Charlie in the rear of the aircraft had four machine guns to cover the area from which German fighters were most likely to attack. Although RAF bombers flew in huge streams, they seldom saw each other unless lit up by searchlights or enemy gunfire, which might end in a spectacular explosion or a long burning dive to destruction. The gunners were more useful as spotters, for their guns were outranged by the cannon on the German night fighters, and ultimately the crew depended on the courage and skill of the pilot. In the event of a fighter attack, he had to take the evasive action known as a corkscrew, which sent the aircraft into a sequence of dives and turns rather like a train on a fairground white-knuckle ride. If the plane suffered catastrophic damage, seven men bulked out with thick layers of underwear and sweaters beneath their flying suits, and further encumbered with oxygen masks, had to get out of the small spaces into which they were wedged, find and clip on their parachutes, and try to reach the few exits – difficult enough if the aircraft was flying stright and level, well-nigh impossible if the plane was falling out of control and crew were pinned to the sides by G-forces. Rear gunners were the least likely and bomb aimers located right next to the forward hatch were the most likely to survive. Fifty-five thousand of these British and Commonwealth heroes did not.[3]

All air crew held the rank of sergeant or higher, and were well remunerated relative to other services. The bomber crews were all volunteers, many of them the public or grammar school boys who in other circumstances would have been going to university. We should not overlook those who aged fifteen had become technical apprentices at the Halton Aircraft Apprentice School, where after training as electricians, fitters or riggers they then volunteered for flight training to capture some of the romance of flying.[4] A significant number of volunteers also came from Australia, Canada, South Africa and New Zealand, although their home governments had about as much say in directing the war effort as Britain does in the higher counsels of the US today. By January 1943, some 37 per cent of Bomber Command pilots were Canadians, Australians or New Zealanders, and the figure was 45 per cent by the war's end. There were so many Canadians that they were formed into their own 6 Group. A third of these young men would not reach the end of the thirty missions comprising a tour, with trips to anywhere nearer than Germany counting as only a third of a sortie for these lethal accounting purposes. That meant six or seven missions a month, with any curiosity extinguished by the first trip and raw courage thereafter in the face of hazards that were well understood. Rituals and superstition were rife, from the practice of collectively pissing on the rear wheel to having to play the hit record 'The Shrine of St Cecilia' before take off. Pets were another consolation, including Sammy the cocker spaniel, who on fifty (wholly illegal) occasions accompanied his master Squadron Leader Tommy Blair on sorties to Berlin or the Ruhr, curled up under the wireless operator's table. When the aircraft came into land Sammy would rush to the bomb aimer's Perspex cone to watch the descent and touchdown.[5]

This was lethal work, with casualty rates that approximated to those of Gallipoli or the Somme during the Great War. Aircraft collided, burst into flames or disappeared in a puff of smoke as if victims of a conjuror's trick. Pieces of aircraft, such as the wing or tail, tumbled to the ground, sometimes accompanied by the bodies of the crew, while the lucky few floated down in parachutes, although some were lynched by cowardly German mobs when they reached the ground. One hundred and twenty thousand men served in Bomber Command, of whom 55,573 perished in action during the war. Another 9,838 were shot down and captured alive, and a further 8,403 wounded, whether from gunfire, frostbite, or burns of a horrific nature. A bomber base consisted of a constant influx of fresh new faces to replace those who had disappeared. The new faces, no longer fresh, disappeared in turn.

Nuremberg established that offences committed in the heat of battle could not be considered in the same light as cold-blooded crimes against humanity, or what nowadays is called genocide, which is the deliberate attempt to exterminate an ethnic group or race, activities irrelevant to the strategic outcome of the war. Genocide involved the diversion of war materials – from transport capacity to bullets – away from conventional military operations. War crimes also involve deliberately killing defenceless people, which was clearly not the case in Nazi Germany, where Bomber Command had to fly through prodigious defences to reach their targets. Air crew were convinced of the military necessity of what they were doing. Killing a large number of German civilians was not their primary objective, and indeed would have been greatly reduced if the Nazis had evacuated non-essential personnel from the cities. The Germans were confident that as a police state they could deal with any of the morale consequences of Allied bombing. The Allied aim was to destroy military and industrial targets, their workforces included, to defeat an evil system that enjoyed overwhelming popular support. The German people had to share the fate of the regime they supported so enthusiastically when it was crushing the liberty and lives of others, so that when the war ended the peace would not merely become another armistice before a third conflict. That does not mean that every action undertaken by Bomber Command or the USAAF was what nowadays most reasonable people would regard as morally desirable, particularly towards the end of the war, although it is easy to under-

[handwritten at top: B172 + 44,000 dead]

estimate how much fight the Germans still had left in them when their cause was objectively lost. *[handwritten: Just like Japan]*

No serious person can compare the hard-fought bombing campaign with slaughtering innocent civilians in circumstances where the only risk the perpetrators ran was to be splashed with blood and brains in some ditch in the Ukraine. The attempt to criminalise retroactively RAF or USAAF air crews is not merely tendentious as history, it also ignores the moral awareness, the *mens rea*, of those involved. This most technological means of warfare meant that the crew necessarily had to concentrate on getting in and out to their target in one piece, while trying to avoid catastrophic mid-air collisions. The Germans did not respond passively to this assault, putting in place ever more effective defences. The need to focus on the job in hand, all those dials, levers and sights, while beset by fear of the fighters and anti-aircraft guns meant that very few of the young air crew could expend much thought on the fate of civilians thousands of feet below, in target cities which, when not obscured by clouds, were a pyrotechnic blizzard of pink, orange and white explosions. In some cases guilt set in with age, a reaction that may also be related to delayed post-traumatic stress in individual cases, or to the increasing emphasis civilian suffering has received in the last few decades. It remains invidious to judge what people did seventy years ago by the far from perfect light of utterly different modern circumstances where in each conflict the media and human rights lawyers are effectively an independent non-combatant arm. This author neither approves nor disapproves of this development.

The desire to survive also created a certain frame of mind in the grim-faced young men who went on these missions, namely a carapace of hardness. Even in normal times, people do not approach life with the measured, rational weighing up of cause and effect, actions and consequences, proportionality and so on, that historians or moral philosophers can bring to the task. Undoubtedly philosophers apply a special professional rigour to these issues, but the space and time for such deliberations was not available to men fighting a war. The airmen thought about the forty-four thousand British lives lost in the Blitz and the threat to their families and the freedom of their country. They knew about police states and concentration camps and did not want them in Britain. They were part of a military machine that had been developed at enormous cost, and they wanted it used in battle. So did the government, which had spent so much treasure developing this arm of warfare. RAF leaders encouraged this tendency towards focus rather than the philosopher's reflection, by presenting every

[handwritten at bottom: Then what about those who sent them on their missions?]

mission in terms of the military–industrial importance of the targets selected, even though they knew it was technically impossible to guarantee that only factories or transport targets would be hit. For this was a matter not of individual moral psychology but of policy for winning the war. Alan Cranswick explained to his mother shortly before being killed on a raid on a French railway yard in 1944: 'I don't like what I have to do, but I think of you and my country and know I must carry on and do all I can. I must do what my pals who have not returned would have done. I shall try to forget the horrors we are committing.'[6] Destroying cities began unintentionally but ended up as the intended object, though this was publicly denied by the politicians and service chiefs who planned it.[7]

II THE PATH TO PROMISCUOUS BOMBING

Most Second World War air forces were tactical adjuncts to the clash of huge armies, although the Luftwaffe certainly used low-level terror strikes against several cities in the course of land invasions, bringing death and destruction to Warsaw, Rotterdam, Belgrade and several cities in the Soviet Union. There were two exceptions to this trend, the British and US, who regarded strategic bombing as a rapid way of striking at the nerve centres and vital organs of the enemy, rather than hacking at his military limbs. Bombing exercised a natural attraction for the British. The nation that had made the Maxim machine gun a general weapon of colonial wars was tantalised by the cost- and labour-saving virtues of modern technology. This approach continued after the Great War in the shape of air control or policing, which meant the bombs dropped on the villages of mutinous tribesmen in Mesopotamia or India's North West Frontier during the 1920s so as to obviate the need to deploy large numbers of ground troops in messy counter-insurgency operations. Bombing would also avoid the horrific rates of attrition recently experienced on the Western Front, massacres which some bomber commanders had witnessed at first hand during their service in the Royal Flying Corps. It might even be construed as a more humane method of warfare, as bombing promised to achieve a quick result. Bombing would allegedly work more rapidly than naval blockade, a vice that was slow to tighten. True, civilians would die – but the Allied naval blockade of Germany in 1914–18 had been indirectly responsible for the deaths of three-quarters of a million civilians from starvation

[handwritten: morality of blockade not 8.]

and attendant epidemics. Nobody questioned the morality of blockade, or of the economic sanctions which would have mostly affected the weakest and most helpless members of the sanctioned societies. *[handwritten: cf WJ + Iran]*

The British did, however, quietly bury research conducted after the Great War by the Royal Naval Air Service, which had merged into the new RAF in 1918. The RNAS had developed precision-bombing techniques to use against maritime targets, but it had also undertaken feasibility studies of the effects of hitting oil, steel and other industrial targets.[8] The research concluded that precision targeting was extremely difficult and likely to achieve very little. *[handwritten: NB]* Bomber Command developed despite this research as a cheaper way of waging warfare, then as now the defining feature of British defence policy, and because the RAF was able to argue that technological advances had rendered the RNAS's findings obsolete. When a new war revealed that the findings were still valid, there was a large investment to justify and remarkably few alternatives to hand, so those who advocated area bombing without actually calling it that tended to have their own way. The more extravagant boosters of bombing saw it as a decisive instrument of war, which would not only obliterate economic targets, but crack enemy civilian morale. In 1927 a retired British barrister gave an interview to the *Daily Mail* about how he had treated warfare in a futuristic novel he had written entitled *1944*. He said:

> The girl filling a shell in a factory is just as much part of the machinery of war as the soldier who fires it. She is much more vulnerable and will certainly be attacked. It is impossible that such an attack would be unjustified. The matter does not end with mere munitions workers. The central organisations essential to modern warfare are carried on in 'open towns' and largely by civilians. An attempt to paralyse them would be perfectly legitimate. The first conclusion, therefore, that emerges is that an attack will be made upon the civilian population.

The novelist, Lord Tiverton, was the former head of the Royal Naval Air Service's operational research and of the Air Ministry's directorate of flying operations.[9] The argument he advanced was to be fundamental to the survival of the RAF as an independent force. Its commander, Major General Sir Hugh 'Boom' Trenchard, alleged on the basis of no evidence whatever that the moral effects of bombing were twenty times greater than the physical damage caused. Such evidence as there was suggested that

Hague draft rules 1922-23
Confusion in int'l. law
re civs

aerial bombing might generate as much defiance as demoralisation. Ironically, what some thought had happened in Germany in November 1918 gave Trenchard's claim some substance. Although the Germans were still ensconced in northern France, it appeared to be a mysterious domestic collapse – the crisis of morale known on the German right as the stab in the back – which led them to throw in the towel. Anecdotal studies of how civilians had panicked in the Gotha raids on the East London docks, or of Mesopotamian and Pashtun tribesmen fleeing when their villages were bombed, reinforced the view that bombing could bring about a sudden collapse in enemy morale. The 1926 General Strike also suggested that mass discontent could have a paralysing effect on a society.[10] All of these calculations were completely useless in considering the likely effects of bombing on a police state like Nazi Germany, where discontent could never acquire critical mass. In addition, Nazi Germany was a thoroughgoing welfare state with ramified organisations of people bent on doing good by ethnic comrades. The sustained bombing of civilians was to demonstrate the worth of formations like the National Socialist People's Welfare or NSV, since it led the way in looking after those injured or bombed out.[11]

Initially, both the British and Germans were punctilious in not deliberately targeting each other's civilians. That was the view of J. M. Spaight, the informal legal adviser within the Air Ministry, who recommended that *Hague* Britain respect the 1922–3 Hague draft rules on air war, even though no country had ratified them. Spaight revealed as much when he entitled an article he published in 1939 'The Chaotic State of Law Governing *defense* Bombardment'. One key point, almost universally ignored today, is that *allows* the moment any objective was defended, it was liable to bombardment. *bombing?* Despite this, in 1938 Chamberlain falsely told the House of Commons that targeting civilians was against international law. In practice, politicians tried to maintain civilised standards, mainly to avoid retaliation, although indiscriminate reprisals against civilians were illegal under the existing laws of war. Private property was also regarded as sacred, even when the factories bore the name of Krupp. President Roosevelt sought and received guarantees from Britain, Germany and France that they would not indiscriminately bomb civilians. In 1940 the Permanent Secretary at the Air Ministry personally assured Cosmo Lang, the Archbishop of Canterbury, that 'the intentional bombing of civilian populations is illegal'.[12]

On the eve of war the head of RAF Bomber Command, Edgar Ludlow Hewitt, acknowledged that accuracy was not a strong point. In August 1939 over 40 per cent of bombers could not find a target in a friendly city in broad daylight. In the two years before war erupted, 478 aircraft had had to make forced landings after getting lost and running out of fuel.[13] Worse, with extraordinary complacency, small formations of aircraft ventured in broad daylight into heavily defended German air space. For example, on 18 December 1939 twenty-four Wellington bombers attacked Wilhelmshaven. Twelve of them were shot down by Luftwaffe fighters and three crashed on their home run to England. That represented a casualty rate of 63 per cent.[14]

Once the phoney war ended, the propaganda leafleting of Germany gave way to concerted attempts to destroy German oil installations. From May 1940 until February 1943, RAF Bomber Command dropped an average of 1,500 to 2,000 tons of bombs a month on Germany, occasionally rising to 4,000 or 6,000 tons in a good month. Portal determined that on moonlit nights Bomber Command would target oil installations, while on moonless nights cities were to be attacked so as to cause 'very heavy material destruction'. Waves of aircraft were to use a combination of high-explosive bombs and incendiaries to start fires while preventing German civil defences from putting them out. This policy was enshrined in a new Bombing Directive issued on 30 October 1940, when Sir Richard Peirse was head of Bomber Command and long before the arrival of Sir Arthur Harris, *bête noire* of the moral-equivalence claque.[15]

The effects of this strategy were limited, partly because bombers were also needed to combat the U-boat menace and in the Middle East. But it was in addition a case of too many cooks. Target priorities were discussed within the Air Ministry and then referred through the Chiefs of Staff to the War Cabinet. Target categories were chosen by a Targets Committee, into which the Ministry of Economic Warfare, the Admiralty and the War Office had input, and which were then translated into Air Directives. Quite apart from poor weather experienced in the winter of 1940–1, Germany was a big place, which meant that raids were too dispersed. Moreover target priorities kept shifting between oil installations, tactical objectives and military–industrial facilities within urban centres. Moonlight was a double-edged factor, for it made it easier not only to identify targets on the ground but also for the defenders to see the bombers. Specific targeting within a darkened city on a moonless night was a practical impossibility, and the bombers either had to bomb blind or return home with their bombs.[16] While continuing to pay lip-service to precision bombing, in practice the effect of collateral damage on civilian morale became the new paradigm. The emphasis on military objectives served to veil what was actually happening, namely a slippage towards bombing urban areas for their own sake. That was never admitted, for as the War Cabinet decided on 24 March 1941, 'it was better that actions should speak louder than words in this matter'.[17]

Many critics of area bombing question its military necessity, which they narrowly construe as what contributed to Allied victory. This is less clear-cut than it may seem. Any war is a constant process of trial and error, of commanders adapting what they have learned to constantly changing circumstances. From the perspective of the political and military decision-makers, necessity included: whatever prevented large numbers of military losses; maintaining domestic civilian morale through retaliation against an apparently invincible opponent; and giving tangible support to allies who were making far greater human sacrifices. Bombing was Britain's sole way of hitting back at Germany on the continent after Dunkirk. It was also a demonstration of the country's Churchill-inspired dogged determination to fight on, with important echoes across the Atlantic. 'We are hitting that man hard,' Churchill cabled Roosevelt in July 1940.[18] 'You have no idea of the thrill and encouragement which the Royal Air Force bombing has given us over here,' wired back Harry Hopkins. The theme would be played with even greater brio for the benefit of Stalin, as he became increasingly exasperated by the staggering losses of the Red Army while the British hardly seemed to be fighting the Germans at all. These considerations were as necessary to winning the war as the large number of dual-purpose 88mm guns the Germans had to withdraw from the Eastern Front to shoot at RAF bombers, or the huge numbers of otherwise productive people who might have been involved in more aggressive war fighting who were tied up in anti-aircraft and civil defence. There were also such imponderable effects as the exhaustion which resulted from having to go to shelters at night, to say nothing of being evacuated and having to undertake a long commute to work, or having to find new sources of food because the nearby butchers and bakers had been destroyed.

Initially, the British were lucky to hit anything at all. Navigational aids were poor, and the aircraft were capable only of modest payloads of low-powered bombs, many of which failed to explode. The Luftwaffe bombed London by accident on 24 August 1940, to which the British responded with raids on the industrial periphery of Berlin a day later. The Germans were left puzzled by what the RAF sought to achieve with attacks that were so wide of the mark that they almost went unnoticed. However, after five such attacks, Hitler responded with a retaliatory fury that resulted in a sustained assault on London and several British cities. While the Blitz caused massive loss of life, the Luftwaffe's lack of a heavy bomber fleet meant that things could have been a lot worse. The public clamoured for hard retaliation, which also suited the temperament of the belligerent British Prime Minister, who exchanged words like 'extermination' with the German Führer. After seeing the devastation an indiscriminate German aerial mine had caused in Wandsworth in south London, Churchill talked 'about castrating the lot ... There will be no nonsense about a "just peace".' After the Germans had achieved a firestorm in Coventry on 14–15 November, Churchill insisted on retaliatory strikes, which began with Mannheim on 16 December. John Colville noted that 'The moral scruples of the Cabinet on this subject have been overcome.'[19]

The inaccuracy of British bombing contributed to the move to area bombing. Even Bomber Command leaders admitted that they were 'exporting' bombs in a general direction rather than hitting much of industrial or military substance. Air Minister Archibald Sinclair's parliamentary under-secretary acknowledged the disparity between claims and effects in a confidential memo to his boss. The criticisms were taken up by other services, which resented the resources lavished on the RAF. The Royal Navy thought the sums expended on strategic bombers could be better spent on the Fleet Air Arm. RAF Coastal Command, which came under joint Admiralty operational control, was starved of the long-range aircraft needed to protect the Atlantic convoys. The army wanted airpower used tactically in the Middle and Far East, leading Alan Brooke to contemplate setting up a separate Army Air Arm. Meanwhile the forty-nine squadrons of Wellingtons, Whitleys, Halifaxes and Hampdens kept up their desultory raids on Germany. It was indefensible that the last three aircraft continued to be produced when they were manifestly not up to the task, but the murky history of British military procurement has produced countless other examples of young lives being wasted to ensure directorships and other rewards for retiring senior officials and officers.

In August 1941, a civil servant called David Butt subjected the RAF's extravagant claims to precise statistical analysis by comparing 633 bomb-damage photos with the payloads carried by bombers. One aircraft in three had got within five miles of its target – one in ten in the smog obscuring the Ruhr on an otherwise good night. Forty-nine per cent of the bombs dropped between May 1940 and May 1941 fell on unbuilt-up countryside. In March 1942 even Churchill felt moved to tell Portal that 'bombing is not decisive, but better than doing nothing', which hardly constituted ringing endorsement.[20] That month the Directorate of Bombing Operations responded to these criticisms with an analysis based on the destruction caused in Britain by the Blitz. Prepared by Churchill's scientific adviser Frederick Lindemann, ennobled as Lord Cherwell, the memorandum used data derived from damage to Birmingham and Hull, whose findings Cherwell outrageously falsified, to argue that each heavy bomber coming on stream could drop forty tons of bombs during its service life, which would render four to eight thousand people homeless.[21] Cherwell argued that losing one's home was worse than having family and friends killed, a dubious finding anyway, and overlooking the fact that Germany was a nation of renters rather than owners. He calculated that it would be possible with the additional aircraft to 'dehouse' a third of the German population, resulting in a crisis of morale. There was no mention of how this would be objectively measured, or how it could contribute to the collapse of the totalitarian Nazi political system.

Portal used this dubious intervention to go on the attack against those who wanted the resources devoted to the RAF reallocated to the navy and army. He claimed that with a bomber force of four thousand aircraft he could win the war within six months. When Churchill responded that this was overly optimistic, Portal objected that Churchill himself had urged the bombing offensive and that future production was geared to it. If things were to be changed then the War Cabinet must make a ruling 'without delay'. Portal came up with a number of recommendations designed to improve accuracy, while the Air Staff modified their line, arguing that they could so weaken Germany that Allied ground forces would be able to occupy continental Europe with little serious fighting. In a fresh Air Directive issued on 14 February 1942, Portal's deputy, Norman Bottomley, reversed the priority given to precision attacks over area bombing, while claiming that this would bring relief to the hard-pressed Soviets.[22] None of this stopped informed criticism of the bombing campaign, although objective scientific observation has to be balanced with consideration of how retaliatory bombing played to British domestic morale. Professor Patrick Blackett, the chief scientist of the Royal Navy, was sceptical about the casualties of bombing:

The average number of bomber sorties per month, then, mainly by Wellingtons, was 1,000, and of these some 40 were lost with their crews of five men, giving a loss of airmen, all highly skilled men, at the rate of 200 per month. Comparing this with the estimated

debate in uk

number of enemy killed, that is 400 men, women and children [in fact the real figure was 200] ... it was concluded that in the matter of personnel casualties the 1941 bombing offensive had been nearly a dead loss.[23]

A professor MP representing Cambridge University further twisted the knife when in the Commons he remarked that the Blitz had damaged British war production by about the same degree as the long Easter-weekend vacation, the implication being that Britain's more dispersed efforts were both costly and hopeless. The most powerful critic of Bomber Command, Sir Henry Tizard, Rector of Imperial College London, queried the mathematical basis behind the optimistic forecasts for dehousing, while acknowledging that bombers did subtract a proportion of German guns and manpower from the front line. The dispute was resolved by a High Court judge, Mr Justice Singleton, whose report concluded, 'If Russia can hold Germany on land I doubt whether Germany will stand 12 or 18 months' continuous, intensified and increased bombing, affecting, as it must, her war production, her power of resistance, her industries and her will to resist (by which I mean morale).' In reality, it was not easy to reduce or reverse the resources allocated to bombing in a planning phase that had entertained quite unrealistic expectations of what strategic bombing could achieve. Nor were the airmen easily diverted from their focus on Germany, since they believed that dispersion explained why bombing was not succeeding.[24]

Stalin

During Churchill's visit to Moscow in August 1942, Stalin stressed that British soldiers needed to spill German blood, according to Churchill asking: 'Why were we so afraid of the Germans?' Later Stalin grew bolder: 'he said a great many disagreeable things, especially about our being too much afraid of fighting the Germans, and if we tried it like the Russians we should find it not so bad'. Churchill responded by regaling the Soviet leader with lurid talk of the devastation the RAF could mete out to German cities, a theme Stalin warmed to immediately. As Averell Harriman noted, by the night's end they had destroyed most of the cities in Germany from their armchairs.[25] Thereafter Churchill regularly supplied Stalin with photos of aerial devastation consisting of images of houses reduced to empty boxes with their lids blown off.

After mollifying the Soviet leader, Churchill had little alternative other than to step up the strategic bombing campaign, boosting the Air Ministry's funding for 1943 by a third more than it had requested. Portal issued a stream of directives which emphasised that attacks on the morale or psychological health of industrial workers were as important as attacks on factories, power grids and transport infrastructures. That was a way of indirectly acknowledging that, although it was possible to blow down a factory's walls, damaging heavy machinery inside was harder, while it was much easier to wreck rows of residential buildings with a combination of fire and explosives.

So far we have not considered the personalities involved in making British bombing policy. The Air Minister, Sinclair, was an affable Liberal politician, who was no match for the Chief of the Air Staff, Charles Portal, one of the most popular service chiefs of the war. Portal was aloof, quiet, driven, efficient and possessed of considerable political nous. A taciturn man, who talked to no one when he broke for lunch at the Travellers Club, he worked a fifteen- or sixteen-hour day, catching four hours' sleep in a glorified bedroom at the supposedly bomb-proof Dorchester Hotel. If he gave an order, he meant it. When he once returned early from lunch to find his papers locked in a secure cabinet, as he had instructed, he insisted it be forced open rather than wait five minutes for his secretary to return with the key. If he said he wanted twenty cigarettes, he was not satisfied when an office whip round produced ten, and moreover he was not happy when they appeared arrayed on a plate rather than in a packet. He never visited air bases on the grounds that if he went to one, he would have to visit them all.

Sinclair and Portal had a more difficult relationship with the man who, perhaps unfairly, has become the personification of Bomber Command, for he merely inherited a policy they had established and which they pursued as ruthlessly as he. In February 1942, the lacklustre Peirse was despatched to India and replaced by Arthur Harris at Bomber Command's High Wycombe HQ. While he and Portal differed in manner, they saw eye to eye on one matter, when they stood together on the Air Ministry roof where one night they had surveyed London under Luftwaffe attack. Harris remarked, 'Well they are sowing the wind.' Harris claimed that it was the only moment when he felt vengeful during the entire war.[26] He was a tough little man with an angry face, hard stare and brusque manner, made worse by an untreated duodenal ulcer and the alimony payments to his first wife that diminished the lifestyle of the second family he had with a beautiful woman who was twenty years his junior. His greatest admirers included the Soviets, whose London ambassadors decorated and fêted him at receptions; by contrast, Harris became a figure of hate among the Germans.

As a teenager Harris had sought his fortune tobacco farming in Rhodesia, before fighting in the Great War in southern Africa. He joined the Royal Flying Corps in 1916, becoming a night fighter pilot shooting down Zeppelins over England, before transferring to France where he shot down five German planes, a feat which made him an ace. What he saw flying above the battlefield at Passchendaele convinced him for life that bombing was a more humane method of warfare than infantry engagements. As a regular officer in the newly constituted RAF, he undertook aerial policing on India's North West Frontier and then in Mesopotamia.[27] Harris had a remarkable grasp of all the technical issues related to aerial warfare, and he understood the needs of both pilots and ground crew. This colonial service was followed by staff postings at the Air Ministry, missions to the US and, from September 1939, command of 5 Group of Bomber Command based at Grantham in Lincolnshire. In November 1940 he became deputy chief of Air Staff. Striding into the Air Ministry he would greet senior civil servants with such observations as 'Morning Abrahams, and what have you done to impede the war effort today?' He disliked operational interference from the desk-bound warriors in the Ministry, on one occasion chiding Sir Norman Bottomley, 'Dear Norman, I note that in your last directive you have failed to indicate at which precise moment my pilots should blow their noses. Yours ever, Bert'.[28]

Harris has become a controversial figure, for he was not given to the hypocrisy and indirection that characterises most political utterances. Defence procurement has always been a murky area in Britain, and one that military historians often eschew lest it upset their own and their readers' moral universe. One of Harris's first actions was to write to Sinclair claiming that the corrupt influence of arms manufacturers – one of whom he dismissed as a drunk – was the only plausible explanation for why the British kept churning out such sub-standard aircraft as the Avro Manchester, Short Stirling and early Handley Page Halifax. Harris wrote of Handley Page, 'not an aircraft manufacturer, just a financier, with all that implies, and more'.[29] Just before Christmas 1942, Harris let rip against the captains of the aviation industry in a letter to Sinclair:

> The Stirling Group has now virtually collapsed. They make no worth-while contribution to our war effort in return for their overheads ... There should be a wholesale sacking of the incompetents who have turned out approximately 50% rogue aircraft from S&H Belfast [Short and Harland's manufacturer], and Austins, not forgetting the

supervisories responsible in the parent firm. Much the same applies to the Halifax issue. [Sir Frederick] Handley Page is always weeping crocodile tears in my house and office, smarming his unconvincing assurances all over me and leaving me with a mounting certainty that nothing whatever ponderable is being done to make his deplorable product worthy for war or fit to meet those jeopardies which confront our gallant crews. Nothing will be done until Handley Page and his gang are also kicked out, lock, stock and barrel. Trivialities are all they are attempting at present, with the deliberate intent of postponing the main issue until we are irretrievably committed.[30]

Harris was impatient of the usual lies and excuses about how retooling delayed production of better products. Evidently he was not interested in being on the boards of defence companies, the usual manner in which military men are corrupted. Introspection was not his strong suit and he was certainly a philistine, more interested in mules than Monet. He was dismissive of those who affected concern for the fine china produced in Dresden, but would one seriously want Bernard Berenson or Roger Fry running a war? He saw much of Churchill because his official residence at Springfield House was only a few miles from Chequers, which he occasionally visited in a horse-drawn trap rather than by chauffeured Bentley. He lived and breathed bombing, but was able to sleep like a log despite constant telephoned updates of how operations were progressing. He was intensely concerned about the wellbeing of his air crew and ground staff, but did not make a practice of visiting them, except under rather forced circumstances. Unlike admirals or generals, he had the constant strain of committing his entire command to battle almost daily for three years.[31] Although his men called him 'Butch', short for Butcher, rather than the 'Bomber' which has stuck to him, but which Churchill alone essayed face to face, veterans of his command defend Harris's reputation with the same intense loyalty he showed to them. For military men, that is the ultimate accolade. He galvanised Bomber Command, giving it the intense esprit de corps necessary to carry out its grimly demanding task. In war, commanders like Harris must exhibit absolute tenacity of purpose; a more sensitive character would never have coped with the enormous losses sustained by Bomber Command. A rather revealing moment came when in 1943 he visited a mixed Anglo-Polish squadron at RAF Scampton. He told the men in the briefing room that he knew it was rough, adding that it was going to get rougher. He said: 'I want you to look at the man on either side of you.

In six months' time only one in three will be left, but if you are the lucky one I promise you this. You will be two ranks higher.' As he left the room, the men banged appreciatively on the tables and the Poles rose to cheer. Harris half turned in the doorway and started to speak, but no words came out. Instead he smartly saluted ᵗhem.³² Although Harris did order raids which through ill-luck, notably over Nuremberg, resulted in horrific RAF casualties towards the end of the war, it was Portal who wrote that losses of ten per cent would be justified on attacks against oil targets, with Harris responding that if losses of 5–10 per cent were acceptable, then raids on oil would be the last mission undertaken by his command.³³

Harris was not as entirely insensible to questions of morality as the caricature of him suggests. Reflecting on the bombing firestorm that had engulfed Hamburg, he argued that bombing was more humane than either the military casualties sustained on the Western Front or the civilian losses due to the British naval blockade of Germany between 1914 and 1918. These losses dwarfed those due to 'even the most ruthless exponents of air frightfulness'. As for international law, Harris merely remarked that this 'can always be argued pro and con, but in this matter of the use of aircraft in war there is, it so happens, no international law at all'. While one may speculate whether it was tenacity of purpose or dogmatic obstinacy to pursue a course of action whose effects were at best indirect, and which many regard as morally repugnant, one cannot argue that it was criminal by the standards of contemporary legal norms.³⁴

The tactics of area bombing evolved from trial and error, while the total operational bomb lift of the RAF increased fortyfold. It began with 520 tons of bombs delivered by twenty-three squadrons in 1940, rising to 10,000 tons of bombs, dropped by a hundred operational squadrons in 1944–5. The USAAF contribution, after January 1943 when it first bombed Germany, doubled the last total to 20,000 tons by the closing months of the war.³⁵ The RAF's targets were chosen at meetings, known as 'morning prayers', held in the operations room at Bomber Command HQ, known as 'the Hole'. Harris would arrive, study target reports in the lavatory and then conduct his conferences with senior officers. The general target parameters were set by the latest Air Ministry Directive pinned to the wall. The likely weather over northern Europe ultimately determined which city was to be attacked. Surveying a map table, the names of cities would be tersely identified and deliberately mispronounced – Wysbaden rather than Wiesbaden. Staff officers worked up the detailed plans of attack and used a secure teleprinter to relay these instructions to the bomber groups, which then passed the night's target to individual squadrons. We began this chapter with air crew preparations after that.[36]

Incendiary bombs had extremely little application against industrial establishments or transport infrastructure. Usually four pounds in weight, they were intended to start uncontrollable fires in residential areas, while the high-explosive bombs dropped with them were intended to rip off roofs and blow in windows in order to make the incendiaries more effective. Weapons experts based at Woolwich in south-east London discovered that these munitions worked better when grouped in clustered casings which dispersed them at a lower altitude. Combinations of chemicals were tried to improve combustion, to keep the incendiaries burning for as long as possible and to make them resistant to firefighting efforts, including some designed to look like duds, but which blew up when handled. At the Building Research Department in Watford, technicians built mock German buildings, filled with 1930s-style furnishings, to find the best way of creating the most voracious fires.[37] Other scientists pondered why German bombs were more powerful than the 'scrap iron' dropped by the British, coming up with lighter casings and new explosives like amatol and cyclonite which were then rendered more forceful by the addition of aluminium powder.[38] Meanwhile, Bomber Command's own Operational Research Service sought to maximise the damage to a target with the greatest economy of means. This meant calculating that, to demolish a large railway marshalling yard, it would take four 500-pound bombs per acre, or for a fifty-acre site, as the scientists had it: '1 short ton per acre 50x100=100÷11=450 short tons must be dropped; and since 30% of the sorties would be abortive, 500 short tons or 110x18 bomb sorties must be despatched.'[39]

On 9 March 1942, over two hundred aircraft attacked the Renault plant at Billancourt. The first aircraft dropped flares which provided target markers for the main force of bombers. Although more accurate than most raids up to this time, a large number of French civilians were killed or injured and production at the plant fell only by the equivalent of two months' output. At the end of March, Harris decided to attack Lübeck. This was an ancient Hansa port, encircled by the Rivers Trave and Wakenitz, which had docks, industry and a training school for U-boat crews. Today, everything in the historic centre looks plausibly medieval, until one realises that it has been entirely reconstructed. The water features made Lübeck easy to identify on H2S, and the densely packed timber-framed buildings were like kindling.[40] The city was bombed by 234 aircraft on the 28 March, although only 191 planes made the final runs in two waves separated by a half-hour interval. The fires started by the first wave guided in the second. Some 1,425 houses were destroyed and 1,976 badly damaged; 312 people were killed, at a loss to the RAF of twelve aircraft. In April the formula was repeated at Rostock, another venerable Hanseatic port further along the coast.[41] By this means Harris had blooded his crews.

The enemy responded from May to June with the so-called Baedeker Raids, in which British cities with three stars in this German guidebook – such as Bath, Exeter and Norwich – were hit in return. Although the RAF raids had minimal impact on German war production – the Heinkel works at Rostock was up and running within weeks – the fact that these attacks resulted in the population's mass flight to the surrounding villages inclined Harris and his bosses to scrape together a thousand bombers for a raid on a single city. Such attacks would saturate and overwhelm anti-aircraft defences, while firefighters would be unable to work under a continuous rain of bombs. The big round number had an instant public relations appeal, for making headlines was important to the business of war. Indeed, much of Harris's time was spent entertaining a total of five thousand visitors to his command, showing them bomb-damage reconnaissance photographs through a stereopticon. On the final day of May 1942, Harris moved his forefinger across a map of Europe, before pressing it down on Cologne and saying 'The 1,000 Plan tonight.' In a colossal act of bluff, this force was cobbled together partly so as to ensure the survival of a free-standing RAF.

For nearly two hours Cologne was ravaged from end to end in a raid that destroyed forty-five thousand houses and cost 469 people their lives. The *New York Times* inaccurately inflated the number of dead to twenty thousand. The London *Times*, which repeated this inaccuracy, reported that Churchill had congratulated Sinclair and Harris; Sinclair saluted Harris; and Harris congratulated his men. There were follow-up raids of similar strength on Bremen and Essen. The raid on Bremen saw the debut of an elite Pathfinder Force – whose formation Harris had initially resisted – of experienced pilots whose job was to light up the target in all weathers by dropping different-coloured flares. This was not entirely foolproof since on one occasion they illuminated Saarlouis rather than Saarbrücken, and in their first month of existence the Pathfinders suffered casualties of 9 per cent.[42]

Buoyed by these successes, in November 1942 Portal requested a force growing to six thousand first-line bombers to carry out huge area-bombing raids in 1943 and 1944. Massively exaggerating the impact of the raid on

Cologne, he argued that ten such attacks on every German city with more than fifty thousand people, dropping one and a quarter million tons of bombs, would destroy six million homes, kill six hundred thousand people and injure another million, while making twenty-five million homeless. Attempts to co-opt the USAAF into this project ran into the Americans' belief in daylight precision bombing of a narrow range of vital industrial targets, although it should be stressed that Harris had exceptionally cordial relations with his US air baron colleagues Fred Anderson, 'Hap' Arnold and Ira Eaker, who before US entry into the war had made available to Bomber Command a third of their training facilities under the Arnold–Towers flying training scheme. The Americans were encouraged to mute these tactical objections lest they indirectly benefit the two Allied navies, which were jealous of the resources being poured into bombers, or, in the case of the US naval chief Admiral Ernest King, thought the war's entire emphasis should be shifted to the Pacific.

A combined bombing offensive also represented the minimum consensus, for at least it would soften up the Germans as the Allies internally clashed over where and when to open a second European front. These complex considerations were reflected in the Combined Bomber Offensive directive issued during the January 1943 Casablanca Conference of Allied leaders. This artfully fused the night area bombing favoured by the RAF with the daylight raids on precise economic targets which the Americans over-confidently thought they could deliver. Inevitable imprecision by either was disguised by two qualifications regarding tactical feasibility and northern European weather.[43]

Armed with this directive, from March to July 1943 the RAF launched the Battle of the Ruhr – a protracted and punishing series of raids against Germany's major industrial conurbation in which 58,000 tons of bombs fell. It included a daring attempt to interdict riverine traffic and to drown the industrial workforce through the Dambusters Raid in May, a raid Harris had initially regarded as a waste of time. When Goebbels visited Essen on 10 April after the third major raid, he had to walk around the ruins as the roads were impassable. As he surveyed the wrecked Krupp arms factory, engineers explained to the Minister that it would take twelve years to repair the damage. After two thousand people were killed in Wuppertal in June, the Propaganda Minister acknowledged in his diary that morale was fraying under these relentless assaults.[44] When in June 1943 the Pointblank directive incorporated into the overall strategy industrial targets which sustained Luftwaffe fighter defences, the RAF insisted on area bombing of these cities by night, while the Americans struck by day.[45]

With much of the Ruhr reduced to rubble, Harris turned his attention to Germany's second largest city. In the attacks on Hamburg in late July and early August 1943, Bomber Command employed a device it had possessed for at least a year. Window consisted of strips of metallic foil which confused the radars that directed German fighters. On this occasion, German radar operators saw a blizzard of static rather than the RAF aircraft speeding to effect Hamburg's fiery doom. Hamburg was home to the shipyards Blohm und Voss, Howaldtswerke, Deutsche Werft and Stülken und Sohn, which accounted for most of Germany's U-boat production. These were the vessels that were taking a devastating toll on Britain's Atlantic merchant shipping. There were also oil refineries and aircraft-parts manufacturers. Because of this, the city had ample anti-aircraft provision, notably over fifty batteries of heavy flak, as well as sophisticated civil defence measures. Harris's decision 'to destroy Hamburg' had been reached by 27 May 1943, when he wrote to that effect to his six operational group commanders. The codename for the attack was Operation Gomorrah, the name of the city destroyed by heavenly fire in the Old Testament. The raids fortuitously coincided with a heatwave and the resultant firestorms devastated eight and a half square miles of the city, while high explosives produced fifty-six million cubic yards of rubble. About forty-two thousand people were killed, most of them burned alive or suffocated by carbon monoxide in cellars, and a million survivors fled the city. Thanks to Window, Bomber Command lost only eighty-seven aircraft of the 3,095 sent in four night raids against Hamburg between 24 July and 3 August 1943. The USAAF lost thirty-nine of 337 bombers sent in two daylight raids.[46] It was after seeing film of the raid on Hamburg that Churchill exclaimed, 'Are we beasts? Are we taking this too far?', although a few days later he was all for pummelling Berlin.

Harris became obsessed with wrecking German cities, resenting any attempts to divert Bomber Command resources against what he dismissed as panacea targets or on maritime missions or those supporting SOE. He made such large claims as 'We can wreck Berlin from end to end if the USAAF will come in on it. It will cost between 400–500 aircraft. It will cost Germany the war' (3 November) or 'The Lancaster force alone should be sufficient, but only just sufficient, to produce in Germany by 1 April 1944 a state of devastation in which surrender is inevitable' (7 December). His men had virtually destroyed forty-five of sixty major cities, and he wanted completion, specifically the 'Big City' of Berlin, thereby underplaying the facts that the capital was vast in area, far away and well defended. Its large parks and wide thoroughfares nullified the impact of incendiary bombs.

Nonetheless, Berlin it was to be, on sixteen occasions between November 1943 and March 1944, with RAF casualties mounting as the campaign intensified. So did the number of early returns for alleged mechanical malfunction, or instances of crews dumping bombs rather than venturing to that dreadful target. While Harris insisted that his strategy would work if aircraft were not constantly diverted to what he regarded as peripheral targets, others began to wonder about this obsessive bomber. They included Portal, whose relations with Harris involved counterbalancing the latter's public celebrity with the beady eye Portal himself cast on posterity. Harris did not help his own case by almost resenting orders for the tactical deployment of bombers before and after D-Day or to emulate the Americans in focusing on fuel-related targets in Germany. He argued that such a focus would alert the German defenders and hence result in higher air-crew losses. He also doubted whether the Germans were stupid enough to concentrate essential production in a few places, his obtuseness perhaps influenced by the fact that he was not entitled to see top secret Ultra evidence derived from decryption of the German Enigma coding device, which revealed internal German assessments of the effects of the bombing campaign. He was openly contemptuous of 'ball-bearing experts', admirals who had 'resuscitated the U-boat threat', not to speak of 'the nearly defunct SOE which has raised its bloody head and produced what I hope is its final death rattle'. This may have been right about SOE, but it was unwise of 'Butch' to be so dismissive of cloak-and-dagger romantics. In a protracted correspondence, Portal accused Harris of half-heartedly obeying orders concerning a strategy he did not believe in, while Harris accused Portal of diverting resources away from a strategy that given time and concentrated resources might have worked. This was to overlook the aircraft shot down over Berlin, and the effects the USAAF was having on German oil targets. Harris eventually called Portal's bluff by threatening to resign, calculating correctly that he was so popular with the British public, at a time when American ground commanders filled the news, that Portal (or Churchill) would never concur. In the end Harris's value as a charismatic commander trumped Portal's attempts to make him see reason. The devastation went on, while Portal deftly stepped away from Harris. Ironically, while Harris would take the blame for bombing Dresden, it was actually Churchill and Portal who came up with this target group before the February 1945 Yalta Summit Conference.[47]

III BLOTS ON OUR ESCUTCHEON

Harris made no pretence that his purpose was anything other than the destruction of Germany's cities. They had no value in his eyes; adapting a comment once made by German Chancellor Bismarck, he said that none of them was worth 'the bones of a British Grenadier'. That view was a little too stark for his political masters, who sought to avoid any public impression of sowing terror. The official government position, as usually represented in the Commons by Sinclair, was that the primary objectives were military targets, although there would be inevitable civilian collateral casualties. Opposition to the RAF bombing campaign came from a variety of sources, all benefiting from the fact that Britain was a democracy, which even in wartime allowed public debate and press comment about the conduct of warfare. The very different response to conscientious objectors in 1939–45 to that in 1914–18 was more generally indicative of how times had changed. The hyper-patriotism of the Church of England and the press during the Great War had moderated into a more considered and sometimes critical stance during the Second World War, even though there was surely a better argument for fighting Hitler than there had been for going to war with the Kaiser.

Outright pacifists were opposed to all violence rather than simply area bombing, and would logically have led to the swastika fluttering over Whitehall together with all the attendant evils Nazism brought in its wake. They should ponder Kevin Brownlow's 1966 film called *It Happened Here*. Moralistic arguments that selected some but not all aspects of war fighting were more common. The upper-class author Vera Brittain had lost a brother and a lover in the Great War, during the latter part of which she worked as a nurse tending wounded British and German troops near the front. With considerable moral courage, she relentlessly attacked the area-bombing campaign. The consequences for her were extremely scathing reviews of her books and some degree of social ostracism, although Home Secretary Herbert Morrison rejected a request by a Conservative MP that she should be interned. Her bright lamp was slightly tarnished by her insistence that stories of German atrocities in concentration camps were exaggerated, and that in any case they were morally no different from incinerating people by bombing.[48]

Another critic of bombing was Alfred Salter, the Labour MP for West Bermondsey, much of which had been ravaged by the Luftwaffe in 1940, including Salter's own home, which was destroyed. Perhaps because of what he had suffered, but also because the poor man was dying, the Commons heard him respectfully when he said: 'No apologies are now offered for the indiscriminate bombing of women and children ... In the early days of the war only strictly military targets were said to be the objectives of our Air Force. Now we have photographs showing whole streets of working class houses being blown sky high by our bombs ... Every day the war continues it will become harder, not only materially but spiritually, to build a new and better world.' A further thorn in the government's side was the Labour MP Richard Stokes. Stokes was no pacifist. He had won the Military Cross and Croix de Guerre in 1914–18 and fully supported the tactical use of airpower. In the Commons, he probed Sinclair about the concealed aims of area bombing, calling it 'morally wrong and strategic lunacy'. In a statement startlingly at variance with the public's support for paying the Germans back in their own coin, he said, 'It fills me with absolute nausea to think of the filthy task that many of our young men are being invited to carry out.' He tried to force Sinclair to admit a specific switch in policy to indiscriminate bombing, which the Minister denied, while invidiously inquiring why the Soviet air force, which he knew had no heavy bombers, did not attack cities. Sinclair was precluded by considerations of diplomatic secrecy from rebutting Stokes by telling him how enthusiastically Stalin applauded the bombing offensive.

Among those who condemned the policy of area bombing was Bomber Command's own dedicated chaplain, based at High Wycombe. The Reverend John Collins went on to his apotheosis as a leading light of the post-war Campaign for Nuclear Disarmament, after finding the High Wycombe HQ 'the most soul destroying, the most depressing of the ... places in which I had to serve'. The Church of England endeavoured to combine the role of Established state Church with the duty of Christian witness and guardian of the nation's moral and spiritual health. It did so within the limits of a system in which the Prime Minister's ecclesiastical patronage secretary presented nominations to the King for all archbishoprics and episcopal sees. Individual churchmen privately opposed to area bombing on moral grounds were a small band whose ranks included Cosmo Lang, until 1942 the Archbishop of Canterbury. However, Lang also had the good sense to know that clerics had no special competence to comment on these issues, a humility lost on some of his contemporaries and successors. There were also a few churchmen, notably Bishop Mervyn Haigh of Coventry and later of Winchester, who advocated reprisal attacks and bought the government's line on waging ethical air war.[49]

One cleric stood out from the rest in his public criticism of the bombing campaign: George Bell, the Bishop of Chichester. Bell was a protégé and biographer of Randall Davidson, the Archbishop of Canterbury who had opposed the use of gas and reprisal bombing in the Great War. Bell had an honourable record of helping the vulnerable, including German refugees and the starving people of Greece, as well as fostering ecumenical contacts that took him into the shallows of the German resistance to Hitler inspired by Pastor Dietrich Bonhoeffer. He was fastidious in distinguishing between Germans and National Socialists, becoming a leading booster of the notion of 'the good German', an idea that primarily appealed to those who had hobnobbed at All Souls with well-mannered aristocratic Germans rather than with Nazi thugs. Bell forcefully rejected the suggestion that the Church was the 'state's spiritual auxiliary', let alone 'the Tory party gathered at prayer'. In reality it had long since ceased to be Tory, and William Temple, who succeeded Lang as Archbishop of Canterbury in 1942, was a former member of the Labour Party. Bell opened his campaign in a speech to the 1941 Canterbury Convocation, which included a potted history of area bombing that blamed the British for starting it, a bizarre interpretation he picked up from his friend the military historian Basil Liddell Hart. From being an exponent of bombing, Liddell Hart had become a convinced opponent, partly because he thought it did not work, partly because he thought the British were adopting methods more worthy of the Nazis, but also because he detested Churchill and thought a compromise peace with Hitler would preserve Europe from the Soviets.[50]

While Archbishop Temple respected the views of pacifists, he did not share them. However he was also unwilling to echo the Germanophobes in government, press and society. When Bell lobbied him to join in the criticism of area bombing, Temple declined on the perfectly coherent grounds that he was not qualified to express an opinion on the complex issues involved, although he did understand all too well how total war blurred the distinction between combatants and civilians. He also believed that the 'worst of all things is to fight and to do it ineffectively'. As the ferocity of the bombing campaign mounted over Hamburg, Temple – who accepted Sinclair's version of policy – deflected critics with the argument that 'it does not necessarily follow that acts which horrify us are wrong'. At the same time he refused to pray for victory unless the phrase 'if it be Thy will' was inserted. Despite being warned to leave the subject alone, Bell persisted and finally made a major speech attacking area bombing in the House of Lords in February 1944. Part of Bell's concern was that indiscriminate bombing was causing a general 'lowering of moral tone', by which he meant the casual brutality with which bombing was discussed by such as Home Secretary Morrison. But he was also concerned with the more practical matter that the claims of bombing's exponents did not correspond with their less than impressive results, and with how area bombing detracted from the fundamental justness of the Allied cause. Here he had a serious point, although his high moral tone floated over the inconvenient alliance with the murderous Soviets:

> The Allies stand for something greater than power. The chief name inscribed on our banner is 'Law'. It is of supreme importance that we, who, with our Allies, are the Liberators of Europe, should so use power that it is always under the control of law. It is because the bombing of enemy towns – this area bombing – raises this issue of bombing unlimited and exclusive that such immense importance is bound to attach to the policy and action of His Majesty's Government.[51]

Speaking for the government, Lord Cranborne, whose father was a discreet critic of area bombing, promised that Bomber Command would redouble its efforts. Cosmo Lang lent Bell his qualified support, especially with regard to the falsehoods being told about the objectives of bombing: 'We were always told that that policy was to limit attacks to definite military objectives or their immediate neighbourhood ... I do not think it can be said that that policy has been adhered to in these apparently deliberate attempts to destroy whole cities, and I venture to think there is some force ... in the plea that either the hitherto declared policy is to be changed or this new policy is to be definitely adopted.'[52]

Bell was more than slightly in love with his self-image as a brave dissenter, which did indeed cost him promotion to the bishopric of London. But his vanity does not devalue the informed criticism he made of the military rationale for bombing, however it must have grated on those who bore the daily burden of life-and-death decisions. A more thoughtful, perhaps more traditionally Anglican position was expressed by Cyril Garbett, the Archbishop of York. Declining Bell's invitation to join his moral crusade, in 1943 Garbett wrote: 'Often in life there is no clear choice between absolute right and wrong; frequently the choice has to be made of the lesser of two evils, and it is the lesser evil to bomb a war-loving Germany than to sacrifice the lives of our fellow-countrymen who long for peace, and to delay delivering millions now held in slavery.' The Bishop of Oxford also dismissed Bell's concern with German civilisation, saying that to stop the bombing would prolong the war by years and sacrifice 'twenty times – fifty times – perhaps a hundred times as many lives, not merely of Germans, but of the allies and of the enslaved populations as well. This is neither common sense nor Christianity.' Hensley Henson, the former Bishop of Durham, wisely commented that 'if Hitler is victorious, what value any longer can attach to the few sacred monuments of European civilisation, which henceforth can only be intelligible as memorials and epitaphs of a perished culture? In the interest of the human spirit and its intellectual, artistic and, above all, its ethical potencies and promises, we dare not lose this Crusade.' These statements had a breadth of common-sense realism, tinged with a theologically coherent pessimism about the human condition, denied to such as Bell and Collins.[53]

CHAPTER 20

Is That Britain? – No, It's Brittany

I EUROPE

The RAF alone bombed Germany until January 1943, three years and four months after the war in Europe started. Two Americans of German (or Pennsylvanian Dutch) ancestry were prominent in the USAAF campaign in Europe, along with Ira Eaker, the second head of Eighth Air Force. The USAAF commanding general, Henry 'Hap' Arnold, and the commander of Eighth Air Force, Carl 'Tooey' Spaatz, were both from a background in which a paternal grandparent still spoke German. Arnold was nicknamed 'Hap' because this otherwise taciturn man bore a permanent faint smile which made him seem happy. Spaatz was nicknamed 'Tooey' because he had similar red hair to another West Point cadet called Toohey; in 1937 Mrs Spaatz insisted on including the second 'a' in their surname, to show that it was pronounced Spahtz not Spats.

Spaatz spent sixty days in Britain in 1940, as assistant military attaché (air) or, as he recalled it, 'a high-class spy'. A British Home Guard volunteer arrested Spaatz in Dover when, dressed in crumpled tweeds, he wandered into a restricted area while witnessing an RAF dogfight with the Germans. Thereafter Spaatz signed himself into RAF bases as 'Colonel Carl A. Spaatz, German spy'. Afforded total access, even to radar, Spaatz made his cool appraisals of RAF Bomber Command, while deducing from Luftwaffe tactics that it could never bomb Britain into submission. With Colonel 'Wild Bill' Donovan, head of the OSS he played a crucial part in persuading Roosevelt that Britain would survive.[1]

Eaker set up shop in Wycombe Abbey School for Girls near Harris's command. The RAF practised a sort of reverse Lend–Lease, giving the Americans everything from air bases – mostly in East Anglia – to RAF and

WAAF support staff. Spaatz was named commander of Air Forces Combat Command in January 1942 and in May he became commander of the Eighth Air Force, transferring his headquarters to England in July. Spaatz was in overall command of the USAAF in Europe, while remaining the CO of Eighth Air Force. In December 1942 he was appointed commander of the Twelfth Air Force in North Africa. He became commander of the Allied Northwest African Air Force in February 1943, of the combined Fifteenth Air Force and Royal Air Force in Italy in November 1943 and of US Strategic Air Forces in Europe in January 1944. Finally, he was given overall command of USAAF efforts in the Pacific.

Like their British peers, the US air barons believed that airpower would prevent attritional stalemate of the kind experienced on the Western Front in the Great War. There was a similar belief that it could deliver a quick and decisive outcome, more humane than either the endless slogging in the trenches or the slow starvation of civilians by naval blockade. Some US airmen agreed with Trenchard's view that massive air attacks on cities would deliver victory. However, experts at the Army Air Corps Tactical School argued that, rather than simply pulverising cities, civilian morale could be collapsed by destroying the critical infrastructure on which modern urban life depended. That meant power generation and transmission, energy sources such as oil, and industrial sites crucial to the enemy war effort. It also meant taking the war to the Luftwaffe by obliterating aircraft factories.

After studying the impact of indiscriminate Japanese bombing in China, the Americans concluded that it consolidated rather than subverted civilian morale. The majority of American air force experts did not have moral objections to bombing civilians; they simply thought that it did not achieve its objectives. This dovetailed with the moral objections to indiscriminate bombing made by Roosevelt's government while the US was uninvolved in the air war in Europe, although the Air War Plans Division strategic plan issued in the summer of 1941 left open direct attacks on German civilians once the infrastructural blows had brought their morale to breaking point.[2] The result was the division of labour agreed at the Casablanca Conference in early 1943, by which time Eighth Air Force was fully established at its bases in East Anglia. The RAF would continue with its nocturnal area bombing while the USAAF would undertake daylight precision strikes. The working relationship was complementary rather than antagonistic, and partly reflected the type of aircraft the USAAF deployed. They cost a great deal, flew fast and high and were equipped with a sophisticated Norden bombsight, which had been demonstrated to be extraordinarily accurate – in the clear blue skies over Arizona or Texas. The B-17 heavy bombers also bristled with heavy machine guns, with which it was expected they would take on and destroy any German fighters that intercepted them.

In order to play itself in, Eighth Air Force was initially deployed attacking targets located within occupied countries rather than undertaking the altogether more arduous task of deep raids into Germany. It was also hoped that precision bombing would minimise civilian casualties in countries with whose populations the Allies were not at war. In northern European flying conditions, precision quickly revealed itself as a chimera. In January 1943, the USAAF undertook its first raids into Germany itself. In difficult conditions it raided aircraft production plants at Oschersleben and Halberstadt near Brunswick. Although it caused these targets significant damage, it also lost 13 per cent of the attacking force – forty-two heavy bombers. For about a year it continued mounting precision strikes against critical infrastructure or military targets, with mixed results. During the joint series of raids on Hamburg, it claimed that the pall of smoke left over the city by the RAF obscured its crews' view of submarine yards and factories, to excuse the fact that they did little damage to these installations. Adverse weather conditions grounded the vision-dependent Eighth Air Force more than they did Bomber Command, leading to a slower learning curve for the American air crew. Although the B-17s were much more heavily armed than RAF bombers, their crews found that even in tight defensive formation they were outgunned by battle-hardened Luftwaffe fighter pilots, who quickly discovered their Achilles heel, which was that the bombers had only a single, medium machine gun firing forward.

In mid-August 1943 the Americans launched two large raids against the Messerschmitt works at Regensburg and three ball-bearing plants at Schweinfurt. The attack on Regensburg was led by Colonel Curtis LeMay, commander of the 3rd Air Division. Like Eaker who sometimes flew on combat missions, LeMay did not have to be there, but on occasions he joined in 'whenever it seemed that my actual presence and physical direction and command of the mission – simultaneously with the activity of others – would result in a benefit to the Group at large … something new in the way of enemy defences, enemy fighter tactics, enemy ground to air bombardment, something new somewhere. Then I'd go.'[3] The two raids were tactically interconnected, with the Regensburg bombers intended to exhaust the German defences, allowing the Schweinfurt crews to follow relatively unscathed in their wake. Since the Regensburg attackers were to fly south to North Africa after the mission, the Schweinfurt raiders would take the heat on their return to Britain.[4]

Although the bombers had long-range fighter coverage, with planes equipped with supplementary fuel tanks, the last three hundred miles of their mission deep into the German south were unescorted. Arriving over Regensburg with 122 of the 139 B-17s that had taken off, the Americans successfully bombed the Messerschmitt plant, even managing to avoid hitting a nearby hospital. The attack on Schweinfurt was less successful and caused more collateral damage, since the three small factories were embedded in residential areas. Annihilation threatened on the return leg to Britain, until Colonel Hubert Zemke's long-range P-47s came to their rescue. During these raids, the USAAF lost sixty aircraft, fifty-five crews with 552 crewmen, about half of whom were killed, with five more crews rescued after ditching at sea. The Regensburg Messerschmitt factory was wrecked, but the machine tools inside survived, so the plant lost only the equivalent of eight to ten weeks' output. At Schweinfurt, the impact of the raids on the three allegedly neuralgic ball-bearing plants was minimal: the Germans had stockpiled ball-bearings and could easily purchase more from Sweden. Harris was right to refuse to pursue it, in defiance of the Air Ministry and his boss, Portal. The raids did encourage the Germans to disperse production, not least to camouflaged outdoor sites within forests, rendering the possibility of hitting so-called bottleneck targets even more remote.

The onset of consistently bad winter weather led Eaker to take the conscious decision to conduct area raids on German cities rather than have his bombers languishing on British airfields. A by no means secondary benefit was to force the Luftwaffe to do battle in defence of those cities and to suffer irreparable attrition from the USAAF's long-range fighters. For all these good and sufficient reasons, the USAAF embarked on indiscriminate area bombing of Germany, even as it continued to carry out a limited number of precision raids on targets in German-controlled parts of Europe. The policy was never publicly admitted or announced, and became controversial when in March 1944 the British pacifist Vera Brittain's condemnation of area bombing was reported on the front page of the *New York Times*, always a paper that can be relied on to question US motives and methods. The criticism undermined the USAAF public relations image of engaging in clean surgical strikes while RAF Bomber Command bludgeoned the Germans to death, which in turn called into question the more general US self-image as God's chosen force for good in the world.

enemy morale

Moralistic posturing aside, the USAAF did conduct internal debate about bombing strategy, much of it turning on the imprecise notion of enemy morale. In June 1944, Spaatz ordered American air intelligence officers and psychological warfare experts to study the impact of area bombing on German civilian morale. They concluded that it was inevitably limited under a totalitarian dictatorship, for the secret police could crush any dissent: people may have been exhausted but they were not restive. Rather than simply bashing away at big cities, they recommended raiding a hundred smaller towns, with important government or party offices, minor industries or significant transport facilities. The idea behind this Operation Shatter was to expose the Nazis' inability to protect the population, rather than annihilating civilians for its own sake. Psychological warfare experts dreamed up the idea of using white propaganda to warn some towns of imminent raids, which would trigger mass flight from raids that never happened. Black propaganda, meanwhile, posed as mocking Nazi defiance of the Allies' capacity to hit certain towns, putting the Nazi authorities in a quandary: they could not rebut the black broadcasts without admitting that the towns in question were vulnerable, nor could they be seen to strengthen their defences. Accordingly, when the raids did come, the psychological impact was maximised.

Shatter was opposed by Colonel Richard Hughes, an English-born officer serving at the USAAF Enemy Objectives Unit, which selected USAAF bombing targets. A former infantry officer in the Great War and commander of the Gurkhas, Hughes was no softie. His naval-officer brother had died when the Germans sank a British aircraft carrier off Norway. He considered himself a steely realist, but one who thought it was important for the US to maintain the moral high ground or 'an urge towards decency and better treatment of man by man'. He astutely argued that just because the enemy committed such atrocities as shooting POWs, this did not oblige the Allies to emulate them. Hughes argued that weather conditions would nullify the elaborations of psychological warfare experts, so that the USAAF would be reduced to issuing idle threats against specific towns, only to invite the charge of terror bombing when it had to find somewhere else. Looking towards the future, he thought that indiscriminate bombing would make it harder for the Americans to win German civilian support for reconstruction in the post-war era, when the US would clearly assume the lead role given that Britain was bankrupt. Area bombing would merely convince German civilians that they were going to be treated harshly after the war and so stiffen their resolve to fight on. Hughes was predictably derided by Lowell Weicker, the USAAF Director of Intelligence, for his lack of killer instinct: 'you cannot always use the Marquess of Queensberry's rules against a nation brought up on doctrines of unprecedented cruelty, brutality, and disregard of basic human decencies'.[5]

In the event, Spaatz took a dispassionate look at the issues and came out against the psychological bombing campaign. It would divert resources from more militarily vital objectives like the ongoing assault against Germany's dwindling oil supplies and refineries. Morale was too imprecise a quantity to be assessed in this way. Even when the air force consulted eminent academic psychologists, they were not much help. The Germans would have few difficulties in neutralising the propaganda effects with broadcasts purporting to come from the Americans, whose effect would be to call their bluff. Finally, Eisenhower disliked terror weapons, arguing, 'For God's sake let's keep our eyes on the ball and use some sense.' Spaatz ordered his forces to continue precision attacks, although he left some leeway by authorising blind bombing of city-centre targets should there be impenetrable cloud cover over industrial or military facilities.

This was not the end of the matter, for in late 1944 the RAF invited the USAAF to participate in Operation Thunderclap. This was to be a massed combined strike on the German capital, which the RAF believed might kill a quarter of a million people, in addition to striking terror into the Nazi elite in their bunkers. While US commanders found this idea repugnant, suspecting a British attempt to inculpate the Americans in their own dubious deeds, Eisenhower had the operation deferred rather than rejected outright. The USAAF also investigated the possibility of using clapped-out B-17s as robot weapons. They could be packed with up to twenty thousand pounds of high explosives and then automatically guided on to cities after the crew had set the instrumentation and baled out. This was an entirely indiscriminate weapon, akin to the German V1 and V2, although with a far greater explosive payload. While this weapon proved to be of limited utility, at the highest level the US was still interested in undermining German civilian morale by creating airborne pandemonium. Roosevelt was especially interested in anything that created more streams of refugees, as they would overburden whatever already strained infrastructure they alighted upon. The result, on 22–23 February 1945, was Operation Clarion. This was a series of combined RAF and USAAF low-level bomber and fighter raids, ostensibly on the transport system, but involving bomb, cannon and rocket attacks on anything that walked or crawled, whether in major cities or sleepy little places. While publicly the Americans were keen to avoid any impression of terrorising civilians, their ordnance now also included the first routine deployment of napalm.

By now attacking an enemy largely bereft of fighter cover, the Allies launched huge raids on Berlin. On 3 February a thousand B-17s attacked Berlin, killing three thousand Berliners. The problem was that the relentless raids on the capital were tantamount to thumping a punch-drunk boxer; they rarely stay down. The limited impact of this punishment on the German capital was one of the reasons why Allied air planners were keen to hit relatively unscathed targets in the deepest eastern corners of Germany. Another was the desire to do something to relieve the pressure of German counter-attacks against the advancing Soviets. Those with an eye to the immediate future may have seen no harm in demonstrating to the Russians what Allied airpower could do, although there is little to support that Cold War reading of things. Three cities came under consideration: Chemnitz, Dresden and Leipzig. Harris had wanted to bomb Dresden as early as November 1944, but it became a priority target only at the Yalta Conference, where the Soviets expressed a general desire for their Western allies to bomb transport hubs which the Germans were using to move troops from Italy and Norway to the contracting Eastern Front. They did not specify Dresden, but that city would certainly have been among those they had in mind. Dresden also recommended itself, not only because it contained around 130 war-related factories, but because it was already crowded with civilian refugees fleeing from further east. An attack on the city would cause sufficient confusion to paralyse the trans-shipment of German troops to fight the Red Army.

At around 10 p.m. on Tuesday 13 February, an advance group of Lancasters dropped green markers and magnesium parachute flares on Dresden, illuminating the general target before more precise red marking began. Next Mosquitoes from 627 Squadron swept low to drop 1,000-pound canisters packed with red target indicators, which burst at 700 feet. Circling the city at three thousand feet was Wing-Commander Maurice Smith, the Master Bomber for the night, who after checking the visibility of all the red and green markers gave the order: 'Controller to Plate Rack Force: Come in and bomb glow of Red TI as planned. Bomb the glow of Red TIs as planned.' This launched the main Lancaster force, 240 aircraft flying at twelve to thirteen thousand feet, on its final bombing run, a difficult bit of flying, because the aircraft were synchronised in a fan shape so that the bombs fell sequentially a few degrees from each other. Some 881.1

tons of ordnance of various types fell on to the city centre, 57 per cent high-explosive bombs, and 43 per cent incendiary devices. While the fire brigades endeavoured to deal with a conflagration that could be seen from fifty miles away, a second wave of 525 bombers hit the burning city between 1.21 and 1.45 in the morning.

Since there was no point in bombing where the main fires burned, this force sought out fresh areas which were duly marked out. This included the main rallying point for those displaced from their homes by the earlier raid. At noon on the 14th a huge force of USAAF B-17s appeared over the burning city to bomb its marshalling yards. The impact of this was minimal, as most of the city lay in ruins, while a significant part of the force wandered off course and hit Prague instead. On the 15th a USAAF bomber force was diverted by impenetrable cloud cover from its primary target – the hydrogenation plant at Böhlen – to hit Dresden instead. This caused limited damage, although it did blow a hole in the wall of the main prison, enabling some escapes. In sum, these raids may have killed between twenty-five and thirty-five thousand people, some of them simply vaporised. There was extensive damage to the city's many arms-related industries, especially those engaged in manufacturing optical instruments, but the vital railway system was quickly restored.[6]

Churchill decided to go on the record as saying that the bombing of Dresden was a raid too far, even though he had specifically authorised it. In a memorandum drafted on 28 March, which the Air Staff persuaded him to retract, Churchill wrote: 'The destruction of Dresden remains a query against the conduct of Allied bombing.' This implied more than his pragmatic concern that the British would be inheritors of a costly wasteland when they occupied Germany, for the Prime Minister referred to Dresden as an 'act of terror and wanton destruction'. In other words he was criticising Bomber Command for carrying out a policy he had repeatedly endorsed. Harris thought the criticism the raid had attracted was due to sentimentality about Dresden's glorious past, as epitomised by Meissen porcelain – which the city did not, in fact, produce. He was right, however, to point out that the raid was an operation that went conspicuously right on the night, against a target of both industrial and strategic value, as requested by Britain's ally Russia. Nonetheless, both Churchill and Portal used the opportunity to pose as having moral qualms about a policy they had repeatedly urged on Harris. Admittedly Harris needed no urging, but he was to receive only grudging recognition under Britain's Ruritanian honours system, while Portal became a peer of the realm and a well-paid

not war crimes (at Time) – 1977
He skips over Hague 190:
that did forbid aerial bombing

514 · MORAL COMBAT

director on the boards of the British aviation companies that owed him so much.

The raids on Dresden were not a war crime, since the relevant international laws on aerial bombing were not codified or ratified until 1977, and they cannot be equated with Nazi crimes against humanity, though some historians have certainly endeavoured to do so with more or less malign intent. Ironically, those who made the 1977 laws relied upon figures for the death toll at Dresden that ultimately came from the Nazis' own propagandists, via the dubious mediation of David Irving, a prominent Holocaust revisionist who incorporated the Nazis figure of 125,000 dead in his book on Dresden, when the reality was more like 25,000–30,000, considerably less than at Hamburg a year earlier. The fact that Dresden was a much loved pre-war cultural centre may have contributed to the facility with which its suffering has been elided with Hiroshima, Nagasaki and, equally outrageously, Auschwitz. What these raids may suggest is that by this stage in the war Bomber Command was engaged in kicking to death the drunken boxer mentioned earlier, although the German offensive in the Ardennes indicated that the Nazis had a lot of fight left. The brutal reality was that Dresden was just another name on a target board, to which much unjustified retrospective significance has been attached.[7]

According to pacifists like Vera Brittain, who chronicled and opposed area bombing, it was the routineness of the Dresden operation that pointed to its morally deleterious effects. It engendered 'a process of deterioration which displays itself in a loss of sensitivity, and in words and actions showing callous indifference to suffering'. There is no good reason to question that verdict, for by then RAF bombing had been reduced to graphs and tables showing that x tons of bombs meant y millions of lost man hours, which after a couple of raids covered the cost of an aircraft delivering z tons of bombs.[8]

II 'HAD TO BE DONE': THE USAAF OVER JAPAN 1944–1945

From late 1943 onwards, USAAF planners turned their minds to targets in Japan. The weather over the Japanese home islands was one justification for not resorting to precision bombing. Planes would encounter vast banks of cloud while the 100–200 mph jet stream played havoc with air speeds and the ability to hold an aircraft steady at high altitudes. The effects of precision raids on the Japanese aircraft industry were less than impressive, leading to calls to disperse the USAAF bomber fleet to where it could be tactically useful to the army. The pressure was on to find a way of making the air force decisive in this theatre.

Experts working for the Committee of Operations Analysts concentrated on firebombing as the surest route to crippling Japanese industry, while sowing class division and mass panic. Japanese urban housing stock was dense, flimsy and easily combustible. The experts consulted insurers who had worked in pre-war Japan to establish how well the authorities coped with fires like the one that had attended the 1923 Tokyo earthquake. Chemists employed by Standard Oil tested new incendiary devices such as M-69 canisters whose contents squirted out a hundred-foot jet of the jellified petrol called napalm. They scoured the 'Orientalist' photographic archives of the motion-picture giant RKO for interiors of Japanese houses and then took floor mats from ethnic Japanese homes in Hawaii. They built mock 'little Tokyos' to test the right combination of incendiaries and high explosives, not forgetting fragmentation bombs which were designed to kill Japanese firefighters. That included a large number of civilians, for every Japanese family was supposed to spring into action to put incendiaries out or to knock down their own homes to create firebreaks. Academic psychologists and so-called experts on Japan opined on the alleged propensity of the Japanese to irrational mass panic when anyone so much as cried 'fire' in a theatre.

See 496

This developed into a campaign to burn down six major cities on the main island of Honshu, including Tokyo. The task devolved upon Twenty-First Air Force based on Guam, and its new commander Curtis LeMay, who had first been transferred from Europe to command 20th Bomber Command in India and China. Relatively youthful, LeMay had a podgy, slightly dishevelled demeanour, complete with five-o'clock shadow and a cigar clenched in his mouth. Appearances were deceptive. After a very troubled childhood, with a drifter father, he had risen by exemplary merit to high command in a profession he loved, and to which he brought a practical mind. As a hands-on commander, LeMay flew on a B-29 Superfortress mission over the Himalayas from India to study the new aircraft's capabilities, which included dealing with a radio operator wounded by Japanese flak.[9] He found that, regardless of the bombing-accuracy factor, operating at high altitudes placed excessive stress on B-29 engines. He decided to strip out the heavy defensive armament to reduce fuel consumption and to maximise the bombloads the aircraft could carry, operating at lower levels. He reasoned that they would fly over too fast for light flak and too low for heavy flak. Air crews thought he was mad. LeMay customarily flew with big missions, but shortly after arriving on Guam he was briefed about the atomic bomb and thereafter could not go on further operations. He sat up all night in his HQ, with his Havanas and a Coca-Cola bottle in hand.[10] Perhaps he and his crews heard the New Orleans-born jazz singer and saxophonist Louis Prima, of 'Angelina', 'Just a Gigolo' and 'Jungle Book' fame nowadays, singing 'I Want to Go to Tokyo'. The lyrics are just about discernible from the 1944 recording. 'Sing a High / Sing a Lee / Sing a Low / We're Off to Tokyo ... Where the Yanks are going / The lanterns are blowing / Down they'll zoom / Down they boom' captures the spirit of the times pretty well.[11]

Tokyo

By early 1945 the population of Tokyo was five million, after nearly two million non-essential people, many of them children, had been evacuated to the countryside. Primitive shelters had been dug and firebreaks smashed out to limit any conflagration. On 9 March 1945, over three hundred huge B-29s took off from Guam, Saipan and Tinian heading for Tokyo. They arrived over the city after midnight on the 10th, with the last bombing run taking place at 3.45 a.m. In that three-hour period they dropped 1,665 tons of bombs which caused a fire that destroyed over fifteen square miles of the city, killing 87,793 people and making more than a million homeless. The entire working-class residential area of Asakusa was destroyed. In the following days nearly three million people fled the city.[12]

The Tokyo raid was the opening salvo of an area-bombing campaign designed 'not to leave one stone lying on another'. Leaflets were showered on eleven cities warning them of potential attack, shortly before half of them were hit by equally enormous B-29 raids. The target was 'the Japanese mind'. US propaganda assured the Japanese that they were not deliberately targeting civilians, but that bombs were blind; at the same time, however, US pilots were reminded that most Japanese were enrolled in the Volunteer Defence Corps: 'THERE ARE NO CIVILIANS IN JAPAN.' After a temporary diversion to support the invasion of Okinawa, LeMay returned to razing Japanese cities, which he thought might decide the war within six months. In April, he despatched two more big raids against Tokyo, the second of which gutted over ten square miles of the already reeling city. Four raids hit Nagoya, home to the Mitsubishi aircraft factory. Among the fatalities were sixty-two captive B-29 crew members, who were left to burn inside the city's prison. On 25–26 May a massive raid on Tokyo focused on the government quarter south of the imperial palace. The fire spread to the palace, puncturing the myth that it was immune to enemy assault. Raids involving five hundred aircraft devastated Kobe, Osaka and Yokohama. When the campaign ended on 15 June, US analysts calculated that 126,762 people had been killed, nearly one and a half million homes destroyed and 105 square miles of cityscape erased.

US air war commanders were a notoriously tough-minded group of men, but they were not insensible to moral issues. Even LeMay, who like Harris came to epitomise callousness, especially after becoming strategic air commander in the Cold War, thought there was 'no point in slaughtering civilians for the sake of slaughter'. The US air commanders were keenly aware of Japanese war crimes, not only against captured US air crew, but also more generally in China and the Philippines. They also believed that a distinction between soldiers and civilians was meaningless in this context, since every home seemed to have been converted into a mini-workshop. LeMay claimed that his dehousing campaign revealed endless mechanical drills sticking up from the dying embers. That fact recommended an altogether more radical solution to the problem of ongoing Japanese resistance.

III PUMPKINS AND GADGETS:
LITTLE BOY AND FAT MAN 1944–1945

In both Britain and the US, émigré scientists were not allowed to work on militarily sensitive projects such as radar. That left many of them available to work in the more rarefied field of nuclear physics within university laboratories. The émigrés Otto Frisch and Rudolf Peierls, working at Birmingham University, were the first to postulate that a single kilogram of uranium 235 would be required to trigger a massive chain reaction, although they also warned about the lingering effects of radiation, which brought use of such a bomb into question. This last issue was ignored by the MAUD Committee responsible for British nuclear research, though it still haunted Peierls when this author talked about this with him at dinner one night at New College in the 1980s. He suffered from optical shingles and scrutinised the menu with a pocket torch as he expressed regret that in 1945 there had been no demonstrative air burst over an uninhabited island.

Once the possibility of nuclear chain reaction and explosive fission had been established, leading scientists alerted Roosevelt to the prospect of Germany acquiring a super-weapon. Initially, therefore, the nuclear threat was from Germany, with the Allies responding with what would come to be called a deterrent. Ironically Hitler's suspicious attitude towards 'Jewish' theoretical physics meant that German scientists were never in a position to lobby intensively for a bomb. By contrast, Roosevelt grasped the implications of such a device, and in 1941 set in place the budgets and organisational structures needed to develop an Allied version of such a weapon. Vannevar Bush, James Conant and an army engineer called Leslie Groves played key roles in co-ordinating academic physicists, industrial engineers and the US military in what evolved into the Manhattan Engineering Project, although the British insisted on calling it Tube Alloys. Eventually the bomb project employed 130,000 people and cost around US$2 billion, or about US$28 billion at current values. Groves, who had supervised construction of the Pentagon, gave the project its anodyne codename by the standard practice of calling an engineering division by its geographical location, for initially the project was housed in over a dozen locations scattered throughout New York City. The city had a high concentration of foreign-born scientists at Columbia University, as well as a port through which uranium could be imported without attracting much notice. The Columbia University football team was co-opted to shift tons of uranium ore imported from Africa by a Belgian.

On 5 May 1943 Bush, Conant, Groves and others, meeting as the Military Policy Committee, formally switched the atomic target from Germany to Japan. They reasoned that, since Japan lacked what they mistook for a German active nuclear-bomb project, there was less chance of the Japanese learning anything should the US drop a dud weapon. A more bizarre consideration was that it was safer to assemble the weapon on a Pacific island rather than in England, although that probably also reflected a desire to keep it an all-American show. The Committee also discussed whether to use the bomb as a naval mine, against the imperial fleet at Truk, so that a failed bomb could not be salvaged by naval divers, or whether to detonate it as an air burst over Tokyo, the only Japanese target they mentioned. That option was subsequently erased by Curtis LeMay's firestorms. They would need an intact city, not one reduced to ashes and rubble.

The development of the bomb and the decision to use it was a complicated and protracted process which tended to minimise the role of any single individual, including the President. Individual and team choices were made, but they were cumulative rather than individually critical. That in turn tended to marginalise any arguments made from general moral principles. Moral philosophers also note that their own academic community shared indirect blame, as they were largely engaged in a conversation with one another rather than engaging with public policy in wartime. Perhaps that was so, but one doubts whether anyone would have paid them any attention.[13]

The project's emphasis shifted from scientists working at Chicago or Columbia to the engineers and scientists who weaponised such a device after 1943 at the Nuclear Weapons Laboratory at Los Alamos in the New Mexican desert. Of course there were theoretical physicists at Los Alamos too; indeed the project's scientific director, Lieutenant Colonel Robert Oppenheimer, a left-wing scientist interested in Hinduism and literature, persuaded the US government to purchase the site. It was only forty-five miles from where he had long rented a cottage called Perro Caliente (Hot Dog in English), his base for riding in the desert mountains. A lonely, precocious child, Oppenheimer's best scientific work was already behind him by this stage in his life, but he had undoubted talents as a scientific impresario or entrepreneur. Fenced in behind barbed wire, the Los Alamos complex became a cross between a military base and a corporate town. The inmates combined hard graft with hard partying: dry martinis (Mrs Kitty Oppenheimer was an alcoholic as well as a Marxist) and square dancing in cowboy gear were the highlights. Eighty babies were born there in the first year of the camp's existence, indicating that it was not just fertile in ideas.[14] Work combined the regularity of a factory, with schedules and siren blasts to add a sense of urgency that limited moral reflection, and the timelessness of a modern campus-style enterprise like Google or Microsoft, where the enthusiastic can work through the night.[15]

Bomb design and potential targets were the province of, respectively, Oppenheimer, and Captain William Parsons, the head of the Los Alamos Ordnance Section. Although very different in temperament, both men rejected a demonstration over uninhabited ground. They preferred to see what the weapon would do to humans and the materials of civilisation. There were tensions at Los Alamos, but they only fitfully concerned morality.[16] There were acute cultural misunderstandings between scientists who wished to communicate freely with the wider, if highly exclusive, community of acknowledged experts, and the military, represented by Groves, who attached a higher priority to security (Groves regarded his task as akin to herding crackpots rather than cats). Scientists also have politics. Although

Einstein had initially alerted Roosevelt to the possibility of such a weapon, his flaky pacifism and Zionism ensured that he was kept at arm's length from the entire project. Many scientists, including Oppenheimer, seemed to regard the bomb as a way of making future conflicts unthinkable, ignoring the fact that for any human a rock or stone will do. Groves had more of a point than he realised, since many of the idealistic scientists thought that the best way to avert future war was to share the secret technology with the Soviets, a happy prospect especially if they were covert Communists or Red Army intelligence spies. Much of the security was aimed at preventing penetration by Nazi agents; in fact it should have been more focused on Soviet sympathisers and spies among their own scientists. One of the latter, the Anglo-German spy Klaus Fuchs, was to play a key role in the US, British and Soviet bomb projects.[17]

There were other, more exalted tensions. Although the project began as a joint Anglo-US enterprise – a reflection of the contribution of Frisch and Peierls – this quickly changed. A bankrupt Britain could not cover the vast cost of the project, nine-tenths of which came from the US. That fed into another set of questions about the bomb and the post-war world. How far should the US share knowledge of the bomb with the British and the Soviet Union? Would it be best to retain a monopoly, thereby determining if and when the weapon would be used, or should the knowledge be shared in the interests of maintaining future international peace? In January 1943 co-operation with the British was abruptly curtailed. British persistence, which owed much to Churchill's anxieties about a future Soviet threat, and his implied threats about not co-operating in opening a second European front, led Roosevelt to reverse this policy at the August 1943 Anglo-US summit in Quebec. The decision reflected the President's view that in a post-war world dominated by four great powers, the US, Britain, France and the USSR, only the first two should have the bomb. Efforts by the Danish physicist Niels Bohr, who had been extracted from Denmark to prevent the Nazis using him, to persuade the leaders to share information with the Soviets were scotched by Roosevelt's and Churchill's Hyde Park September 1944 memorandum, which kept the bomb secret from the rest of the world, and Churchill rapidly decided that Bohr was dangerous and insisted that MI5 investigate him. Given the scale of their investment, the Americans typically reserved the lion's share of future commercial development to themselves. To that end the US had already established a Combined Development Trust to buy up secretly the world's uranium supplies with a budget of US$12.5 million. As Germany collapsed, secret agents in the Alsos Project beavered away around the sacred groves of liberated Europe, making off with 1,100 tons of uranium from a field at Stassfurt in the area allotted to the Soviets. It took two to have an arms race.

On 12 April 1945, following the death of President Roosevelt, these weighty matters fell on the shoulders of a former haberdasher turned machine politician called Harry Truman. In vital respects he lived down to his average-man image. He was 'an instinctive, common, hearty-natured man'. Given his lack of experience, Truman was a prisoner of Roosevelt's core advisers, who had deliberately withheld knowledge of the bomb when the then Missouri Senator was chairman of a Senate inquiry into national defence and was stonewalled by Secretary of War Stimson. After the first meeting of Truman's cabinet on the day of his inauguration, Stimson informed him of a 'new explosive ... of almost unbelievable destructive power'. Stimson patronisingly regarded Truman as like a little boy eager to use a toboggan. Truman also inherited a rapidly deteriorating relationship with the Soviets, whose land-based forces were at the zenith of their power in Europe. Although the US noted the grey brutal army of secret policemen that the Soviets brought with them, they also hoped that Soviet forces would be redeployed eastwards to help force surrender on Japan. While the Soviets had soaked up the punishment for three years, vainly waiting for a second European front, now it was America's turn to face the prospect of horrendous casualties if forced to invade Japan, and a Soviet offensive into Japanese Manchuria might make it unnecessary. Truman's advisers differed over how to influence Soviet behaviour, which included reneging on assurances given at Yalta regarding a democratic Poland by foisting the unrepresentative Lublin-based Communist government on the Poles. The US held three trump cards: Lend–Lease aid (which so far had totalled US$10 billion); the Soviet's desire for US$6 billion to help them with post-war reconstruction; and the mystery weapon being developed at Los Alamos. All of which is to say that conflicting perceptions governed US relations with the Soviets at a time when the world was on the cusp between the Second World War and the world that would come after.

As the inner circle had long known, the development of an atomic bomb – with a much more powerful hydrogen bomb more than a theoretical possibility in the mind of physicist Edward Teller – raised huge questions about the international architecture of the post-war world, including the possibility that the US and USSR could be brought together to contain and manage these weapons of mass destruction. But what is called atomic diplomacy, that is using possession of the bomb as a form of leverage, was not the foremost concern of the US government in its war with Germany and Japan.

That was plain from the crucial meetings which decided to use the bomb. The dominant issue was to end a war that had dragged on for four years for the US, not with how to manage a post-war nuclear armed peace. After Germany's unconditional surrender in May 1945, these questions solely concerned Japan. That the US was capable of adjusting the notion of unconditional surrender was already evident from its dealings with Darlan's Vichy regime in North Africa and with the army and monarchy in Italy after the deposition of Mussolini. Japan amounted to more than they, but it did not represent the same order of evil as Nazi Germany, which all agreed had to be utterly destroyed. Throughout the weeks before the atomic bombs were dropped, the prospect of settling for something short of Japan's unconditional surrender was occasionally mooted, the guarantee being that the US would maintain the imperial system. That it did not come to this was largely because of the financial and technical momentum the Manhattan Project itself had created, although the decisions were made by a few men rather than by abstract forces.

By one of history's ironies the decision to use the most destructive weapon ever invented fell on Stimson, known to detractors as 'a New England conscience on legs'. An alternative nickname was 'the human icicle'. Aged seventy-seven when these decisions were taken, Stimson's life encompassed Andover, Yale's Skull & Bones society and the wealth and distinction that came from being a corporate lawyer turned distinguished public servant. He was a typical Wasp, who on one occasion objected to having a 'Hebrew' working anywhere near him. After service in France as a fifty-year-old major, he became secretary of war under Taft and Secretary of State under Hoover. A teetotal Presbyterian Republican, Stimson was a great believer in disarmament, international law and a World Court, ideals of 'organized self-control' which came to naught in the world of the 1930s. Nonetheless, in June 1940 he was appointed secretary of war for a second time, partly to weaken the Republican Party before an election. Leaving aside his importance in swinging the US behind Britain, Stimson was a quintessential American silver fox, capable of ruthless decisions dextrously veiled in the preachy moralism he had acquired at Yale.

In early May 1945 Stimson set up an Interim Committee to deliberate all questions concerning the bomb's deployment. He chaired it, although he had to accommodate Secretary of State-designate James Byrnes as

Truman's spy in the cab. The other members included representatives of the navy, the State Department, project experts Bush and Conant, and Karl Compton, president of the Massachusetts Institute of Technology. Oppenheimer and the Italian Enrico Fermi were members of a Scientific Panel that the Interim Committee could consult. After writing a physics undergraduate paper that merited a doctorate, Fermi had won the 1938 Nobel Prize for his work on nuclear piles or reactors, and was the only scientist to be both a brilliant experimenter and a theoretician, as much at home cutting up tin sheets as at a blackboard. He fled Italy after the prize ceremony in Stockholm in protest against anti-Semitic laws that affected his wife Laura. He was a great deal more talented than the increasingly egoistical and tortured Oppenheimer. Since April there had also been a separate Target Committee, consisting of mid-level USAAF officers and Los Alamos scientists, which convened first in the Pentagon and then in Oppenheimer's office. Its decision to include historic Kyoto on a list of possible targets inadvertently provided a key safety valve for anyone harbouring reservations about the morality of what was being discussed. Groves and others insisted on its inclusion, since as a large city of a million people, it would enable them to assess the full potential of the bomb as its effects diminished in the suburbs. Stimson, however, had visited Kyoto in 1928–9 en route to the Philippines to take up the governorship, to which he had been appointed by Calvin Coolidge, and made it clear he would never accept its targeting. On one occasion he summoned General Marshall from his nearby lair to ensure that Groves got the message. No one knew for certain what the effects of the two atomic bombs would be, which is why the Target Committee also suggested a conventional follow-up raid to ensure maximum destruction.[18]

So much of the literature on the bomb concentrates on the consciences of scientists that one can forget that its use was part of grand military strategy. The Joint Chiefs had to decide a plan to achieve Japan's unconditional surrender, which was the precondition for the US being able to reorder Japanese society. The navy was most sceptical about being able to project sufficient force for an invasion of the Home Islands, where it felt the army would encounter seriously adverse terrain. The army believed it could pull off an invasion, once blockade and bombardment had softened up the defenders. In April the Joint Chiefs agreed on a two-stage invasion in November 1945 called Operation Downfall. It would start with an invasion of southern Kyushu, codenamed Operation Olympic, followed by Operation Coronet in the Tokyo region in March 1946.

Okinawa Stats + projections
monthly deaths in Asia = 100k
of slave labor —
524 • MORAL COMBAT

Since the Japanese had never surrendered in their 2,600-year history, and no military unit had surrendered in the current conflict, the Chiefs worried that even if the government surrendered, the 5.5 million troops in the field might not. Anticipated casualties loomed large too. The Joint Chiefs grimly established how many casualties the US would suffer when they launched Olympic and Coronet. Their projections were based on the three months it took to subdue the Japanese on Okinawa: 107,539 Japanese soldiers had died in this operation, with a further 27,769 entombed in caves; 75,000 civilians also perished, while the US lost 7,374 dead and 31,807 wounded.[19] There were various projections of US casualties. The lowest was of 31,000 dead in the first thirty days after the invasion, but Pacific Commander Chester Nimitz believed 49,000 would be more likely, while MacArthur's staff suggested 55,000. In Britain, Major M.R.D. Foot was tasked with similar calculations: he reckoned there would be 600,000 Allied and 900,000 Japanese service fatalities. During this period the Japanese were not idle. They established that since the US air force was dependent on land bases, the invasion would come from Okinawa towards southern Kyushu, where they therefore deployed extra troops and aircraft. They also reinforced their troops around Tokyo. This was part of a strategy called Ketsu Go or Operation Decisive. They also established a vast national militia consisting of all males aged fifteen to sixty and women of seventeen to forty, armed with old guns and bamboo spears.

Leaving aside this militia, the US army and Marines would hit the beaches on a ratio of 1:1 with the defenders. This intelligence, which meant that all casualty figures had to be revised upwards, was crucial, since US leaders had to reckon with how the American public would react to huge losses, perhaps greater than the three hundred thousand combat deaths previously suffered in the entire war. There was also the not inconsiderable matter of the hundreds of thousands of civilians (and Allied POWs) who continued to languish under Japanese overlordship throughout China and South-east Asia, as well as the Asian slave labourers the Japanese had taken to Japan from Indonesia or Korea. The prodigious death rate among these foreign helots has never attracted the notice of the casualties of the atomic bombs, but it is likely to have exceeded a hundred thousand every month. Those who object to the dropping of two atomic bombs might ask themselves how many Americans (and Russians) they would have preferred to see killed. Would they prefer that LeMay's fleets continued to burn their way through cities? How many civilian Japanese would they prefer to have been slaughtered or starved to death by a tightening naval blockade that had cut all food imports, while, as in Europe, conventional bombing wrecked the entire transport infrastructure? This would lead to starvation in a country dependent on moving home-grown rice around. How many more millions of Asian helots would they prefer to have been starved and beaten to death while the war dragged on?[20]

Last but not least, the Americans had come to hate this enemy. In April 1943 the White House released news that the Japanese had tried and executed so-called Doolittle flyers for war crimes. In 1944 their torture and trial became the basis for the movie *The Purple Heart*. In October 1943 the US government released extracts from the diary of a fallen Japanese soldier who had beheaded and disembowelled a US airman the previous March. This was splashed on the front page of the *New York Times*. In January 1944 the US authorities released information on the Bataan death march, which had taken place in spring 1942. Then came news of suicidal Japanese missions in the Aleutian Islands, and in April 1945 the first release of information on kamikaze planes, which had been used since October 1944. Polls of American attitudes to the Japanese revealed that 13 per cent of the sample wanted the Japanese exterminated entirely, with another 33 per cent wanting Japan extinguished as a functioning state. Bombing would purify the blood (something the Japanese were themselves keen on) or sear a permanent scar into the nation's soul.[21]

The key decision-makers were not insensitive to moral questions, defined more narrowly than any of the above considerations. Outside formal contexts, both Marshall and Stimson talked about the bomb. They had moral reservations about indiscriminately killing civilians rather than about the precision bombing of important military–industrial targets. Stimson in particular had been horrified by news of Dresden, which he called 'terrible and probably unnecessary'. Both men were worried about how Dresden might affect the US's future image as a symbol of hope for mankind. Marshall thought that if the bomb were used, it should be preceded by a warning to evacuate civilians. These moral reservations went into abeyance when on 31 May the main Committee met with the scientists to discuss a range of diplomatic and technical questions. Oppenheimer mounted his own rhetorical show of shock and awe. He explained that these were not ordinary weapons. The existing bomb would have a blast of 2,000–20,000 tons of TNT, something that came within the imaginations of men who had seen the conventional raids on Tokyo. However, Oppenheimer then mentioned a second generation of bombs, which were 'considered a scientific certainty', that would explode with the equivalent force of 50,000–100,000 tons of TNT. Finally, he said that a further generation of weapons, using fission to trigger an explosion based on nuclear fusion, was only three years away. These would have the equivalent power of 10,000,000–100,000,000 tons of TNT.

Much of the morning discussion before they broke for lunch concerned how to deal with the Soviets in what was about to become the nuclear age. As one of the paladins of the Grand Alliance, Marshall was most sensitive to the Soviets' concerns about their own security, going so far as to suggest inviting two Russian scientists to witness the test which was shortly to happen at Alamogordo in New Mexico. Byrnes from State was the most vehemently opposed to this view, arguing that surprise use of the bomb would have the maximum effect in terms of inducing Soviet post-war compliance with US will. He indicated that the US was engaged in an arms-research race with the Russians. During the lunch break a matter was raised that had been bothering some of the scientists and engineers involved in developing the bomb, notably Leo Szilard and Oswald Brewster. Would it be possible to demonstrate the weapon's power without dropping it on a city, or what about giving the Japanese advance warning?

This option was systematically shut down by Groves and Oppenheimer. They knew the capacity of the Japanese to deny cold facts and their ability to fight to the last man standing. Intelligence intercepts of Japanese coded messages were indeed revealing that if the US invaded the mainland the Japanese military were planning an Armageddon-style final showdown. If the Japanese were given prior warning, they might frustrate any plane seeking to deliver a high air burst or move Allied POWs into the target area. They would contrive not to be impressed by an explosion on some uninhabited neutral site where the crater would not be especially large (although in point of fact the Hiroshima and Nagasaki bombs left no crater at all). Presumably satisfied with Oppenheimer's reassurance that the bomb would not be that different to the devastating raids already carried out on Tokyo, the Committee's focus narrowed to whether to launch simultaneous or sequential atomic attacks. The optimum results could be achieved by bombing the centre of cities with vital war industries and adjacent workers' homes. The Interim Committee recommended use of the bomb; there would be no prior warnings. That settled most of the essentials.

Although the fiction was maintained that the bomb was being put down over an industrial or military target, in practice such facilities were on the peripheries of the designated cities and, as such, the air force could not guarantee hitting them with the bombs available. That meant the bombs were going straight down on the residential centres. As well as the awe with which Oppenheimer had begun, there was much talk of shock. The problem was no one knew how the total demoralisation of a couple of cities could be translated into the capitulation of the Japanese oligarchy. At a meeting with Truman on 6 June, Stimson tried to square his opposition to the conventional firebombing of Japanese cities with his recommendation to drop atomic bombs. Truman chuckled at the contradiction.

The Alamogordo test explosion of a plutonium bomb was expedited so that the intelligence and performance reports would reach Truman during the Potsdam Conference in July, an urgency clearly dictated by a desire to impress Stalin. The test bomb was reported to be so powerful that a blind woman was able to see the light, while a mushroom cloud reached over forty thousand feet into the sky. Four hours after this Trinity test, the USS *Indianapolis* slipped out of San Francisco harbour heading towards the Marianas islands with the components of the bomb codenamed Little Boy on board.

At Potsdam Truman adopted a bullish stance with Stalin, who was bidding high for Soviet support against the Japanese, while his legions and secret policemen took over half of Europe. After he had received reports on the test, Truman then overplayed his hand, hinting darkly to Stalin that the US had 'a new weapon of unusual destructive force'. Stalin, who knew all about it from Soviet agents within the Manhattan Project and in Washington, calmly said he was 'glad to hear it and hoped he would make good use of it against the Japanese'. He agreed to unleash 1.5 million men against the Kwantung Army in Manchuria. US intelligence indicating that the Japanese might want to surrender, based on intercepted Japanese government communications to their embassy in Moscow concerning a request to the Soviets to mediate a ceasefire, was ignored by the US government. As Ambassador Sato sought clarification from his masters in Tokyo, he paradoxically hardened US belief that the Japanese were never going to give up, for his masters categorically rejected unconditional surrender. Nor did they indicate that they might make peace if the US guaranteed the survival of the Emperor. That was never mentioned in any of these internal Japanese communications. Meanwhile intelligence on Japanese military dispositions hardened the US naval chiefs in their view that an invasion would be very costly.[22]

Truman decided to issue one final warning to the Japanese, after which the bombs would be dropped. He hoped this would pre-empt a Soviet invasion of mainland Japan, with all the opportunities for expansionism that entailed. On 26 July the US, China and Britain released the Potsdam declaration, giving the Japanese the choice of unconditional surrender or 'prompt and utter destruction'. The Japanese were divided over how to respond, but they collectively decided to reject it 'with contempt' on the 28th.

The means of judgement were at hand. *Indianapolis* dropped off the bomb and then was sunk by a Japanese submarine; many of the survivors who spent a week huddled together in the ocean were snatched by cruising sharks. Meanwhile C-54 transport aircraft delivered the components for the second bomb. The uranium bomb (Little Boy) would be available by 1 August, followed by a plutonium implosion device (Fat Man) two weeks later, with another ready by the 24th. The rate of production would accelerate, with three more bombs in September and seven in December.

A special team of airmen, the 509th Composite Group, had been formed in September 1944 under the twenty-nine-year-old pilot Paul Tibbets. It was initially based in the salt flats of Utah, where the group took delivery of modified long-range B-29 bombers. These were immense aircraft designed to take 20,000 pounds of bombs on a 4,000 mile round trip. The propellers were over 16 feet high, and the plane required an 8,000-foot runway to take off. The group's training consisted of dropping a single orange-painted mock-up made of concrete and nicknamed 'Pumpkin', and then executing a diving turn to speed away. The Pumpkins were surrogates for what were referred to as 'gadgets'. The best crews were then sent to Cuba for six weeks to practise using radar navigation over water. Four cities were to be hit as soon after 3 August as weather allowed: Hiroshima, Kokura, Niigata and Nagasaki. On 24 July Marshall and Stimson received a communication from Groves containing draft authorisation to use the bomb. Truman agreed with Stimson that Kyoto was not a desirable target, and he swallowed the fiction that the bombs were being used against vital industrial and military objectives rather than women and children. On 25 July Marshall wired the Acting Chief of Staff, 'Reference your WAR 37683 of July 24, [the Secretary of War] approves Groves directive.' That turned things over to Spaatz. His last-minute concern for US prisoners of war held in the four cities was parried by Groves: 'Targets previously assigned ... remain unchanged.'[23] Their fate was in the hands of LeMay.

In his memoirs, LeMay dismissed the moral qualms of 'aged beatniks, savants and clergymen': 'I suppose they believe that a machine gun is a hundred times wickeder than a bow and arrow ... we in the bombardment business were not at all concerned about this ... We just weren't bothered about the morality of the question. If we could shorten the war, we wanted to shorten it.' LeMay thought it more immoral to use less rather than more force, for the former would merely protract any conflict. Believing that an atom bomb was the modern equivalent of hitting an enemy over the head with a rock in the Stone Age, LeMay equated the radiation after-effects with the Romans sowing the site of Carthage with salt.[24]

Actually, the US could have simply continued the conventional bombing of Japan, which had already caused thirty times the devastation of the bombs dropped on Hiroshima and Nagasaki, though without the long-term radiological harm to the population. How many that would have killed can be surmised, although the survivors would not have been dying from obscure cancers decades after the event.[25] Neither Eisenhower back in Europe nor MacArthur, Leahy or Nimitz was in favour of this way of ending the Pacific war. Eisenhower had seen enough death and destruction for one lifetime. MacArthur wanted to have his moment of glory as the Marines stormed ashore in Japan. The two admirals thought Japan could be starved into submission by naval blockade, an alternative scenario which critics of the bomb usually do not deal with. Morality did not have much to do with this rehearsal of the same range of issues that had recurred throughout the history of warfare in the twentieth century.

During the afternoon of 4 August the B-29 officers were briefed on their missions, with Captain Parsons on hand to explain that the bomb would wipe out about three square miles of the target area. The target was Hiroshima, the base for the Second Imperial Army which defended southern Japan. There were 43,000 soldiers and 280,000 civilians in the city. The atmosphere in the briefing room was described as weird.

On 5 August at 2.45 in the morning the *Enola Gay* (or Dimples Eight Two to use its call sign) took off from Tinian air base. It was named in honour of Tibbets's mother, who had encouraged him to join the air force. The crew were told that an atomic bomb was on board only as they got under way. Over Iwo Jima they rendezvoused with two aircraft, one called *Necessary Evil*, the other *Great Artiste*, loaded with observers and monitoring equipment. The B-29 climbed to thirty thousand feet as it made landfall, by which time Little Boy had been fully armed by Parsons, nervously inserting the triggers that activated the detonators. At twelve miles out from Hiroshima the bombardier took over the *Enola Gay*, with the bombsight making corrections to the automatic pilot called 'George'. A T-shaped bridge was the aiming point as the bomb doors opened. Little Boy was emblazoned with such slogans as 'Greetings to the Emperor from the men of the *Indianapolis*' as well as a few obscenities. It exploded at 1,900 feet above a hospital. As the B-29 made a steep turn, it was filled with a bright light and shaken when a hazy rippling mass of nothing hit it nearly twelve miles from where the bomb had detonated. The crew tasted lead in the air and worried about being sterilised. Most of them had not donned polarised goggles because these cut down their vision. Hiroshima seemed engulfed in a bubbling black cauldron which the tail gunner photographed as *Enola Gay* sped away, dwarfed by a towering mushroom cloud.

On the ground, an all-clear had sounded at 7.30 a.m. after the mission's advance weather plane had passed overhead. People were splashing the sleep from their eyes with water, while bare-chested soldiers were already performing callisthenics on their parade grounds. It was a still summer morning, already a pleasant 27 degrees Celsius. Some witnesses saw the aluminium undercarriage of *Enola Gay* glint in the sunlight, before the city was blasted with a light momentarily brighter than several suns. According to John Hersey, who the following summer wrote the finest account of the bombing and its aftermath, based on eyewitness accounts, people speculated that the city had been engulfed by some form of fuel-air explosive after being sprayed with petrol. The effects were more radical than that.

Birds combusted in mid-air and the shadows of vaporised people were etched on to stone. The shockwave hurled people through buildings from which their corpses emerged studded with broken glass. Those who were not shrivelled to a crisp wandered around with their blackened skin hanging from their faces and limbs, although injury was so great it was impossible to tell back from front. Since eighteen hospitals were destroyed and 90 per cent of medical personnel killed, there was no one to treat the living dead except a few doctors who quickly fell into a somnambulant trance so great were the numbers of casualties. Then the survivors began to notice that, in addition to feeling deeply enervated, their hair came out in clumps and superficial wounds failed to heal. Carcinomic lumps grew back even after being surgically removed. These people were dying of radiation sickness, something the incoming American experts observed but did not treat. There are no reliable figures for how many died on the day, or in the years to come. Somewhere between 70,000 and 120,000 seems plausible. One man who survived, though he was burned down one side, returned home to Nagasaki. He was the only person to experience and survive two atomic blasts.[26]

The Japanese government prevaricated as it absorbed the shocking news, even as Soviet mechanised forces attacked in Manchuria. The

Russians' experiences during the ensuing Battle of Mutachiang seemed to confirm the US desire to avoid launching Olympic, because Soviet tanks were destroyed by firemen carrying suicide satchels packed with 15 kilograms of explosives. The Japanese miscalculated that the US had only one bomb so they resolved to tough it out. Even those who thought of surrender were busy devising conditions which the US would never accept, as they would have prevented the wholesale reconstruction of Japanese society.

On 8 August a B-29 called *Bock's Car* after its commander left the base at Tinian carrying Fat Man towards Kokura. Over the city the aircraft encountered dense cloud and sporadic flak, prompting the pilot to divert to the secondary target of Nagasaki, Japan's main southern port and home to the Mitsubishi torpedo plant and shipyards. This was also obscured by cloud, but a sudden window of opportunity saw Fat Man launched, and it imploded at 1,600 feet above the Urakami Catholic cathedral. Seventy thousand people died either then or by the end of the year, for certain topographical features mitigated the effects of the nuclear implosion. On the 10th the Japanese offered to surrender, even as Spaatz was planning to concentrate their minds with a third bomb on Tokyo. Meanwhile, on the 13th, conventional raids dropped twelve million pounds of explosives and incendiaries on two further cities. Secretary of State Byrnes told the Japanese that while they could retain the Emperor, if that was their wish, he was not going to be the final arbiter of any occupation arrangements. That was as far as the US was prepared to go. Meanwhile, Soviet forces battled through Manchuria to the Kuril Islands; of the 2.7 million Japanese who fell into their hands, four hundred thousand died, not including combatant deaths. Two major Japanese commands also declined their own government's order to surrender. On the 15th Emperor Hirohito broadcast a message of surrender. Since he had lost faith in the military, they lost faith in him, claiming that in war it was always the upper classes that first crumbled.[27]

Having clasped his hands over his head and pumped them back and forth like a sporting hero when he spoke to his team at Los Alamos on the day Hiroshima was destroyed, Oppenheimer developed doubts about what had been done. These contributed to his general celebrity, something that he ardently craved. He got a little above himself. On the morning of 25 October 1945 Truman granted him a brief audience. The conversation did not flow. Oppenheimer eventually said, 'Mr President, I feel I have blood on my hands.' Truman's response has been variously reported. He said,

'The blood was on my hands – let me worry about that' or 'Never mind, it'll all come out in the wash.' Another version the President liked to relate was that he offered Oppenheimer a handkerchief and said: 'Well, here, would you like to wipe your hands?' After encountering the 'cry-baby scientist' Truman told under-secretary of State Dean Acheson, 'I don't want to see that son-of-a-bitch in this office ever again.'[28] Although this did not impede Oppenheimer's rise to global celebrity, his security clearance was revoked after revelations concerning his dubious contacts before and during his Los Alamos phase with Communist fellow-travellers, about which he had lied.

CHAPTER 21

The Predators at Bay

I MUSSOLINI'S DOUBLE DOWNFALL

Retribution rather than justice caught up first with the earliest Fascist dictator, whom many Italians contemptuously called 'Baldie' or 'Big Head'. Even his erstwhile Fascist accomplices referred to him as *il pazzo* (the madman) or, worse, *il vecchio* (the old man), for this last stressed the dictator's declining virility. He no longer resembled a man of extraordinary will.

Mussolini's downfall was complicated and protracted, as both disgruntled Fascists and members of Italy's old elites connived to oust him. This was the price of his having so personalised the war by becoming commander-in-chief in addition to occupying all three service ministries. When the war went disastrously wrong, who else was to blame? A majority of both old elites and the more flexible Fascists, such as Giuseppe Bottai and Dino Grandi, realised that Mussolini was the main obstacle to a negotiated Italian exit from the war. Before the end of 1942 these senior Fascists began sounding out the dictator's son-in-law Ciano, with a view to replacing the Duce with a less notorious figure, with whom the Allies might cut a deal, enabling the Italians either to achieve neutrality or to switch sides. There were also rumblings of discontent within the army, notably from Badoglio, who Mussolini had dismissed as chief of staff. His replacement, Vittorio Ambrosio, proved equally disaffected. In January 1943 Mussolini sacked Bottai, Ciano and Grandi, a miscalculation that drove them into open revolt. Meanwhile, the Vatican had sounded out the Americans about whether the Allies would make a separate peace with a non-Fascist government headed by Badoglio. By contrast, Fascist hardliners hoped that once Mussolini – or Canute as they also called him – had been ditched, Italy could more wholeheartedly join the Nazi war effort.

The backdrop to these calculations was ominous. A major Allied air raid on Rome on 19 July indicated that the Allies were willing to extend the strategic bombing campaign to Italy. Acute sensitivities about Pius XII and the city's rich artistic heritage meant that the destruction was inflicted elsewhere. Most Italians regarded that as a pity, because they identified the regime's capital with the miasma of corruption that the regime had come to signify. The major Allied raids focused on the northern industrial triangle and the southern city ports. Air-raid protection was not the regime's strong point. A plan to fund shelters from the national lottery had been rejected. Mussolini unhelpfully suggested that people with unusually acute hearing would be able to hear incoming bombers and warn everyone else with shouts. While the rich could escape by tarrying in their country second homes, the poor working class had to languish in lice-ridden shelters or wear themselves out tramping from temporary suburban accommodation to the docks and factories. Sixty-four thousand Italians perished in such Allied raids.

The Fascist Grand Council held its only meeting of the war on the night of 24 July. It promised to be so fractious that some of the participants slipped hand grenades into their briefcases beforehand and, at one moment of extreme drama, surreptitiously passed them around under the conference table. Grandi led the way in proposing that Mussolini step down as head of the armed forces in favour of King Victor Emmanuel. The acrimonious meeting dragged on to 3 a.m., when there was a vote. Nineteen voted that Mussolini should go; seven voted against and there were two abstentions, including the veteran Florentine Fascist Roberto Farinacci. On the evening of the 25th Mussolini went for his fortnightly audience with the king he called 'the little sardine'. The monarch told the dictator that he was the most hated man in Italy and had to go. Mussolini left the Villa Savoia and boarded a police ambulance, which he mistakenly thought had been laid on for his protection.

He was taken to a naval base at La Maddalena, an island off the northeast coast of Sardinia, whither Hitler despatched the complete works of Nietzsche as a sixtieth-birthday present to a colleague with time on his hands. After discovering that Mussolini had been the victim of two interconnected coups – one Fascist, the other royalist – Hitler decided that he could not accept the downfall of the first Fascist dictator. Although his instincts were to storm southwards to round up what he had long regarded as a degenerate elite rabble, senior German army commanders prevailed on him stealthily to increase the troop numbers deployed in the peninsula. The Germans were going to defend the Reich not on the Alps but with a series of fortified lines across Italy.

On 26 August Mussolini was moved to a ski resort called Campo Imperatore at Gran Sasso, in the Abruzzi Apennines not far from L'Aquila, where he whiled away the time reading and playing cards with his guards. After Italian forces had surrendered to the Allies on 3 September, the guards removed anything the Duce could use to kill himself, since the Allies had demanded his surrender as part of the armistice arrangements. However, on 12 September even he was surprised to see a German glider land a hundred yards from his quarters, the first of several which debouched German troops and a token Italian general brought along to confuse the guards. Otto Skorzeny, the strapping Austrian SS officer leading this daring raid, allowed Mussolini to bid farewell to the hotel staff before he was whisked off the mountain top in a Fieseler Storch light aircraft. After a rest in Vienna, where Hitler phoned to inquire about his welfare, Mussolini was moved to Munich for a reunion with his wife Rachele and their younger children. In September, he had an audience with Hitler at Rastenburg. It was not congenial. Although he wished to retire from public life, the Führer insisted that Mussolini return to northern Italy to run a new Fascist regime under German aegis. The first Fascist should demonstrate that there was still life in Fascism, which should rise like a phoenix from the ashes. Hitler also took the opportunity to strip Italy of the South Tyrol, Trieste and the Trentino, the territorial claims he had forsworn in the early interests of an Italian alliance. Meanwhile German forces had declared Italy a war zone. Italian troops who were obliged to surrender to them became seven hundred thousand military internees, many of whom were horribly abused as 'Badoglio swine' when they were deployed as forced labour in Germany in flagrant violation of the laws of war. On the Greek island of Cephalonia, the Germans murdered five thousand Italian soldiers who decided not to go without a fight.

Ailing from a duodenal ulcer, the gaunt dictator was moved to the Villa Feltrinelli at Gargnano, a town on Lake Garda, where SS guards kept him at a remove from the new Italian Social Republic at Salò. The words 'social' and 'republic' indicated that this regime was based on hostility to treacherous plutocrats and monarchists. It was peopled with violent middle-aged *squadristi* who had been marginalised under the Fascist regime, but who now got a fresh wind, as well as the products of that regime's totalitarian youth organisations. This meant that it relied on the over-forties and the under-twenty-fives.[1] Mussolini and Donna Rachele plotted vengeance on the few traitors who had fallen into their clutches. Both Ciano and the general commanding the war in Abyssinia, Marshal Emilio de Bono, were tried at Verona and shot, despite the tearful intercessions of Ciano's wife, Mussolini's daughter Edda. Relations in Gargnano were fraught because the Germans had thoughtfully installed Clara Petacci, Mussolini's mistress, in a nearby house, enabling Rachele to give vent to her sense of betrayal face to face. The dictator escaped this marital hell by going for long bicycle rides around Lake Garda followed by a truckload of SS troops. In July he ventured again to Rastenburg, in the hope of persuading his erstwhile friend to reverse the recent acquisitions of Italian territory. He arrived shortly after Hitler had nearly been killed in the Stauffenberg bomb plot, and the Führer was deafened and singed, with one of his arms hanging slackly at his side. There was no opportunity to discuss the territorial issues in an interview dominated by Hitler raving against traitors and screaming for vengeance.

The government of the Salò Republic was scattered throughout northern Italy – the Foreign Ministry was in Venice – and the single telephone connection between the separate ministries was controlled by the Germans. The Social Republic engaged in some sham radicalism, as represented by the Verona Manifesto of February 1944, which introduced worker participation in the management of factories. Although it also abolished the monarchy, the Manifesto was more like an attempt to sow multiple divisions, which did indeed come to haunt post-war Italian society. Meanwhile, the army was forced into an unhappy merger with the Guardia Nazionale Repubblicana militia, and so-called Black Brigades fought a dirty war against the ever more emboldened partisans. Nearly forty-five thousand partisans fell in action between September 1943 and April 1945, together with fifteen thousand civilians killed in German or Fascist reprisals. No one knows how many Germans and Fascists were killed in these encounters. Of course, life is never morally simple. Many Italian veterans of the Eastern Front were so disgusted by the Germans that they switched to the partisans after reaching home. So did some of those who had raped and burned their way through the Balkans. As one veteran remarked: 'I had been in Yugoslavia, and I too had burned villages, shot hostages, raped women. When my eyes were opened, what could I do? I became a partisan.'[2]

At the end, Mussolini could have surrendered to the partisan leader Raffaele Cadorna at a meeting brokered by Cardinal Schuster in Milan, but he decided to act as if he was still a free agent. He then hesitated between such options as flight to Argentina or Spain, before eventually making a dash across the border to neutral Switzerland. He left his villa for the last time, pausing to listen to his eighteen-year-old pianist son Romano playing Duke Ellington's 'Saddest Tale' in an upstairs room. Donning a German helmet and a Luftwaffe greatcoat he attached himself to a German convoy retreating towards Austria. Early on the morning of 27 April 1945 the convoy was halted by partisans at Dongo. The Germans negotiated their own safe passage, the sole proviso being that they hand over any Fascists they had on board. The partisan commander recognised Mussolini, who was pretending to be a German in a drunken stupor under a blanket, and shouted, 'We've got Big Head.' Reunited with Clara Petacci, Mussolini was taken to a remote farmstead, then to the Villa Belmonte on Lake Como, where they were both shot at close range. Their corpses were taken to Milan where they were hung by their ankles from the gantry of a petrol station on the Piazzale Loreto. After being buried in a numbered grave, the Duce's corpse was spirited away to a monastery near Milan. In 1957 the government permitted the reburial of his remains near Predappio, his birthplace.

Of all the predator regimes, Italy's Fascists got off most lightly in formal judicial terms. There was, however, a protracted and messy bloodbath of random reprisals against them that claimed between ten and fifteen thousand lives. As belated 'co-belligerents' of the Allies, who even declared war on Japan, the royal armed forces were not held accountable for war crimes in Abyssinia and the Balkans, a stance aided by the refusal (maintained to the present day) of the Italian Ministry of Defence fully to open its wartime archives. In some provinces, tribunals were established, but the Italian appeals system meant that of the thousand death sentences handed down, only forty to fifty were carried out. In mid-1946 the Communists and Christian Democrats colluded in passing a general amnesty – for imprisoned Fascists and partisans who had committed murder – which meant that all but four thousand Fascists were released from jail. The Communists were keener to shed their bloodily sectarian image to broaden their middle-class support than they were to uphold bourgeois justice. The Allies were so focused on their desire to defeat and deNazify the Germans that they devoted little thought to Hitler's former Axis ally, while soberly realising that mass dismissals of public officials would bring chaos in a country that was always on the brink of it anyway.[3]

Victor Emmanuel abdicated in favour of his son Umberto, but the monarchy failed to survive a referendum in June 1946 by a couple of million votes and Umberto joined Dino Grandi in exile in Portugal. Attempts to purge the bureaucracy were complicated by the fact that all civil servants had been compelled to join the Fascist Party. Even the head of the Duce's OVRA secret police was acquitted of all charges on the grounds that he had merely been a public official. There was massive continuity in the administration. In Naples, only twenty-three former Fascists were fired from a public sector that employed 128,837 officials. In Palermo the number was five out of more than twenty-six thousand bureaucrats.[4] Nationally, sixty-two of the sixty-four prefects in 1960 were former Fascists, as were all 135 police chiefs and their 139 deputies. Much the same was true of the judiciary and many professions. This had little to do with the forgiveness enjoined by the Catholic Church, almost everything to do with the Allies' awareness that sacking these men would have left the door ajar to the Communists. The new democratic Republic may have adopted anti-Fascism as its public creed, but during the Cold War this was eclipsed by the real local menace of Stalin's Italian supporters. At one point the US planned to pull its troops back on Sicily and Sardinia should the Communists win power on the mainland in the 1948 elections, but Pope Pius XII mobilised the Catholic Church against them and the Christian Democrats began their long monopoly of political office. A persistent strain of neo-Fascism endured, which mutated into the post-Fascism of the Alleanza Nazionale of Gianfranco Fini, the current speaker of Italy's parliament. Of the three predator nations, Italy has suffered from the least national neurosis about the Fascist past, partly because the army redeemed itself in the final years of the war, but also because the Germans behaved so badly towards their erstwhile ally that the crimes of both sides during the civil war that took place in those years have been seen, perhaps rightly, as minor by comparison.[5]

NB

G Losses 1944–45

II GERMANS AS VICTIMS

The ten months between July 1944 and Germany's unconditional surrender on 8 May 1945 resulted in the deaths of more Germans than in the five years 1939–44. Every month during that eleven-month period, between 300,000 and 400,000 German soldiers and civilians lost their lives, many of them through relentless aerial bombardment. According to ongoing SS monitoring of popular opinion, bombing was widely regarded as retribu-

Russia lost 200 K / mo. (soldiers) every month from June 1941 – May

tion for what the Germans had done to the Jews, which indicates how widespread awareness of the Final Solution was among the general population. Anti-Semites still claimed that Allied airmen were mere tools of an Anglo-American Jewish conspiracy to destroy the Germans, although as we have seen the fate of the Jews counted for little in the counsels of those who despatched the bombers. Of the 5.3 million German combat fatalities, 2.6 million of them were killed between July 1944 and May 1945. On the contracting Eastern Front, lives were squandered in senseless battles to the last man, engagements which lacked any justification save desperation. Important towns were defended with whatever cannon fodder could be cobbled together from army stragglers to adolescent boys and elderly men. In January 1945, some fifteen thousand poorly trained troops sought to defend Posen; ten thousand of them died in the ensuing battle, which ended only when the colonel in charge shot himself. Breslau was virtually destroyed in a battle that cost the lives of twenty-nine thousand German soldiers and eighty thousand civilians. The Luftwaffe formed a kamikaze squadron named the 200, which vainly attempted to stem the onslaught of Allied bombers by ramming. The U-boats fought to the bitter end, suffering the highest proportion of fatal casualties of any branch of the Wehrmacht.[6]

Vast Allied armies converged on Germany from east and west, as even the tenacious defence of Italy collapsed. The Soviet regime encouraged its legions to rape and plunder an enemy whose wartime standard of living embarrassed many Red Army soldiers to the point of fury.[7] Entire towns, such as Allenstein, Insterburg, Stolp and Zoppot, were set ablaze and an estimated one hundred thousand people were killed in wanton acts of murder. There was a rough method in this reckoning. A Red Army captain once remarked that the first-echelon troops stole the watches, the second wave raped the women and the third echelon made off with household goods.[8] The Soviets went through the homes of Germans like locusts, demanding watches at gunpoint, ('Urri, urri!') and anything that was not bolted down, including water closets, and raped women of all ages. The slightest equivocation, let alone resistance, meant instant death. Solzhenitsyn caught the dread momentum of this army in his poem *Prussian Nights*, which skilfully incorporates contemporary Soviet propaganda in the penultimate two lines:

> Zweiundzwanzig Horingstrasse.
> It's not been burned, just looted, rifled.
> A moaning, by the walls half muffled:

The mother's wounded, still alive.
The little daughter's on the mattress,
Dead. How many have been on it?
A platoon, a company perhaps?
A girl's been turned into a woman,
A woman turned into a corpse.
It all comes down to simple phrases:
Do not forget! Do not forgive!
Blood for blood! A tooth for a tooth!
The mother begs, Tote mich, Soldat![9]

While the Western allies did not engage in systematic rape and robbery on this epic scale, even military necessities posed difficult moral questions for their commanders. One of these was the collateral damage done by, for example, the massive aerial attacks against rail communications in northern France before D-Day and the pulverising of Caen afterwards. Another harsh choice was made in the case of Holland, where the Germans cut off the country's food imports, while looting the meagre supplies that were still there. Under pressure from Pieter Gerbrandy, the Prime Minister of the exiled Dutch government, Churchill was prevailed upon to allow limited seaborne relief provided by the Swedes. The Allies were not keen to slow down their push across the Rhine by diverting troops to the liberation of Holland north of the Maas and Waal, where there was an eighty-thousand-strong German garrison behind a waterlogged operational hell created by the demolition of dykes and pumping stations. Persistent Dutch pressure on Churchill at least led Brooke and the Chiefs of Staff to consider the diversionary option: 'there is no doubt', wrote Brooke, 'that we should work for the destruction of Germany and not let any clearing up of Holland delay our dispositions'. Eisenhower readily concurred on the main objective of a breakout into Germany to link up with the Soviets. As Canadian troops ground their way into Holland, the Nazi Reich Commissioner Seyss-Inquart offered the Allies a truce through clandestine talks with the Dutch resistance. The deal was that after the truce the Allies would be allowed to provision the starving Dutch population. While Churchill hated being dictated to by Seyss-Inquart, he commented, 'It is a terrible thing to let an ancient nation like the Dutch be blotted out ... I would rather be blackmailed in a matter of ceremony than be haughty and see a friendly nation perish.' Seyss-Inquart held a parley with Generals Walter Bedell Smith and Freddie de Guingand in April 1945, after which thousands of tons of food were airdropped into Holland. The German garrison did not interfere, but did not surrender to the Allies until the end of hostilities on 5 May.[10]

As the Allies converged on their rendezvous at Torgau, an army of a different sort was being herded from the outer ring of hell to the inner. In January 1945 there were 714,211 prisoners in concentration camps. As Soviet artillery grew audible, the SS resolved to evacuate the surviving inmates to the original network of camps within Germany proper. They had erased all trace of the Aktion Reinhard death camps in 1943, when a special SS unit disinterred the dead and burned them on huge pyres, using a crusher to shred the bones. In the winter of 1944–5, the SS decided to move any ambulant survivors back to the Reich, mainly with a view to cobbling together a further reserve army of slave labour, but also to ensure there were no living witnesses. Especially incriminating groups of victims – such as those who had been subjected to vile medical experimentation – were systematically murdered to leave no trace. A major consideration was to prevent a recurrence of what had happened at Majdanek, whose facilities and documentary records had fallen intact into Soviet hands.

The SS began evacuating surviving inmates from Auschwitz, Gross-Rosen and Stutthof in the depths of a very severe winter with only the vaguest idea of how to get to their designated destinations. The miserable survivors were herded back and forth through the snows, their routes punctuated by the bodies of those shot because they were unable to keep up, and by large-scale massacres like the one at Gardelegen, where a thousand prisoners were crammed into a barn, shot and incinerated. A single group of three thousand (of the sixty thousand Auschwitz inmates evacuated) spent nearly a fortnight in transit by train and on foot, with a mere four hundred completing their 120-mile journey to a small labour camp.[11] In the case of smaller satellite camps in the vicinity of Königsberg, from which it was impossible to evacuate the inmates, they were shot by their guards, including three thousand machine-gunned on the seashore at Palmnicken. Many evacuees were housed in appalling conditions at Gross-Rosen, where up to fifteen hundred people were forced into huts designed for one or two hundred. These unfortunates were in turn evacuated westwards to Buchenwald, Dora-Mittelbau and Flossenbürg, journeys during which forty-four thousand died.

In March 1945 Himmler, who up to that point had concurred with Hitler's insistence that the camps and their inmates be blown up to stop them falling into Allied hands, reversed track and issued orders that all killings of Jews cease and that the survivors should be adequately fed pending their liberation. The parallel decision to continue evacuating prisoners from the diminishing ring of camps meant that a third of those evacuated from Buchenwald to Theresienstadt or Dachau perished en route. If many of the prisoners were beaten to death or shot by experienced SS or Ukrainian guards, it was also the case that elderly members of the Volkssturm militia who were conscripted as escorts, murdered those who could march no longer. It is important to note that many if not most of the victims of these death marches were not Jews, but rather various kinds of political prisoner. The rationale for killing them had become the real danger they represented to the German population, after the liberated inmates of Buchenwald had run amok in Goethe's Weimar.[12]

Imminent defeat brought a rash of suicides, although never on a scale that matched the regime's desire for general immolation. Hitler killed himself on 30 April, his final testament focused obsessively on the Jews, hatred of whom was the animating principle of his adult life. Even as he was on the brink of death, they crowded into his thoughts, though so many Jews had become ghosts. He was shortly followed by Goebbels, who with his wife first murdered their six children. The deaths of the regime's leaders signified the end of the world to their most dedicated followers, logical enough by the fiery light of an ideology that celebrated Wagnerian heroic sacrifice. Of the forty-three Nazi Gauleiters in office at the end of the war, eleven killed themselves. So did seven of the forty-seven Higher SS and Police Leaders, as well as leading personalities from the Reich Main Security Office. Himmler and Globocnik were among those who committed suicide in Allied captivity. Thirty-five army generals, six Luftwaffe generals, eight admirals, thirteen generals of the Waffen-SS and five from the police also took their own lives. Especially in the former German eastern territories there were large-scale instances of communal suicide. A thousand people killed themselves in Pomeranian Demmin, six hundred in Neubrandenburg, 120 in Stargard, 681 in Neustrelitz and 230 in Penzlin. There were cases of entire families being killed by one of their own number. Their motives were various. Among women it could have been well-motivated fear of being raped and killed by Soviet soldiers, or the despair and shame that gang rape by the Red Army had already engendered. How many mothers tried to assure their daughters that 'it was just an act of violence that did not change anything in a person'? Others feared reprisals and retribution for crimes in which they had been complicit, a fear that in many cases proved unwarranted.[13]

At one point so many leading Nazis had killed themselves, or had been summarily shot, that the British Foreign Office official Alexander Cadogan wrote in his diary: 'The question of the major war criminals seems to be settling itself, as they seem to be getting bumped off satisfactorily one way or another.'[14] Cynics argue that war crimes trials are a matter of 'who gets who' first, and dismiss them as examples of victors' justice. There have also been claims that German prisoners were subjected to torture by, among others, their British captors at a secret interrogation centre in Kensington, but such claims were made as part of their defence by men facing capital war crimes charges, and there is no evidence that the undoubtedly rigorous regime run by a Colonel Scotland had any sort of official sanction. All this ignores noble attempts from the Middle Ages onwards to mitigate the horrors of war and, from the late nineteenth century onwards, a determination to hold such criminals to account. The Allies had signalled their intention to bring German war criminals to book with the 13 January 1942 St James's Declaration. The recent history of war crimes trials was not encouraging. After the First World War, the US had stymied efforts to try German war criminals before an international tribunal, while the Dutch had refused to relinquish the Kaiser from his exile at Doorn. Instead, the Germans themselves held trials in 1921 at Leipzig, generally regarded as a farce since only thirteen of the accused received sentences, all of them light. Similar prosecutions could have been mounted against many servicemen from the Entente, not least those who had shot prisoners taken in the trenches. Ironically, the Ottoman Sultanate, which was also obliged to hold war crimes trials by the Treaty of Sèvres, set a better precedent, holding sixty-three members of the Young Turk regime to account for the massacre of Armenians, and the provincial governor Kemal Bey was publicly hanged in Constantinople after being found guilty. His defence that he had only been obeying orders was rejected: 'It is true that everyone is obligated to carry out orders from the highest offices, but he must judge and weigh in the balance whether the issued order does not violate justice and law, and whether one must obey it or not.' Four wartime leaders who had fled abroad were also sentenced to death *in absentia*. Ironically, the successor republican regime in Turkey persists to this day in denying the Armenian genocide perpetrated under the sultanate.[15]

From October 1943 onwards, the United Nations War Crimes Commission began gathering evidence and producing lists of suspects that included 36,529 names. The Moscow foreign ministers' conference of November 1942 had determined that, while the main culprits would be tried by an intra-Allied tribunal, the majority would face justice in the countries where they had committed their crimes. It was touch and go whether there would be trials at all. After all, Allied leaders had the alternative precedent of Napoleon, who was bundled off without a trial to St Helena.[16] As we saw, Churchill favoured declaring a small core of fifty to a hundred German leaders 'outlaws', to be summarily shot on apprehension. That was the view of the Foreign Office, which thought trials too cumbersome and likely to result in sympathy for the accused.[17] Yet at the Tehran summit, when Stalin 'jokingly' ventured the thought that they might need to shoot fifty thousand leaders of the German armed forces to extirpate German militarism, Churchill took offence and walked out after Roosevelt quipped that they might have to settle for forty-nine thousand.

Neither Stalin nor, surprisingly, Roosevelt was joking. The US had its own advocates of extreme measures. Roosevelt's Secretary of the Treasury, Henry Morgenthau, had produced a plan to pastoralise Germany, following the summary execution of many of its wartime leaders. Roosevelt inclined to this view but Secretary of War Stimson, the saviour of Kyoto, bitterly opposed it. As far as the topmost Nazi leaders were concerned, Churchill seems to have agreed with the Americans that their fate lay outside the law. Oddly enough, it was Stalin who became the staunchest advocate of trials of the senior Nazi leaders. Interestingly, the Soviets mandated war crimes trials in April 1943, a couple of months after the Germans gave maximum publicity to the murders at Katyń. It is likely that public show trials of captured Germans and Russian collaborators were designed to distract from the unwelcome attention Katyń had attracted. Commencing with trials in Krasnodar (July 1943) and Kharkov (December 1943), those found guilty – usually without either defence counsel or interpreters – were strung up in public. Rings were put around the corpses to leave them hanging for days, reminiscent of the gibbets in which hanged criminal were hung in an earlier age, as an example and a warning.[18]

Although the US government had not swung decisively behind trials, jurists outlined what form they might take. Since some of the American legal team had a background in prosecuting stock exchange and securities fraud, they favoured charges of criminal conspiracy, which was common enough on Wall Street but alien to the world of diplomacy. In this case, Germany's leaders would be charged with conspiracy to wage aggressive war and other crimes against peace. The US also decided that entire institutions and organisations should be indicted, although the guilt of individuals convicted of belonging to them would have to be established in connection with specific allegations of war crimes or crimes against humanity. In May 1945 the Western allies and the Soviets, gathered in San Francisco, agreed on the principle of judicial proceedings. The framework was settled at a conference in London in August, although it proved difficult to reconcile the adversarial defence and prosecution model of the Anglo-Saxons with the inquisitorial practices of continental law, in which judges pose all the questions and interrogate the witnesses. 'What is meant in the English by cross-examine?' asked a Soviet judge, to whom a trial whose results were not preordained was clearly unfamiliar. All the Allies agreed lists in advance of subjects concerning their own policies and actions that the defence was to be prohibited from raising in court such as area bombing and the Molotov–Ribbentrop 'annexations'.[19]

The major war criminals were indicted on four counts before the trials opened at the Palace of Justice in Nuremberg on 14 November 1945, the courts adjacent to a prison with capacity for twelve hundred inmates. Counts one and two concerned a conspiracy to commit crimes against peace and to wage aggressive war 'in violation of international treaties, agreements and assurances'. This involved elevating the Pact of Paris, otherwise known as the 1928 Kellogg–Briand Pact, to a canonical status it had wholly lacked. The British chief prosecutor, Sir Hartley Shawcross, was notably pompous in dismissing 'some small-town lawyers' who questioned the existence of a coherent corpus of international law. The Soviets were unhappy about this emphasis on aggressive war, since this might cover what they called revolutionary wars of liberation. It raised a large question mark over the Soviet invasions of Poland and Finland, and indeed British and French plans for a pre-emptive invasion of Norway. The defence could legitimately argue *tu quoque*. Count three concerned a plan or conspiracy to commit war crimes against civilians and prisoners of war, which encompassed hostage taking and reprisals. The Soviets found themselves in difficulties when, after they had insisted that Katyń be included as a Nazi crime, some German defendants attributed it to their accusers. Although the British and Americans savoured their embarrassment, they colluded in the Soviets' denial of responsibility. The fourth count concerned 'crimes against humanity', namely murder, extermination, deportation and enslavement of civilians, especially 'persecution on political, racial and religious grounds'. This encompassed what in 1944 the Polish jurist Raphael Lemkin called genocide, a crime only recognised by the United Nations three years later, although Turkish treatment of the

Armenians had established an important precedent for this legally novel offence.[20]

There were problems with what the Allies undertook at Nuremberg, although they do not invalidate the exercise as a whole. Common law was far more accommodating, by way of natural law, of retroactive criminalisation than continental Roman law with its principle of *nullum crimen sine lege, nulla poena sine lege*. The defence lawyers had only limited access to the reams of German evidence being assembled by the prosecution, and lacked the small armies of researchers and secretaries available to the prosecution. They had no access to the records of foreign governments, which might have revealed the complex dialectic of foreign relations. They got their hands on the secret protocol appended to the Nazi–Soviet pact only after someone on the US prosecution team leaked it. Quite correctly, the defence lawyer acting for Ribbentrop argued that if there had been a Nazi conspiracy to wage wars of aggression, then between 1939 and 1941 the Soviets had surely been party to it.[21] The Soviets had despatched Nikolai Zoria, a senior military lawyer, to ensure that this subject was never aired in court, and he was found shot dead in his Nuremberg hotel room shortly after it became evident that he had failed.[22]

More seriously, the charges of conspiracy exaggerated the coherence of the Nazi decision-making process, a point eloquently made by Göring in his account of the *ad hoc* circumstances that led to the remilitarisation of the Rhineland: 'It was never the case that from the beginning, as has often been represented here, we got together and, conspiring, laid down every point of our plans for decades to come. Rather, everything arose out of the play of political forces and interests, as has always been everywhere the case, the whole world over, in matters of state policy.'[23] The coherence of the Nazi regime was not established at Nuremberg, and the debate on this subject has occupied historians ever since. Not unnaturally, the Allies were determined to make someone pay for war crimes, not simply involving their own servicemen, but also against civilians in general. Although there was plenty of airing of atrocities committed against Europe's Jews under the umbrella of crimes against humanity, some Jews thought that there should have been more exclusive focus on this category of atrocity. In fact, judges and prosecutors representing the major Allies gave ample consideration to the murder of nearly six million Jews, the figure accepted at the time, with the horrors shown on documentary film and in the harrowing testimony of eyewitnesses. The focus on the regime's surviving leaders also had implications for the civic role the trials were designed to play. As the prosecution painted the twenty-four accused in ever darker colours, with the French senior prosecutor freely using words like 'diabolic' to describe them, so the average German felt the burden of personal responsibility grow a little lighter.[24] Those who argue that the defendants should have been tried in German courts, for offences that were criminal under existing German law, underestimate the total permeation of the German legal profession with Nazis.[25]

The hearings themselves lasted nine months and consisted of over four hundred open sessions. There were four judges from the US, Britain, France and the Soviet Union. The physical record of the proceedings is enormous, since the transcripts and a brief selection of the documentary evidence and witness testimony runs to forty-two printed volumes. In so far as it produced the first comprehensive snapshot of what had happened in Germany and occupied Europe under the Nazis, the undertaking was of enormous historical significance. The trials themselves created a model of how similar tribunals might function in future, notably in Tokyo where, as we shall see, a similar format was adopted to try Japanese major war criminals. One needs only to imagine a war crimes trial conducted by Nazis to reach the conclusion that Nuremberg was fair by the lights of the day. Defendants would have been softened up by torture before being harangued by Party jurists, sentenced by Party judges and then bundled off to be executed. Nuremberg and Tokyo also established a series of legal precedents which have been followed to this day by courts dealing with atrocities and genocide in former Yugoslavia and Rwanda, although there is legitimate scepticism about the universal and perpetual reign of activist fat-cat lawyers desired by devotees of an International Criminal Court. At their conclusion in early October 1946, twelve of the defendants – including Martin Bormann, who was tried *in absentia* – were sentenced to death by hanging. With the exception of Göring, who committed suicide on the 15th, the rest were duly executed the following day.

In addition to the intra-Allied tribunal at Nuremberg, each of the four occupying powers conducted separate prosecutions of war criminals. A War Crimes Group accompanied the US army into Germany, which by March 1947 disposed of a staff of 1,165 investigators. If their initial remit concerned the lynching or shooting of downed Allied airmen, it quickly expanded to the surviving personnel of Dachau (the Americans had shot some of them already) and other major concentration camps such as Buchenwald, Dora-Mittelbau, Flossenbürg and Mauthausen. Availing themselves of twelve and a half tons of evidence, an American military court tried 1,672 people at hearings held within Dachau, transformed in the interim into a giant internment camp for former Nazis. Of these accused, some 1,416 were found guilty and 426 sentenced to death, although only 268 of these sentences were eventually carried out within the main prison for war criminals at Landsberg. Those convicted included those who had murdered Allied airmen as well as seventy-three SS men accused of the Malmedy massacres in the Ardennes offensive. A striking forty-three death sentences were passed in the Malmedy trial, a figure reduced to twelve after the courts seemed to accept that some of these defendants had been beaten into confessing. In the event, none of the Malmedy murderers was executed, after the intercession from afar of Wisconsin Senator Joseph McCarthy, who had many German constituents.[26]

Parallel with these military tribunals the US authorities organised the twelve Nuremberg successor trials which involved symbolic samples of Nazi inhumanity from various sectors. There were separate trials of medical personnel, commanders of the four Einsatzgruppen, of the corporations IG Farben and Flick for their exploitation of slave labour, Foreign Ministry diplomats, judges and lawyers, and two trials of generals involved in war crimes in the Balkans and the Soviet Union. These trials produced an impressive amount of documentary evidence, which is still useful to any historian working on these areas today.[27] In total there were 177 accused at these twelve trials; twenty-four were sentenced to death. They included Dr Karl Rudolf Brandt, one of the architects of the euthanasia programme who had essayed an idealistic defence that failed to disconnect him from the grim realities of murdering mentally ill and disabled people. It would be quite misleading to imply, however, that such trials encompassed more than a fraction of those who were culpable, many of whom went on to be lynchpins of post-war German society.[28]

The British also held war crimes trials within Bergen-Belsen concentration camp, whose liberation had so shocked the British public, even though the emaciated survivors had been shipped in from the eastern death camps, about which the British public still knew nothing. These hearings commenced on 17 September 1945 and involved forty-five defendants, including Josef Kramer, 'the Beast of Belsen', and his female subordinate Irma Grese. Their sadistic exploits gave rise to a quasi-pornographic Nazi crimes literature, which had the bizarre effect of distracting attention from the dispassionate, industrialised killing that had taken place by demonising individual perpetrators. Eleven of the defendants were sentenced to death and executed on 12 December 1945. Some Jewish survivors of the camp were appalled at the latitude granted to the defence lawyers, but it could not have been done otherwise if the trial was to be seen to be fair.[29]

The Allies were also assiduous in repatriating about four thousand of the worst criminals to countries like Belgium, France, the Netherlands and Poland. They included Hanns Rauter, who was tried in Holland and then hanged. Kurt Daluege, the Order Police chief who replaced Heydrich in Bohemia-Moravia and ordered the murders at Lidice, was tried and executed in Prague. After Rudolf Höss had testified for the prosecution at Nuremberg, he was tried in Poland and hanged outside his former home within the main camp at Auschwitz. By this time, 1947, the Germans themselves had been allowed to conduct their own trials of Nazi criminals. Until 1950, some five thousand people were convicted in connection with such crimes as the Röhm purge, the *Kristallnacht* and the T-4 euthanasia programme. The burden of proof for murder was set much higher than for manslaughter, and there was no satisfactory reckoning with those who were at various removes from physical killing but whose words and deeds had facilitated it. There were similar tribunals in the Soviet Occupied Zone of Germany, although these were increasingly used to weed out democratic opponents of the Communists.

Meanwhile, from June 1945 onwards, the Soviets turned an unforgiving eye towards more than three million POWs, including seventy thousand officers, four hundred generals and three field marshals. They paid special attention to former members of the various branches of the SS. Thirty-seven thousand of these men were convicted of war crimes by Soviet courts. This was rough justice, which ended with either public hanging or very long sentences of hard labour in the gulags. While some of the accused, like Friedrich Jeckeln, were notorious murderers, eight Germans were also executed after a trial in Leningrad for their alleged role in the Katyn massacre. There was no attempt to establish individual guilt in the case of many German POWs sent to labour camps; their rank or role – notably military intelligence officers – sealed their fate. Confessions were the result of extremely brutal interrogation methods. Among those hanged in the Lubyanka prison in Moscow was General Helmuth von Pannwitz, commander of the Wehrmacht's Cossack cavalry. The Cossacks themselves were among the thousands of previously Soviet citizens repatriated by the British, who were subject to mass executions on arrival. Quite rightly that piece of Realpolitik has left a nasty taste in the mouth, especially since the new post-war Labour government blithely allowed most of the SS Galicia

Gas *victims* from harsh postwar
cf. Japan, see Dower's
list

Division soldiers whom British troops had corralled at Rimini to settle in Britain as coalminers.[30]

However incomplete and unsatisfactory the reckoning with Nazi war criminals may seem in retrospect, the wider political effects of total and unconditional German defeat are not hard to enumerate. The experience of defeat, which included the forced repatriation of eleven million ethnic Germans from eastern Europe under the terms of the Yalta Agreement, meant that many Germans considered themselves among the war's primary victims. Among these were former members of the Wehrmacht, whose wartime experiences were compounded in the case of POWs taken by the Red Army with the horrors of Soviet labour camps. Survivors were eventually released in 1955 and fêted as returning heroes. Ironically, a West German poster lamenting the plight of German POWs still behind barbed wire in Soviet labour camps prominently displayed the word 'Accuse', though the title *I Accuse* had been used for a 1941 German propaganda film about the Nazi euthanasia programme.[31] The Western Allies also colluded in the fiction of a decent but simple soldiery led astray by Nazi ideologues. This reflected sheer ignorance and wishful thinking, particularly in the case of officers like Manstein and Kesselring, but also the need to integrate West Germany into the NATO alliance.

The Federal Republic of Germany (FDR), created in May 1949, rejoined the democratic Western mainstream, to be followed, after five decades, by the so-called German Democratic People's Republic (DDR) in the east. The FDR was transformed by the economic miracle symbolised by the emergence of industrial giants like AEG, BMW, Bosch, Mercedes-Benz, Siemens and VW, while the DDR languished under a centrally planned economy which, as everywhere else, totally failed to produce the rational allocation of resources that its advocates all over the world still believe in with near-religious fervour. The FDR's prosperity took a hit when it had to absorb the DDR in the 1990s, while achieving a muted reckoning with the DDR's own Gestapo-like secret police organisation. Although it is untrue to say that the Germans did not face up to the lessons of the Nazi era in its immediate aftermath, this often took the form of allusive religious or philosophical ruminations rather than the denunciatory moralising that became commonplace to a less cultivated and more uncouth generation of academics and journalists in the 1960s.

What one might unkindly call the guilt industry culminated in a massive proliferation of Holocaust memorials and museums and an enthusiasm for Yiddish folk culture. Many Jews now feel entirely comfort-

was a long way from Britain's
finest Hour

able living among the Germans, where philo-Semitism is a public doctrine, with the only licensed anti-Semitism – if that is what it is – directed by the liberal left against Israel and Zionist 'racism' which they strenuously associate with apartheid and Nazism. A society whose historic identity owed much to militarism has become so averse to war that the only German soldier to kill a member of the Afghan Taliban after the 2003 Nato invasion was flown home for counselling, although in Kunduz province the Germans have become involved in heavier fighting. So deeply has Germany imbibed the disasters of Nazism and Allied conquest, to the point where its people's ostentatious self-repudiation is parodied by foreign comedians, that it seems highly improbable that it will ever again represent a menace to its neighbours. Ironically, Germany's wartime opponents in the West now seek increased signs of German belligerence, at least in the case of NATO engagements outside its traditional area. They are also discombobulated by the close relationship a united democratic Germany has with the quasi-democratic regime in contemporary Russia. While Nazi Germany as history episodically impinges on mass consciousness, it is less remarked how it has become an export commodity for bright young Germans who have acquired jobs in British academia and television on the basis of their historical or linguistic expertise in an area where British interest is still strong. As Goebbels once accurately predicted, the Nazis have largely monopolised the spot reserved for human evil in the Western contemporary imagination.[32]

III CHRYSANTHEMUMS: THE LONG-LIVED FLOWER

On 15 August 1945 wireless listeners in Japan strained to separate the high-pitched voice of Emperor Hirohito from the ambient static. The language was in the stilted, high-court manner, so an announcer had to re-read it in the vernacular when the Emperor had finished. Hirohito explained that 'The war situation has developed not necessarily to Japan's advantage.' Cruel new bombs had threatened the 'total extinction of human civilisation'. His sole expression of regret was for those other peoples who had assisted Japan in 'the liberation of Asia'. He enjoined his subjects to 'endure the unendurable, bear the unbearable', which was that 'Our Empire accepts the provisions of their Joint Declaration,' an unconditional surrender. A desperate minority could not. They included the Army Minister, Major

a "memorably meiotic" locution

General Korechika Anami, Vice-Admiral Takijiro Onishi (the man responsible for the kamikaze), General Shigeru Honjo, Field Marshal Hajime Sugiyama and about a thousand officers who committed suicide. On 15 August the ageing admiral Matome Ugaki left his fleet and clambered into a dive-bomber beside a kamikaze pilot, clutching a short sword. The aircraft crashed into the sea after failing to find a US ship to ram. Ugaki had wanted the Japanese to fight a guerrilla war against the Americans. The admiral left a note which read, 'Having a dream, I will go up into the sky.'[33] Former premier Hideki Tojo shot himself inexpertly when the Americans came to arrest him; a blood transfusion from a US soldier ensured that he survived to face trial and execution.[34]

In the fortnight between the capitulation and the arrival of General Douglas MacArthur's occupation forces, Japan's leaders were highly energetic. Huge bonfires blazed outside official buildings and industrial concerns to erase any record of wartime illegalities. On 14 August 1945, the War Ministry sent a telegram instructing all servicemen that 'the confidential documents held by every troop should be destroyed by fire immediately'. Telephone calls instructed troops outside Japan to burn this telegram. On 20 August the chief of prisoner-of-war camps told the Japanese armies overseas: 'Personnel who mistreated prisoners of war and internees or who are held in extremely bad sentiment by them are permitted to take care of it by immediately transferring or by fleeing without trace. Moreover, documents which would be unfavourable to us in the hands of the enemy are to be treated in the same way as secret documents and destroyed when finished with.' According to a Japanese Defence Agency estimate made in 2003, some 70 per cent of the army's wartime records were destroyed in the last weeks of the war.[35] This policy also extended to the prisoners themselves, whether they were alive or dead. The bodies of ninety-six US POWs who had been murdered by the naval garrison on Wake Island in 1943 were disinterred and distributed on a beach that had more recently been shelled by US warships. On 16 August, the day after Hirohito's broadcast, sixteen US POWs were taken from Fukuoka prison camp and hacked to death by guards who brought their girlfriends along to the spectacle. They then falsified the prison records to claim the men had died of natural causes.[36]

The elites also secured their financial future at the expense of their starving fellow countrymen and women. Vast quantities of war materials, stockpiled for the final showdown, were handed over to army commanders, local government and private enterprises. While millions of Japanese were homeless or faced starvation, a black market with seventeen thousand open-air emporia flourished, as did a new class of spivs and gangsters. Exhausted people turned to home-brewed alcohol that increased their depressed tiredness, when it did not leave them blind. Demobilised soldiers sold bits of their kit until they resembled peeled onions, bereft even of their clothes. The wounded and disfigured, like the victims of the atomic bombs, found themselves shunned in a society that prized physical wholeness. Around 125,000 orphans similarly found themselves alone in a society whose much vaunted solidarity and spirit of sacrifice had disappeared.[37]

Into this swung General Douglas MacArthur and a quarter of a million US occupation troops. His title, Supreme Commander for the Allied Powers, was a fiction, as the voices of the other Allies counted for little in a nation solely occupied by US troops. The HQ of SCAP in downtown Tokyo was vast, with the 1,500 personnel in early 1946 becoming 3,200 two years later. Generously provisioned from the ubiquitous PXs, the Americans settled in with their wives and families in apartments and houses with central heating, refrigerators, showers, cooks, maids and houseboys. A must-have souvenir was a photo of GIs being carted around by former Japanese soldiers earning a living as rickshaw pullers.[38] This all made it hard for the Japanese to see the Americans as having been among the victims of barbarity, for how could such prosperous, strapping fellows ever have been the emaciated wrecks of wartime prison camps? They were to be envied rather than pitied.[39]

MacArthur embodied the confident virility of the victorious Americans, represented elsewhere by the GIs who frequented the licensed brothels the Japanese authorities had established to reduce the likelihood of Soviet-style mass rape. He was a physically imposing man, much given to orotund declarations of the 'as history shows' variety. Although a self-considered expert on the childishness of the 'oriental mind', MacArthur hardly visited the Japanese, whose progress to maturity he preferred to view on newsreel film. In effect, the general became a surrogate emperor, to whom the aggrieved or sentimental addressed an enormous range of written petitions. However, he was also obliged to execute policies formulated in Washington, where there was a constant tussle between rival factions in the State Department, between those sympathetic to the Japanese, like former ambassador Joseph Grew, and those like Dean Acheson who shared the hostile perspective of the Chinese. The former wanted little change, the latter believed in radical reconstruction. Radical reconstruction proved to be the dominant trend until the outbreak of the Korean War in 1950 meant that change was sacrificed in favour of integrating Japan into the Western camp against Communism.

Ironically the real Emperor, Hirohito, was concurrently rebranding himself to obliterate the wartime image he had presented in uniform astride a handsome white charger. He seems to have brushed up on the House of Windsor, those quintessential experts on dynastic survival. From 1946 Hirohito embarked on a marathon nationwide tour, in the course of which with some strain he doffed his trilby to his bowing subjects and famously talked to a survivor of Hiroshima on his death bed. Illustrated books and magazines, all obviously licensed by the occupiers, refashioned Hirohito as a retiring, peace-loving marine biologist and family man, for peaceful pursuits, along with the scientific prowess represented by Canon, Nikon, Sony and Toyota, were the nation's new vocations. Although it was not tolerated by the Americans, there was also a powerful parallel trend to reconfigure the Japanese as war's ultimate victims because of Hiroshima and Nagasaki, which would be unthinkingly coupled with Auschwitz. The refashioning of the Emperor suited the Americans, whose psychological warfare experts had long sought to isolate him from the Fascist–militarist clique who had surrounded him, as if he had merely attended wartime meetings for reasons of protocol in the capacity of honorary bystander. The written record never captured the inclinations of the head, nods and hand gestures that could have been as determining as words. In the most positive construction, Hirohito would be a useful symbol of national continuity and stability when the Americans embarked on radical reconstruction.

The two emperors first met at MacArthur's residence in the former US embassy on 27 September 1945. The court circle regarded this encounter with some trepidation, unaware that the US government had already decided to use Hirohito for its own purposes. MacArthur arrived in open-neck shirt and slacks, without any of his many decorations. Hirohito wore formal court dress. As MacArthur swept in, he exclaimed, 'You are very, very welcome, sir!', the only recorded occasion when he said 'sir' to anyone. They exchanged compliments for forty minutes, as they headed ineluctably to the conclusion that war was horrid and peace a desirable goal. America's eagle-like plenipotentiary extended his protective wings over the man whom many US allies – especially the Australians – regarded, with reason, as a war criminal. Popular sentiment in the Allied nations ensured that Hirohito was not granted immunity from possible war crimes charges; in practice the US busied itself to ensure that his role in the war was moved off limits. Although photographs of the MacArthur–Hirohito meetings – there would be ten more – convey an immense physical disparity between these embodiments of conqueror and conquered, in fact relations were more nuanced than the visual images suggest.

Initially, the US arrived with intentions so radical that they won the admiration of the resurgent Japanese left as its remnants emerged from wartime confinement. The Americans dissolved the country's armed forces, including the four million troops overseas, who, with the exception of those in Soviet captivity, were to be repatriated as soon as possible. They abolished the Special Higher Police and purged some two hundred thousand Japanese in the bureaucracy and business whom they held responsible for Japan's militaristic rampage. The Americans introduced the separation of Church and state by abolishing Shinto as a state religion. That had implications for the Emperor, who while explicitly rejecting the claim that the Japanese were superior to other races managed to avoid through elaborate translation any direct denial of descent from ancient gods. Hirohito was prepared to have himself redesigned as the symbolic figleaf for the US occupation, if that was the price of survival for the institution he embodied.

US administrators sought to break the structures that they felt had given rise to imperialism and aggression, while granting the Japanese rights they had never enjoyed before. They introduced basic rights of assembly and of the press, while encouraging the formation of trades unions. They went to great lengths to improve the rights of women in what was a highly patriarchal society. Women acquired the right to divorce, inheritance and property. Feudal landowners were compelled to sell land to their tenants. A new constitution was promulgated in November 1946, coming into effect the following May. In addition to these rights, the constitution solemnly committed the Japanese people to 'forever renounce war as a sovereign right of the nation and the threat or use of force as a means of settling international disputes'.

As part of the act of surrender, the Japanese agreed that the Allies would mete out stern retribution to wartime malefactors. Prosecutors acting for the International Military Tribunal for the Far East commenced work in May 1946. They largely copied the Nuremberg model, although in the Tokyo case there were initially twenty-eight rather than twenty-four major war criminals. The trial was held in a purpose-built structure in the former Japanese military academy at Ichigaya in central Tokyo.

About two thousand Japanese attended the trials as spectators. It is doubtful whether either this or copious coverage in the licensed newspapers had the desired pedagogical effect, for most Japanese believed the defendants should have killed themselves before surrendering. Eleven countries sent judges and prosecutors, including China, India and the Philippines. Although nationalist Japanese like to think that this was a case of Western victors' justice, the presence of Burmese, Indonesian and Filipino experts attached to the prosecution team meant that it was more a matter of victims' justice. Of course, things are never that tidy. While Koreans and Taiwanese suffered grievously at the hands of the Japanese, and no more so than the Korean comfort women, the fact that 148 Koreans and 173 Taiwanese were tried for war crimes committed while serving in the imperial armed forces meant that they were left unrepresented in a prosecution effort that otherwise cannot be accused of institutionalised racism.

Much of the evidence for war crimes and crimes against humanity was garnered from fifty parallel national war crimes trials which were conducted by Australian, Chinese, Dutch and French courts across East and South Asia. These trials concerned Class B or C war criminals – that is, men who had carried out barbarities, or who had commissioned or had been negatively or vicariously responsible for such acts higher up the civil and military hierarchies. The trial in the Philippines of Generals Yamashita and Homma established the legal principle of command responsibility, or the criminal liability of a senior commander for atrocities committed by his subordinates. Yamashita was found guilty of being indirectly responsible for the deaths of a hundred thousand civilians in Manila after he retreated from the city and turned it over to Rear Admiral Sanji and army security troops. He was hanged on 23 February 1946. He dictated his last testament to a Buddhist prison chaplain, saying: 'The people of Japan must develop a sense of individual duty, based on moral judgement.'[40] Around 5,700 Japanese were indicted by these parallel courts, of whom 984 were sentenced to death and around 920 hanged, a far higher proportion of executed death sentences than in Europe. The Soviets may also have executed a further three thousand war criminals, including twelve personnel of Unit 731, whose colleagues the Americans were otherwise discreetly rescuing for their own chemical- and germ-warfare programmes.

The enormous volume of evidence generated by these subsidiary national trials was incorporated into the main prosecution case at Tokyo. Since the material was in several different languages, it was decided to introduce it in synoptic form, which may have diminished its power to shock, for these trials were intended to have the same national-pedagogical function as Nuremberg. The impact of the evidence was also diminished by the relative absence of film footage concerning atrocities committed in obscure jungle camps or on islands throughout an enormous theatre that mainly consisted of water. The issue of language was an obstacle to comprehension and expeditiousness, since at Tokyo every utterance had to be simultaneously translated for the benefit of the accused, the lawyers and judges. Labyrinthine Japanese sentences came out in attenuated English, losing any subtlety in the process. Two of the non-Anglo-Saxon judges – the French and the Soviet – understood neither English nor Japanese, the main languages of the proceedings, although the Soviet representative could stretch to 'Bottoms up' when he had a glass in hand. The Filipino judge, Delfin Jaranilla, had survived the Bataan death march, although he did recuse himself when the hearings concerned crimes on the Philippines. Sir William Webb, the Australian presiding judge, had been a war crimes investigator in New Guinea. Webb argued that since not all eleven judges were present at each session, there was little point deciding as they went along which items of evidence were admissible, which opened the way for hearsay and such subjective testimony as diary extracts and copies of documents whose originals had been lost. Because Japanese law lacked an adversarial system, the defence was at some disadvantage, and had to be bolstered by US lawyers.

The twenty-eight main accused were allegedly a representative sample of the Japanese ruling elites stretching back into recent history, signalling that the symbolic importance of the accused bulked larger than their individual guilt. It was a very deliberate choice since the key charge against these Class A war criminals was that they had conspired, for the eighteen years 1928–45, to wage serial wars of aggression. The accused included four former prime ministers, five war ministers, three ministers without portfolio, two Greater East Asia ministers, two education ministers, two chiefs of army general staff and thirteen other officers, one lord keeper of the privy seal, four ambassadors, a finance minister and two navy ministers. By the time the proceedings commenced, two of the accused had died and one had gone mad. Their ranks included no representatives of big business or the ubiquitous academics, intellectuals and journalists who had materially contributed to the hysterical public climate. The sole person who represented continuity throughout 1928–45 was not in the dock, but behind the chrysanthemum curtain the Americans had lowered over him.

MacArthur decreed that Hirohito was never to be interrogated, would never be asked for private papers and would not be appearing as a witness.[41] Oddly, the chief prosecutor did his utmost to shield the Emperor on the rare occasions when, breaking a conspiracy of silence, one of the accused inadvertently alluded to Hirohito's involvement. In Sugamo prison the defendants wept with joy on the night they learned that the US had decided not to prosecute the Emperor. The US also kept all mention of the role of major industrial concerns or chemical warfare and medical experiments off limits.

The main charge concerned the conspiracy to wage aggressive war against international peace. The fact that this was supposed to be precedent-setting indicated one of its weaknesses, since the international law was being made on the hoof at the time. No international law covered naked conspiracy to commit aggression, so effectively this was a matter of the retroactive criminalisation of actions that were not crimes at the time. A robust assertion of high principles could not quite conceal the legally dubious nature of what was afoot. The prosecution argued that the 1928 Pact of Paris – better known as the Kellogg–Briand Pact – had made waging aggressive war not simply unlawful but criminal, although that last point nowhere figured in the Pact itself, which Japan had signed. They circumvented this omission by suggesting that there was a large body of internationally recognised custom which had the same effect as codified law. They also dispensed with the notion of state or sovereign immunity (the latter had some ironies in the Tokyo context) by arguing that official positions did not absolve anyone from responsibility for criminal acts. A major effort went into proving criminal complicity or negligence of cabinet ministers for crimes committed by the armed forces. Throughout the view was taken that individual men, rather than abstract entities, commit or sanction crimes, and as such are accountable for them.

The charges of conspiracy were difficult to prove against members of successive governments stretching over nearly two decades, moreover involving men who were sometimes political opponents and rivals, or who had never met one another. Unlike Nazi Germany, there was no single dictatorial leader whose aberrant vision had been converted into plans for aggression. Some of the key ideologists had been executed long before the Pacific war started. There was no Japanese equivalent to the SS, for the Kempeitai were more like the Gestapo than a surrogate army. Although the accused were convicted of a single conspiracy, as in the German case, the reality was of improvisation or successive governments meandering through a welter of war plans, which often had competing objectives, depending on the service involved in drafting them. The judges also had to ponder the defence arguments that Japanese policy was often *ad hoc* and reactive to the aggressive moves of others, for in some respects the trial resembled a chess board with only one team present. How did the Mukden Incident of 1931 relate to more expansive military aggression in northern China six years later? In 1939, had the Japanese fought border skirmishes with the Soviets and Mongolians, or were they planning a full-scale invasion of both those countries? What was the difference between Japanese conduct and the Soviet invasion of Finland? Where did the armistices and the 1941 Japanese–Soviet neutrality pact fit into this alleged pattern of continuous aggression? Had not Vichy in 1940 accorded the Japanese the right to enter Indo-China under the Matsuoka–Henri Agreement, and was this an act of aggressive war since the Japanese had not fired a shot? The prosecutors were on firmer ground with the 1941 rampage throughout South Asia following Pearl Harbor. In this narrative of aggression, it was Japan's desire to deny the Chinese external assistance that led Tokyo's leaders to attack the European colonial powers and the US.

Throughout, the defendants and their Japanese and US lawyers were denied the right to mount a counter-narrative involving their defence of Japan, or more grandly Asia, against the imperialist onslaught of the Europeans and Americans. They were accused of naked imperialism by judges from nations that were busily reimposing their dominance in Indo-China, Indonesia and Malaya. Ironically, in Malaya, the ethnic Chinese guerrilla forces the British orchestrated against the Japanese were metamorphosing into the 'Communist terrorists' the British fought until the early 1960s. It took two dissenting judges, the Indian Radhabinod Pal and the Dutchman Bert Röling, to broach the indelicate subject of where the firebombing of Japanese cities or the dropping of two atomic bombs might sit in any catalogue of war crimes. Pal was an unfortunate choice, as he had been a fervent supporter of the pro-Axis Indian nationalist Chandra Bose. On the days when he deigned to appear in court, he first bowed deeply towards the defendants. Unsurprisingly, Pal became a great favourite of Japanese nationalists and extreme leftists. His hatred of Western racism led him to discount the no less pernicious racism of the Japanese, whom he would exculpate of every charge in his bizarre dissenting judgement.

If it was hard to make the charges of conspiracy stick, there was no doubt about Japanese war crimes and crimes against humanity. Evidence and testimony from China and the Philippines were used to paint a picture of systematic atrocities by the Japanese armed forces. The most moving testimony concerned Japanese mass murder and rape in Nanking, and both the Bataan death march and the Manila massacres in the Philippines. Shang Teh-yi came from Nanking to testify that he, his brother, a cousin and five neighbours had been among the thousand men whom the Japanese had roped together on the banks of the Yangtze before opening fire on them with machine guns. He had survived under a pile of corpses. An American priest recounted the story of a fifteen-year-old girl. Japanese soldiers had killed her brother, believing him to be a fleeing soldier, then killed the brother's wife and the girl's elder sister when they resisted rape. They bayoneted the girl's parents. She was dragged off to a barracks where she was gang-raped every day for a month, until she was so ill and diseased the Japanese grew afraid of her. Even though General Iwane Matsui claimed to have been ill and bed-ridden 140 miles away from the scene of these atrocities, as commander-in-chief of the Central China Area Army he was convicted of a failure to exercise command responsibility over his subordinates. The former Prime Minister and Foreign Minister, Koki Hirota, was also convicted of doing nothing to prevent atrocities about which he received constant information. To be more precise, although he had complained to the War Minister, he had not followed this up by ensuring that counter-measures were being taken. Instead of raising the matter in cabinet, Hirota had accepted the verbal assurances of the War Ministry that action was being taken. This reaffirmed the Nuremberg principle that 'individuals have international duties which transcend the national obligations of obedience imposed by the individual State'.[42]

As we have seen, whereas 4 per cent of British and US prisoners of war died in German captivity, the equivalent figure for those held by the Japanese was 27 per cent.[43] Most of these prisoners had had to endure long sea voyages in the hellish holds of Japanese troopships, which bore no markings that POWs were on board. Those who died or were executed on deck were tossed overboard to the sharks. The main atrocities against Allied prisoners of war included the 1942 Bataan death march, as a result of which fifteen hundred US servicemen and twenty-six thousand Filipinos died during a nine-day sixty-five-mile forced march. Sometimes passing Japanese troops leaned out of trucks and used bayonets to slit their throats. Anyone who fell exhausted was bayoneted or shot. Secondly, the Japanese had illegally used POWs as slave labour on the construction of the Burma–Siam Railway, a 258-mile line designed to connect Bangkok with

Rangoon. Some 61,800 Allied prisoners of war were used to work on the Death Railway, which deserved its name because 12,300 of them perished, or roughly one in five. There were also two hundred thousand Asian workers, of whom between forty-two and seventy-four thousand died from disease or maltreatment. Their fate was given equal attention during the trial, even though the Japanese had not even recorded their names.

The main accused in this section of the trial was General Tojo, who was prime minister and war minister from 1941 to 1944. He sat picking his nose and taking notes while evidence of the utmost cruelty was delivered. Several of his fellow defendants removed their earphones so as not to hear it any more. Several witnesses testified about conditions in jungle camps linked to the railway-construction project. The general policy was 'no work, no food', and there was ample evidence that this had originated with Tojo, who had enjoined camp personnel 'not to be obsessed with a mistaken idea of humanitarianism'. That alone proved that cruelty was not culturally determined, since the camp personnel were clearly cognisant of other options. Jocular sadism was evident among the camp personnel who made a prisoner band play the dwarfs' song from Snow White – 'Hi-ho, hi-ho, It's off to work we go' – each morning. Prisoners had nothing but the uniforms they were wearing when they were captured, clothes which turned to papery rags under the incessant monsoon rains. The Asian labourers were given hessian sacks in place of clothes, items which soon crawled with lice. They slept in huts with mud floors, which turned to slush when the rains came. Diseases like beriberi, cholera and malaria were rampant, and medical supplies virtually non-existent. The Japanese also purloined most Red Cross parcels. Several former prisoners testified that the Japanese were obsessed with completing the railway, and that if the project fell behind schedule they 'became insane with rage'. That included beating people unconscious and then leaving them bound in a water-logged slit trench, with only mosquitoes for company. There were instances of men being bound to trees and burned alive.[44]

Further court sessions chronicled atrocities committed the length and breadth of the Pacific theatre, including massacres of tiny tribes like the Suluks on Borneo as well as female Australian nurses on Banka Island east of Sumatra. It revealed airmen who were deliberately killed so that the Japanese could cook and eat them, for the Japanese seem to have practised cannibalism on a wide scale. Some of this may have been because they were starving, but there are instances where it seems to have had a more symbolic significance. A B-29 crew were subjected to live, unanaesthetised vivisection in a university hospital, where their organs were removed one by one until they died. There were several instances of crucifixion and so many instances of prisoners being beheaded or bayoneted that they were impossible to count. To economise on food, the Japanese occupiers had sought to drown the entire population of the Andaman Islands, by taking them out in boats, and then throwing them overboard, killing them if they tried to crawl back. The native population of the Dutch East Indies had been abused as forced labourers or sex slaves, a practice forensically exposed by Dutch war crimes investigators.[45]

On 12 November 1948 the verdicts were read by Webb. There were no acquittals. Sentencing took place in the afternoon. Fifteen of the accused were sentenced to life imprisonment, and two more to seven- and twenty-year terms. Seven were sentenced to death, all of them generals apart from Hirota.

The Sugamo Seven were held in individual cells while their appeals were considered and rejected. They were hanged shortly after midnight on 22 December, their bodies cremated in the municipal crematoria and the ashes scattered to the winds. In the decades since, Japan has become a prosperous, multi-party democracy. As in the case of West Germany the Korean War hastened its economic recovery and integration into US alliance systems. Recently it has pursued a more independent foreign policy, like Germany seeking a place on the permanent UN Security Council. While Japan has embraced the uniqueness of being history's only victim of a double nuclear attack, it has stubbornly refused to apologise publicly or to give compensation for the atrocities it committed. When Shiro Azuma, a veteran of the Japanese forces in Nanking, used his wartime diary for a 1987 book, he was subjected to defamation suits by fellow veterans as well as abusive letters and telephone calls. His case is still being discussed after he appealed to the UN Commission on Human Rights. He died in 2006 and the book has not appeared in Japan. The fifteen million Chinese killed by the Japanese may prove to be, in the long-term general trend of the world, the deed that will prove to have turned most notably against Japan's interest, for there can be little doubt about who is going to be the super-power of the twenty-first century.[46] For although the events of the Second World War seem so far behind us, in many ways they continue to structure mentalities in the contemporary world.

LIST OF ILLUSTRATIONS

Heinrich Himmler consults with commanders of a Waffen-SS cavalry brigade in the eastern territories. (United States Holocaust Memorial Museum, courtesy of James Blevins)

Officers of Einsatzgruppe D. (Bundesarchiv Ludwigsberg, B 162/363, Anhang I, Bild 20)

The Japanese Imperial Council meets under the Presidency of the Emperor. (*Picture Post*, 17 January 1942)

General Tadamichi Kuribayashi, *c.* 1944. (Getty Images)

Letter from Kuribayashi to his son Taro. (Collection of Fumiko Kuribayashi, reproduced from *Letters From Iwo Jima* by Kumiko Kakehashi, courtesy of Shinchosa Publishing Co. Ltd.)

General Tomoyuki Yamashita in Malaya. (Australian War Memorial, neg. no. 127913)

General Gotthard Heinrici in conference with Field Marshal Günther von Kluge, September 1943. (Bundesarchiv Ludwigsberg, Bild 146-1977-12-09)

Field Marshal William 'Bill' Slim in Burma. (Imperial War Museum, London, IND 4545)

SECOND PLATE SECTION

German soldiers attending a show in Paris, September 1942. (Roger-Viollet/Topfoto)

Danny Kaye entertains 5th Marine Division occupation troops in Japan, October 1945. (US National Archives/CORBIS)

Zarah Leander on the cover of *Signal* magazine, 1941/42. (Photo Scala, Florence/BPK, Bildagentur für Kunst, Kultur und Geschichte, Berlin)

George Formby entertaining troops in Northern England, 1939. (Hulton Archive/Getty Images)

Crossing the Rhine under enemy fire at St. Goar, March 1945. (US National Archives/CORBIS)

25 Brigade advancing along Kokoda Trail near Templeton's Crossing, oil on canvas on plywood by George Browning, 1944. (Australian War Memorial, ART23615)

Sappers from 73rd Field Company Royal Engineers queue for food at a field kitchen in Germany, March 1945. (Imperial War Museum, London, BU 2658)

German paratroopers land during the invasion of Crete, 1941. (Getty Images)

An accordionist leads a sing-along for SS officers at their retreat at Solahuette outside Auschwitz. (United States Holocaust Memorial Museum, courtesy of Anonymous Donor)

Staff from the Belzec extermination camp in Poland. (Courtesy of Muzeum Regionalne im J. Petera, Tomaszow Lubelski, Poland)

Elderly Jewish men pronounced unfit for labour waiting to be exterminated at Birkenau, Poland. (Yad Vashem Archive, Israel)

Clothing for children on display for an internal exhibition of articles manufactured in the Łódź ghetto, c. 1944. (Photograph by Walter Genewein/Jüdisches Museum, Frankfurt am Main)

Nazi graphic showing 'before' and 'after' views of a Polish economy removed of Jewish middlemen. (From *Das Vorfeld*, Folge 3/4, 1940, reproduced in *Beiträge zur Nationalsozialistischen Gesundheits- und Sozialpolitik*, vol. 5, Rotbuch Verlag, Berlin, 1987)

Air Chief Marshall Sir Arthur Harris. (From Henry Probert, *Bomber Harris. His Life and Times*, London 2001)

Graph showing devastation of German industrial towns, from Sir Arthur Harris's report on war operations 23 February 1942 to 8 May 1945. (National Archives)

Armourers make final checks on the bomb load of an Avro Lancaster B Mark I of No. 207 Squadron RAF at Syerston, Nottinghamshire, September 1942. (Imperial War Museum, London, CH 17458)

General Curtis LeMay of the USAAF. (Bettman/CORBIS)

Victims of an Allied bombing raid laid out for identification, Germany 1943. (Imperial War Museum, London, HU 12143)

Vermork hydroelectric plant at Rjukan, Norway. (National Archives)

Lieutenant Knut Haukelid. (National Archives)

Arrest of civilians by German and Italian troops following the bomb attack in the via Rasella in Rome, 13 March 1944. (Bundesarchiv Ludwigsberg, Bild 1011-312-0983-03/Photo: Koch)

While every effort has been made to trace the owners of copyright material reproduced herein, the publishers would like to apologise for any omissions and would be pleased to incorporate missing acknowledgements in future editions.

NOTES

Chapter 1: The Predators

1 A. J. Rhodes, *The Poet as Superman. A Life of Gabriele D'Annunzio* (London 1959) and M. A. Ledeen, *The First Duce: D'Annunzio at Fiume* (Baltimore 1977)

2 For this important insight see Adrian Lyttelton, *The Seizure of Power. Fascism in Italy 1919–1929* (London 1987) p. 44

3 Donald Sassoon, *Mussolini and the Rise of Fascism* (London 2007) p. 98

4 For Italian Fascism as a political religion see especially Emilio Gentile, *The Sacralisation of Politics in Fascist Italy*; for the mixed success of Fascism in altering the character of Italian life see R. J. B. Bosworth, *Mussolini's Italy. Life under the Dictatorship* (London 2005) especially pp. 249–76

5 Alfred Cobban, *Dictatorship in History and Theory* (London 1939) p. 128

6 As argued by MacGregor Knox, *Common Destiny. Dictatorship, Foreign Policy and War in Fascist Italy and Nazi Germany* (Cambridge 2000) pp. 145–147

7 Richard Lamb, *Mussolini and the British* (London 1997) p. 120

8 For the latest archival revelations see Robert Mallett, *Mussolini and the Origins of the Second World War 1933–1940* (London 2003) pp. 32–47

9 Richard Overy with Andrew Wheatcroft, *The Road to War* (London 1999) p. 183

10 For a good history of colonial Abyssinia see Alberto Sbacchi, *Ethiopia under Mussolini. Fascism and the Colonial Experience* (London 1985)

11 Angelo Del Boca, *The Ethiopian War 1935–1941* (Chicago 1969) pp. 78–9

12 Alberto Sbacchi, *Legacy of Bitterness. Ethiopia and Fascist Italy 1935–1941* (Lawrenceville, New Jersey 1997) pp. 55ff.

13 Antony Beevor, *The Battle for Spain. The Spanish Civil War 1936–1939* (London 2006) p. 333

14 Herbert Bix, *Hirohito and the Making of Modern Japan* (New York 2000) pp. 186ff. for Hirohito's coronation

15 See Marius Jansen, *Japan and China. From War to Peace 1894–1972* (Chicago 1975)

16 Andrew Gordon, *A History of Modern Japan. From Tokugawa Times to the Present* (Oxford 2003) pp. 162–7 for these remarks on Japanese politics

17 Courtney Browne, *Tojo. The Last Banzai* (London 1967) p. 42

18 See Akire Iriye, *The Origins of the Second World War in the Pacific* (London 1987) p. 12

19 Louise Young, *Japan's Total Empire. Manchuria and the Culture of Wartime Imperialism* (Berkeley 1998) pp. 77–8

20 Jonathan Fenby, *The Penguin History of Modern China. The Fall and Rise of a Great Power 1850–2008* (London 2008) pp. 236–47 is vivid and valuable

21 R. A. C. Parker, *The Second World War. A Short History* (Oxford 1997) p. 74

22 Jonathan R. Adelman, 'German–Japanese Relations 1941–1945', in Jonathan R. Adelman (ed.), *Hitler and his Allies in World War II* (London 2007) pp. 63–5

23 Bob Tadashi Wakabayashi (ed.), *The Nanking Atrocity 1937–38. Complicating the Picture* (New York 2007) pp. 32 and 36 for the two decrees cited

24 Bernd Martin, 'Japanische Kriegsverbrechen und Vernichtungspraktiken während des Pazifischen Krieges (1937–1945), in Dittmar Dahlmann and Gerhard Hirschfeld (eds) *Lager, Zwangsarbeit, Vertreibung und Deportation* (Essen 1999) pp. 142ff.

25 On Japanese (military) values see Meirion and Susie Harris, *Soldiers of the Sun. The Rise and Fall of the Imperial Japanese Army* (New York 1991) especially pp. 222ff.

26 Martin, 'Japanische Kriegsverbrechen', p. 142

27 Michael Bloch, *Ribbentrop* (London 1992) p. 81

28 Fritz Stern, *The Politics of Cultural Despair. A Study in the Rise of Germanic Ideology* (Berkeley 1961) is the classic study

29 Adolf Hitler, *Mein Kampf*, trans. by Ralph Manheim (London 1974) pp. 139–41

30 See Christopher Clarke, *Iron Kingdom. The Rise and Downfall of Prussia, 1600–1947* (London 2006) pp. 655ff. But see also Wolfgang Wippermann's *Der Ordensstaat als Ideologie* (Göttingen 1979) and his 'Nationalsozialismus und Preussentum', *Aus Politik und Zeitgeschichte* (1981) pp. 13–22

31 See the very suggestive remarks of Sebastian Haffner writing originally in 1940 in his *Germany. Jekyll & Hyde. A Contemporary Account of Nazi Germany* (London 2005) pp. 81–2

32 There are very few studies of ethics under the Nazis, although virtually every book or source contains material for such a venture. Two exceptions are Raimond Reiter, *Nationalsozialismus und Moral. Die 'Pflichtenlehre' eines Verbrecherstaates* (Frankfurt am Main 1996) and Harald Ofstad, *Our Contempt in Weakness. Nazi Norms and Values – and our Own* (Stockholm 1989). A useful essay is Raphael Gross and Werner Konitzer, 'Geschichte und Ethik. Zum Fortwirken der nationalsozialistischen Moral', *Mittelweg* (1999) 36 pp. 44–67. The best English-language book on philosophy in general under the Nazis is Hans Sluga, *Heidegger's Crisis. Philosophy and Politics in Nazi Germany* (Cambridge, Massachusetts 1993)

33 Michael Burleigh, *Death and Deliverance. 'Euthanasia' in Germany 1900–1945* (London 2003, originally Cambridge 1994) highlights this economistic theme and contains a long bibliography of other relevant works

34 Ian Kershaw, *Hitler 1889–1936. Hubris* (London 1998) pp. 121–5 corrects Hitler's own selective autobiographical story

35 Hitler, *Mein Kampf*, p. 28

36 Ibid., p. 124

37 The journalist Roy Howard was one of those to spot the problem – so much so that Hitler refused to answer a question on the subject and prohibited Howard from publishing any reference to this awkwardness. See William E. Dodd Jr and Martha Dodd (eds) *Ambassador Dodd's Diary 1933–1938* (London 1941) pp. 334–5

38 Hitler, *Mein Kampf*, pp. 604ff. for Hitler's rejection of a Russian alliance

39 See the still fundamental Wolfgang Wippermann, *Der 'Deutsche Drang nach Osten'. Ideologie und Wirklichkeit eines politischen Schlagwortes* (Darmstadt 1981)

40 Jonathan Wright, *Germany and the Origins of the Second World War* (Basingstoke 2007) p. 20 for Hitler's thoughts on foreign policy, and Gerhard L. Weinberg (ed.), *Hitler's Second Book. The Unpublished Sequel to Mein Kampf* (New York 2003) pp. 232–3 for the quotation from Hitler

41 Richard Bessel, *Nazism and War* (London 2004) p. 28. See also his earlier *Political Violence and the Rise of Nazism* (New Haven 1984)

42 For an eyewitness account of this process see Victor Klemperer, *The Language of the Third Reich. LTI–Lingua Tertii Imperii. A Philologist's Notebook* (London 2000)

43 Edward Timms, *Karl Kraus. Apocalyptic Satirist. The Post-War Crisis and the Rise of the Swastika* (New Haven 2005) p. 510

44 See the still useful essay 'National Socialism as Temptation', in Fritz Stern's *Dreams and Delusions. The Drama of German History* (New Haven 1999) pp. 147–91

45 Notably the German Christians – see Doris L. Bergen, *Twisted Cross. The German Christian Movement in the Third Reich* (Chapel Hill, North Carolina 1996)

46 Ian Kershaw, *The 'Hitler Myth'. Image and Reality in the Third Reich* (Oxford 1987)

47 Sebastian Haffner, *Geschichte eines Deutschen. Die Erinnerungen 1914–1933* (Stuttgart/Munich 2003) pp. 307–8

48 Thomas Mann, *Tagebücher 1933–1934*, ed. Peter de Mendelssohn (Frankfurt am Main 1977) pp. 46 and 54

49 Max Domarus (ed.), *Hitler. Speeches and Proclamations 1932–1945*, vol. 1 1932–1934 (London 1990) p. 233, 1 February 1933

50 Ibid., pp. 324–33

51 For an intelligent discussion of the Rhineland Crisis see Peter Neville, *Hitler and Appeasement. The British Attempt to Prevent the Second World War* (London 2006) pp. 69–73

52 Jeremy Noakes and Geoffrey Pridham (eds), *Nazism 1919–1945. A Documentary Reader* (Exeter 1988) vol. 3. doc. no. 501 p. 677

53 For the Hossbach memorandum see Ibid., doc. no. 503 pp. 680–687

54 *Documents of German Foreign Policy* Series D vol. 1 (London 1949) pp. 240ff.

Chapter 2: Appeasement

1 Neville Chamberlain, *Norman Chamberlain. A Memoir* (London 1923)

2 The Siegfried Sassoon line at the top of Churchill's chapter 7 on 'The Somme' in his *World Crisis* (London 1923–31)

3 Keith Feiling, *The Life of Neville Chamberlain* (London 1946) p. 321

4 Robert Skidelsky, 'In the Führer's Face', *New York Review of Books*, 24 February 2005

5 Peter Neville, *Hitler and Appeasement. The British Attempt to Prevent the Second World War* (London 2006) pp. 15–16

6 Robert Rhodes James (ed.), *Winston S. Churchill. His Complete Speeches 1897–1963* (London 1974) vol. 5 p. 5262, 13 April 1933

7 Benny Morris, *The Roots of Appeasement. The British Weekly Press and Nazi Germany during the 1930s* (London 1991) p. 181; Feiling, *Life of Neville Chamberlain*, p. 321

8 John Julius Norwich (ed.), *The Duff Cooper Diaries 1915–1951* (London 2005) entry dated 20 September 1938, p. 262

9 On the Legion and Germany see John Ramsden, *Don't Mention the War. The British and Germans since 1890* (London 2006) pp. 164–5

10 Ben Pimlott, *Hugh Dalton* (London 1995) p. 234

11 The American foreign correspondent John Gunther noted the sporting approach to foreign policy in Britain at the time; see his *Inside Europe* (London 1938) p. 247

12 Richard Overy with Andrew Wheatcroft, *The Road to War* (London 1999) p. 77

13 See Andrew Stewart, *Empire Lost. Britain, the Dominions and the Second World War* (London 2008) for the latest thought on these important imperial relationships, and Keith Robbins, 'Experiencing the Foreign: British Foreign Policy Makers and the Delights of Travel', in Michael Dockrill and Brian McKercher (eds), *Diplomacy and World Power. Studies in British Foreign Policy 1890–1950* (Cambridge 1996) pp. 19–42 for the overseas experience of the British elite

14 Anita Prazmowska, *Eastern Europe and the Origins of the Second World War* (London 2000) pp. 11ff.

15 Eugen Weber, *The Hollow Years. France in the 1930s* (London 1995) p. 145

16 Henri Nogueres, *Munich or the Phoney Peace* (London 1965) p. 46

17 Christopher Thorne, *The Limits of Foreign Policy. The West, the League and*

the Far Eastern Crisis of 1931–1933 (London 1972) p. 162

18 Ibid., pp. 283–4

19 R. A. C. Parker, *Chamberlain and Appeasement. British Policy and the Coming of the Second World War* (London 1993) p. 45

20 Martin Gilbert, *Winston S. Churchill*, vol. 5 (London 1976) pp. 224–225

21 For an excellent discussion see Richard Lamb, *Mussolini and the British* (London 1997) pp. 129ff.

22 Parker, *Chamberlain and Appeasement*, pp. 52–7

23 Peter Neville, *Appeasing Hitler. The Diplomacy of Sir Nevile Henderson 1937–39* (London 2000) pp. 20–6

24 Martin Gilbert, *Churchill and the Jews* (London 2007) p. 139. Writing in the *Evening Standard* on 17 September 1937 Churchill declared: 'We cannot say that we admire your [Hitler's] treatment of the Jews or of the Protestants and Catholics of Germany, but these matters, so long as they are confined inside Germany, are not our business.'

25 P. H. M. Bell, *The Origins of the Second World War in Europe* (London 1986) pp. 205–6

26 The speeches referred to are from Rhodes James (ed.), *Winston S. Churchill. His Complete Speeches*, vol. 5 pp. 5199 (1932) and 5263 (1933)

27 Parker, *Chamberlain and Appeasement*, pp. 62–5

28 R. J. Q. Adams, *British Politics and Foreign Policy in the Age of Appeasement 1935–39* (London 1993) pp. 43–5

29 Niall Ferguson, *The War of the World. History's Age of Hatred* (London 2006) pp. 339–41

30 David Carlton, *Anthony Eden* (London 1981) p. 79

31 Nevile Henderson, *Failure of a Mission. Berlin 1937–1939* (London 1940) pp. 94–5

32 David Reynolds, *Summits. Six Meetings that Shaped the Twentieth Century* (London 2007) p. 32

33 Prazmowska, *Eastern Europe*, pp. 33–4

34 Ian Kershaw, *Making Friend's with Hitler. Lord Londonderry, the Nazis and the Road to World War II* (London 2005)

35 Alfred Duff Cooper, *Old Men Forget* (London 1953) p. 200

36 Feiling, *Life of Neville Chamberlain*, p. 324

37 Rhodes James (ed.), *Winston S. Churchill. His Complete Speeches* vol. 6 p. 6017. Voigt was the author of *Unto Caesar* (London 1938), one of the key contemporary texts that treated totalitarianism as a species of political religion

38 Frederick Raphael was father to this helpful thought in our correspondence in the summer of 2008 on appeasement

39 Lord Halifax, *The Fulness of Days* (London 1957)

40 See Karina Urbach, 'The British Aristocracy', in her edited collection *European Aristocracies and the Radical Right 1918–1939* (Oxford 2007) pp. 70–1

41 Norwich (ed.), *Duff Cooper Diaries*, entry dated 25 September 1938, p. 266

42 Reynolds, *Summits*, p. 48

43 Andrew Roberts, '*The Holy Fox*'. *The Life of Lord Halifax* (London 1991) p. 72

44 Robert Self (ed.), *The Neville Chamberlain Diary Letters*, vol. 4 (Aldershot 2005) p. 287, letter to Ida Chamberlain dated 26 November 1937

45 Rhodes James (ed.), *Winston S. Churchill. His Complete Speeches*, vol. 6 p. 6008, House of Commons, 5 October 1938

46 Michael Bloch, *Ribbentrop* (London 1992) pp. 170–3

47 Self (ed.), *Neville Chamberlain Diary Letters*, vol. 4 p. 307, letter to Ida Chamberlain dated 20 March 1938

48 Rhodes James (ed.), *Winston S. Churchill. His Complete Speeches*, vol. 6 pp. 5955ff. for Churchill's 'Arm, and Stand by the Covenant' speech at the Free Trade Hall, Manchester on 9 May 1938, and R. A. C. Parker, *Churchill and Appeasement* (London 2000) pp. 158ff.

49 Self (ed.), *Neville Chamberlain Diary Letters*, vol. 4 p. 307, letter to Ida Chamberlain dated 20 March 1938

50 Joachim Fest, *Hitler* (London 1974) p. 817

51 See Mark Cornwall '"A Leap into Ice-Cold Water". The Manoeuvres of the

Henlein Movement in Czechoslovakia 1933–1938' in Mark Cornwall and R. J. W. Evans (eds), *Czechoslovakia in a Nationalist and Fascist Europe 1918–1948* (Oxford 2007) pp. 123ff.

52 Jeremy Noakes and Geoffrey Pridham (eds), *Nazism 1919–1945. A Documentary Reader* (Exeter 1988) vol. 3 doc. no. 517 p. 708

53 Nogueres, *Munich*, pp. 52–5

54 David Vaughan, *Battle for the Airwaves. Radio and the 1938 Munich Crisis* (Prague 2008) pp. 28–9. As well as also being in Czech, the book has a CD with all the relevant broadcasts

55 Vaughan, *Battle for the Airwaves*, p. 88

56 Harold Macmillan, *Winds of Change 1914–1939* (London 1966) p. 573

57 David Dilks (ed.), *The Diaries of Sir Alexander Cadogan 1938–1945* (London 1971) entry dated 10 September 1938, p. 128

58 For Kleist's visit see Klemens von Klemperer, *German Resistance against Hitler. The Search for Allies Abroad 1938–1945* (Oxford 1992) pp. 97–100

59 Max Domarus (ed.), *Hitler. Speeches and Proclamations 1932–1945*, vol. 2: 1935–1938 (London 1992) p. 1154

60 Self (ed.), *Neville Chamberlain Diary Letters*, vol. 4 p. 344, letter to Ida Chamberlain dated 11 September 1938

61 Roberts, 'Holy Fox', p. 70

62 Goebbels diary entry 18 September 1938 in Elke Fröhlich (ed.), *Die Tagebücher von Joseph Goebbels 1923–1941*, vol. 6 (Munich 1998)

63 Martin Broszat, 'Das sudetendeutsche Freikorps', *VfZ* (1961) 9 pp. 30–49

64 Callum A. MacDonald, *The United States, Britain and Appeasement 1936–1939* (London 1981) pp. 73–4

65 E. L. Woodward et al. (eds), *Documents on British Foreign Policy 1919–1939*, (hereafter DBFP), Third Series vol. 2 (1938) doc. no. 928, Record of Anglo-French Conversations, 18 September 1938, p. 396

66 Reynolds, *Summits*, pp. 61–2

67 *DBFP*, Third Series vol. 2 (1938) doc. no. 1033 pp. 463–73 for the record of their meeting

68 Roberts, 'Holy Fox', pp. 116–18

69 *DBFP*, Third Series vol. 2 (1938) doc. no. 1093, Record of Anglo-French Conversation, 25 September 1938, pp. 528–9

70 Ibid., pp. 527–35

71 Ibid., doc. no. 1118, Notes of Conversation between Sir Horace Wilson and Hitler, 26 September 1938, pp. 554–7

72 Louis MacNeice, *Autumn Journal* (London 1988 originally 1939) pp. 22–3

73 Galeazzo Ciano, *Diary 1937–1943*, ed. Robert Miller and Stanislao Pugliese (London 2002) entry dated 29–30 September 1938, p. 134

74 *DBFP*, Third Series vol. 2 (1938) doc. no. 1228, Note of a Conversation between the Prime Minister and Herr Hitler on 30 September 1938, pp. 635–40

75 Self (ed.), *Neville Chamberlain Diary Letters*, vol. 4 p. 351, letter to Hilda Chamberlain dated 2 October 1938

76 For a fair summary of these positions see Reynolds, *Summits*, pp. 92–4

77 Pimlott, *Hugh Dalton*, p. 257

78 Vaughan, *Battle for the Airwaves*, p. 76

79 Ibid., p. 81

80 Helmut Krausnick, *Tagebücher Groscurths* (Stuttgart 1970) p. 127

81 Anonymous note, 12 October 1938, *ADAP* D4 doc. no. 53 p. 68 (Göttingen 1982–95)

82 Fröhlich (ed.), *Tagebücher von Joseph Goebbels*, vol. 6, entry dated 10 November 1938, for the four references to the Stosstrupp Adolf Hitlers. See also Saul Friedländer, *Nazi Germany and the Jews. The Years of Persecution 1933–39* (London 1997) pp. 69ff. for a classic interpretation, and Angela Hermann, 'Die Vorkriegsphase. Quellenkritische Studien zu den Tagebuchern von Jospeh Goebbels', PhD dissertation, Ludwig-Maximilians University, Munich 2008, pp. 291ff. for a detailed discussion of Goebbels's role in the events

83 Minute of their conversation, 21 January 1939, *ADAP* D4 doc. no. 158 p. 170

84 *Ciano Diaries*, pp. 176–7, 11–14 January 1939

85 Hermann, 'Vorkriegsphase', pp. 374–5

86 Noakes and Pridham (eds), *Nazism. A Documentary Reader,* vol. 3 doc. no. 533 p. 727

87 Vaughan, *Battle for the Airwaves,* p. 84

88 Nogueres, *Munich,* pp. 337–41

89 Dilks (ed.), *Alexander Cadogan Diaries,* p. 167, subsequent interpolated comment on entry dated 30 March 1939

90 Richard Overy, *1939. Countdown to War* (London 2009) especially pp. 119–23

Chapter 3: Brotherly Enemies

1 Robert Rhodes James (ed.), *Winston S. Churchill. His Complete Speeches 1897–1963* (London 1974) vol. 6 p. 5823

2 For a self-serving example of how left-wing British and US historians of Nazism simply ignore the contemporary French, German, Italian and Polish (non-left-wing) historians who use these models see Neil Gregor's 'Nazism – A Political Religion? Rethinking the Voluntarist Turn', in Neil Gregor (ed.), *Nazism, War and Genocide* (Exeter 2005) pp. 1–21. Mr Gregor has apparently not read an enormous literature from Raymond Aron, Norman Cohn and Alain Besançon to Hans Maier and Tzvetan Todorov that regards the millenarian social utopianism of Communism and Nazism as the motor force behind their improving exterminations. But then these eminent thinkers would not have used such academic jargon as 'voluntarist turn' and would have read books before criticising them

3 See the important papers in Horst Möller (ed.), *Der rote Holocaust und die Deutschen. Die Debatte um das 'Schwarzbuch des Kommunismus'* (Munich 1999), and also the related debate between François Furet and Ernst Nolte, *Fascism and Communism* (Lincoln, Nebraska 2001)

4 Wacław Długoborski, 'Das Problem des Vergleichs von Nationalsozialismus und Stalinismus', in Dittmar Dahlmann and Gerhard Hirschfeld (eds), *Lager, Zwangsarbeit, Vertreibung und Deportation. Dimensionen der Massenverbrechen in der Sowjetunion*

und in Deutschland 1933 bis 1945 (Essen 1991) p. 26

5 Steve Aschheim, 'Imagining the Absolute. Mapping Western Conceptions of Evil', in Helmut Dubiel and Gabriel Motzkin (eds), *The Lesser Evil* (London 2003) pp. 78ff.

6 I am grateful to Frederic Raphael for exchanges of views we had on this subject in August 2008

7 For this point see Tzvetan Todorov, 'What Went Wrong in the Twentieth Century?', in his *Hope and Memory in the Twentieth Century* (London 2003) pp. 35ff.

8 Lord Ismay, *The Memoirs of General the Lord Ismay* (London 1960) p. 234

9 For numerous examples see Robert Conquest, *Reflections on a Ravaged Century* (London 1999) and his *The Dragons of Expectation. Reality and Delusion in the Course of History* (London 2005)

10 Martin Malia, 'Nazism–Communism. Delineating the Comparison', Dubiel and Motzkin (eds), *Lesser Evil* pp. 7–24

11 Robert Conquest, *Kolyma. The Arctic Death Camps* (London 1978) is the classic account

12 Robert Gellately, *Backing Hitler. Consent and Coercion in Nazi Germany* (Oxford 2001) pp. 58–63 is excellent on the evolution of the camp system

13 *I Shall Bear Witness. The Diaries of Victor Klemperer 1933–45,* trans. Martin Chalmers (London 1998) vol. 1 p. 43

14 Ian Kershaw, 'Working towards the Führer. Reflections on the Nature of Hitler's Dictatorship', in Ian Kershaw and Moshe Lewin (eds), *Stalinism and Nazism. Dictatorships in Comparison* (Cambridge 1997) pp. 90–5

15 For a thoughtful comparison of the two men and their regimes see Richard Overy, *The Dictators. Hitler's Germany, Stalin's Russia* (London 2004) pp. 6ff., and Alan Bullock, *Hitler and Stalin. Parallel Lives* (London 1992)

16 Robert Service, *Stalin. A Biography* (London 2004) p. 230

17 Simon Sebag Montefiore, *Young Stalin* (London 2007) is masterly on Stalin's early years

18 For a good discussion of this see Leonid Luks, 'Zur "Herrschaftslogik" im Stalinismus und im Nationalsozialismus', in Jürgen Zarusky (ed.), *Stalin und die Deutschen. Neue Beiträge der Forschung* (Munich 2006) p. 226

19 Anne Applebaum, *GULAG. A History of the Soviet Camps* (London 2003) pp. 76ff.

20 Service, *Stalin*, pp. 272–4

21 Robert Conquest, 'Into the Planned Economy', in his *Dragons of Expectation*, p. 102 for the quotations from Molotov and the Politburo resolution. For the terror famine see his monumental *Harvest of Sorrow. Soviet Collectivization and the Terror-Famine* (New York 1986)

22 Christel Lane, *The Rites of Rulers. Ritual in Industrial Society – the Soviet Case* (Cambridge 1981); Robert Tucker, 'The Rise of Stalin's Personality Cult', *American Historical Review* (1984) 79 pp. 347–66 and Nina Tumarkin, *Lenin Lives! The Lenin Cult in Soviet Russia* (Cambridge, Massachusetts 1997)

23 J. Arch Getty and Oleg Naumov, *Yezhov. The Rise of Stalin's 'Iron Fist'* (New Haven 2008) pp. 179ff.

24 Applebaum, *GULAG*, pp. 106–9 for examples

25 Marc Jansen and Nikita Petrov, *Stalin's Loyal Executioner. People's Commissar Nikolai Ezhov 1895–1940* (Stanford, California 2002) pp. 66–68

26 Robert Conquest, *Stalin. Breaker of Nations* (London 1991) pp. 208–9

27 Anne E. Gorsuch, *Youth in Revolutionary Russia. Enthusiasts, Bohemians, Delinquents* (Bloomington, Indiana 2000) pp. 20ff.

28 Sebastian Haffner, *Germany. Jekyll & Hyde. A Contemporary Account of Nazi Germany* (London 2005) pp. 87–8

29 Aaron Solts, 'Communist Ethics', in William G. Rosenberg (ed.), *Bolshevik Visions. First Phase of the Cultural Revolution in Soviet Russia* (Ann Arbor, Michigan 1990) p. 31

30 For most of these examples of Communist practice see Simon Sebag Montefiore's brilliant *Stalin. The Court of the Red Tsar* (London 2003)

31 Arkady Vaksberg, *Stalin's Prosecutor. The Life of Andrei Vyshinsky* (New York 1990) pp. 86–93

32 See Ian Kershaw, *The 'Hitler Myth'. Image and Reality in the Third Reich* (Oxford 1987) especially pp. 83–104

33 Frank Bajohr, *Parvenüs und Profiteure. Korruption in der NS-Zeit* (Frankfurt am Main 2004) pp. 34ff.

34 Niall Ferguson, *War of the World. History's Age of Hatred* (London 2006) p. 148

35 Richard Pipes, *Russia under the Bolshevik Regime 1919–1924* (Cambridge, Massachusetts 1994) pp. 328–9

36 Geoffrey Hosking, *Rulers and Victims. The Russians in the Soviet Union* (Cambridge, Massachusetts 2006) pp. 200–3

37 Mikhail Heller, *Cogs in the Wheel. The Formation of Soviet Man* (New York 1988), p. 173

38 As far as I know, George Steiner is one of the few, other than Orthodox Jews, to make this important point about moral excellence aggravating the Torah-less, although in a television religious programme discussion chaired by Melvyn Bragg many years ago rather than in print. The pathology was evident during the 2009 Gaza operation where the Israeli Defence Force's claims to be waging a uniquely ethical war seemed to incite even more anti-Semitic responses across Europe

39 Claudia Koonz, *The Nazi Conscience* (Cambridge, Massachusetts 2003) p. 5

40 Daniel Peris, *Storming the Heavens. The Soviet League of the Militant Godless* (Ithaca, New York 1998)

41 Karl Dietrich Bracher, *The German Dictatorship* (London 1973) p. 343

42 Max Domarus (ed.), *Hitler. Speeches and Proclamations 1932–1945*, vol. 2: *1935–1938* (London 1992) p. 700

43 Heller, *Cogs in the Wheel*, p. 149

44 Michael Burleigh and Wolfgang Wippermann, *The Racial State. Germany 1933–1945* (Cambridge 1991) pp. 206–7 for an extract from this 1938 speech

45 Catriona Kelly, *Comrade Pavlik. The Rise and Fall of a Soviet Boy Hero* (London 2005) p. 34

46 Orlando Figes, *The Whisperers. Private Life in Stalin's Russia* (London 2008) pp. 29 and 38

47 Geoffrey Hosking, *A History of the Soviet Union 1917–1991* (London 1992) pp. 175–6

48 Heller, *Cogs in the Wheel*, p. 151

49 Figes, *Whisperers*, p. 47

50 See Lisa Pine's *Nazi Family Policy 1933–1945* (Oxford 1999)

51 See Jill Stephenson, 'Women, Motherhood and the Family in the Third Reich', in Michael Burleigh (ed.), *Confronting the Nazi Past. New Debates on Modern German History* (London 1996) pp. 172ff.

52 *Deutschland-Berichte der Sozialdemokratischen Partei Deutschlands (Sopade) 1934–1940*, vol. 1: *1934* (Frankfurt am Main 1980) p. 117

53 Michael Kater, *Hitler Youth* (Cambridge, Massachusetts 2004) p. 29

54 Franz-Lothar Kroll, 'Geschichte und Politik im Weltbild Hitlers' *VfZ* (1996) 44 p. 337

55 Getty and Naumov, *Yezhov*, p. 9

56 For an excellent discussion of anti-Comintern see Walter Z. Laqueur, *Russia and Germany. A Century of Conflict* (New Brunswick, New Jersey 1990) pp. 194ff.

57 Aleksandr M. Nekrich, *Pariahs, Partners, Predators. German–Soviet Relations 1922–1941* (New York 1997) p. 70

58 Domarus (ed.), *Hitler. Speeches and Proclamations*, vol. 2 p. 736

59 Roger R. Rees, 'The Red Army and the Great Purges', in J. Arch Getty and Roberta T. Manning (eds), *Stalinist Terror. New Perspectives* (Cambridge 1993) p. 213

60 Ian Kershaw, *Fateful Choices. Ten Decisions that Changed the World 1940–1941* (London 2007) p. 247

61 Geoffrey Roberts, *The Soviet Union and the Origins of the Second World War. Russo-German Relations and the Road to War 1933–1941* (London 1995) pp. 65–8

62 Nekrich, *Pariahs, Partners, Predators*, p. 115

63 Rolf Ahlmann, 'Der Hitler–Stalin-Pakt. Nichtsangriffs- und Angriffsvertrag?', in Erwin Oberländer (ed.), *Hitler–Stalin-Pakt 1939. Das Ende Ostmitteleuropas?* (Frankfurt am Main 1989) pp. 36–7

64 Michael Bloch, *Ribbentrop* (London 1992) pp. 233ff. for a good discussion of the signing of the Pact

Chapter 4: The Rape of Poland

1 Jeremy Noakes and Geoffrey Pridham (eds), *Nazism 1919–1945. A Documentary Reader* (Exeter 1988) vol. 3 doc. no. 541 pp. 739–42, and Joachim C. Fest, *Hitler* (London 1974) pp. 884–5

2 Max Domarus (ed.), *Hitler. Speeches and Proclamations 1932–1945*, vol. 3: *1939–1940* (London 1997) p. 1745

3 Karol Marian Pospieszalski, 'The Bomb Attack at Tarnow', *Polish Western Affairs* (1986) 27 pp. 241ff.

4 Bob Graham, 'Was This the First Victim of the War?', *Daily Telegraph* 29 August 2009 p. 21

5 Alfred Spiess and Heiner Lichtenstein, *Das Unternehmen Tannenberg* (Munich 1979)

6 *ADAP* Series D (1937–45) vols. 1–13 (Baden-Baden 1950–70) vol. 7 doc. no. 496 p. 400

7 Heinz Boberach (ed.), *Meldungen aus dem Reich. Die geheimen Lageberichte des Sicherheitsdienstes der SS 1938–1945* (Herrsching 1984) vol. 2 p. 331, report dated 9 October 1939

8 Domarus (ed.), *Hitler. Speeches and Proclomations*, vol. 3 pp. 1750–6

9 Michael Bloch, *Ribbentrop* (London 1992) pp. 260–2

10 Andrew Stewart, *Empire Lost. Britain, the Dominions and the Second World War* (London 2008) p. 24

11 Ribbentrop to the Foreign Ministry and Secret Additional Protocol, both dated 28 September 1939, in *Documents of German Foreign Policy 1918–1945* Series D (1937–45) vol. 8 (London 1954) doc. nos. 152, pp. 159–161, and 159, p. 166 (hereafter *DGFP*), Jan T. Gross, 'Die Sowjetisierung Ostpolens 1939–1941', in Bernd Wegner (ed.), *Zwei Wege nach Moskau. Vom Hitler–Stalin-Pakt zum*

'*Unternehmen Barbarossa*' (Munich 1991) pp. 57–8

12 Horst Rohde, 'Hitlers erster Blitzkrieg und seine Auswirkungen auf Nordosteuropa', in Klaus Maier, Horst Rohde, Bernd Stegemann and Hans Umbreit (eds), *Die Errichtung der Hegemonie auf dem europäischen Kontinent*, vol. 2 of Militärgeschichtlichen Forschungsamt (ed.), *Das Deutsche Reich und der Zweite Weltkrieg* (Stuttgart/Munich 1979) pp. 92ff.

13 Shmuel Krakowski, 'The Fate of Jewish Prisoners of War in the September 1939 Campaign', *Yad Vashem Studies* (1977) 12 pp. 296–333

14 Tomasz Szarota, 'Germans in the Eyes of Poles during World War II', *Acta Poloniae Historica* (1983) 47 pp. 151ff.

15 See Michael Burleigh, *Germany Turns Eastwards. A Study of 'Ostforschung' in the Third Reich* (London 2003, originally Cambridge 1988) for an archive-based account of the contribution German scholars made to these animosities throughout the Weimar and Nazi eras

16 Noakes and Pridham (eds), *Nazism. A Documentary Reader*, 3 doc. no. 542 p. 743

17 Ulrich Herbert, *Best. Biographische Studien über Radikalismus, Weltanschauung und Vernunft 1903–1989* (Bonn 1996) pp. 237ff. is thorough

18 Christian Janssen and Arno Weissbecker, *Der 'Volksdeutsche Selbstschutz' in Polen 1939/40* (Munich 1992)

19 Alexander B. Rossino, *Hitler Strikes Poland. Blitzkrieg, Ideology, and Atrocity* (Lawrence, Kansas 2003) pp. 30ff.

20 Klaus-Michael Mallmann, Jochen Böhler and Jürgen Matthäus (eds), *Einsatzgruppen in Polen. Darstellung und Dokumentation* (Darmstadt 2008) p. 72

21 Alexander B. Rossino, *Hitler Strikes Poland* p. 14

22 Jochen Böhler, *Auftakt zum Vernichtungskrieg. Die Wehrmacht in Polen 1939* (Frankfurt am Main 2006) pp. 150–3 for examples of differing orders licensing illegal acts

23 Mallmann, Böhler and Matthäus (eds), *Einsatzgruppen in Polen* doc. no. 118 Lagebericht SD-Einsatzkommando Bromberg, dated 11 November 1939, and doc. no. 120, Lagebericht Sicherheitspolizei-Einsatzkommando Bromberg, dated 17 November 1939, pp. 191–3

24 Böhler, *Auftakt zum Vernichtungskrieg*, pp. 213–14

25 Helmuth Krausnick, *Hitlers Einsatzgruppen. Die Truppen des Weltanschauungskrieges 1938–1942* (Frankfurt am Main 1985) pp. 71–2

26 Ulrich von Hassell, *The von Hassell Diaries. The Story of the Forces against Hitler Inside Germany* (Boulder, Colorado 1994) entry dated 11 October 1939, p. 79

27 Mallmann, Böhler and Matthäus (eds), *Einsatzgruppen in Polen*, pp. 60–7

28 International Military Tribunal (IMG) vol. 26 pp. 255ff. doc. no. PS-686

29 Noakes and Pridham (eds), *Nazism. A Documentary Reader*, vol. 3 doc. no. 646 p. 928

Chapter 5: Trampling the Remains

1 Klaus-Michael Mallmann, Jochen Böhler and Jürgen Matthäus (eds), *Einsatzgruppen in Polen. Darstellung und Dokumentation* (Darmstadt 2008) pp. 87–8

2 Hitler's decree on the consolidation of ethnic Germandom dated 7 October 1939, vol. 1 of Werner Röhr (ed.), *Die faschistische Okkupationspolitik in Polen (1939–1945)* Wolfgang Schumann and Ludwig Nestler (eds), *Europa unterm Hakenkreuz 1938–1945*, vols. 1–8 (Berlin 1989) doc. no. 19 pp. 126–7

3 Hitler's decree on the administration of occupied Polish territory in Röhr (ed.), *Die faschistischen Okkupationspolitik in Polen*, doc. no. 22 clause 3 p. 129

4 Notes of this conference in Ibid., doc. no. 25 pp. 133–4

5 Decree for Combating of Violent Acts in the General Government dated 31 October 1939 in Jeremy Noakes and Geoffrey Pridham (eds), *Nazism*

1919–1945. A Documentary Reader vol. 3
doc. no. 688 p. 975

6 Czesław Madajczyk, *Polityka III Rzeszy w okupowanej Polsce* (Warsaw 1970) vol. 1 p. 400 for this document, which is not included in the German edition cited in note 7 below

7 'The legal framework for German policy towards Poland from a racial-political perspective' issued by the Academy of German Law dated January 1940, in Röhr (ed.), *Die faschistischen Okkupationspolitik in Polen,* doc. no. 47 p. 157

8 Stephan Lehnstaedt, 'Okkupation im Osten. Besatzeralltag in Warschau und Minsk 1939–1944', PhD dissertation, Institut für Zeitgeschichte, Munich (2008) pp. 8off. Subsequently published as *Okkupation im Osten* (Munich 2009)

9 Tomasz Szarota, *Warschau unter dem Hakenkreuz. Leben und Alltag im besetzten Warschau 1.10.1939–31.7.1944* (Paderborn 1985) p. 35

10 See Markus Roth, *'Herrenmenschen'. Die deutschen Kreishauptleute im besetzten Polen* (Göttingen 2009)

11 For example a police order regarding the hours of grocers in Posen dated 8 November 1940, in Noakes and Pridham (eds), *Nazism. A Documentary Reader,* vol. 3 doc. no. 669 pp. 951–2

12 Lehnstaedt, 'Okkupation im Osten', pp. 212ff. has some interesting thoughts on this subject

13 Dieter Schenk, *Hans Frank. Hitlers Kronjurist und Generalgouverneur* (Frankfurt am Main 2008) pp. 165ff.

14 See my earlier work including *Germany Turns Eastwards. A Study of Ostforschung in the Third Reich* (London 2003, originally Cambridge 1988) which has an extensive discussion of the IdO

15 Christoph Klessmann, *Die Selbstbehauptung einer Nation. NS-Kulturpolitik und polnische Widerstandsbewegung* (Düsseldorf 1971) pp. 45–6

16 Czesław Madajczyk, *Die Okkupationspolitik Nazideutschlands in Polen 1939–1945* (Cologne 1988) pp. 305–6

17 Ibid., pp. 343ff.

18 Volker Riess, *Die Anfänge der Vernichtung 'lebensunwerten Lebens' in den Reichsgauen Danzig-Westpreussen und Wartheland 1939/40* (Frankfurt am Main 1995) pp. 21–106

19 Arthur Greiser to the district councillors of Posen regarding place name changes dated 8 November 1939, in Röhr (ed.), *Die faschistischen Okkupationspolitik in Polen,* doc. no. 28 p. 136

20 See the still useful Volker Kellermann, *Schwarzer Adler, Weisser Adler. Die Polenpolitik der Weimarer Republik* (Cologne 1970)

21 Confidential Protocol dated 28 September 1939, in *DGFP* Series D (1937–45) vol. 8 (London 1954) doc. no. 158 p. 165

22 Report on experience of the Office for Resettling Poles and Jews dated 26 January 1940, in Röhr (ed.), *Die faschistischen Okkupationspolitik in Polen* doc. no. 46 pp. 154–6

23 Bogdan Musial, *Deutsche Zivilverwaltung und Judenverfolgung im Generalgouvernement. Eine Fallstudie zum Distrikt Lublin 1939–1944* (Wiesbaden 1999) pp. 129–30

24 See Peter Black, 'Odilo Globocnik–Himmlers Vorposten im Osten', in R. Smelser, E. Syring and R. Zitelmann (eds), *Die braune Elite II* (Darmstadt 1993) pp. 103ff.

25 Joseph Poprzeczny, *Odilo Globocnik. Hitler's Man in the East* (Jefferson, North Carolina 2004) pp. 148–9

26 Pavel Polian, 'Hätte der Holocaust beinahe nicht stattgefunden?', in Johannes Hürter and Jürgen Zarusky (eds), *Besatzung, Kollaboration, Holocaust. Neue Studien zur Verfolgung und Ermordung der europäischen Juden* (Munich 2008) pp. 1–19

27 See Magnus Brechtken, *'Madagascar für die Juden'. Antisemitische Idee und politische Praxis 1885–1945* (Munich 1997) especially pp. 221ff.

28 Report by Waldemar Schön on the establishment of the Warsaw Ghetto dated 20 January 1941, in Noakes and Pridham (eds), *Nazism. A Documentary Reader,* vol. 3 doc. no. 784 pp. 1063–7

29 T. Berenstein (ed.), *Faschismus-Getto-Massenmord. Dokumentation über Aurottung und Woderstand der Juden in Polen während des zweiten Weltkrieges* (Frankfurt 1960) pp. 152–3

30 Musial, *Deutsche Zivilverwaltung und Judenverfolgung*, p. 190

31 Stephan Lehnstaedt, 'Alltägliche Gewalt. Die deutschen Besatzer in Warschau und die Ermordung der jüdischen Bevölkerung', in Hürter and Zarusky (eds), *Besatzung, Kollaboration, Holocaust*, pp. 90–4

32 Rosenberg report in Noakes and Pridham (eds), *Nazism. A Documentary Reader*, doc. no. 787 p. 1069

33 Ralf Georg Reuth (ed.), *Joseph Goebbels. Tagebücher 1924–1945* vols. 1–4 (Munich 1992) vol. 3 entry dated 2 November 1939, p. 1340

34 Saul Friedlander, *The Years of Extermination. Nazi Germany and the Jews 1939–1945* (London 2007) p. 39

35 Heinrich Himmler, 'Some Thoughts on the Treatment of the Alien Population in the East', in Noakes and Pridham (eds), *Nazism. A Documentary Reader*, vol. 3 doc. no. 651 p. 933

36 Chief of Protocol German Foreign Ministry to Ambassador von der Schulenburg dated 19 October 1939, in *DGFP* Series D (1937–45) vol. 8 (London 1954) doc. no. 283 pp. 323–4

37 Jan T. Gross, 'Die Sowjetisierung Ostpolens', in Bernd Wegner (ed.), *Zwei Wege nach Moskau. Vom Hitler–Stalin-Pakt zum 'Unternehmen Barbarossa'* (Munich 1991) p. 71

38 Secret Protocol dated 28 September 1939, in *DGFP* Series D doc. no. 160 p. 166

39 Beria memorandum to Stalin proposing the execution of the Polish officers, gendarmes, military settlers and others in the three special POW camps dated 5 March 1940, in Anna M. Cienciala, Natalia S. Lebedeva and Wojciech Materski (eds), *Katyń. A Crime without Punishment* (New Haven 2007) doc. no. 47 pp. 118–20

40 Cienciala, Lebedeva and Materski (eds), *Katyń. A Crime without Punishment* pp. 124–5

41 See Allen Paul, *Katyń. The Untold Story of Stalin's Polish Massacre* (New York 1991) and George Sanford, *Katyń and the Soviet Massacres of 1940. Truth, Justice and Memory* (London 2005)

42 Robert Edwards, *White Death. Russia's War on Finland 1939–40* (London 2006) p. 98

43 Ibid., p. 231

Chapter 6: Not Losing: Churchill's Britain

1 Gerhard Weinberg, *A World at Arms. A Global History of World War II* (Cambridge 1994) pp. 113ff.

2 Churchill speeches to the House of Commons on 11 April and 8 May 1940, in Robert Rhodes James (ed.), *Winston S. Churchill. His Complete Speeches 1897–1963* (New York 1974) vol. 6 pp. 6201–11 and pp. 6212–18

3 Roy Jenkins, *Churchill* (London 2001) p. 579

4 Ben Pimlott, *Hugh Dalton* (London 1995) pp. 275–6

5 Lynne Olson, *Troublesome Young Men. The Rebels Who Brought Churchill to Power and Helped Save England* (New York 2008)

6 Andrew Roberts, 'The Holy Fox'. The Life of Lord Halifax* (London 1991) pp. 197–209

7 For some of the above see Carlo D'Este, *Warlord. Churchill at War 1874–1945* (London 2009) and Geoffrey Best *Churchill and War* (London 2005)

8 D'Este, *Warlord*, pp. 242ff.

9 Best, *Churchill and War*, pp. 80–4

10 Martin Gilbert (ed.), *The Churchill War Papers*, vol. 2: *Never Surrender May 1940–December 1940* (London 1994) p. 1017, Winston Churchill to Private Office dated 31 October 1940

11 John Colville, *The Fringes of Power. Downing Street Diaries 1939–1955* (London 2004) entry dated 13 December 1940 p. 268

12 See the discussion in Eliot Cohen, *Supreme Command. Soldiers, Statesmen, and Leadership in Wartime* (New York 2002) pp. 118ff. and now Max Hastings, *Finest Years. Churchill as Warlord 1940–45* (London 2009)

13 Gilbert (ed.), *Churchill War Papers*, vol. 2: pp. 580–2

14 For an example on 15 August (at the height of the Battle of Britain) involving hostile responses to the Swinton Committee's search for fifth columnists see Rhodes James (ed.), *Winston S. Churchill. His Complete Speeches*, vol. 6 pp. 6255–60

15 Martin Gilbert (ed.), *The Churchill War Papers*, vol. 3: *The Ever-Widening War 1941* (London 2000) p. 775, debate on 10 June 1941

16 Andrew Roberts, 'The Religious Sense of Sir Winston Churchill', Lambeth Palace Library Lecture 2004

17 Gilbert (ed.), *Churchill War Papers*, vol. 3: p. 797, speech on the BBC on 12 June 1941

18 Most obviously Nicholson Baker, *Human Smoke* (London 2008) and Patrick J. Buchanan, *Churchill, Hitler, and the Unnecessary War* (New York 2008)

19 Cited by Stephen A. Garrett, *Ethics and Airpower in World War II. The British Bombing of German Cities* (New York 1993) pp. 26–9

20 Max Hastings, *Bomber Command* (London 1979) p. 48 cites the document extensively

21 Gilbert (ed.), *Churchill War Papers*, vol. 2: Harold Nicolson diaries entry dated 17 October 1940, p. 960

22 Colville, *Fringes of Power. Downing Street Diaries* entries dated 8 July 1940, p. 154, and 8 March 1941, p. 313

23 Ibid., entry dated 20 September 1940, p. 206

24 Gilbert (ed.), *Churchill War Papers*, vol. 2: p. 839, Churchill to Ismay 19 September 1940

25 Rhodes James (ed.), *Winston S. Churchill. His Complete Speeches*, vol. 6 p. 6248, speech dated 14 July 1940

26 David Cannadine, 'Churchill as the Voice of Destiny', in his *In Churchill's Shadow. Confronting the Past in Modern Britain* (Oxford 2003) pp. 104–8

27 Colville, *Fringes of Power. Downing Street Diaries* is littered with colour and incident

28 Gilbert (ed.), *Churchill War Papers*, vol. 3: p. 302 in an article from the *Canberra Times* dated 18 July 1942

29 John Lukacs, *Blood, Toil, Tears and Sweat. The Dire Warning. Churchill's First Speech as Prime Minister* (New York 2008) p. 47; the speech is in Rhodes James (ed.), *Winston S. Churchill. His Complete Speeches,* vol. 6 pp. 6218–20

30 See John Lukacs, *The Duel. Hitler vs. Churchill. 10 May–31 July 1940* (London 1990) pp. 90–6

31 John Lukacs, *Five Days in London. May 1940* (New Haven 1999) pp. 108ff.

32 Ben Pimlott (ed.), *The Second World War Diary of Hugh Dalton 1940–45* (London 1986) entry dated 28 May 1940, p. 29

33 Rhodes James (ed.), *Winston S. Churchill. His Complete Speeches*, vol. 6 p. 6238

34 Lukacs, *Blood, Toil, Tears and Sweat*, p. 120

35 Max Domarus (ed.), *Hitler. Speeches and Proclamations 1932–1945*, vol. 3: *1939–1940* (London 1997) p. 2062

36 Jeremy Noakes and Geoffrey Pridham (eds), *Nazism 1919–45. A Documentary Reader* (Exeter 1988) vol. 3 doc. nos. 572, 573, 574 pp. 787–91 illustrate the evolution of German thinking about Britain and Russia

37 Richard Overy, *The Battle* (London 2000) pp. 36–7

38 Richard Overy, *The Air War 1939–45* (London 1980) p. 37

39 Robert Wright, *Dowding and the Battle of Britain* (London 1969) does his best with this colourless character

40 Tim Vigors, *Life's Too Short to Cry* (London 2006) pp. 142–3

41 Rhodes James (ed.), *Winston S. Churchill. His Complete Speeches* vol. 6 p. 6266

42 See the very vivid account by Patrick Bishop, *Fighter Boys. Saving Britain 1940* (London 2004), as well as Laddie Lucas (ed.), *Voices in the Air 1939–1945* (London 2003) and Matthew Parker, *The Battle of Britain July–October 1940. An Oral History of Britain's 'Finest Hour'* (London 2000)

43 Vigors, *Life's Too Short to Cry* p. 132

44 David Ross, *Richard Hillary* (London 2003) p. 160 gives a very full account of a pilot who suffered severe burns

45 Patrick Bishop, *Bomber Boys. Fighting Back 1940–1945* (London 2007) p. 4

46 Overy, *Battle* pp. 90–2

47 Klaus A. Maier, 'Die Luftschlacht um England', in Klaus Maier, Horst Rohde, Bernd Stegemann and Hans Umbreit, *Die Errichtung der Hegemonie auf dem europäischen Kontinent*, vol. 2 of Militärgeschichtlichen Forschungsamt (eds), *Das Deutsche Reich und der Zweite Weltkrieg* (Stuttgart/Munich 1979) p. 390

48 Peter Stansky, *The First Day of the Blitz* (New Haven 2007) pp. 81–2

49 Pimlott (ed.), *Second World War Diary of Hugh Dalton,* entry dated 14 October 1940, p. 90

50 George Orwell, *A Patriot for All 1940–1941* in *Complete Works of George Orwell,* ed. Peter Davison (London 1998), diary entries in August and September 1940 interpolated with his writings and broadcasts from p. 237 onwards

51 Lukacs, *Duel,* p. 226

52 Warren Kimball, *Forged in War. Churchill, Roosevelt and the Second World War* (London 1997) p. 58

53 David Gordon, 'America First: The Anti-War Movement, Charles Lindbergh and the Second World War, 1940–1941', *Historical Society and the New York Military Affairs Symposium* (2003)

54 George C. Herring, *From Colony to Superpower. US Foreign Relations since 1776* (Oxford 2008) pp. 506–7

55 Gilbert (ed.), *Churchill War Papers*, vol. 3 pp. 44–45

56 Nicholas John Cull, *Selling War. The British Propaganda Campaign against American 'Neutrality' in World War II* (Oxford 1995) pp. 170–3

57 Herring, *From Colony to Superpower*, p. 528

58 Kimball, *Forged in War,* p. 83

59 Richard Overy, *Why the Allies Won* (London 1995) p. 30

60 For an excellent account of Operation Compass see Adrian Fort, *Archibald Wavell: The Life and Times of an Imperial Servant* (London 2009) pp. 153–75

61 D'Este, *Warlord*, pp. 584–9

62 Fort, *Archibald Wavell,* pp. 210ff.

63 Ibid., p. 240

Chapter 7: 'Give Me your Watch and I'll Tell You the Time': Nazi Occupied Europe

1 Nigel Nicolson (ed.), *The Harold Nicolson Diaries 1907–1963* (London 2004) 10 April 1939 p. 186 note 1

2 Frederick Spotts *The Shameful Peace. How French Artists and Intellectuals Survived the Nazi Occupation* (New Haven 2008) p. 55

3 Jørgen Haestrup, *European Resistance Movements 1939–1945. A Complete History* (Westport, Connecticut 1981) p. 211

4 Richard Petrow, *The Bitter Years. The Invasion and Occupation of Denmark and Norway April 1940–May 1945* (London 1974) pp. 46–7

5 Guidelines for the troops issued by General Nikolaus von Falkenhorst dated 13 March 1940, in Fritz Petrick (ed.), *Die Okkupationspolitik des deutschen Faschismus in Dänemark und Norwegen 1940–1945* vol. 7 of Bundesarchiv (ed.), *Europa unterm Hakenkreuz* (Berlin 1992) p. 76

6 Fritz Petrick, 'Dänemark, das "Musterprotektorat"?', in Robert Bohn (ed.), *Die deutsche Herrschaft in den 'germanischen' Ländern 1940–1945* (Stuttgart 1997) pp. 120ff.

7 Telegram from Renthe-Fink to the Foreign Ministry dated 14 June 1941, in Petrick (ed.), *Die Okkupationspolitik des deutschen Faschismus in Dänemark und Norwegen,* p. 111

8 Annual Political Report by Cecil von Renthe-Fink dated 22 March 1941, in Petrick (ed.), *Die Okkupationspolitik des deutschen Faschismus in Dänemark und Norwegen,* p. 107

9 Hans Frederik Dahl, *Quisling. A Study in Treachery* (Cambridge 1999) p. 182; see also Oddvar Hoidal's massive *Vidkun Quisling. A Study of Treason* (London 1989)

10 See the standard work by Alan S. Milward, *The Fascist Economy in Norway* (Oxford 1972)

11 Robert Bohn, 'Die Instrumenten der deutschen Herrschaft im Reichskommissariat Norwegen', in Bohn (ed.), *Die deutsche Herrschaft in den 'germanischen' Ländern*, pp. 71–94

12 Tore Gjelsvik, *Norwegian Resistance 1940–1945* (London 1979) p. 19

13 Martin Moll, 'Die deutsche Propaganda in den besetzten "germanischen" Staaten' in Bohn (ed.), *Die deutsche Herrschaft in den "germanischen" Ländern*, pp. 230–1

14 Petrow, *Bitter Years*, pp. 111–3

15 Stein Ugelvik Larsen, Beatrice Sandberg and Volker Dahm (eds), *Meldungen aus Norwegen 1940–1945. Die geheimen Lageberichte des Befehlshabers der Sicherheitspolizei und des SD in Norwegen* (Munich 2008) vol. 1, p. 232, report dated 3 April 1941 (Café Viking incident); p. 301 report dated 11 June 1941 (shit and swine country); p. 319 report dated 30 June 1941 (Hitler an idiot); p. 15, report dated 30 July 1940 (suicide attempt); p. 83, report dated 26 August 1940 (moral injunctions 'what we must never forget')

16 Ibid., p. 351 report dated 28 July 1941

17 Gerhard Hirschfeld, *Nazi Rule and Dutch Collaboration. The Netherlands under German Occupation 1940–1945* (Oxford 1988) pp. 57–86

18 Alan Clinton, *Jean Moulin 1899–1943. The French Resistance and the Republic* (London 2002) pp. 88–91

19 For an account which emphasises the fate both of prisoners of war and refugees see Richard Vinen, *The Unfree French. Life under the Occupation* (London 2006)

20 Yves Durand, 'Collaboration French-style. A European Perspective', in Sarah Fishman, Laura L. Downs, Ioannis Sinanoglu, Leonard V. Smith and Robert Zaretsky (eds), *France at War. Vichy and the Historians* (Oxford 2000) p. 63

21 David Bidussa and Denis Peschanski (eds), *La France de Vichy* (Milan 1996) p. 160

22 Alan S. Milward, *War, Economy and Society 1939–1945* (London 1987) p. 138

23 Harry Roderick Kedward, *Resistance in Vichy France. A Study of Ideas and Motivation in the Southern Zone 1940–1942* (Oxford 1978) p. 45

24 Robert Paxton, *Vichy France. Old Guard and New Order 1940–1944* (New York 1972) p. 68 for Laval's offer of pilots

25 Ibid., p. 374

26 Robert Frank, 'Die französische Kollaboration', in Bundesarchiv (ed.), *Europa unterm Hakenkreuz,* supplementary volume *Okkupation und Kollaboration (1938–1945)* (Berlin 1994) p. 90

27 Julian Jackson, *France. The Dark Years 1940–1944* (Oxford 2001) p. 99

28 Jean Guéhenno, *Journal des années noires 1940–1944* (Paris 1947) entry dated 7 August 1941, p. 137

29 Stanley Hoffmann, *Decline and Renewal? France since the 1930s* (New York 1974) pp. 26ff. is still very pertinent on this distinction

30 Jackson, *Dark Years*, pp. 143–4

31 Maurice Larkin, *France since the Popular Front. Government and People 1936–1996* (Oxford 1997) p. 98

32 Robert Gildea, *Marianne in Chains. In Search of the German Occupation 1940–1945* (London 2002) p. 142

33 From a vast literature see most recently Shannon L. Fogg, *The Politics of Everyday Life in Vichy France. Foreigners, Undesirables and Strangers* (Cambridge 2008)

34 Don and Petie Kladstrup, *Wine & War. The French, the Nazis, and France's Greatest Treasure* (London 2001) p. 128

35 There is an interesting discussion of these issues by W. D. Halls, 'Catholics, the Vichy Interlude, and After', in Fishman et al. (eds), *France at War. Vichy and the Historians*, especially pp. 234ff.

36 For examples drawn from several regions see Philip W. Whitcomb (ed.), *France during the German Occupation 1940–1944. A Collection of 292 Statements on the Government of Maréchal Pétain and Pierre Laval* (Stanford, California 1958) vol. 1 pp. 411ff.

37 Michael R. Marrus and Robert O. Paxton, *Vichy France and the Jews* (New York 1983)

38 Susan Zuccotti, *The Holocaust, the French and the Jews* (Lincoln, Nebraska 1993) pp. 60–1

39 Agnès Humbert, *Résistance. Memoirs of Occupied France* (London 2008) entry dated 6 August 1940, p. 9

40 For examples see Gildea, *Marianne in Chains*, p.72

41 For a vivid evocation of this world by a highly informed commentator see David Pryce-Jones, *Paris in the Third Reich. A History of the German Occupation 1940–1944* (London 1981)

42 Spotts, *Shameful Peace*, pp. 36–9

43 Walter Bargatzky, *Hotel Majestic. Ein Deutsche im besetzten Frankreich* (Freiburg 1987) is evocative

44 None of these questions is even posed in Mark Mazower's *Hitler's Empire. How the Nazis Ruled Europe* (London 2008) which seems otherwise dedicated to smearing the record of various colonial empires through association with Nazism. The French art world is depicted as synonymous with Jean Cocteau, who was hardly a typical case

45 Most recently in Spotts's acerbic *The Shameful Peace. How French Artists and Intellectuals Survived the Occupation* although see also Michèle Cone, *Artists under Vichy. A Case of Prejudice and Persecution* (Princeton 1992) and Alice Kaplan, *The Collaborator. The Trial and Execution of Robert Brasillach* (Chicago 2000)

46 The Taittinger Champagne house did this with labels marked 'Reserved for the Wehrmacht' even though one Taittinger was a prominent collaborator; see Don and Petie Kladstrup, *Wine & War*, p. 91. See also a report on a historical conference on delation at Caen, 'Petty disputes led to Nazi denunciation in WWII France', *Daily Telegraph* 3 December 2008

47 (Jean Bruller) Vercors, *The Silence of the Sea*, trans. Cyril Connolly (New York 1944) pp. 38–9

48 Whitcomb, *France during the German Occupation*, vol. 2 pp. 593ff. for Gabolde's testimony

49 Rab Bennett, *Under the Shadow of the Swastika. The Moral Dilemmas of Resistance and Collaboration in Hitler's Europe* (London 1999) pp. 100–4

50 For this important contrast see Ulrich Herbert, *Best. Biographisches Studien über Radikalismus, Weltanschauung und Vernunft 1903–1989* (Bonn 1996) pp. 300–2

51 Gildea, *Marianne in Chains*, pp. 243–4

52 Herbert, *Best*, pp. 303–5

Chapter 8: Barbarossa

1 Johannes Hürter, *Hitlers Heerführer. Die deutschen Oberbefehlshaber im Krieg gegen die Sowjetunion 1941/42* (Munich 2006) p. 175

2 See Adam Tooze, *The Wages of Destruction. The Making and Breaking of the Nazi Economy* (London 2006) pp. 461ff.

3 Jürgen Förster and Evan Mawdsley, 'Hitler and Stalin in Perspective. Secret Speeches on the Eve of Barbarossa', *War in History* (2004) 11 pp. 61ff.

4 Halder, *Kriegstagebuch tägliche Aufzeich-hungen des Chefs des Generalstabes des Heeres 1939–42* ed. Hans-Adolf Jacobsen (Stuttgart 2004) vol. 2 entry dated 30 March 1941, p. 337

5 Hermann Graml, 'Am Beispiel meines Bruders. Oberleutnant Bernhard Graml', in Christian Hartmann (ed.), *Von Feldherren und Gefreiten. Zur biographischen Dimension des Zweiten Weltkriegs* (Munich 2008) pp. 57–68

6 Gerd R. Ueberschär, 'Die Einbeziehung Skandinaviens in die Planung "Barbarossa"', in Horst Boog, Jürgen Förster, Joachim Hoffmann, Ernst Klink, Rolf-Dieter Müller and Gerd R. Ueberschär (eds), *Der Angriff auf die Sowjetunion* (Frankfurt am Main 1991) p. 463, and Thomas Schlemmer (ed.), *Die Italiener an der Ostfront 1942/43. Dokumente zu Mussolinis Krieg gegen die Sowjetunion* (Munich 2005)

7 Jürgen Förster, 'Die Gewinning von Verbündeten in Südosteeuropa' in *Der Angriff auf die Sowjetunion*, in Boog et al. (eds), pp. 396ff.

8 Manfred Menger, 'Deutschland und der finnische "Sonderkrieg" gegen die Sowjetunion', in Bernd Wegner (ed.), *Zwei Wege nach Moskau. Vom Hitler–Stalin-Pakt zum 'Unternehmen Barbarossa'* (Munich 1991) pp. 548–54

9 Evan Mawdsley, *Thunder in the East. The Nazi–Soviet War 1941–1945* (London 2005) pp. 42–3

10 Klaus Schüler, 'Der Ostfeldzug als Transport-und Versorgungsproblem', in Wegner (ed.), *Zwei Wege nach Moskau*, p.220 for these statistics

11 Geoffrey Megargee, *Barbarossa 1941. Hitler's War of Annihilation* (Stroud 2008) p. 53

12 Andreas Hillgruber, 'Das Russland-Bild der führenden deutschen Militärs vor Beginn des Angriffs auf die Sowjetunion', in Wegner (ed.), *Zwei Wege nach Moskau*, p. 180; John Colville, *The Fringes of Power. Downing Street Diaries 1939–1955* (London 2004) entry dated 21 June 1941, p. 350

13 On planning for Operation Barbarossa see Ernst Klink, 'Die militärische Konzeption des Krieges gegen die Sowjetunion', in Boog et al. (eds), *Der Angriff auf die Sowjetunion*, pp. 246ff.

14 'Brauschitsch Regelung des Einsatzes der Sicherheitspolizei und des SD im Verbande des Heeres' dated 28 April 1941, in Gerd R. Ueberschär and Wolfram Wette (eds), *Der deutsche Überfall auf die Sowjetunion. 'Unternehmen Barbarossa' 1941* (Frankfurt am Main 1991) doc. no. 4 pp. 249–50

15 Boog, Förster, Hoffman, Klink, Müller, Üeberschar (eds), *Der Angriff auf die Sowjetunion* (Frankfurt am Main 1983), p. 509

16 'Erlass über der Kriegsgerichtsbarkeit im Gebiet "Barbarossa" und über besondere Massnahmen der Truppe' dated 13 May 1941, in Ueberschär and Wette (eds), *Der deutsche Überfall auf die Sowjetunion*, doc. no. 5 pp. 252–3

17 See Jürgen Förster, 'Das Unternehmen "Barbarossa" als Eroberungs- und Vernichtungskrieg', in Boog et al. (eds), *Der Angriff auf die Sowjetunion*, pp. 498–525

18 Christian Streit, *Keine Kameraden. Die Wehrmacht und die sowjetischen Kriegsgefangenen 1941–1945* (Stuttgart 1980)

19 Hürter, *Hitlers Heerführer*, p. 290

20 Menger, 'Deutschland und der finnische "Sonderkrieg" gegen die Sowjetunion', pp. 554–60

21 Stefan Schmitz (ed.), *Willy Peter Reese. Mir selber seltsam fremd. Die Unmenschlichkeit des Krieges. Russland 1941–44* (Munich 2003) pp. 85–6

22 Halder, *Kriegstagebuch*, vol. 3 entry dated 11 August 1941, p. 170

23 Mawdsley, *Thunder in the East*, p. 110

24 For a very interesting account of these operations see Robert M. Citino, *Death of the Wehrmacht. The German Campaigns of 1942* (Lawrence, Kansas 2007) especially pp. 152ff.

25 Rolf-Dieter Müller, '"Was wir an Hunger ausstehen müssen, könnt Ihr Euch gar nicht denken". Eine Armee verhungert', in Wolfgang Wette and Gerd R. Ueberschär (eds), *Stalingrad. Mythos und Wirklichkeit einer Schlact* (Frankfurt am Main 1993) pp. 131ff. for these vivid examples

26 Anthony Beevor, *Stalingrad* (London 1998) is the classic account; see also the earlier Wette and Ueberschär (eds), *Stalingrad: Mythos und Wirklichkeit*

27 Wette, Uberschär (eds) *Stalingrad*, p. 181

28 Johannes Hürter '"Es herrschen Sitten und Gebräuche, genauso wie im 30-Jährigen Krieg". Das erste Jahr des deutsch–sowjetischen Krieges in Dokumenten des General Gotthard Heinrici', *VfZ* (2000) 48 doc. no. 3, letter to his wife dated 22 April 1941 p. 367

29 Ibid., doc. no. 12 p. 371

30 Ibid., doc. no. 15, letter to his wife dated 11 July 1941, pp. 372–3

31 Ibid., doc. no. 18, letter to his wife dated 1 August 1941, p. 374

32 Ibid., doc. no. 27, letter to his family dated 8 October 1941, p. 380

33 Ibid., doc. no. 28, war report to his family dated 23 October 1941, p. 381

34 Ibid., doc. no. 35, war report to his family dated 19 November 1941, pp. 385–6

35 Ibid., doc. no. 42, letter to his wife dated 12 December 1941, p. 391

36 See the sensible discussion by Horst Möller, the director of the Institut für Zeitgeschichte, in the foreword to the informed collection of essays Christian Hartmann, Johannes Hürter and Ulrike Jureit (eds), *Verbrechen der Wehrmacht. Bilanz einer Debatte* (Munich 2005) p. 12, a corrective to the controversial book Hannes Heer and Klaus Naumann (eds) *Vernichtungskrieg. Verbrechen der Wehrmacht 1941–1944* (Hamburg 1995) and the exhibition catalogue Hamburg Institute for Social Research (ed.), *The German Army and Genocide. Crimes against War Prisoners, Jews and Other Civilians 1939–1944* (New York 1999)

37 General Manstein, 'Armeebefehl der Oberbefehlshabers der 11 Armee', dated 20 November 1941, in Ueberschär and Wette (eds), *Der deutsche Überfall auf die Sowjetunion*, doc. no. 22 p. 289

38 Oberkommando der Wehrmacht (ed.), *Mitteilungen für die Truppe*, June 1941 doc. no. 112

39 Krisztián Ungváry, 'Das Beispiel der ungarischen Armee', in Hartmann, Hürter and Jureit (eds), *Verbrechen der Wehrmacht*, pp. 98ff.

40 Felix Römer, 'Truppenführer als Täter. Das Beispiel des Majors Günther Drange', in Hartmann (ed.), *Von Feldherren und Gefreiten*, pp. 69ff.

41 Dieter Pohl, *Die Herrschaft der Wehrmacht. Deutsche Militärbesatzung und einheimische Bevölkerung in der Sowjetunion 1941–1944* (Munich 2008) p. 205

42 Bogdan Musial, *'Konterrevolutionaere Elemente sind zu erschiessen'. Die Brutalisierung des deutsch–sowjetischen Krieges im Sommer 1941* (Berlin 2000) p. 114

43 Ibid., p. 138

44 Franz W. Seidler (ed.), *Verbrechen an der Wehrmacht. Kriegsgruel der Roten Armee 1941/42* (Selent 1997) case 039 Gericht der 4 Gebirgsdivsion dated 9 July 1941, p. 115

45 Ibid., case 065 p. 162

46 Reichenau telegram dated 24 December 1941 which began, 'STALIN HAT AM JAHRESTAGE DER BOLSHEWISTISCHEN REVOLUTION BEFOHLEN, DASZ JEDER DEUTSCHE AUF RUSSISCHEN BODEN GETOETET WERDEN MUESSE, HAT ALSO DEN ABSOLUTEN VERNICHTUNGSKRIEG VERKUENDET' – in Ueberschär and Wette (eds), *Der deutsche Überfall auf die Sowjetunion*, doc. no. 23 p. 291

47 Hürter, 'Es herrschten Sitten und Gebräuche', doc. no. 13, Heinrici letter to his wife dated 6 July 1941, p. 371

48 Ibid., doc. no. 34, diary entry dated 7 November 1941, p. 385, and doc. no. 35, report to his family dated 19 November 1941, p. 385

49 Ibid., doc. no. 36, diary entry dated 19 November 1941, p. 387

50 Pohl, *Die Herrschaft der Wehrmacht,* p. 208

51 Streit, *Keine Kameraden. Die Wehrmacht und die sowjetischen Kriegsgefangenen*

52 Helmut Krausnick, *Hitlers Einsatzgruppen. Die Truppen des Weltanschauungskrieges 1938–1942* (Frankfurt am Main 1985) pp. 225–6

53 Hermann Hoth, 'Armeebefehl des Oberbefehlshabers der 17 Armee', dated 17 November 1941, in Ueberschär and Wette (eds), *Der deutsche Überfall auf die Sowjetunion*, doc. no. 21 p. 287

54 Ibid., p. 289

55 Krausnick, *Hitlers Einsatzgruppen*, pp. 226–7

56 Hürter, *Hitlers Heerführer*, p. 519

57 Krausnick, *Hitlers Einsatzgruppen*, p. 179

58 Hürter, *Hitlers Heerführer*, pp. 540–1

59 'Polizeilicher Tätigkeitsbericht der Einsatzgruppe B für das H.Gr.Kdo Mitte für die Zeit von ca. 9 bis 16.7.1941', in Johannes Hürter, 'Auf dem Weg zur Militäropposition. Tresckow, Gersdorff, der Vernichtungskrieg und der Judenmord. Neue Dokumente über das Verhältnis der Heeresgruppe Mitte zur Einsatzgruppe B im Jahre 1941', *VfZ* (2004) 52 pp. 552–6

60 Wolfram Wette, *Die Wehrmacht. Feindbilder, Vernichtungskrieg, Legenden* (Frankfurt am Main 2002) p. 119

61 Pohl, *Die Herrschaft der Wehrmacht*, pp. 259–61

62 'Verhalten der Truppe im Osten', issued 10 October 1941 by Field Marshal von Reichenau in Ueberschär, and Wette (eds), *Der deutsche Überfall auf die Sowjetunion*, doc. no. 83 pp. 284–6, including Rundstedt's order to generalise it throughout Army Group South

63 Andrej Angrick, 'Das Beispiel Charkow. Massenmord unter deutscher Besatzung', in Hartmann, Hürter and Jureit (eds), *Verbrechen der Wehrmacht*, pp. 117–24

64 For the above see Oliver von Wrochem, *Erich von Manstein. Vernichtungskrieg und Geschichtspolitik* (Paderborn 2006) pp. 71–8

65 Krausnick, *Hitlers Einsatzgruppen*, p. 240

66 Wrochem, *Erich von Manstein*, p. 78

Chapter 9: Global War

1 Robert Rhodes James (ed.), *Winston S. Churchill. His Complete Speeches 1897–1963* (New York 1974) vol. 6 p. 6429

2 David Carlton, *Churchill and the Soviet Union* (Manchester 2000) pp. 87–8

3 David Dilks (ed.), *The Diaries of Sir Alexander Cadogan 1938–1945* (London 1971) entry dated 17 December 1941, p. 422, and David Carlton, *Anthony Eden* (London 1981) pp. 191ff.

4 See the lucid discussion in Nicholas Tarling, *A Sudden Rampage. The Japanese Occupation of Southeast Asia 1941–1945* (London 2001) pp. 61–8

5 Richard Overy with Andrew Wheatcroft, *The Road to War* (London 1999) p. 292

6 Akira Iriye, *The Origins of the Second World War in Asia and the Pacific* (London 1987) pp. 150–1

7 Herbert Bix, *Hirohito and the Making of Modern Japan* (New York 2000) p. 401

8 Ibid., pp. 411–12

9 Tarling, *Sudden Rampage*, p. 77

10 Ian Kershaw, *Fateful Choices. Ten Decisions that Changed the World 1940–1941* (London 2007) p. 353

11 Overy with Wheatcroft, *Road to War*, p. 296

12 Tarling, *Sudden Rampage*, p. 80

13 S. Tonnesson, *The Vietnamese Revolution of 1945* (Oslo 1991) p. 34

14 Jonathan R. Adelman, 'German–Japanese Relations 1941–1945', in Jonathan R. Adelman (ed.), *Hitler and his Allies in World War II* (London 2007) p. 47

15 Norman Dixon, *On the Psychology of Military Incompetence* (London 1976) p. 136

16 Keith Simpson, 'Lieutenant-General Arthur Percival', in John Keegan (ed.), *Churchill's Generals* (London 1991) pp. 265–6 is coolly devastating

17 For this and much more of learning and sense see Christopher Bayly and Tim Harper, *Forgotten Armies. Britain's Asian Empire and the War with Japan* (London 2005) p. 68

18 See the obituary of 'Lieutenant-Commander Geoffrey Brooke 1920–2009', *The Times* 4 March 2009 p. 58. Brooke was on the *Prince of Wales* when she was sunk. After returning to Singapore, he fled on a junk on what turned out to be a 1,600-mile voyage to Ceylon

19 Nigel Nicolson (ed.), *The Harold Nicolson Diaries 1907–1963* (London 2004) entry dated 27 February 1942, p. 258

20 For some vivid Japanese accounts of the fighting in Burma see John Nunneley and Kazuo Tamayama (eds), *Tales by Japanese Soldiers of the Burma Campaign 1942–1945* (London 2000)

21 Robert Lyman, *Slim, Master of War. Burma and the Birth of Modern Warfare* (London 2004)

22 Tarling, *Sudden Rampage*, pp. 95–100

23 Ibid., p. 55

24 Bayly and Harper, *Forgotten Armies*, pp. 114–5

25 For the above see Raymond Lamont-Brown, *Kempeitai. Japan's Dreaded Secret Police* (Thrupp 1998) pp. 149ff.; Bayly and Harper, *Forgotten Armies*, pp. 211ff.; and A. Frank Reel, *The Case of General Yamashita* (Chicago 1949)

26 Louis de Jong, *The Collapse of a Colonial Society. The Dutch in Indonesia during the Second World War* (Leiden 2002) p. 43

27 Tarling, *Sudden Rampage*, pp. 125–33

28 Bayly and Harper, *Forgotten Armies*, p. 120

29 Ibid., p. 128

30 Lewis Gann, 'Western and Japanese Colonialism', in Ramon Myers and Mark Peattie (eds), *The Japanese Colonial Empire 1895–1945* (Princeton 1984) p. 518

Chapter 10: The Resistance

1 Roderick Kedward, *Resistance in Vichy France. A Study of Ideas and Motivation in the Southern Zone 1940–1942* (Oxford 1978) p. 186

2 Ibid., p. 275

3 Julian Jackson, *France. The Dark Years 1940–1944* (Oxford 2001) pp. 419ff.

4 Kedward, *Resistance in Vichy France*, pp. 251–252

5 The psychology of resisters is perfunctorily treated by Roderick Kedward in *La Vie en Bleu. France and the French since 1900* (London 2005) pp. 282–3

6 Henri Frenay, *The Night Will End. Memoirs of the Resistance* (London 1976) pp. 27–8 for Frenay's political evolution and p. 245 on the arrest of Renouvin

7 See Lucie Aubrac, *Outwitting the Gestapo* (Lincoln, Nebraska 1993) with its often luminous descriptions of family life

8 Frenay, *Night Will End*, p. 158

9 Dominique Veillon, 'The Resistance and Vichy', in Sarah Fishman, Laura L. Downs, Ioannis Sinanoglu, Leonard V. Smith and Robert Zaretsky (eds), *France at War. Vichy and the Historians* (Oxford 2000) pp. 161ff.; see also Olivier Wieviorka, *Une Certaine Idée de la Résistance. Défense de la France 1940–1949* (Paris 1995)

10 On the different strands in Resistance see Kedward, *Resistance in Vichy France*, pp. 32–3 and Frenay, *Night Will End*, p. 13 for his 1938 lecture

11 Agnès Humbert, *Résistance. Memoirs of Occupied France* (London 2008) pp. 11–12

12 Harry Stone, *Writing in the Shadow. Resistance Publications in Occupied Europe* (London 1996)

13 Jackson, *France. The Dark Years*, p. 408

14 Frenay, *Night Will End*, p. 155

15 Jackson, *France. The Dark Years*, p. 479

16 Rab Bennett, *Under the Shadow of the Swastika. The Moral Dilemmas of Resistance and Collaboration in Hitler's Europe* (London 1999) p. 148

17 Nigel Perrin, *Spirit of Resistance. The Life of SOE Agent Harry Peulevé* (Barnsley 2008) pp. 95–6

18 William Jordan, *Conquest without Victory. A New Zealander's Experiences in the Resistance in Greece and France* (London 1969) pp. 229–32

19 For what follows see mainly Tzvetan Todorov, *A French Tragedy. Scenes of Civil War, Summer 1944* (Hanover, New Hampshire 1996)

20 Robert Gildea, 'Resistance, Reprisals and Community in Occupied France', *Transactions of the Royal Historical Society* 13 (2003) pp. 168–70, and Jean-Marie Mocq, *La 12 SS-Panzer-Division. Massacre: Ascq. Cité martyre* (Bordeaux 1994)

21 Max Hastings, *Das Reich. The March of the 2nd SS Panzer Division through France June 1944* (London 1981) pp. 118ff. is indispensable as an account

22 See Jean-Jacques Fouché and Gilbert Beaubatie, *Tulle. Nouveaux regards sur les pendaisons et les événements de juin 1944* (Paris 2008) and Peter Lieb, 'Répression et massacres. L'occupant allemand face à la résistance française 1943–1944', in Gaël Eismann and Stefan Maertens (eds), *Occupation et répression militaires allemandes 1939–1945* (Paris 2006) pp. 169–85

Chapter 11: Moral Calculus

1 David Stafford, *Churchill and Secret Service* (London 1995) p. 218

2 David Stafford, *Britain and European Resistance 1940–1945. A Survey of the Special Operations Executive, with Documents* (Oxford 1980) p. 24

3 M. R. D. Foot, *SOE. The Special Operations Executive 1940–1946* (London 1999) p. 18

4 Stafford, *Britain and European Resistance*, p. 56

5 Ben Pimlott, *Hugh Dalton* (London 1995) pp. 317–18

6 See Nigel Perrin, *Spirit of Resistance. The Life of SOE Agent Harry Peulevé* (Barnsley 2008) pp. 15–16

7 Knut Haukelid, *Skis against the Atom* (Minot, North Dakota 1989) p. 43

8 M. R. D. Foot, 'SOE in the Low Countries', in Mark Seaman (ed.), *Special Operations Executive. A New Instrument of War* (London 2006) p. 87

9 Roderick Bailey (ed.), *Forgotten Voices of the Secret War. An Inside History of Special Operations during the Second World War* (London 2008) pp. 121–3

10 Knud V. Jespersen, 'SOE and Denmark', in Seaman (ed.), *Special Operations Executive*, pp. 196–199

11 Marcus Binney, *Secret War Heroes. Men of the Special Operations Executive* (London 2005) pp. 201–7

12 'The Distant Future', Joint Planning Staff Review of Future Strategy dated 14 June 1941, in Stafford, *Britain and European Resistance*, Appendix 4 pp. 234–9

13 Rab Bennett, *Under the Shadow of the Swastika. The Moral Dilemmas of Resistance and Collaboration in Hitler's Europe* (London 1999) p. 243

14 Ibid., p. 133

15 Henri Frenay, *The Night Will End. Memoirs of the Resistance* (London 1976) p. 162

16 For some of these complications see Roderick Bailey, *The Wildest Province. SOE in the Land of the Eagle* (London 2008) pp. 149ff.

17 Foot, *SOE. The Special Operations Executive* pp. 177ff.

18 Ibid., 'Special Operations Executive', Joint Planning Staff report dated 9 August 1941, pp. 240–5

19 Richard Petrow, *The Bitter Years. The Invasion and Occupation of Denmark and Norway April 1940–May 1945* (London 1974) pp. 126–9

20 Lieutenant Jens Anton Poulsson cited in Bailey (ed.), *Forgotten Voices of the Secret War*, p. 137

21 Ibid., testimony of Lieutenant Joachim Rønneberg, p. 140

22 For this and the following paragraph see Haukelid's *Skis against the Atom*, pp. 97ff.

23 Ibid., p. 187

24 For some of these details see Richard Rhodes, *The Making of the Atomic Bomb* (New York 1986) pp. 512–17

25 Jørgen Haestrup, *European Resistance Movements 1939–1945. A Complete History* (Westport, Conecticut 1981) p. 453

26 See Chad Bryant, *Prague in Black. Nazi Rule and Czech Nationalism* (Cambridge, Massachusetts 2007) pp. 41–5

27 Ibid., pp. 168–9 for this exchange of views

28 Stanislaw Berton, 'Das Attentat auf Reinhard Heydrich vom 27 Mai 1942. Ein Bericht des Kriminalrats Heinz Pannwitz', *VfZ* (1985) 33 p. 688

29 Bennett, *Under the Shadow of the Swastika*, p. 261

30 Michal Burian, Aleš Knížek, Jiří Rajlich and Eduard Stehlík, *Assassination. Operation Anthropoid 1941–1942* (Ministry of Defence, Prague 2002) is the best recent study, although the older study by Callum MacDonald, *The Killing of Obergruppenführer Reinhard Heydrich* (London 1990) is still useful

31 James Holland, *Italy's Sorrow. A Year of War 1944–5* (London 2008) pp. xxxiiiff.

32 Steffen Prauser, 'Mord in Rom? Der Anschlag in der Via Rasella und die deutsche Vergeltung in den Fosse Ardeatine im März 1944', *VfZ* (2002) 50 pp. 269ff.

33 Richard Lamb, *War in Italy 1943–1945. A Brutal Story* (New York 1994) pp. 65–6 for this document

34 Holland, *Italy's Sorrow*, pp. 264–6

Chapter 12: Beneath the Mask of Command

1 Walter Warlimont, *Inside Hitler's Headquarters 1939–45* (London 1964) p. 315

2 Jonathan Adelman, 'German–Japanese Relations 1941–1945', in Jonathan Adelman (ed.), *Hitler and his Allies in World War II* (London 2007) p. 50

3 Galeazzo Ciano, *Diary 1937–1943*, ed. Robert Miller and Stanislao Pugliese (London 2002) entries dated 31 May 1941, p. 431; 30 June 1941, p. 440; 25 February 1942, p.497

4 Bernd Wegner, 'Japan und der Krieg in Europa', in H. Boog, W. Rahn, R. Stumpf and B. Wegner (eds), *Die Welt im Krieg 1941–1943*, vol. 1: *Von Pearl Harbor zum Bombenkrieg in Europa* (Frankfurt am Main 1992) pp. 195–9

5 Robert Lyman, *The Generals. From Defeat to Victory, Leadership in Asia 1941–45* (London 2008) pp. 23–24

6 F. W. Deakin, *The Brutal Friendship. Mussolini, Hitler and the Fall of Italian Fascism* (New York 1968) pp. 27–31 is still fundamental

7 Alex Danchev, *Very Special Relationship* (London 1986) and John Keegan, *Churchill's Generals* (London 1991) p. 62

8 Ciano, *Diary*, entry dated 3 November 1941, p. 461

9 Ibid., entry dated 13 October 1941, p. 454

10 Davide Rodogno, *Fascism's European Empire. Italian Occupation during the Second World War* (Cambridge 2006) pp. 34–6

11 Jürgen Förster, 'Die Entscheidung der "Dreierpaktstaaten"', in Horst Boog, Jürgen Förster, Joachim Hoffmann, Ernst Klink, Rolf-Dieter Müller and Gerd R. Ueberschär (eds), *Der Angriff auf die Sowjetunion* (Frankfurt am Main 1991) pp. 1065–8

12 Thomas Schlemmer, 'Giovanni Messe. Ein Italienischer General zwischen Koalitions-und Befreiungskrieg', in Christian Hartmann (ed.), *Von Feldherren und Gefreiten. Zur biographischen Dimension des Zweiten Weltkriegs* (Munich 2008) pp. 33–8

13 Philip Morgan, *The Fall of Mussolini* (Oxford 2008) pp. 52–5 is fascinating on the Italians in Russia

14 Albert Kesselring, *The Memoirs of Field-Marshal Kesselring* (London 2007) pp. 121 and 178

15 'Gefechtsbericht des Deutschen Verbindungskommandos bei der Division "Ravenna"', dated 20 March 1943, in Thomas Schlemmer (ed.), *Die Italiener an der Ostfront 1942/43.*

Dokumente zu Mussolinis Krieg gegen die Sowjetunion (Munich 2005) doc. no. 9 p. 125

16 Report by Colonel Francesco Polito to the Commander of the 'Cosseria' Infantry Division dated 28 March 1943 in Schlemmer (ed.) *Die Italiener an der Ostfront 1942/43*, doc. no. 24 pp. 223–34

17 Rolf-Dieter Müller, *An der Seite der Wehrmacht. Hitlers ausländische Helfer beim 'Kreuzzug gegen den Bolshewismus' 1941–45* (Berlin 2007) pp. 81ff.

18 Brian Sullivan, 'The Italian Soldier in Combat, June 1940–September 1943: Myths, Realities and Explanations', in Paul Addison and Angus Calder (eds), *Time to Kill. The Soldier's Experience of War in the West 1939–45* (London 1997) pp. 177ff. is excellent on the problems of the Italian army

19 Kesselring, *Memoirs*, pp. 107–8

20 Rodogno, *Fascism's European Empire*, pp. 179–81

21 Jonathan Steinberg, *All or Nothing. The Axis and the Holocaust 1941–1943* (London 1990) p. 60. Although Steinberg's book is rather rosy-tinted about the Italians, he was one of the first to undertake comparative studies of the two Axis partners

22 Ibid., p. 46

23 Ibid., pp. 74–5, and Rodogno, *Fascism's European Empire*, p. 390

24 MacGregor Knox, 'Das faschistische Italien und die "Endlösung" 1942/43', *VfZ* (2007) 55, pp. 84ff.

25 *Hitler's Table Talk 1941–1945* (Oxford 1988)

26 Richard Overy, *Why the Allies Won* (London 1995) p. 276

27 Warlimont, *Inside Hitler's Headquarters*, p. 13

28 Ibid., p. 244

29 Helmut Heiber and David Glantz (eds), *Hitler and his Generals. Military Conferences 1942–1945* (New York 2003) p. 575

30 Ibid., pp. 580–1

31 Warlimont, *Inside Hitler's Headquarters*, pp. 244–245

32 Heiber and Glantz (eds), *Hitler and his Generals*, pp. 583–4

33 Steven H. Newton, *Hitler's Commander. Field Marshal Walter Model – Hitler's Favorite General* (Cambridge, Massachusetts 2006) p. 177

34 Warlimont, *Inside Hitler's Headquarters*, p. 250

35 Ibid., p. 252

36 Heiber and Glantz (eds), *Hitler and his Generals*, p. 62

37 Robert Gellately (ed.), *The Nuremberg Interviews. An American Psychiatrist's Conversations with the Defendants and Witnesses* (London 2006) p. 292

38 Johannes Hürter '"Es herrschen Sitten und Gebräuche, genauso wie im 30-Jährigen Krieg". Das erste Jahr des deutsch–sowjetischen Krieges in Dokumenten des Generals Gotthard Heinrici', *VfZ* (2000) 48 doc. nos. 50, 11 January 1942; 52, 21 January 1942; 54, 6 February 1942; 55, 28 February 1942, pp. 395–8

39 James Holland, *Together We Stand. North Africa 1942–1943. Turning the Tide in the West* (London 2006) pp. 113 and 366

40 Johannes Hürter, *Hitlers Heerführer. Die deutschen Oberbefehlshaber im Krieg gegen die Sowjetunion 1941/42* (Munich 2006) p. 352

41 Newton, *Hitler's Commander*, pp. 200–4

42 Christian Gerlach, 'Männer des 20 Juli und der Krieg gegen die Sowjetunion', in Hannes Heer and Klaus Naumann (eds), *Vernichtungskrieg. Verbrechen der Wehrmacht 1941–1944* (Hamburg 1995) pp. 427–46. See also Johannes Hürter, 'Auf dem Weg zur Militäropposition. Tresckow, Gersdorff, der Vernichtungskrieg und der Judenmord. Neue Dokumente über das Verhältnis der Heeresgruppe Mitte zur Einsatzgruppe B im Jahr 1941', *VfZ* (2004) 52 pp. 527–62

43 Lyman, *Generals,* p. 49

44 Kumiko Kakehashi, *Letters from Iwo Jima* (London 2007). I strongly recommend Clint Eastwood's eponymous film, in which the quality of the acting far surpasses its tandem piece *Flags of our Fathers*

Chapter 13: Antagonistic Allies

1 The man at the heart of these mechanisms has left the best description of them; see Lord Ismay, *The Memoirs of General the Lord Ismay* (London 1960) pp. 158ff.

2 David Carlton, *Anthony Eden* (London 1981) pp. 202–6

3 Max Hastings, *Finest Years. Churchill as Warlord 1940–45* (London 2009) explores this theme in a subtle way

4 Ismay, *Memoirs of Lord Ismay,* p. 187

5 Carlo D'Este, *Warlord. Churchill at War 1874–1945* (London 2009) pp. 443ff. has many details of Churchill's working habits, as has Roy Jenkins, *Churchill* (London 2001) pp. 630ff.

6 John Colville, *The Fringes of Power. Downing Street Diaries 1939–1945* (London 2004) entry dated 8 March 1941, p. 313

7 Carlo D'Este gets this all wrong in his *Warlord*

8 Geoffrey Best, *Churchill and War* (London 2005) p. 288

9 Major-General Sir John Kennedy, *The Business of War* (London 1957) p. 274

10 Notably Hastings, *Finest Years*

11 Ismay, *Memoirs of Lord Ismay,* p. 271

12 Colville, *Fringes of Power. Downing Street Years,* entry dated 13 May 1944, p. 467

13 Ismay, *Memoirs of Lord Ismay,* p. 209

14 Alex Danchev and Daniel Todman (eds), *Field Marshal Lord Alanbrooke. War Diaries 1939–1945* (London 2001) entry dated 26 May 1944, p. 551

15 Ibid., entry dated 19 November 1941, p. 201

16 Andrew Roberts, *Masters and Commanders. How Roosevelt, Churchill, Marshall and Alanbrooke Won the War in the West* (London 2009) pp. 12–15

17 Danchev and Todman (eds), *Field Marshal Lord Alanbrooke. War Diaries,* entry dated 8 May 1945, p. 689

18 Ibid., entry dated 19 June 1944, p. 560

19 Kennedy, *Business of War,* p. 275

20 Danchev and Daniel Todman (eds), *Field Marshal Lord Alanbrooke. War Diaries,* entry dated 10 April 1942, p. 247

21 Ibid., entry dated 25 December 1941, p. 214 (Churchill was in the US)

22 Ibid., entry dated 26 June 1942, p. 273
23 Kennedy, *Business of War,* p. 106
24 Ibid., pp. 104–8
25 Danchev and Daniel Todman (eds), *Field Marshal Lord Alanbrooke. War Diaries,* entry dated 28 February 1944 p. 526
26 Ibid., entry dated 19 January 1944, p. 515
27 Ibid., entry dated 8 March 1944, p. 530
28 Ibid., entry dated 8 October 1941, p. 188
29 Ibid., entry dated 23 October 1941, p. 193
30 Ibid., entry dated 17 February 1942, p. 230
31 Ibid., entry dated 8 May 1943, p. 400
32 Ibid., entry dated 19 May 1943, p. 407
33 Ibid., entry dated 27 May 1944, p. 551
34 Ibid., entry dated 31 March 1944, p. 536
35 Ibid., entry dated 5 April 1944, p. 538
36 Ibid., entry dated 2 May 1944, p. 542
37 John Keegan (ed.), *Churchill's Generals* (London 1991) pp. 7–12
38 James Holland, *Together We Stand. North Africa 1942–1943. Turning the Tide in the West* (London 2006) pp. 260ff.
39 Carlo D'Este, *Eisenhower. Allied Supreme Commander* (London 2004) p. 484
40 Ibid., p. 409
41 Robert Lyman, *Slim, Master of War. Burma and the Birth of Modern Warfare* (London 2004) p. 249
42 Kennedy, *Business of War,* p. 165
43 Chris Bellamy, *Absolute War. Soviet Russia in the Second World War* (London 2007) pp. 214–15
44 Evan Mawdsley, *Thunder in the East. The Nazi–Soviet War 1941–1945* (London 2005) pp. 21–2
45 Dmitri Volkogonov, *Stalin. Triumph and Tragedy* (London 1991) pp. 418–19
46 Adam Ulam, *Stalin. The Man and his Era* (Boston, Massachusetts 1989) p. 592
47 Robert Service, *Stalin. A Biography* (London 2004) p. 437
48 Ibid., p. 420
49 Volkogonov, *Stalin,* p. 423
50 For these biographical details see Aleksandr Maslov, *Fallen Soviet Generals. Soviet General Officers Killed in Battle 1941–1945,* trans. and ed. David M. Glantz (London 1998) p. 55
51 Robert Conquest, *Stalin. Breaker of Nations* (London 1991) p. 243

52 A. A. Maslov, 'How were Soviet Blocking Detachments Employed?', *Foreign Military Studies Office Fort Leavenworth* (2009), translation of a Russian paper originally published in 1988
53 John Erickson, 'Red Army Battlefield Performance 1941–45. The System and the Soldier', in Paul Addison and Angus Calder (eds) *Time to Kill. The Soldier's Experience of War in the West 1939–1945* (London 1997) p. 244
54 Richard Overy, *Why the Allies Won* (London 1995) p. 271
55 Ismay, *Memoirs of Lord Ismay,* pp. 233–4
56 Conquest, *Stalin,* pp. 243–4
57 Robert Sherwood, *The White House Papers of Harry L. Hopkins* (London 1948) vol. 1 pp. 328–9
58 See the marvellous account by my late friend Amos Perlmutter, *FDR and Stalin. A Not So Grand Alliance 1943–1945* (Columbia, Missouri 1993) pp. 65–87
59 Keith Sainsbury, *Churchill and Roosevelt at War* (London 1994) p. 75
60 Conquest, *Stalin,* p. 263
61 Carlton, *Anthony Eden,* pp. 213–6
62 Frank Field (ed.), *Attlee's Great Contemporaries. The Politics of Character* (London 2009) p. 87
63 Mark Perry, *Partners in Command. George Marshall and Dwight Eisenhower in War and Peace* (London 2007) p. 10
64 Roberts, *Masters and Commanders,* pp. 24ff. evokes Marshall's character very well
65 D'Este, *Eisenhower,* pp. 200–1
66 Ed Cray, *General of the Army. George C. Marshall, Soldier and Statesman* (New York 1990) pp. 314–15 for the financial costs
67 Marshall to Allen Merriam letter dated 7 March 1943, in Larry Bland and Sharon Ritenour Stevens (eds), *The Papers of George Catlett Marshall* (Baltimore 1996) vol. 3 pp, 581–2
68 Ibid., Marshall memo dated 11 September 1942, pp. 354–5
69 D'Este, *Eisenhower,* p. 327, and Cray, *General of the Army,* p. 338
70 D'Este, *Eisenhower,* p. 316
71 Ibid., p. 353

72 Perry, *Partners in Command*, p. 176
73 Ibid., p. 162
74 D'Este, *Eisenhower*, p.421
75 I am grateful to James Kurth for his paper 'The US Navy in World War II', Foreign Policy Research Institute Paper (2009) 14 no. 24 which alerted me to Michael Bess's excellent book *Choices under Fire. Moral Dimensions of World War II* (New York 2006) especially pp. 136–65

Chapter 14: 'We were Savages': Combat Soldiers

1 Meirion and Susie Harries, *Soldiers of the Sun. The Rise and Fall of the Imperial Japanese Army* (New York 1991) p. 369
2 James Holland, *Together We Stand. North Africa 1942–1943. Turning the Tide in the West* (London 2006) p. 24. Unlike much of the 'new history' of the German army, historians like Holland give due attention to the largely logistic nature of modern warfare
3 John Ellis, *Cassino. The Hollow Victory. The Battle for Rome January–June 1944* (London 1984) p. 356
4 John Ellis, *The Sharp End. The Fighting Man in World War II* (London 2009) is fundamental
5 Max Hastings, *Armageddon. The Battle for Germany 1944–45* (London 2004) pp. 241–2
6 I have relied on a very informative discussion of this subject, Lieutenant Colonel Dave Grossman's *On Killing. The Psychological Cost of Learning to Kill in War and Society* (New York 1995) especially pp. 97ff.
7 Günther K. Koschorrek, *Blood Red Snow. The Memoirs of a German Soldier on the Eastern Front* (Minneapolis 2002) pp. 63–4
8 Ellis, *Sharp End*, p. 102
9 'Lieutenant Garry Maufe', *Daily Telegraph* 25 April 2009. I am grateful to the obituaries editor, David Twiston-Davies, for this information, and to Mrs Maufe for sending me her late husband's handwritten account of this action
10 Catherine Merridale, *Ivan's War. The Red Army 1939–45* (London 2005) p. 191
11 Norman Davies, *Europe at War 1939–1945. No Simple Victory* (London 2006) p. 232
12 Evan Mawdsley, *Thunder in the East. The Nazi–Soviet War 1941–1945* (London 2005) p. 215 for these statistics
13 Eugene B. Sledge, *With the Old Breed. At Peleliu and Okinawa* (New York 2007) p. 70
14 Ibid., pp. 129–30
15 Ibid., pp. 160–1
16 Ibid., pp. 218–9
17 Anthony Beevor and Luba Vinogradova (eds), *A Writer at War. Vasily Grossman with the Red Army 1941–1945* (London 2005) p. 86
18 Merridale, *Ivan's War*, p. 174
19 Ibid., p. 207 for examples of Russian 'marching field wives'
20 Antony Beevor, *D-Day. The Battle for Normandy* (London 2009) p. 205
21 Hastings, *Armageddon*, pp. 86–7
22 Gerald F. Linderman, *The World within War. America's Combat Experience in World War II* (New York 1997) pp. 269–70
23 Beevor and Vinogradova (eds), *Writer at War*, p. 218
24 Sledge, *With the Old Breed*, p. 21
25 Meirion and Susie Harries, *Soldiers of the Sun*, pp. 330–1
26 Stefan Schmitz (ed.), *Willy Peter Reese. Mir selber seltsam fremd. Die Unmenschlichkeit des Krieges. Russland 1941–44* (Munich 2003)
27 Merridale, *Ivan's War*, p. 209
28 Ellis, *Cassino*, p. 379
29 Schmitz (ed.) *Willy Peter Reese. Mir selber seltsam fremd*, p. 164
30 Ibid., p. 130
31 Richard Holmes, 'The Italian Job. Five Armies in Italy 1943–45', in Paul Addison and Angus Calder (eds), *Time to Kill. The Soldier's Experience of War in the West 1939–1945* (London 1997) p. 208
32 Stephen G. Fritz, *Frontsoldaten. The German Soldier in World War II* (Lexington, Kentucky 1995) p. 68
33 Ibid., p. 144
34 Schmitz (ed.), *Willy Peter Reese. Mir selber seltsam fremd*, p. 132

35 Holmes, 'Italian Job', p. 217

36 Merridale, *Ivan's War*, p. 187

37 Paul Ham, *Kokoda* (Sydney 2005) p. 433

38 Keith Douglas, 'How to Kill' (1943), in Victor Selwyn (ed.), *The Voice of War. Poems of the Second World War* (London 1996) pp. 34–5

39 Beevor and Vinogradova (eds), *Writer at War*, p. 157

40 On this see James Bowman's thoughtful *Honor. A History* (New York 2006) pp. 138ff.

41 Samuel Stouffer (ed.), *The American Soldier* (Princeton 1949)

42 Richard Holmes, *Acts of War. The Behaviour of Men in Battle* (London 1985) pp. 313–14. Holmes's book is easily the most intelligently persuasive on these subjects

43 Evelyn Waugh, *Men at Arms* (London 1952) pp. 48–9

44 'Lieutenant-Colonel Jack Churchill', in David Twiston-Davies (ed.), *The Daily Telegraph Book of Military Obituaries* (London 2003) pp. 194–9

45 Ellis, *Sharp End*, pp. 282ff. seems persuasive

46 James Holland, *Italy's Sorrow. A Year of War 1944–1945* (London 2008) p. 324

47 Ellis, *Sharp End*, p. 304

48 Meirion and Susie Harries, *Soldiers of the Sun*, p. 331

49 Ellis, *Sharp End*, p. 90

50 Ibid., p. 92

51 Ham, *Kokoda*, p. 47

52 Paul Fussell, *The Boys' Crusade. American G.I.s in Europe. Chaos and Fear in World War Two* (London 2003) p. 77

53 Grossman, *On Killing*, p. 118

54 Ham, *Kokoda*, p. 449

55 Schmitz (ed.), *Willy Peter Reese. Mir selber seltsam fremd*, p. 131

56 Merridale, *Ivan's War*, p. 168

57 Cited by Niall Ferguson, *The Pity of War* (London 1998) p. 365

58 Ellis, *Cassino*, p. 102

59 Brian R. Sullivan, 'The Italian Soldier in Combat, June 1940–September 1943. Myths, Realities and Explanations', in Addison and Calder (eds), *Time to Kill*, pp. 197–8

60 Sidney Keyes, 'Sand' (1943), in Selwyn (ed.), *Voice of War*, pp. 47–8

61 Holland, *Together We Stand*, pp. 201ff.

62 Linderman, *World Within War*, pp. 91ff.

63 Holland, *Together We Stand*, p. 644 for Frost, p. 406 for Montgomery's dinner with Thoma, and p. 88 for Harper and Rommel

64 C. P. S. Denholm-Young, 'Grave near Sirte' (1942), in Selwyn (ed.), *Voice of War*, p. 32

65 Rick Atkinson, *An Army at Dawn. The War in North Africa 1942–1943* (London 2004) p. 461

66 Ibid., pp. 497–8

67 Rick Atkinson, *The Day of Battle. The War in Sicily and Italy 1943–1944* (New York 2007) pp. 116–21

68 Koschorrek, *Blood Red Snow*, p. 69

69 Beevor, *D-Day. The Battle for Normandy*, pp. 67–8

70 See the very careful discussion in Peter Leib, *Konventioneller Krieg oder NS-Weltanschauungskrieg? Kriegsführung und Partisanenbekämpfung in Frankreich 1943/44* (Munich 2007) pp. 154ff.

71 Ham, *Kokoda*, p. 517

72 Ibid., pp. 189–90

73 Major Misao Sato in John Nunneley and Kazuo Tamayama (eds), *Tales by Japanese Soldiers of the Burma Campagn 1942–1945* (London 2000) doc. no. 15 pp. 63–4

74 Linderman, *World within War*, pp. 112–13

75 John W. Dower, *War without Mercy. Race & Power in the Pacific War* (New York 1986) pp. 203ff.

76 Meirion and Susie Harries, *Soldiers of the Sun*, p. 479

77 Max Hastings, *Nemesis. The Battle for Japan 1944–45* (London 2007) pp. 393–9 has a sensitive discussion of this issue

78 Linderman, *World Within War*, pp. 172–3

79 Dower, *War without Mercy*, p. 91

80 Merridale, *Ivan's War*, p. 164

81 Mawdsley, *Thunder in the East*, p. 213

82 Veljko Vujačić, 'Stalinism and Russian Nationalism', in Marlene Laruelle (ed.), *Russian Nationalism and the National Reassertion of Russia* (London 2009) pp. 58ff.

83 Geoffrey Hosking, *Rulers and Victims. The Russians in the Soviet Union* (Cambridge, Massachusetts 2006) p. 192

84 Ibid., p. 226

85 Ibid., pp. 193–5 is excellent on these themes

86 Michael H. Kater, *Hitler Youth* (Cambridge, Massachusetts 2004) is good on pre-military training

87 Fritze, *Frontsoldaten*, pp. 13ff.

88 Ellis, *Cassino*, p. 465

89 Fritz, *Frontsoldaten*, p. 204

90 Ibid., p. 196

91 Schmitz (ed.), *Willy Peter Reese. Mir selber seltsam fremd*, p.137

92 Fritz, *Frontsoldaten*, pp. 84–6

93 Theo Schulte, *The German Army and Nazi Policies in Occupied Russia* (Oxford 1989) is notably fair-minded on the German army's dropouts

94 Omer Bartov, 'Von unten betrachtet. Überleben, Zusammenhalt und Brutalität an der Ostfront', in Bernd Wegner (ed.), *Zwei Wege nach Moskau. Vom Hitler-Stalin-Pakt zum 'Unternehmen Barbarossa'* (Munich 1991) pp. 328–9, and Bartov, *Hitler's Army. Soldiers, Nazis and War in the Third Reich* (Oxford 1991)

95 See the useful essay collection by Norbert Haase and Gerhard Paul (eds), *Die anderen Soldaten. Wehrkraftzersetzung, Gehorsamsverweigerung und Fahnenflucht im Zweiten Weltkrieg* (Frankfurt am Main 1995)

96 Schmitz (ed.), *Willy Peter Reese. Mir selber seltsam fremd*, p. 68

97 Berward Dörner, '"Der Krieg ist verloren!" "Wehrkraftversetzung" und Denunziation in der Truppe', in Haase and Paul (eds), *Die anderen Soldaten*, pp. 105–22

Chapter 15: Massacring the Innocents

1 Martin Cüppers, *Wegbereiter der Shoah. Die Waffen-SS, der Kommandostab Reichsführer-SS und die Judenvernichtung 1939–1945* (Darmstadt 2005) p. 119

2 Ibid., p. 117

3 See the fundamental work of Ruth Bettina Birn, *Die Höheren SS und Polizeiführer. Himmlers Stellvertreter im Reich und in den besetzten Gebieten* (Düsseldorf 1986)

4 Martin Cüppers, 'Gustav Lombard – ein engagierter Judenmörder aus der Waffen-SS', in Klaus-Michael Mallmann and Gerhard Paul (eds), *Karrieren der Gewalt. Nationalsozialistische Täterbiographien* (Darmstadt 2005) pp. 146–7

5 Andrej Angrick, 'Erich von dem Bach-Zelewski. Himmlers Mann für alle Fälle', in Ronald Smelser and Enrico Syring (eds), *Die SS. Elite unter dem Totenkopf. 30 Lebensläufe* (Paderborn 2000) pp. 28–35

6 Cüppers, *Wegbereiter der Shoah*, p. 165

7 Peter Longerich, *Heinrich Himmler. Biographie* (Munich 2008) pp. 553–4

8 Ibid., p. 551

9 On Jeckeln see Richard Breitman, 'Friedrich Jeckeln. Spezialist für die "Endlösung" in Osten', in Smelser and Syring (eds), *Die SS. Elite unter dem Totenkopf*, pp. 267–75

10 Ibid., pp. 267–269

11 Klaus-Michael Mallmann, 'Der qualitative Sprung im Vernichtungsprozess. Das Massaker von Kamenez-Podolsk Ende August 1941' in Wolfgang Benz (ed.), *Jahrbuch für Antisemitismusforschung* (Frankfurt am Main 2001) pp. 239–64

12 See Johannes Heil and Rainer Erb (eds), *Geschichtswissenschaft und Öffentlichkeit. Der Streit um Daniel J. Goldhagen* (Frankfurt am Main 1998)

13 For a pioneering discussion of these matters see Herbert Jäger, *Verbrechen unter totalitärer Herrschaft. Studien zur nationalsozialistischen Gewaltkriminalität* (Frankfurt am Main 1982, originally 1967)

14 Klaus-Michael Mallmann, 'Die Sicherheitspolizei und die Shoah in Westgalizien', in Gerhard Paul (ed.), *Die Täter der Shoah. Fanatische Nationalsozialisten oder ganz normale Deutsche?* (Göttingen 2002) p. 118

15 Jürgen Matthäus, 'An vorderster Front. Voraussetzung für die Beteiligung der Ordnungspolizei an der Shoah', in Paul (ed.), *Die Täter der Shoah*, pp. 137ff.; on the police and SS, see Edward B. Westermann, *Hitler's Police Battalions. Enforcing Racial War*

in the East (Lawrence, Kansas 2005) pp. 92ff.

16 Klaus-Michael Mallmann, Volker Riess and Wolfram Pyta (eds), *Deutscher Osten 1939–1945. Der Weltanschauungskrieg in Photos und Texten* (Darmstadt 2003) p. 138

17 Andrej Angrick, *Besatzungspolitik und Massenmord. Die Einsatzgruppe D in der südlichen Sowjetunion 1941–1943* (Hamburg 2003) pp. 248–9

18 Angrick, 'Erich von dem Bach-Zelewski', p. 40

19 For a very fair summary of the Browning–Goldhagen debate see Christopher Browning, 'Die Debatte über die Täter des Holocaust', in Ulrich Herbert (ed.), *Nationalsozialistische Vernichtungspolitik 1939–1945. Neue Forschungen und Kontroversen* (Frankfurt am Main 1998) pp. 148–69

20 Classic works include Shmuel Spector, *The Holocaust of Volhynian Jews 1941–1944* (Jerusalem 1990)

21 Christopher Browning, *Ordinary Men. Reserve Battalion 101 and the Final Solution in Poland* (London 2001) p. 213

22 Jäger, *Verbrechen unter totalitärer Herrschaft*, p. 69

23 Mallmann, Riess and Pyta (eds), *Deutscher Osten*, p. 37

24 Jäger, *Verbrechen unter totalitärer Herrschaft*, p. 282

25 Westermann, *Hitler's Police Battalions*, p. 172

26 Harald Welzer, *Täter. Wie aus ganz normalen Menschen Massenmörder werden* (Frankfurt am Main 2005) pp. 30–40

27 Jäger, *Verbrechen unter totalitärer Herrschaft*, p. 280

28 Mallmann, Riess and Pyta (eds), *Deutscher Osten*, p. 148

29 Angrick, *Besatzungspolitik und Massenmord*, p. 447

30 Dieter Pohl, 'Ukrainische Hilfskräfte beim Mord an den Juden', in Paul (ed.), *Die Täter der Shoah*, p. 214 for examples

31 Browning, *Ordinary Men*, pp. 72–3

32 For these examples see Welzer, *Täter*, p. 160, and Mallmann, Riess and Pyta (eds), *Deutscher Osten*, p. 139

33 Angrick, *Besatzungspolitik und Massenmord*, p. 435

34 Ibid., 131–3

35 Browning, *Ordinary Men*, p. 60

36 Angrick, *Besatzungspolitik und Massenmord*, pp. 389–93 for the poem

37 Jürgen Matthäus in Christopher Browning's *The Origins of the Final Solution. The Evolution of Nazi Jewish Policy September 1939–March 1942* (London 2005) p. 315

38 Saul Friedländer's monumental *The Years of Extermination. Nazi Germany and the Jews 1939–1945* (London 2007) especially pp. 331ff. has a useful running reminder of Hitler's increasingly unrestrained remarks about Jews

39 *Hitler's Table-Talk. Hitler's Conversations Recorded by Martin Bormann* (Oxford 1988) entry dated 25 October 1941, p. 87

40 See Michael Burleigh, *Death and Deliverance. 'Euthanasia' in Germany 1900–1945* (London 2003, originally Cambridge 1994), and Henry Friedlander, *The Origins of Nazi Genocide. From Euthanasia to the Final Solution* (Chapel Hill, North Carolina 1995)

41 Gudrun Schwarz, *Die nationalsozialistischen Lager* (Frankfurt am Main 1996)

42 Most of the relevant literature is mentioned in Rolf-Dieter Müller, *Hitlers Ostkrieg und die deutsche Siedlungspolitik. Die Zusammenarbeit von Wehrmacht, Wirtschaft und SS* (Frankfurt am Main 1991)

43 Longerich, *Heinrich Himmler*, p. 567

44 Matthäus in Browning's *Origins of the Final Solution*, p. 421; see also Yitzhak Arad, *The Operation of the Reinhard Death Camps* (Bloomington, Indiana 1987) and Bogdan Musial (ed.), *Aktion Reinhardt. Der Völkermord an den Juden in Generalgouvernement 1941–1944* (Frankfurt am Main 2004)

45 For the protocol see Jeremy Noakes and Geoffrey Pridham (eds), *Nazism 1919–1945. A Documentary Reader* (Exeter 1988) vol. 3 doc. no. 849 p. 1131; see also Dieter Pohl, *Nationalsozialistische Judenverfolgung in Ostgalizien. Organisation und Durchführung eines staatlichen*

Massenverbrechens (Munich 1996) and
Thomas Sandkühler, '*Endlösung' in
Galizien: Der Judenmord in Ostpolen
und die Rettungsinitiativen von Berthold
Beitz 1941–1944* (Bonn 1996)

46 Shmuel Krakowski, *Das Todeslager
Chelmno/Kulmhof. Der Beginn der
'Endlösung'* (Göttingen 2007) pp. 31–5

47 Gunnar Boehnert, 'Rudolf Höss –
Kommandant von Auschwitz', in
Smelser and Syring (eds), *Die SS. Elite
unter dem Totenkopf*, p. 261

48 Gitta Sereny, *Into that Darkness*
(London 1974) pp. 191–2, which
describes a visit to Treblinka of high-
ranking SS men from Berlin

49 Hannah Arendt, *Eichmann in Jerusalem.
Ein Bericht von der Banalität des Büsen*
(Munich 1964)

50 Hans Safrian, *Eichmann und seine
Gehilfen* (Frankfurt am Main 1995)
pp. 41–5

51 Alfred C. Mierzejewski, 'A Public
Enterprise in the Service of Mass
Murder. The Deutsche Reichsbahn and
the Holocaust', in David Cesarani (ed.),
*Holocaust. Critical Concepts in
Historical Studies* (London 2004) vol. 3
pp. 285ff., and Klaus Hildebrand, 'Die
Deutsche Reichsbahn in der
nationalsozialistischen Diktatur
1933–1945', in Lothar Gall and Hans
Pohl (eds), *Die Eisenbahnen in
Deutschland. Von den Anfängen bis zur
Gegenwart* (Munich 1999) pp. 237–41

52 Yaacov Lozowick, 'Malice in Action', in
Cesarani (ed.), *Holocaust. Critical
Concepts in Historical Studies*, vol. 3,
pp. 241ff.

Chapter 16: Journeys through Night

1 Rab Bennett, *Under the Shadow of the
Swastika. The Moral Dilemmas of
Resistance and Collaboration in Hitler's
Europe* (London 1999) p. 192

2 Martin Gilbert (ed.), *Avraham Tory.
The Kovno Ghetto Diary* (Cambridge
Massachusetts 1990) entry dated 12
February 1943, p. 209

3 Gordon J. Horwitz, *Ghettostadt: Łódź and
the Making of a Nazi City* (Cambridge,
Massachusetts 2009) pp. 14–21

4 Ibid.

5 On this see Christopher R. Browning,
'Nazi Ghettoization Policy in Poland
1939–41', *Central European History*
(1986) 19 pp. 343–68, and his 'German
Technocrats, Jewish Labour and the
Final Solution', in *Remembering for the
Future. The Impact of the Holocaust on
the Contemporary World* (Oxford 1988)
vol. 2 pp. 2199–208

6 Shmuel Krakowski, *Das Todeslager
Chelmno/Kulmhof. Der Beginn der
'Endlösung'* (Göttingen 2007) pp. 45–6

7 The economics of the ghetto are
explained by Götz Aly and Susanne
Heim, *Vordenker der Vernichtung.
Auschwitz und die deutschen Pläne für
eine neue europäische Ordnung*
(Hamburg 1991) pp. 300ff.

8 Isaiah Trunk, *Judenrat. The Jewish
Councils in Eastern Europe under Nazi
Occupation* (New York 1972) p. 49

9 US Holocaust Memorial Museum (ed.),
Hidden History of the Kovno Ghetto
(Washington DC 1997) p. 80 for
illustrated examples of designs for
armbands for firemen and so forth

10 Horwitz, *Ghettostadt: Łódź and the
Making of a Nazi City*, p. 150

11 See the documents in Isaiah Trunk,
Łódź Ghetto. A History (Bloomington,
Indiana 2008) e.g. doc. no. 74 'What's
Being Delivered to US' dated 2 July
1942, p. 134

12 Trunk, *Judenrat*, p. 88

13 Trunk, *Łódź Ghetto*, pp. 172–183

14 Ibid., p. 347

15 Trunk, *Judenrat*, p. 401

16 Sascha Feuchert, Erwin Leibfried and
Jörg Riecke (eds), *Die Chronik des
Gettos Łódź/Litzmannstadt* (Göttingen
2001) vol. 1 p. 301ff.

17 Bennett, *Under the Shadow of the
Swastika*, p. 212

18 Krakowski, *Das Todeslager
Chelmno/Kulmhof*, p. 116

19 Gilbert (ed.), *Avraham Tory. The Kovno
Ghetto Diary*, entry dated 28 October
1941, pp. 43–60

20 US Holocaust Memorial Museum (ed.),
Hidden History of the Kovno Ghetto, p. 83

21 Krakowski, *Das Todeslager Chelmno/
Kulmhof*, pp. 127–30 for these debates

22 Filip Müller, *Eyewitness to Auschwitz. Three Years in the Gas Chambers* (New York 1979) p. 114

23 Margarete Buber-Neumann, *Under Two Dictatorships. Prisoner of Stalin and Hitler* (London 2008) p. 250

24 Ibid., quotations from p. 213

25 The best physical descriptions of what the camp environment was supposed to do are by Wolfgang Sofsky, *The Order of Terror* (Princeton 1999)

26 Paul Steinberg, *Speak You Also. A Survivor's Reckoning* (London 2001) pp. 88–9

27 Ibid., p. 88

28 Ibid., pp. 223–4

29 Anna Pawelczynska, *Values and Violence in Auschwitz. A Sociological Analysis* (Berkeley 1979) is indispensable

30 Tzvetan Todorov, *Facing the Extreme. Moral Life in the Concentration Camps* (London 1999) pp. 82ff. is sharp on this subject

31 Steinberg, *Speak You Also*, p. 48

32 Buber-Neumann, *Under Two Dictatorships*, pp. 232–3

33 Saul Friedländer, *The Years of Extermination. Nazi Germany and the Jews 1939–1945* (London 2007) p. 308

34 Ibid., pp. 306ff.

35 For 'indifference' see Ian Kershaw, 'Popular Opinion and the Extermination of the Jews', in his *Hitler, the Germans, and the Final Solution* (New Haven 2008) p. 198, and the preceding essay in the collection with its famous observation that 'the road to Auschwitz was built by hate, but paved with indifference', p. 186

36 Frank Bajohr and Dieter Pohl, *Massenmord und schlechtes Gewissen. Die deutsche Bevölkerung, die NS-Führung und der Holocaust* (Frankfurt am Main 2008) pp. 45–9

37 Ibid., p. 54

38 Götz Aly, *Hitler's Beneficiaries. How the Nazis Bought the German People* (London 2007) p. 123

39 Karl Ley, *Wir glauben Ihnen* (Siegen-Volnsberg 1973) p. 115

40 Herbert and Sibylle Obenaus, '*Schreiben, wie es wirklich war!' Aufzeichnungen Karl Dürkefälder aus den Jahren 1933–1945* (Hanover 1985)

41 Sönke Neitzel, 'Deutsche Generäle in britischer Gefangenschaft 1942–1945' *VfZ* (2004) 52 doc. nos. 5, pp. 313–4, and 12, pp. 322–3

42 Kershaw, 'Popular Opinion and the Extermination of the Jews', p. 203

43 Neitzel, 'Deutsche Generäle in britischer Gefangenschaft', doc. nos. 5, p. 314, and 15, p. 327

44 Frank Bajohr, 'Vom antijüdischen Konsens zum schlechten Gewissen. Die deutschen Gesellschaft und die Judenverfolgung 1933–1945', in Bajohr and Dieter Pohl (eds), *Massenmord und schlechtes Gewissen. Die deutsche Bevölkerung, die NS-Führung und der Holocaust* (Frankfurt am Main 2008) p. 70

Chapter 17: Observing an Avalanche

1 Richard Breitman, *Official Secrets. What the Nazis Planned, What the British and Americans Knew* (London 1998) pp. 57ff.

2 Ibid., p. 92

3 Richard Breitman, 'Intelligence and the Holocaust', in David Bankier (ed.), *Secret Intelligence and the Holocaust* (New York 2006) pp. 22–31

4 Robert Rhodes James (ed.), *Winston S. Churchill. His Complete Speeches 1897–1963* (London 1974) vol. 6 pp. 6472–8 for the full text of his broadcast

5 As pointed out by Gerhard Weinberg, 'The Allies and the Holocaust', in David Cesarani (ed.), *Holocaust. Critical Concepts in Historical Studies* (London 2004) vol. 5 pp. 144–5

6 Theodore S. Hamerow, *Why We Watched. Europe, America, and the Holocaust* (New York 2008) pp. 406–7

7 See the very fair-minded and interesting essay by David Cesarani, 'Mad Dogs and Englishmen. Towards a Taxonomy of Rescuers in a "Bystander" Country – Britain 1933–45', in David Cesarani and Paul Levine (eds), *'Bystanders' to the Holocaust. A Re-evaluation* (London 2002) pp. 41–2

8 Martin Gilbert, *Auschwitz and the Allies* (London 1981) p. 312

9 Breitman, 'Intelligence and the Holocaust', p. 39

10 Meredith Hindley, 'Constructing Allied Humanitarian Policy', in Cesarani and Levine (eds), *'Bystanders' to the Holocaust*, p. 88

11 Hamerow, *Why We Watched*, p. 323 for Ben Gurion's own words

12 Gilbert, *Auschwitz and the Allies*, p. 40

13 For a marvellous biography see E. Thomas Wood and Stanislaw M. Jankowski, *Karski. How One Man Tried to Stop the Holocaust* (New York 1994) pp. 120ff.

14 Gilbert, *Auschwitz and the Allies*, pp. 106–7

15 Ibid.

16 Arieh Kochavi, 'Britain and the Establishment of the United Nations War Crimes Commission', in Cesarani (ed.), *Holocaust. Critical Concepts in Historical Studies*, pp. 135–8

17 See Priscilla Dale Jones, 'British Policy towards German Crimes against German Jews 1939–1945', *Leo Baeck Institute Yearbook* (1991) 36 pp. 339ff. for these issues

18 See the important article by Edward B. Westermann, 'The Royal Air Force and the Bombing of Auschwitz. First Deliberations January 1941', in Cesarani (ed.), *Holocaust. Critical Concepts in Historical Studies*, vol. 5 pp. 195–211

19 See Tammi Davis Biddle, 'Allied Air Power. Objectives and Capabilities' and Williamson Murray, 'Monday Morning Quarterbacking and the Bombing of Auschwitz', both in Michael J. Neufeld and Michael Berenbaum (eds), *The Bombing of Auschwitz. Should the Allies Have Attempted It?* (Lawrence, Kansas 2003) pp. 35–51 and 204–14

20 For some of these points see Stuart Erdheim, 'Could the Allies Have Bombed Auschwitz-Birkenau?', in Cesarani (ed.), *Holocaust. Critical Concepts in Historical Studies*, vol. 5 pp. 212ff.

21 See the instructive article by Dino Brugioni, 'The Aerial Photos of the Auschwitz-Birkenau Extermination Complex', in Neufeld and Berenbaum (eds), *Bombing of Auschwitz*, pp. 52–7

22 Gilbert, *Auschwitz and the Allies*, plate 28

23 See the fair-minded account by David Cesarani in his edited collection *Genocide and Rescue. The Holocaust in Hungary 1944* (Oxford 1997) pp. 14–16

24 Aide-memoire that Chaim Weizmann and Moshe Shertok left for Eden dated 6 July 1944, in Neufeld and Berenbaum (eds), *Bombing of Auschwitz*, doc. no. 3.4 pp. 263–4

25 John McCloy to John W. Pehle (War Refugee Board) dated 18 November 1944, in Neufeld and Berenbaum (eds), *Bombing of Auschwitz*, doc. no. 4.10 pp. 279–80

26 See James H. Kitchens III, 'The Bombing of Auschwitz Re-examined', in Neufeld and Berenbaum (eds), *Bombing of Auschwitz*, pp. 80ff. I like Mr Kitchens's robust defence of Allied air forces

27 Henry Feingold, 'Bombing Auschwitz and the Politics of the Jewish Question during World War II', in Neufeld and Berenbaum (eds), *Bombing of Auschwitz*, p. 200 at least raises the Soviet issue

28 Simon Sebag Montefiore, *Stalin. The Court of the Red Tsar* (London 2003) pp. 310–12 is much more astute on these issues than Zvi Gitelmann, 'The Soviet Union', in David Wyman (ed.), *The World Reacts to the Holocaust* (Baltimore 1996) pp. 295ff.

29 Richard Pipes, *Russia under the Bolshevik Regime 1919–1924* (Cambridge, Massachusetts 1994) p. 281

30 Antony Beevor and Luba Vinogradova (eds), *A Writer at War. Vasily Grossman with the Red Army 1941–1945* (London 2006)

31 Joshua Rubenstein, *Tangled Loyalties. The Life and Times of Ilya Ehrenburg* (London 1996) p. 205

32 William Korey, 'Soviet Treatment of the Holocaust: History's "Memory Hole"', in *Remembering for the Future. The Impact of the Holocaust on the Contemporary World* (Oxford 1988) vol. 2, pp. 1360–1

33 Joshua Rubenstein and Vladimir Naumov (eds), *Stalin's Secret Pogrom. The PostWar Inquisition of the Jewish Anti-Fascist Committee* (New Haven 2001)

Chapter 18: Tenuous Altruism

1 Norbert Haase, 'Oberleutnant Albert Battel und Major Max Liedtke', in Wolfram Wette (ed.), *Retter in Uniform. Handlungsspielräume im Vernichtungskrieg der Wehrmacht* (Frankfurt am Main 2002) pp. 181–208

2 Arno Lustiger, 'Feldwebel Anton Schmidt. Judenretter aus Vilna 1941–1942' Wette (ed.), *Retter in Uniform*, pp. 45–63

3 P. M. Oliner and S. P. Oliner, 'Rescuers of Jews during the Holocaust. Justice, Care and Religion', in *Remembering for the Future. The Impact of the Holocaust on the Contemporary World* (Oxford 1988) vol. 1 pp. 506–16

4 Nechama Tec, 'Theoretical Analysis of Altruistic Rescue during the Holocaust', in John D. Michalczyk (ed.), *Resisters, Rescuers and Refugees. Historical and Ethical Issues* (Kansas City 1997) p. 158

5 Gunnar Paulsson, 'The "Bridge over the Oresund". The Historiography on the Expulsion of the Jew from Nazi-occupied Denmark', and the rebuttal by Hans Kirschhoff, 'Denmark: A Light in the Darkness of the Holocaust?', both in David Cesarani (ed.), *Holocaust. Critical Concepts in Historical Study* (London 2005) vol. 5 pp. 99–139

6 Much of the recent revisionist literature on Pius XII is cited in Michael Burleigh, *Sacred Causes. Religion and Politics from the European Dictators to Al Qaeda* (London 2006)

7 Eva Fogelman, *Conscience and Courage. Rescuers of Jews during the Holocaust* (London 1995) p. 172

8 Antony Polonsky, 'Beyond Condemnation, Apologetics, and Apology. On the Complexity of Polish Behaviour towards the Jews during the Second World War', in Cesarani (ed.), *Holocaust. Critical Concepts in Historical Studies*, vol. 5, p. 46

9 Ibid., pp. 57–8 for the full text

10 For numerous examples see Martin Gilbert, *The Righteous. The Unsung Heroes of the Holocaust* (New York 2003) pp. 101ff.

11 Fogelman, *Conscience and Courage*, p. 176

12 Ibid., p. 96

13 Bob Moore, *Victims and Survivors. The Nazi Persecution of the Jews in the Netherlands 1940–1945* (London 1997) pp. 91ff.

14 Ruth Bettina Birn, 'Hanns Rauter – Höhere SS-und Polizei Führer in den Niederlanden', in Ronald Smelser and Enrico Syring (eds), *Die SS. Elite unter dem Totenkopf. 30 Lebensläufe* (Paderborn 2000) pp. 408–17 for the only biography

15 Gerhard Hirschfeld, *Nazi Rule and Dutch Collaboration. The Netherlands under German Occupation 1940–1945* (Oxford 1988) p. 174

16 Ibid., p. 179 n. 173

17 Guus Meershoek, 'The Amsterdam Police and the Persecution of the Jews', in Cesarani (ed.), *Holocaust. Critical Concepts in Historical Study*, vol. 3 pp. 537–56

18 Ad van Liempt, *Hitler's Bounty Hunters. The Betrayal of the Jews* (Oxford 2005) pp. 19ff.

19 Ibid., pp. 40–2

20 These figures are mentioned by Dieter Pohl in the investigation 'Der dunkle Kontinent', *Der Spiegel* no. 21, 18 May 2009, pp. 82ff.

Chapter 19: 'The King's Thunderbolts are Righteous': RAF Bomber Command

1 Chris Ward, *5 Group Bomber Command. An Operational Record* (Barnsley 2007) p. 129

2 For these technical observations see Jarrod Cotter and Paul Blackah, *Avro Lancaster 1941 Onwards. Owners' Workshop Manual* (Yeovil 2008). There are only two operational Lancasters, one in Britain, the other in Canada

3 Peter Jacobs and Les Bartlett, *Bomb Aimer over Berlin. The Wartime Memoirs of Les Bartlett DFM* (Barnsley 2007) pp. 36–47, and Patrick Bishop, *Bomber Boys. Fighting Back 1940–1945* (London 2007) are both excellent accounts of life and death for RAF bomber crews

4 For numerous examples from among the best pilots see Chaz Bowyer, *Bomber Barons* (London 1983)

5 Ibid., p. 190

6 Ibid., p. 48

7 Stephen A. Garrett, *Ethics and Airpower in World War II. The British Bombing of German Cities* (London 1993) pp. 78–84

8 Geoffrey Best, *Humanity in Warfare. The Modern History of the International Law of Armed Conflict* (London 1980) pp. 266–7

9 Huw Strachan, 'Strategic Bombing and the Question of Civilian Casualties up to 1945', in Paul Addison and Jeremy Crang (eds), *Firestorm. The Bombing of Dresden 1945* (London 2006) pp. 6–7. This essay is easily the most intelligent contribution to this difficult subject

10 Richard Overy, *The Air War 1939–1945* (London 1980) pp. 13–14

11 Armin Nolzen, '"Sozialismus der Tat?" Die Nationalsozialistische Volkswohlfahrt (NSV) under der allierte Luftkrieg gegen das Deutsche Reich', in Dietmar Süss (ed.), *Deutschland im Luftkrieg. Geschichte und Erinnerung* (Munich 2007) pp. 57ff.

12 Tammi Davis Biddle, 'Air Power', in Michael Howard, George J. Andreopoulos and Mark Shulman (eds), *The Laws of War. Constraints on Warfare in the Western World* (New Haven 1994) p. 151

13 Geoffrey Best, *Humanity in Warfare*, pp. 273–4

14 Bowyer, *Bomber Barons*, p. 19

15 Denis Richards, *Portal of Hungerford* (London 1977) p. 301

16 This rather convoluted argument is made in 'The Phase of Preparation and the Start of the Bombing War: 11 May 1940–9 July 1941', in British Bombing Survey Unit (ed.), *The Strategic Air War against Germany 1939–1945* (London 1998) pp. 2–3

17 Richards, *Portal of Hungerford*, p. 301

18 Richard Overy, *Why the Allies Won* (London 1995) p. 108

19 John Colville, *The Fringes of Power. Downing Street Diaries 1939–1955* (London 1985) entries dated 20 September 1940, p. 206, and 13 December 1940, p. 265

20 John Ellis, *Brute Force. Allied Strategy and Tactics in the Second World War* (London 1990) p. 178

21 See the excellent analysis in Max Hastings, *Bomber Command* (London 1979) especially pp. 130–2

22 Richards, *Portal of Hungerford*, p. 305

23 Ellis, *Brute Force*, p. 172

24 Overy, *Air War*, pp. 116–17

25 Jonathan Glover, *Humanity. A Moral History of the Twentieth Century* (London 1999) pp. 71–2

26 Arthur Harris, *Bomber Offensive* (London 1998) p. 52

27 Henry Probert, *Bomber Harris. His Life and Times* (London 2006) pp. 33–64

28 Richards, *Portal of Hungerford*, p. 314

29 Probert, *Bomber Harris*, p. 222

30 Roy Irons, *The Relentless Offensive. War and Bomber Command 1939–1945* (Barnsley 2009) p. 116

31 Richards, *Portal of Hungerford*, pp. 72–3

32 Probert, *Bomber Harris*, pp. 199–200

33 Ibid., pp. 309–10

34 Richards, *Portal of Hungerford*, pp. 176–7. This is also the conclusion of A. C. Grayling, *Among the Dead Cities. Was the Allied Bombing of Civilians in WWII a Necessity or a Crime?* (London 2006)

35 British Bombing Survey Unit (ed.), *Strategic Air War against Germany*, p. 40

36 Martin Middlebrook, *The Battle of Hamburg. The Firestorm Raid* (London 1984) pp. 243ff.

37 Frederick Taylor, *Dresden. Tuesday 13 February 1945* (London 2004) pp. 114–15

38 Irons, *Relentless Offensive*, pp. 190–1

39 Randall Wakelaw, *The Science of Bombing. Operational Research in RAF Bomber Command* (Toronto 2009) p. 186 for these calculations

40 Jörg Friedrich, *The Fire. The Bombing of Germany 1940–1945* (New York 2006) pp. 70–1

41 Hastings, *Bomber Command*, pp. 147–8

42 Simon Read, *The Killing Skies. RAF Bomber Command at War* (Stroud 2006) p. 120

43 British Bombing Survey Unit (ed.), *Strategic Air War against Germany*, pp. 10–11

44 Ralf Georg Reuth (ed.), *Joseph Goebbels. Tagebücher 1924–1945* (Munich 1992) vol. 5, entries dated 10 April 1943, p. 1921, and 5 June 1943, p. 1936

45 British Bombing Survey Unit (ed.), *Strategic Air War against Germany*, pp. 10–11

46 Middlebrook, *Battle of Hamburg. The Firestorm Raid* is definitive

47 Hastings, *Bomber Command*, p. 341

48 On Vera Brittain's wartime writing see her *One Voice. Pacifist Writings from the Second World War* (London 2005). I am grateful to Mark Bostridge for giving me this book

49 Andrew Chandler, 'The Church of England and the Obliteration Bombing of Germany in the Second World War', *English Historical Review* (1993) 108 p. 926–8

50 Garrett, *Ethics and Airpower* pp. 105–8

51 Ibid., p. 113

52 Hansard vol. 130 cols. 747–50, 9 February 1944

53 Chandler, 'Church of England', p. 941

Chapter 20: Is That Britain? – No, It's Brittany

1 Richard G. Davis, *Carl A. Spaatz and the Air War in Europe* (Washington DC 1993) pp. 41–56

2 Ronald Schaffer, *Wings of Judgment. American Bombing in World War II* (Oxford 1985) pp. 32–3

3 Curtis LeMay with Kantor MacKinlay, *Mission with LeMay. My Story* (New York 1965) p. 280

4 See Martin Middlebrook, *The Schweinfurt–Regensburg Mission. American Raids on 17 August 1943* (London 1983)

5 Schaffer, *Wings of Judgment* p. 77

6 Frederick Taylor, *Dresden. Tuesday 13 February 1945* (London 2004) is the best recent account

7 See Paul Addison and Jeremy Crang (eds), *Firestorm. The Bombing of Dresden 1945* (London 2006) and especially the essays by Donald Bloxham and Richard Overy on the wider significance of the Dresden raids.

I disagree with Bloxham's conclusion that they were a war crime

8 Vera Brittain, *One Voice. Pacifist Writings from the Second World War* (London 2005) p. 159

9 LeMay, *Mission with LeMay*, pp. 330–1

10 Richard B. Frank, *Downfall. The End of the Imperial Japanese Empire* (London 1999) pp. 58ff.

11 *Louis Prima and his Orchestra 1944–1945* (Classic Record CD 2002)

12 Schaffer, *Wings of Judgment*, pp. 130ff.

13 Jonathan Glover, *Humanity. A Moral History of the Twentieth Century* (London 1999) p. 103 makes this telling point

14 See Kai Bird and Martin J. Sherwin, *American Prometheus. The Triumph and Tragedy of J. Robert Oppenheimer* (London 2008) pp. 256ff.

15 Charles Thorpe, *Oppenheimer. The Tragic Intellect* (Chicago 2006) pp. 128ff.

16 Sean L. Malloy, *Atomic Tragedy. Henry L. Stimson and the Decision to Use the Bomb against Japan* (Ithaca, New York 2008) pp. 60–1

17 Martin J. Sherwin, *A World Destroyed. Hiroshima and the Origins of the Arms Race* (New York 1987) pp. 58ff.

18 Richard Rhodes, *The Making of the Atomic Bomb* (New York 1986) p. 632

19 John Costello, *The Pacific War* (London 1981) p. 578

20 Frank, *Downfall*, pp. 337–43

21 John W. Dower, *War without Mercy. Race & Power in the Pacific War* (New York 1986) pp. 46–57

22 Richard B. Frank, 'Ending the Pacific War: Harry Truman and the Decision to Drop the Bomb', *Footnotes*, newsletter of the Foreign Policy Research Institute Wachman Center (2009) 14 pp. 1–14

23 Malloy, *Atomic Tragedy*, pp. 136–7

24 LeMay, *Mission with LeMay*, pp. 380–4 for his moral reflections

25 Overy, *Air War*, p. 100

26 John Hersey, *Hiroshima* (London 2008, originally New York 1946)

27 Frank, *Downfall*, pp. 285–7 for a careful discussion of these statistics

28 Bird and Sherwin, *American Prometheus* p. 332

Chapter 21: The Predators at Bay

1 Philip Morgan, *The Fall of Mussolini* (Oxford 2007) pp. 168ff. is useful

2 Ibid., p. 57

3 Hans Woller, '"Ausgebliebene Säuberung?"' Die Abrechnung mit dem Faschismus in Italien', in Klaus-Dietmar Henke and Hans Woller (eds), *Politische Säuberung in Europa. Die Abrechnung mit Faschismus und Kollaboration nach dem Zweiten Weltkrieg* (Munich 1991) p. 180

4 R. J. B. Bosworth, *Mussolini's Italy. Life under the Dictatorship* (London 2005) p. 543

5 Christopher Duggan, *The Force of Destiny. A History of Italy since 1796* (London 2007) p. 546 is an exemplary history of that complex country

6 Wolfram Wette, *Militarismus in Deutschland. Geschichte einer kriegerischen Kultur* (Darmstadt 2008) p. 211

7 Antony Beevor, *Berlin. The Downfall 1945* (London 2002) pp. 28ff. is the best account

8 Manfred Zeidler, 'Die Rote Armee auf deutschem Boden' in Horst Boog et al (eds) *Der Zusammenbruch des deutschen Reiches 1945* (Munich 2008) vol. 10 part I p. 718

9 Alexander Solzhenitsyn, *Prussian Nights. A Poem* (New York 1977) pp. 38–9

10 See the exceptionally interesting discussion in William I. Hitchcock, *The Bitter Road to Freedom. A New History of the Liberation of Europe* (New York 2008) pp. 102–22

11 Daniel Blatman, 'The Death Marches January–May 1945', in David Cesarani (ed.), *Holocaust. Critical Concepts in Historical Studies* (London 2004) vol. 6 pp. 69–70

12 See the thoughtful discussion in Robert Gellately, *Backing Hitler. Consent and Coercion in Nazi Germany* (Oxford 2001) pp. 242–52

13 Richard Bessel, *Nazism and War* (London 2004) p. 180 for the striking quotation

14 David Dilks (ed.), *The Diaries of Sir Alexander Cadogan 1938–1945* (London 1971) entry dated 3 May 1945, p. 738

15 See Edward Alexander, *A Crime of Vengeance. An Armenian Struggle for Justice* (New York 1993)

16 Arieh Kochavi, 'Britain and the Establishment of the United Nations War Crimes Commission', in Cesarani (ed.), *Holocaust. Critical Concepts in Historical Studies*, vol. 6 p. 130

17 Michael Marrus, *The Nuremberg War Crimes Trial 1945–46. A Documentary History* (New York 1997) p. 23

18 Gerd R. Ueberschär, 'Die sowjetischen Prozesse gegen deutsche Kriegsgefangene 1943–1952', in Gerd R. Ueberschär (ed.), *Der Nationalsozialismus vor Gericht. Die alliierten Prozesse gegen Kriegsverbrecher und Soldaten 1943–1952* (Frankfurt am Main 2008) pp. 240–4

19 Marrus, *Nuremberg War Crimes Trial*, p. 28

20 See Robert Gellately (ed.), *The Nuremberg Interviews. An American Psychiatrist's Conversations with the Defendants and Witnesses* (London 2006) pp. xvi–xvii

21 Marrus, *Nuremberg War Crimes Trial*, pp. 133ff.

22 Anna M. Cienciala, Natalia S. Lebedeva and Wojciech Materski (eds), *Katyń. A Crime without Punishment* (New Haven 2007) pp. 233–5

23 Marrus, *Nuremberg War Crimes Trial*, p. 128

24 See the very balanced account by Michael Marrus, 'The Holocaust at Nuremberg', in Cesarani (ed.), *Holocaust. Critical Concepts in Historical Studies*, vol. 6, pp. 158–84

25 For example Istvan Deak, 'Misjudgement at Nuremberg', *New York Review of Books* 7 October 1993, 40 pp. 1–17

26 Thomas Raithel, *Die Strafanstalt Landsberg am Lech und der Spöttinger Friedhof (1944–1958)* (Munich 2009) pp. 26–35

27 Apart from the Einsatzgruppen trial, the medical trial has proved fertile ground for historians. See, for example, Ulf Schmidt, *Karl Brandt. The Nazi Doctor. Medicine and Power in the Third Reich* (London 2007)

28 See Ernst Klee, *Was sie taten. Was sie wurden. Ärzte, Juristen und andere Beteiligte am Kranken- oder Judenmord* (Frankfurt am Main 1988) for how many doctors and lawyers evaded justice

29 Hitchcock, *Bitter Road to Freedom*, pp. 355–65

30 Ueberschär, 'Sowjetischen Prozesse gegen deutsche Kriegsgefangene', pp. 246ff.

31 The poster is in Robert Moeller, *War Stories. The Search for a Usable Past in the Federal Republic of Germany* (Berkeley 2001) Fig. 11 after p. 122

32 Stéphane Courtois, Nicolas Werth, Jean-Louis Panné, Andrzej Paczkowski, Karel Bartošek and Jean-Louis Margolin, *The Black Book of Communism. Crimes – Terror – Repression* (Cambridge, Massachusetts 1999)

33 Donald Goldstein and Katherine Dillon (eds), *Fading Victory. The Diary of Admiral Matome Ugaki 1941–1945* (Annapolis, Maryland 1991) entry dated 15 August 1945, pp. 663–6

34 Arnold C. Brackman, *The Other Nuremberg. The Untold Story of the Tokyo War Crimes Trials* (London 1989) pp. 46–8

35 Yuma Totani, *The Tokyo War Crimes Trial. The Pursuit of Justice in the Wake of World War II* (Cambridge, Massachusetts 2008) p. 106

36 Brackman, *Other Nuremberg*, p. 45

37 Frank Dikotter, *The Discourse of Race in Modern China* (Stanford 1992)

38 For the above see mainly John W. Dower's brilliant *Embracing Defeat. Japan in the Aftermath of World War II* (London 1999) pp. 289ff.

39 See John W. Dower, "An Aptitude for being Unloved". War and Memory in Japan', in Omar Bartov, Atina Grossman and Mary Nolan (eds), *Crimes of War. Guilt and Denial in the Twentieth Century* (New York 2002) p. 229

40 'Last words of the Tiger of Malaya. General Yamashita Tomoyuki', http://www.japanfocus.org

41 Herbert Bix, *Hirohito and the Making of Modern Japan* (New York 2000) p. 596

42 Totani, *Tokyo War Crimes Trial*, pp. 64–5

43 Ibid., pp. 131–41

44 Dower, *Embracing Defeat*, p. 446

45 For a vivid account of Japanese mistreatment of POWs and civilian internees see Max Hastings, *Nemesis. The Battle for Japan 1944–45* (London 2007) pp. 373ff.

46 Brackman, *Other Nuremberg*, pp. 450–3

Hastings:
published in USA as
"Retribution..."
I own a copy. Believe
Burleigh means ch. 15,
p 345 ff

SELECT BIBLIOGRAPHY

I have omitted many specialist titles which can be found in my earlier books on Nazism.

Adams, R. J. Q. *British Politics and Foreign Policy in the Age of Appeasement 1935–39* (London 1993)

Adelman, Jonathan (ed.) *Hitler and his Allies in World War II* (London 2007)

Adelson, Alan and Lapides, Robert (eds) *Łódź Ghetto. Inside a Community under Siege* (New York 1989)

Addison, Paul and Calder, Angus (eds) *Time to Kill. The Soldier's Experience of War in the West 1939–1945* (London 1997)

Addison, Paul and Crang, Jeremy (eds) *Firestorm. The Bombing of Dresden 1945* (London 2006)

Aly, Götz *Hitler's Beneficiaries. How the Nazis Bought the German People* (London 2007)

Angrick, Andrej *Besatzungspolitik und Massenmord. Die Einsatzgruppe D in der südlichen Sowjetunion 1941–1943* (Hamburg 2003)

Applebaum, Anne *GULAG: A History of the Soviet Camps* (London 2003)

Arad, Yitzshak, Krakowski, Shmuel and Spector, Shmuel (eds) *The Einsatzgruppen Reports. Selections from the Dispatches of the Nazi Death Squads' Campaign against the Jews in Occupied Territories of the Soviet Union July 1941–January 1943* (Jerusalem 1989)

Atkinson, Rick *An Army at Dawn. The War in North Africa 1942–1943* (London 2003)

—— *The Day of Battle. The War in Sicily and Italy 1943–1944* (New York 2007)

Aubrac, Lucie *Outwitting the Gestapo* (Lincoln, Nebraska 1993)

Azéma, Jean-Pierre and Bédarida, François (eds) *Vichy et les français* (Paris 1992)

Bailey, Roderick *The Wildest Province. SOE in the Land of the Eagle* (London 2008)

Bajohr, Frank 'Unser Hotel ist Judenfrei'. Bäder-Antisemitismus im 19. und 20. Jahrhundert (Frankfurt am Main 2003)

—— Parvenüs und Profiteure. Korruption in der NS-Zeit (Frankfurt am Main 2004)

—— and Pohl, Dieter Der Holocaust als offenes Geheimnis. Die Deutschen, die NS-Führung und die Allierten (Munich 2006)

—— Massenmord und schlechtes Gewissen. Die deutsche Bevölkerung, die NS-Führung und der Holocaust (Frankfurt am Main 2008)

Baker, Nicholson Human Smoke (London 2008)

Bankier, David (ed.) Secret Intelligence and the Holocaust (New York 2006)

Bardach, Janusz and Gleeson, Kathleen Man is Wolf to Man. Surviving the Gulag (Berkeley 1998)

Barnett, Correlli (ed.) Hitler's Generals (London 1989)

Barr, Niall Pendulum of War. The Three Battles of El Alamein (London 2004)

Beck, Earl Under the Bombs. The German Home Front 1942–1945 (Lexington, Kentucky 1986)

Beevor, Antony Berlin. The Downfall 1945 (London 2002)

—— D-Day. The Battle for Normandy (London 2009)

—— Stalingrad (London 1998)

—— and Vinogradova, Luba (eds) A Writer at War. Vasily Grossman with the Red Army 1941–1945 (London 2006)

Bellamy, Chris Absolute War. Soviet Russia in the Second World War (London 2007)

Bennett, Rab Under the Shadow of the Swastika. The Moral Dilemmas of Resistance and Collaboration in Hitler's Europe (London 1999)

Bess, Michael Choices under Fire. Moral Dimensions of World War II (New York 2006)

Bessel, Richard Nazism and War (London 2004)

Best, Geoffrey Humanity in Warfare. The Modern History of the International Law of Armed Conflict (London 1980)

—— Churchill and War (London 2005)

Bierman, John and Smith, Colin Alamein. War without Hate (London 2003)

Binney, Marcus Secret War Heroes. Men of the Special Operations Executive (London 2005)

Bird, Kai and Sherwin, Martin J. American Prometheus. The Triumph and Tragedy of J. Robert Oppenheimer (London 2008)

Bishop, Patrick Fighter Boys. Saving Britain 1940 (London 2004)

—— Bomber Boys. Fighting Back 1940–1945 (London 2007)

Bix, Herbert Hirohito and the Making of Modern Japan (New York 2000)

Bland, Larry (ed.) The Papers of George Catlett Marshall (Baltimore 1996) vols 1–4

Böhler, Jochen *Auftakt zum Vernichtungskrieg. Die Wehrmacht in Polen 1939* (Frankfurt am Main 2006)

Bohn, Robert (ed.) *Die deutsche Herrschaft in den 'germanischen' Ländern 1940–1945* (Stuttgart 1997)

Bönisch, Georg 'Der dunkle Kontinent' *Der Spiegel* 18 May 2009 pp. 82–92

Boog, Horst, Rahn, Werner, Stumpf, Reinhard and Wegner, Bernd (eds) *Die Welt im Krieg 1941–1943* (Frankfurt am Main 1992) vols 1–2

Bosworth, R. J. B. *Explaining Auschwitz and Hiroshima. History Writing and the Second World War 1945–1990* (London 1993)

—— *Mussolini's Italy. Life under the Dictatorship* (London 2005)

Bowman, James *Honor. A History* (New York 2006)

Brechtken, Magnus *'Madagascar für die Juden'. Antisemitische Idee und politische Praxis 1885–1945* (Munich 1997)

Breitman, Richard *Official Secrets. What the Nazis Planned, What the British and Americans Knew* (London 1998)

British Bombing Survey Unit (ed.) *The Strategic Air War against Germany 1939–1945* (London 1998)

Brittain, Vera *One Voice. Pacifist Writings from the Second World War* (London 2005)

Broszat, Martin and Schwabe, Klaus (eds) *Die deutschen Eliten und der Weg in den Zweiten Weltkrieg* (Munich 1989)

Bryant, Chad *Prague in Black. Nazi Rule and Czech Nationalism* (Cambridge, Massachusetts 2007)

Buber-Neumann, Margarete *Under Two Dictators. Prisoner of Stalin and Hitler* (London 2008)

Burdick, Charles and Jacobsen, Hans-Adolf (eds) *The Halder War Diary 1939–1942* (Novato, California 1988)

Burleigh, Michael *Germany Turns Eastwards. A Study of 'Ostforschung' in the Third Reich* (London 2003, originally Cambridge 1988)

—— *Death and Deliverance. 'Euthanasia' in Germany 1900–1945* (London 2003, originally Cambridge 1994)

—— *The Third Reich: A New History* (London 2000)

—— *Sacred Causes. Politics and Religion from the European Dictators to al-Qaeda* (London 2006)

—— (ed.) *Confronting the Nazi Past. New Debates on Modern German History* (London 1996)

—— and Wippermann, Wolfgang *The Racial State. Germany 1933–1945* (Cambridge 1991)

Burrin, Philippe *Living with Defeat. France under German Occupation 1940–1944* (London 1996)

Butcher, Harry C. *Three Years with Eisenhower* (London 1946)

Butow, Robert *Tojo and the Coming of the War* (Stanford, California 1969)

Carlton, David *Anthony Eden* (London 1981)
—— *Churchill and the Soviet Union* (Manchester 2000)
Cesarani, David (ed.) *The Final Solution. Origins and Implementation* (London 1994)
—— (ed.) *Genocide and Rescue. The Holocaust in Hungary 1944* (Oxford 1997)
—— (ed.) *Holocaust. Critical Concepts in Historical Studies* (London 2004) vols 1–6
—— and Levine, Paul (eds) *'Bystanders' to the Holocaust. A Re-evaluation* (London 2002)
—— *Eichmann. His Life and Crimes* (London 2005)
Chandler, Andrew 'The Church of England and the Obliteration Bombing of Germany in the Second World War' *English Historical Review* (1993) 108, pp. 920–46
Churchill, Winston S. *The Second World War* (London 1948–55) vols 1–6
Ciano, Galeazzo *Diary 1937–1943* (London 2002)
Cienciala, Anna M., Lebedeva, Natalia J. and Materski, Wojciech (eds) *Katyń. A Crime without Punishment* (New Haven 2007)
Citino, Robert M. *The Path to Blitzkrieg. Doctrine and Training in the German Army 1920–39* (Mechanicsburg, Pennsylvania 1999)
—— *Death of the Wehrmacht. The German Campaigns of 1942* (Lawrence, Kansas 2007)
Clinton, Alan *Jean Moulin 1899–1943. The French Resistance and the Republic* (London 2002)
Cobb, Matthew *The Resistance. The French Fight against the Nazis* (London 2009)
Coffey, Thomas *Iron Eagle. The Turbulent Life of General Curtis LeMay* (New York 1986)
Cohen, Eliot *Supreme Command. Soldiers, Statesmen, and Leadership in Wartime* (New York 2002)
Cointet, Michèle *L'Eglise sous Vichy 1940–1945* (Paris 1998)
Connelly, Mark *Reaching for the Stars: A New History of Bomber Command in World War Two* (London 2001)
Conquest, Robert *The Great Terror* (London 1968)
—— *Stalin. Breaker of Nations* (London 1991)
Cornwall, Mark and Evans, R. J. W. (eds) *Czechoslovakia in a Nationalist and Fascist Europe 1918–1948* (London 2007)
Costello, John *The Pacific War* (London 1981)
Cotter, Jarrod and Blackah, Paul *Avro Lancaster 1941 Onwards. Owners' Workshop Manual* (Yeovil 2008)

Cowling, Maurice *The Impact of Hitler. British Politics and British Policy 1933–1940* (Cambridge 1975)

Cray, Ed *General of the Army. George C. Marshall, Soldier and Statesman* (New York 1990)

Cull, Nicholas John *Selling War. The British Propaganda Campaign against American 'Neutrality' in World War II* (Oxford 1995)

Cüppers, Martin *Wegbereiter der Shoah. Die Waffen-SS, der Kommandostab Reichsführer-SS und die Judenvernichtung 1939–1945* (Darmstadt 2005)

Dahl, Hans Frederik *Quisling. A Study in Treachery* (Cambridge 1999)

Dallin, Alexander *German Rule in Russia* (London 1981)

Davies, Norman *Europe at War 1939–1945. No Simple Victory* (London 2006)

Davis, Richard G. *Carl A. Spaatz and the Air War in Europe* (Washington DC 1993)

Del Boca, Angelo *The Ethiopian War 1935–1941* (Chicago 1969)

D'Este, Carlo *Patton* (London 1996)

—— *Eisenhower* (London 2002)

—— *Warlord. Churchill 1874–1945* (London 2009)

Dilks, David (ed.) *The Diaries of Sir Alexander Cadogan 1938–1945* (London 1971)

Dodd, William E., Jr, and Dodd, Martha (eds) *Ambassador Dodd's Diary 1933–1938* (London 1941)

Dower, John W. *War without Mercy. Race & Power in the Pacific War* (New York 1986)

—— *Embracing Defeat. Japan in the Aftermath of World War II* (London 1999)

Du Réau, Elizabeth *Edouard Daladier 1884–1970* (Paris 1993)

Edwards, Robert *Cassino. The Hollow Victory. The Battle for Rome January-June 1944* (London 1984)

Ellis, John *The Sharp End. The Fighting Man in World War II* (London 2009)

—— *Brute Force. Allied Strategy and Tactics in the Second World War* (London 1990)

—— *White Death. Russia's War on Finland 1939–40* (London 2006)

Fenby, Jonathan *The Penguin History of Modern China. The Fall and Rise of a Great Power 1850–2008* (London 2008)

Ferguson, Niall *War of the World. History's Age of Hatred* (London 2006)

Field, Frank (ed.) *Attlee's Great Contemporaries. The Politics of Character* (London 2009)

Figes, Orlando *The Whisperers. Private Life in Stalin's Russia* (London 2008)

Fogelman, Eva *Conscience and Courage. Rescuers of Jews during the Holocaust* (London 1995)

Foot, M. R. D. *SOE. The Special Operations Executive 1940–1946* (London 1999)

Förster, Jürgen and Mawdsley, Evan 'Hitler and Stalin in Perspective. Secret Speeches on the Eve of Barbarossa' *War in History* (2004) 11 pp. 61–103

Frank, Richard B. *Downfall. The End of the Imperial Japanese Empire* (London 1999)

Freedman, Lawrence (ed.) *War* (Oxford 1994)

Frei, Norbert (ed.) *Hitlers Eliten nach 1945* (Frankfurt am Main 2007)

Frenay, Henri *The Night Will End. Memoirs of the Resistance* (London 1976)

Friedländer, Saul *The Years of Extermination. Nazi Germany and the Jews 1939–1945* (London 2007)

Fritz, Stephen G. *Frontsoldaten. The German Soldier in World War II* (Lexington, Kentucky 1995)

Furet, François, and Nolte, Ernst *Fascism and Communism* (Lincoln, Nebraska 2001)

Gellately, Robert *Backing Hitler. Consent and Coercion in Nazi Germany* (Oxford 2001)

—— (ed.) *The Nuremberg Interviews. An American Psychiatrist's Conversations with the Defendants and Witnesses* (London 2006)

Getty, J. Arch and Manning, Roberta T. (eds) *Stalin's Terror. New Perspectives* (Cambridge 1993)

—— and Naumov, Oleg V. *Yezhov. The Rise of Stalin's 'Iron Fist'* (New Haven 2008)

Gilbert, Martin *Churchill's Political Philosophy* (Oxford 1981)

—— *Auschwitz and the Allies* (London 1981)

—— *The Righteous. The Unsung Heroes of the Holocaust* (New York 2003)

—— (ed.) *Avraham Tory. The Kovno Ghetto Diary* (Cambridge, Massachusetts 1990)

—— and Churchill, Randolph *Winston S. Churchill* (London 1966–88) vols 1–8

Gildea, Robert *Marianne in Chains. In Search of the German Occupation 1940–1945* (London 2002)

Glantz, David *Soviet Military Deception in the Second World War* (London 1989)

—— *The Role of Intelligence in Soviet Military Strategy in World War II* (Novato, California 1990)

—— *From the Don to the Dnepr* (London 1991)

—— *The Military Strategy of the Soviet Union: A History* (London 1992)

—— *A History of Soviet Airborne Forces* (London 1994)

—— (ed.) *The Initial Period of War on the Eastern Front 22 June–August 1941* (London 1993)

—— and Orenstein, Harold S. (eds) *The Battle for Kursk 1943* (London 1999)

Glover, Jonathan *Humanity. A Moral History of the Twentieth Century* (London 1999)

Goldstein, Donald and Dillon, Katherine (eds) *Fading Victory. The Diary of Admiral Matome Ugaki 1941–1945* (Annapolis, Maryland 1991)

Golovchansky, Anatoly et al. (eds) *'Ich will raus aus diesem Wahnsinn': Deutsche Briefe von der Ostfront 1941–1945. Aus sowjetischen Archiven* (Hamburg 1993)

Gordon, Andrew *A Modern History of Japan. From Tokugawa Times to the Present* (New York 2003)

Gorsuch, Anne E. *Youth in Revolutionary Russia. Enthusiasts, Bohemians, Delinquents* (Bloomington, Indiana 2000)

Graml, Hermann *Hitler und England. Ein Essay zur nationalsozialistischen Aussenpolitik 1920 bis 1940* (Munich 2010)

Grayling, A. C. *Among the Dead Cities. Was the Allied Bombing of Civilians in WWII a Necessity or a Crime?* (London 2006)

Gruhl, Werner *Imperial Japan's World War Two* (New Brunswick, New Jersey 2007)

Guéhenno, Jean *Journal des années noires 1940–1944* (Paris 1947)

Gunther, John *Inside Europe* (London 1938)

Guthrie, Charles and Quinlan, Michael *Just War. The Just War Tradition. Ethics in Modern Warfare* (London 2007)

Haase, Norbert and Paul, Gerhard (eds) *Die anderen Soldaten. Wehrkraftzersetzung, Gehorsamsverweigerung und Fahnenflucht im Zweiten Weltkrieg* (Frankfurt am Main 1995)

Haestrup, Jørgen *European Resistance Movements, 1939–1945. A Complete History* (Westport, Connecticut 1981)

Haffner, Sebastian *Germany. Jekyll & Hyde. A Contemporary Account of Nazi Germany* (London 2005, originally 1940)

—— *Geschichte eines Deutschen. Die Erinnerungen 1914–1933* (Stuttgart and Munich 2003)

Halifax, Lord *The Fulness of Days* (London 1957)

Halls, W. D. *Politics, Society and Christianity in Vichy France* (Oxford 1995)

Ham, Paul *Kokoda* (Sydney 2005)

Harris, Arthur *Despatch on War Operations. 23rd February 1942 to 8th May 1945* (London 1995)

—— *Bomber Offensive* (London 1998)

Hartmann, Christian *Wehrmacht im Ostkrieg. Front und militärisches Hinterland 1941/42* (Munich 2009)

—— (ed.) *Von Feldherren und Gefreiten. Zur biographischen Dimension des Zweiten Weltkriegs* (Munich 2008)

——, Hürter, Johannes and Jureit, Ulrike (eds) *Verbrechen der Wehrmacht. Bilanz einer Debatte* (Munich 2005)

——, Hürter, Johannes, Lieb, Peter and Pohl, Dieter (eds) *Der deutsche Krieg im Osten 1941–1944. Facetten einer Grenzüberschreitung* (Munich 2009)

Hassell, Ulrich von Hassell *The von Hassell Diaries. The Story of the Forces against Hitler inside Germany 1938–1944* (Boulder, Colorado 1994)

Hastings, Max *Bomber Command* (London 1979)

—— *Das Reich. The March of the 2nd SS Panzer Division through France June 1944* (London 1981)

—— *Overlord. D-Day and the Battle for Normandy* (London 1984)

—— *Armageddon. The Battle for Germany 1944–45* (London 2004)

—— *Nemesis. The Battle for Japan 1944–45* (London 2007)

—— *Finest Years. Churchill as Warlord 1940–45* (London 2009)

Haukelid, Knut *Skis against the Atom* (Minot, North Dakota 1989)

Havens, Thomas *Valley of Darkness. The Japanese People in World War Two* (Lanham, Maryland 1986)

Haynes, John Earl, Klehr, Harvey and Vassiliev, Alexander *Spies. The Rise and Fall of the KGB in America* (New Haven 2009)

Headland, Ronald *Messages of Murder. A Study of the Reports of the Einsatzgruppen of the Security Police and the Security Service 1941–1943* (London 1992)

Heer, Hannes and Naumann, Klaus (eds) *Vernichtungskrieg. Verbrechen der Wehrmacht 1941–1944* (Hamburg 1995)

—— 'Extreme Normalität. Generalmajor Gustav Freiherr von Mauchenheim gen. Bechtolsheim. Umfeld, Motive und Entschlussbildung eines Holocaust-Täters' *Zeitschrift für Geschichtswissenschaft* (2003) 51 pp. 729–53

Heiber, Helmut and Glantz, David (eds) *Hitler and his Generals. Military Conferences 1942–1945* (New York 2003)

Henderson, Nevile *Failure of a Mission. Berlin 1937–1939* (London 1940)

Herbert, Ulrich (ed.) *Nationalsozialistische Vernichtungspolitik 1939–1945. Neue Forschungen und Kontroversen* (Frankfurt am Main 1998)

Hersey, John *Hiroshima* (London 1985, originally New York 1946)

Hillary, Richard *The Last Enemy* (London 1950)

Hirschfeld, Gerhard *Nazi Rule and Dutch Collaboration. The Netherlands under German Occupation 1940–1945* (Oxford 1988)

Hitchcock, William I. *The Bitter Road to Freedom. A New History of the Liberation of Europe* (New York 2008)

Hitler, Adolf *Mein Kampf* trans. Ralph Manheim (London 1974)

Hoffmann, Stanley *Decline and Renewal? France since the 1930s* (New York 1974)

Holland, James *Italy's Sorrow. A Year of War 1944–1945* (London 2008)

—— *Together We Stand. North Africa 1942–1943. Turning the Tide in the West* (London 2006)

Holmes, Richard *Acts of War. The Behaviour of Men in Battle* (London 1985)

Holmes, Robert L. *On War and Morality* (Princeton 1989)

Hore, Peter (ed.) *Patrick Blackett. Sailor, Scientist and Socialist* (London 2003)

Hosking, Geoffrey *A History of the Soviet Union 1917–1991* (London 1985)

—— *Rulers and Victims. The Russians in the Soviet Union* (Cambridge, Massachusetts 2006)

Humbert, Agnès *Résistance. Memoirs of Occupied France* (London 2008)

Hürter, Johannes *Hitlers Heerführer. Die deutschen Oberbefehlshaber im Krieg gegen die Sowjetunion 1941/42* (Munich 2006)

—— '"Es herrschen Sitten und Gebräuche, genauso wie im 30-Jährigen Krieg". Das erste Jahr des deutsch–sowjetischen Krieges in Dokumenten des Generals Gotthard Heinrici' *VfZ* (2000) 48 pp. 329–403

—— 'Auf dem Weg zur Militäropposition. Tresckow, Gersdorff, der Vernichtungskrieg und der Judenmord. Neue Dokumente über das Verhältnis der Heeresgruppe Mitte zur Einsatzgruppe B im Jahr 1941' *VfZ* (2004) 52 pp. 527–562

—— and Zarusky, Jürgen (eds) *Besatzung, Kollaboration, Holocaust. Neue Studien zur Verfolgung und Ermordung der europäischen Juden* (Munich 2008)

Ibuse, Matsuji *Black Rain* (Tokyo 1969)

Ioanid, Radu *The Holocaust in Romania. The Destruction of the Jews and Gypsies under the Antonescu Regime 1940–1944* (Chicago 2000)

Iriye, Akira *Power and Culture. The Japanese–American War 1941–1945* (Cambridge, Massachusetts 1981)

—— *The Origins of the Second World War in Asia and the Pacific* (London 1987)

—— *Japan and the Wider World. From the Mid-Nineteenth Century to the Present* (London 1997)

Irons, Ray *The Relentless Offensive. War and Bomber Command 1939–1945* (Barnsley 2009)

Jackson, Julian *France. The Dark Years 1940–1944* (Oxford 2001)

—— *The Fall of France. The Nazi Invasion of 1940* (Oxford 2003)

Jacobs, Peter and Bartlett, Les *Bomb Aimer over Berlin. The Wartime Memoirs of Les Bartlett DFM* (Barnsley 2007)

Jäger, Herbert *Verbrechen unter totalitärer Herrschaft. Studien zur nationalsozialistischen Gewaltkriminalität* (Frankfurt am Main 1982, originally 1967)

Jansen, Marc and Petrov, Nikita *Stalin's Loyal Executioner. People's Commissar Nikolai Ezhov 1895–1940* (Stanford, California 2002)

Jones, F. C. *Japan's New Order in East Asia. Its Rise and Fall 1937–1945* (Oxford 1954)

Jong, Louis de *The Collapse of a Colonial Society. The Dutch in Indonesia during the Second World War* (Leiden 2002)

Jordan, William *Conquest without Victory. A New Zealander's Experiences in the Resistance in Greece and France* (London 1969)

Kaplan, Alice *The Collaborator. The Trial and Execution of Robert Brasillach* (Chicago 2000)

Karlsch, Rainer *Hitlers Bombe. Die geheime Geschichte der deutschen Kernwaffenversuche* (Munich 2005)

Kater, Michael *Hitler Youth* (Cambridge, Massachusetts 2004)

Kedward, Harry Roderick *Resistance in Vichy France. A Study of Ideas and Motivation in the Southern Zone 1940–1942* (Oxford 1978)

—— *Occupied France. Collaboration and Resistance 1940–1944* (Oxford 1985)

—— *In Search of the Maquis. Rural Resistance in Southern France 1942–1944* (Oxford 1993)

—— *La Vie en bleu. France and the French since 1900* (London 2005)

Kellermann, Volkmar *Schwarzer Adler, Weisser Adler. Die Polenpolitik der Weimarer Republik* (Cologne 1970)

Kelly, Catriona *Comrade Pavlik. The Rise and Fall of a Soviet Boy Hero* (London 2005)

Kennedy, Major-General Sir John *The Business of War* (London 1957)

Kershaw, Ian *The 'Hitler Myth'. Image and Reality in the Third Reich* (Oxford 1987)

—— *Hitler 1889–1936. Hubris* (London 1998)

—— *Hitler 1936–1945. Nemesis* (London 2000)

—— *Fateful Choices. Ten Decisions that Changed the World 1940–1941* (London 2007)

—— *Hitler, the Germans, and the Final Solution* (New Haven 2008)

—— and Lewin, Moshe (eds) *Stalinism and Nazism. Dictatorships in Comparison* (Cambridge 1997)

Kesselring, Field Marshal Albert *The Memoirs of Field-Marshal Kesselring* (London 2007)

Kettenacker, Lothar (ed.) *Ein Volk von Opfern? Die neue Debatte um den Bombenkrieg 1940–45* (Berlin 2003)

Kimball, Warren *Forged in War. Churchill, Roosevelt and the Second World War* (London 1997)

Kindelberger, Charles *The World in Depression 1929–1939* (London 1987)

Kittel, Manfred *Nach Nürnberg und Tokyo. 'Vergangenheitsbewältigung' in Japan und Westdeutschland 1945 bis 1968* (Munich 2004)

Kladstrup, Don and Petie *War & Wine. The French, the Nazis and France's Greatest Treasure* (London 2001)

Knox, MacGregor *Common Destiny. Dictatorship, Foreign Policy and War in Fascist Italy and Nazi Germany* (Cambridge 2000)

—— *Hitler's Italian Allies. Royal Armed Forces, Fascist Regime, and the War of 1940–1943* (Cambridge 2000)

Koonz, Claudia *The Nazi Conscience* (Cambridge, Massachusetts 2003)

Kozak, Warren *LeMay. The Life and Wars of General Curtis LeMay* (Washington DC 2009)

Krakowski, Shmuel *Das Todeslager Chelmno/Kulmhof. Der Beginn der 'Endlösung'* (Göttingen 2007)

Kushner, Barak *The Thought War. Japanese Imperial Propaganda* (Honolulu 2006)

Lamb, Richard *War in Italy 1943–1945. A Brutal Story* (New York 1994)

—— *Mussolini and the British* (London 1997)

Laqueur, Walter Z. *The Political Psychology of Appeasement. Finlandization and Other Unpopular Essays* (New Brunswick, New Jersey 1980)

Larsen, Stein Ugelvik, Sandberg, Beatrice and Dahm, Volker (eds) *Meldungen aus Norwegen 1940–1945. Die geheimen Lageberichte des Befehlshabers der Sicherheitspolizei und des SD in Norwegen* (Munich 2008) vols 1–3

Laruelle, Marlene (ed.) *Russian Nationalism and the National Reassertion of Russia* (London 2009)

Ledig, Paul *Payback* (London 2003)

Lehnstaedt, Stephan *Okkupation im Osten. Besatzeralltag in Warschau und Minsk 1939–1944* (Munich 2009)

LeMay, Curtis with MacKinlay, Kantor *Mission with LeMay. My Story* (New York 1965)

Levine, Joshua (ed.) *Forgotten Voices of the Blitz and the Battle of Britain* (London 2007)

Li, Lincoln *The Japanese Army in North China 1937–1941. Problems of Political and Economic Control* (Oxford 1975)

Lieb, Peter *Konventioneller Krieg oder NS-Weltanschauungskrieg? Kriegsführung und Partisanenbekämpfung in Frankreich 1943/44* (Munich 2007)

—— 'Täter aus Überzeugung? Oberst Carl von Andrian und die Judenmorde der 707 Infanteriedivision 1941/42' *VfZ* (2002) 50 pp. 523–57

Liempt, Ad van *Hitler's Bounty Hunters. The Betrayal of the Jews* (Oxford 2005)

London, Louise *Whitehall and the Jews 1933–1948. British Immigration Policy and the Holocaust* (Cambridge 2000)

Longerich, Peter *Heinrich Himmler. Biographie* (Munich 2008)

Lucas, Laddie (ed.) *Voices in the Air 1939–1945* (London 2003)

Lukacs, John *The Last European War September 1939–December 1941* (New Haven 1976)

—— *The Duel. Hitler vs. Churchill 10 May–31 July 1940* (London 1990)

—— *Five Days in London. May 1940* (New Haven 1999)

—— *Blood, Toil, Tears and Sweat. The Dire Warning. Churchill's First Speech as Prime Minister* (New York 2008)

Lukes, Igor and Goldstein, Erik (eds) *The Munich Crisis 1938. Prelude to World War* (London 1999)

Lyman, Robert *Slim, Master of War. Burma and the Birth of Modern Warfare* (London 2004)

Lyttelton, Adrian *The Seizure of Power. Fascism in Italy 1919–1929* (London 1987)

—— (ed.) *Liberal and Fascist Italy* (Oxford 2002)

Lytton, Neville *Life in Unoccupied France* (London 1942)

MacDonald, Callum A. *The United States, Britain and Appeasement 1936–1939* (London 1981)

MacNeice, Louis *Autumn Journal* (London 1988, originally 1939)

Malia, Martin *The Soviet Tragedy. A History of Socialism 1917–2000* (New York 1994)

Mallett, Robert *Mussolini and the Origins of the Second World War 1933–1940* (London 2003)

Mallmann, Klaus-Michael and Paul, Gerhard (eds) *Karrieren der Gewalt. Nationalsozialistische Täterbiographien* (Darmstadt 2005)

——, Böhler, Jochen, Matthäus and Jürgen *Einsatzgruppen in Polen. Darstellung und Dokumentation* (Darmstadt 2008)

——, Riess, Volker and Pyta, Wolfram *Deutscher Osten 1939–1945. Der Weltanschauungskrieg in Photos und Texten* (Darmstadt 2003)

Malloy, Sean L. *Atomic Tragedy. Henry L. Stimson and the Decision to Use the Bomb against Japan* (Ithaca, New York 2008)

Markusen, Eric and Kopf, David *The Holocaust and Strategic Bombing. Genocide and Total War in the 20th Century* (Boulder, Colorado 1995)

Marshall, S. L. A. *Men against Fire. The Problem of Battle Command* (Norman, Oklahoma 2000)

Maslov, Aleksandr *Fallen Soviet Generals. Soviet General Officers Killed in Battle 1941–1945* trans. and ed. David M. Glantz (London 1998)

Masson, Madeleine *Christine. SOE Agent & Churchill's Favourite Spy* (London 1975)

Mawdsley, Evan *Thunder in the East. The Nazi–Soviet War 1941–1945* (London 2005)

May, Larry *War Crimes and Just War* (Cambridge 2007)

Mazower, Mark *Hitler's Empire. How the Nazis Ruled Europe* (London 2008)

Megargee, Geoffrey *Barbarossa 1941. Hitler's War of Annihilation* (Stroud 2008)

Merridale, Catherine *Ivan's War. The Red Army 1939–45* (London 2005)

Meyer, Klaus and Wippermann, Wolfgang (eds) *Der Vernichtungskrieg gegen die Sowjetunion 1941–1945* (Frankfurt am Main 1992)

Michalczyk, John (ed.) *Resisters, Rescuers and Refugees. Historical and Ethical Issues* (Kansas City 1997)

Middlebrook, Martin *The Schweinfurt–Regensburg Mission. American Raids on 17 August 1943* (London 1983)

—— *The Battle of Hamburg. The Firestorm Raid* (London 1984)

—— *The Berlin Raids. RAF Bomber Command Winter 1943–44* (London 1988)

Militärgeschichtlichen Forschungsamt (ed.) *Das Deutsche Reich und der Zweite Weltkrieg* (Stuttgart/Munich 1979–2005) vols 1–9

Milosz, Czeslaw *Legends of Modernity. Essays and Letters from Occupied Poland 1942–1943* (New York 2005)

Milward, Alan *War, Economy and Society 1939–1945* (London 1987)

Moeller, Robert *War Stories. The Search for a Usable Past in the Federal Republic of Germany* (Berkeley 2001)

Möller, Horst (ed.) *Der rote Holocaust und die Deutschen. Die Debatte um das 'Schwarzbuch des Kommunismus'* (Munich 1999)

Moore, Bob *Victims and Survivors. The Nazi Persecution of the Jews in the Netherlands 1940–1945* (London 1997)

Moorehead, Alan *The Desert War* (London 1944)

Morgan, Philip *The Fall of Mussolini* (Oxford 2007)

Müller, Rolf-Dieter *Hitlers Ostkrieg und die deutsche Siedlungspolitik. Die Zusammenarbeit von Wehrmacht, Wirtschaft und SS* (Frankfurt am Main 1991)

—— *Kriegsende 1945. Die Zerstörung des Deutschen Reiches* (Frankfurt am Main 1994)

—— *An der Seite der Wehrmacht. Hitlers ausländische Helfer beim 'Kreuzzug gegen den Bolshewismus' 1941–1945* (Berlin 2007)

—— and Ueberschär, Gerd (eds) *Hitlers Krieg im Osten 1941–1945. Ein Forschungsbericht* (Darmstadt 2000

Musial, Bogdan *Deutsche Zivilverwaltung und Judenverfolgung im Generalgouvernement. Eine Fallstudie zum Distrikt Lublin 1939–1944* (Wiesbaden 1999)

—— 'Konterrevolutionaere Elemente sind zu erschiessen'. Die Brutalisierung des deutsch–sowjetischen Krieges im Sommer 1941 (Berlin 2000)

Myers, Ramon and Peattie, Mark (eds) The Japanese Colonial Empire 1895–1945 (Princeton 1984)

Neitzel, Sönke 'Deutsche Generäle in britischer Gefangenschaft 1942–1945. Eine Auswahledition der Abhörprotokolle des Combined Services Detailed Interrogation Centre UK' VfZ (2004) 52 pp. 289–438

Neufeld, Michael J. and Berenbaum, Michael (eds) The Bombing of Auschwitz. Should the Allies Have Attempted It? (Lawrence, Kansas 2003)

Neville, Peter Hitler and Appeasement. The British Attempt to Prevent the Second World War (London 2006)

Nicolson, Nigel (ed.) The Harold Nicolson Diaries 1907–1963 (London 2004)

Norwich, John Julius (ed.) The Duff Cooper Diaries 1915–1951 (London 2005)

Nossiter, Adam France and the Nazis. Memories, Lies and the Second World War (London 2001)

Nunneley, John and Tamayama, Kazuo (eds) Tales by Japanese Soldiers of the Burma Campaign 1942–1945 (London 2000)

Ory, Pascal Les Collaborateurs 1940–1945 (Paris 1976)

Ottmer, Hans-Martin 'Weserübung'. Der deutsche Angriff auf Dänemark und Norwegen im April 1940 (Munich 1994)

Overy, Richard The Air War 1939–1945 (London 1980)

—— The Origins of the Second World War (London 1987)

—— Why the Allies Won (London 1995)

—— The Battle (London 2000)

—— The Dictators. Hitler's Germany, Stalin's Russia (London 2004)

—— 1939. Countdown to War (London 2009)

—— with Wheatcroft, Andrew The Road to War (London 1999)

Parker, Matthew The Battle of Britain July-October 1940. An Oral History of Britain's 'Finest Hour' (London 2000)

Parker, R. A .C. Chamberlain and Appeasement. British Policy and the Coming of the Second World War (London 1993)

—— Struggle for Survival. The History of the Second World War (Oxford 1989); 2nd ed The Second World War. A Short History (Oxford 1997)

—— Churchill and Appeasement (London 2000)

Paul, Gerhard Bilder des Krieges. Krieg der Bilder. Die Visualisierung des Modernen Krieges (Paderborn 2004)

—— (ed.) Die Täter der Shoah. Fanatische Nationalsozialisten oder ganz normale Deutsche? (Göttingen 2002)

Paxton, Robert *Vichy France. Old Guard and New Order 1940–1944* (New York 1972)

Perlmutter, Amos *FDR and Stalin. A Not So Grand Alliance 1943–1945* (Columbia, Missouri 1993)

Perrin, Nigel *Spirit of the Resistance. The Life of SOE Agent Harry Peulevé* (Barnsley 2008)

Perry, Mark *Partners in Command. George Marshall and Dwight Eisenhower in War and Peace* (New York 2007)

Petrow, Richard *The Bitter Years. The Invasion and Occupation of Denmark and Norway April 1940–May 1945* (London 1974)

Pimlott, Ben *Hugh Dalton* (London 1995)

—— (ed.) *The Second World War Diary of Hugh Dalton 1940–45* (London 1986)

Pipes, Richard *Russia under the Bolshevik Regime 1919–1924* (Cambridge, Massachusetts 1994)

Poel, Jean van der (ed.) *Selections from the Smuts Papers* (Cambridge 1973) vol. 6 December 1934–August 1945

Poewe, Karla *New Religions and the Nazis* (Abingdon 2006)

Pohl, Dieter *Die Herrschaft der Wehrmacht. Deutsche Militärbesatzung und einheimische Bevölkerung in der Sowjetunion 1941–1944* (Munich 2008)

Poprzeczny, Joseph *Odilo Globocnik. Himmler's Man in the East* (Jefferson, North Carolina 2004)

Prazmowska, Anita *Eastern Europe and the Origins of the Second World War* (London 2000)

Probert, Henry *Bomber Harris. His Life and Times* (London 2006)

Pryce-Jones, David *Paris in the Third Reich. A History of the German Occupation 1940–1944* (London 1981)

Ramsden, John *Don't Mention the War. The British and the Germans since 1890* (London 2006)

Read, Simon *The Killing Skies. RAF Bomber Command at War* (Stroud 2006)

Rees, Laurence *Horror in the East* (London 2001)

Reuth, Ralf Georg (ed.) *Joseph Goebbels. Tagebücher 1924–1945* (Munich 1992) vols 1–5

Reynolds, David *Summits. Six Meetings that Shaped the Twentieth Century* (London 2007)

Rhodes, Richard *The Making of the Atomic Bomb* (New York 1986)

Rhodes James, Robert *Winston S. Churchill. His Complete Speeches 1897–1963* (London 1974) vols 1–8

Richards, Denis *Portal of Hungerford* (London 1977)

Robbins, Keith *Appeasement* (Oxford 1997)

Roberts, Andrew '*The Holy Fox'. A Life of Lord Halifax* (London 1991)

—— *Masters and Commanders. How Roosevelt, Churchill, Marshall and Alanbrooke Won the War in the West* (London 2008)

—— *The Storm of War. A New History of the Second World War* (London 2009)

Roberts, Geoffrey *The Soviet Union and the Origins of the Second World War. Russo-German Relations and the Road to War 1933–1941* (London 1995)

Rodogno, Davide *Fascism's European Empire. Italian Occupation during the Second World War* (Cambridge 2006)

Rogalla von Bieberstein, Johannes *'Jüdischer Bolshewismus'. Mythos und Realität* (Dresden 2002)

Rolfe, Mel *Flying into Hell. The Bomber Command Offensive as Recorded by the Crews Themselves* (London 2001)

Rosenberg, William G. (ed.) *Bolshevik Visions. First Phase of the Cultural Revolution in Soviet Russia* (Ann Arbor, Michigan 1990)

Ross, David *Richard Hillary* (London 2003)

Rossino, Alexander B. *Hitler Strikes Poland. Blitzkrieg, Ideology, and Atrocity* (Lawrence, Kansas 2003)

Roth, John (ed.) *Ethics after the Holocaust* (St Paul, Minnesota 1999)

Roth, Markus *'Herrenmenschen'. Die deutschen Kreishauptleute im besetzten Polen* (Göttingen 2009)

Rubenstein, Joshua *Tangled Loyalties. The Life and Times of Ilya Ehrenburg* (London 1996)

—— and Naumov, Vladimir (eds) *Stalin's Secret Pogrom. The Postwar Inquisition of the Jewish Anti-Fascist Committee* (New Haven 2001)

Rubenstein, William *The Myth of Rescue. Why the Democracies Could Not Have Saved More Jews from the Nazis* (London 1997)

Sainsbury, Keith *Churchill and Roosevelt at War* (London 1994)

Sbacchi, Alberto *Ethiopia under Mussolini. Fascism and the Colonial Experience* (London 1985)

Schaffer, Ronald *Wings of Judgment. American Bombing in World War II* (Oxford 1985)

Schlemmer, Thomas *Die Italiener an der Ostfront 1942/43. Dokumente zu Mussolinis Krieg gegen die Sowjetunion* (Munich 2005)

Schmitz, Stefan (ed.) *Willy Peter Reese. Mir selber seltsam fremd. Die Unmenschlichkeit des Krieges. Russland 1941–44* (Munich 2003)

Schwarz, Gudrun *Die Nationalsozialistischen Lager* (Frankfurt am Main 1996)

Seaman, Mark (ed.) *Special Operations Executive. A New Instrument of War* (London 2006)

Sebag Montefiore, Simon *Stalin. The Court of the Red Tsar* (London 2003)

—— *Young Stalin* (London 2007)

Self, Robert (ed.) *The Neville Chamberlain Diary Letters 1869–1940* (Aldershot 2005) vols 1–4

Service, Robert *Stalin. A Biography* (London 2004)

Sherwin, Martin J. *A World Destroyed. Hiroshima and the Origins of the Arms Race* (New York 1987)

Simpson, J. S. M. *South Africa Fights* (London 1941)

Slim, Hugo *Killing Civilians. Method, Madness and Morality in War* (London 2007)

Sluga, Hans *Heidegger's Crisis. Philosophy and Politics in Nazi Germany* (Cambridge, Massachusetts 1993)

Smelser, Ronald and Syring, Enrico (ed.) *Die SS. Elite unter dem Totenkopf. 30 Lebensläufe* (Paderborn 2000)

Smith, Alice Kimball and Weiner, Charles (eds) *Robert Oppenheimer. Letters and Recollections* (Cambridge, Massachusetts 1980)

Smith, Michael *Foley. The Spy Who Saved 10,000 Jews* (London 1999)

Solzhenitsyn, Alexander *Prussian Nights. A Poem* (New York 1977)

Spotts, Frederick *The Shameful Peace. How French Artists and Intellectuals Survived the Nazi Occupation* (New Haven 2008)

Stafford, David *Britain and European Resistance 1940–1945. A Survey of the Special Operations Executive, with Documents* (Oxford 1980)

—— *Churchill and Secret Service* (London 1995)

—— *Roosevelt and Churchill. Men of Secrets* (London 1999)

—— *Endgame 1945. Victory, Retribution, Liberation* (London 2007)

Stansky, Peter *The First Day of the Blitz* (New Haven 2007)

Steinberg, Paul *Speak You Also. A Survivor's Reckoning* (London 1996)

Stern, Fritz *Dreams and Delusions. The Drama of German History* (New Haven 1999)

—— *The Politics of Cultural Despair. A Study in the Rise of Germanic Ideology* (Berkeley 1961)

Stewart, Andrew *Empire Lost. Britain, the Dominions and the Second World War* (London 2008)

Stone, Dan *Responses to Nazism in Britain 1933–1939* (London 2003)

Stone, Harry *Writing in the Shadow. Resistance Publications in Occupied Europe* (London 1996)

Sweets, John *Choices in Vichy France. The French under German Occupation* (Oxford 1986)

Szarota, Tomasz *Warschau unter dem Hakenkreuz. Leben und Alltag im besetzten Warschau 1.10.1939–31.7.1944* (Paderborn 1985)

Szepamsky, Gerda *'Blitzmädel – Heldenmutter – Kriegerwittwe'. Frauenleben im Zweiten Weltkrieg* (Frankfurt am Main 1993)

Tarling, Nicholas *A Sudden Rampage. The Japanese Occupation of Southeast Asia 1941–1945* (London 2001)

Taylor, Frederick *Dresden. Tuesday 13 February 1945* (London 2004)

Thompson, Julian (ed.) *Call to Arms. Great Military Speeches from Ancient Greece to the Modern World* (London 2009)

Thorne, Christopher *The Limits of Foreign Policy. The West, the League and the Far Eastern Crisis of 1931–1933* (London 1972)

Thorpe, Charles *Oppenheimer. The Tragic Intellect* (Chicago 2006)

Timms, Edward *Karl Kraus. Apocalyptic Satirist. The Post-War Crisis and the Rise of the Swastika* (New Haven 2005)

Todorov, Tzvetan *A French Tragedy. Scenes of Civil War, Summer 1944* (Hanover, New Hampshire 1996)

—— *Facing the Extreme: Moral Life in the Concentration Camps* (London 1999)

Tooze, Adam *The Wages of Destruction. The Making and Breaking of the Nazi Economy* (London 2006)

Totani, Yuma *The Tokyo War Crimes Trial. The Pursuit of Justice in the Wake of World War II* (Cambridge, Massachusetts 2008)

Tournier, Michel *The Ogre* (Baltimore 1997)

Trunk, Isaiah *Judenrat. The Jewish Councils in Eastern Europe under Nazi Occupation* (New York 1972)

—— *Łódź Ghetto. A History* (Bloomington, Indiana 2006)

Twiston-Davies, David (ed.) *The Daily Telegraph Book of Military Obituaries* (London 2003)

Ueberschär, Gerd (ed.) *NS-Verbrechen und die militärische Widerstand gegen Hitler* (Darmstadt 2000)

—— (ed.) *Der Nationalsozialismus vor Gericht. Die alliierten Prozesse gegen Kriegsverbrecher und Soldaten 1943–1952* (Frankfurt am Main 2008)

—— and Wette, Wolfram (eds) *'Unternehmen Barbarossa'. Der deutsche Überfall auf die Sowjetunion 1941* (Paderborn 1984)

Unger, Michal (ed.) *The Last Ghetto. Life in the Łódź Ghetto 1940–1944* (Jerusalem 1995)

Urbach, Karina (ed.) *European Aristocracies and the Radical Right 1918–1939* (Oxford 2007)

Vaksberg, Arkady *Stalin's Prosecutor. The Life of Andrei Vyshinsky* (New York 1990)

Vaughan, David *Battle for the Airwaves. Radio and the 1938 Munich Crisis* (Prague 2008)

Vigors, Tim *Life's Too Short to Cry* (London 2006)

Vinen, Richard *The Unfree French. Life under Occupation* (London 2006)

Volkmann, Hans-Erich (ed.) *Das Russlandbild im Dritten Reich* (Cologne 1994)

Volkogonov, Dmitri *Stalin. Triumph and Tragedy* (London 1991)

Vonnegut, Kurt *Armageddon in Retrospect* (London 2008)

Vyšný, Paul *The Runciman Mission to Czechoslovakia 1938. Prelude to Munich* (London 2003)

Wakabayashi, Bob Tadashi (ed.) *The Nanking Atrocity 1937–38. Complicating the Picture* (New York 2007)

Wakelaw, Randall *The Science of Bombing. Operational Research in RAF Bomber Command* (Toronto 2009)

Walker, Jonathan *Poland Alone. Britain, SOE and the Collapse of the Polish Resistance 1944* (Stroud 2008)

Walzer, Michael *Arguing about War* (New Haven 2004)

Waugh, Evelyn *Unconditional Surrender* (London 2001, originally 1961)

Wegner, Bernd (ed.) *Zwei Wege nach Moskau. Vom Hitler–Stalin-Pakt zum 'Unternehmen Barbarossa'* (Munich 1991)

Weinberg, Gerhard *A World at Arms. A Global History of World War II* (Cambridge 1994)

—— (ed.) *Hitler's Second Book. The Unpublished Sequel to Mein Kampf* (New York 2003)

Welzer, Harald *Täter. Wie aus ganz normalen Menschen Massenmörder werden* (Frankfurt am Main 2005)

Werth, Alexander *Russia at War 1941–1945* (London 1964)

Westermann, Edward *Hitler's Police Battalions. Enforcing Racial War in the East* (Laurence, Kansas 2005)

Wette, Wolfram *Militarismus in Deutschland. Geschichte einer kriegerischen Kultur* (Darmstadt 2008)

—— *Die Wehrmacht. Feindbilder, Vernichtungskrieg, Legenden* (Frankfurt am Main 2002)

—— (ed.) *Retter in Uniform. Handlungsspielräume im Vernichtungskrieg der Wehrmacht* (Frankfurt am Main 2002)

—— and Ueberschär, Gerd (eds) *Stalingrad. Mythos und Wirklichkeit einer Schlacht* (Frankfurt am Main 1993)

Whitcomb, Philip W. (ed.) *France during the German Occupation 1940–1944. A Collection of 292 Statements on the Government of Maréchal Pétain and Pierre Laval* (Stanford, California 1958) vols 1–3

Wood, E. Thomas and Jankowski, Stanislaw M. *Karski. How One Man Tried to Stop the Holocaust* (New York 1994)

Wright, Jonathan *Germany and the Origins of the Second World War* (Basingstoke 2007)

Wright, Robert *Dowding and the Battle of Britain* (London 1969)

Wrochem, Oliver von *Erich von Manstein. Vernichtungskrieg und Geschichtspolitik* (Paderborn 2006)

Young, Louise *Japan's Total Empire. Manchuria and the Culture of Wartime Imperialism* (Berkeley 1998)

Zarusky, Jürgen (ed.) *Stalin und die Deutschen. Neue Beiträge der Forschung* (Munich 2006)

INDEX